Lecture Notes in Artificial Intelligence   1531

Subseries of Lecture Notes in Computer Science
Edited by J. G. Carbonell and J. Siekmann

Lecture Notes in Computer Science

Edited by G. Goos, J. Hartmanis and J. van Leeuwen

Springer
Berlin
Heidelberg
New York
Barcelona
Hong Kong
London
Milan
Paris
Singapore
Tokyo

Hing-Yan Lee   Hiroshi Motoda (Eds.)

PRICAI'98: Topics in Artificial Intelligence

5th Pacific Rim International Conference
on Artificial Intelligence
Singapore, November 22-27, 1998
Proceedings

Springer

Series Editors

Jaime G. Carbonell, Carnegie Mellon University, Pittsburgh, PA, USA
Jörg Siekmann, University of Saarland, Saarbrücken, Germany

Volume Editors

Hing-Yan Lee
Knowledge Lab., Kent Ridge Digital Labs
21 Heng Mui Keng Terrace, Singapore 119613
E-mail: hingyan@krdl.org.sg

Hiroshi Motoda
The Institute of Scientific and Industrial Research
Osaka University
8-1 Mihogaoka, Ibaraki, Osaka 57, Japan
E-mail: motoda@ar.sanken.osaka-u.ac.jp

Cataloging-in-Publication Data applied for

Die Deutsche Bibliothek - CIP-Einheitsaufnahme

Topics in artificial intelligence : proceedings / PRICAI '98, 5th
Pacific Rim International Conference on Artificial Intelligence,
Singapore, November 22 - 27, 1998. Hing-Yan Lee ; Hiroshi Motoda
(ed.). - Berlin ; Heidelberg ; New York ; Barcelona ; Hong Kong ;
London ; Milan ; Paris ; Singapore ; Tokyo : Springer, 1998
  (Lecture notes in computer science ; Vol. 1531 : Lecture notes in
  artificial intelligence)
  ISBN 3-540-65271-X

CR Subject Classification (1998): I.2

ISBN 3-540-65271-X Springer-Verlag Berlin Heidelberg New York

Preface

The Fifth Pacific Rim International Conference on Artificial Intelligence (PRICAI'98) being held in Singapore continues the successful series of AI conferences that have visited Cairns (Australia), Beijing (China), Seoul (Korea), and Nagoya (Japan) in 1996, 1994, 1992, and 1990 respectively.

The PRICAI conference series are biennial international events that concentrate on AI technologies and their applications in areas of social and economic importance for countries in the Pacific Rim. The objective of PRICAI is to promote research and development of AI in Pacific Rim countries by:
- providing a forum for the introduction and discussion of new research results, concepts, and technologies;
- providing practising engineers exposure to and an evaluation of evolving research, tools, and practices;
- providing the research community exposure to the problems of practical applications of AI; and
- encouraging the exchange of AI technologies and experience within Pacific Rim countries.

This conference attempts to meet the needs of a large and diverse constituency, which includes practitioners, researchers, educators, and users. The focus of the conference is on areas of AI that of particular importance in Pacific Rim countries.

Amidst the currency and economic turmoil that has plagued the Asian region the past year, PRICAI'98 received over 197 paper submissions from 25 countries, with strong representation and support from Pacific Rim countries. The Program Committee members and their qualified reviewers have worked diligently to ensure that the conference quality is maintained through stringent refereeing. The papers have each had the benefit of three reviews on average. A total of 56 papers were accepted for presentation and inclusion in the conference proceedings. Another 14 were accepted for poster presentations and were published separately.

The technical paper program is accompanied by three days of pre-conference activities comprising tutorials and workshops. Noteworthy of these is the Pacific-Rim Knowledge Acquisition Workshop (PKAW). PRICAI'98 invited speakers, Dr. Hiroaki Kitano (Sony Computer Science Lab, Japan), Prof. Robert Kowalski (Imperial College, UK), and Dr. Usama Fayyad (Microsoft Research, USA), are all distinguished authorities in their respective fields.

At PRICAI'98, the RoboCup Pacific Rim series makes its debut with a workshop and football playing robot competitions. The PRICAI Steering Committee has agreed to include RoboCup Pacific Rim series workshops and competitions as a regular feature of future PRICAI conferences.

We thank the Program Committee members and reviewers for refereeing the great number of papers. The generous contributions of many people and cooperating organizations are gratefully acknowledged in the following pages.

November 1998

Hing-Yan Lee & Hiroshi Motoda
Program Co-Chairs

Sponsors

PRICAI'98 gratefully acknowledges financial support from the following sponsors:

Center of the International Cooperation for
    Computerization (CICC Singapore)
Microsoft Singapore
Sony Corporation

Cooperating Organizations & Conferences

PRICAI'98 is held in cooperation with:

American Association on Artificial Intelligence (AAAI)
Australian Computer Society (ACS) National Committee on
    Expert Systems & Artificial Intelligence
Canadian Society for Computational Studies of Intelligence
    (CSCSI)
Computer Association of Thailand (CAT)
Instrumentation and Control Society of Malaysia (ICSM)
Intelligent Automation Society of the Chinese Association of
    Automation International Society for Applied Intelligence
    (ISAI)
Japanese Society for Artificial Intelligence (JSAI)
National Computer Board (NCB)
National Science & Technology Board (NSTB)
Singapore Computer Society (SCS)
Taiwanese Association for AI (TAAI)

PRICAI Standing Steering Committee

Chair:
 Michael Georgeff   Australian Artificial Intelligence
           Institute, Australia

Committee:
Ruwei Dai	Chinese Academy of Sciences, China
Randy Goebel	University of Alberta, Canada
Young Hwan Lim	Soongsil University, Korea
Fumio Mizoguchi	Science University of Tokyo, Japan
Juzar Motiwalla	Kent Ridge Digital Labs, Singapore
Setsuo Ohsuga	Waseda University, Japan
Zhongzhi Shi	Chinese Academy of Sciences, China
Saburo Tsuji	Osaka University, Japan
Benjamin Wah	University of Illinois, USA
Vilas Wuwongse	Asian Institute of Technology, Thailand
Wai Kiang Yeap	University of Otago, New Zealand

Conference Committee

General Chair:
 Juzar Motiwalla   Kent Ridge Digital Labs

Program Co-Chairs:
 Hing-Yan Lee   Kent Ridge Digital Labs
 Hiroshi Motoda   Osaka University, Japan

Local Arrangements Chair:
 Hwee-Leng Ong   Kent Ridge Digital Labs

Workshop Chair:
 Jane Hsu   National Taiwan University, Taiwan

Tutorial Chair:
 Phan Minh Dung   Asian Institute of Technology, Thailand

Organizing Committee:
Soo-Hye Goh	Kent Ridge Digital Labs
Kwok-Leong Hui	Kent Ridge Digital Labs
Paramasiwan Kalaselvi	Kent Ridge Digital Labs
Fon-Lin Lai	Kent Ridge Digital Labs
Khee-Erng Lau	Kent Ridge Digital Labs
Siew-Choo Tay	Kent Ridge Digital Labs
Rina Wang	Kent Ridge Digital Labs

Program Committee

Randy Goebel	University of Alberta, Canada
Jieh Hsiang	National Taiwan University, Taiwan
David Israel	SRI International, USA
Joxan Jaffar	National University of Singapore
Marzuki Khalid	Universiti Teknologi Malaysia, Malaysia
Hing-Yan Lee	Kent Ridge Digital Labs
Richiiro Mizoguchi	Osaka University, Japan
Hiroshi Motoda	Osaka University, Japan
Hwee-Tou Ng	DSO National Labs, Singapore
Masayuki Numao	Tokyo Institute of Technology, Japan
Yung-Hwan Oh	KAIST, Korea
Young-Tack Park	Soongsil University, Korea
Claude Sammet	University of New South Wales, Australia
Abdul Sattar	Griffith University, Australia
Ah-Hwee Tan	Kent Ridge Digital Labs
Sek-Wah Tan	Kent Ridge Digital Labs
Takao Terano	Tsukuba University, Japan
Ian Witten	Waikato University, New Zealand
Daniel Yeung	Hong Kong Polytechnic, Hong Kong
Zhang Bo	Tsinghua University, China

Workshop Organizers

Aditya Ghose	University of Wollongong, Australia
Toru Ishida	Kyoto University, Japan
Takashi Kido	NTT MSC, Malaysia
Hiroaki Kitano	Sony Computer Science Laboratory, Japan
Mun-Kew Leong	Kent Ridge Digital Labs
Bing Liu	National University of Singapore
Fumio Mizoguchi	Science University of Tokyo, Japan
Hiroshi Motoda	Osaka University, Japan
Roland Yap	National University of Singapore

Tutorial Presenters

Robert Dale	Macquarie University, Australia
Martin Henz	National University of Singapore
Mark Klein	Massachusetts Institute of Technology, USA
Bing Liu	National University of Singapore
Huan Liu	National University of Singapore
Chris Manning	University of Sydney, Australia

PRICAI'98 Reviewers

Noboru Babaguchi
Shuanhu Bai
Peter van Beek
Chung Chen Chen
Chung-Min Chen
Eng-Siong Chng
Sidney Chong
Yeow Chong Chuah
Shou King Foo
Kok Wee Gan
R.G. (Randy) Goebel
Russ Greiner
Ping Gu
Jin Guo
David Harmanec
Martin Henz
Tadashi Horiuchi
Gohuo Huang
Guan Shieng Huang
Zhiyi Huang
Kwok Leong Hui
Jieh Hsiang
Md. Farhad Hussain
Ryutaro Ichise
Mitsuru Ikeda
David Israel
Yoshinobu Kitamura
Ken Kuriyama
Hoong-Chuin Lau

Khee-Erng Lau
Hing-Yan Lee
Jae-Sung Lee
Yumi Iwasaki
Joxan Jaffar
Andreas Junghanns
Akihiro Kashihara
Ji-Hyung Lee
Sangho Lee
Mun Kew Leong
Haizhou Li
Churn-Jung Liau
Bing Liu
Huan Liu
Oscar Ortega Lobo
Yingwei Lu
Kim Teng Lua
Ho Chung Lui
Riichiro Mizoguchi
Hiroshi Motoda
Tsuyoshi Murata
Sivakumar Nagarajan
Hwee Tou Ng
Masayuki Numao
Kozo Ohara
Young-Tack Park
Francis Jeffry Pelletier
Kim-Leng Poh
M.R.K. Krishna Rao

Kanagasabai
Rajaraman
Hae Chang Rim
Byung-Sun Ryu
Claude Sammut
Abdul Sattar
Dennis Seah
Rudy Setiono
Simon Shiu
Raymund Sison
Eleni Stroulia
Jang-Won Suh
Ah Hwee Tan
Chew Lim Tan
Sek-Wah Tan
John Thornton
Loong Cheong Tong
Eric Tsang
Ke Wang
Takashi Washio
Hock-Soon Wee
Paul Wu Horng Jyh
Wu Xi
Roland Yap
Tralvex Yeap
Jane You
Bo Zhang
Tong Zheng

Table of Contents

Induction (Improving Classifier's Accuracy)

Multi Agent Architecture

Knowledge Acquisition, Modeling and Validation

Reasoning (Non-monotonic Reasoning, Default Logic, Commonsense Reasoning)

Knowledge Discovery and Data Mining

Knowledge Management (Ontology, Individual and Collective Knowledge)

**Induction (Decision Tree Pruning, Feature Selection,
Feature Discretization)**

Application of Fuzzy Logic

Reasoning (Temporal Reasoning, Event Calculus)

Application of Neural Network

Search (Constraint Satisfaction, Heuristic Search)

Bayesian Network

Intelligent Systems

Foundation of AI

Stochastic Process

Abduction (Explanation, Hypothetical Reasoning)

Image Retrieval and Speech Recognition

Repechage Bootstrap Aggregating for Misclassification Cost Reduction

Mike Cameron-Jones and Linda Richards

School of Computing
University of Tasmania
Launceston
Tasmania 7250
Australia
Michael.CameronJones@utas.edu.au

Abstract. This paper examines the use of bootstrap aggregating (bagging) with classifier learning methods based upon hold-out pruning (or growing) for misclassification cost reduction. Both decision tree and rule set classifiers are used. The paper introduces a "repechage" variation of bagging, that uses, as the hold-out data for cost reduction, the "out of bag" items, which would be unused in standard bagging. The paper presents experimental evidence that, when used with the hold-out cost reduction methods, the repechage method can achieve better misclassification cost results than the straightforward use of standard bagging used with the same hold-out cost reduction method. Superior results for the repechage method on some problems with previously defined cost matrices are shown for a cost reduction decision tree method and two cost reduction rule set methods.

1 Introduction

The most common task addressed in machine learning is that of learning a classifier from attribute-value data. The resulting classifier predicts to which of a predefined set of disjoint categories, or classes, an item belongs, on the basis of the values of the item's attributes. The classifier is learned from items for which the classes are known, and is intended to predict well the classes of items for which it has not been given the true classes.

While the most common definition of predicting well is simply that few errors are made, i.e. the classifier is accurate, there is also interest in the case where there are different costs for different types of error, e.g. [13] and [20]. For example, it is more expensive for a bank to make the mistake of lending a million dollars to someone who does not repay the loan or pay any interest, than to make the mistake of not lending a million dollars to someone who would have repaid the loan with interest. In the case of non-uniform misclassification costs, the standard goal is low expected misclassification cost, which might be achieved with a higher error rate than the maximal accuracy goal, as expected costs may be reduced by avoiding a few high cost errors at the expense of making many low cost errors. For example, a bank may choose to exercise caution in its loans, missing out on many potential small profits in order to avoid a few large losses. This paper examines an approach to learning classifiers that are measured in terms of their expected misclassification cost.

There has long been interest in learning different types of single classifier, such as sets of rules (e.g. [8]) and decision trees (e.g. [15]), and recently there has been renewed interest in methods which learn multiple component classifiers and combine their results, e.g. learning many decision trees and combining them as in [16]. This paper looks at the use of one of these multiple classifier methods, bootstrap aggregating (bagging), due to Breiman [2], and attempts to use it with some methods for learning classifiers in the misclassification cost context, rather than the common use in which accuracy is the goal. Ting and Zheng [18] have recently successfully used another multiple classifier method, "boosting", in the misclassification cost context.

The methods used here for learning the component classifiers are all based on "hold-out" methods, of which reduced error decision tree pruning [14] is the best known, but the methods here are reduced cost rather than reduced error methods. Hold-out methods test some possible classifiers on a hold-out portion of the training data – a portion not used to form the classifiers – and choose from amongst these possible classifiers, that which performs best on this hold-out portion of the data.

This paper considers the straightforward use of bagging with these hold-out methods, and then introduces a new variation of bagging, "repechage" bootstrap aggregating, in which the bagging and hold-out pruning are more closely integrated. The repechage method uses as the hold-out data, a portion of the data that has been referred to as the "out of bag" data by Breiman when using the data for other purposes, [3]. The out of bag data is that training data not in the bootstrap sample used to learn a classifier in the standard form of bagging, hence the repechage method can potentially benefit from the fact that the component classifiers are learned with more data. The hold-out data is also more independent of the data used to form the classifiers compared on it, a further potential advantage.

The rest of the paper consists of a description of the types of misclassification cost reduction learning methods examined, a description of the forms of bagging used including the new repechage method, a description of some experiments with results supporting the advantage of the repechage method when compared against straightforward bagging with the hold-out methods, and finally the paper ends with some conclusions and further work.

2 Misclassification Cost Reduction Learning Methods

Many learning approaches that consider some forms of costs have been examined, including some that are affected by costs such as those involved in measuring attributes, for example see [19]. However, the most common form of cost considered is that of misclassifying an item. A range of methods for learning classifiers with the goal of having low misclassification costs was examined in [13]. These approaches included various decision tree methods, including adjusting the priors to take into account classes' average misclassification costs as done in CART [4], some Naive Bayes methods, and some rule set methods. (Interestingly, the straightforward use of a cost heuristic when growing a decision tree produced generally poor results.) The classifier learning methods used in this paper are decision tree and rule set methods, related to the decision tree and rule set hold-out cost reduction methods of [13], but based upon decision tree and rule set implementations to hand.

2.1 Decision Tree Methods

Cost reduction methods for decision trees are based upon straightforward variations of the reduced error decision tree pruning of [14], an approach to reducing overfitting. Like other hold-out methods, it forms potential classifiers using one part of the training data, and selects the potential classifier that performs best when evaluated on another, hold-out, part of the training data. In such reduced error pruning (REP), the training data available is split into two parts, a growing part (in this work 2/3 of the training data) and a hold-out pruning part (the remaining 1/3).

A decision tree is then grown, using the growing part of the data, to the point where the tree classifies the growing data correctly (barring the existence of items with duplicate attribute values and different classes, which are bound to end up in the same leaf). During the growing phase a record is kept for each decision node, of which class it would predict if it were a leaf, i.e. what is the most common class in the growing data that reaches that node. The potential classifiers to be evaluated are then the full tree and all pruned versions of it, where pruning replaces a decision node and the rest of the tree below it with a leaf.

The full tree grown is then pruned back to the point at which it has fewest errors on the pruning data, pruning a decision node to a leaf, if the leaf (with the class recorded in the growing phase) will make as few errors on the pruning data reaching it as the decision node and the pruned subtrees below it. The pruning process consists of a post-order traversal of the decision tree, pruning the subtrees below a decision node, then determining whether to prune the decision node given the error rates of the pruned subtrees.

Cost reduction decision tree pruning simply alters the pruning criterion to minimise *costs* rather than errors, and the potential leaf class assigned to a node is altered to be that which minimises costs rather than errors. However the methods described in [13] redetermine the appropriate class for a leaf during pruning, choosing that class which minimises cost on the pruning data at the node. This change to the class conflicts with the notion that the pruning data is simply being used to choose from amongst possible classifiers defined by the growing data, i.e. the original tree or a pruned version thereof. Our initial experiments [17] have confirmed that it is better not to change the class during the pruning phase, so the work reported here does not. However, it does adopt from [13] the approach of labelling the *final* pruned tree using all the training data, both growing and pruning.

The reduced cost pruning decision tree method has been implemented as a modification to Quinlan's C4.5 [15], which normally grows and prunes using all the training data and Quinlan's own error criterion. C4.5's classification method is based upon choosing at classification time the most common class from a frequency distribution estimated for the item, as opposed to simply using a leaf class label. (This frequency distribution can be estimated over more than one leaf due to the handling of missing values.) The classification code has been adjusted in the reduced cost version, so that the class chosen is the least expected cost class given the frequency distribution, rather than the most common class. However, aspects such as C4.5's splitting criterion – gain ratio by default – have been left unchanged.

2.2   Rule Set Methods

The reduced cost rule set methods used in this work are versions of Cohen's reduced error methods [9], whose computational efficiency we previously studied in [6]. These methods are based upon an adaptation to FOIL [7] to apply it to multiple class classifier problems. The basic approach consists of using FOIL to learn a set of rules for each class, regarding all the instances of the class as positive examples of the concept "is a member of that class", and all instances of other classes as negative examples. (In the work here FOIL's standard minimum description length criterion for limiting rule growth is retained, not dropped as per the previous work.) The rule sets are then used as a decision list with a default added, which is chosen to minimise errors on the training examples, (or to be the most common class of the training examples if there are no such errors).

The reduced cost methods split the original training data as per the decision tree method, and grow an initial set of rules upon the growing part. Unlike the straightforward decision list approach, which always uses the first rule in the list that fires, Cohen's approach to conflict resolution chooses, from amongst rules that fire, the most accurate of them. (This accuracy is assessed on the growing data for use in the pruning phase, then reassessed on the whole of the training data once the final rule set has been selected – similarly to the use of the whole of the training data on the final pruned tree in our reduced cost tree implementation.) There are then two approaches to using the hold-out "pruning" data.

Reduced Cost Pruning The pruning approach of Cohen was a form of REP for rule sets, as also considered in e.g. [5]. Cohen's method went through a process of considering all single step changes to the current rule set, evaluating the possible resulting rule sets in terms of errors on the pruning data, then made the best single step change, and repeated the process on the new rule set, progressively reducing the rule set to the default rule. The two types of single step changes considered were firstly deleting one or more conditions from the end of a rule (and adjusting the default to minimise errors), and secondly deleting an entire rule (and adjusting the default to minimise errors). The classifier chosen from the repeated pruning process was the smallest of those with least error on the pruning data.

In this work the above REP method has been adapted to choose the best single step change where best is determined in terms of the *cost* on the pruning data, as opposed to the number of errors on the pruning data, and the final classifier is chosen to be best in terms of cost rather than errors.

Reduced Cost Growing Cohen's Grow method is similar to the Reduced Cost Ordering method of [13]. The Grow method rather than pruning an initially large rule set uses the hold-out ("pruning") data to grow a rule set based upon the initial rule set. A set of candidate rules is initially formed which consists of prefixes of the rules found from the growing data. The Grow method, starting from a rule set containing only a default rule, went through a process of considering the addition of a candidate rule to the existing rule set, evaluating the resulting rule set (with appropriately adjusted default) in terms of errors on the pruning data, then added the best rule, and repeated the process on the new rule set, building up the rule set until no single addition improved the rule set. As the Grow method starts from an empty rule set and stops building when no single addition will improve the rule set, it tends to produce smaller final rule sets than pruning, which can be beneficial on some problems.

Similarly to the reduced cost pruning, the reduced cost growing method used here alters the choice of rule to add to be that which most improves the *cost* of the rule set on the pruning data, rather than that which most improves the error rate. The implementation is based upon the FastGrow method we proposed in [6], which is more efficient than a naive implementation, although as explained in that paper the method is still cubic in the number of training items on data that is purely noise, hence not efficient by comparison with e.g. the decision tree method.

3 Bootstrap Aggregating

There has been recent interest in various methods for reducing classification error by learning and combining multiple classifiers. While some of these methods involve learning different types of classifiers, others learn different classifiers of the one type through perturbing the classifier learning process, e.g. choosing randomly amongst greedy choices which perform similarly according to the method's heuristic [1] enables different classifiers to be learned from exactly the same training data.

Bootstrap aggregating (bagging), due to Breiman [2], enables different classifiers to be learned by learning each upon a different sample of the training data. During learning a series of bootstrap samples are taken from the training data and a classifier grown on each. (A bootstrap sample is a sample of the same size as the original formed by sampling with replacement; thus roughly 37% of the items in the original are omitted, and some items in the sample are duplicates.) At classification time the classifiers are combined by taking a simple vote amongst them.

Bagging has been shown to be effective for error reduction in both classification and regression problems, when using "unstable" [2] learning methods for which the perturbation of the data can produce large changes to the learned classifiers. Here it is applied to classification with the goal being misclassification cost reduction rather than error reduction. As we are considering its use with methods that predict a single class attempting to reduce misclassification cost, the classifiers used are combined by a simple vote as usual. However, an alternative approach worth considering is to use classifiers that attempt to predict class probabilities, and to combine the class probabilities, then predict the least cost class given those probabilities.

The straightforward application of bagging with the hold-out reduced cost learning methods results in the bootstrap sample being split into a growing part and a hold-out "pruning" part. This has two potentially undesirable aspects. Firstly, as is inherent in the bootstrap method, the number of distinct items being used to train each classifier is less than in the original training data (approximately 63%), and when combined with the approach of splitting the data (2/3, 1/3) into growing and hold-out parts, only about half the original data items will be used in the growing phase. Secondly, as the hold-out part is formed from a bootstrap sample, it may contain duplicates of items in the growing part and thus give less reliable estimates of the costs of different classifiers considered. While both of these aspects also contribute to the variety of the classifiers, which is essential to the success of bagging, this paper suggests that the repechage method proposed below can perform better.

3.1 Repechage Bootstrap Aggregating

The repechage method is proposed as a means of tackling the two problems identified with the straightforward use of bagging with the hold-out reduced cost methods, firstly the reduction in the number of distinct data items used in the growing phase, and secondly the lack of independence of the hold-out "pruning" data. The repechage method follows the standard approach of taking a series of bootstrap samples and learning a classifier on each. However, it integrates the bagging and hold-out approaches by learning each classifier using the bootstrap sample as the growing data, and the data not in the bootstrap sample (the "out of bag" data [3]) as the hold-out data. (Note that the number of hold-out data items, approximately 37% of the training data, will vary between bootstrap samples.) The term "repechage" is used by analogy with the competition procedure of that name, which lets first round losers participate further in an event – in this case the out of bag items are the first round losers through not being in the bootstrap sample, but are allowed to participate further, not eliminated.

Thus all the data is used, the hold-out data is genuinely independent of the growing data, and yet a different classifier is being learned for each bootstrap sample, as required for the benefits of bagging. There is a trade-off in that the variation between classifiers might be reduced by the fact that the whole of the data is used to learn each classifier – the results of the experiments will show that the trade-off can be favourable to the repechage method.

4   Experiments

This section presents the results of some experiments comparing the repechage method against the straightforward application of bagging with the reduced cost learning methods used. As previous work, e.g. [16], has suggested that the benefits of bagging may be seen by combining 10 classifiers, and the reduced cost rule set pruning implementation is fairly inefficient (e.g. approximately a CPU minute on a Sparcstation 10 to produce a final rule set for the German credit data set, that on which it was slowest), a repechage or standard bagged classifier is always based upon 10 simple classifiers. (Our initial experiments with the reduced cost pruned trees, which are found more efficiently than the rule sets, showed that further improvements in the repechage results were gained by combining more classifiers as reported in [17].)

The data sets used for the experiments were chosen because they had been used before to report the results of misclassification cost based work. Three of the four data sets used by Pazzani et al., [13], were used here – the fourth was unavailable due to commercial confidentiality.

The first of these was the Cleveland heart disease data set (used with the original 5 classes, rather than the 2 commonly used in machine learning experiments), for which we used the cost matrix defined by Pazzani et al., in which underdiagnosing the degree of heart disease costs twice the amount by which it is in error, but overdiagnosing costs only the amount by which it is in error. For example if an item is truly of class 2, predicting that it is class 0 costs 4, and predicting that it is class 4 costs 2.

The second data set was the Pima Indians Diabetes data set, for which the cost matrix defined by Pazzani et al was also used – diagnosing disease when absent costs 1, failing to diagnose when present costs 2.

The third was the mushroom data set, for which again the previous cost matrix was used – classifying an edible mushroom as poisonous costs 1, and the reverse costs 10.

The final data set used was the German credit data used in the Statlog project [12] with the cost matrix previously defined – classifying a good customer as bad costs 1, and the reverse 5.

The training / test splits were chosen to match Pazzani et al. for the first three data sets – training sizes of 200 (out of 303), 440 (out of 768), and 500 (out of 8124). A training size of 500 (out of 1000) was chosen for the last data set.

All the data sets were obtained from the UCI Repository of Machine Learning Databases [11]. Unfortunately, despite the commercial interest in misclassification cost reduction, the issue of commercial confidentiality seems to result in few data sets with identified cost matrices. It might be preferable for evaluation purposes to use more data sets and generate the cost matrices randomly as done in [18].

All experimental results reported are the average of 50 trials, as per [13]. In each trial a portion of the original data set was randomly selected as the training data and the rest kept as test data, all learning methods were then applied to the training data set, and their resulting classifiers evaluated on the test data set. Thus each trial involves a different subset of the data being used as training data (and the remainder being used as test data), and within a trial all learning methods are being compared on the same training and test data as each other – a series of paired trials. (The standard bagging and the repechage methods were also using the same bootstrap samples of the training data within a trial, and thus also paired in this respect.)

Table 1 shows the average costs of the classifiers learned by the different methods applied:

1. Default method that simply predicts the single class that gives least cost on the test data.
2. C4.5 (using full, not bootstrap-sampled training data)
3. Bagged C4.5
4. Reduced cost pruned decision tree method (using full, not bootstrap-sampled training data)
5. Bagged reduced cost pruned decision tree method
6. Repechage bagged reduced cost pruned decision tree method
7. Decision list with rules produced by adapted FOIL (using full, not bootstrap-sampled training data)
8. Bagged decision lists with rules produced by adapted FOIL
9. Reduced cost pruned rule set method (using full, not bootstrap-sampled training data)
10. Bagged reduced cost pruned rule set method
11. Repechage bagged reduced cost pruned rule set method
12. Reduced cost grown rule set method (using full, not bootstrap-sampled training data)
13. Bagged reduced cost grown rule set method
14. Repechage bagged reduced cost grown rule set method

Entries not separated by a horizontal line were compared by a significance test and are in bold if a two-tailed paired t-test (90% significance level) suggests that they differ significantly from the entry above.

The comparison between the repechage and straightforward bagging method always favours the repechage methods, across all the data sets, for all the hold-out reduced cost methods used: pruned tree, pruned rule set and grown rule set. While not all the individual comparisons are statistically significant, the overall comparison is 12 favourable results to none unfavourable. The repechage method is also never worse than the non-bagged results, whereas the straightforward bagged method sometimes is.

Table 1. Average costs of learned classifiers

Method	Heart	Diabetes	Mushroom	German
Default	1.4918	0.6430	0.5183	0.6965
C4.5	1.1402	0.4089	0.1051	1.0052
Bag C4.5	1.1357	0.4109	0.1049	1.0151
Tree	1.0480	0.3970	0.0602	0.6440
Bag Tree	1.0249	**0.3692**	0.0696	**0.6714**
Rep Tree	**0.9734**	**0.3595**	**0.0549**	**0.5994**
DList	1.2074	0.4132	0.0405	0.9561
Bag DList	**0.9955**	**0.3618**	**0.0333**	**0.6241**
Prune	1.0569	0.4059	0.0795	0.7872
Bag Prune	1.0699	**0.3829**	0.0849	**0.8572**
Rep Prune	**1.0400**	**0.3666**	**0.0679**	**0.6704**
Grow	1.0781	0.3946	0.0708	0.6888
Bag Grow	1.1016	**0.3767**	0.0757	0.6875
Rep Grow	1.0765	**0.3699**	**0.0574**	**0.6030**

A check of the results of the (unbagged) reduced cost methods against previously published results [13] for corresponding methods on the first three data sets shows that their performance is credible. However, it is clear that the pruned rule set method performs very poorly on the German credit data set, and examination of the rule sets suggests that there may be a problem with overfitting, despite the use of a pruning process. As pointed out in our previous work [6], hold-out methods are not immune to rule set growth in the presence of noise.

Table 2 shows the fractional error rates of the various methods to illustrate the point that improvements in cost may frequently occur at a cost in accuracy, e.g. sometimes the repechage method has done worse in accuracy while meeting the goal of improving costs. (The default in this table is the most common class, as is appropriate for the accuracy goal.)

5   Conclusions and Further Work

This paper has looked at the use of bootstrap aggregating (bagging) with hold-out methods for cost reduction. It has proposed that the straightforward application of bagging may have potential problems in this context and suggested a new repechage approach which uses the out of bag data as the hold-out data. It has tested this approach with two types of classifier, decision trees and rule sets, with the rule sets being determined by two alternative approaches, pruning and growing, and found that on the data sets tried, the new repechage method was superior in cost terms to the standard method. Thus the repechage method and related approaches seem worth further investigation.

Two reasons were suggested for why the repechage method might prove preferable, firstly the use of more of the original training data when learning a classifier, and secondly the genuine independence of the hold-out data. An

Table 2. Average fractional error rates of learned classifiers

Method	Heart	Diabetes	Mushroom	German
Default	0.4608	0.3512	0.4817	0.3035
C4.5	0.4757	0.2688	0.0112	0.2909
Bag C4.5	**0.4441**	**0.2520**	0.0109	**0.2695**
Tree	0.4996	0.2988	0.0088	0.4085
Bag Tree	**0.4491**	**0.2507**	**0.0075**	**0.3387**
Rep Tree	0.4517	**0.2616**	**0.0061**	**0.3957**
DList	0.4854	0.2818	0.0050	0.3111
Bag DList	**0.4383**	**0.2471**	**0.0063**	**0.2662**
Prune	0.4515	0.2904	0.0135	0.3848
Bag Prune	**0.4216**	**0.2482**	0.0091	**0.2801**
Rep Prune	0.4188	0.2482	**0.0074**	**0.3384**
Grow	0.4524	0.2789	0.0228	0.4092
Bag Grow	**0.4159**	**0.2480**	**0.0101**	**0.3235**
Rep Grow	0.4239	**0.2538**	**0.0081**	**0.3825**

attempt to determine the relative importance of these factors seems worth pursuing. It was also suggested that the reduction in variation of the data seen by a learning method, due to using the whole of the data might be disadvantageous. This would also seem worth investigating. In general the question of how important the variation due to bootstrap sampling is by comparison with other methods, e.g. simply repeatedly randomly splitting the data (2/3, 1/3), seems worth study. This might open the door to multiple uses of incremental reduced cost pruning methods which could be developed from Cohen's incremental reduced error pruning method RIPPER, [10], which is much more computationally efficient than the batch methods used here, and has proved very effective in practice.

Acknowledgements

Thanks are due to Ross Quinlan for the original C4.5 code that was adapted for this work, which also used code adapted from that written by the first author as part of a project made possible by grants from the Australian Research Council (J.R.Quinlan, Principal Investigator) and assisted by research agreements with Digital Equipment Corporation.

References

1. K.M. Ali and M. Pazzani. Error reduction through learning multiple descriptions. *Machine Learning*, 24:173–202, 1996.
2. L. Breiman. Bagging predictors. *Machine Learning*, 24:123–140, 1996.
3. L. Breiman. *Out-of-bag Estimation*. available from ftp.stat.berkeley.edu as /users/pub/breiman/OOBestimation.ps, 1996.

4. L. Breiman, J.H. Friedman, R.A. Olshen, and C.J. Stone. *Classification and Regression Trees.* Wadsworth, 1984.

5. C.A. Brunk and M.J. Pazzani. An investigation of noise-tolerant relational concept learning algorithms. In *Proceedings of the Eighth International Workshop of Machine Learning*, pages 389–393. Morgan Kaufmann, 1991.

6. R.M. Cameron-Jones. The complexity of batch approaches to reduced error rule set induction. In *Proceedings of the Fourth Pacific Rim International Conference on Artificial Intelligence*, pages 348–359. Springer Verlag, 1996.

7. R.M. Cameron-Jones and J.R. Quinlan. Efficient top-down induction of logic programs. *SIGART*, 5:33–42, 1994.

8. P. Clark and R. Boswell. Rule induction with CN2: Some recent improvements. In *Machine Learning - EWSL91: Proceedings of the Fifth European Working Session on Machine Learning.* Springer-Verlag, 1991. Lecture Notes in Artificial Intelligence, 482.

9. W.W. Cohen. Efficient pruning methods for separate-and-conquer rule learning systems. In *Proceedings of the Thirteenth International Joint Conference on Artificial Intelligence*, pages 988–994. Morgan Kaufmann, 1993.

10. W.W. Cohen. Fast effective rule induction. In *Proceedings of the Twelfth International Conference on Machine Learning (ML95)*, pages 115–123. Morgan Kaufmann, 1995.

11. C.J. Merz and P.M. Murphy. UCI repository of machine learning databases, 1996. http://www.ics.uci.edu/~mlearn/MLRepository.html.

12. D. Michie, D.J. Spiegelhalter, and C.C. (eds.) Taylor. *Machine learning, neural and statistical classification.* Ellis Horwood, 1994.

13. M. Pazzani, C. Merz, P. Murphy, K. Ali, T. Hume, and C. Brunk. Reducing misclassification costs. In *Proceedings of the Eleventh International Conference on Machine Learning (ML94)*, pages 217–225. Morgan Kaufmann, 1994.

14. J.R. Quinlan. Simplifying decision trees. *International Journal of Man-Machine Studies*, 27:221–234, 1987.

15. J.R. Quinlan. *C4.5: Programs for Machine Learning.* Morgan Kaufmann, 1993. The Morgan Kaufmann Series in Machine Learning.

16. J.R. Quinlan. Bagging, boosting and C4.5. In *Proceedings of the Thirteenth American Association for Artificial Intelligence National Conference on Artificial Intelligence*, pages 725–730. AAAI Press, 1996.

17. L.M. Richards. Reduced cost pruning and classifier combination, 1997. Honours thesis, School of Computing, University of Tasmania.

18. K.M. Ting and Z. Zheng. Boosting trees for cost-sensitive classifications. In *Proceedings of the Tenth European Conference on Machine Learning*, pages 190–195. Springer-Verlag, 1998. Lecture Notes in Artificial Intelligence, 1398.

19. P.D. Turney. Cost-sensitive classification: Empirical evaluation of a hybrid genetic decision tree induction algorithm. *Journal of Artificial Intelligence Research*, 2:369–409, 1995.

20. G.I. Webb. Cost-sensitive specialization. In *Proceedings of the Fourth Pacific Rim International Conference on Artificial Intelligence*, pages 23–34. Springer Verlag, 1996.

Generating Classifier Committees by Stochastically Selecting both Attributes and Training Examples

Zijian Zheng

School of Computing and Mathematics
Deakin University, Geelong
Victoria 3217, Australia
zijian@deakin.edu.au

Abstract. Boosting and Bagging, as two representative approaches to learning classifier committees, have demonstrated great success, especially for decision tree learning. They repeatedly build different classifiers using a base learning algorithm by changing the distribution of the training set. SASC, as a different type of committee learning method, can also significantly reduce the error rate of decision trees. It generates classifier committees by stochastically modifying the set of attributes but keeping the distribution of the training set unchanged. It has been shown that Bagging and SASC are, on average, less accurate than Boosting, but the performance of the former is more stable than that of the latter in terms of less frequently obtaining significantly higher error rates than the base learning algorithm. In this paper, we propose a novel committee learning algorithm, called SASCBAG, that combines SASC and Bagging. It creates different classifiers by stochastically varying both the attribute set and the distribution of the training set. Experimental results in a representative collection of natural domains show that, for decision tree learning, the new algorithm is, on average, more accurate than Boosting, Bagging, and SASC. It is more stable than Boosting. In addition, like Bagging and SASC, SASCBAG is amenable to parallel and distributed processing while Boosting is not. This gives SASCBAG another advantage over Boosting for parallel machine learning and datamining.

1 Introduction

Much recent research effort has been exerted to study classifier committee learning [1, 2, 3, 4, 5, 6, 7, 8, 9, 10, 11, 12]. With this type of approach, a set of classifiers is generated using a single base learning algorithm to form a committee. The committee members vote to decide the final classification.

Bagging [5] and Boosting [13, 2, 3, 1, 11], as two representative methods of this type, can significantly decrease the error rate of decision tree learning [4, 3, 12]. They repeatedly build different classifiers using a base learning algorithm, such as a decision tree generator, by changing the distribution of the training set. Bagging generates different classifiers using different bootstrap samples. Boosting builds different classifiers sequentially. The weights of training examples used for creating each classifier are modified based on the performance of the previous classifiers. The objective is to make the generation of the next classifier concentrate on the training examples that are misclassified by the previous classifiers. The main difference between Bagging and Boosting is that the latter adaptively changes the distribution of the training set based on the performance of previously created classifiers and uses a function of the performance of a classifier as the weight for voting, while the former stochastically changes the distribution of the training set and uses equal weight voting.

While much recent attention has focused on Boosting and Bagging, other classifier committee learning approaches have also been developed, including generating multiple trees by manually changing learning parameters [14], error-correcting output codes [15], generating decision tree committees by stochastically selecting attributes [7, 8, 16], learning option trees [17, 18], training a committee of neural networks by manually selecting attribute subsets [19, 20], learning naive Bayesian classifier committees by randomly choosing attribute subsets [21], creating Gaussian classifier committees by varying attribute sets [22], and creating committees for first-order learning by adding random selection of conditions to FOIL [10]. Finally, different base learning algorithms can be used for learning different classifiers in committees [23, 24]. A collection of recent research in this area and reviews of related methods can be found in [9, 25, 8].

As an alternative approach to creating classifier committees, the stochastic attribute selection committee learning method can also significantly reduce the error rates of decision tree learning [7, 8, 16]. It builds different classifiers by stochastically modifying the set of attributes considered during induction, while the distribution of the training set is kept unchanged. We have shown that SASC, a variant of this stochastic attribute selection committee learning method,[1] and Bagging are more stable than Boosting, although the latter is, on average, more accurate than the former [16]. This is consistent with the previous findings regarding the relative performance of Bagging and Boosting [4, 12].

In this paper, we propose a novel committee learning approach by combining Bagging and SASC. The new method, called SASCBAG, generates different classifiers in a committee through stochastically changing both the attribute set and the distribution of the training set. We expect that SASCBAG can keep the stable behavior of Bagging and SASC, since different individual classifiers are also built in a stochastic manner for SASCBAG. In addition, we expect that SASCBAG is more accurate than either Bagging or SASC alone, since the diversity and independence of committee members are increased due to the change of the attribute set and the distribution of the training set at the same time. Consequently, we expect that the shortcoming of Bagging and SASC being less accurate than Boosting on average can be overcome through the combination.

We briefly present Bagging, SASC, and Boosting for decision tree learning in the following section, and then describe the SASCBAG algorithm in Section 3.

---

[1] The idea of SASC is very close to that of other two variants of this type of method proposed by Dietterich and Kong [7] and Ali [8]. We do not expect that they perform significantly differently. Therefore, we only use SASC in this study.

Section 4 reports experiments for evaluating SASCBAG. The final section summarizes our findings and discusses some directions for future research.

2 Bagging, SASC, and Boosting

Since SASCBAG can be thought of as a combination of Bagging and SASC, we briefly describe Bagging and SASC in this section. In addition, Boosting is used as a comparison algorithm for empirically evaluating SASCBAG, so we briefly discuss Boosting in this section as well. The classification process of these three committee learning algorithms is presented in Section 2.4. Further details are available from [5] for Bagging; [16] for SASC; [13, 4, 11, 12] for Boosting.

2.1 Bagging

The primary idea of Bagging [5] is to generate a committee of classifiers with each from a bootstrap sample of the original training set. BAG, our implementation of Bagging, uses C4.5 [26] as its base classifier learning algorithm.

Given a committee size T and a training set D consisting of m instances, BAG generates $T - 1$ bootstrap samples with each being created by uniformly sampling m instances from D with replacement. It, then, builds one decision tree using C4.5 from each bootstrap sample. Another tree is created from the original training set.

2.2 SASC

During the growth of a decision tree, at each decision node, a decision tree learning algorithm searches for the best attribute to form a test based on some test selection functions [26]. The key idea of SASC is to vary the members of a decision tree committee by stochastic manipulation of the set of attributes available for selection at decision nodes. This creates decision trees that each partition the instance space differently.

We use C4.5 [26] with the modifications described below as the base classifier learning algorithm of SASC. When building a decision node, by default C4.5 uses the information gain ratio to search for the best attribute to form a test [26]. To force C4.5 to generate different trees using the same training set, we modified C4.5 by stochastically restricting the set of attributes available for selection at a decision node. This is implemented by using a probability parameter P.[2] At each decision node, an attribute subset is randomly selected with each available attribute having the probability P of being selected. The available attributes refer to those attributes that have non-negative gain values. For nominal attributes, they must not have been used in the path from the root to the current node. Numeric attributes are always available for selection. This stochastic attribute subset selection process will be repeated, if no attribute was selected and there are some attributes available at this node. The objective is to make sure that at

---

[2] The value of P does not change during induction.

least one available attribute is included in the subset if possible. After attribute subset selection, the algorithm chooses the attribute with the highest gain ratio to form a test for the decision node from the subset. A different random subset is selected at each node of the tree.

The modified version of C4.5 is called **C4.5SAS** (**C4.5** Stochastic Attribute Selection). The only difference between C4.5SAS and C4.5 is that when growing a tree, at a decision node, C4.5SAS creates an attribute subset and uses the best attribute in it to form a test as described above. All other parts are identical for these two algorithms. With $P = 1$, C4.5SAS generates the same tree as C4.5.

Having C4.5SAS, the design of SASC is very simple. SASC invokes C4.5SAS T times to generate T different decision trees to form a committee. Here, all the trees are pruned trees. As in Boosting, the first tree produced by SASC is the same as the tree generated by C4.5. For further details about C4.5SAS and SASC, see [16].

2.3 Boosting

Boosting is a general framework for improving base learning algorithms, such as decision tree learning, rule learning, and neural networks. The key idea of Boosting was presented in Section 1. Here, we describe our implementation of the Boosting algorithm with decision tree learning, called BOOST. It follows the Boosted C4.5 algorithm (AdaBoost.M1) [4] but uses a new Boosting equation as shown in Equation 1, derived from [11].

Given a training set D consisting of m instances and an integer T, the number of trials, BOOST builds T pruned trees over T trials by repeatedly invoking C4.5 [26]. Let $w_t(x)$ denote the weight of instance x in D at trial t. At the first trial, each instance has weight 1; that is, $w_1(x) = 1$ for each x. At trial t, decision tree H_t is built using D under the distribution w_t. The error ϵ_t of H_t is, then, calculated by summing up the weights of the instances that H_t misclassifies and divided by m. If ϵ_t is greater than 0.5 or equal to 0, $w_t(x)$ is re-initialized using bootstrap sampling, and then the Boosting process continues. Note that the tree with $\epsilon_t > 0.5$ is discarded,[3] while the tree with $\epsilon_t = 0$ is accepted by the committee. Otherwise, the weight $w_{t+1}(x)$ of each instance x for the next trial is computed using Equation 1. These weights are, then, renormalized so that they sum to m.

$$w_{(t+1)}(x) = w_t(x)exp((-1)^{d(x)}\alpha_t), \tag{1}$$

where $\alpha_t = \frac{1}{2}ln((1 - \epsilon_t)/\epsilon_t)$; $d(x) = 1$ if H_t correctly classifies x and $d(x) = 0$ otherwise.

2.4 Decision Making in BAG, SASC, and BOOST

At the classification stage, for a given example, BAG, SASC, and BOOST make the final prediction through committee voting. In this paper, a voting method that

---

[3] This step is limited to $10 \times T$ times.

uses the probabilistic predictions produced by all committee members without voting weights is adopted. With this method, each decision tree returns a distribution over classes that the example belongs to (see [16], for the computation of class distributions). The decision tree committee members vote by summing up the class distributions provided by all trees. The class with the highest score (sum of probabilities) wins the voting, and serves as the predicted class of BAG, SASC, and BOOST for this example. Class distribution provides more detailed information than is obtained when each committee member votes for a single class, and this information is meaningful for committee voting.

There are three other approaches to voting. One is using the categorical predictions provided by all trees, without voting weights. In this case, each tree produces a single predicted class for an example. Then, the committee predicts the most frequent class returned by all trees. This voting method corresponds to the method used in the original Bagging [5].

The other two methods are the same as the two mentioned above but each tree is given a weight α_t for voting, which is a function of the performance of the decision tree on the training set, and is defined in Equation 1. The last of these alternatives, weighted voting of categorical predictions, corresponds to the original AdaBoost.M1 [13, 2, 3, 1, 11]. These three voting methods perform either worse than or similarly to the method that we use here.[4] See [16] for a detailed empirical study on this issue.

3 SascBag: A Combination of Sasc and Bag

To generate accurate committees, individual classifiers in the committees should be as diverse, independent, and accurate as possible. Bagging and SASC create committee members in different manners. Combining them should be able to increase the diversity and independence of committee members. There is no reason to believe that this combination will considerably reduce the accuracy of each individual classifier. As Geoffrey Webb suggested,[5] we expect that the combination will improve the accuracy of learned committees.

We implemented SASCBAG for decision tree learning by combining BAG and SASC. Figure 1 presents its details. SASCBAG builds each decision tree, except the first one, by invoking C4.5SAS on a bootstrap sample of the original training set. The only difference between SASC and SASCBAG is that the former builds each tree on the original training set. Note that SASCBAG builds the first tree using the original training set and without stochastically selecting attributes. The reason is to follow the idea of Bagging and Boosting to make the committee contain a tree that is the same as the one created by C4.5. It is worth mentioning that, like SASC and BAG, SASCBAG is amenable to parallel and distributed

---

[4] Quinlan [4] uses categorical predictions with the confidence with which a tree classifies a test instance as the weight of this tree for voting in the Boosted C4.5 algorithm. In effect, this treatment is similar to using probabilistic predictions without weights discussed here.

[5] Personal communication, 1998.

SASCBAG(*Att*, *D*, *P*, *T*)
    INPUT: *Att*: a set of attributes,
                D: a training set represented using *Att* and classes,
                P: a probability value,
                T: the number of trials.
    OUTPUT: a committee, *H*, consisting of *T* trees.

H_1 := **C4.5SAS**(*Att*, *D*, 1)
FOR each *t* from 2 to *T*
{ D' = generating a bootstrap sample from *D*
    H_t := **C4.5SAS**(*Att*, D', *P*)   }
RETURN *H*

Fig. 1. The SASCBAG learning algorithm

processing while Boosting is not, since the generation of each tree in SASCBAG is independent from that of another while it must occur sequentially for Boosting.

At the classification stage, SASCBAG makes the final classification through voting. As BAG, SASC, and BOOST, by default SASCBAG also uses the probabilistic predictions without weights method for voting, since it performs either better than or similarly to the other three voting methods on average [16].

4 Experiments

In this section, we empirically evaluate SASCBAG using a representative collection of natural domains. The objective is to examine whether it can significantly reduce the error rate of C4.5, and how it performs relatively to BAG, SASC, and BOOST with respect to accuracy.

4.1 Experimental Domains and Methods

Forty natural domains from the UCI machine learning repository [27] are used. They include all the domains used in [4] for studying Boosting and Bagging. This test suite covers a wide variety of different domains with respect to dataset size, the number of classes, the number of attributes, and types of attributes.

In every domain, two stratified 10-fold cross-validations [28] are carried out for each algorithm. The result of each algorithm in each domain reported is an average value over 20 trials. All the algorithms are run on the same training and test set partitions with their default option settings except when otherwise indicated. All of BOOST, BAG, SASC, and SASCBAG use probabilistic predictions (without voting weights) for voting to decide the final classification. The number of trials (the parameter *T*) is set at 100 for BOOST, BAG, SASC, and SASCBAG. The probability of each attribute being selected into the subset (the parameter *P*) is set at the default, 33%, for SASC and SASCBAG.

4.2 Results

Table 1 shows the error rates of the five algorithms. To facilitate the pairwise comparisons among these algorithms, error ratios are derived from Table 1 and presented in Table 2. An error ratio, for example for BOOST vs C4.5, presents a result for BOOST divided by the corresponding result for C4.5 – a value less than 1 indicates an improvement due to BOOST. To compare the error rates of two algorithms in a domain, a two-tailed pairwise t-test on the error rates of the 20 trials is carried out. The difference is considered as significant, if the significance level of the t-test is better than 0.05. In Table 2, **boldface** (*italic*) font, for example for BOOST vs C4.5, indicates that BOOST is significantly more (less) accurate than C4.5. The second last row in Table 2 presents the numbers of wins, ties, and losses between the error rates of the corresponding two algorithms in the 40 domains, and the significance levels of a one-tailed pairwise sign-test on these win/tie/loss records. The last row presents similar comparison results but treating insignificant wins and losses as ties.

From Tables 1 and 2, we have the following four observations.

(1) All the four committee learning algorithms can significantly reduce the error rate of the base decision tree learning algorithm, with SASCBAG achieving the lowest average error rate.

The average error rate of C4.5 in the 40 domains is 19.18%. BOOST, BAG, and SASC reduce it to 15.97%, 16.35%, and 16.10% respectively, while SASCBAG further reduces it to 15.55%. The average relative error reduction of SASCBAG over C4.5 is 19% in the 40 domains. It is 20%, 14%, and 16% for BOOST, BAG, and SASC respectively. A one-tailed pairwise sign-test shows that all of these error reductions are significant at a level better than 0.0001. Note that although the average error rate of SASCBAG is 0.42 percentage points lower than that of BOOST, the average relative error reduction of the former over C4.5 is 1 percentage point lower than that of the latter. The reason is that BOOST performs better than SASCBAG in domains where C4.5 has low error rates, and vice versa in domains where C4.5 has high error rates.

(2) On average, BOOST is more accurate than BAG and SASC, but the latter are more stable than the former in terms of less frequently obtaining significantly higher error rates than C4.5. However, a one-tailed sign-test shows that error difference between BOOST and either BAG or SASC is not significant at a level of 0.05. For detailed comparison among BOOST, BAG, and SASC, see [16].

(3) Combining SASC and BAG can further significantly reduce the error rates of decision trees. SASCBAG is also more accurate than BOOST on average.

The average relative error reductions of SASCBAG over BAG and SASC in the 40 domains are 6% and 4% respectively. SASCBAG obtains significantly lower error rates than SASC in 12 out of the 40 domains, and significantly higher error rates in 3 domains. It achieves significantly lower error rates than BAG in 13 domains, and in no domains does the latter obtain significantly lower error rates than the former. A one-tailed sign-test shows that SASCBAG is significantly more accurate than either SASC or BAG alone at a level better than 0.02.

SASCBAG is more accurate than BOOST in 25 out of the 40 domains, and is

Table 1. Error rates (%)

Domain	C4.5	Boost	Bag	Sasc	SascBag
Annealing	7.40	4.90	5.73	5.85	5.68
Audiology	21.39	15.41	18.29	18.73	17.64
Automobile	16.31	13.42	17.80	14.35	16.11
Breast (W)	5.08	3.22	3.37	3.44	3.08
Chess (KR-KP)	0.72	0.36	0.59	0.67	0.70
Chess (KR-KN)	8.89	3.54	7.80	9.26	8.35
Credit (Aust)	14.49	13.91	13.84	14.71	13.04
Credit (Ger)	29.40	25.45	24.95	25.10	23.35
Echocardiogram	37.80	36.24	33.57	37.01	33.19
Glass	33.62	21.09	27.38	25.27	23.17
Heart (C)	22.07	18.80	18.45	16.65	16.65
Heart (H)	21.09	21.25	20.38	18.88	18.85
Hepatitis	20.63	17.67	18.73	18.40	17.42
Horse colic	15.76	19.84	15.77	17.39	16.84
House votes 84	5.62	4.82	4.71	4.59	4.59
Hypo	0.46	0.32	0.45	0.46	0.44
Hypothyroid	0.71	1.14	0.71	0.76	0.81
Image	2.97	1.58	2.62	2.06	2.23
Iris	4.33	5.67	5.00	5.00	5.33
Labor	23.67	10.83	14.50	18.83	16.00
LED 24	36.50	32.75	31.00	29.00	30.00
Letter	12.16	2.95	5.93	3.74	3.92
Liver disorders	35.36	28.88	27.43	29.90	25.40
Lung cancer	57.50	53.75	42.50	45.83	50.00
Lymphography	21.88	16.86	18.50	18.48	15.43
NetTalk(Letter)	25.88	22.14	22.98	21.98	20.71
NetTalk(Ph)	18.97	16.01	17.33	18.03	16.49
NetTalk(Stress)	17.25	11.91	14.97	12.44	11.29
Pima	23.97	26.57	23.37	23.76	23.37
Postoperative	29.44	38.89	30.00	28.89	28.89
Primary tumor	59.59	55.75	55.46	54.72	55.02
Promoters	17.50	4.68	9.32	7.09	7.00
Sick	1.30	0.92	1.18	1.42	1.39
Solar flare	15.62	17.57	15.91	15.70	16.20
Sonar	26.43	14.64	21.12	16.32	19.68
Soybean	8.49	6.22	6.80	5.42	5.27
Splice junction	5.81	4.80	5.18	4.50	4.30
Vehicle	28.50	22.40	25.30	25.12	24.70
Waveform-21	23.83	18.33	19.67	19.83	17.33
Wine	8.96	3.35	5.29	4.48	1.96
average	19.18	15.97	16.35	16.10	15.55

Table 2. Error rate ratios

Domain	Boost	Bag	Sasc	SascBag	SascBag vs		
	vs C4.5				Boost	Bag	Sasc
Annealing	**.66**	**.77**	**.79**	**.77**	1.16	.99	.97
Audiology	**.72**	**.86**	**.88**	**.82**	1.14	.96	.94
Automobile	**.82**	1.09	.88	.99	*1.20*	.91	1.12
Breast (W)	**.63**	**.66**	**.68**	**.61**	.96	.91	.90
Chess (KR-KP)	**.50**	.82	.93	.97	*1.94*	1.19	1.04
Chess (KR-KN)	**.40**	.88	1.04	.94	*2.36*	1.07	.90
Credit (Aust)	.96	.96	1.02	**.90**	.94	.94	.89
Credit (Ger)	**.87**	**.85**	**.85**	**.79**	**.92**	.94	.93
Echocardiogram	.96	.89	.98	.88	.92	.99	**.90**
Glass	**.63**	**.81**	**.75**	**.69**	1.10	**.85**	**.92**
Heart (C)	**.85**	**.84**	**.75**	**.75**	.89	.90	1.00
Heart (H)	1.01	.97	.90	.89	.89	.92	1.00
Hepatitis	.86	.91	**.89**	**.84**	.99	**.93**	.95
Horse colic	*1.26*	1.00	1.10	1.07	**.85**	1.07	.97
House votes 84	.86	.84	.82	.82	.95	.97	1.00
Hypo	**.70**	.98	1.00	.96	1.38	.98	.96
Hypothyroid	*1.61*	1.00	1.07	1.14	**.71**	1.14	1.07
Image	**.53**	.88	**.69**	**.75**	*1.41*	**.85**	1.08
Iris	1.31	1.15	1.15	1.23	.94	1.07	1.07
Labor	**.46**	**.61**	.80	**.68**	1.48	1.10	.85
LED 24	.90	.85	.79	.82	.92	.97	1.03
Letter	**.24**	**.49**	**.31**	**.32**	*1.33*	**.66**	*1.05*
Liver disorders	**.82**	**.78**	**.85**	**.72**	**.88**	**.93**	.85
Lung cancer	.93	.74	.80	.87	.93	1.18	1.09
Lymphography	**.77**	**.85**	.84	**.71**	.92	**.83**	**.83**
NetTalk(Letter)	**.86**	**.89**	**.85**	**.80**	**.94**	**.90**	**.94**
NetTalk(Ph)	**.84**	**.91**	**.95**	**.87**	1.03	**.95**	**.91**
NetTalk(Stress)	**.69**	**.87**	**.72**	**.65**	**.95**	**.75**	**.91**
Pima	*1.11*	.97	.99	.97	**.88**	1.00	.98
Postoperative	*1.32*	1.02	.98	.98	**.74**	.96	1.00
Primary tumor	**.94**	**.93**	**.92**	**.92**	.99	.99	1.01
Promoters	**.27**	**.53**	**.41**	**.40**	1.50	**.75**	.99
Sick	**.71**	.91	1.09	1.07	*1.51*	1.18	.98
Solar flare	*1.12*	1.02	1.01	*1.04*	**.92**	1.02	*1.03*
Sonar	**.55**	**.80**	**.62**	**.74**	*1.34*	.93	*1.21*
Soybean	**.73**	**.80**	**.64**	**.62**	.85	**.77**	.97
Splice junction	**.83**	**.89**	**.77**	**.74**	**.90**	**.83**	.96
Vehicle	**.79**	**.89**	**.88**	**.87**	*1.10*	.98	.98
Waveform-21	**.77**	**.83**	**.83**	**.73**	.95	**.88**	**.87**
Wine	**.37**	**.59**	**.50**	**.22**	**.59**	**.37**	**.44**
average	.80	.86	.84	.81	1.08	.94	.96
w/t/l	33/0/7	34/1/5	32/1/7	35/0/5	25/0/15	30/1/9	26/3/11
p. of wtl	< .0001	< .0001	< .0001	< .0001	.0769	.0005	.0100
significant w/t/l	27/8/5	23/17/0	23/17/0	25/14/1	11/21/8	13/27/0	12/25/3
p. of sign. wtl	< .0001	< .0001	< .0001	< .0001	.3238	.0001	.0176

less accurate in the other 15 domains. If only considering significant differences, the former is better than the latter in 11 domains, and worse in 8 domains. However, a one-tailed sign-test fails to show that the frequency of SASCBAG being more accurate than BOOST is significant at a level of 0.05. The average relative error increase of SASCBAG over BOOST in the 40 domains is 8%. As mentioned before, this is because BOOST performs better than SASCBAG in domains in which they have relative low error rates, and vice versa in domains in which they have relatively high error rates. It might be thought a serious disadvantage of SASCBAG that the average error ratio compared to BOOST is greater than 1. However, we argue that this is a statistical anomaly, due to BOOST's superior performance when C4.5 has lower error rates. Increasing accuracy is as important as decreasing error. The average *accuracy ratio*, a measure that favors better performance at large error rates, of SASCBAG against BOOST (the accuracy for SASCBAG divided by the corresponding accuracy for BOOST) is 1.01. While a 1% gain in accuracy may not appear as dramatic as a 8% gain in error, the average accuracy of BOOST is 84.03%, but its average error rate is 15.97%. The latter is much smaller than the former. The 8% of 15.97% is 1.28%, while 1% of 84.03% is 0.84%. It can be seen that the difference in these two results is not great. In addition, when considering absolute error rate differences, SASCBAG is 0.42 percentage points lower than BOOST on average over the 40 domains. When considering absolute accuracy differences, SASCBAG is 0.42 percentage points higher than BOOST on average. In addition, the win/tie/loss records show that SASCBAG performs better than BOOST.

(4) Like SASC and BAG, SASCBAG is more stable than BOOST.

BOOST significantly increases the error rates of C4.5 in five out of the 40 domains, while SASCBAG does so only in one domain. Note that SASC and BAG obtain significantly higher error rates than C4.5 in no domains. The biggest relative error increase of BOOST over C4.5 in the 40 domains is 61%, which is significant, whereas it is 23% for SASCBAG, which is not significant. Therefore, SASCBAG is more stable than BOOST in terms of less frequently obtaining significantly higher error rates than C4.5 and obtaining lower error rate increases over C4.5. Our analysis suggests that the stochastic component of SASC, BAG, and SASCBAG contributes to their stable behavior.

5 Conclusions and Future Work

We have presented a new classifier committee learning algorithm, namely SASCBAG, that combines Bagging and SASC. It generates different classifiers to form a committee by stochastically changing both the attribute set and the distribution of the training set. Like Bagging and SASC, SASCBAG is amenable to parallel and distributed processing. This is an advantage of SASCBAG over Boosting for parallel machine learning and datamining.

Boosting, Bagging, and SASC use different manners to create different classifiers as members of a committee. In this paper, we have shown that combining Bagging and SASC can further improve the performance of classifier committee learning. Other types of combination technique of these three basic committee learning methods (other methods can also be considered) could also produce promising results, and are currently under investigation.

The empirical evaluation using a representative collection of natural domains shows that SASCBAG can significantly reduce the error rates of decision tree learning. Combining Bagging and SASC can achieve significantly lower error rates, on average, than either Bagging or SASC alone. On average, SASCBAG is also more accurate than Boosting. Additionally, like Bagging and SASC, SASCBAG is more stable than Boosting in terms of less frequently obtaining significantly higher error rates than C4.5 and obtaining lower error rate increases over C4.5.

Acknowledgements

The author is grateful to Ross Quinlan for providing C4.5. Many thanks to Geoffrey Webb for his helpful comments that improved the ideas and earlier versions of this paper.

References

1. Freund, Y.: Boosting a weak learning algorithm by majority. *Information and Computation* **121** (1996) 256-285.
2. Freund, Y. and Schapire, R.E.: A decision-theoretic generalization of on-line learning and an application to Boosting. Unpublished manuscript (1996a) (available at http://www.research.att.com/~yoav).
3. Freund, Y. and Schapire, R.E.: Experiments with a new Boosting algorithm. *Proceedings of the Thirteenth International Conference on Machine Learning.* San Francisco, CA: Morgan Kaufmann (1996b) 148-156.
4. Quinlan, J.R.: Bagging, Boosting, and C4.5. *Proceedings of the Thirteenth National Conference on Artificial Intelligence.* Menlo Park, CA: AAAI Press (1996) 725-730.
5. Breiman, L.: Bagging predictors. *Machine Learning* **24** (1996a) 123-140.
6. Breiman, L.: Arcing classifiers. Technical Report (available at: http://www.stat.Berkeley.EDU/users/breiman/). Department of Statistics, University of California, Berkeley, CA (1996b).
7. Dietterich, T.G. and Kong, E.B.: Machine learning bias, statistical bias, and statistical variance of decision tree algorithms. Technical Report, Dept of Computer Science, Oregon State University, Corvallis, Oregon (1995) (available at ftp://ftp.cs.orst.edu/pub/tgd/papers/tr-bias.ps.gz).
8. Ali, K.M.: *Learning Probabilistic Relational Concept Descriptions.* PhD. Thesis, Dept of Info. and Computer Science, Univ. of California, Irvine (1996).
9. Chan, P., Stolfo, S., and Wolpert, D. (eds): *Working Notes of AAAI Workshop on Integrating Multiple Learned Models for Improving and Scaling Machine Learning Algorithms* (available at http://www.cs.fit.edu/~imlm/papers.html), Portland, Oregon (1996).
10. Ali, K.M. and Pazzani, M.J.: Error reduction through learning multiple descriptions. *Machine Learning* **24** (1996) 173-202.

11. Schapire, R.E., Freund, Y., Bartlett, P., and Lee, W.S.: Boosting the margin: A new explanation for the effectiveness of voting methods. *Proceedings of the Fourteenth International Conference on Machine Learning.* Morgan Kaufmann (1997) 322-330.

12. Bauer, E. and Kohavi, R.: An empirical comparison of voting classification algorithms: Bagging, Boosting, and variants. To appear in *Machine Learning* (1998) (available at: http://reality.sgi.com/ronnyk/vote.ps.gz).

13. Schapire, R.E.: The strength of weak learnability. *Machine Learning* 5 (1990) 197-227.

14. Kwok, S.W. and Carter, C.: Multiple decision trees. Schachter, R.D., Levitt, T.S., Kanal, L.N., and Lemmer, J.F. (eds) *Uncertainty in Artificial Intelligence.* Elsevier Science (1990) 327-335.

15. Dietterich, T.G. and Bakiri, G.: Solving multiclass learning problems via error-correcting output codes. *Journal of Artificial Intelligence Research* 2 (1995) 263-286.

16. Zheng, Z. and Webb, G.I.: Stochastic attribute selection committees. Technical Report (TR C98/08), School of Computing and Mathematics, Deakin University, Australia (1998) (available at http://www3.cm.deakin.edu.au/~zijian/Papers/sasc-tr-C98-08.ps.gz).

17. Buntine, W.: *A Theory of Learning Classification Rules.* PhD. Thesis, School of Computing Science, University of Technology, Sydney (1990).

18. Kohavi, R. and Kunz, C.: Option decision trees with majority votes. *Proceedings of the Fourteenth International Conference on Machine Learning.* San Francisco, CA: Morgan Kaufmann (1997) 161-169.

19. Cherkauer, K.J.: Human expert-level performance on a science image analysis task by a system using combined artificial neural networks. Chan, P., Stolfo, S., and Wolpert, D. (eds) *Working Notes of AAAI Workshop on Integrating Multiple Learned Models for Improving and Scaling Machine Learning Algorithms* (available at http://www.cs.fit.edu/~imlm/papers.html), Portland, Oregon (1996) 15-21.

20. Tumer, K. and Ghosh, J.: Error correction and error reduction in ensemble classifiers. *Connection Science* 8 (1996) 385-404.

21. Zheng, Z.: Naive Bayesian classifier committees. *Proceedings of the Tenth European Conference on Machine Learning.* Berlin: Springet-Verlag (1998) 196-207.

22. Asker, L. and Maclin, R.: Ensembles as a sequence of classifiers. *Proceedings of the Fifteenth International Joint Conference on Artificial Intelligence.* San Francisco, CA: Morgan Kaufmann (1997) 860-865.

23. Wolpert, D.H.: Stacked generalization. *Neural Networks* 5 (1992) 241-259.

24. Zhang, X., Mesirrov, J.P., and Waltz, D.L.: Hybrid system for protein secondary structure prediction. *Journal of Molecular Biology* 225 (1992) 1049-1063.

25. Dietterich, T.G.: Machine learning research. *AI Magazine* 18 (1997) 97-136.

26. Quinlan, J.R.: *C4.5: Program for Machine Learning.* San Mateo, CA: Morgan Kaufmann (1993).

27. Merz, C.J. and Murphy, P.M.: UCI Repository of machine learning databases [http://www.ics.uci.edu/~mlearn/MLRepository.html]. Irvine, CA: Univ of California, Dept of Info and Computer Science (1997).

28. Kohavi, R.: A study of cross-validation and bootstrap for accuracy estimation and model selection. *Proceedings of the Fourteenth International Joint Conference on Artificial Intelligence.* San Mateo, CA: Morgan Kaufmann (1995) 1137-1143.

Multi-layer Incremental Induction

Xindong Wu and William H.W. Lo

School of Computer Science and Software Ebgineering
Monash University
900 Dandenong Road
Melbourne, VIC 3145, Australia
Email: xindong@computer.org

Abstract. This paper describes a multi-layer incremental induction algorithm, MLII, which is linked to an existing nonincremental induction algorithm to learn incrementally from noisy data. MLII makes use of three operations: data partitioning, generalization and reduction. Generalization can either learn a set of rules from a (sub)set of examples, or refine a previous set of rules. The latter is achieved through a redescription operation called reduction: from a set of examples and a set of rules, we derive a new set of examples describing the behaviour of the rule set. New rules are extracted from these behavioral examples, and these rules can be seen as meta-rules, as they control previous rules in order to improve their predictive accuracy. Experimental results show that MLII achieves significant improvement on the existing nonincremental algorithm HCV used for experiments in this paper, in terms of rule accuracy.

1 Introduction

Existing machine learning algorithms can be generally distinguished into two categories [Langley 1996], nonincremental algorithms which process all training examples at once, and incremental algorithms which handle training examples one by one. When an example set is not a static repository of data, for example, an example set may be added, deleted, or changed over a span of time, the learning on the example set cannot be an one-time process, so nonincremental learning has a problem dealing with changing example populations.

However, processing examples one by one in existing incremental algorithms is a very tedious process when the example set is extraordinary large. In addition, when some of the examples are noisy, the results learned from them must be reverted at a later stage. As stated in [Schlimmer and Fisher 1986], incremental learning provides predictive results that depend on the particular order of the data presentation.

This paper designs a new incremental learning algorithm, multi-layer induction, which divides an initial training set into subsets of approximately equal size, runs an existing induction algorithm on the first subset to obtain a first set of rules, and then processes each of the remaining data subsets at a time by incorporating the induction results from the previous subset(s). This way, multi-layer induction accumulates discovered rules from each data subset at each layer and produces a final integrated output which represents the original data more accurately. Any noisy data contained in the original data set can be partitioned and diminished in multi-layer induction into the small data subsets, thus the effects of noise would be diluted and induction efficiency can be increased. The existing algorithm used in this paper for experiments is HCV (Version 2.0) [Wu 1995], a nonincremental rule induction system that in many cases performs better than other induction algorithms in terms of rule complexity and predictive accuracy.

2 MLII: Multi-Layer Incremental Induction

Multi-layer incremental induction (MLII) applies three learning operations, data partitioning, rule reduction and rule generalization into a self-developed process. Generalization and reduction work together with sequential incrementality in order to learn and refine rules incrementally. After data partitioning, MLII handles example subsets sequentially through the generalization-reduction process. The sequential incrementality is particularly useful in cases of huge amount of data, in order to avoid exponential explosion.

2.1 Algorithm Outline

In the first step, the initial data set is partitioned into a number of data subsets of approximately equal size in a random shuffled way.

In the second step, a set of rules is learned from a first subset of examples by a generalization algorithm. The only assumption we make here is that the generalization algorithm is able to produce deliberately under-optimal solutions (rules are redundant). This way, the learning problem is given an approximate rule set, and this rule set will be refined with other data subsets.

The third step performs the transition toward another learning problem, namely the refinement of the previous set of rules. This transition is performed by a redescription operator called reduction, which derives a new set of behavioral examples by examining the behavior of the rule set from Step 2 over a second data subset.

From these behavioral examples, generalization can extract new rules, which are expected to correct defects and inconsistencies of previous rules. A sequence of rule sets is so gradually built. Successive applications of the above generalization-reduction process allow more accurate and more complex (because of disjunctive) rules to be discovered, by sequentially handling the subsets of examples.

2.2 Data Partitioning

Data partitioning affects the quality of information in each data subset and in turn affects the performance of multi-layer induction. Our main design aim here is to dilute the noise in the original data set and evenly distribute examples of different classes. The partitioning process is designed as follows.

1. Shuffle all examples in the training set randomly.
2. Put examples of each class into one separate group.
3. Count the number of examples in each class group and get the ratio of the numbers of each class.
4. Randomly select examples from each class group according to the above ratio and put them into a subset. This process performs for N times (where N is the number parameter adjusted by the user).

In some cases, the example ratio from different class groups cannot be integers and for the last subset some class groups may still have examples while other class groups do not have any examples. In these cases, we do not form the last subset, but insert the remaining examples randomly into the existing subsets.

2.3 Generalization

Generalization compresses initial information. It involves observing a (sub)set of training examples of some particular concept, identifying the essential features common to the positive examples in these training examples, and then formulating a concept definition based on these common features. The generalization process can thus be viewed as a search through a space of possible concept definitions for a correct definition of the concept to be learned. Because the space of possible concept definitions is vast, the heart of the generalization problem lies in utilizing whatever training data, assumptions and knowledge are available to constrain the search.

In MLII, discriminant generalization by elimination [Tim 1993] is adapted. A discriminant description specifies an expression (or a logical disjunction of such expressions) that distinguishes a given class from a fixed number of other classes. The minimal discriminant descriptions are the shortest expressions (i.e., with the minimum number of descriptors) distinguishing all objects in the given class from objects of other classes. Such descriptions specify the minimum information sufficient to identify the given class among a fixed number of other classes. These discriminant descriptions will be converted into generalization rules.

A generalization rule is a transformation of a description into a more general description that tautologically implies the initial description. Generalization rules are not truth-preserving but falsity preserving, which means that if an event falsifies some description, then it also falsifies a more general description. This is immediately seen by observing that $H \Rightarrow F$ is equivalent to $\neg F \Rightarrow \neg H$ (the law of contraposition).

Generalization by Elimination Generalization by elimination lies on the concept of the *star* methodology [Michalski 1984]. Its main originality is a logical pruning of counter-examples, based on the near-miss notion [Kodratoff 1984].

Let s be an example of an example (sub)set A. Any counter-example t of A gives a constraint over the generalization of s: the descriptors which discriminate t from s cannot be dropped simultaneously. The constraint $C(s, t)$ is a subset of integers, given by

$$C(s,t) = \{i | attribute\ i\ discriminates\ s\ and\ t\}.$$

A counter-example t_0 is a *maximal near-miss* to s in A if the constraint $C(s, t0)$ is minimal for the set inclusion, among all $C(s, t)$.

We search all maximal near-miss counter-examples to find such an integer set M that intersects every constraint $C(s,t)$. From M, a rule $R_{s...M}$ is defined as follows: its premises are the conjunction of all conditions in s. We prove that $R_{s...M}$ is a maximally discriminant generalization of s. By construction, for any counter-example t discriminated from s, there exists an element in $C(s,t)$ which belongs to M: the corresponding attribute allows to discriminate s and t; this condition is kept from s to $R_{s...M}$, hence $R_{s...M}$ still discriminates t.

The search for M can be achieved by a graph exploration, which is exponential with respect to the number of constraints. However, it is enough for a subset M to intersect all $C(s,t)$ for t maximally near-miss to s. This generalization by elimination therefore reduces the size of exponential exploration by a preliminary (polynomial) pruning.

Predicate Calculus for Reduction On the discriminant rules obtained above, we apply predicate calculus [Leung 1992] to generate more general rules. The following is a list of formulae (where X, Y and Z each represent a conditional statement and $\neg$ represents complement (*not*)) we have used in our MLII system.

1. $\neg(\neg(X)) \equiv X$
2. $X \wedge Y \equiv Y \wedge X$
   (the commutative law of conjunction)
3. $X \wedge (Y \wedge Z) \equiv (X \wedge Y) \wedge Z$
   (the associative law of conjunction)
4. $X \vee X \equiv X$
5. $X \vee Y \equiv Y \vee X$
   (the commutative law of disjunction)
6. $X \vee (Y \wedge Z) \equiv (X \vee Y) \wedge (X \vee Z)$
   (the distributive law)
7. $X \wedge (Y \vee Z) \equiv (X \wedge Y) \vee (X \wedge Z)$
   (the distribute law)
8. $\neg(X \vee Y) \equiv (\neg X) \wedge (\neg Y)$ (De Morgan's law)
9. $\neg(X \wedge Y) \equiv (\neg X) \vee (\neg Y)$ (De Morgan's law)

These laws are useful to combine different conditional rules together by *symbolic resolution* in order to get generalized conditional rules (meta-rules).

2.4 Reduction

Let Ω denote the description space of the learning domain, B be the set of rules expressed within Ω, and L be the number of rules in B. For any rule in B, we say an example in Ω fires the rule if the description of the example satisfies the premises of the rule.

Definition 1. Reduction, denoted by ΠB, is a redescription operator defined as follows.

$$\Pi B: \Omega \longrightarrow [0,1]^L$$
$$\Pi B: s \in \Omega \longrightarrow \Pi B(s) = [\ r_j(s), j = 1, \cdots, L]$$

where the *reduced descriptor* r_j is given by:

$$r_j(s) = \begin{cases} 1 \ if \ s \ fires \ the \ \text{j-th} \ rule \ in \ B \\ 0 \ otherwise \end{cases}$$

The redescription transforms each example in Ω into an L-dimension description. The class of the example does not change.

Definition 2. From a learning set A and a rule set B, the reduced learning set, denoted by A_B, is generated as follows.

$$A_B = [(\Pi_B(s_i), Class(s_i)) | (s_i, Class(s_i)) \in A]$$

where $Class(s_i)$ indicates the class information of the s_i example.

The reduced learning set A_B describes the behaviour of B on the examples in A. It is expressed in boolean logic, whatever the initial representation of A and B are. Generalization can be carried out on the reduced learning set to produce a refined set of rules. The refined set of rules is applied to a new subset of the original training examples to obtain a new learning set for further generalization, and so on.

The number of examples in the reduced learning set A_B is generally less than the number of examples in the initial learning set A. But the reduced learning set must still contain enough information in order to enable a further generalization. So the number of examples in each data subset should not decrease too much.

2.5 Refinement of Previous Rules

At each learning layer, generalization on a reduced learning set A_B refines the rule set B from previous layer(s).

First, if a rule in B has a good predictive accuracy, this information is implicitly available from the reduced learning set A_B: it is often fired by the examples in A and consequently, the corresponding descriptor in A_B takes the value 1, and the class of these examples is often the same as the rule class. Hence, there is a correlation in A_B between a value of this descriptor and a value of the class information, and rules with a good predictive accuracy will be discovered again by next generalization. This process is stable, as good rules in B are carried on.

Second, the same argument above ensures that irrelevant rules are dropped: if a rule is irrelevant, the associated reduced descriptor is irrelevant with respect to A_B too. As generalization is supposed to detect and drop irrelevant descriptors, the rules learned from A_B do not keep previous irrelevant rules.

Third, generalization discovers links among descriptors and classes. In the reduced learning set A_B, examples are described according to the rules in B they trigger. Hence, the triggering of rules can be generalized from A_B: the generalization solves conflicts arising among previous rules.

	Expermnt 1	**Expermnt 2**	**Expermnt 3**	**Expermnt 4**
Database	Person 1	Person 2	Labor-Neg 1	Labor-Neg 2
No of training examples	100	300	100	300
Number of attributes	4	4	5	5
Number of classes	2	2	2	2
Missing values	10	15	23	10
Misclassifications	3	7	17	7
Level of noise	low	low	high	low
No of test examples	30	50	50	80
No of HCV rules	8	12	16	10
Accuracy of HCV rules	88.92%	77.33%	81.71%	87.77%
No of MLII rules	6	7	10	8
Accuracy of MLII rules	98.88%	90.73%	92.57%	94.61%

Table 1. Summary of Experiments 1-4.

3 Experiments

MLII has been implemented in C++ on Unix workstations. In this section, we set up a few experiments to compare the predictive accuracy of MLII rules with the HCV induction program [Wu 1995].

3.1 Experiments 1 to 4

Table 1 provides a summary of the data sets used in our first four experiments and the results.

The 4 databases were all copied from the University of California at Irvine machine learning database repository [Murphy & Aha 95], and each contains certain level of noise. These databases have been selected because each of them consists of two standard components when created or collected by the original providers: a training set and a test set. The databases have been used "as is". Example ordering has not been changed, neither have examples been moved between the sets. For each database, we ran each of HCV (Version 2.0) and MLII (with 4 layers) 10 times on the training set, and the accuracies listed in Tables 1 are average results from the test set.

For all the 4 databases, MLII (with 4 layers) performs better than HCV (Version 2.0). The accuracy difference on each database between MLII and HCV is statistically significant. Therefore, we conclude that with a carefully selected number of layers, MLII achieves significant improvement on HCV in terms of rule accuracy.

3.2 Experiment 5

The purpose of this experiment is to check the change of accuracy of MLII rules generated on each layer in a n-layer induction. The data set used is labor-neg1, the same as used in Experiment 3.

Layer No.	Rule Set	Test Set Accuracy
1	B	73.331%
2	C1	63.214%
	C2	69.643%
3	D1	54.123%
	D2	70.813%
	D3	80.771%
4	E1	45.634%
	E2	60.811%
	E3	75.123%
	E4	92.512%

Table 2. Results of Experiment 5.

Table 2 shows the results, and Figure 1 provides a visual illustration of the same results.

From the graph in Figure 1, it is obvious that at the first layer, the accuracy of the induced rules on the same test data decreases when the number of layers increases in MLII. The highest is HCV induction (just one layer) and lowest is the 4-layer MLII. The reason is that HCV uses the whole 300 training examples to generate rules, while MLII uses only a subset (one-Nth of the training set) at the first layer for HCV to generate an initial rule set.

We have tried up to 4 layers with MLII, and the rule accuracy on the test set is always increasing at the last layer. A question arise here. What is the optimal number of layers for MLII on a training set? Based on various experiments we have carried out, it depends on the size and the noise level of the training set. If the size of the training set is very large (e.g. 5000 examples or more) and there exists high-level noise, more layers of learning allows deeper rule refinement to dilute the noise. Otherwise, if we use a large number of layers on a small data set, MLII can not gain enough information to generate approximate (redundant) rules for later successive refinement, and this in turn affects the completeness and consistency of the final generated rules.

For each curve in Figure 1, we can find that the test set accuracy increases significantly from the first to second layer rules, still increases from the second to third layer and the improvement decreases as the number of layers increases. This indicates that the approximate rules generated at the first layer are successively refined at the following learning layers (i.e., rules become more consistent and accurate) and finally achieve an optimal level and are no longer redundant. Therefore, the successive learning should be stopped and the optimal rules be taken as the final rules. In general, it is not the case that the more layers we use, the more accurate final rules we will get.

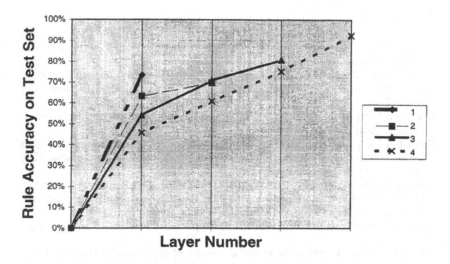

Fig. 1. Rule Accuracy at Each Induction Layer of Experiment 5.

4 Conclusions

Multi-layer induction learns accurate rules in an incremental manner. It handles subsets of training examples sequentially. Compared to handling training examples one by one in existing incremental learning algorithms, this sequential incrementality is more flexible, because the size of data subsets is controlled by data partitioning in multi-layer induction. Multi-layer induction suits noisy domains, because data partitioning dilutes the effects of noise into data subsets. Five experiments were carried out in this paper to quantify the gains of MLII, and significant improvement of rule accuracy has been achieved.

Multi-layer induction is designed for handling large and/or noisy data sets. With medium-sized, noisefree data sets, we have not found much improvement of MLII on HCV induction in rule accuracy. The information quality of the data sets is a critical factor to determine the number of layers in MLII. The noise level, number of training examples, numbers of attributes and classes, and value domains of attributes are all contributing factors when applying MLII to a particular data set.

Future work will involve applying MLII to other induction programs, such as C4.5 [Quinlan 1993], extending the experiments to larger data sets and comparing with other incremental learning methods such as case-based learning [Ram 1990] which learns incrementally case by case and treats each case as a chunk of partially matched rules.

References

[Kodratoff 1984] Kodratoff, Y. (1984). Learning complex structural descriptions from examples. *Computer vision, graphics and image processing 27*.

[Langley 1996] Langley, P. (1996). *Elements of Machine Learning*. Morgan Kaufmann.

[Leung 1992] Leung, K. T. (1992). *Elementary Set Theory* (3 Ed.). Hong Kong University Press.

[Michalski 1984] Michalski, R. S. (1984). A theory and methodology for inductive learning. *Artificial Intelligence 20*(2).

[Michalski 1985] Michalski, R. S. (1985). Knowledge repair mechanisms: Evolution versus revolution. In *Proceedings of the Third International Machine Learning Workshop*, 116–119. Rutgers University.

[Murphy & Aha 95] Murphy, P.M. & Aha, D.W. (1995). UCI Repository of Machine Learning Databases, Machine-Readable Data Repository. University of California, Department of Information and Computer Science, Irvine, CA.

[Quinlan 1993] Quinlan, J. R. (1993). *C4.5: Programs for Machine Learning*. Morgan Kaufmann.

[Ram 1990] Ram, A. (1990). Incremental learning of explanation patterns and their indices. In *Proceedings of the Seventh International Conference on Machine Learning*, 49–57. Morgan Kaufmann.

[Schlimmer and Fisher 1986] Schlimmer, J. and Fisher, D. (1986). A case study of incremental concept induction. In *Proceedings of the Fifth National Conference on Artifical Intelligence*, pp. 496–501. Morgan Kaufmann.

[Tim 1993] Tim, N. (1993, Feb). Discriminant generalization in logic program. *Knowledge Representation and Organization in Machine Learning 14*(3), 345–351.

[Wu 1995] Wu, X. (1995). *Knowledge Acquisition from Databases*. Ablex.

An Adaptive Agent Oriented Software Architecture[*]

Babak Hodjat   Christopher J. Savoie   Makoto Amamiya

Department of Intelligent Systems
Graduate School of Information Science and Electrical Engineering
Kyushu University
6-1 Kasugakoen, Kasuga-shi
Fukuoka 816, Japan
http://www_al.is.kyushu-u.ac.jp/~bobby/index.html

Abstract. A new approach to software design based on an agent-oriented architecture is presented. Unlike current research, we consider software to be designed and implemented with this methodology in mind. In this approach agents are considered adaptively communicating concurrent modules which are divided into a white box module responsible for the communications and learning, and a black box which is the independent specialized processes of the agent. A distributed Learning policy is also introduced for adaptability.

Topics: Agent Architectures, Agents Theories.

Keywords: Agent-oriented systems, Multi-Agent Software architectures, Distributed Learning,

1. Introduction

The classic view taken with respect to *Agent Oriented Systems* is to consider each agent an autonomous individual the internals of which are not known and that conforms to a certain standard of communications and/or social laws with regard to other agents [5]. Architectures viewing agents as such have had to introduce special purpose agents (e.g., broker agents, planner agents, interface agents...) to shape the structure into a unified entity desirable to the user [2]. The intelligent behavior of these key agents, with all their complexities, would be vital to the performance of the whole system.

---

[*] This paper describes a new adaptive, multi-agent approach to software architecture, currently being investigated as an on going project at Kyushu University.

Another trend in this view is to give the possibility to the agents to query each other's internal knowledge and states through the communications protocols, while at the same time conserving the black-box view of the agents. Inevitably, defining and controlling such issues as conflicts of interest between agents, honesty, helpfulness, and gullibility, have had to be taken into account and dealt with [4]. The most important aspect of this dominant view is that agent architectures are considered to be unifiers of pre-written, separate modules (heterogeneity) [3]. Each of these modules was probably designed without having this higher structure in mind, and is completely different (be it in the code, the machine it is implemented upon, the designer, or the purpose of design). Agent-based Software Engineering was originally invented to facilitate the creation of software able to interpolate in such settings and application programs were written as software agents [6]. On the other hand, methodologies dealing with the internal design of agents tend to view them primarily as intelligent, decision-making beings. In these methodologies, techniques in Artificial Intelligence, Natural Language Processing, machine learning, and adaptive behavior seem to overshadow the agent's architecture, in many cases undermining the main purpose of the agent [7][13].

For instance, one can view agents as reinforcement learning agents with a set of tools to be chosen with respect to environmental senses. Such a view, however well suited for agent learning techniques, may not be readily applied to more algorithmic applications, thus misleading one to assume that such applications should not be or could not be implemented as agents.

In this paper, we wish to present an agent-oriented methodology, which can be universally applied to any software design. The Adaptive Agent Oriented Software Architecture (AAOSA) builds upon and extends the widely accepted object oriented approach to system design. The primary difference sited between Agent-oriented and Object oriented programming has been the language of the interface [6]. In this paper we will suggest an approach in which communication between agents can be done independent of language. This language independent communication will still hold as the main difference with the Object oriented methodology. Another aspect that makes agents more attractive to use in software than objects is their quality of volition. Using AI techniques, adaptive agents are able to judge their results, then modify their behavior (and thus their internal structure) to improve their perceived fitness. First we will clarify our definition of agents, which is somewhat relaxed with respect to the classic definitions. Then the steps by which software should be designed using AAOSA methodology are described. Some suggestions as to how adaptive learning and communication language independence can be achieved are briefly presented next. To clarify the AAOSA methodology, we present an example application in the form of a simple multimodal map program and show some of the resulting features.

2. Our Definition of Agents

Our definition of agents is more in line with the ones given by [12] and [2], and we classify our agents as having the following properties [5]: reactivity, autonomy, temporal continuity, communicative capabilities, team orientation, mobility, learning (adaptive), and flexibility. The resulting multi-agent system we have in mind is a partially connected one [5]. A direct communication specification-sharing approach is taken here to enhance collaboration. Instead of using assisted coordination, in which agents rely on special system programs (facilitators) to achieve coordination [2], in our approach new agents supply other agents with information about their capabilities and needs. To have a working system from the beginning, the designers preprogram this information at startup. This approach is more efficient because it decreases the amount of communication that must take place, and does not rely on the existence, capabilities, or biases of any other program [6].

Adaptive agents are adaptively communicating, concurrent modules. The modules therefore consist of three main parts: A communications unit, a reward unit, and a specialized processing unit. The first two units we will call the white box and the third the black box parts of an agent (Figure 1). The main responsibilities of each unit follow:

The communications unit: This unit facilitates the communicative functions of the agent and has the following sub-systems:
- *Input of received communication items:* These items may be in a standard agent communication language such as KQML. Later in this paper we will see that only a small subset is needed here.
- *Interpreting the input:* Decides whether the process unit will need or be able to process certain input, or whether it should be forwarded to another agent (or agents). Note that it is possible to send one request to more than one agent, thus creating competition among agents.
- *Interpretation Policy:* (e.g., a table) Determines what should be done to the input. This policy could be improved with respect to the feedback received for each interpretation from the rewards unit. Some preset policy is always desirable to make the system functional from the beginning. In the case of a system reset, the agent will revert to the basic hard-coded startup information. The interpretation policy is therefore comprised of a preset knowledge base, and a number of learned knowledge bases acquired on a per-user basis. A *learning* module will be responsible for conflict resolutions in knowledge base entries with regard to feedback received on the process of past requests. Past requests and what was done with them are also stored until in anticipation of their feedback.
- *Address-Book:* keeps an address list of other agents known to be useful to this agent, or to agents known to be able to process input that can not be processed by this agent. Requests to other agents may occur when:
  - ➢ The agent has received a request it does not know how to handle,
  - ➢ The agent has processed a request and a number of new requests have been generated as a result.
This implies that every agent have an address and there be a special name server unit present in every system to provide agents with their unique addresses (so that new agents can be introduced to the system at run time). This address list should be dynamic, and therefore adaptive. It may be limited; it may also contain

information on agents that normally send their requests to this agent. In many cases the Address-book could be taken as an extension of the Interpretation Policy and therefore implemented as a single module.

- *Output:* Responsible for sending requests or outputs to appropriate agents, using the Address-book. A confidence factor could be added to the output based on the interpretations made to resolve the input request or to redirect it. We shall see later in the paper that this could be used when choosing from suggestions made by competing agents by output agents.

The rewards unit: Two kinds of rewards are processed by this module: outgoing and incoming. An agent is responsible for distributing and propagating rewards being fed back to it*. This unit will determine what portion of the incoming reward it deserves and how much should be propagated to requesting agents. The interpreter will update its interpretation policy using this feedback. The rewards will also serve as feedback to the Address-book unit, helping it adapt to the needs and specifications of other agents. The process unit could also make use of this feedback.

The rewards may not be the direct quantification of user states and in most cases will be interpretations of user actions made by an agent responsible for that. We will further clarify this point later in the paper.

The process unit: This unit is considered a black box by our methodology. The designer can use whatever method it deems more suitable to implement the processes unique to the requirements of this agent. The only constraints being that the process unit is limited to the facilities provided by the communications unit for its communications with other agents. The process unit also may use the rewards unit to adapt its behavior with regard to the system. Note that each agent may well have interactions outside of the agent community. Agents responsible for user I/O are an example of such interactions. These agents generally generate requests or initiate reward propagation in the community, or simply output results.

The white box module can easily be added to each program module as a *transducer*. According to definition [6] the transducer mediates between the existing program (the process unit) and other agents. The advantage of using a transducer is that it requires no knowledge of the program other than its communication behavior.

We mentioned the process unit as being able to conduct non-agent I/O. It is easy to consider I/O recipients (e.g. files or humans) as agents and make the program redirect its non-agent I/O through its transducer. Other approaches to agentification (wrapper and rewriting) are discussed in [6].

---

* A special purpose agent is responsible for the interpretation of user input as feedback to individual user requests. This agent will then initiate the reward propagation process.

3. Software design

The software as a whole should be thought of as a society, striving to accomplish a set of requests. The input requests are therefore propagated, processed by agent modules that may in turn create requests to other agents. Again, it is up to the designers to break down the system, as they feel suitable. Hierarchies of agents are possible and agents can be designed to be responsible for the minutest processes in the system. It is advisable that each agent be kept simple in its responsibilities and be limited in the decisions it needs to make to enhance its learning abilities. The overhead of the required units (the white box) should be taken into consideration.

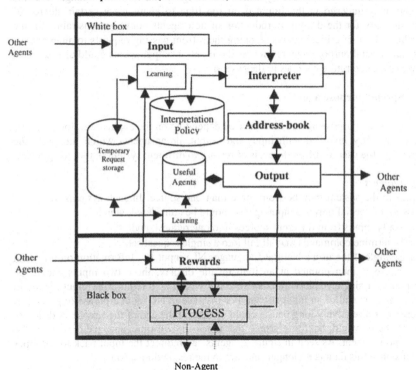

Non-Agent

Fig. 1. Each agent is comprised of a black box section (specialties) and a white box section (communications).

Agents can be replaced at run-time with other more complete agents. The replacement can even be a hierarchy or network of new agents breaking down the responsibilities of their predecessor. This feature provides for the incremental design and evaluation of software.

We recommend each agent's responsibilities and actions to be clearly defined at design time. As stated in the previous section, many aspects of the white box units should also be preset for each agent according to its definition. To have a working system from the beginning, it is also necessary to define the preliminary communication links between the agents at design time. It should be noted that these communications might change through time, for instance in the case of the introduction of newer agents. Thus, the most important phase in the design of software with this methodology will be to determine the participating agents and their capabilities, although the precise details of how they will eventually communicate with each other may not be known at design time.

There are a number of ways by which the designer can limit the changes that his design may undergo in the future or at run time to guarantee a certain degree of functionality for the design. Introduction of new agents could be constrained in the Address Book of critical agents stopping them from passing requests to alien agents. Certain special purpose agents such as the input or output agents could also serve to limit unwanted future changes to the system.

3.1. Special purpose agents

Some special purpose agents may be used depending on the application, for example, agents directly involved with input and output, or an agents which interprets the actions of the user as different levels of reward to different system output[*] (Figure 2)

Input Agents
Inputs to the system may be from more than one source. In such systems, one, or a network of special purpose input agents should be considered, which:
• Unify inputs from different sources into one request, and/or
• Determine commands that all fall into a single request set.
For example if the user's Natural Language (NL) input is: "Information on this" and the mouse is then pointed at an item on the display, these two inputs should be unified as a single request. Interactive input would also require the input agents to determine the end of an input stream. For instance in NL input a phrase (e.g., Do! or Please!) or a relatively long pause, could determine the end of the stream. A different policy here would be to interpret the input in real-time and redirect it to the appropriate agent. As seen in figure 2, agents can redirect the input back to the input agents once this data is no longer relevant to the responding agent.

Output Agents
This special purpose agent decides which response suggested by various agents should be actuated, thus ensuring competition between agents. The decision may be made based on a combination of different criteria and may depend on a specific request. The criteria may be speed, confidence, or other checks that could in turn be made by quality assurance agents. After the final choice has been made, the output agent will ask the specific suggesting agent to actualize its suggestion, or the decision may be redirected to actuator agents. The output agents may be more than one, thus

---

[*] One of these agents may be the reward agent itself, thus tuning itself with the user.

breaking the decision making process into a hierarchy. For instance, competing agents could have an output agent decide between them and the output agents in turn could have a higher-level output agent. Safety mechanisms to ensure the requests will not be stuck in cycles of infinite deadlock loops between the agents could be another responsibility of the output agents. Special purpose safeguard agents could also be used.

Feedback Agents
Any adaptive system needs a reward feedback that tells it how far from the optimum its responses have been. This reward could be explicitly input to the system, or implicitly judged from input responses by the system itself. In the case of implicit rewarding, an agent could be responsible for the interpretation of the input behavior and translating it into rewards. The criteria that could be used depend on the system. For instance in an interactive software application a repeat of a command, remarks indicating satisfaction or dissatisfaction, user pause between requests or other such input could be translated into rewards to different output. The feedback agents could also be more than one depending on the different judgement criteria and a hyper-structure [8] or hierarchy might be designed to create the rewards. One way of propagating the feedback reward through the system would be to be aware of the different output and to pass the interpreted reward to the final (output) layer, which will, in turn, pass it back to the previous agents involved in that particular output.

A name server unit is also required to make possible the dynamic introduction of new agents to the system. Each new agent will have to obtain its name (or address) from this name server so that conflicts do not occur and so agents can be referred to throughout the system. Input requests (commands) to the system should be tagged with the user-id that has issued them because interpretation is done on a per-user basis. Reward fed back to the system should also incorporate the request-id to which the reward belongs.

4. Communication Language

In Agent-Based Software Engineering [6], Agents receive and reply to requests for services and information using a declarative knowledge representation language KIF (Knowledge Interchange Format), a communication language KQML (Knowledge Query and Manipulation Language) and a library of formal ontologies defining the vocabulary of various domains. KQML [4] is a superset of what is needed as a communication language between the AAOSA agents and may well be used effectively. The stress on adaptability eliminates the need for elaborate languages and even a simple message passing protocol between the agents should be sufficient.

The main request string may be made of different types of information (e.g., Character strings, voice patterns, images, etc...). Various standard information may be passed along with the main request string including: The originator agent, sender agent, the user initiating this request, request id, and/or a time stamp. The request string itself could be comprised of any item of information ranging from natural language requests from the user, to specialized inter-agent messages. Introductory messages sent by new agents (introduced to the system at run time), could also be incorporated in the request string, or sent under preset standards such as those provided by KQML. Other specialized (and possibly standardized) information that should be passed includes the reward propagation data.

5. An Example: A multimodal map [1]

Multiple input modalities may be combined to produce more natural user interfaces. To illustrate this technique [1] presents a prototype map-based application for a travel-planning domain. The application is distinguished by a synergistic combination of handwriting, gesture and speech modalities; access to existing data sources including the World Wide Web; and a mobile handheld interface. To implement the described application, a distributed network of heterogeneous software agents was augmented by appropriate functionality for developing synergistic multimodal applications. We will consider a simplified subset of this example to show the differences of the two approaches. A map of an area is presented to the user and she is expected to give view port requests (e.g., shifting the map or magnification), or request information on different locations on the map. For example, a user drawing an arrow on the map may want the map to shift to one side. On the other hand the same arrow followed by a natural language request such as: "Tell me about this hotel." May have to be interpreted differently.

[Cheyer et al 96] use the Open Agent Architecture (OAA) [2] as a basis for their design. In this approach, based on a "federation architecture" [9], the software is comprised of a hierarchy of facilitators and agents. The facilitators are responsible for the coordination of the agents under them so that any agent wanting to communicate with any other agent in the system must go through a hierarchy of facilitators (starting from the one directly responsible for it). Each agent, upon introduction to the system, provides the facilitator above it with information on its capabilities (Figure 3). No explicit provision is given for learning.

An example design based on AAOSA is shown in figure 4. It must be noted here that the design shown in figure 4 is not rigid and communication paths may change through time with the agents adapting to different input requests. The NLP and pointer input agents determine the end of their respective inputs and pass them on to the input regulator. This agent in turn determines whether these requests are related or not. It then passes it down to the agent it considers more relevant to the request. The output agents hierarchically sift the outputs suggested by the shifting, magnification, hotels, restaurants and general information agents. Note that combinations of these output suggestions could also be chosen for actuation. The feedback agent provides the system with rewards interpreted from user input. Some of the differences in the two designs are given below:

• The AAOSA design is much more distributed and modular by nature and many of the processes concentrated in the facilitator agents in figure 3 are partitioned and simplified in figure 4.

- AAOSA is more of a network or hyper-structure [8] of process modules as opposed to the hierarchical tree like architecture in the OAA design.
- AI behavior such as natural language processing and machine learning are incorporated on the architecture rather than introduced as new agents (as is the case with the natural language macro agent in figure 3).

It must be stressed that AAOSA like architectures could be achieved with an OAA if we take each OAA facilitator and its macro agents as one agent and add learning capabilities to each facilitator. Another point worth mentioning is that agents in OAA are usually pre-programmed applications linked together through facilitators. The designers have a lesser say over the software architecture as a whole because they are forced to use what has already been designed, possibly without the new higher-level framework in mind.

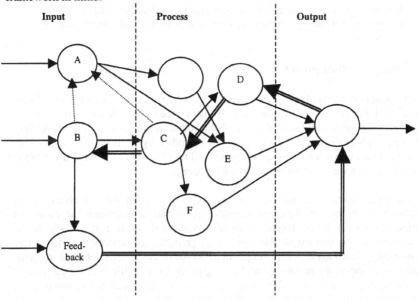

Fig. 2. Example of agent-oriented software architecture. Input agent B may redirect input that does not belong to it to agent A (dotted arrow). This redirection may even happen in later stages (e.g., from C to A). Output suggestions from agents D, E, and F are considered in the output agent and one (in this case D's) is chosen for actuation. The feedback agent uses input directives or indirect behavioral assumptions to calculate a numerical representation of the reward for each output. This reward is then fed back to the agents (e.g., double line arrows).

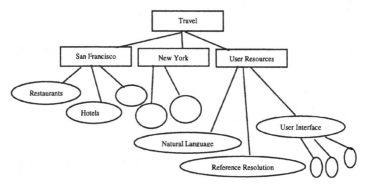

Fig. 3. A structural view of the multimodal map example as designed using OAA in [1]. Boxes represent Facilitators, ellipses represent macro agents and circles stand for modality agents.

6. Interpretation policy

Each agent matches the input pattern with its stored key patterns and finds the closest match and a degree of confidence for it. If this degree of confidence is lower than a threshold, the agent will forward the request to other agents for whom it is confident of their ability to process the request. If no other agent is known with these specifications, either a random action (weighted by the confidence on that action) is chosen, or the request is forwarded to another agent.

In the simplest case the pattern matching process is comprised of checking the presence or absence of certain segments (e.g., words) to determine the course of action that needs to be taken. In more complicated forms patterns should be discovered in the context of the input (e.g., grammar or semantics). This is one reason why if each agent is kept simple in the range of the decisions it needs to make based on its input, the matching and learning process is simplified. A simple pattern matching may be enough to determine the course of action needed. For instance the occurrence of a pointer drag or word patterns including such phrases as "go", or "shift" could cause the map agent in our example (Figure 4) to redirect the request to the shifting agent. Whereas words such as "bigger", "smaller", "magnify", "I can't see" may cause it to send the request to the magnification agent (Figure 5).

Techniques such as those given in [10] could help sort the patterns according to their information value. The nature of the information depends on the application and the agent specializing in it. For example such information as the time between inputs and the loudness or general pattern of the input speech wave could be useful for the feedback agent. The information value of patterns varies depending on the agent (Figure 5).
We will not offer any solutions as to how the interpretation policy of each agent should be stored and updated. Some points that should be taken into consideration while pondering a solution follow:

- It is very important for the interpreter agent to be able to load pre-defined policies at start-up. These are not learned, but hard wired by the engineers. The engineers also determine how much of this initial policy could be undermined through learning.
- It is of equal importance for other agents to be able to contribute to this policy, for instance introducing themselves to the Address-book as possible references.
- The interpretation policy should be dynamic to allow learning of new interpretation rules.
- In many cases the learned policies should be stored on a per-user basis.

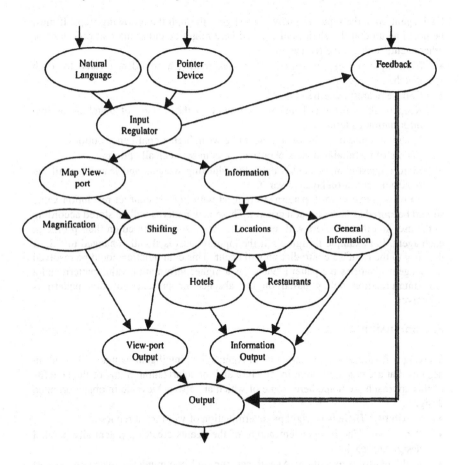

Fig. 4. The multimodal map example as designed based on AAOSA.

7. Learning

Adaptability in AAOSA materializes in three forms:
- The ability of the system to accept new agents at run time,
- The ability of each agent to accept unexpected input or requests,
- The ability of each agent to adapt its behavior according to the feedback it receives (i.e., learning).

Some features of a pattern learning algorithm that may be suitable for AAOSA are briefly mentioned in this section.

Each agent upon the input of a new request goes through the following steps. It must be noted again that the choices mentioned here might be either internal processes or other agents to direct the request to.
- Scan input request for stored patterns estimating a confidence value for each match.
- Choose nearest pattern's choice.
- Keep track of patterns being thrown away in the process of matching as low information patterns [10].
- In case of close ties, choose at random between higher confidence options.
- In case of no reliable match, choose at random between all options*.
- Store request-choice decided upon for adjusting weights and learning until the feedback arrives (delayed reward).

In case of negative reward, patterns in request with highest conflict resolution value should be stored as new decision criteria. These new patterns will be stored according to the user so different users will receive different responses based on their profile in each agent. For example in figure 5 if the input request is slightly changed to: "Shift the *view* to the right", a contradiction will occur. This contradiction could be resolved if the agent identifies the pattern "view" as a higher information value pattern and a new interpretation policy based on the absence or presence of this pattern is conceived.

8. Conclusion

Viewing software as a hyper-structure of Agents (i.e., intelligent beings) will result in designs that are much different in structure and modularization. Some of the benefits of this approach are noted here, some of which are also achievable in object oriented design.
- Flexibility: There is no rigid predetermination of valid input requests.
- Parallelism: The independent nature of the agents creates a potentially parallel design approach.
- Multi platform execution: Agents can run and communicate over networks of computers (on the Internet for instance).
- Runtime addition of new agents and thus incremental development of software.

---

* Random functions may be weighted according to confidence.

- Software additions by different designers: Different designers can introduce different agents to compete in the software, making this design methodology attractive for commercial applications.

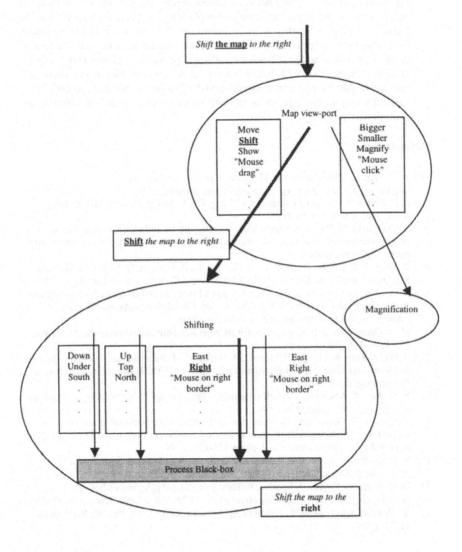

Fig. 5. Each agent needs to identify a small subset of the information in the request and act upon that. This is also an example of distributed Natural Language Processing. Low information (throwaway) patterns (shown in *italic*) vary depending on the agent.

- Reusability of agents.
- Incremental design and evaluation.
- Learning and Intelligence: The distributed nature of learning introduced in this paper suggests a powerful adaptive software design that potentially breaks down an application to a hyper-structure of simple learning modules [8]. Another AI technique that could readily be incorporated into the agents is *artificial evolution* [11]. The mere presence of a reward for each agent makes the introduction of death (removal of an agent from the software) possible. This will make way for other agents, perhaps with better learning techniques, to take over. There will also inevitably be numerous variables to be fine-tuned for each agent. These variables may be thought of as the agent's genes and optimized through this evolutionary process.

References

1. A. Cheyer, L. Julia, Multimodal Maps: An Agent-based Approach, http://www.ai.sri.com/~cheyer/papers/mmap/mmap.html, 1996.
2. P. R. Cohen, A. Cheyer, M. Wang, S. C. Baeg, OAA: An Open Agent Architecture, AAAI Spring Symposium, 1994.
3. S. Cranefield, M. Purvis, An agent-based architecture for software tool coordination, in *the proceedings of the workshop on theoretical and practical foundations of intelligent agents*, Springer, 1996.
4. T. Finin, J. Weber, G. Wiederhold, M. Genesereth, R. Fritzson, D. McKay, J. McGuire, S. Shapiro, C. Beck, Specification of the KQML Agent-Communication Language, 1993.
5. S. Franklin, A. Graesser, Is it an Agent or just a Program? A Taxonomy for Autonomous Agents, in: *Proceedings of the Third International Workshop on Agents Theories, Architectures, and Languages*, Springer-Verlag, 1996.
6. M. R. Genesereth, S. P. Ketchpel, Software Agents, Communications of the ACM, Vol. 37, No. 7, July 1994.
7. B. Hayes-Roth, K. Pfleger, P. Lalanda, P. Morignot, M. Balabanovic, A domain-specific Software Architecture for adaptive intelligent systems, IEEE Transactions on Software Engineering, April 1995.
8. B. Hodjat, M. Amamiya, The Self-organizing symbiotic agent, http://www_al.is.kyushu-u.ac.jp/~bobby/1stpaper.htm, 1998.
9. T. Khedro, M. Genesereth, The federation architecture for interoperable agent-based concurrent engineering systems. In *International Journal on Concurrent Engineering, Research and Applications*, Vol. 2, pages 125-131, 1994.
10. R. R. Korfhage, Information Storage and Retrieval, John Wiley & Sons, June 1997.
11. M. Mitchell. An Introduction to Genetic Algorithms. MIT Press, 1996.
12. D. C. Smith, A. Cypher, J. Spohrer, KidSim: Programming Agents without a programming language, Communications of the ACM, Vol. 37, No. 7, pages 55-67, 1994.
13. Y. Shoham, Agent-oriented programming, Artificial Intelligence, Vol. 60, No. 1, pages 51-92, 1993.

An Architecture for Multi-agent Negotiation Using Private Preferences in a Meeting Scheduler

Toramatsu Shintani and Takayuki Ito

Department of Intelligence and Computer Science,
Nagoya Institute of Technology
Gokiso, Showaku, Nagoya, 466-8555, JAPAN
E-mail: {tora itota}@ics.nitech.ac.jp

Abstract. We present an architecture for multi-agent negotiation for implementing a distributed meeting scheduler. In the scheduling system, an agent is assigned to an user who plans private schedules and events. An agent negotiates with other agents about making an public schedule by referring user's private schedules and preferences. The multi-agent negotiation we proposed here facilitates reaching an agreement among agents effectively. A characteristic function based on a game theory is used for reflecting users' preferences in the negotiation process. We have implemented a distributed meeting scheduler to see how effectively the multi-agent negotiation can be used. The result shows that the multi-agent negotiation based on private preferences is an effective method for a distributed meeting scheduler.

1 Introduction

The negotiation problem in a multi-agent system is being investigated very actively[10]. A distributed scheduler for a meeting[4] is an application of multi-agent systems. In this paper, we present an architecture for multi-agent negotiation for implementing a distributed meeting scheduler[13]. The meeting scheduler plans schedules (such as a meeting) based on a multi-agent system. The reason we propose the distributed meeting scheduler is that a meeting scheduler requires us to invent new methods to develop an efficient system on multi-agent environments.

In social decision making, there is a coalition formation problem that we need to clarify a trade-off between "reaching a consensus" and " maximizing own expected payoffs". During the past few years, several solutions to the coalition formation problem have been presented by researchers in DAI(Distributed Artificial Intelligence)[11][15]. Cooperation among autonomous agents may be mutually beneficial even if membership in the coalition may maximize a personal outcome. In Japanese social decision making, some of solutions for the coalition can be based on persuasion[8] (that is, "Settoku" in Japanese) . In agent negotiation, the persuasion mechanism can be defined as follows[7] . When agent A persuades agent B, agent A sends a persuasion message to agent B. Then, according to the message, agent B tries to change its belief. If agent B is able to change its belief, the persuasion is a success. However, if agent B cannot change its belief, the persuasion is a failure. A concrete method for implementing the persuasion mechanism based on private preferences is given in section 3.

In the meeting scheduler, an agent is assigned to an user who plans private schedules and events in a calendar. A supervisor manages to plan schedules and events. We call the supervisor the host user. An agent assigned to a host user is called a host agent. Candidates invited to an event are called attendee users. An agent assigned to an attendee user is called an attendee agent. In order to schedule a public event, a host agent negotiates with other attendee agents by using the users' private schedules and preferences[3]. Agents can reach an agreement about a public event. The point is that agents need to clarify a trade-off between an agreement about scheduling a public event and users' private schedules. We improve the trade-off by using a persuasion process[6][7] and by controlling negotiation among agents by means of an characteristic function. The characteristic function is used in a coalition game concerned with game theory[9]. The multi-agent negotiation we proposed here facilitates reaching an agreement among agents effectively. The characteristic function we introduced can reflect the users' preferences in a negotiation process among agents.

Multi-agent meeting scheduling has been a current topic of research and has been studied widely. Sen and Durfee[12] has been focused on solving meeting scheduling problem using a central host agent. However, user preferences are not taken into account. Ephrati and Zlotkin[4] presented an alternative approach which is economic in flavor. They introduced the Clark Tax mechanism as a method for removing manipulability from agents. Garrido and Sycara[5] has been focused on decentralized meeting scheduling with user preferences taking into account. They did not, however, establish how to reach an agreement among agents and compromise with other agents.

The aim of this paper is to present a new architecture for multi-agent-negotiation for realizing a best coalition formation algorithm in a distributed meeting scheduler based on the persuasion mechanism. The paper consists of five sections. In section 2, we show the architecture of reflecting private preferences and the coalition formation in our system. In section 3, we present the persuasion process based on private preferences. In section 4, we show an example the persuasion mechanism and discuss the results of the multi-agent negotiation. Some concluding remarks are presented in section 5.

2 Reflecting Private Preferences

2.1 Multi-agent Problem Solving

In order to improve the multi-agent problem solving, DAI researchers develop and employ negotiation protocols, e.g., the contract net protocol[14], the multi-stage negotiation[2], and the unified negotiation protocol[11]. The contract net protocol is a well known protocol for assigning subtask to agents involved in multi-agent problem solving. In the contract net protocol two kinds of agent, manager and contractor, exist. The contract net protocol is based on a human activity metaphor. The most significant feature of the contract net protocol is that both managers and contractors "award" or "bid" according to their own standard. Namely, a manager uses an evaluation function to evaluate the bids made by the "bidders". Each constructor will select a task that matches its own standard. By using a framework of the contract net protocol, the targets, here, are to clarify a new multi-agent negotiation mechanism for realizing a distributed meeting scheduler, and implement a persuasion mechanism for coordinating actions and forming a coalition.

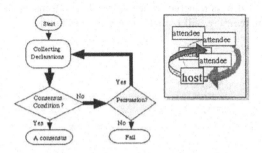

Fig. 1. The outline of the persuasion protocol

Fig.1 shows a new idea for realizing a persuasion protocol for a distributed meeting scheduler. In this protocol, two kinds of agent, host and attendee, exist. This protocol is also based on a human activity metaphor. That is a persuasion for reaching consensus among attendee. In this persuasion protocol, agents negotiate with other agents using user's private preferences and attributes decided by a host user. At the beginning of negotiation, a host agent collects attendee agents' declarations. Then the host agent checks whether the declarations fill a consensus condition. A consensus condition is filled if a size of a certain coalition is larger than a size decided by a host user. If a consensus condition is filled, agents reach a consensus. After agents reach a consensus, a host agent broadcasts the result to all attendee agents. If the consensus conditions is not filled, agents negotiate using the persuasion process to reach a consensus. If the persuasion process is not satisfied the cooperation for meeting scheduling fails.

2.2 The Distributed Meeting Scheduler

Fig.2 shows a scheduling process we used in a distributed meeting scheduler. Before scheduling meetings, each user has inputted their private schedules into their own calendar. The meeting scheduler has four phases. In the first phase, an user requests for scheduling a meeting. The user becomes a host user. In the second phase, a host user decides attributes as condition for a meeting.

Attributes of a meeting involves length and size. The length of a meeting is the number of hours. This length means how long the meeting is held. The size of a meeting is the number of attendee. A host user choices time intervals that satisfy the attributes of the meeting. We call these time intervals candidate time intervals. A host agent proposes candidate time intervals in the beginning of the third phase. In the third phase, by using a persuasion protocol, agents negotiate with other agents using users' private preferences (i.e., schedules and attributes) of the meeting that are decided by a host user. In the forth phase, a host agent broadcasts the result of the agent negotiation. If agents can not reach a consensus, the result of a negotiation is that a schedule for a meeting proposed by a host user is rejected. If agents reach a consensus, the result is that a schedule for the meeting will be held as a public schedule.

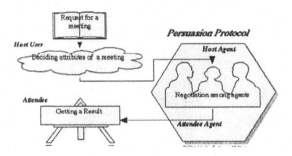

Fig. 2. A process in a meeting scheduler

Fig.3 shows the outline of a calendar used in the meeting scheduler. The calendar has information about events. An event is represented by using an event slot that includes an event name, a date, time and a weight (that is, a weighting value) for an event . For example, in Fig.3 "xyz-12/12/1996-9:00to12:00-weight(5)" is an event, in which "xyz" is an event name, "12/12/1996" shows a date(that is, month/date/year), "9:00to12:00" shows a time interval and "weight(5) " is a weight. A time interval is a set of contiguous time slots. In the example, the time interval 9:00to12:00 is composed of contiguous time slots "10:00", "11:00", and "12:00". Users input information of their private events into their calendar. Users can attach weights (their preferences) to events. The information of a private event involves a length of the event. For example, if an event needs 3 time slots, the event's length is 3. A weight of an event takes an integer which is less 9. The larger the number, the more importantly the judgment is agreed upon. 1, 3, 5, 7, 9 represent "slightly important", " important", "strongly important", "very strongly important", " extremely important" respectively (2,4,6,8 are used for intermediate values). 0 represents "unimportant". Fig.3 shows that an user has a strongly important event held for 3 hours from "12:00" on "12/12/1996". As the result, the user inputs the weight 5 at the time slot "12:00", "13:00", and "14:00" in the calendar.

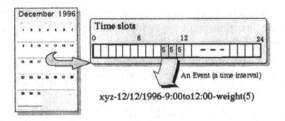

Fig. 3. The example of a calendar

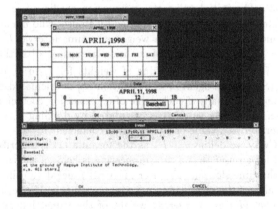

Fig. 4. The example of the user interface

Fig.4 shows the user interface of the distributed meeting scheduler. The programming language used for the current implementation is Java language[1]. Two calendar windows, the window labels are "APRIL, 1998", "MAY, 1998", are at the top of Fig.4. The window placed at the center of Fig.4, that window label is "Date", shows the time slots. At the bottom the window that window label is "Event", shows details of a private event on the time slot . In this example, the user has an event "Baseball" from the "13:00" to "17:00" on "11 APRIL, 1998". The weighting value is 4.

2.3 The Coalition Formation

In the multi-agent negotiation, agents play a coalition game. In a coalition game, $N = \{a_1, a_2, \ldots, a_n\}$ is a set of agents. A coalition is a subset of agents $S_{I_j} \subset N$. The coalition S_{I_j} is formed by agents who declare a candidate time interval I_j. $v(S_{I_j})$ is the value of the coalition S_{I_j}, which is the total utility that the members of S_{I_j} can achieve by coordinating together. The $v(S_{I_j})$ is calculated by a characteristic function. In our system, we define the characteristic function that reflects users' preferences as follows:

$$W_{a_i}(I_j) = \frac{1}{|I_j|} \times \sum_{t_{jk} \in I_j} \{9 - w_{a_i}(t_{jk})\} \tag{1}$$

$$v(S_{I_j}) = \sqrt{(\frac{g}{n} \times |S_{I_j}| \times \overline{W(I_j)})^2 + \sum_{a_i \in S_{I_j}} (p_{a_i} \times W_{a_j}(I_j))^2} \tag{2}$$

$$u_{a_i}(S_{I_j}) = \frac{p_{a_i}}{\sum_{a_k \in S_{I_j}} p_{a_k}} \times v(S_{I_j}) \tag{3}$$

where a_i is an agent $(i = 1, 2, \ldots, n)$, p_{a_i} is a persuasion coefficient for agent a_i, and S_{I_j} is a coalition for a time interval $I_j = \{t_{ji}, t_{j2}, \ldots, t_{jl}\}, (j = 1, 2, \ldots, m)$. t_{jk} is a time slot. The initial value of a persuasion coefficient is 1. $w_{a_i}(t_{jk})$ is subjective weight for the time slot t_{jk} decided by an user who manages an agent a_i . In the formula $w_{a_i}(I_j)$ denotes a weight of a time interval I_j that is used by an agent a_i . The g is the size of coalition groups. $|S_{I_j}|$ is the size of the coalition S_{I_j} . $\overline{W(I_j)}$ is the mean value of weights for I_j in a coalition S_{I_j} . The utility $u_{a_i}(S_{I_j})$ for an agent a_i in a coalition S_{I_j} is calculated by dividing a coalition value $v(S_{I_j})$ equally if each value of a persuasion coefficient for agents is 1. Otherwise, the utility $u_{a_i}(S_{I_j})$ is calculated by dividing a coalition value $v(S_{I_j})$ in proportion to a value of a persuasion coefficient p_{a_i}.

The reason why we define $w_{a_i}(I_j)$ as the formula (1) is described below. It is inconvenient for an user that a certain meeting is held on the time interval I_j that includes the time slot t_{jk}. The user must get a negative utility $-w_{a_i}(t_{jk})$. We hope the value of the utility becomes a positive value. Hence, we define the interval weight $w_{a_i}(I_j)$ as an average weight of the value that subtracted the weight $w_{a_i}(t_{jk})$ from the maximum value of the weight 9 in the time interval I_j.

The reason why we define $v(S_{I_j})$ as the formula (2) is described below. We use the size of the coalition $|S_{I_j}|$ and the agent's interval weight $w_{a_i}(I_j)$ as the main factors in the $v(S_{I_j})$. Firstly, we think that when a group makes a decision, minorities in the group tend to follow majority's opinions, because individuals in the majority get benefit more than individuals in the minority. To realize this idea, we use the size of the coalition $|S_{I_j}|$ in the $v(S_{I_j})$. By using $|S_{I_j}|$, agents can get more utilities in the larger coalition, in other words, agents in the minority tend to move into the majority. Secondly, we think that when a group schedules a meeting, if a member scheduled a private event on a time slot, the member hopes that the meeting should not be scheduled on the time slot. In the system, if the agent a_i has an event scheduled in the time interval I_j, then the value of the $w_{a_i}(I_j)$ reduces. Agents avoid to reduce the $w_{a_i}(I_j)$, because the agents try to get more utilities, namely, the agents are selfish. Therefore, by using the agent's time interval weight $w_{a_i}(I_j)$ in the $v(S_{I_j})$, a meeting on the time interval that includes less private events is apt to be agreed by the agents.

In social decision making, there is a trade-off between "reaching a consensus" and "reflecting private preferences in the social decision". At first, we make the value of the persuasion coefficient p_{a_i} to 1. Thereby, the value of the $v(S_{I_j})$ is affected by the time interval weight $w_{a_i}(I_j)$. In this condition, agents participate in coalitions according to their time interval weight rather than according to the size of coalitions. In other words, we can reflect private preferences in group decision (that is, "reflecting private preferences in the social decision" of the trade-off), because a time interval weight associates with private preference.

However, it is difficult to reach a consensus in the condition mentioned above. To facilitate reaching a consensus (that is, "reaching a consensus" of the trade-off), we increase the value of the persuasion coefficient P_{a_i} in the persuasion process (described in the section 3). In the persuasion process, agents try to change the coalitions by changing the persuasion coefficient. To change the value of the coefficient, an agent needs to compromise with other agents by using own heuristics.

3   The Persuasion Process

Fig. 5 shows the persuasion process for a negotiation among agents. At the beginning of negotiation, a host agent inputs attributes of an event (such as a meeting, candidate time intervals, and so on) into an electrical message-passing board. We call the board the circulation board. In order to collect attendee agents' declarations for their choices, a host agent starts to circulate a circulation board. A circulation board is circulated among agent in a predesignatory order. When an attendee agent receives a circulation board, an attendee agent declares his/her preferences as follows: (1)At first, an attendee agent calculates his/her expected utility of each candidate time intervals by using the characteristic function. (2)The attendee agent inputs an candidate time interval that maximizes his/her expected utility into a circulation board. In other words, the attendee agent declares his/her preferences. (3)At last, the attendee agent sends the circulation board to the next agent in a circulating order. The circulating order depends on user's status. For example, in a laboratory professor's agent can declare prior to a student's agent. In this case, a professor can affect a student's declaration and other users who declare after a professor.

A circulation board is circulated among all attendee agents and returned to a host agent. A host agent checks whether declarations described in the board satisfy a condition for reaching an agreement. The condition is satisfied if a number of agents in a coalition is larger than that of participants decided by a host user. A coalition is a subset of agents who enter for an candidate event. The size of a collation means the number of agents in the coalition. If the condition is satisfied, agents reach an agreement, and a host agent broadcasts the result of an agreement to all attendee agents.

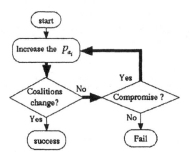

Fig. 5. The framework of the persuasion process

If a condition for an agreement is not satisfied, a host agent checks whether the size of a coalition can be changed or not. In order to change the size, a host agent starts to circulate a circulation board again. A host agent continues to circulate a circulation board until sizes of any coalitions does not change or does not satisfy conditions for any agreements. If the sizes of any coalitions can be changed or do not satisfy conditions for any agreements, the host agent try to negotiate with other agents by using a persuasion process we proposed here.

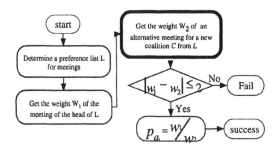

Fig. 6. The outline of a compromise process

In the persuasion protocol, at first, the value of the persuasion coefficient p_{a_i}

is checked. If the value of the p_{a_i} is increased in a compromise process, the value of the $v(S_{I_j})$ is increased more effectively compared with the previous calculation. The change of the value of the $v(S_{I_j})$ gives an opportunity for changing the size of a coalition among agents. After increasing the value of the p_{a_i}, a host agent collects attendee agents' declarations. Attendee agents declare their preferences based on the newest persuasion coefficient. After collecting the declarations, a host agent checks whether a condition for an agreement is satisfied or not. If the condition is satisfied, agents reach an agreement. To increase the value of the persuasion coefficient, an agent needs to be compromised by using own heuristics.

Fig.6 illustrates the outline of a compromise process based on heuristics. The process can be shown as follows: (1)Determine a preference list L for candidate meetings. In the list L, the meetings are arranged in descending order of importance. (2)Get the weight W_1 of the meeting of the first element of the preference list L. (3)Get the weight W_2 of the alternative meeting of the preference list L. In order to revise a coalition, an agent compares the size of the weight W_1 and the weight W_2. The agent can accept the alternative meeting(that is, a new coalition) if the range of the change (that, is from W_1 to W_2) is small (namely, takes ±2), because we assume that the verbal scale for weighting meetings is not so precise. The change of the weight corresponds to changing the persuasion coefficient P_{a_i} in which we use the ratio of W_1 to W_2 (that is, W_1/W_2).

4 Discussions

4.1 An Example

In this section, we show an example for the multi-agent negotiation we proposed here. Suppose that the candidate time intervals are I_0, I_1, I_2, the host agent is a_{host} and the invitee agents are $a_i = \{a_0, a_1, a_2, a_3, a_4\}$. Table 1 shows the agents' time interval weights $w_{a_i}(I_j)$.

In the table 1, the agent a_0's time interval weights for the time interval I_0 (that is, $W_{a_i}(I_0)$) is 5. Suppose that the time interval I_0 consists of the time slots, t_1(e.g., 5/1/1996-12:00), t_2(e.g., 5/1/1996-13:00), t_3(e.g., 5/1/1996-14:00). In this case, the user, who manages the agent a_0, has weighted events in the time interval as follows: t_1 is weighted to 3, t_2 is weighted to 3, t_3 is weighted to 6. The value of the $W_{a_0}(I_0)$ is 5 by following the formula (1). In the same way, the other agent's interval weights are calculated.

The agents negotiate by using these interval weights. Suppose the order for the circulation is a_0, a_1, a_2, a_3, a_4, the initial value of the persuasion coefficient p_{a_i} is 1 and the consensus condition is that more than 4 agents participate in a coalition. At first, the agent a_0 received the circulation board from the host agent. The agent a_0 calculates his/her own expected utility for each time intervals following the formula (1). The expected utility for an agent is calculated on each coalitions by supposing that the agent participates in the coalition. In this case, because the size of all coalitions is 1, $u_{a_0}(S_{I_1}) > u_{a_0}(S_{I_2}) > u_{a_0}(S_{I_0})$. Because the $u_{a_0}(S_{I_1})$ is the highest expected utility, the agent a_0 takes part in the coalition S_{I_1}. The other agents calculate the expected utility in the same way. After all agents declare their preferences, the coalitions are $S_{I_0} = \{a_2\}, S_{I_1} = \{a_3, a_1, a_0\}$, $S_{I_2} = \{a_4\}$. In this time, any coalitions do not change. However, the consensus condition is not filled. In order to satisfy the consensus condition, at first, the host agent a_{host} tries to adopt the coalition S_{I_1} by using his/her own private preferences. The host agent a_{host} starts to negotiate with the agent a_2 and a_4 by using the persuasion process. To increase the value of the persuasion coefficient p_{a_i} for the agent a_2 and a_4, the agents a_{host} circulate the circulation board iteratively. In this case, the agent a_4 can increase the value of the p_{a_4} by using the compromise process. The agent a_2 fails to increase the value of the p_{a_2} in the process. By increasing the value of the p_{a_4} the agent a_4 takes part in the coalition S_{I_1}. Namely, the coalitions are $S_{I_0} = \{a_2\}, S_{I_1} = \{a_3, a_1, a_0, a_4\}$, $S_{I_2} = \{\}$ ($\{\}$ means an empty set). Because the coalition $|S_{I_1}| = 4$, the consensus condition is filled and the agents reach a consensus. The host agent broadcasts to the users that the meeting is held on the time interval I_1.

Table 1. An Example of time interval weights

agents	I_0	I_1	I_2
a_0	5	9	8
a_1	4	9	0
a_2	7	0	0
a_3	4	5	3
a_4	3	5	6

4.2 Some Features of the Multi-agent Negotiation

In this section, we discuss some features of the multi-agent negotiation protocol we proposed. We can summarize the features as follows:

(1) The agent negotiation protocol can facilitate reaching a consensus among agents. Because the persuasion coefficient is increased until the consensus condition is filled, the agents can reach a consensus certainly.

(2) The agent negotiation protocol can reflect group's preference. In an example, when we take a preference order of the agents into consideration, according to the simple majority rule, the group of agents selects the time interval I_1. The preference order means the set of time intervals in order of weight. In the example, the agent a_0's preference order is $I_1 \geq_{a_0} I_2 \geq_{a_0} I_0$. $x \geq_i y$ means that i prefers x to y. Table 2 shows all agents' preference orders in the example.

In the simple majority rule, if a majority of agents in a group prefer x to y, the group prefers x to y. In this example, the number of agents who prefer I_0 to I_1 is 1, while the number of agents who prefer I_1 to I_0 is 4. Thereby, the group prefers I_1 to I_0 according to the simple majority rule. The other preference order of the group is decided in the same way. Then, the group's preference order is $I_1 \geq_{group} I_0 \geq_{group} I_2$. This means that the group prefers I_1 to I_0 and I_0 to I_2. In our agent negotiation protocol, the agents reach a consensus on the time interval I_1 also in the example. The selection by the simple majority rule corresponds with the selection by our agent negotiation protocol. Thereby, the agent negotiation protocol reflects a group's preference into a group decision validly.

Table 2. Preference orders of an example

agents	preferences
a_0	$I_1 \geq_{a_0} I_2 \geq_{a_0} I_0$
a_1	$I_1 \geq_{a_1} I_0 \geq_{a_1} I_2$
a_2	$I_0 \geq_{a_2} I_1 \geq_{a_2} I_2$
a_3	$I_1 \geq_{a_3} I_0 \geq_{a_3} I_2$
a_4	$I_2 \geq_{a_4} I_1 \geq_{a_4} I_0$

(3) The agent negotiation protocol can reflect users' individual preferences. In the example, the agent a_2 declares the time interval I_0 iteratively until the other agents reach a consensus. On the other hand, table 2 shows that the agent a_2 prefers I_0 to I_1 and I_2 strongly. This means that because the agent a_2 prefers the time interval I_0 and does not prefer the time intervals I_1 and I_2, the agent a_2 declares the time interval I_0 and does not move to the other coalitions until reaching a consensus. Hence, we can interpret that the user related to the agent a_2 has a private event scheduled on the time intervals I_1 and I_2 and the event is very important for the user. Therefore, the agent a_2 does not compromise his/her preference in the negotiation. As a result, the user assigned the agent a_2 does not participate in the meeting, because the user have an important event on the time interval I_1.

5 Conclusions

In social decision, we need to clarify a trade-off between "reaching a consensus" and "reflecting private preferences in the social decision". In order to improve the trade-off, we proposed a new multi-agent negotiation protocol that has an effective characteristic function and the persuasion protocol. We have implemented a distributed meeting scheduler to see how effectively the multi-agent negotiation can be used. In the scheduling system, an agent is assigned to an user who plans private schedules and events. An agent negotiates with other agents about making an public schedule by referring the user's private schedules and preferences. The multi-agent negotiation we proposed here facilitates reaching an agreement among agents effectively. A characteristic function based on a game theory is used for reflecting users' preferences in the negotiation process. The result shows that the multi-agent negotiation based on private preferences is an effective method for a distributed meeting scheduler.

References

1. Arnold, K. and Gosling, J.: The Java Programming language. Addison-Wesley, 1996.
2. Corny, S., Meyer, R.A., and Lesser, V.R. : Multistage Negotiation in Distributed Planning, Readings in Distributed Artificial Intelligence (Bond, A.H. and Gasser, L. (eds.)), Morgan Kaufman, pp. 367-384, 1988.
3. Ephrati, E., and Rosenschein, J.S. : Distributed Consensus Mechanisms for Self-interested Heterogeneous Agents, Proc. of International Conference on Intelligent and Cooperative Information Systems, pp.71-79, 1993.
4. Ephrati, E., Zlotkin, G., and Rosenschein, J.S. : A Non-manipulable Meeting Scheduling System, The Thirteenth International Distributed Artificial Intelligence Workshop, pp.105–125 ,1994.
5. Garrido, L. and Sycara, K. : Multi-Agent Meeting Scheduling: Preliminary Experiment Results, Proc. of Second International Conference on Multi-Agent Systems(ICMAS-96), AAAI Press, pp. 95–102,1996.
6. Ito, T. and Shintani, T. : An Agenda-scheduling System Based on Persuasion Among Agents, Proceedings of IPSJ International Symposium on Information Systems and Technologies for Network Society, pp.287-294, World Scientific, 1997.
7. Ito, T. and Shintani, T. : Persuasion among Agents : An Approach to Implement a Group Decision Support System Based on Multi-Agent Negotiation, Proceedings of the 15th International Joint Conference on Artificial Intelligence(IJCAI-97), Morgan Kaufmann, pp. 592–597, 1997.
8. Kusano, K. : Negotiation As a Game, in Japanese, Maruzen Library, 1994.
9. Luce, R.D., and Raiffa, H. : Games And Decisions, Dover Publications, 1989.
10. Rosenschein, J.S. : Consenting agents: Negotiation mechanisms for multi-agent systems, Proceedings of the 13th International Joint Conference on Artificial Intelligence(IJCAI-93), pp. 792–779, 1993.
11. Rosenschein, J.S. and Zlotkin, G. : Rules of Encounter, The MIT Press, 1995.
12. Sen, S. and Durfee, E.H. : On the design of an adaptive meeting scheduler, In The Tenth IEEE Conference on Artificial Intelligence for Applications, pp. 40–46,1994.
13. Shintani, T. and Ito, T. : Distributed Scheduling based on a Multi-Agent System, Proc. of 4th International Conference on Control & Automation, Robotics and Vision (ICARCV-96), pp.1313–1317, 1996.
14. Smith, R.G. : The contract net protocol: High-level communication and control in a distributed problem solver, In IEEE Trans. on Comp., No.12 in C-29, pp. 1104–1113, 1980
15. Zlotkin, G. and Rosenschein, J.S. : Coalition, cryptography, and stability: Mechanism for coalition formation in task oriented domains, Proceedings of the 12th National Conference on Artificial Intelligence(AAAI-94), pp.432–437, 1994.

Towards Agent-Oriented Smart Office Based on Concurrent Logic Languages

Hiroyuki Nishiyama, Hayato Ohwada and Fumio Mizoguchi

Faculty of Sci. and Tech.
Science University of Tokyo
Noda, Chiba, 278-8510, Japan

Abstract. This paper presents an AI architecture for multiple robots working collaboratively in a future smart office. This architecture integrates the control, communication, planning, and learning necessary to agentify office robots. Such integration is based on our multiagent robot language (MRL), which is an extension of concurrent logic programming languages (CCL). While the behavior of an agent is specified within guarded Horn clause logic, the communication and concurrency controls are amenable to the operational semantics of CCL. Our planning module provides well-balanced coordination between single agent planning and supervisor-level planning, yielding the minimum interaction for multiagent communication and control. Furthermore, inductive learning is incorporated into the planning module and is applied to produce empirical rules for action selection, providing the utility of multiagent problem solving. These features allow a unified view of both low- and high-level computation, which enables intelligent collaboration between robotic agents and provides a powerful framework for distributed AI and agent-oriented programming in the real world.

1 Introduction

This paper describes our smart office design project, wherein future offices will include robots that collaboratively work together to support office operations. Unlike traditional approaches to distributed machine control, we regard physical robots and sensors in the office as intelligent agent s (*i.e.*, robotic agents) and focus on semantic-level communication (negotiation) between them. Robotic agents thus have their own knowledge source (for rules and procedures), perform a desired task while communicating with each other, and update behavioral rules autonomously using learning facilities.

This agent approach to robot control has been characterized as distributed AI; Smith's contract net [9] was a representative framework that provided semantic-level protocol between distributed problem solvers. A more agenthood approach was taken by Shoham, who presented agent-oriented programming within which the mental state of the agent was formalized and processed using its agent language and interpreter [7]. Our approach is close to those on a conceptual level, but provides a spectrum from low-level control to high-level communication in a unified computational framework. This framework results in an AI design that

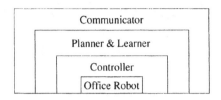

Fig. 1. Agentification of an office robot

integrates concurrency control, communication, planning and learning for robotic agents. This integration agentifies physical robots and sensors for future office environments.

The proposed framework is based on our multiagent robot language (MRL) [5]. Its computation model is an extension of committed-choice concurrent logic programming languages [6], and the behavior of an agent is specified by a set of guarded Horn clauses that are executed in parallel. In this sense, the multiagent robots are defined declaratively and controlled procedurally based on parallel processes, such as concurrency and synchronization. This is quite different from traditional robot languages, which have concurrent facilities based on semaphore provided within the operating system programming. Such languages are not suitable for agent-oriented programming. In contrast, logic-based specifications are abstract and expressive in describing logical concurrency.

The distinct purpose of this study is to clarify the agentification process of a physical robot. MRL allows this process by using the following subsystems.

- The module controller sends action commands to the robot. The commands are executed sequentially or concurrently using control variables. Emergent event handling allows cancellation of actions already sent to the robot.
- The module's planner and learner generate and select reasonable action sequences. The module provides well-balanced planning coordination for both a single agent and its supervisor agent. It also produces useful rules to enable multiagent problem solving.
- The module communicator handles negotiation protocols between agents. The module achieves effective collaboration by using broadcast and incomplete message communication within the MRL programming framework.

These modules wrap a robot as shown in Fig 1 and direct the process from distributed machine control to intelligent agent design. This demonstrates that MRL provides a definitive description for the agentification of physical robots and represents a powerful tool for distributed AI and agent-oriented programming in the real world.

While this paper focuses on the computational framework, the above modules are implemented in MRL. MRL programs are compiled into KL1 programs, which are then compiled, using the KLIC system, into C programs running on

UNIX-based systems such as workstations, parallel UNIX systems, and even DOS-based computers [1].

The paper is organized as follows. Section 2 shows how to describe agents in CCL. Section 3 describes MRL and its features for robot control. Section 4 presents the negotiation protocol for communication with agents. Section 5 describes planning for both a single agent and its supervisor agent. Section 6 introduces inductive learning to improve the performance of the planning module. Section 7 has concluding remarks.

2 Specifying agents in CCL

We start with an informal description of committed-choice concurrent logic programming languages (CCL). A CCL program consists of the following guarded Horn clause:

$$H \; : - \; G_1, ..., G_m \mid B_1, ..., B_n. \qquad (1)$$

where H, G_i and B_j are atomic formulas and the clause means that "H is implied by G_i and B_j." In operation, the clause indicates that "to prove H, prove G and B." Such semantics are just logic programming, except for the operational semantics of guard. Guard is used for clause selection to prove an atomic formula. Once a clause is selected, no other clauses are selected. Another use of guard is in the synchronization rule "execute B when sufficient information to entail G is obtained; otherwise wait until G is entailed." Thus, guard has blocking statements being checked for activation of a clause and the body is executed in an active manner. If there are a number of atomic formulas (goals in logic programming) in a body, they are executed in parallel.

2.1 Declarative semantics

Our multiagent model structures agents as a hierarchy. An agent has only one super-agent as its supervisor. This structure can be easily described in CCL:

$$\text{SuperAgent} \; :- \; \text{true} \mid \text{Agent}_1, \; ..., \; \text{Agent}_m$$

$$\text{SAgent}_i \; :- \; \text{true} \mid \text{SubAgent}_1, \; ..., \; \text{SubAgent}_n$$

where SuperAgent has m Agent$_i$ and each agent has a finite set of sub-agents. An agent invokes its sub-agents as CCL goals, setting all guards are true.

An agent is regarded as a task to be processed. Such a task can be divided into several sub-tasks and is defined in a hierarchical manner [2]. If SuperAgent is given as a desired task, its sub-tasks Agent$_i$ are solved. Thus, an agent is divided into a set of sub-agents and such a fact can be described simply in a logic programming framework.

2.2 Procedural semantics

Owing to the autonomous nature, an agent changes its state over time. This is described in the following recursive clause:

```
agent(State) :- G |
    new_state(State, NewState),
    agent(NewState).
```

where the predicate **new_state** generates the new state (**NewState**) from the current state (**State**). State change is defined by invoking the agent predicate with the new state. Guard **G** is an invocation condition for state change.

Termination or deletion of an agent behavior are simply described as follows:

```
agent(State) :- terminate_condition(State) |
                true.
```

The state of an agent meets the termination condition, the agent terminates, setting a pseudo goal **true**.

2.3 Communication via shared variables

Logical variables are used for agent communication in CCL. Suppose that we have two agents, **vision** and **mobile_robot**. A shared variable **Com** is assigned to the goals:

```
vision(Com), mobile_robot(Com)
```

The two agents are defined within the following clauses:

```
vision(Com) :- person_exists(Man) |
    Com = [Man|Next],
    vision(Next).
mobile_robot(Com)   :- Com = [Man|Next] |
    navigate(Man),
    mobile_robot(Next).
```

where the **vision** agent detects the occurrence in the guard **Person_exists(Man)** and put the information on the communication channel **Com**. In contrast, the **mobile_robot** agent receives the information using the guard **Com=[Man|Next]** and navigates for the man. The **mobile_robot** agent waits until an information is sent from the **vision** agent, but the **vision** agent can send at any time regardless with the state of **mobile_robot** (asynchronous communication).

Synchronization can be implemented in the following clauses:

```
vision(Com) :- person_exists(Man) |
    Com = [exec(Man,Ret)|Next],
    wait_vision(Ret,Next).
wait_vision(ok,Com) :- true |
```

```
    vision(Com).
  mobile_robot(Com) :- Com = [exec(Man,Ret)|Next] |
    navigate(Man,Ret),
    mobile_robot(Next).
```

The **vision** agent sends **mobile_robot** the message **exec(Man,Ret)** where **Ret** is a unbound variable and is used to receive the reply from the **mobile_robot**. The **mobile_robot** agent executes a **navigate** action and instantiates the variable **Ret** to constant **ok**. This instantiation activates the **vision** agent which detects the next occurrence. Such a message with variables allows various patterns of agent communication.

3 Multiagent robot language

MRL extends CCL to control multiagent robots. This section includes agent specification, communication and control.

3.1 Agent specification

An agent consists of the following predicates:

new instantiates an agent.
init instantiates its sub-agents.
run specifies the behavior of the agent.

The **new** predicate normally invokes the **init** and **run** predicates. After instantiates the sub-agents, the **run** and other predicates manage the behavior of the agent.

3.2 Message handling

Message specification in MRL is simple enough to describe multiagent communication. It is based on the agent hierarchy and has the following two notations:

- Message **m** for a super-agent is described as ^m.
- Message **m** for sub-agents is described as *m.

where the message recipient is abbreviated. For communication with the super-agent, this abbreviation is straightforward. In contrast, MRL provides broadcast communication between an agent and its all sub-agents. By merging messages from the sub-agents, the agent receives the messages one by one via a communication channel. The agent does not sends a message to a particular sub-agent. Instead, each sub-agent checks whether the message is material. Sibling agents that have the same super-agent indirectly communicate with each other; the super-agent acts as a router between sibling agents.

This communication model may be too restrictive and may violate the nature of multiagent systems. However, agents are hierarchically structured and excessive centralization can be avoided. An agent should have a manageable number of sub-agents.

Based on the guarded Horn clause semantics, the above message notations are handled as follows:

- A message notation in guard is for receiving its message.
- A message notation in body is for sending its message.

3.3 Action control

An agent at the lowest position sends an action command to a physical robot or a process controlling the robot directly. Such an action can not be controlled within MRL; it is regarded as an atomic action. It is possible for MRL to activate the atomic action and receive the result of the action execution. To handle an atomic action, the following message pattern is introduced:

$$do(\text{<Command>, [Start, End]})$$

where two variables (control variables) are attached. The robot executes the action when the variable **Start** is instantiated to the constant **ok**. After executing the action, the variable **End** is instantiated to **ok** [1].

4 Negotiation patterns between agents

4.1 Agent structure

Shoham's AOP defines the components of mental state for a single agent. We provide simple but expressive negotiation patterns in a multiagent setting. In particular, our agent records negotiation processes to maintain tasks to request, accept and execute. The components of our agent are defined as follows:

- **Facts** stating information the agent possesses,
- **Process** stating the current process the agent handles,
- **Action** stating a list of actions to be executed,
- **Requested** stating a list of agents that requested tasks, and
- **Task** stating a list of tasks to be requested by other agent.

Our MRL-based framework consists of several agents that solve multiple tasks in parallel. This means that a task is assigned to and solved by a single agent at a time. The agent solves several tasks sequentially. The component **Process** records either the current task solved by the agent, the latest message the agent sent or the action the agent is executing now, identifying what is going on the agent. The component **Requested** records a list of agents that the agent should

---

[1] **ok** means the success of the action execution. If the execution fails, the variable is instantiated to **no**.

reply some messages in the future. When releasing from the busy state, the agent eventually solves the requested task. The components `Fact`, `Action` and `Task` are information the agent have, corresponding to *fact* and *capability* in the AOP framework. The component `Task` is a kind of *obligation* in AOP, but dealing with *obligation* is unclear.

4.2 Negotiation protocol

The following messages show the negotiation protocol which is classified into messages for communication or control. + and − indicate input and output.

For communication

- `request(+Agent, +Task, +Info)` sends a task to an agent with task information.
- `accept(+Agent, +Task,+Cost,-Com)` replies a request message and send the agent the cost of task execution. `Com` is used to handle a commit message.
- `commit(+Task, +Info,-Rep)` replies to an accept message and indicate the commitment of a task execution which is reported on `Rep`.

For control

- `before(+Act,-Rep)` inquires the permission of an action to the super-agent. The result is reported on `Rep`.
- `do(+Act,+Control, -Time)` performs an action using control variables and return its action time.
- `after(+Act)` notifies the super-agent regarding the end of an action.

The communication messages are task requesting (**request**), accept to the request (**accept**), and commitment to task execution (**commit**). Using the **request** message, the agent announces a task to all its sibling agents and receives replies through **accept** messages. The agent then selects an agent from the replies and sends the agent the commitment message.

The control messages mainly handle mutually exclusive control. For example, the multiple mobile robots can not move the same node at the same time. This problem can be avoided to request the action permission to the super-agent that manages consistency among the agents. The **before** message is such a request-type one and the after message notifies the end of the action to the super-agent.

5 Planning in an agent and its supervisor

Planning in an agent individually is not compatible with planning in the set of agents, resulting in an introduction of social laws to the keep distributed nature of multiagent planning [8]. We provide an intuitive and more practical approach in which well-balanced coordination between distributed and centerized planning can be done by using the agent hierarchy. We put the following definitions:

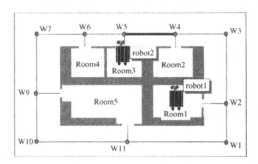

Fig. 2. Two mobile robots.

Definition 1 *Let A be a set of actions executable within a single agent. We are suppose to select a sequence P of elements of A in a sequential order. If task T is achieved executing P, we say P an executable plan for T.*

Definition 2 *Let P_1 and P_2 be executable plans of two agents. If there is no actions in P_1 and P_2 that derive contradictly facts over time, we say that P_1 is compatible with P_2.*

As a typical example, two mobile robots moving to the destinations are illustrated in Fig 2. A contradictly fact can be found in robot collision on the route between $W4$ and $W5$. The following plans are not compatible.

```
robot1 : mp(W2),...,mp(W6),in(Room4)
```

```
robot2 : mp(W5),mp(W4),in(Room2)
```

We aim to produce multiagent plans that are compatible with all executable plans of the agent. The judgment for this compatibility is requested to the superagent. If the plan P is compatible, it is possible for the agent to execute P. Otherwise, a compatible plan is generated .

The compatibility of a set of plans can be done by adjusting the execution time for each plan. A temporal notation is introduced to specify the time interval the agent executes an action. $\Box_{I/d}A$ states that the agent is executing action A on the time interval I whose duration is d. We focus on the following rule which represents the next action to be executed:

$$\Box_{I_A/d_A}A \rightarrow \Box_{next(I)/d_B}B \tag{1}$$

where the term $next(I)$ is the next time interval. The rule expresses the conditional statement to execute the action. A special rule with no condition to execute action B is described as follows:

$$\Box_{I=[0,0]/0}true \rightarrow \Box_{next(I)/d_B}B$$

Each agent produces a set of the conditional rules that may be incompatible with plans of other agents.

We define the safety operation to transform a single agent plan to a compatible plan. Intuitively, the compatibility is guaranteed to wait actions until the actions are not conflict.[2] The priority order for the agents is supposed to be specified. The following safety operation performs compatibility transformation from the second order agent.

Definition 3 (Safety operation) *A conditional rule the agent with priority i produces is of the form (1). Suppose that there is an action in the rule conflicting with the consequent part of (1), and let the action be $\Box_{I_j/d_j} A_j$. The safety operation transforms rule (1) to the following:*

$$\Box_{I_A/d_A} A \wedge \Box_{I_1/d_1} A_1 \wedge ... \wedge \Box_{I_j/d_j} A_j \rightarrow \Box_{I'_B/d_B} B$$

where the following equality holds:

$$I'_B = next(I_A \cup I_1 \cup ... \cup I_j)$$

Theorem 1 *The safety operation produces no conditional rules conflicting with any other rules.*

Proof: *Any potentially conflict actions are safely executed after executing the action in the consequent part. This completes the proof.*

Definition 4 (Priority transfer) *Suppose that a set of facts $\Box_{I/d} A$ are a model of a set of rules produced by the safety operation, and for two facts $\Box_{I_i/d_i} A_i$ and $\Box_{I_j/d_j} A_j$ of agents i and j, A_i is in conflict with A_j. For all A_i and A_j such that $after(I_i) = I_j$, [3] the following transformation is defined:*

(1) Delete condition $\Box_{I'_j/d_j} A_j$ from the rule whose consequent part is $\Box_{I'_i/d_i} A_i$.

(2) Add $\Box_{I'_i/d_i} A_i$ as a condition of the conditional rule whose consequent part is $\Box_{I'_j/d_j} A_j$.

Theorem 2 *A transformed conditional rule has no action conflicting any other rules. In addition, for the original consequent $\Box_{I/d} A$ and the transformed consequent $\Box_{I'/d'} A$, the equality $after(I) = I'$ does not hold.*

Proof: *After transformation, the time intervals of the conditional actions and the consequent action remains disjoint. Deletion of the condition yields the equality $I = after(I')$. In contrast, a newly added condition does not change the interval of the consequent, yielding $I = I'$. This completes the proof.*

Owing to the above operations, the procedure for planning and execution is specified as follows:

---

[2] In case of two agents, this is true. For the general case in which we have n agents, more complex conditions are needed to guarantee the compatibility.

[3] For all $t_i \in I_i, t_j \in I_j, t_i < t_j$.

Step1 Planning for a single agent

A plan is generated for each agent to achieve a give task.

Step2 Using default priority

The priority order is prespecified and repeat the safety operation in this order. While no transformation occurs for the agent with the highest priority, the super-agent refers the plans of sub-agents with higher priority to do the safety operation.

Step3 Priority transfer

This step generates more efficient plans that remain compatible.

Step4 Reconfirming compatibility using negotiation between agents

This step is done by checking the difference from the actual execution state of an agent.

These steps except for Step 2 are done for each agent. After producing a set of executable plans, the agent sends the super-agent a **before** message and receives compatible plans. In Step 3, the agent sends all conflict agents a **request** message to execute the priority transfer. For Step 4, a **commit** message is used after replying to the **request** message. These messages are based on the same negotiation protocol shown in the previous section. The resulting framework provides a well-balanced planning between distributed and centerized processing.

In MRL, $\Box_{I/d}A$ is expressed in the term:

$$do(\texttt{<AgentID>, I, d, A, [Start, End]})$$

where the variables in the fifth argument allow action control. The super-agent assigns these control variables to each sub-agent where the variables are used to communicate with the sub-agent directly. This means that conflict resolution in action execution is done locally for each agent.

6 Incorporating inductive learning into planning

This section describes a method for incorporating inductive learning into planning. Although explanation-based learning has been used for planning problems, we focus on producing somewhat general rules that are applicable to unseen cases in various multiagent settings. In such cases, prespecified rules for each agent are not sufficient, and an inductive and predictive nature of the agent is needed for multiagent programming. In general, it is needed to select some collaborators that are more reliable, efficient or cooperative agents based on accumulated experiences. For our negotiation patterns, a reasonable agent is selected from a set of agents that accept the task requirement.

Our learning module was developed on the basis of Inductive Logic Programming (ILP). ILP is defined as an intersection of machine learning and logic programming, and provides a framework for producing clausal rules that covers given examples using background knowledge [4]. Due to space limitation, this section outlines how to apply ILP to our multiagent setting.

Inductive learning is used to select the best agent for action commitment and we used our ILP system (GKS) [3] implemented in MRL.

The learning task here is to extract the relationship between agent actions and environment states. This relationship expresses good or bad actions under what environment states. If some executed actions are good, common conditions of the states are empirical ones to select a good action.

We introduce a measure for doing task t. The measure has the following criteria: (1) minimizing the finishing time for completing the task, (2) load balance, (3) the degree of parallelism for action execution, and (4) tradeoff between the finishing time and load balance. The resulting measure is in the following equation:

$$f_k(r,t) = \lambda \frac{min(r)}{T(r,t)} + (1-\lambda) \left(1 - \prod_{i=1,k} \frac{w(r,t,i)}{T(r,t)} \right)$$

where $0 \leq \lambda \leq 1, w(i) > 0, 0 \leq f_k(r,t) \leq 1$ and

- k : number of agents,
- $T(r,t)$: finishing time for completing task t requested to agent r,
- $min(r)$: minimum value of $T(r,t)$ for all tasks, and
- $w(r,t,i)$: the action execution time for each agent i on the time interval $[0, T(r,t)]$.

where λ indicates the tradeoff between the finishing time and load balance.

For $\frac{min(r)}{T(r,t)}$, $min(r)$ is constant[4] and a shorter finishing time is better. $\frac{w(i)}{T(r,t)}$ indicates the working ratio of agent r. If r increases, $\left(1 - \prod_{i=1,k} \frac{w(i)}{T(r,t)} \right)$ decreases, resulting in heavy load. Since $\frac{w(i)}{T(r,t)} < 1$, $\prod_{i=1,k} \frac{w(i)}{T(r,t)}$ is a monotonically decreasing function. This means that $f_k(r,t)$ increases according to the number of agents.

The measure allows classification of executed actions into two sets. The first set includes good actions that are regarded as positive examples for ILP, and the other covers bad actions as negative examples. Let E^+ and E^- be positive and negative examples that are input to the GKS system. The two set is defined as follows: $E^+ = \{t_j | f(t_i) > f(t_j)\}$, $E^- = \{t_j | f(t_i) \leq f(t_j)\}$.

Given the above example sets, our learning procedure has the following steps:

Step 1. Sort the actions using the measure in an increasing order and the sequence is $t_1, ..., t_n$.

Step 2. for $i=2$ to n-1

Let positive and negative examples be $t_1, ..., t_i$ and $t_{i+1}, .., t_n$, respectively. Invoke GKS to produce rules R_i that cover as many positive examples as possible and as few negative examples as possible.

---

[4] Since $f_k(r,t)$ is relatively important, the value of $min(r)$ may be unknown.

The obtained rules are applied in the order of $R_2, ..., R_{n-1}$ and potentially illegal actions are eliminated.

The learning and planning modules run in parallel and the learned rules are transferred to the planning module and used for future decisions. Since priority clause selection in MRL is used within the planning module, there is no need to synchronize the two modules.

An experimental result of our robot cooperation problem shows that the obtained rules improve the efficiency of solving tasks where each action execution takes from 6 to 20 % shorter time, resulting in the great reduction of the total execution time.

7   Conclusions

We have described an integrated agent architecture to design collaborative robotic agents in a future smart office. This integration comes from the underlying concurrent logic language and our multiagent robot language and provides a clear computational framework for control, communication, planning and learning.

References

1. T. Chikayama, A KL1 Implementation for Unix Systems, *New Generation Computing 12*, pp. 123-124, 1993.
2. M. Minsky, *The Society of Mind*, Simon and Schuster, 1986.
3. F. Mizoguchi and H. Ohwada, Constrained Relative Least General Generalization for Inducing Constraint Logic Programs, *New Generation Computing*, Vol 13, pp. 335-368, 1995.
4. Mugglenton, S., Inverse Entailment and Progol, *New Generation Computing*, Vol. 13, 1995.
5. H. Nishiyama, H. Ohwada and F. Mizoguchi, A Multiagent Robot Language for Communication and Concurrency Control, *International Conference on Multiagent Systems(ICMAS)*, 1998.
6. Saraswat, V. A., *Concurrent constraint programming*, MIT Press, 1993.
7. Y. Shoham, Agent-oriented Programming, *Artificial Intelligence*, pp. 51-92, 1993.
8. Y. Shoham and M. Tennenholtz, On social laws for artificial agent societies: off-line design, *Artificial Intelligence 73*, pp. 231-252, 1995.
9. R. Smith, The Contract Net Protocol: High-Level Communication and Control in a Distributed Problem Solver, *IEEE Transactions on Computers*, Vol. C-29, No. 12, 1980.
10. K. Ueda, Guarded Horn Clauses, Concurrent Prolog, Vol. 1, MIT Press, 1987.

Analyzing the Roles of Problem Solving and Learning in Organizational-Learning Oriented Classifier System *

○ **Keiki Takadama** *1, **Shinichi Nakasuka** *2 and **Takao Terano** *3

*1 The University of Tokyo, 4-6-1 Komaba, Meguro-ku, Tokyo 153-8904 Japan
Tel:+81-3-3481-4486 Fax:+81-3-3481-4585
Email: `keiki@ai.rcast.u-tokyo.ac.jp`
*2 The University of Tokyo, 4-6-1 Komaba, Meguro-ku, Tokyo 153-8904 Japan
Tel:+81-3-3481-4452 Fax:+81-3-3481-4452
Email: `nakasuka@space.t.u-tokyo.ac.jp`
*3 The University of Tsukuba, 3-29-1, Otsuka, Bunkyo-ku, Tokyo 112-0012 Japan
Tel:+81-3-3942-6855 Fax:+81-3-3942-6829
Email: `terano@gssm.otsuka.tsukuba.ac.jp`

Abstract. This paper analyzes the roles of problem solving and learning in Organizational-learning oriented Classifier System (OCS) from the viewpoint of organizational learning in organization and management sciences, and validates the effectiveness of the roles through the experiments of large scale problems for Printed Circuit Boards (PCBs) re-design in the Computer Aided Design (CAD). OCS is a novel multiagent-based architecture, and is composed of the following four mechanisms: (1) reinforcement learning, (2) rule generation, (3) rule exchange, and (4) organizational knowledge utilization. In this paper, we discuss that the four mechanisms in OCS work respectively as an individual performance/concept learning and an organizational performance/concept learning in organization and management sciences. Through the intensive experiments on the re-design problems of real scale PCBs, the results suggested that four learning mechanisms in individual/organizational levels contribute to finding not only feasible part placements in fewer iterations but also the shorter total wiring length than the one by human experts.
Keywords: organizational learning, learning classifier system, multiagent system, print circuit board design

1 Introduction

In multiagent environments, there are a lot of types or levels of learning and they affect each other. From this factor, a lot of researches are investigated with several viewpoints. As typical researches, reinforcement learning [14], evolutionary computation [6] and distributed artificial intelligence [2] address problems in multiagent environments. However, these researches are studied in each independent area, and few of them investigate the effectiveness of integrated methods.

From this background, we have proposed Organizational-learning oriented Classifier System (OCS) which composes four methods to show the effectiveness of integrated methods. [15, 16]. In our previous work, we have applied OCS to one of the most complex, practical and engineering problems: Printed Circuit

---

* Paper submitted to the 5th Pacific Rim International Conference on Artificial Intelligence (PRICAI '98)

Boards (PCBs) re-design in Computer Aided Design (CAD) domain, and have shown its effectiveness in terms of both the total wiring length and the iteration counts. However, we have not identified what and how components in OCS effect the performance. Therefore, this paper analyzes the roles of problem solving and learning in OCS from the viewpoint of organizational learning in organization and management sciences, and validates the effectiveness of the roles.

This paper is organized as follows. Section 2 starts to explain the details of OCS, and Section 3 analyzes OCS from the viewpoint of organization and management science. An example of an automated parts placement on PCBs is given in Section 4, and Section 5 discusses the experimental results in the PCBs re-design problems. Finally, the conclusion is given in Section 6.

2 Organizational-learning oriented Classifier System

2.1 Architecture of OCS

Organizational-learning oriented Classifier System (OCS) is a novel multiagent-based architecture with Learning Classifier System (LCS) [6], and is composed of (1) reinforcement learning, (2) rule generation, (3) rule exchange and (4) organizational knowledge utilization. In OCS, agents acquire their own appropriate functions through the local interaction among their neighbors, and form an organizational structure which solves the given problems without explicit control mechanisms. From the viewpoints of the conventional LCS, OCS is an extension and modification of both Michigan approach [8] and Pittsburgh approach [13] with introducing the concept of the organizational learning [1, 3, 4, 10] as follows.

- As shown in Fig. 1, agents do not employ the explicit global evaluation mechanism, but employ their own local evaluation mechanism composed of the following five parts: (1) Organizational knowledge on the division of work, (2) Individual knowledge as a rule base composed of a lot of rules (CFs: Classifiers), (3) Working Memory (WM) for storing information on the environmental state, (4) Memory for storing a sequence of fired rules, and (5) Evaluation Mechanism to evaluate a sequence of fired rules.
- Agents obtain their partial environmental states, but they cannot obtain the total environmental states. This distributed recognition indicates that agents must determine their behaviors according to their partial states. Actually in OCS, the rule in an agent is selected according to the partial environmental state with a roulette selection used in an usual LCS, and an agent performs one behavior according to the selected rule.
- At the beginning, FIRST_CF number of rules in each agent are generated at random, and each strength of rules is set to the same value. In this case, FIRST_CF is defined as the number of rules which are provided to each agent.

2.2 Four Mechanism in OCS

(1) Reinforcement Learning: In OCS, Profit Sharing [5] which is one of methods for reinforcement learning is employed as an evaluation mechanism in Fig. 1. Among various methods of Profit Sharing, OCS distributes positive

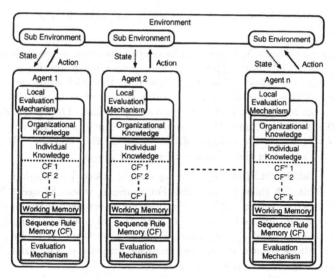

Fig. 1. Architecture of OCS

rewards to all fired rules according to a geometrical decreasing function as shown in Fig. 2 when agents solve given problems. Actually, the strength of CF which agents have is calculated according to Eq. (1). After the rewards distribution, agents in OCS clear their memory for storing a sequence of fired rules in Fig. 1.

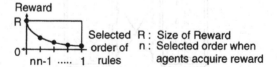

Fig. 2. Profit Sharing

$$ST(i) = ST(i) + R \cdot G^{n-i}, where \ i = n, n - 1, \cdots, 1 \qquad (1)$$

In the above figure, the vertical and horizontal axes indicate the size of reward and the selected order of rules, respectively. Furthermore, in the equations, ST represents the strength of CF, i represents the selected order of CF, n represents the max number of the selected CFs, R represents the max size of the rewards, and G represents the geometric ratio with the range of $0 < G < 1$. From this definition, CF(i) which i is small indicates CF selected in the first several selections.

(2) Rule Generation Mechanism: To adapt to dynamical environments, rule generation mechanism in OCS creates rules when an agent encounters a new environment. Especially when the number of the rules is more than **MAX_CF** which defines the max number of the rules, the rule with the lowest strength is removed and a new rule is generated. Concerning with the strength, OCS decrease the strength temporary when the selected CF is selected again. In the rule generation, the condition part is created to reflect the current situation, and the action part is determined at random. In this case, the strength of the rule is set to the same initial value.

(3) Rule Exchange Mechanism: Instead of the elite selection principle in conventional evolutionary approaches, the rule exchange mechanism in OCS replaces the rules whose strength are low with the rules whose strength are high between two arbitrary agents according to the following mechanism. This rule exchange mechanism works as crossover operations. The **CROSSOVER_TIME**, **CROSSOVER_NUM** and **BORDER_ST** are respectively defined as the interval steps for crossover operations, the number of the replaced rules, and the rule strength which decides whether the rule must be replaced or not.

- Every **CROSSOVER_TIME** step, two agents are selected at random, and the **CROSSOVER_NUM** rules are replaced. For example, when the agent X and Y are selected as shown in Fig. 3, the rules whose strength is low in the agent X and Y are replaced respectively with the rules whose strength is high in the agent Y and X. This method not only prevents agents from getting into deadlock situations, but also improves organizational performance by propagating effective rules among agents.
- In order to avoid the unnecessary crossover operations, the rules are not replaced when their strength value are higher than the **BORDER_ST**. This method contributes to quick problem solving.

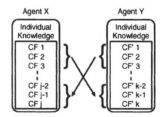

Fig. 3. Rule Exchange Mechanism

(4) Organizational Knowledge Utilization: In OCS, organizational knowledge is defined as a method for the division of work, and is represented by a set of LCS. OCS store LCSs of all agents when they solve given problems most effectively. Since each LCS contributes to reproducing the same effective results by dividing given problems, these LCSs work as knowledge for the division of work. For example, when we assume x number of agents solve problems most effectively with using their LCSs, organizational knowledge is represented by the set of LCSs $(LCS(1), LCS(2), \cdots LCS(x))$. In this case, LCS(x) indicates LCS for the x-th agent and all agents memory the same total LCSs. This kind of knowledge contributes both to reducing the iterations and to solving given problems which cannot be solved without organizational knowledge.

2.3 Definition in OCS

In OCS, the following technical terms are defined.

- **Function:** A sequence of behaviors determined by rules.

– **Organizational Structure:** A structure in which agents acquire their own functions as shown in Fig. 4.

From this definition, the aim of agents in OCS is defined to acquire their own functions as a sequence of behaviors to solve given problems. This function acquisition is implemented by dividing given problems. Actually, agents generate/delete/exchange their rules according to the rule generation/exchange mechanisms, and learn adaptive strategies as the order of using the rules according to reinforcement learning.

Next, the organizational structure as shown in Fig. 4 is flat unlike the hierarchical structure, but this structure changes dynamically when agents acquire their new functions. This implies that agents address the same problem and aim to form an organizational structure which solves given problems by acquiring their own appropriate functions.

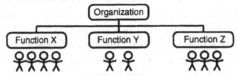

Fig. 4. Organizational Structure

3 Analysis of OCS

3.1 Organizational Learning

The research on organizational learning has been developed in the context of organization and management sciences (OMS), and a lot of researches focus on human organizations [1, 3, 4, 10]. In OMS, organizational learning is generally defined as follows: "Organizational learning occurs when members of the organization act as learning agents for the organization, responding to changes in the internal and external environments of the organization by detecting and correcting errors in organizational theory-in-use [1]". Although this definition is too general to analyze OCS, this paper operationalizes it from more detailed viewpoints. According to Kim, organizational learning is composed of the following four kinds of learning [9]:

– **Individual single-loop learning:**
  In this learning, an agent improves its performance not by changing the contents or the amount of individual rules/knowledge, but by utilizing them.
– **Individual double-loop learning:**
  In this learning, an agent extends the range of problem solving ability by creating/modifying/deleting individual rules/knowledge.
– **Organizational single-loop learning:**
  In this learning, agents improve their performance not by changing the contents or the amount of total individual rules/knowledge in organization, but by exchanging/referring to them among agents.
– **Organizational double-loop learning:**
  In this learning, agents extend the range of problem solving ability as a whole organization by creating/modifying/deleting organizational knowledge which is shared by agents.

3.2 Comparing OCS with Four-loop Learning

From the viewpoints of organization and management sciences discussed in the previous section, we summarize that four mechanisms in OCS work as follows.

- **Reinforcement learning:**
  Reinforcement learning in OCS improves individual performance by learning the order of using individual rules. From this way of learning, reinforcement learning works as one of individual single-loop learning.
- **Rule Generation Mechanism:**
  Rule generation mechanism enables agents to solve given problems by creating/deleting individual rules. From this way of learning, rule generation mechanism works as one of individual double-loop learning.
- **Rule Exchange Mechanism:**
  Rule exchange mechanism improves organizational performance by propagating effective rules among agents. From this way of learning, rule generation mechanism works as one of organizational single-loop learning.
- **Organizational Knowledge on Division of Work:**
  Organizational knowledge in OCS is defined as the knowledge on the division of work and contributes to solving given problems which cannot be solved without organizational knowledge. From this way of learning, organizational knowledge utilization works as one of organizational double-loop learning.

4 PCBs Design

4.1 Problem Description

To investigate the effectiveness of four mechanisms in OCS, this paper applies them to the part addition problems in printed circuit boards (PCBs) re-design as one of the real problems for a practical and engineering use, and evaluate the total wiring length, steps for finding appropriate placement and iterations counted until the value of wiring length is converged. In this PCBs re-design, the problem is difficult because (1) the original parts layout should be remained as much as possible, (2) the severe constraints are added to the original design when new parts are placed, (3) it is impossible to clearly define an explicit evaluation mechanism in advance, and (4) heuristic knowledge is not enough. Although various methods such as the knowledge-base system [17], Simulated Annealing [7, 12] or Genetic Algorithms [18] for PCBs design problems which are easier to be solved than re-design problems are proposed in the literature, even these conventional methods have not been able to place effectively the parts as done by human experts. Furthermore, the supports of human experts are intrinsically required to satisfy the constraints and to optimize the layout of parts placement.

4.2 Part

In the parts addition as an one of PCBs re-design problem, new parts are added to the original parts according to the circuit design which decides the connection of parts electrically. Actually, additional parts are placed on initial parts placement as shown in Fig. 5-1 to make the total wiring length shorter, and thus new parts overlap with the original parts as shown in Fig. 5-2. After parts placement, each part moves or rotates to reduce the overlapping areas of other parts as shown in Fig. 5-3. Finally, all parts are placed with keeping some space between parts as shown in Fig. 5-4.

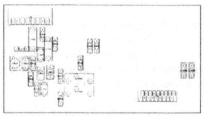

(5-1) Step 0: Initial Parts Placement

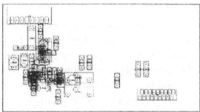

(5-2) Step 1: Parts Addition

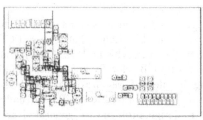

(5-3) Step 10: Parts Movement

(5-4) Final Step: All Parts Placement

Fig. 5. Snapshot of Parts Placement

In this task domain, the parts are intelligent agents, and acquire their own functions to minimize the total wiring length without explicit control mechanisms. As an assumption, the parts can recognize the overlapping areas, but they do not know the total wiring length and their effective behaviors beforehand. Furthermore, each part has some primitive actions: move, rotation, and so on. Rewards are distributed to a sequence of fired rules of each parts according to reinforcement learning in OCS when all parts are placed. Due to this reward, the functions of the parts are changed.

4.3 Design of OCS and Task Environment

In this task, we design OCS and a task environment as follows.

- In OCS, the condition part of CF (classifier) is designed as following: (1) Previous action (10 types, for example, move, rotation); (2) Previous condition on overlap and space between parts (4 types); (3) Overlap condition (1 or 0); (4) Space condition (1 or 0); (5) Flag which distinguishes whether the location is changed or not by a previous behavior (1 or 0). Furthermore, the action part of CF indicates some primitive behaviors (10 types). According to this design, one example of CF is represented as 2 1 1 # 1 6. This rule indicates that *if* previous **action is 2 & previous condition is 1 & overlap & location change** *then* act **6**. In this case, the mark of # indicates "don't care".

– An action is indicated by a discrete number, but a movement distance is indicated by a real number. This implies that the task environment is not a grid world.

5 Experiments

5.1 Method

In the experiments, this paper applies the following four mechanisms in OCS to to PCB re-design problem: (a) reinforcement learning, (b) rule generation mechanism, (c) rule exchange mechanism and (d) organizational knowledge utilization. Actually, the following 15 cases are tested on a PCB in which 40 parts are added to the 52 original parts (we name this PCB as PCB1).

– **Case 1,2,3,4**   : (a), (b), (c), (d)
– **Case 5,6,7,8,9,10** : (a)+(b), (a)+(c), (a)+(d), (b)+(c), (b)+(d), (c)+(d)
– **Case 11,12,13,14** : (a)+(b)+(c), (a)+(b)+(d), (a)+(c)+(d), (b)+(c)+(d)
– **Case 15**   : (a)+(b)+(c)+(d)

Furthermore, organizational knowledge is generated as the set of LCSs in advance. In this case, 20 parts are added to the 25 original parts on a PCB which is different in type and size from PCB1 (we name this PCB as PCB2). One example of difference types shows that a certain PCB is for TV and another PCB is for audio. PCB2 is used for investigating the effect of organizational knowledge utilization by transferring the knowledge acquired in PCB2 to PCB1. Actually, 45 (=20+25) LCSs which divide PCB2 re-design problem are generated and utilized for 92 (=40+52) parts in PCB1. The way of utilization is describes as follows: $LCS(x)$ in $PCB1$ *utlizes* $LCS((x-1) \% 45 + 1)$ in $PCB2$, *where* $x = 1, 2, \cdots, 92$. In this case, % indicates the mod function.

In the above cases, all agents continue to solve the same given PCB re-design problem dozens of times, and aim to acquire their own function as a sequence of behaviors which find appropriate placement with reducing the overlapping area and minimizing the total wiring length. Furthermore, as a definition, we count one step when all parts perform one behavior such as rotation, and count one iteration when the parts are all placed. The variables are set as follows: **FIRST_CF** is 50, **MAX_CF** is 100, **CROSSOVER_TIME** is 100, **CROSSOVER_NUM** is 5, **BORDER_ST** is -50.0, R is 1, and G is 0.5,

5.2 Results

Table 1 shows the results of PCB re-design. In this table, the attribute of horizontal and vertical axes indicate the learning in an organizational and individual level, respectively. "—" in the left-up side box indicates that there is no experiment, and "×" in each box indicates that agents cannot solve given problems. Furthermore, the number in upper, middle and lower side of each box indicate the total wiring length, the steps and the iteration counts, respectively.

From this table, we found that (1) reinforcement learning minimizes the total wiring length, but increases both the steps and the iteration counts; (2) rule generation mechanism enable agents to solve given problems; (3) rule exchange mechanism contributes to minimizing the total wiring length and reducing the steps; and (4) organizational knowledge utilization finds the minimum total wiring length with reducing both the steps and the iteration counts by integrating other mechanisms in OCS.

Table 1. Total Wiring Length, Steps and Iteration Counts

Learning in Organizational Level / Learning in Individual Level	None	Rule Exchange (c)	Organizational Knowledge (d)	Rule Exchange & Organizational Knowledge (c)+(d)
None	—	X	X	X
Reinforcement Learning (a)	X	X	X	X
Rule Generation (b)	24858 580 12	24208 423 25	31218 2752 27	24616 130 19
Reinforcement Learning & (a)+(b) Rule Generation	24503 750 128	23663 626 89	25490 820 24	23206 138 38

- - - → Effect of Reinforcement Leaning   ——→ Effect of Rule Exchange Mechanism
—·—→ Effect of Rule Generation Mechanism   ·······→ Effect of Organizational Knowledge

5.3 Findings and Discussions

From the experimental results in the automated parts placement on PCBs, we summarized the following points:

-- **Effectiveness of OCS:**
 Although PCBs re-design problems must satisfy a lot of constrains, OCS enables agents to find an appropriate placement without explicit control mechanisms. Furthermore, the total wiring length of OCS is shorter than that of human experts, even if appropriate rules are not prepared beforehand. From these results, OCS is effective for the following problems: (1) the problem which is difficult to design an appropriate global evaluation mechanism, (2) the problem which is difficult to prepare appropriate rules beforehand, (3) the problem which must satisfy a lot of constrains, and (4) the domain where heuristic knowledge is not enough.

-- **Effectiveness of Reinforcement learning:**
 In multiagent environments, the results is easy to be evaluated, but the learning process is generally difficult to be evaluated. This is because behaviors of some agents affect the learning of other agents, and the results are changed according to this kind of interaction among agents. Even this kind of environment, reinforcement learning in OCS enables agents to acquire their own appropriate functions which solve given problems by evaluating the learning process. Therefore, the total wiring length with reinforcement learning is shorter than that without reinforcement learning. However, reinforcement learning has a tendency to increase both the steps for solving given problems and the iterations counted until the result is converged.

– **Effectiveness of Rule Generation Mechanism:**
A lot of conventional multiagent researches focus on (1) the method for
finding optimal solutions, (2) the improvement of speed in problem solving
or (3) the accuracy in the distributed environments. However, these methods
cannot be applied to the practical problems, because it is generally difficult to
prepare appropriate rules/knowledge in advance. Comparing these research,
OCS solves given problems by generating rules, even if appropriate rules
cannot be prepared in advance. This implies that rule generation mechanism
is necessary for the practical problems.

– **Effectiveness of Rule Exchange Mechanism:**
In order to solve the problems which cannot be solved by one agent, agents
must communicate to cooperate with each other. However, it is difficult
for agents to decide what partner/contents must be communicated, when
communication must be started, or how much communication is needed for
cooperation. Although rule exchange mechanism in OCS just makes agents
tell the effective rules among agents without considering the above decision,
both the total wiring length and the steps become short or small. This implies
that the way of rule exchange contributes to the problems which must be
solved by multiagent systems.

– **Effectiveness of Organizational Knowledge Utilization:**
Organizational knowledge created in PCB2 not only minimizes the total
wiring length more than human experts, but also reduces both the steps
and the iteration counts in the case of PCB1. This result suggests that (1)
Organizational knowledge explores the search space in the first few iterations. This is because the utilized knowledge may not be effective and thus
the agents learn how to utilize the knowledge with extending search space.
Furthermore, the result also suggests that (2) Organizational knowledge enable agents to exploit the effective rules of LCSs in another problems and
this exploitation reduces the overlapping areas as quickly as possible. From
these factors, organizational knowledge utilization addresses effectively the
trade-off between exploration and exploitation, and finds the minimum total
wiring length with reducing both the steps and the iteration counts.

– **Effectiveness of Integration of Four Mechanisms:**
Fig. 6 shows the total wiring length of both human experts and OCS. In these
figures, the x-axis indicates the number of iterations and the y-axis indicates
the total wiring length. Furthermore, Fig. 6-1 $\sim$ 6-4 show the results respectively with rule generation mechanism, both reinforcement learning and rule
generation mechanism, both reinforcement learning and rule generation &
exchange mechanisms, and all mechanism in OCS. From Fig. 6-1, the total
wiring length is converged in OCS and is shorter than than that of human
experts (27913). Next, Fig. 6-2 shows the large and wide vibrations, but
the total wiring length is converged at 24503 which is shorter than that in
Fig. 6-1. Third, Fig. 6-3, not only the range of vibrations becomes small,
but also the total wiring length (23663) is shorter than that in the previous
figures. Finally, Fig. 6-4 shows that agents find the minimum total wiring
length (23206) with fewer iteration counts.

From these results, the integration of four mechanisms in OCS not only makes up for the defects of a single mechanism, but also contributes to finding the minimum total wiring length with reducing the iteration counts. This implies that local interaction in four mechanisms is important for a practical and engineering use. Furthermore, since organizational knowledge utilization must not be employed as a singe mechanism but be employed with other mechanism from the result in Table 1, this way of integration is important for multiagent environments.

In addition, the total wiring length of human experts in each figure is not improved even if the iteration counts increase. This is because it takes a half day for human experts to optimize the layout of parts placement and there is no more time for optimizing a lot of PCBs re-design.

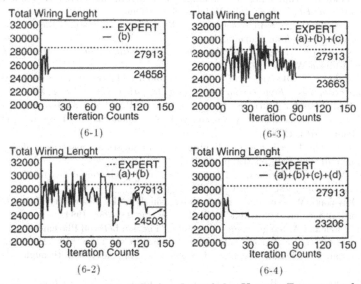

Fig. 6. Iteration versus Total Wiring Length by Human Experts and OCS

6 Conclusion

This paper has analyzed four mechanisms in OCS from the viewpoint of organizational learning in organization and management sciences, and has validated the effectiveness of the four mechanisms through the experiments of real scale PCBs re-design problems in the CAD domain. From the experimental results, we have concluded that (1) Four mechanisms in OCS respectively work as an individual single-/double-loop learning and an organizational single-/double-loop learning in organization and management sciences, and (2) The integration of four mechanisms in OCS compensate the defects of a single mechanism each other and contributes to finding the minimum total wiring length with reducing both the steps and the iteration counts. Future researches include:

– Theoretical analysis in our model OCS.
– Verification of the effectiveness of OCS in other domain problems.
– Verification of the effectiveness of OCS in the reconstruction of organization not only when new parts are added, but also when some parts are removed.

References

1. C. Argyris and D.A. Schon: *Organizational Learning*, Addison-Wesley, 1978.
2. A.H. Bond and L.Gasser: *Reading in Distributed Artificial Intelligence*, Morgan Kaufmann Publishers, 1988.
3. R. Duncan and A. Weiss: "Organizational Learning:Implications for organizational design", in *Research in organizational behavior*, B.M. Staw (Ed.), Vol. 1, JAI Press, pp. 75-123, 1979.
4. R. Espejo, W. Schuhmann, M. Schwaninger and U. Bilello: *"Organizational Transformation and Learning"*, John Wiley & Sons, 1996.
5. J.J. Grefenstette: "Credit Assignment in Rule Discovery Systems Base on Genetic Algorithms", *Machine Learning*, Vol. 3. pp. 225–245, 1988.
6. D.E. Goldberg: *"Genetic Algorithms in Search, Optimization, and Machine Learning"*, Addison-Wesley, 1989.
7. M. Hirahara, N. Oka and K. Yoshida:, "Automatic placement using static and dynamic groupings", *Engineering Design & Automation*, Vol. 3, No. 2, 167-178, 1997.
8. J.H. Holland and J. Reitman: "Cognitive Systems Based on Adaptive Algorithms", in *Pattern Directed Inference System*, D.A. Waterman and F. Hayes-Roth (Eds.), Academic Press, 1978.
9. D. Kim: "The Link between individual and organizational learning", *Sloan Management Review*, Fall, pp. 37–50, 1993.
10. J.G. March: "Exploration and Exploitation in Organizational Learning", *Organizational Science*, Vol. 2, No. 1, pp. 71–87, 1991.
11. K. Miyazaki, M. Yamamura and S. Kobayashi: "On the Rationality of Profit Sharing in Reinforcement Learning", *IIZUKA '94*, pp. 285–288, 1994.
12. C. Sechen and A. Sangiovanni-Vincentelli: "The TimberWolf Placement and Routing package" *IEEE Journal Solid-State Circuits*, SC-20,2, pp. 510–522, 1985.
13. S.F. Smith: "Flexible learning of problem solving heuristics through adaptive search", *IJCAI '83*, pp. 422–425, 1983.
14. R.S. Sutton, A.G. Bart: *Reinforcement Learning - An Introduction* –, The MIT Press, 1998.
15. K. Takadama, S. Nakasuka and T. Terano: "Printed Circuit Board Design via Organizational-Learning Agents", *Applied Intelligence: Special Issue on Intelligent Adaptive Agents*, 1998, to appear.
16. K. Takadama, K. Hajiri, T. Nomura, M. Okada, S. Nakasuka and K.Shimohara : "Learning Model for Adaptive Behaviors as an Organized Group of Swarm Robots", *International Journal of Artificial Life and Robotics*, 1998, to appear.
17. H. Yoshimura: "Knowledge-based placement and routing system for printed circuit board", *PRICAI '90*, pp. 116–121, 1990.
18. T. Yoshikawa, T. Furuhashi and Y. Uchikawa: "Coding Methods for Automatic Placement of Parts on Printed Circuit Boards" (in Japanese), *Trans. of The Institute of Electrical Engineers of Japan*, Vol. 115-D, No. 5, pp. 642–651, 1995.

Simultaneous Modelling and Knowledge Acquisition Using NRDR

Ghassan Beydoun and Achim Hoffmann

School of Computer Sciences and Engineering
University of New South Wales
Sydney, NSW 2052, Australia
Email: {ghassan, achim}@cse.unsw.edu.au

Abstract. Incremental refinement methods of knowledge bases ease maintenance but fail to uncover the underlying domain model used by the expert. In this paper, we propose a new knowledge representation formalism for incremental acquisition and refinement of knowledge. It guides the expert in expressing his model of the domain during the actual knowledge acquisition process. This knowledge representation scheme, Nested Ripple Down Rules, is a substantial extension to Ripple Down Rule (RDR) knowledge acquisition framework. This paper introduces a theoretical framework for analysing the structure of RDR in general and NRDR in particular. Using this framework we analyse the conditions under which RDR converges towards the target knowledge base. Further, we analyse the conditions under which NRDR offers an effective approach for domain modelling. We discuss the maintenance problems of NRDR as a function of this convergence. We show that the maintenance of NRDR requires similar effort to maintaining RDR for most of the knowledge base development cycle. We show that when an NRDR knowledge base shows an increase in maintenance requirement in comparison with RDR during its development, this added requirement can be automatically handled.

1 Introduction

Incremental construction and refinement of knowledge bases have proved successful in building many useful applications [4,5,13]. Ripple Down Rules (RDR)[4] is a knowledge acquisition methodology relying on incremental refinement of acquired domain expert's knowledge. RDR proved successful for developing large knowledge bases for classification tasks [4]; also in [13], RDRs were successfully used for the acquisition of complex control knowledge. With RDR, knowledge maintenance is a simple process that can be done by the user without a knowledge engineer [5]. However, RDRs have two shortcomings: Firstly, RDR knowledge bases may have repetition [10], and further RDR do not convey the expert's model of the domain directly [9].

In this paper, we describe a knowledge representation formalism, Nested RDR, that preserves the strength of RDR, their ease of maintenance, and also addresses those two shortcomings. Further, there have been little theoretical analysis of RDR structures, most noted are [7,8,12]. This paper provides a theoretical framework for analysing RDR in general and NRDR in particular. The paper is organised as follow: We first introduce NRDR and compare them to simple RDR. In section 2 we discuss the development and maintenance of NRDR. In section 3, we give a theoretical framework of RDR structures. The framework will be used to prove convergence of RDR and NRDR. We will also show that maintaining NRDR knowledge bases throughout most of its development is as simple as maintaining RDR. In section 4, we will prove that any extra effort of NRDR maintenance can be handled automatically without an expert. Finally, section 5 discusses results and possible directions of this research.

1.1 Introducing Nested RDR

An RDR tree is a collection of simple rules organised in a tree structure. Every rule can have two branches to two other rules: A false and a true branch. Examples are shown in figure 2, where every block represents a simple RDR. When a rule fires a true branch is taken, otherwise a false one is taken. If a 'true-branch' leads to a terminal node t and the condition of t is not fulfilled the conclusion of the rule in the parent node of t is taken. If a 'false-branch' leads to a leaf node t and the condition of t is not fulfilled the knowledge base is said to fail and requires modification. An important strength of RDRs is that they can be easily modified in order to become consistent with a new case without becoming inconsistent with previously classified cases.

In their simple form, RDRs use simple attribute-value in conditions of rules [5]. In [2,3], we extended RDRs into NRDR to allow the expert to use abstract attributes which he can explain using simpler attributes. The extension was intended for search domains where the attributes were not known a priori [2,3]. The general utility of NRDR was first noted in [1]. In this paper, we view NRDR as a tool allowing simultaneous knowledge acquisition and modelling. We provide a theoretical treatment of this knowledge representation scheme, and extend part of the work in [3] by analysing the maintenance of NRDR and automating part of the involved effort.

Using NRDR, the expert can introduce her vocabulary, she has more freedom to express herself naturally than using normal RDRs. She uses an RDR structure to define a conceptual hierarchy during the KA process. Every concept is defined as a simple RDR tree. Conclusions of rules within a concept definition have a boolean value indicating whether the concept is satisfied by a case or not. Defined concepts can in turn be used as higher order attributes by the experts to define other concepts. The elementary level is the level of domain primitives. Clearly, the evolving concept hierarchy depends not only on the given domain but also on the expert and will reflect his/her individual way of conceptualising his/her own thought process.

Richards and Compton proposed an approach for removing RDR repetitions using machine learning [10] after a knowledge base is developed. In contrast, using NRDR some of these repetitions is avoided during the actual knowledge acquisition process.

NRDR can condense the size of RDRs as the same concept defined by a lower order RDR tree may be used multiple times in higher order trees.

In addressing the limitations of using RDRs in modelling domain terms used by the expert, their relationships and abstraction hierarchies, Richards and Compton [9] developed a technique to uncover conceptual structures from RDR knowledge bases. Their method relied on eliminating unused attributes. This method is limited to domains where not all attributes are always used with every case. For instance, this method cannot be used when the conditions are based on relational attributes between the elements of the feature vector representations of classified cases. Opposed to uncovering models after the knowledge acquisition process, NRDR is a solid framework to capture the relationships between terms used by the expert and acquire abstraction hierarchies during the actual knowledge acquisition process. Further, this is possible while preserving the ease of maintenance of RDRs.

Note that simple RDR as proposed by Compton and Jansen [5] discriminate input objects into a set of mutually exclusive classes. In the rest of this paper, when referring to simple RDR embedded within NRDR we mean a binary conclusion RDR which classify input into two sets, positive objects belonging to a given class and negative objects falling outside the class definition. In the next section we discuss the maintenance issues of NRDR.

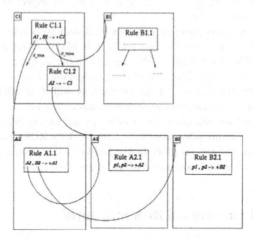

Fig. 1. A simple example of nested ripple down rules. An update in concept A2 can cause changes in the meaning of rules knowledge base.

2. NRDR Technicalities

This hierarchical structure of NRDR causes problems for keeping the entire knowledge base consistent when a single concept definition needs to be altered (see figure

1). In section 4, we sketch two approaches in maintaining this consistency. We first describe a typical update process.

Given a case x that requires the knowledge base to be modified, the modification can occur in a number of places. For example –referring to figure 1 say case x satisfies conditions A1 and B1 in rule C1.1 but the expert thinks that case x is not C1. Hence, the knowledge base needs to be modified to reflect this. A rule can be added as an exception for the RDR tree describing C1, or alternatively, the meaning of attribute A1 can be changed by updating the definition A1, or, the meaning of A2 in rule A1.1 can be changed; and so forth. The number of possibilities depends on the depth of the concept hierarchy in the knowledge base. This is where the user interface must provide assistance to the expert [2]. This is also where the general intelligence of the expert is needed as he deals with the knowledge base as a holistic interconnected system of beliefs. A more serious maintenance problem is dealing with inconsistencies[1] due to localised updates in the hierarchical knowledge base. For instance, if the expert updates the meaning of A1 by changing the meaning of attribute A2 in rule A1.1, he may inadvertently cause a change in the meaning of rule C1.2 that contains A2. Generally, When a condition X is defined in terms of lower order RDR, and X is repeatedly used in different rules, the update of X- by adding an extra rule or an exception to an existing rule- has an effect everywhere it's used. Hence, the update locality property of simple RDR- where the effect of the change has no impact on the rest of the knowledge base- is compromised.

In simple RDRs, a *corner stone case* is associated with every rule. The rule is the justification for the classification for this case [10]. In NRDR, every rule has a set of corner stone cases. This set contains all the cases that a rule classified correctly under the verification of an expert. These verified classifications must always hold. The cases travel between sets because of the interactions within an NRDR knowledge base. During check for inconsistencies, some of those sets of cases are classified again. In section 4, we will discuss two approaches to deal with such inconsistencies.

In the next section, we provide a theoretical framework for RDR structures. We will also show that the inconsistencies problem discussed above is primarily of theoretical interest. Its impact on the knowledge base development is minimal.

3. Theoretical Framework of RDR Structures

In this section, we first introduce a theoretical framework for dealing with RDRs, we then show that the depth of exceptions in an RDR is a quantity mainly dependent on the quality of expertise used. This framework will be then be used to derive a mathematical model for RDR trees. Using that model we will show that the problem of inconsistencies is primarily of theoretical interest. Further, the final part of this section deals with the convergence of NRDR knowledge bases and *inconsistencies*.

The following definitions follow [12]:

---

[1] In the rest of this paper, given a case c classified by the knowledge base, if this classification is inconsistent with respect to a correct past classification, then c is called an *inconsistency*.

Definition 1: The scope of a rule r, *scope(r)* is the set of objects that the rule fires for and no exception or preceding rule fired for. Note, a rule *fires* for a given case *c*, if *c* satisfies all its conditions.

Definition 2: The context of a rule r, *context(r)* is the set of objects that reach that rule when being classified.

Definition 3: The domain of a rule r, *dom(r)* is the set of objects that reach that rule and for which the condition of r is satisfied. Note, domain of an exception of a rule is a subset of its domain. Note, $scope\ (r) \subseteq dom(r) \subseteq context\ (r)$

In RDR, the context and domain of rules does not change during maintenance and extension of the knowledge base. This is the reason behind RDRs'ease of maintenance and extensibility.

We extend the above set of definitions by the following notions:

Definition 4: A rule *r* is *complete* when all the objects in its *domain* are classified correctly by *r* or one of its exceptions.

Definition 5: The predictivity measure *p* of a rule *r* is the ratio of objects in its domain that are correctly classified. That is $pred\ (r) = |\ scope\ (r)\ |\ /\ |\ dom\ (r)\ |$.

Normally, an RDR tree starts with a default rule *"if true then default conclusion"*. The context and the domain of this rule are the whole domain the knowledge base is being built for. In binary domains where there are only two classes, the predictivity of this rule is fairly high as it classifies many cases correctly.

Definition6: The *granularity g* of a domain *D* is the number of rules with disjoint domains the expert requires, such that the union of the domain of these rules is *D*. ie. In an RDR tree this is the length of a false link chain covering *D*.

Definition7: The *initial granularity G* of a concept definition is the number of rules in the most outer target false links chain. This is the longest false links chain in an RDR tree. The union of the domains of this chain is the super-set of the domains of all rules within the tree- except the default rule.

Definition8: A rule's depth, *depth(r)* is the number of true links taken to get to the rule starting from the root node.

Definition9: A rule's *rank* is the number of false links taken after the last true link.

Definition10: The *coverage ratio* R is the ratio of the scopes of an RDR tree to the scope of the default rule. It is equal to: *1 – predictivity (default rule)*.

For a given domain *D*, the objective of a knowledge acquisition process using RDRs is to come up with a set of *complete* rules R, such that $\forall\ r_i \in R,\ U_i\ dom(r_i) = D$. The more predictive the rules, the faster the completion. The expert's role is to come up with the most predictive rules for a given domain. Thus, one can assume that under normal circumstances of building a knowledge base, a competent expert chooses rules that are most predictive for their *domain*. When an exception *e* for a rule *r* is added, the context and the domain of *r* remains the same, however, a subset of its scope becomes that of *e*. Because of the predictivity of *r* we have: $|scope(r\ )| > |scope(e)|$. Furthermore, $|scope(r)| > total\ scopes\ of\ all\ its\ exceptions$. The predictivity assumption applies recursively to all rules added by the expert. Hence, the stated inequalities also apply to all exception rules. That is, the scope of an exception rule is larger than the scope of all its exceptions put together. This leads us to *Theorem 1*.

Theorem 1: The depth of exception for a rule *r* is bounded by:

$$\frac{(1- pred(r))\ ln\ |dom(r)|}{g\ pred(r)}$$ *(ln is the natural log, g is the granularity).*

Proof: We denote *pred(r)* by *p*. At a level of exception *i*, we denote the scope of an exception rule is S_i, and the domain is denoted by D_i. Note D_i is the set of objects which were satisfied by D_{i-1} but didn't belong to S_{i-1}. Assuming a uniform granularity *g* for the rule exceptions, we have the following identity:

$$g\ |D_i| = |D_{i-1}|\ - |S_{i-1}| \qquad (1)$$

Using *definition 4*, we can rewrite (1) as:

$$g\ |Di| = (\ 1- p)\ |D_{i-1}| \qquad (2)$$

Let's define a function *Size:* $N \rightarrow N$ which takes the depth of exception of a rule and returns the number of objects in its domain. So, we can rewrite (2) as:

$$Size(i) = \frac{1-p}{g}\ Size(i-1) \qquad (3)$$

The first derivative: $Size'(i) = \frac{-p}{g(1-p)}\ Size\ (i)$

So, the *Size* function is a decaying function of decay rate *(-p/1-p)* which can be rewritten as: $Size\ (i) = Size\ (0)\ Exp(\frac{-p}{g(1-p)}\ i\ )$. The initial condition *Size(0)* is $|dom(r)|$. The decay of the size of the scope must stop when the scope of the exception rule is 1 case [in reality it stops earlier than this]. So, to find an upper bound on the depth of exceptions i_{max} we set size of the domain to 1, i.e:

$Size(i_{max}) = 1$

$$1 = |dom(r)|\ Exp\ (\frac{-p}{g(1-p)}\ i_{max}) \qquad \rightarrow \qquad i_{max} = \frac{1-p}{pg}\ ln\ |\ dom(r)|$$

If *p* is not uniform, the upper bound is in terms of the minimum value for *p*. **QED**

From *Theorem 1*, the dominating term of the expression *(1-pred (r))/pred(r)* depends primarily on the quality of the expertise. Hence, this quality primarily determines the depth of exception. The poorer the expertise (the smaller *pred(r)*) the deeper the exception hierarchy. However, given the same level of expertise, the depth of exception will be a function of the size of the domain.

3.1. Modelling NRDR concepts

Theorem1 applies to only a single rule. To model an RDR tree we note that the whole domain is presented for the expert at the outer level false link. There are lots of cases to be covered at the outer level in comparison with the number of cases to be covered at the first exceptions level. The gap between the granularity of the first and second level in the exception hierarchy is greatest in an RDR knowledge base, this is empirically evident in [4]. For our modelling purpose we assume that the granularity at the outer level is available independently of the granularity at the first exception level. However, we note that as we move inside the exceptions hierarchy the domain presented to the expert to cover shrinks quickly (by the predictivity assumption), the expressiveness of the language used by the expert stays the same. Consequently, the granularity decreases, because generally the smaller the domain the more possible it becomes for the expert to cover it with less rules. This is evident in large RDR knowledge bases [4] developed for medical classifications. So in our model we assume granularity is a monotonically decreasing function where granularity g decays inversely with depth i. i.e^2. $g = c/i$. The predictivity p is also assumed uniform for a given concept definition RDR tree. The coverage ratio is R. We previously defined a function *Size* which takes the depth of an exception of a rule and returns the number of objects in its domain. We had: $Size(i) = (1 - p)(Size(i-1))/g$. Under our current model $g=c/i$ so the first derivative of this function is:

$$Size'(i) = (\frac{-p}{1-p}) (\frac{i}{c}) \; Size \,(i) \qquad (see\ footnote\ ^3)$$

$$Size(i) \; = Size \,(0) \; Exp \,((\frac{-p}{2(c-cp)}) \; i^{\,2} \,)$$

So under this model, assuming that the initial granularity of the domain is G, the domain of a rule r with depth d is given by:

$$dom \,(r) \; = (R/G) \; |D| \; Exp \,((\frac{-p}{2(c-cp)}) \, d^{\,2} \,) \;, for \; d > 1$$

$$= (R/G) \; |D| \,, for \; d = 1 \; \{\textit{ decay of the granularity starts at depth 2 }\}$$

Observation 1: Given a rule r_2 in a concept definition C_2, and r_2 uses a concept definition X that gets modified by the addition of a rule r_1. A case becomes an *inconsistency* as a result of this update only if it falls simultaneously in the scope of the new rule r_1 and the context of r_2.

Clearly, not all objects in this intersection will become *inconsistencies*. Some cases may migrate to new rules where they are correctly classified[4], and furthermore not all cases within the intersection will migrate. So, the upper bound can be further tight-

---

[2] c is a constant made of the product of the decay ratio of granularity as we move down the exception hierarchy and the granularity at the first exception level.

[3] $d/\,dx \,(exp \,(\,1/2 \;\; x^2)) = x \; exp \; ½\,x^2)$

[4] We have shown that the probability of a migrating case moving the domain of a rule of correct conclusion is bounded by ½. Lack of space does not permit the inclusion of the proof.

ened. However, under our model, the probability of an arbitrary case becoming an *inconsistency* under this model as a result of a single update r_1 is[5] bounded by:

$P (x \in dom(r_1)) P (x \in context(r_2)$ { see footnote 6 }

$$= (c_2/d_2 - rank(r_2)+1) \ (R/ G_2 G_1) \ Exp \ [- \ p_1/ (2(c_1\text{-}p_1)) \ d_1^{\ 2} + \ \text{-}p_2/ (2(c_2\text{-}p_2)) \ d_2^{\ 2}]$$

For illustration, we apply the above model to two typical interacting RDR trees, each of size 150 rules, and depth 5, and a coverage Ratio R of 0.1; the probability of a case becoming an *inconsistency* over the entire development cycle of an NRDR knowledge base is: $0.146 \ R \ x \ 0.0109 = 1.59 \ x \ 10 \ exp \ \text{--}4$. So, we need on average about 6500 cases to expect to detect one *inconsistency*. So, the *inconsistencies* problem has a small impact on the knowledge base development. This will also be seen from calculating the upper bound on the average probability $\mathcal{P}$ of an arbitrary case belonging to a domain.

The upper bound can be calculated by observing the exception hierarchy on a level by level basis. The probability for a case to belong to the first level false chain in the knowledge base is ≤ 1, to belong to the second is $\leq 1\text{-}p$. Generally, the probability that a case is classified by a rule on the nth level exception is $\leq (1\text{-}p)^{n\text{-}1}$. The number of rules on a the nth exception level is given by: $g_0 \ g_1 \ g_2 \ ..... g_n$, where g_i is the granularity at level i. For a complete knowledge base [where all exceptions are handled], we have:

$$\mathcal{P} = R \ [1 + (1\text{-}p) +(1\text{-}p)^2 + ..\ .... + (1\text{-}p)^{n\text{-}1}] \ / \ [g_0 + g_0 g_1 + \ .... + .(g_0 g_1 g_2 ..... g_n)]$$

In a growing knowledge base, as new rules are added, the denominator increases much faster than the numerator. So substituting the current size of the knowledge base in the denominator yields the following upper bound on the average probability that a case belongs to a domain of a rule (excluding the default rule)[6]:

$$R \ [1 +(1\text{-} p) +(1\text{-}p)^2 + ... + (1\text{-}p)^{n\text{-}1}]/ \ S \ < R \ [1+ \frac{1\text{-}p}{p} \ ]/ \ S$$

The above result is independent of the shape or the depth of the RDR tree. For a typical RDR tree with varying values of p, the lowest value of p can be taken to derive the upper bound (In practice, p is larger than ½). In the above, as S increases, the numerator hardly increases. Hence, the above upper bound decreases as the knowledge base matures. More importantly, the probability (hence the frequencies) of *inconsistencies* occurring decreases as the knowledge base matures.

---

[5] For a rule with rank r, its context is the set of objects that get tested for the membership of its domain and the domains of all its antecedents. Therefore we have: $|Context \ (r)| = 1/R \ (g - rank(r)+1 \ )|dom(r)|$.
[6] $(1\text{-} p) +(1\text{-}p)^2 + ... + (1\text{-}p)^{n\text{-}1} < (1\text{-}p)/p \ [because \ 1\text{-}p < 1]$

3.2. Knowledge base convergence and *inconsistencies*

During its development cycle, an RDR tree shows two types of inaccuracies, type I includes cases incorrectly classified by the default rule, type II includes cases incorrectly classified by an expert entered rule because of imperfect predictivity. Inaccuracies of type I lead to addition of new false links on the outer chain, while inaccuracies of type II lead to addition of new exception rules. So given the coverage ratio, the target initial granularity, the current structure of the knowledge base we can calculate both inaccuracies as a function of *predictivity*.

Completion of rules on the first false link increases accuracy by p, completion of exception level n rules increases this accuracy by p^n. The addition of a rule at a level $n-1$ is $1/(1-p)$ more likely than the addition of a rule at level n, simply because the former has $1/(1-p)$ times larger domain. An arbitrary case belonging to the domain of a target rule at level $n-1$ is $1/(1-p)$ more likely to be met than a case belonging to the domain of a rule on level n. So an RDR tree development occurs in a breadth first manner where false branches develop faster than true branches. Hence, plotting accuracy of the knowledge of the base versus its size yields the graph in figure 2. In [4], Compton etal empirically observed this relationship. As the RDR tree becomes more accurate, the number of cases required to cause an addition of a rule increases, hence changing the horizontal axis to #cases instead #rules would yield an exponential function with a sharper rise and flatter top. Also, as the knowledge base develops the domain size of newly added rules shrinks exponentially. So we also expect the inconsistencies to decrease exponentially as shown in figure 2, this is also observed from the upper bound derived in section 3.1 tightening as the knowledge base gets larger.

We end this section by noting the following: The depth of a conceptual hierarchy expressed by a human expert is limited by cognitive strain [14], typically values are 4 to 5 [2]. Indirect dependencies between concepts in the conceptual hierarchy have minimal effect on the knowledge base consistency. The probability of an arbitrary case becoming inconsistent as a result of such indirect dependency is bounded by the probability of a case belonging to the domain a chain of rules simultaneously. This probability is exponential to the length of the chain, for our current purpose, it's too small to be considered. Further, different orders of presentation of cases to the expert simply permute the same rules within a given exception level to which the cases belong. This is because when an exception case is presented before its parent false branch is added, the case is correctly classified by the default rule. This implies that the semantics of the knowledge base generated is independent of the order of examples seen. Hence, the discussion in this paper is independent of the order of cases seen.

4. NRDR maintenance

In this section, we use decision lists (DL) to demonstrate the problems and solutions for maintaining the consistency of our hierarchical NRDR. Methods or results obtained using DLs can easily be mapped back to NRDR.

A decision list [11] is a list of rules. A rule applies if none of its predecessors apply, ie. The first applicable rule classifies the input. Sheffer [12] discussed the techniques of converting RDR into decision lists. Briefly, exception rules overshadowing their parent rules are removed and placed in front of their parents. The condition of a removed rule becomes a conjunction of its previous condition with its parent condition. Obviously, an RDR containing no exceptions is a decision list. We will be discussing interacting decision lists because NRDR is a collection of interacting RDRs. Note, for a rule r within a decision list, definitions 1 to 4 in section 3 still apply. Further, because rules within a DL have no exceptions, *scope = domain* for all rules.

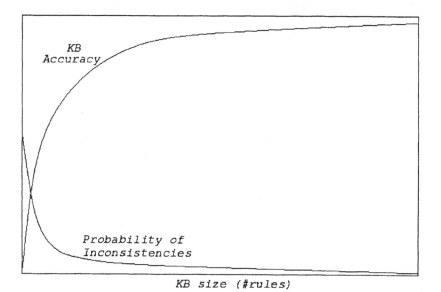

Fig 2. Inconsistencies frequency versus knowledge base correctness: As the KB gets larger, the incremental accuracy of the rules decreases. As the KB size increases the domain of the rules shrinks rapidly, taking down the probability of past cases becoming inconsistent close to 0. Hence, most of the inconsistencies occur in the early stages of developing an RDR concept.

To convert RDRs to decision lists, we introduce Nested Decision Lists (NDL). In NDL, corresponding to NRDR, a condition in a given list can be defined and calculated as lower order decision list. A Nested RDR knowledge base can be represented as: $\{C|\ R_1^s, R_2^s,\ R_3^s,\ ....,\ R_n^s$ *default rule* $\}$ where C is the concept name. R_i^s is a rule with condition R and conclusion $_sC$ where $s \in \{+,-\}$ (That is R_i^s is a shorthand for $R_i \rightarrow _sC$). In NDL this condition is a conjunct of lower order concepts which are in turn defined in forms of decision lists.

4.1 Maintaining NRDR

In section 3, we noted that the context and domain of rules during maintenance of RDRs is stable and this stability eases their maintenance. In Nested RDR, this stability no longer exists. Consider a concept representation $C = \{C| R_1^s, R_2^s, R_i^s, ..., R_n^s$ *default rule* $\}$, if the expert updates a concept definition within the conjunction expression of a R_i^s for some i, then $scope(R_i^s)$ changes. This change is the set of cases that were satisfied by the rule initially and ceased to be satisfied as a result of the update. These cases migrate to the first satisfied rule R_j^s for some j where $j > i$. Another source of the change of the context may come from intercepting cases from the context of antecedent rules. This change in rule contexts may create *inconsistencies*. The set of corner stone cases constituting the scope of a *suspect rule*[7] is retested to detect *inconsistencies*. By *observation 1* only those cases in common between the context of the suspect rule and the domain of the new rule need to be rechecked.

We propose two methods for fixing the *inconsistencies*. The first method shields a rule from any lower order updates that create inconsistencies. It virtually stops cases leaving the scope of the rule classifying them, unless they migrate to a rule of same conclusion. In the second method, the expert adds extra rules to account for the migrating or intercepted cases. He creates new rules with conclusion same as the class of the inconsistencies. The first method can be done automatically while the second method requires expert intervention.

We discuss formal framework for the first method. In this method, if a concept X is used to define another concept Y, and if the change in X causes inconsistencies within Y, then new terms are automatically added within Y to shield it from effects of the change within X. This is based on the following:

Theorem 2: Let a concept X get updated by adding a rule R_i^s to become:
$\{ X | R_1^s, R_2^s, ..., R_i^s, ..., R_n^s$ *default rule* $\}$; If X is used by a rule Q_i' within a concept Y defined by $\{ Y | Q_1', Q_2', ..., Q_i', ..., Q_m'$ *default rule* $\}$ then to shield Y from any impact the update may have on Y, we can rewrite Y *as (bold font indicates new additions)*: $\{ Y | Q_1', Q_2', ..., \mathbf{R_i}R_i Q_x'^s\backslash\{x\}, ..., \mathbf{R_i}R_{i-1} Q_x'^s\backslash\{x\}, \sim \mathbf{R_i}Q_x', ... Q_m'$ *default rule* $\}$ Where $s' = s \oplus t$ ($\oplus$ *is exclusive or*) and $Q_x'\backslash\{x\} = Q_x'$ without the X.

We prove the above theorem using the following observations:
Observation 2: If the condition of a rule r is always false within a decision list L, r will never be used, and hence such R can be safely deleted from L.
Observation 3: The positions of two consecutive rules R_1 and R_2 within L with mutually exclusive conditions can be swapped over without altering the semantics of L.
Observation 4: Making replicates of a rule R does not change the semantics of a decision list, as long as the replicates follow R.
Observation 5: A rule $R \rightarrow +C$, can be rewritten as $(R X \lor \sim\!XR) \rightarrow +C$, which can be rewritten within a decision list as two mutually exclusive consecutive rules: $\{C| ...,RX \rightarrow +C, R\sim X \rightarrow +C, ...\}$.

---

[7] A rule r is a suspect if it uses concept X in its conditions, and X is being updated.

Observation 6: Given a concept X defined by $\{ X \mid R_1^s,..., R_n^s$ *default rule* $\}$ and a rule r: $X \to {}^t Y$ within the definition of a concept Y, then within Y this rule can rewritten as: $\{ Y \mid ..., R_1 \to {}^{s'} Y..., R_n \to {}^{s'} Y, ... \}$ *where* $s' = s \oplus t$. The conclusion of r is reached if X is true. The sign of the conclusion of r depends on its sign t and the sign s of the satisfied R, for some $R \in X_{definition}$.

For the proof, we need to show that the initial rule using concept X within $Y = \{ Y \mid Q_1', Q_2', ..., Q_x', ..., Q_m'$ *default rule* $\}$, i.e. Q_x' before the addition of R_i^s to concept X is equivalent to the following sub-list of rules substituted within the adjusted Y:

$$R_1 R_i Q_x{}^{'} \backslash \{x\}, \quad ....., R_i R_{i-1} Q_x{}^{'} \backslash \{x\}, \sim R_i Q_x{}^{'} \qquad (1)$$

Using *observation 6* initial Q_x' can be rewritten as:

$$R_1 Q_x{}^{'} \backslash \{x\}, \quad ....., R_n Q_x{}^{'} \backslash \{x\} \qquad (2)$$

Using *observation 6* and noting that $Q_x{}^{'}$ within (1) uses the modified X :

$R_1 R_i Q_x{}^{'} \backslash \{x\}, \quad ....., R_{i-1} R_i Q_x{}^{'} \backslash \{x\}, \sim R_i \{ R_1 Q_x{}^{'} \backslash \{x\}, \quad ..., R_i Q_x{}^{'} \backslash \{x\}, ..., R_n Q_x{}^{'} \backslash \{x\} \} =$

$R_1 R_i Q_x{}^{'} \backslash \{x\}, \quad ....., R_{i-1} R_i Q_x{}^{'} \backslash \{x\}, \sim R_i R_1 Q_x{}^{'} \backslash \{x\}, ..., \sim R_i R_i Q_x{}^{'} \backslash \{x\}, ..., \sim R_i R_n Q_x{}^{'} \backslash \{x\}$

By the definition of a decision list the $\sim R_i$ can be deleted from all terms after the point of insertion of R_i, to get:

$R_1 R_i Q_x{}^{'} \backslash \{x\}, \quad ....., R_{i-1} R_i Q_x{}^{'} \backslash \{x\}, \sim R_i R_1 Q_x{}^{'} \backslash \{x\}, \quad ..., False\ rule, ..., R_n Q_x{}^{'} \backslash \{x\} ==$

$R_1 R_i Q_x{}^{'} \backslash \{x\}, \quad ....., R_{i-1} R_i Q_x{}^{'} \backslash \{x\}, \sim R_i R_1 Q_x{}^{'} \backslash \{x\}, ..., \sim R_i R_{i-1} Q_x{}^{'} \backslash \{x\}, R_{i+1} Q_x{}^{'} \backslash \{x\}, ..., R_n Q_x{}^{'} \backslash \{x\}$

Note, any two rules containing complementing conditions are mutually exclusive, so the first i-1 rules in the above are mutually exclusive from the second i-1 rules, so using *observation 3*, we can rewrite the above in pairs as follow:

$R_1 R_i Q_x{}^{'} \backslash \{x\}, \sim R_i R_1 Q_x{}^{'} \backslash \{x\}, .., R_{i-1} R_i Q_x{}^{'} \backslash \{x\}, \sim R_i R_{i-1} Q_x{}^{'} \backslash \{x\}, R_{i+1} Q_x{}^{'} \backslash \{x\}, .., R_n Q_x{}^{'} \backslash \{x\}$

Using *observation 5*, the above can be rewritten as:

$R_1 Q_x{}^{'} \backslash \{x\}, ..., R_{i-1} Q_x{}^{'} \backslash \{x\}, R_{i+1} Q_x{}^{'} \backslash \{x\}, ..., R_n Q_x{}^{'} \backslash \{x\}$

The above is exactly equivalent to (2); and hence (1) is equivalent to (2) and *Theorem 2* is proved. **QED**

During the maintenance of the knowledge base the conversion done due to *Theorem 2* is automatic. As we proved in the theoretical section, the expected number of inconsistencies is extremely low, so we would expect most of the rules in $R_1 R_i Q_x{}^{'} \backslash \{x\}$, ..., $R_i R_{i-1} Q_x{}^{'} \backslash \{x\}$ to have an empty scope, and get automatically deleted. Note also, that if a concept X occurs in more than one rule within Y, the above conversion is only needed where inconsistencies are detected. However, unless every occurrence of X is converted according to *Theorem 2*, then the inconsistencies check needs to be propagated up the conceptual hierarchy in the knowledge base.

5. Discussion and future work

In this paper we presented a substantial extension to Ripple Down Rules, our Nested Ripple Down Rules. This extension is a novel approach to allow modelling and knowledge acquisition concurrently. NRDR have a hierarchical structure that is a natural representation of the way humans give their explanations in many domains such as circuit analysis[6], chess[2],.. This knowledge representation scheme allows the expert to view the knowledge base as a holistic model of his knowledge. Concepts are allowed to interact, but to ease the maintenance updates are localised within a concept. We have shown that these interactions add very little burden on the expert. Further, in section 4 we showed that these interactions can be handled automatically. In section 3, we showed that the number of fixes is indeed small. Thus, the automatically generated terms derived in section 4 are an upper bound on the size of an actual fix. In section 3, we also formally showed that the size of a knowledge base is more dependent on the quality of expertise rather than the size of the domain.

Future extension of the work presented in this paper will deal with the behaviour of the knowledge base as a conceptual structure. This will enable assessment of different properties (size, frequency of use..) which concepts at different layers of the knowledge base would exhibit.

References

[1] G. Beydoun, A. Hoffmann, Building Problem Solvers Based on Search Control Knowledge. *In Proceedings of the 11th Banff Knowledge Acquisition for Knowledge Base System Workshop*, 1998.

[2] G. Beydoun and A. Hoffmann, Acquisition of Search Knowledge. *In Proceedings of the 10th European Knowledge Acquisition Workshop*, 1997.

[3] G. Beydoun and A. Hoffmann, NRDR for the Acquisition of Search Knowledge. *In Proceedings of the 10th Australian Conference on AI*, 1997.

[4] P. Compton, G. Edwards, B. Kang, L.Lazarus, R.Malor, P. Preston, and A. Srinivasan. Ripple Down Rules: Turning knowledge acquisition into knowledge maintenance. *Artificial Intelligence in Medicine*, 4:463-475, 1992.

[5] P. Compton, R. Jansen. Knowledge in context: a strategy for expert system maintenance. In *Proceedings of AI'88: 2nd Australian Joint Artificial Intelligence Conference*, pages:292-306, 1988.

[6] D. E. Kieras. Learning Schemas From Explantions in Practical Electronics. In *Foundations of Knowledge Aquisition*, Kluwer Academic 1993.

[7] J. Kivinen, H. Mannila and E. Ukkonen. Learning Hierarchical Rule Sets. *In Proceedings of the fifth annual ACM workshop on Computational Learning Theory*, p37-44, 1992.

[8] J. Kivinen, H. Mannila and E. Ukkonen. Learning Rules with Local Exceptions.*In Proceedings of the European Conference on Computational Theory*, 1993.

[9] D. Richards and P. Compton. Uncovering the conceptual models in RDR KBS.*In Proceedings of the International Conference on Conceptual Structures* ICCS'97 Seattle, August 4-8 1997, Springer Verlag.

[10] D. Richards, V. Chellen, P. Compton. The Reuse of RDR Knowledge Bases: Using Machine Learning to Remove Repetition. *In Proceedings of the Pacific Knowledge Acquisition Workshop*, 1996.

[11] R. L. Rivest. Learning Decision Lists. *In Machine Learning*, 2 (1987), pp. 229-246.

[12] T. Scheffer.Algebraic foundations and improved methods of induction or ripple-down rules. *In Proceedings of the 2nd Pacific Rim Knowledge Acquisition Workshop*, 1996.

[13] G. Shiraz and C. Sammut. Combining Knowledge Acquisition and Machine Learning to Control Dynamic Systems. *In Proceedings of the 15th IJCAI*, 1997.

[14] J. F. Sowa. *Conceptual Structures, Information Processing in Mind and Machine*. Addison and Wesley, 1984.

Model Building and Program Specification
· In a Case of Enterprise Design

Setsuo Ohsuga[1] and Takanori Nishio [2]

[1] Department of Inf. and Comp. Science, Waseda University,
3-4-1 Ohkubo Shinjyuku-ku, Tokyo 169-8555, JAPAN
ohsuga@ohsuga.info.waseda.ac.jp
[2] Data Storage & Retrieval Division, Hitachi Ltd.
322-2 Nakazato, Odawara-shi, Kanagawa-ken 250, JAPAN
nishio-t@red.an.egg.or.jp

Abstract. A formal way of modeling complex objects such as enterprises is discussed. Information system is indispensable in every enterprise to accomplish various activities required there and, therefore, must be defined as a part of an enterprise model. Programs of information systems are specified based on this model representation. It enables automation of the following programming process. A new modeling scheme named multi-strata modeling is introduced as a key concept to make computer system intelligent.

1 Introduction

Problems are expected to glow very large and complex in future [1]. A traditional human-centered method of problem solving can no more be effective but a computer-centered method is needed. Computer systems used there must be an intelligent system based on AI.

In this paper a formal way of modeling complex objects including persons are discussed using an enterprise modeling as an example. A new modeling method is necessary for the purpose. It must be general enough so that it covers the different types of problems in the different domains. F.H.Ross discussed its importance and difficulty in [7].

Generality however tends to make AI systems impractical. A method to select a small subset of rules instead of using large knowledge base before entering the actual problem solving is needed. This subset is specific to the problem. In [5, 6] the author showed a way of realizing this idea and generating a problem solving system specific to the problem on the basis of a new modeling scheme for representing a problem solving process. It includes not only an object but one or more subjects who concern the object. These subjects are given the requirements what to do for this object or to the other subject(s). It is called multi-strata model in this paper.

Generation of automatic problem solving system leads us further to generation of programs because program is a special form of an automatic problem solver. Programs of an information system in an enterprise are to accomplish some of its activities and, therefore, must be defined as a part of an enterprise model. Ways of representing enterprises and also of specifying programs of information systems based on this model representation are discussed. It enables automation of the following programming process.

In section 2 multi-strata model are discussed first. Then in section 3, it is shown that a problem solving system specific to a problem can be generated by using this model. Ways of building an enterprise model and specifying programs on the model are discussed in section 4. In section 5 an approach to automatic programming is discussed. Section 6 is a conclusion.

2 Multi-Strata Model as Problem Model

Problem model must be defined in an intelligent system. It plays many roles. First of all, it is a representation of a problem as a requirement to be satisfied. It must be comprehensive for persons, especially for those not the specialist of computers, and at the same time it must be processed in computer systems. It is modified in a computer system until a representation is reached which is accepted by the person as a solution. Thus the model represents a state of problem solving process at every instance of time and a solution in its final state. Every decision is made on the basis of the model representation.

Modeling procedure is different by the maturity of problem domain. In an immature domain, model representation method is not fixed. Few things are formalized and most of the things must be invented. In a matured problem domain on the other hand, model representation method of an object is almost fixed and many activities with respect to the object are formalized. These activities can be programmed in the conventional style. Making such programs however is another problem not matured yet. This paper deals with the latter case.

2.1 Object Model

An object model is a representation of an object which a person has interest in and wishes to know about. A modeling scheme to represent it must be defined. It is desirable that a single modeling scheme can represent different objects. In general, such information as the following is necessary to represent an object correctly and therefore be included in an object model, (1) structural information to represent a structural organization of the object from its components, (2) functionality to represent attribute, property, function, behavioral characteristic of the object and of its components, relation with the other entity, each of which is represented by a predicate in relation with the object structure, and (3) relation or constraint among the representations of functionality to define specific functional capability of the object. For the detail of this object modeling scheme and an example of its application, refer to [4,6].

2.2 Multi-Strata Model

Problem is created when a person has an intention to do something with an object. Different object models may be created depending on personal interests even if the object is the same. Building only an object model therefore is not adequate for representing problems correctly. In order to describe problems correctly, a modeling scheme that describe not only an object but a subject in the context of a relation between subjects and object is necessary.

Everything in the world can be an object of human interests. It can even be a problem solving process by others. Then a problem solving process forms a nested structure in which the inside process is for obtaining a solution directly on the lower level object and the outside process is for obtaining a way of obtaining the solution in the inside process. Sometimes the more number of strata must be considered (Figure 1(a)). Let it be called a multi-strata object. A new modeling scheme is necessary to represent such multi-strata objects as shown in Figure 1(b). Requirements are given not only to object but to subjects too at any stratum in this model. For example, "design an object to satisfy the given object-level requirements" may be given to S1 of Figure 1. It specifies the activity of S1 as to find an object model structure to satisfy the requirement.

This scheme represents many different cases by the different combination of the specific requirements given to the higher- and lower-stratum entities. Among a number of possibilities realizable with this scheme, an attempt to generate autonomous systems has been described in [6]. It was formalized as a process of making a multi-strata model and then generating a system that can replace a person as the lower stratum subject. Automatic programming has been discussed as its extension.

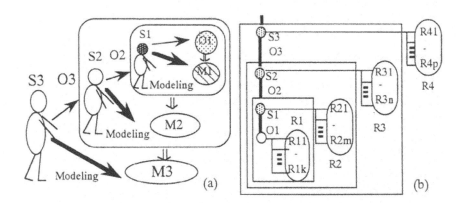

Fig. 1. Multi-strata object and multi-strata model

3 System Generation Based On Multi-Strata Model

3.1 Generation of Problem Solving Systems

Every problem requires its own problem solving method. This method must be found and represented as a problem-specific structure of knowledge chunk. Because of its problem dependency, the key information to find this structure must be included in the problem representation.

Multi-strata model is suited for this purpose. Requirements in this model are processed from the top in order to identify and retrieve the problem-specific knowledge chunk from a large knowledge bases. For example, let a requirement 'automateActivity (subject2, subject1, system)' (automate the activity of subject1) be given to the top subject, where 'subject2', 'subject1', and 'system' denote respectively the subject to which this requirement is given, the subject of which the activity is to be automated, and an automatic problem solving system to replace the activity of the designated subject (subject1). This is interpreted to generate the necessary problem solving system for automating the activity of the lower stratum subject. Only an outline is shown in this paper. Refer to [6] for the detail.

Knowledge is provided for this purpose. As an example, let the requirement given to the subject1 be 'exploration(subject1, model, domain)' to mean that the 'subject1' has to solve the problem by exploration in the specified domain. In this case the requirement for 'subject2' is satisfied by generating an exploratory problem solving system which can do every operation required by 'subject1' to solve the given problem. The following rule can be used for this purpose.

Rule for generating automation system :

automateActivity (Subject2, Subject1, System):-
  getSubjectRequirement(Subject1,Requirement1),   --- (*1)
  generateSystem (Requirement1, System),   --- (*2)
  evokeSubject (Subject1, System).   --- (*3)
  The predicates 'generateSystem' and 'evokeSubject' are expanded further.

Rule for system generation :

generateSystem (exploration(Subject1, Model, Domain), System):-
  getObjectRequirement(Model, Requirement'),   --- (*1)
  problemType(Reqirement', Type),   --- (*2)
  makeRetrieveKey(Subject1, Model, Domain, Type, Key),   --- (*3)
  retrieveKnowledge(Subject1, Domain, Key, KnowledgeStructure), --- (*4)
  makeSystem(System, KnowledgeStructure).   --- (*5)

There must be the different rules for 'generateSystem' by the requirements substituted in 'Requirement1' included therein. The above rule is the one for which 'Requirement1' is substituted by 'exploration (Subject1, Model, Domain)'. Thus this is the rule for generating an exploratory problem solving system. KnowledgeStructure represents a problem-specific structure of knowledge. The type of problem must be identified from the representation of the requirement on object.

Rule for evoking subject :

evokeSubject (Subject, System) :-
  getSubjectRequirement(Subject, Requirement1),   --- (*1)
  getSolution(Requirement1, System).   --- (*2)

The structure of knowledge chunks can be retrieved by the following rule.

Rule for retrieving knowledge chunk for design problem :

retrieveKnowledge(Subject1, Domain, Key, KnowledgeStructure)

getTaskKnowledge(Key, TaskKnowledge),   --- (*1)

getDomainKnowledge(Domain, DomainKnowledge),   --- (*2)

includeKnowledge(KnowledgeStructure, TaskKnowledge,

DomainKnowledge).   --- (*3)

3.2 Program generation

Generation of problem solving system leads us further to program generation. In general an exploratory problem solving system may include irrelevant knowledge. Even if the same knowledge is used, the different results may be produced by the different order of the using the knowledge. If , (1) irrelevant knowledge is deleted from the system, and (2) an order of using knowledge is specified, then the problem solving system becomes equivalent to a procedural program which accepts the input to generate a corresponding output. Thus, a program is a special form of an automatic problem solving system. The problem of program generation therefore must be represented in the similar way as the problem of generating problem solving systems as shown in 3.1. An original problem model is made explicitly and programs are defined as a system to solve the problem automatically. The multi-strata modeling scheme is used for the purpose. This idea holds true to very wide class of programming but the discussion is focused to a case of developing business systems hereafter.

4 Enterprise Model Building and Program Specification

Programs of an information system must be defined as a part of an enterprise model. The way of representing enterprise model and also of specifying programs in this model representation are discussed.

4.1 Making Problem Model - A case of An Enterprise Model

Person starts a program specification by making an original problem model, in this case an enterprise model. Every enterprise has a corporate vision or objective. In order to fulfill the objective various activities must be performed such as; to offer services according to the request from the clients, to collect information to make decision, to design new models for the future goods, etc. To make an enterprise model is first to clarify the objective and all necessary activities performed there. Every enterprise treats some goods for business. It may not necessarily be physical objects but information. But these are not discriminated here.

Every activity, related with the goods either directly or indirectly, is further broken down as is composed of basic operations such as, business planning, sales planning, production planning, sales management, material arrangement, stock order arrangement, production direction, making estimate, production management, production process planning, shipment instruction, purchase management and so on.

All of them have been well defined through the experiences so that any activity can be represented as a compound of some of them. Let each of these be called a function. A function is defined and is given a name, if it's operation is almost independent from the others and is used for defining some other function(s) and/or activity. There are some dependency relations among them. For example, production planning needs work planning and resource investment planning as the lower functions. Finally an enterprise model structure is made. The main frame is made based on this dependency relations. Then persons are assigned to perform these functions and a structure of the pairs of the functions and the persons is made.

Thus an enterprise model is made by defining the functions and making this structure. Then activities are specified on this model in such a way that the given corporate objective can be achieved in an optimal way. This is a design problem and is called in this paper an enterprise design.

Enterprise models are different depending on the goal, goods treated there, the scale of activity, various social regulations, etc. It is not an easy task to build this model from scratch. But some functions and their relations are common to many enterprises. These are defined formally and refined through the long term experiences of management. Then a general pattern can be made as a collection of these formalized functions and their relations. This is shown in Figure 2. Every function and relation between functions are represented in the form of knowledge. Thus the general pattern is a visualization of existing knowledge on modeling and can be used by an enterprise designer. This is not for restricting the designer but for reference.

There are some functions which can be defined formally but cannot be decided off-line. Then knowledge not for representing but for creating the functions can be made. An example is shown in 4.2.

The designer builds an enterprise model by using the general pattern. He/she extracts only the necessary functions and their relations. But some special function are not included in the general pattern. Accordingly some activities cannot be specified. The necessary functions must be defined and added. Some of them are created by using a domain specific knowledge.

In general a rule to represent a function must be of such a simple form as,

functionName (Var-1, Var-2, --, Var-M) :-
    primitiveOp1(Var-i1, --, Var-ir),

    --

    primitiveOpn (Var-k1, --, Var-ks).

where 'functionName' is a predicate to represent the function, Var-1, Var-2, --, and Var-M are the variables included in the function, primitiveOpn is the other predicate to represent the primitive operation to construct the function such as, for example, to access a database. Var-k1, --, and Var-ks are the variables included in this primitive operation. (Var-k1, --, Var-ks) are a subset of (Var-1, Var-2, --, Var-M). This representation must be simple enough so that a simple language expression such as, "function is achieved by executing operation-1, then operation-2, ---, and operation-n"

102

can define the rule, so that even a novice user can make this expression and the system translate it into the form of rule. A proper tool must be provided for generating the knowledge. If the function needs the more complex form, then the user needs help of some specialists.

The activities are defined formally on this model as composed of some functions and represented in the form of knowledge.

The enterprise design proceeds as follows.

First, a base structure of an enterprise model is made referring to and extracting only the relevant part from the general pattern. This results in a rough and incomplete model of the specific enterprise.

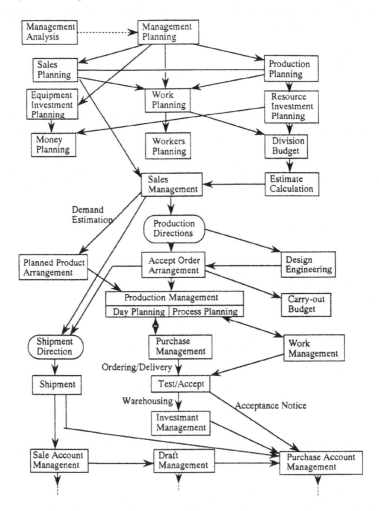

Fig. 2. A general pattern

Second, by referring to generation rules in the knowledge base, some functions which must be defined dynamically are generated and added to the model (ref. 4.2).

Third, the functions which are peculiar to an individual enterprise and cannot be prepared in advance in the form neither of the general pattern nor of creation knowledge, must be created by hand as well as the knowledge to represent it. A tool must be provided for creating the function.

Fourth, knowledge to represent newly created functions are tested for its validity. It must be such that the enterprise activities can be simulated properly by using it in the model. A tool must be provided for testing the knowledge.

Fifth, Every necessary activity which is needed to be performed in this enterprise is specified precisely as a compound of the functions, for example as a chain of the functions (Figure 4). These become the sources of program specification.

Sixth, one or more persons are assigned to every function to perform it, or a person is assigned to do some functions. This assignment depends on the scale of enterprise. The distribution and number of the persons arranged in the enterprise are decided depending on the estimated work load. At this stage, not the real persons but the virtual persons or agents with the average capability of achieving the functions are considered.

Seventh, a real person is assigned to every virtual person and, if necessary, his/her role in achieving the goal is modified from those decided for the virtual person taking his/her estimated capabilities in account.

Eighth, as the final stage of enterprise design, some of the activities are computerized. A hardware system can be decided taking the scale of the enterprise into consideration. This decision is made based on the estimated amount of information to be processed in the computer system referring to the enterprise model created up to the last step. A software system depends directly on the definition of the activities as shown above and, therefore, its specification must be included in this design. This is discussed in 4.3. It is possible to generate programs automatically based on this specification.

The enterprise model created in this way must show the same behavior as the real enterprise and its operational simulation must be possible by making use of the modeling knowledge. If this model shows that the enterprise does not meet the given condition, then the model must be modified.

To start an enterprise design from scratch is rather rare. Instead its restructuring is more frequent. In the latter case only a part of the model is changed. But the process is substantially the same with the design starting from scratch.

4.2 Knowledge-Based Modeling

The modeling based on a general pattern is the first step of a total modeling process. The knowledge-based modeling follows this as the second step. This is discussed below using an example of modeling the sales division as a part of the whole model. The detailed model of the sales division cannot be included in the general pattern because it depends on the goods to be dealt with and, therefore, modeling become possible only after the type of the goods is specified. But the method of creating the model can be formalized and prepared as knowledge and its modeling is performed as a knowledge-based operation.

The top node to represent the sales division is included in the general pattern because a sales division exists in every enterprise. The required activity 'sellGoods' is given to this node. This means to do everything necessary for promoting sales of the given goods. It implies to make a detailed sales plan and also to make an organization of this division. The goods treated in the sales division may be the products either designed and produced in the factory of the enterprise or laid in stock including imports from the overseas, or the else. It depends on the objective of the enterprise. A manager is appointed as a chief of the division.

If the goods are consisted from the different types each of which needs the sales persons with the special knowledge on the goods, then there must be a separate group of sales persons for each type forming the different sales sections under the top sales division. The required activity 'sellGoodsType' is given to this section. This means to do everything necessary for promoting sales of the given type of goods. It implies to make a detailed sales plan and also to form an appropriate group of the sales persons belonging to this section, if necessary. A person is appointed as a chief to each section.

The number of the sales person in this group is decided depending on the number/amount of the goods to be treated and the average capability of the sales person. This is a simple example and there can be different cases. The details are ignored. This process can be represented in the form of knowledge as follows.

Rule for making sales division structure :

sellGoods (Subject, Object) :-
manyTypes (Object),	--- (*1)
classifyGoods (Subject, Goods, TypeGoods, Number),	--- (*2)
createSectionSet (Subject, SectionSet, Number),	--- (*3)
makeTypeTable (Subject, TypeTable ("TypeGoods", "SectionName")),	--- (*4)
(Ax/TypeGoods)(Ey/SectionSet),	--- (*5)
[makeCorrespondence (x, y),	--- (*6)
giveRequirement (SellGoodsType (y, x)),	--- (*7)
addTypeTable (x, y)],	--- (*8)
+singleType (Object),	--- (*9)
sellGoodsType (Subject, Object).	--- (*10)

This rule is for the sales division at the top. This rule says that the object (goods) is tested if it is composed of different types of goods (*1), and if so, the object is classified into the separate types of goods and the number of types is obtained (*2), the same number of the nodes to represent the lower sales sections are created (*3), a table TypeTable for the latter management composed of the type of goods and its corresponding section's name is made (*4), then, for every type and every section (*5), a one-to-one correspondence between these is made (*6), a requirement 'sellGoodsType' meaning to sell the given type of goods is given to every section (*7), the type-and-section pair is registered to the TypeTable (*8). The predicate (*9) shows a case of the goods being of a single type. The symbol '+' represents a disjunction in contrast to the symbol ', ' to represent a conjunction. The predicates after '+' is visited directly from the predicate (*1) when this predicate is proved false, then the sales operation for the single type goods is activated (*10).

<u>Rule for making the sales section structure :</u>

sellGoodsType (Subject, Object) :-

quantityGoods (Object, Quantity),	--- (*1)
averageSalesAmount (Object, Amount),	--- (*2)
numberSalesPerson (Quantity, Amount, Number),	--- (*3)
divideObject (Object, PartObjectSet, Number),	--- (*4)
createNodeSet (Subject, LowerNodeSet, Number),	--- (*5)
makePlan (Subject, PartPlanSet, Number),	--- (*6)

makeSalesTable (Subject, SalesTable ("PartGoods", "SalesPersonName",
"Plan")),   --- (*7)

(Ax/LowerNodeSet)(Ey/PartObjectSet)(Ez/PartPlanSet),	--- (*8)
[makeCorrespondence (x, y),	--- (*9)
giveRequirement (x, SellGoodsPart (x, y, Amount, z)),	--- (*10)
addSalesTable (x, y, z)]	--- (*11)

This rule represents operations necessary for prompting sales of the given type of goods. This rule says that, the quantity of the goods and the average capability of sales person for this type of goods are estimated (*1) and (*2), the necessary number of the salespersons is estimated (*3), the goods is divided to the group of the manageable amount (*4), a set of nodes to represent persons who are to be assigned to the groups are created (*5), a sales plan is made for each group (*6). Making the sales plan depends on the situation. For example, it is assumed that an area to cover the sales of the goods are given. Then this area is divided into sub-areas and information on each area is collected such as population, average income of the people, geographical distribution of the people living in this sub-area, the current state of transportation, etc. The plan is made referring to this information. In the rule above, the plan is made for each sub-area and the set of these plans are referred to PartPlanSet. Then a table SalesTable for the latter management is made (*7). After then, for every sales person (*8), a manageable amount of goods is assigned (*9) and a requirement for selling the goods is given to the sales person with the plan for selling (*10). Finally this triple (sales person, goods, plan) is added to the management table (11). Figure 3 illustrates this process.

4.3 Specifying Program

It has been assumed that all activities to be performed in an enterprise can be represented explicitly in the enterprise model through the modeling process and this model representation is computer-readable. Each activity is a response either to a request from outside of the enterprise such as the money drawing request of a client to a bank, purchase order from some outside personnel or company, carrying material into a factory and so on, or an internal decision such as a new sales plan made in executive board, decision on a development of new products and so on. These stimuli can be considered as queries or problems presented to the enterprise and these activities are the processes for obtaining the solution for them. The system looks for the proper knowledge for solving these problems and is possible to obtain solution by exploratory problem solving method if there is enough knowledge in the knowledge base.

Usually however an exploratory problem solving needs much time and often is not suited for business application which requires the quick response. A procedural program must be provided as far as possible instead of the exploratory problem solving. The eighth step of enterprise modeling is to generate a specification for such procedural programs for some or all activities.

Not necessarily all activities can be represented in the procedural form. There is some conditions for a problem solving system being represented in a procedural form. In general, if the range of the solution of a problem is not fixed nor foreseen, then it is difficult to develop a procedural program for solving the problem. Thus the activities in an enterprise are classified into two classes; programmable and non-programmable.

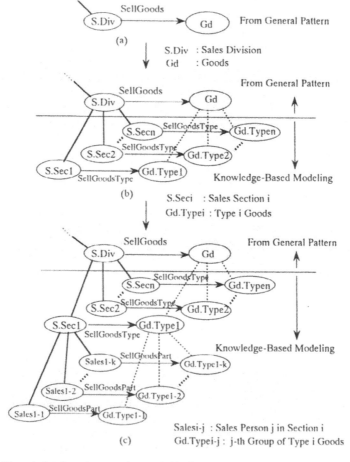

Fig. 3. Knowledge-based enterprise model building

The author discussed in [6] a method of generating a program for the programmable problem from the trace of an exploratory problem solving. This generation process consists of two phases ; creating a deduction tree by exploratory problem solving and the following program generation. But if the domain of problem being considered is matured enough, a modeling method is well established as is the case of general pattern in the enterprise modeling and every programmable activity is specified directly by persons as a chain of the functions. This represents the uppermost part of the deduction tree for the solution. The above example of paying money for the request of 'drawMoney (draw money) is shown in Figure 4. The activity 'drawMoney' is defined by chaining the related functions. This also specifies a program for this activity. The specifications of all programmable activities are made in this way after the decision on what activities should be programmed is made.

A language to represent this modeling scheme is necessary. The author proposed a language named multi-layer logic (MLL). This language has already been developed by the author's group and used in many problem solving [3].

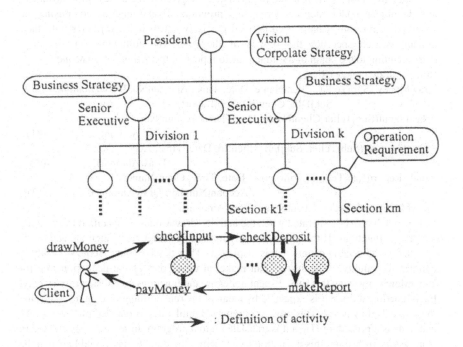

Fig. 4. A simple case of program specification

5. Program Generation

Thus obtained in this way is mere an object model. In order to process this model in various ways, e.g. to make programs, a multi-strata model is formed on this model and the requirement of what to do is represented explicitly. For example in the case of generating programs from the specification, a three-strata model is created of which the top stratum subject is given a requirement 'automateActivity (to automate the activities of the lower-stratum subject)', the second-stratum subject is given the requirement 'makeProgram', and the lowest-stratum subject is given all the required activities such as 'drawMoney' as the above example. The top-stratum subject is responsible to generate a system for generating program with respect to each problem given to the lowest-stratum subject. This is similar to system generation discussed in 3. However it generates not only an exploratory problem solving system for making a deduction tree for the required activity but a system for converting the tree into a program code. The second stratum subject executes 'makeProgram' using this system. It generate a deduction tree first referring to the required activity given to the lowest stratum subject and the object model, then convert it to a program. Every function composing the specified activity must have been defined precisely. It includes variables with their domains which specifies the scopes of the rule. The following rule is made corresponding to the chain of the functions to represent the activity 'drawMoney'.

Rule for draw money (R22) :

drawMoney (SubjTeller, ClientName, Date, Time, AccountNo, DrawAmount,
     SubjDB, ClientID, SubjReport) :-
checkInput(SubjTeller,ClientName, Date, Time,AccountNo,

             DrawAmount),   --(*1)
checkDeposit(SubjTeller, SubjDB, ClientId, Date, Time, AccountNo,

             DrawAmount),   --(*2)
makeReport(SubjTeller, SubjReport , Date, Time, ClientName,

         AccountNumber, DrawAmount),   --(*3)
payMoney(SubjTeller, ClientName, DrawAmount).   --(*4)

This rule has to be generated when the activity 'drawMoney' is specified by chaining the related functions. If this rule is already in the knowledge base, then the activity is included in the general pattern and is displayed. Then the designer is requested only to confirm its validity. The system can make an upper part of the deduction tree for 'drawMoney' by using this rule. Its leaf nodes are the functions composing this activity. Each function at the leaf is expanded by mean of the rule defining its content. Thus the tree expands downward. This process is repeated until a tree is reached of which every leaf node is a procedure. Then it is translated into a program. In reality, a special treaty is necessary in making this deduction tree meeting the conditions to hold between the domain-sets of variables included in the required activities and those of prepared predicates in the knowledge base. For the detail refer to [6].

This is the simplest cases of a single process. In many cases parallel operations are needed. An additional consideration for such an information system architecture as a client-server construct must be considered in this stage.

6 Conclusion

A formal way of modeling a complex object including persons and its computerization were discussed. Modeling procedure is different by the maturity of problem domain. In the immature domain, model representation method is not fixed. Few things are formalized and most of things must be invented. In the matured problem domain on the other hand, model representation method of an object is almost fixed and many activities in the object are formalized. Most of these activities can be programmed in the conventional style. Making such programs is however another problem not formalized yet. This paper discussed this problem of making complex objects using enterprises as an example. Various activities are defined to an enterprise and information system is indispensable. This is a part of the enterprise and must be included in enterprise design.

A way of designing enterprise and specifying programs as a part of the enterprise modeling were discussed. It enables automation of the following programming process. A new modeling scheme named multi-strata modeling was introduced as a key concept to make computer system intelligent. This approach of specifying and generating program can be used not only to enterprises but to many other objects. Ohsuga is developing a programming system for a car electronics system using this method in cooperation with a car production company.

References

1. Gibbs W. Wayt : Software Chronic Crisis, Scientific American, Sept., 1994,
2. Hori, K.: A system for aiding creative concept formation, IEEE Transactions on Systems, Man and Cybernetics, Vol.24, No.6, 1994
3. Ohsuga, S. and Yamauchi, H. : Multi-Layer Logic - A Predicate Logic Including Data Structure As Knowledge Representation Language, New Generation Computing, 1985, 403-439
4. Ohsuga, S. : How Can Knowledge Based Systems Solve Large Scale Problems- Model Based Decomposition and Problem Solving, Knowledge Based Systems, Vol. 5, No.3, 1994
5. Ohsuga, S. : Multi-Strata Modeling to Automate Problem Solving Including Human Activity, Proc. Sixth European - Japanese Seminar on Information Modelling and Knowledge Bases, 1996
6. Ohsuga, S. : Toward Truly Intelligent Systems - From Expert Systems to Automatic Programming, Knowledge Based Systems, Vol. 10, 1998
7. Ross, F. H. : Artificial Intelligence, What Works and What Doesn't ? A· Magazine, Volume 18, No.2, 1997
8. Sumi, Y. et. al. : Computer Aided Communications by Visualizing Thought Space Structure, Electronics and Communications in Japan, Part 3, Vol. 79. No.10, 11- 22, 1996

On the Practicality of Viewpoint-Based Requirements Engineering

Tim Menzies[1], Sam Waugh[2]

[1] AI Department, Computer Science and Engineering, University of NSW, Australia,
tim@menzies.com;
[2] Defence Science and Technology Organisation, Air Operations Division, Melbourne,
Australia, sam.waugh@dsto.defence.gov.au

Abstract. Requirements engineering is often characterised as the management of conflicts between the viewpoints of different stakeholders. This approach is only useful if there is some benefit in moving a specification from one viewpoint to another. In this study, the value of different viewpoints was assessed using a range of different models (ranging from correct to very incorrect), different fanouts, different amounts of data available from the domain, and different temporal linking policies. In all those models, no significant difference was observed between viewpoints.

1 Introduction

Acquiring and consolidating software requirements from different stakeholders is a time-consuming and costly process. If these different viewpoints are poorly managed, the specifications have to be repeatedly reworked or the runtime system has to be extensively modified [9]. Viewpoint-based requirements engineering researchers characterise this process as the management of conflicts between the viewpoints of different stakeholders (e.g. [7,9,18]). Viewpoint-based requirements engineering (hereafter V-RE) assumes that there is some benefit in managing more than one viewpoint. Can we check that assumption?

A core function in viewpoint management is assessing the relative merits of different positions. The limits to this assessment process are the limits to V-RE. One framework for assessing competing options is abduction. Informally, abduction is the inference to the best explanation [19]. More precisely, abduction makes assumptions in order to complete some inference. Mutually exclusive assumptions are managed in separate worlds [17]. That is, given a theory containing contradictions, abduction sorts those contradictions into consistent portions. If the theory is the union of the ideas from different stakeholders, then abduction becomes an V-RE tool. Queries can be written to assess the different worlds. V-RE negotiation then becomes a discussion of the trade-offs between different worlds (an example of this process is given below). Once V-RE has been mapped into abduction, then the limits to V-RE can be found by exploring the limits to abduction. This article will explore those limits as follows. Firstly, an example will show the mapping from V-RE to abduction. Hence, we can show that V-RE is NP-hard. Secondly, an experiment will be defined to find the limits to

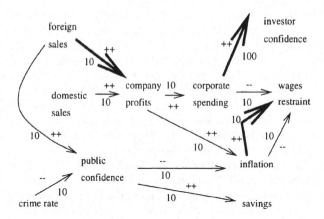

Fig. 1. A model from two experts.

that abductive process. Thirdly, the results of that experiment will show that, at least in the domain studied, different viewpoints are rare and that there is little benefit in moving between them.

2 Example of Abduction

This section offers an example of abductive-based V-RE. Consider the theory shown in Figure 1

This figure is written in the QCM language [17] by two economists: Dr. Thick and Dr. Thin. In QCM, theory variables have three states: *up, down* or *steady*. These values model the sign of the first derivative of these variables and model the rate of change in each value. Dependencies between them can be created as follows. The direct connection between *foreignSales* and *companyProfits* (denoted with plus signs) means that *companyProfits* being *up* or *down* should be connected back to *foreignSales* being *up* or *down* respectively. The inverse connection between *publicConfidence* and *inflation* (denoted with minus signs) means that *inflation* being *up* or *down* should be connected back to *publicConfidence* being *down* or *up* respectively. We assume that, somehow, we have knowledge of the relative costs of each inference step in the model: each edge is the model is annotated with its numeric weight. Dr. Thick's and Dr. Thin's ideas are shown in thick and thin lines respectively. Note that our doctors disagree on the connection between *inflation* and *wagesRestraint*.

How can we test if Dr. Thick or Dr. Thin are saying anything sensible? One method is to use a library of known or desired behaviour. Dr. Thick or Dr. Thin's ideas are sensible if they can reproduce that behaviour. Further, one expert's theory is better than the other theory if that if that theory can explain more known behaviour than its competitors.

This method has at least two problems. Firstly, it may be artificial to demand that (e.g.) Dr. Thick is totally correct and Dr. Thin is totally wrong. A more sensible approach may be to combine portions of Dr. Thick and Dr. Thin's knowledge in order to perform some useful task. Secondly, V-RE researchers such as Easterbrook [6], Finkelstein [9], and Nuseibeh [18] argue that we should routinely expect specifications to reflect different and inconsistent viewpoints. In classical deductive logic, if we can prove a contradiction in a theory, then that theory becomes useless since anything at all can be inferred from that contradiction. Consider the case of *(foreignSales=up, domesticSales=down)* being inputs to the above economics theory. We can now infer two contradictory conclusions: *companyProfits=up* and *companyProfits=down*. In classical deductive logic, we would have to declare our economics theory useless.

A better approach for checking on Dr. Thick and Dr. Thin is graph-based abductive validation [15, 17]. Graph-based abductive validation builds explanations (worlds) for each pair of inputs-outputs in the library of known behaviour. Worlds are built by finding all possible proofs from outputs back to inputs across a directed graph like our economics model. Each maximal consistent subset of those proofs is a world. Worlds are internally consistent. Contradictory assumptions are stored in separate worlds. Each world is scored via its intersection with the total number of outputs we are trying to explain. A theory is then assessed by computing the largest score of its worlds.

This approach to testing was first proposed by Feldman and Compton [8], then generalised and optimised by Menzies [15, 17]. Abductive validation has found a large number of previously unseen errors in models taken from international refereed scientific publications. The errors had not previously been detected and has escaped international peer review prior to publication. To see how graph-based abductive validation contributes to V-RE, consider our economics theory and the case where the inputs are *(foreignSales=up, domesticSales=down)* and the outputs are *(investorConfidence=up, inflation=down, wageRestraint=up)*. The six proofs P which can connect inputs to outputs are:

- P.1: *foreignSales=up, companyProfits=up, corporateSpending=up, investorConfidence=up.*
- P.2: *domesticSales=down, companyProfits=down, corporateSpending=down wageRestraint=up.*
- P.3: *domesticSales=down, companyProfits=down,inflation=down.*
- P.4: *domesticSales=down, companyProfits=down, inflation=down, wagesRestraint=up.*
- P.5: *foreignSales=up, publicConfidence=up, inflation=down.*
- P.6: *foreignSales=up, publicConfidence=up, inflation=down, wageRestraint=up.*

Note that these proofs contain contradictory assumptions; e.g. *corporateSpending=up,* in P.1 and *corporateSpending=down* in P.2. When we sort these proofs into maximal subsets that contain no contradictory assumptions, we arrive at the worlds shown in Figure 2.

Note that world one covers all our output goals while world two only covers two-thirds of our outputs.

V-RE is about facilitating a discussion, not automatically jumping to the next version of the specification. Hence, this abductive approach to V-RE does

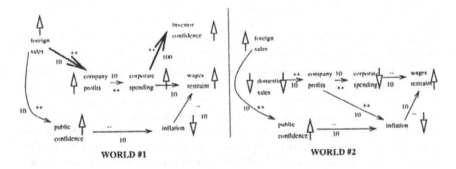

Fig. 2. Worlds from Figure 1.

not offer automatic support for combining the ideas of different experts. However, it does support the automatic generation of reports describing the relative merits of the ideas of Dr. Thick and Dr. Thin. For example, if we combine portions of the ideas from Dr. Thick and Dr. Thin, then we can explain all known behaviour (see world one). Also, Dr. Thin's edges can be found in two worlds; i.e. with respect to the task of inputs *(foreignSales=up, domesticSales=down)* and outputs *(investorConfidence=up, inflation=down, wageRestraint=up)*, a single author's opinions are inconsistent. That is, there is some reason for doubting the view of Dr. Thin. Lastly, we have some evidence that we should endorse the views of Dr. Thin over Dr. Thick since Dr. Thin's ideas are cheaper than Dr. Thick. Consider the cost of world one which can support *investorConfidence=up*. This world contains the very expensive inference proposed by Dr. Thick. If we endorse only Dr. Thin, we get cheaper worlds but lose coverage of all outputs. Such a pragmatic trade off between cost and coverage could inform many debates over conflict resolution.

This abductive approach has technical advantages over other approaches to conflict detection and resolution. Firstly, Easterbrook [6] and Finkelstein [9] require that users enter their requirements into explicitly labeled separate viewpoints. Each viewpoint are assumed to be internally consistent. We have no need for this restrictive (and possibly overly-optimistic) assumption. Recalling the above example, abduction can handle inconsistencies within the opinions of a single user. Further, this approach can check if the explicitly labelled viewpoints are really different: if they don't generate different worlds when they are combined, then they are not truly different.

Secondly, this approach does not demand that we declare (e.g.) Dr. Thick is totally correct and Dr. Thin is totally wrong. This approach can find composite consistent statements that use portions of each expert's knowledge to solve some task (see world one, above).

Thirdly, graph-based abductive validation is not the JTMS-style [5] approach used in other conflict recognition and management systems (e.g. [23]). A JTMS searches for a single set of beliefs. Hence, by definition, a JTMS can only represent a single viewpoint at any one time. This approach is more like the ATMS [4] than a JTMS. An ATMS maintains all consistent belief sets. We believe that an ATMS approach is better suited to V-RE conflict management since the different belief sets are available for reflection.

Fourthly, one striking feature of other systems that support multiple-worlds (e.g. CAKE [23],TELOS [20]) is their implementation complexity. Rich and Waters especially comment on the complexity of their heterogenous architecture [23]. We have found that it is easier to build efficient implementations [15,16] using the above graph-based approach than using purely logical approaches (e.g. [11]). These tools do not suffer from the restrictions of other tools. For example, while Easterbrook's SYNOPTIC tool only permits comparisons of two viewpoints [6] (p113), our approach can compare *N* viewpoints.

Fifthly, the inference procedure described here avoids spurious state assignments. The state assignments proposed by a reasoner are its *envisionments*. Total envisionments are those behaviours which are possible, given some fixed collection of objects in some configuration. Extension generation in default logic [22] systems or the ATMS [4] produce total envisionments. A reasonable restriction on the total envisionments are the attainable envisionments; i.e. all behaviours possible from some given initial state. The QSIM qualitative reasoner uses attainable envisionments [13]. Graph-based abductive validation only finds the relevant envisionments; i.e. state assignments which can lead from inputs to outputs. Relevant envisionments answers the question: *Given some behaviour of interest can these behaviours be reached given certain state assignments?* To answer this question with total or attainable envisionments, one must compute the total or attainable envisionments, then search them for the required behaviour. This approach runs the risk of generating many behaviours that are irrelevant to the process of finding what percentage of known behaviours can be explained by a hypothetical model. For example, given the inputs and outputs of our above example, total envisionments would propose state assignments to *crimeRate* and attainable envisionments would propose state assignments to *savings*, even though these assignments are not relevant to reaching our output goals. To perform relevant envisionments, we restrict the search to the downstream transitive closure of the inputs and the upstream transitive closure of the outputs. For more details, see [17].

Sixthly, the simplicity of this approach can simplify an analysis of the limitations of V-RE (see below).

3   Limits to Abduction

The previous section argued that V-RE can be usefully expressed in an abductive framework. This section explores the computational limits of that abductive framework.

3.1 V-RE is NP-Hard

V-RE can be simply mapped into abduction and abduction is NP-hard. Selman and Levesque show that even when only one abductive explanation is required and the theory is restricted to be acyclic, then abduction is NP-hard [24]. Bylander et.al. make a similar pessimistic conclusion [2].

The specific graph-based abduction validation procedure discussed above is also NP-hard. That procedure grows proofs up from outputs back to inputs. As the proof grows, state assignments (e.g. *domesticSales=up*) is added to the proof. A proof must be consistent; i.e. it must not contain items that contradict other items in the proof. This proof invariant makes this procedure NP-hard. Gabow et.al. [10] showed that finding a directed path across a directed graph that has at most one of a set of forbidden pairs is NP-hard. Our forbidden pairs are assignments of different values to the same variable; e.g. the pairs *domesticSales=up* and *domesticSales=down*.

Pragmatic software engineers often build practical systems for problems that are theoretically NP-hard problems. Hence, merely showing that V-RE is NP-hard is not sufficient reason to abandon that approach. However, the experimental results discussed below are of more practical concern.

3.2 Looking for Multiple Viewpoints

A premise for V-RE is that different viewpoints exist. At first glance, this seems very likely. V-RE is abduction and Kakas et.al. [12] remark that a distinguishing feature of abduction is the generation of multiple explanations (a.k.a. worlds). Researchers into qualitative models (e.g. our economics theory) often comment on the indeterminacy of such models (the generation of too many worlds). Clancy and Kuipers say that qualitative indeterminacy is the major restriction to the widespread adoption of qualitative reasoners [3].

Curiously, and contrary to the experience of Clancy, Kuipers, Kakas, et.al, graph-based abductive validation exhibits very little indeterminacy [14]. That is, when we checked for multiple worlds (a.k.a. viewpoints), we could not find them. This was such a surprising observation that the following experiment was conducted. The aim of the experiment was to try and force graph-based abductive validation to generate numerous worlds.

Firstly, some quantitative equations of a fisheries system was taken from Bossel [1] (pages 135-141) and converted into the QCM-style diagram in Figure 3. Note the two variables *change in boatNumbers* and *change in fishPopulation*. These change variables explicitly model the time rate of change of variables. The simulation data from the quantitative equations offered state assignments at every year. To handle such temporal simulations, the qualitative model was copied, once for every time tick in the simulation. That is, variables like *fishCatch* were copied to become *fishCatch@1*, *fishCatch@2*, etc. Variables at time *i* were connected to variables at time *i+1* using a *temporal linking policy* (discussed below).

Once fisheries was copied, graph-based abductive validation was used to try and reproduce data sets generated from the quantitative equations. Fisheries is only one model. Conclusions drawn from the behaviour of one model are hardly general. Hence, we built several *mutators* to generate 100,000s of problems. The generated problems contained (i) a range of different models (ranging from correct to very incorrect); (ii) models with different fanouts, (iii) different amounts of data available from the domain; (iv) different temporal linking policies.

One mutator added edges to fisheries. Basic fisheries has 12 nodes and 17 edges (fanout=17/12=1.4). This mutator added 0, 5, 10, 15, 20, 25 or 30 new edges at random (checking all the time that the added edges did not exist already in the theory). That is, the model fanout was mutated from 1.4 to (17+30/12=3.9).

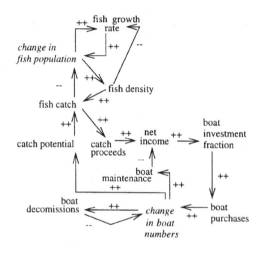

A second mutator corrupted the edges on the original fisheries model. This mutator select *N* links at random in the fisheries model and flipped the annotation (++ to − and visa versa). There are 17 edges in the fisheries model. Note that as the number of edges mutated increases from 0 to 17, the mutated model becomes less and less like the orig-

Fig. 3. The fisheries model. Adapted from [1] (pp135-141).

inal model. That is: at *mutations=0* we are processing the correct fisheries model; at *mutations=17* we are processing a very incorrect fisheries model; at *mutations=2..16* we are processing progressively worse fisheries models.

A third mutator changed the amount data available to graph-based abductive validation. The Bossel equations offered values for all variables at all time points. The third mutator threw away some of that data to produce data sets with 0,10,..,90 percent of the variables unmeasured (denoted as *U* percent unmeasured).

A fourth mutator changed how the variables were connected across time. The XNODE temporal linking policy connects all the explictedly-marked temporal variables from time *i* to time *i+1*; e.g. *change in boatNumbers=up@1* to *change in boatNumbers=up@2*. Note that there are only two explicit time variables in fisheries. It was thought that, since the number of connections were so few, this could artificially restrict world generation. Hence, another time linking policy was defined which made many cross-time links. The IEDGE temporal linking policy took all edges from A to B in the fisheries model and connected $A@i$ to $B@i+1$. XNODE and IEDGE are compared in the following example. Consider the theory *direct(A,B)* and *inverse(B,A)*. If we execute this theory over three time steps, then XNODE and IEDGE describe the search space illustrated in Figure 4.

The above mutators were combined as follows. The Bossel equations were used to generate 105 pairs of inputs and outputs. For statistical validity, the following procedure was repeated 20 times for each of IEDGE and XNODE:

- 0 to 17 edges were corrupted, once for each value of U (0,10,..,90). This lead to 7200 models (20*2*10*18) executed over the 105 input-output pairs (7200*105= 756,000 runs).
- 0, 5, 10, 15, 20, 25 or 30 edges were added, once for each value of U leading to 20*2*10=400 models being executed 105 times (42,000 runs)

The results are shown in Figure 5.

Note the low number of worlds generated. Our reading of the literature (e.g. [3, 12]) lead us the expect far more worlds than those observed here (maximum=5) Also, note the *hump* shape in all the results graphs. As we decrease the amount of data available, there is less information available to constrain indeterminacy. Hence, initially, less data means more worlds. However, after some point (around 50 percent unmeasured), another effect dominants and the number of worlds decreases. We conjecture that relevant envisionments are the cause of the low number of worlds. World-generation is a function of the number of conflicting assumptions made by the reasoner. As the percentage of unmeasured variables increases, the size of the input and output sets decreases. In total envisionments, this has no effect on the number of assumptions made since total envisionments offers assumptions for all variables. However, attainable envisionments make less assumptions while relevant envisionments make even less. Hence, for low-assumption envisionment policies (e.g. relevant envisionments), world-generation is reduced when the amount of data from the domain is reduced.

In summary. only certain interpretations of time (e.g. IEDGE) generate the multiple viewpoints needed for V-RE. How important are those worlds? In the

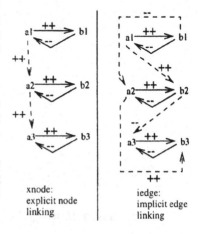

xnode:
explicit node
linking

iedge:
implicit edge
linking

Fig. 4. *Direct(A,B)* and *inverse(B,A)* renamed over 3 time intervals using different time linking policies. Dashed lines indicate time traversal edges.

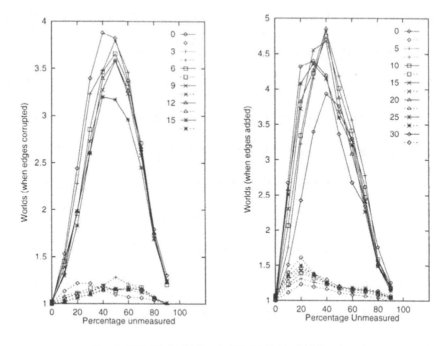

Fig. 5. IEDGE (solid lines), XNODE (dashed lines),

next experiment, we crippled the graph-based abductive validation device. Instead of returning the world(s) that explained the most number of outputs, we returned any single world, chosen at random. The results of that one-world abduction run was compared to the results gained from full multiple-world abduction. The test rig was the same as the edge corruption experiment described above; i.e. another 756,000 runs. A sample of those results are shown in Figure 6.

In these graphs, the percentage of outputs found in the worlds is shown on the y-axis (labelled *percent explicable*). For multiple-world abduction, the maximum percentage is shown; i.e. this is the most explanations that the theory can support. For one-world abduction, the percent of the one-world (chosen at random) is shown. Note that, at most, many-world reasoning was ten percent better than one-world reasoning (in the IEDGE graph for U=40 and 10 edges corrupted). The average improvement of many-world reasoning over one-world reasoning was 5.6 percent. That is, in millions of runs over thousands of models, there was very little difference seen in the worlds generated using one-world and multiple-world abduction.

4 Discussion

There are at least three limits to the above analysis. Firstly, it assumes a definition of the *worth* of a viewpoint along the lines of *what percent of known or*

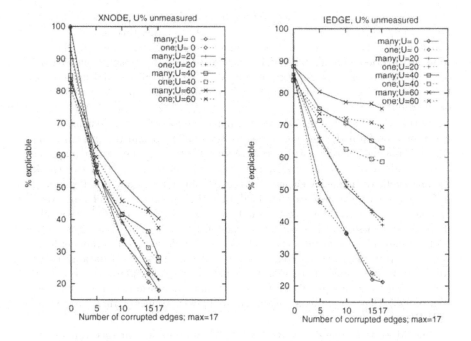

Fig. 6. Multiple-world abduction (solid line) vs one-world abduction (dashed line).

desired behaviour is found in that viewpoint?. Other definitions of testing exist; e.g. the syntactic anomaly detection work of Preece [21]. There is at least one advantage of our approach. If a theory cannot fully reproduce known or desired behaviour, then something *must* be wrong. The same cannot be said for other testing models. For example, Preece stresses that his work does not detect *errors*; rather it only detect *anomalies* which require further human investigation. That is, if a system fails a Preece-style check, it is still possible that nothing is really wrong.

Secondly, our scoring system for the worth of each viewpoint assigns the same score to a viewpoint explaining (e.g.) *a,b* as it does to a viewpoint explaining (e.g.) *c,d*. That is, the analysis here assumes a uniform distribution of goal *utilities* This is an incorrect assumption in domains where certain goals have very high utilities (compared to other goals). For example, two goals might be *healthy* and *well-dressed* and *healthy* might be more crucial than *well-dressed*. We considered experimenting with the effects of different utility distributions. However, that experiment was not conducted since we could not find guidance in the literature on what are reasonable utility distributions in real-world applications.

Thirdly, our analysis is based on mutations to fisheries: a single small theory. Perhaps an analysis of larger, more intricate theories, would offer different conclusions? While we acknowledge this possibility, we note fisheries was just the initial theory that seeded our mutators. Thousands of variants on fisheries were constructed, many of which were more complicated than fisheries (recall the first mutator added edges into the theory). As to larger theories, we showed above that V-RE is NP-hard; i.e. requirements engineering is necessarily limited to small theories. Our analysis of RE hence shares a size restriction with all other RE approaches. In support of this, we note that all the RE models we have ever seen have been small (but we have no data to support this informal observation).

Within the above limitations, we can make the following conclusions. V-RE is can only useful if (i) the viewpoints are truly different and (ii) there is some value in moving a specification from one viewpoint to another. After mapping V-RE to abduction, we have explored these two issues. Abduction can check if some explicitly named viewpoints are truly different: if they don't generate different worlds when they are combined, then they are not truly different. Also, by comparing one-world abductive validation to multiple-world abductive validation, we can assess the merit of exploring multiple viewpoints. Experimentally, we have shown here that for a range of problems (different models ranging from correct to very incorrect, different fanouts, different amounts of data available from the domain, different temporal linking policies) multiple-world reasoning can only generated marginally better results than one-world reasoning (ten percent or less). Hence, the domain explored by these experiments, there is no value in V-RE.

Should we then abandon V-RE? No: V-RE is useful in domains where truly different viewpoints (of significantly different value) can be generated. Alternatively, V-RE may also be of value in domains where increasing the value of a viewpoint by a few extra percent is of vital importance to the application. For example, in a medical domain, *a few percent* could imply saving thousands of deaths. However, what these results show is that even though a domain may *seem* to generate significantly different viewpoints, on average, these different viewpoints may not be worth considering. Multiple-world reasoners are hard to build and understand. Requirements engineers should carefully explore their domains before leaping to the complexity of multiple-world/viewpoint reasoners.

References

1. H. Bossel. *Modeling and Simulations*. A.K. Peters Ltd, 1994. ISBN 1-56881-033-4.
2. T. Bylander, D. Allemang, M.C. M.C. Tanner, and J.R. Josephson. The Computational Complexity of Abduction. *Artificial Intelligence*, 49:25–60, 1991.
3. D.J. Clancy and B.K. Kuipers. Model Decomposition and Simulation: A component based qualitative simulation algorithm. In *AAAI-97*, 1997.
4. J. DeKleer. An Assumption-Based TMS. *Artificial Intelligence*, 28:163–196, 1986.
5. J. Doyle. A Truth Maintenance System. *Artificial Intelligence*, 12:231–272, 1979.
6. S. Easterbrook. *Elicitation of Requirements from Multiple Perspectives*. PhD thesis, Imperial College of Science Technology and Medicine, University of London, 1991. Available from http://research.ivv.nasa.gov/~steve/papers/index.html.

7. S. Easterbrook. Handling conflicts between domain descriptions with computer-supported negotiation. *Knowledge Acquisition*, 3:255-289, 1991.

8. B. Feldman, P. Compton, and G. Smythe. Hypothesis Testing: an Appropriate Task for Knowledge-Based Systems. In *4th AAAI-Sponsored Knowledge Acquisition for Knowledge-based Systems Workshop Banff, Canada*, 1989.

9. A. Finkelstein, D. Gabbay, A. Hunter, J. Kramer, and B. Nuseibe. Inconsistency Handling In Multi-Perspective Specification. *IEEE Transactions on Software Engineering*, 20(8):569-578, 1994.

10. H.N. Gabow, S.N. Maheshwari, and L. Osterweil. On Two Problems in the Generation of Program Test Paths. *IEEE Trans. Software Engrg*, SE-2:227-231, 1976.

11. A. Hunter and B. Nuseibeh. Analysing Inconsistent Specifications. In *International Symposium on Requirements Engineering*, pages 78-86, 1997.

12. A.C. Kakas, R.A. Kowalski, and F. Toni. The Role of Abduction in Logic Programming. In C.J. Hogger D.M. Gabbay and J.A. Robinson, editors, *Handbook of Logic in Artificial Intelligence and Logic Programming 5*, pages 235-324. Oxford University Press, 1998.

13. B. Kuipers. Qualitative Simulation. *Artificial Intelligence*, 29:229-338, 1986.

14. T.J. Menzies. *Principles for Generalised Testing of Knowledge Bases*. PhD thesis, University of New South Wales. Avaliable from http://www.cse.unsw.edu.au/~timm/pub/docs/95thesis.ps.gz, 1995.

15. T.J. Menzies. On the Practicality of Abductive Validation. In *ECAI '96*, 1996. Available from http://www.cse.unsw.edu.au/~timm/pub/docs/96abvalid.ps.gz.

16. T.J. Menzies. Applications of Abduction: Knowledge Level Modeling. *International Journal of Human Computer Studies*, 45:305-355, September, 1996. Available from http://www.cse.unsw.edu.au/~timm/pub/docs/96abkll.ps.gz.

17. T.J. Menzies and P. Compton. Applications of Abduction: Hypothesis Testing of Neuroendocrinological Qualitative Compartmental Models. *Artificial Intelligence in Medicine*, 10:145-175, 1997. Available from http://www.cse.unsw.edu.au/~timm/pub/docs/96aim.ps.gz.

18. B. Nuseibeh. To Be *and* Not to Be: On Managing Inconsistency in Software Development. In *Proceedings of 8th International Workshop on Software Specification and Design (IWSSD-8)*, pages 164-169. IEEE CS Press., 1997.

19. P. O'Rourke. Working Notes of the 1990 Spring Symposium on Automated Abduction. Technical Report 90-32, University of California, Irvine, CA., 1990. September 27, 1990.

20. D. Plexousakis. Semantical and Ontological Considerations in Telos: a Language for Knowledge Representation. *Computational Intelligence*, 9(1), February 1993.

21. A.D. Preece. Principles and Practice in Verifying Rule-based Systems. *The Knowledge Engineering Review*, 7:115-141, 2 1992.

22. R. Reiter. A Logic for Default Reasoning. *Artificial Intelligence*, 13:81-132, 1980.

23. C. Rich and Y.A. Feldman. Seven Layers of Knowledge Represeentation and Reasoning in Support of Software Development. *IEEE Transactions on Software Engineering*, 18(6):451-469, June 1992.

24. B. Selman and H.J. Levesque. Abductive and Default Reasoning: a Computational Core. In *AAAI '90*, pages 343-348, 1990.

Reasoning Without Minimality

Abhaya Nayak[1] and Norman Foo[2]

[1]Information Systems Group
School of Management
University of Newcastle
NSW, Australia 2308

email: abhaya@u2.newcastle.edu.au

[2]Knowledge Systems Group
School of Computer Sci. & Eng.
University of New South Wales
Sydney, Australia 2052

email: norman@cse.unsw.edu.au

Abstract

Various forms of non-monotonic reasoning thrive on minimal change in some form
or other. In general, the principle of minimal change prescribes choosing the best
from a given set of alternatives. A dual of this principle, which has not drawn much
attention from the researchers in the field, is to reject the worst from a given set
of alternatives instead. This paper explores the use of this principle in the context
of belief revision, which has known connections with plausible reasoning. Apart
from arguing that the suggested operation is not excessively weak, we provide a set
of "revision postulates" that demonstrably characterises this "non minimal" belief
revision operation.

1 Introduction

In general, common sense or plausible reasoning allows a reasoner to conclude more
than what is certainly established by the evidence. In jumping to the conclusion that
Tweety is a flier from the evidence that Tweety is a bird, the reasoner
goes beyond evidence. Upon accepting the evidence that Tweety is a bird the
reasoner not only eliminates from consideration the models in which Tweety is not a
bird, she also eliminates from consideration the models in which Tweety is not a flier. It
is through the elimination of this latter set of models that plausible reasoning acquires its
extra inferential power. This situation is pictured in Figure 1 below. The oval represents
the models that satisfy the premise Tweety is a bird. The inference mechanism
eliminates the models in the unshaded part of the oval, whereby the conclusion that
Tweety is a flier is established.

The model elimination in question is not carried out in an arbitrary fashion; otherwise it would not be reasoning at all – plausible or otherwise. Models are eliminated in a
principled, systematic manner. The principle of minimal change (minimality principle)
is one of the principles used to carry out such systematic model elimination.

The minimality principle manifests in different forms in different approaches to reasoning. In the belief *revision* framework [Gär88, AGM85], the reasoner, after receiving
the evidence, entertains as serious possibilities only those models that are, among the
models that satisfy the evidence, minimally different/distant from the set of currently

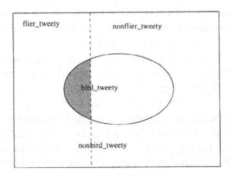

Figure 1: model elimination in common sense reasoning.

entertained models *as a whole*. In belief updates [KM92] and action logics [San94], on the other hand, after an action (a change) in the world has taken place, the agent judges a model to be possible if it is, among those that satisfy the post-condition of the action, minimally different from some model or other that is currently entertained as a possibility. In normality semantics [Sho88, KLM90], on the other hand, all the models are graded in accordance with their (absolute) abnormality, and the reasoner, upon receiving some evidence, considers only those models that are minimally abnormal among those that satisfy the evidence. In counterfactual reasoning and deontic reasoning, similarly, the principle of minimality plays a crucial role.

The general picture that emerges is that by the use of a certain preference relation, the best among the worlds that satisfy the evidence are chosen. In some frameworks the preference is absolute, in some relative. The best models turn out to be minimal under some relation or other.

The minimal change approach is in accordance with the intuition that one should always go for the best. There is an implicit assumption here that the agent (reasoner, buyer, policy maker) already knows what "the best" alternatives are. It is as if the agent has already captured full knowledge of her preference, and for all practical purposes it is static. But that is not always the case. Most often one's preference gets more and more fine grained as one learns from the experience, and the experience comes with acting upon a rough and ready preference in the first place.

This point may be illustrated by a concrete example from John Holland [Hol75, p. 10],

> The problem [of adaptation] is like the problem of adjusting the "height," "vertical linearity," and "vertical hold," controls on a television set. A "best setting" for "height," ignoring the settings of the other two controls, will be destroyed as soon as one attempts to better the settings of either of the other two controls.

The analogy is not quite perfect – but the moral is clear. At the end of the day, the "best setting" is not necessarily the best of any of the factors: height, vertical linearity, and vertical hold. Similarly, the criteria on which the current preference relation is based are not necessarily the ultimate criteria, and should not be treated as such. The minimalist approach, in viewing the current criteria as the ultimate criteria, incurs avoidable epistemic risk; we on the other hand advocate exercise of judicious epistemic restraint. In decision theoretic terms, our approach may be viewed as the maximization of safety within the bounds imposed by nonmonotonic reasoning.

Our approach may be further motivated in light of findings in evolutionary game theory. Robert Axelrod's computer tournament among strategies for playing the iterated game of Prisoners' Dilemma [Axe84] shows that the strategy that pays off best in the long run is not the one that pays off best in a one-shot game. Tit for Tat, the strategy that beats all odds in this iterated game is almost a sure loser in a one-shot game. In the context of a one shot game, it is only a mediocre strategy! It is as if nature eliminates the evolutionary misfits in several eliminative steps. Sure, in the long run, only the fittest survive; that is principally because in each generation (read: iterative step), *the ones that are most unfit lose out.*

In light of this, we suggest that the principle of rejecting of the worst merits attention from researchers in areas that deal with iteration of choices. The basic idea is, if choice in successive steps may use different criteria, it is imprudent to drastically diminish the choice set in one step – for, in doing so, the chooser may be left with what are possibly the worst alternatives from the perspective of future choice criteria. However, in order that the procedure perform its intended function, some alternatives or other, if possible, should be eliminated in each iterative step. Hence, the following principle is deemed plausible:

> *In each eliminative step, using the criterion at hand, eliminate the worst alternatives from the choice-set, given that some alternative are worse than others. Otherwise (if all members of the choice-set are equally preferred), return the current choice-set.*

We maintain that this principle (perhaps with slight modification) is eminently plausible in approaches to non-monotonic reasoning that admit iteration – for instance in belief change and action logics. In this paper we explore the consequences of using this principle in the context of belief change.

2 Minimality Based Belief Change

The AGM system offers a neat model of belief change. A belief state is represented as a theory, new information (epistemic input) is represented as a single sentence, and a state transition function, called revision, returns a new belief state given an old belief state and an epistemic input. If the input in question is not belief contravening, i.e., does not conflict with the given belief state (theory), then the new belief state is simply the consequence closure of the old state together with the epistemic input. In the other case, i.e., when the input is belief contravening, the model utilises a selection mechanism (e.g. an epistemic entrenchment relation over beliefs, a nearness relation over worlds or a preference relation over theories) in order to determine what portion of the old belief state has to be discarded before the input is incorporated into it.

Assume a propositional object language $\mathcal{L}$. (We assume it to be finitary in one of the proofs.) Let its logic be represented by a classical logical consequence operation Cn. The yielding relation $\vdash$ is defined via Cn as: $\Gamma \vdash \alpha$ iff $\alpha \in Cn(\Gamma)$. Let K be a belief set (a set of sentences closed under Cn), the sentence $x \in \mathcal{L}$ be the evidence, $*$ the revision operator, and K_x^* the result of revising K by x. The AGM revision operation satisfies the following rationality postulates:

(1*) K_x^* is a theory
(2*) $x \in K_x^*$
(3*) $K_x^* \subseteq Cn(K \cup \{x\})$
(4*) If $K \not\vdash \neg x$ then $Cn(K \cup \{x\}) \subseteq K_x^*$
(5*) $K_x^* = K_\perp$ iff $\vdash \neg x$
(6*) If $\vdash x \leftrightarrow y$, then $K_x^* = K_y^*$
(7*) $K_{(x \wedge y)}^* \subseteq Cn(K_x^* \cup \{y\})$
(8*) If $\neg y \notin K_x^*$ then $Cn(K_x^* \cup \{y\}) \subseteq K_{(x \wedge y)}^*$

Motivation for these postulates can be found in [Gär88]. We call any revision operation that satisfies the above eight constraints "AGM rational". These postulates can actually be translated into constraints on a non-monotonic inference relation $\vdash\!\!\!\sim$ [GM94]. Roughly, if K represents the background information, then $x \vdash\!\!\!\sim y$ may be taken to mean that $y \in K_x^*$.

There are various constructions of an AGM rational revision operation. The one we will follow is akin to one propounded by Adam Grove [Gro88]. Let $\mathcal{M}$ be the class of maximally consistent set M of sentences in the language in question. (We encourage the reader to think of these maximal sets as worlds or models. We will use the following expressions interchangeably: "$w \models x$", "α allows w" and $w \in [\alpha]$", where w is an element in $\mathcal{M}$ and α is either a sentence or a set of sentences.) We assume a connected, transitive and reflexive relation (total preorder) $\sqsubseteq$ over the set $\mathcal{M}$ such that $[K]$ is exactly the set of $\sqsubseteq$-minimal worlds of $\mathcal{M}$. Intuitively, $w \sqsubseteq w'$ may be read as: w is at least as good/preferable as w' (or, w' is not strictly preferred to w). We define the Grove-revision function $G*$ as: $[K_x^{G*}] = \{w \in [x] |$ for all $w' \in [x], w \sqsubseteq w'\}$, whereby $K_x^{G*} = \bigcap [K_x^{G*}]$. It turns out that the AGM revision postulates characterise the Grove revision operation (see [Gro88] for Grove's systems of spheres approach; our presentation here is different but equivalent to it).

We introduce the following notation for later use.

Definition 1 *A subset $\mathcal{T}$ of $\mathcal{M}$ is said to be $\sqsubseteq$-flat just in case $w \sqsubseteq w'$ for all members w, w' of $\mathcal{T}$. In this case, the members of $\mathcal{T}$ are called $\sqsubseteq$-equivalent. $w \sqsubset w'$, on the other hand, is used as an abbreviation for $(w \sqsubseteq w') \wedge (w' \not\sqsubseteq w)$*

The AGM postulate (2$*$) effectively says that $[K_x^*]$ should be a subset of $[x]$. So the problem of belief revision, from the semantic point of view, is the problem of choosing the right subset of $[x]$. This is what connects belief revision with both rational choice theory and non-monotonic logics. Choice is, in general, non-monotonic in the following sense: any alternative chosen from a subset X is not necessarily chosen from the set X is a subset of. The best horror movie is not, in general, the best movie. This non-monotonicity of choice leads to the non-monotonicity of the non-monotonic inference relation $\vdash$. In fact, minimality based belief change, viewed as a problem of choice, accords well with the established norms of rational choice theory (see [Rot96] for a thorough investigation of this problem). Viewed from this angle, Grove's approach is one of preferential choice: his definition $[K_x^{G*}]$ essentially identifies the subset to be chosen from $[x]$ as the set of worlds that are $\sqsubseteq$-best in $[x]$.

3   A Non-minimal Model of Belief Change

To recapitulate the basic idea of the current paper, the selection mechanism at work rejects the worst alternatives and selects the rest. If strictly followed, this principle would, in general, violate postulate $(4*)$. For the purpose of this paper, we will assume that $(4*)$ holds, and accordingly adjust our definition of the belief change operation.

We motivated this principle by appealing to the problem of iterated choice. Detail study of how our proposed approach deals with it is beyond the scope of this paper. In a sequel to this paper, however, we will replace AGM-expansion by abductive expansion [Pag96] and show, how, our account can handle iterated abductive belief expansion (and revision).

Accordingly, given an appropriate total preorder $\sqsubseteq$ on $\mathcal{M}$ for a belief set K we define the non-minimal revision operation $\boxplus_\sqsubseteq$ (the subscript is henceforth dropped for readability except when the context is confusing) as follows:

Definition 2 (from $\sqsubseteq$ to $\boxplus$) *Where $\sqsubseteq$ be a total preorder on $\mathcal{M}$ and K a belief set such that* $[K] = \{w \mid w \sqsubseteq w' \text{ for all } w' \in \mathcal{M}\}$,

$$[K_x^{\boxplus}] = \begin{cases} [K] \cap [x] & \text{if } [K] \cap [x] \neq \emptyset \\ [x] & \text{else if } [x] \text{ is } \sqsubseteq\text{-flat} \\ \{w \in [x] \mid w \sqsubset w' \\ \quad \text{for some } w' \in [x]\} & \text{otherwise.} \end{cases}$$

This definition separates three distinct cases where the evidence merits different treatments. These cases are separately pictured in Figure 3. The first case is represented by $[z]$. In this case all the models in $[z]$ except those which are also in $[K]$ are eliminated. The area $[y]$ represents the second case. Here, since the models in $[y]$ cannot be discriminated on the basis of $\sqsubseteq$ alone, none of them is eliminated. The principal case, namely the third case, is represented by $[x]$. Here, among the models provided by $[x]$, the most implausible ones are eliminated and the rest are retained, perhaps, for future scrutiny. Note that in the first two cases, $\boxplus$ behaves like the $G*$; only in the case of $[x]$ do they behave differently.

Note that in all the three cases mentioned above, $[K_x^{\boxplus}]$ is a subset of $[x]$ and, when $[K] \cap [x]$ is not empty, $[K_x^{\boxplus}] = [K] \cap [x]$. Accordingly, as readers acquainted with the AGM construction of belief revision from belief contraction via the Levi Identity [Gär88, § 3.6] will recognise, $\boxplus$ as defined from $\sqsubseteq$ via Definition 2 is actually, in the AGM parlance, a partial meet belief revision operation.[1] Hence, by the well known

---

[1] In order to see the connection, one should merely realise that there is a 1-1 mapping between $\mathcal{M}$ and $K \perp \neg x$ where $\neg x \in K$. The rest is folk-lore. Accordingly, a revision operation $\circ$ is partial-meet iff both $[K_x^{\circ}]$ is always a subset of $[x]$ and $[K_x^{\circ}] = [K] \cap [x]$ whenever the RHS is not empty, relational-partial-meet iff it is partial-meet and there exists a binary relation R over $\mathcal{M}$ such that $[K_x^{\circ}]$ is exactly the set of R-best

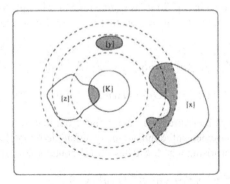

Figure 2: Belief Change without minimality

results from the AGM literature (see Footnote 1) ⊞ will satisfy the (basic) AGM revision postulates (1∗)-(6∗). The more interesting questions are, of course, whether ⊞ will satisfy the (supplementary) revision postulates (7∗)-(8∗).

The first indication that ⊞ will conflict with (7∗) is that in general it is not "relational", i.e., there exists no binary relation ⊑′ over $\mathcal{M}$ such that $K^{⊞}_x$ is, for all sentences x, the set of ⊑′-minimal elements of $[x]$.

Observation 1 *If ⊑ partitions $\mathcal{M}$ into more than three ⊑-equivalent classes, then the operation ⊞ is not relational.*

Proof Sketch: Assume to the contrary. Then there exists some relation ⊑′ such that for every sentence x, the members of $[K^{⊞}_x]$ are exactly the ⊑′-minimal members of $[x]$. Now, pick a sentence x such that no member of $[x]$ is ⊑-minimal in $\mathcal{M}$ and $[x]$ contains members of at least three distinct ⊑-equivalent classes. Then, all its members that are not ⊑-maximal in $[x]$, being ⊑′-minimal in $[x]$, are ⊑′-equivalent. Now choose a sentence y such that both $[y] \subseteq [K^{⊞}_x]$ and $[y]$ contains members of at least two ⊑-equivalent classes. Then $[K^{⊞}_y] \subset [y]$ but all members of $[y]$ are ⊑′-equivalent. ∎

A counter-example to (7∗) can be easily constructed by judiciously choosing the sentences x and y. However, ⊞ satisfies several weaker versions of (7∗), as evidenced by observations (2-4).

Observation 2 *If $K^{⊞}_x \not\subseteq Cn(x \wedge y)$ then $K^{⊞}_{x \wedge y} \subseteq Cn(K^{⊞}_x \cup \{y\})$.*

Proof Sketch: Assume $K^{⊞}_x \not\subseteq Cn(x \wedge y)$. Hence $[x \wedge y] \not\subseteq [K^{⊞}_x]$. Need to show that $[K^{⊞}_x] \cap [y] \subseteq [K^{⊞}_{x \wedge y}]$. Assume that $w \in [K^{⊞}_x]$ and $w \in [y]$. If $[x]$ is ⊑-flat, or $[K] \cap [x] \neq \emptyset$, then the proof is trivial. As to the principal case, assume that $[x]$ is not ⊑-flat and $[K] \cap [x] = \emptyset$. Since $[x \wedge y] \not\subseteq [K^{⊞}_x]$, assume world w' such that $w' \models x \wedge y$

---

elements of $[x]$ and transitively-relational-partial-meet iff it is relational-partial-meet plus the relation R in question is transitive over $\mathcal{M}$. The postulates (1∗)–(6∗) characterise a partial-meet revision operation. A relational-partial-meet revision operation also satisfies (7∗). A revision operation is transitively-relational-partial-meet if and only if it is AGM rational.

and that w' is $\sqsubseteq$-maximal in $[x]$. So w' is $\sqsubseteq$-maximal in $[x] \cap [y]$. Since $w \in [x] \cap [y]$ and w is not $\sqsubseteq$-maximal in $[x]$, it follows that w is not $\sqsubseteq$-maximal in $[x] \cap [y]$. So $w \in [K_{x \wedge y}^{\boxplus}]$. ∎

Observation 3 *If* $K_y^{\boxplus} = Cn(y)$ *then* $K_{x \wedge y}^{\boxplus} \subseteq Cn(K_x^{\boxplus} \cup \{y\})$.

Observation 4 *If* $K_x^{\boxplus} \cap Cn(y) \subseteq Cn(x)$ *then* $K_{x \wedge y}^{\boxplus} \subseteq Cn(K_x^{\boxplus} \cup \{y\})$

In the belief change literature, it is often pointed out that $(8*)$ is rather strong and should possibly be weakened, although not many researchers complain about $(7*)$. It is perhaps some what surprising that $\boxplus$ satisfies $(8*)$ although it fails to satisfy $(7*)$.

Observation 5 *If* $K_x^{\boxplus} \not\vdash \neg y$ *then* $Cn(K_x^{\boxplus} \cup \{y\}) \subseteq K_{x \wedge y}^{\boxplus}$.

Proof Sketch: Again, we prove only the non-trivial case where both $[x]$ is not $\sqsubseteq$-flat and $[K] \cap [x] = \emptyset$. Assume $[K_x^{\boxplus}] \cap [y] \neq \emptyset$ whence there is a member w_0 in $[x] \cap [y]$ that is not $\sqsubseteq$-maximal in $[x]$. Let $w \in [K_{x \wedge y}^{\boxplus}]$. Hence w is chosen from $[x] \cap [y]$. Since w_0 is available in $[x] \cap [y]$, surely w is not $\sqsubseteq$-maximal in $[x]$ whereby $w \in [K_x^{\boxplus}]$. ∎

Another interesting principle that $\boxplus$ satisfies is the following:

Observation 6 *If* $K \vdash \neg x$, $K_x^{\boxplus} \vdash \neg y$ *but* $x \not\vdash \neg y$ *then* $K_{x \wedge y}^{\boxplus} = Cn(x \wedge y)$.

Thus we have seen that the non minimal revision operation $\boxplus_{\sqsubseteq}$ satisfies the following properties:

(1–6$\boxplus$) AGM (1∗-6∗) with ∗ replaced by $\boxplus$
(7.1$\boxplus$) If $K_x^{\boxplus} \not\subseteq Cn(x \wedge y)$ then $K_{x \wedge y}^{\boxplus} \subseteq Cn(K_x^{\boxplus} \cup \{y\})$
(7.2$\boxplus$) If $K_y^{\boxplus} = Cn(y)$ then $K_{x \wedge y}^{\boxplus} \subseteq Cn(K_x^{\boxplus} \cup \{y\})$
(7.3$\boxplus$) If $K_x^{\boxplus} \cap Cn(y) \subseteq Cn(x)$
 then $K_{x \wedge y}^{\boxplus} \subseteq Cn(K_x^{\boxplus} \cup \{y\})$
(8$\boxplus$) If $K_x^{\boxplus} \not\vdash \neg y$ then $Cn(K_x^{\boxplus} \cup \{y\}) \subseteq K_{x \wedge y}^{\boxplus}$
(9$\boxplus$) If $K \vdash \neg x$, $K_x^{\boxplus} \vdash \neg y$ but $x \not\vdash \neg y$
 then $K_{x \wedge y}^{\boxplus} = Cn(x \wedge y)$.

In Section 5 we show that these nine postulates fully characterise the non-minimal belief revision operation. Before that, however, we will examine whether the non-minimal approach we are advocating is not too weak. In the process, we will run through an example which shows how non-minimal belief revision works in practice.

4 Discussion: Modelling Issues

Since non-minimal belief revision is clearly weaker than the minimality based AGM style belief revision, we must ensure that in this process of weakening, we are not throwing away the baby along with the bath water. Although conditions ($1\boxplus - 8\boxplus$) go some way in alleviating this fear, this important issue merits a more detailed examination. In this connection, we consider a possible objection to the view we are advocating.

It seems that given two birds Tweety and Tim, according to the proposed theory we *cannot* infer that they will fly. The reason is, the only state that can be excluded from consideration – namely, the least plausible state – is the one in which *both* birds fail to fly. That is, the state in which Tweety does not fly but Tim does and the state in which Tim flies but Tweety does not, will both be *plausible*.

Let us agree on the following abbreviations for the sake of brevity: x_1: bird(tweety), x_2: bird(tim), y_1: fly(tweety) and y_2: fly(tim). Assuming that these are the only relevant atoms of the language in question, there are sixteen possible worlds/states, named in the following table:

w#	x_1	x_2	y_1	y_2	w#	x_1	x_2	y_1	y_2
1	T	T	T	T	9	F	T	T	T
2	T	T	T	F	10	F	T	T	F
3	T	T	F	T	11	F	T	F	T
4	T	T	F	F	12	F	T	F	F
5	T	F	T	T	13	F	F	T	T
6	T	F	T	F	14	F	F	T	F
7	T	F	F	T	15	F	F	F	T
8	T	F	F	F	16	F	F	F	F

The essence of this objction in question is the following. Suppose we know that typically birds fly. We also know of two objects called Tweety and Tim. For added measure, assume that Tweety and Tim are believed to be non-birds (and non-fliers)[2]. We want to model this situation.

Now, consider the worlds in which both Tweety and Tim are birds, namely, worlds $1-4$. Since we know that typically birds fly, among these four worlds, 1 is most plausible and 4 is least plausible. Hence, if we were to learn that bird(tweety) $\wedge$ bird(tim), i.e., the set $\{1, \ldots, 4\}$, then the least plausible of them, namely 4 is rejected, and we are left with $\{1, 2, 3\}$ which allows the possibility of Tweety (or Tim) being a non-flier. Hence, non-minimal belief change does not allow us to infer that both Tweety and Tim fly from the premise that both of them are birds.

In fact, this objection can be modified to put the theory we are advocating under even worse light. Suppose the new information is simply bird(tweety), represented by the set $\{1, \ldots, 8\}$. It follows that worlds 2 and 3 are not least plausible in $\{1, \ldots, 8\}$ (since they are not least plausible in $\{1, \ldots, 4\}$); hence we cannot infer that Tweety flies. Thus, it appears that non-minimal approach not only disallows inferring that both Tweety and Tim fly from the premise that they are birds, it also disallows the inference that Tweety (or Tim) flies from the premise that Tweety (or Tim) is a bird. Right? Wrong.

This latter case is particularly interesting in that it helps to show what is wrong in this modelling of the situation in question – namely, this particular way of modelling the envisaged situation puts the cart before the horse. What this example establishes is that

---

[2]Without the assumption that Tweety and Tim are non-birds, the situation being described will become a case of AGM-expansion, and is of no interest here.

under this particular modelling of the situation one cannot infer that Tweety (or Tim) flies from the premise that Tweety (or Tim) is a bird. It is little wonder that we cannot infer that Tweety and Tim fly from the premise that Tweety and Tim are birds (under this modelling). This example however does *not* establish that non-minimal approach does not allow one to infer that Tweety and Tim fly from the premise that Tweety and Tim are birds.

The moral to be drawn from this exercise is that modelling of situations are typically different in minimal and non-minimal approaches to belief change. Since the inference relations in question are different, the same situation (e.g. "birds typically fly") will be modelled in different ways in the minimalist and non-minimalist framework. Modelling a situation in the way appropriate for the minimalist approach, and then applying the inference procedure due to the non-minimalist approach will yield unintuitive results. We discuss below the primary difference in the modelling techniques between the minimalist and non-minimalist approaches and demonstrate how the situation referred to in the objection can be modelled in the non-minimalist approach and yet allow us to infer that both Tim and Tweety fly.

Let us denote by $max(S)$, for any set S of worlds, the set of $\sqsubseteq$-maximal elements of S, and by $min(S)$ the set of its $\sqsubseteq$-minimal elements. In general, in the minimality-based approach, $x \hspace{-0.3em}\sim\hspace{-0.3em} y$ leads to the modelling constraint that the set of $\sqsubseteq$-minimal x-worlds is a subset of the set of y-worlds, i.e., $min([x]) \subseteq [y]$. But in the non-minimal approach, the corresponding constraint is different. In the principal case, when $max([x]) \neq [x]$, the constraint in question is that $[x \wedge \neg y] \subseteq max([x]) \not\supseteq [x \wedge y]$. In the special case, when $max([x]) = [x]$, it is simply required that $[x] \subseteq [y]$. Suppose that we

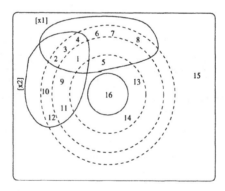

Figure 3: Tweety and Tim, being birds, fly.

would like to conclude fly(tweety) from bird(tweety). In non-minimal approach, this leads to the constraint that $\{3, 4, 7, 8\} \subseteq max(\{1, \ldots, 8\}) \not\supseteq \{1, 2, 5, 6\}$, that is, 3, 4, 7, 8 are maximal, but at least one of 1, 2, 5, 6 is not maximal. Similarly, the other desideratum that we should be able to infer fly(tim) from bird(tim), leads to the the constraint $\{2, 4, 10, 12\} \subseteq max(\{1, \ldots, 4, 9, \ldots, 12\}) \not\supseteq \{1, 3, 9, 11\}$. Thus, together, we are constrained to consider worlds 2,3,4,7,8,10 and 12 to be $\sqsubseteq$-maximal among 1-12, although this list need not be exhaustive. We are furthermore constrained to consider at least one of 1,5,6 and one of 1,9,11 to be non-maximal. There are no constraints on 13-15 to speak of (we assumed that $[K] = \{16\}$ at the beginning). Thus there is a lot of flexibility in their ordering; and the inference behaviour of the situation will depend on that. For instance, in presence of these constraints, $x_1 \wedge x_2 \hspace{0.1em}\vdash\hspace{-0.8em}\sim\hspace{0.2em} y_1 \wedge y_2$ just in case 1 is not $\sqsubseteq$-maximal among 1-12. Figure 4 exemplifies one such ordering. According to this, since both 1 and 5, the non-maximal members of $[x_1]$, satisfy y_1, bird(tweety) $\hspace{0.1em}\vdash\hspace{-0.8em}\sim\hspace{0.2em}$ fly(tweety). Similarly, since each of 1, 9 and 11, the non-maximal members of x_2 satisfies y_2, bird(tim) $\hspace{0.1em}\vdash\hspace{-0.8em}\sim\hspace{0.2em}$ fly(tim). Furthermore, since 1 is the only non-maximal member of $[x_1] \cap [y_1]$, it follows that bird(tweety)$\wedge$ bird(tim) $\hspace{0.1em}\vdash\hspace{-0.8em}\sim\hspace{0.2em}$ fly(tweety)$\wedge$ fly(tim).

5 Completeness Results

In this section we will show that given a revision operation $\boxplus$ that satisfies $(1\boxplus - 9\boxplus)$ and a fixed belief set K we can construct a binary relation $\sqsubseteq_{\boxplus,K}$ with the desired properties. (We will normally drop the subscripts for readability.) In particular, we will show that, where $\sqsubseteq$ is the relation so constructed: (1) $\sqsubseteq$ is a total preorder over $\mathcal{M}$, (2) the SOS (System of Spheres) corresponding to $\sqsubseteq$ is a SOS centred on $[K]$ and (3) $K_x^\boxplus = K_x^{\boxplus\sqsubseteq}$ for any sentence x.

Definition 3 (from $\boxplus$ to $\sqsubseteq$) *Given a revision operation $\boxplus$ and a belief set K, $w \sqsubseteq_{\boxplus,K} w'$ iff $w \in [K_x^\boxplus]$ whenever $w' \in [K_x^\boxplus]$, for every sentence x such that $w \models x$ and $w' \models x$.*

Theorem 1 *Let $\boxplus$ be a revision operation satisfying $(1\boxplus) - (9\boxplus)$ and K a belief set. Let $\sqsubseteq$ be generated from $\boxplus$ and K as prescribed by Definition 3. Then $\sqsubseteq$ is a total preorder on $\mathcal{M}$ such that $[K]$ is the set of $\sqsubseteq$-minimal elements of $\mathcal{M}$.*

The proof of this theorem, in particular, the transitivity of $\sqsubseteq$, presupposes that $\mathcal{M}$ is finite – i.e., the language $\mathcal{L}$ can be divided into a finite number of equivalence classes modulo Cn. We suspect this restriction can be eliminated, but we have no proof for that.

Proof Sketch: The proof that $\sqsubseteq$ is reflexive is trivial and the proof that $[K]$ is the set of $\sqsubseteq$-minimal elements of $\mathcal{M}$ is fairly straightforward. We show the other two properties of $\sqsubseteq$.

Transitivity: For this proof, we assume that $\mathcal{M}$ is finite so that each world w can be represented as a sentence. Assume worlds w_1, w_2 and w_3 such that $w_1 \sqsubseteq w_2$, $w_2 \sqsubseteq w_3$ and $w_3 \in [K_x^\boxplus]$ but $w_1 \notin [K_x^\boxplus]$ for some arbitrary sentence x. If $w_2 \in [x]$, then the proof is trivial; so assume otherwise. Let α and β be sentences such that $[\alpha] = [x] \cup \{w_2\}$ and $[\beta] = \mathcal{M} \setminus \{w_2\}$. Thus $\vdash x \leftrightarrow (\alpha \wedge \beta)$. Case 1. $w_3 \in [K_\alpha^\boxplus]$. Since w_1 and w_2 are also in $[\alpha]$, it follows that they are also in $[K_\alpha^\boxplus]$. Hence $[\alpha] \subseteq [K_\alpha^\boxplus] \cup [\beta]$. By $(7.3\boxplus)$ then, $[K_\alpha^\boxplus] \cap [\beta] \subseteq [K_x^\boxplus]$. Hence $w_1 \in [K_x^\boxplus]$ from which the contradiction easily follows.

Case 2. $w_3 \notin [K_\alpha^\boxplus]$. By $(7.1\boxplus)$ it follows that $[K_\alpha^\boxplus] \cap [\beta] \subseteq [K_{\alpha\wedge\beta}^\boxplus] = [K_x^\boxplus]$. Furthermore, $(8\boxplus)$ applies and we get the converse. So, $[K_x^\boxplus] = [K_\alpha^\boxplus] \cap [\beta]$. But that violates the assumption that $w_3 \in [K_x^\boxplus]$.

Connectedness: Suppose $w \not\sqsubseteq w'$. Let then x be a sentence, $w \models x$, $w' \models x$ such that $w' \in [K_x^\boxplus]$ but $w \notin [K_x^\boxplus]$. Consider an arbitrary sentence y such that $w \models y$,

$w' \models y$ and $w \in [K_y^{⊞}]$ and $w' \notin [K_y^{⊞}]$. It will be sufficient to derive a contradiction. It follows that $w \models x \wedge y$ and $w' \models x \wedge y$. Furthermore, it follows from the assumptions that $K_x^{⊞} \not\vdash \neg y$ whence, by (8⊞) we get $[K_{x \wedge y}^{⊞}] \subseteq [K_x^{⊞}] \cap [y]$. Similarly, we get $[K_{x \wedge y}^{⊞}] \subseteq [K_y^{⊞}] \cap [x]$. Hence neither w nor w' is in $[K_{x \wedge y}^{⊞}]$. On the other hand, $w' \in [K_x^{⊞}] \cap [y]$ but $w' \notin [K_{x \wedge y}^{⊞}]$ whereby $K_{x \wedge y}^{⊞} \not\subseteq Cn(K_x^{⊞} \cup \{y\})$. By (7.1⊞) then $[x \wedge y] \subseteq [K_x^{⊞}]$ whereby $w \in [K_x^{⊞}]$ contradicting the assumption. ∎

Theorem 3 together with Observations 2–6 provide the representation result.

Furthermore, the total preorder $\sqsubseteq_{⊞,K}$ constructed from a given non minimal revision operation ⊞ and belief set K is the desired $\sqsubseteq$ in the sense the non minimal revision operation constructed from it, in turn, behaves like the original operation ⊞ with respect to the belief set K.

Theorem 2 *Let ⊞ be a non minimal belief revision operator satisfying postulates (1⊞ – 9⊞) and K be an arbitrary belief set. Let $\sqsubseteq$ be defined from ⊞ and K in accordance with Definition 3. Let $⊞' = ⊞_{\sqsubseteq}$ be defined from $\sqsubseteq$, in turn, via Definition 2. Then for any sentences x (and the originally fixed belief set K) it holds that $K_x^{⊞} = K_x^{⊞'}$.*

Proof Sketch: If either $K \not\vdash \neg x$ or $[x]$ is $\sqsubseteq$-flat, then the proof is straight forward. So consider only the principal case.
Left to Right. Assume that $w \in [K_x^{⊞}]$. It is sufficient to show that w is not $\sqsubseteq$-maximal in $[x]$. Suppose, to the contrary, that w is $\sqsubseteq$-maximal in $[x]$. Let w' be an arbitrary member of $[x]$. So $w' \sqsubseteq w$. Since $w \in [K_x^{⊞}]$, it follows by Definition 3 then that $w' \in [K_x^{⊞}]$. Hence $[K_x^{⊞}] = [x]$. Since $[x]$ is not $\sqsubseteq$-flat, there exists world $w_0 \in [x]$ and sentence y such that $\{w, w_0\} \subseteq [y]$, $w_o \in [K_y^{⊞}]$ but $w \notin [K_y^{⊞}]$. By (7.3⊞), $[K_x^{⊞}] \cap [y] \subseteq [K_{x \wedge y}^{⊞}] = [K_{y \wedge x}^{⊞}]$. Then, by (8⊞), $[K_{y \wedge x}^{⊞}] \subseteq [K_y^{⊞}] \cap [x]$ whereby $w \in [K_y^{⊞}]$. Contradiction!

Right to Left. Assume that (i) $w \in [K_x^{⊞'}]$ and (ii) $w \notin [K_x^{⊞}]$. It follows from (i) that w is in $[x]$ but not $\sqsubseteq$-maximal in $[x]$. Let w' be $\sqsubseteq$-maximal in $[x]$. So $w \sqsubset w'$. If $w' \in [K_x^{⊞}]$ then result trivially follows. Assume then (iii) $w' \notin [K_x^{⊞}]$. Since $w \sqsubset w'$, let y be a sentence such that $\{w, w'\} \subseteq [y]$, (iv) $w' \notin [K_y^{⊞}]$ but (v) $w \in [K_y^{⊞}]$. Given assumption (ii), by (7.1⊞) it follows that (vi) $[K_x^{⊞}] \cap [y] \subseteq [K_{x \wedge y}^{⊞}]$. Similarly, due to (iv), we get (vii) $[K_y^{⊞}] \cap [x] \subseteq [K_{x \wedge y}^{⊞}]$. From (v) and (8⊞) we get (viii) $[K_{x \wedge y}^{⊞}] \subseteq [K_y^{⊞}] \cap [x]$. From (vi), (vii) and (viii) together, we get (ix) $[K_x^{⊞}] \cap [y] \subseteq [K_y^{⊞}] \cap [x]$. Now, if $K_x^{⊞} \vdash \neg y$ then by applying (9⊞) and (vii)-(viii) we get the contradiction that $[x] \cap [y] = [K_y^{⊞}] \cap [x]$ (w' is in the LHS but not in the RHS). On the other hand, if $K_x^{⊞} \not\vdash \neg y$ then by (8⊞) and (vi)-(vii) we get $[K_x^{⊞}] \cap [y] = [K_y^{⊞}] \cap [x]$ which is contradictory (w not in the LHS but in the RHS). ∎

Conversely, one can start with a total preorder $\sqsubseteq$, construct a revision operation ⊞ from it via Definition 2 and then construct a a total preorder $\sqsubseteq$ from that ⊞ in turn via Definition 3, then one gets back the original relation $\sqsubseteq$.

Theorem 3 *Let $\sqsubseteq$ be a total preorder on $\mathcal{M}$ and $[K]$ the set of $\sqsubseteq$-minimal members of $\mathcal{M}$. Let ⊞ be defined (for K) from $\sqsubseteq$ via Definition 2. Let $\sqsubseteq' = \sqsubseteq_{⊞}$ be defined from ⊞ in turn, via Definition 3. Then $w \sqsubseteq w'$ iff $w \sqsubseteq' w'$ for any two worlds $w, w' \in \mathcal{M}$*

The proof of this claim is straightforward, and omitted.

6 Conclusions and Outlook

In several approaches to commonsense reasoning, the extra power of the inference engine is obtained by eliminating all the models allowed by the evidence except those that are judged to be least implausible in it. Instead, we studied, in the context of belief revision, the consequences of its dual approach, namely retaining all the models allowed by the evidence except those judged to be most implausible.

We observed that although the ensuing belief revision operation is not in general relational, still it satisfies several weakened versions of the AGM postulate (7*). Perhaps somewhat surprisingly, it also satisfies the AGM postulate (8*). We also provided a set of postulates that completely characterise this non minimal belief revision operation.

We suggest that an abductive extension of our proposal can handle the interesting problem of iterated abductive belief change, which has not been dealt in the literature. Research in that direction is currently being pursued.

References

[AGM85] Carlos E. Alchourrón, Peter Gärdenfors, and David Makinson. On the logic of theory change: Partial meet contraction and revision functions. *Journal of Symbolic Logic*, 50:510–530, 1985.

[Axe84] Robert M. Axelrod. *Evolution of Cooperation*. Basic Books, 1984.

[Gär88] Peter Gärdenfors. *Knowledge in Flux: Modeling the Dynamics of Epistemic States*. Bradford Books, MIT Press, Cambridge Massachusetts, 1988.

[GM94] Peter Gärdenfors and David Makinson. Nonmonotonic inference based on expectations. *Artificial Intelligence*, 65:197–245, 1994.

[Gro88] Adam Grove. Two modellings for theory change. *Journal of Philosophical Logic*, 17:157–170, 1988.

[Hol75] John H. Holland. *Adaptation in Natural and Artificial Systems*. The University of Michigan Press, 1975.

[KLM90] S. Kraus, D. Lehmann, and M. Magidor. Nonmonotonic reasoning, preferential models and cumulative logics. *Artificial intelligence*, 44:167–207, 1990.

[KM92] Hirofumi Katsuno and Alberto O. Mendelzon. On the difference between updating a knowledge base and revising it. In Peter Gärdenfors, editor, *Belief Revision*, pages 183–203. Cambridge University Press, 1992.

[Pag96] Maurice Pagnucco. *The Role of Abductive Reasoning within the Process of Belief revision*. PhD thesis, University of Sydney, 1996.

[Rot96] Hans Rott. *Making up one's mind: Foundations, coherence, nonmonotonicity*, To be published by Oxford University Press, 1998.

[San94] Erik Sandewall. *Features and Fluents*. Oxford University Press, 1994.

[Sho88] Yoav Shoham. *Reasoning About Change*. MIT Press, Cambridge, Massachusetts, 1988.

Reasoning with Sets of Preferences in Default Logic

James P. Delgrande[1] and Torsten Schaub[2]

[1] School of Computing Science, Simon Fraser University, Burnaby, B.C., Canada V5A 1S6,
jim@cs.sfu.ca
[2] Institut für Informatik, Universität Potsdam, PF 60 15 53, D-14415 Potsdam,
torsten@cs.uni-potsdam.de

Abstract. We address the problem of representing preferences among sets of properties (outcomes, desiderata, etc.) in default logic. In this approach, an ordered default theory consists of default rules, world knowledge, and preferences on sets of default rules. An ordered theory is transformed into a second, standard default theory wherein the preferences are respected, in that defaults are applied in the specified order and a set of order-equivalent defaults is applied only en masse. This translation is accomplished via the naming of defaults, so that reference may be made to default rules and sets of default rules from within a theory. The approach differs from previous work in that we obtain standard default theories, and do not rely on prioritised versions as do other approaches. In practical terms this means we can immediately use existing default logic theorem provers for an implementation. From a theoretical point of view, this shows that the explicit representation of priorities among sets of defaults adds nothing to the overall expressibility of default logic.

1   Introduction

The notion of *preference* in commonsense reasoning is pervasive. For example, in scheduling not all deadlines may be simultaneously satisfiable, and in configuration various goals may not be simultaneously met. In legal reasoning, laws may apply by default but the laws themselves may conflict; such conflicts may be adjudicated by higher-level principles. Such preferences may be naturally expressed as orderings among defaults in some nonmonotonic reasoning system, the idea being that one wants just the highest-ranked default(s) to apply.

In earlier work [7], we explored preference orderings among default rules in default logic (DL) [11]. In this approach one can state that for colour of a car, red is preferred to blue, which in turn is preferred to green. In the present paper, we extend this work to deal with *sets* of preferences. Thus, in the present paper, one can state that one prefers a car that is safe and efficient over one that is cheap, efficient, and stylish. We begin with an *ordered default theory*, with explicit preferences given on sets of default rules. This theory is translated into a standard default theory, where provably defaults are applied in the appropriate fashion. So with this translation we obtain a theory in "standard" default logic, rather than requiring machinery external to DL, as is found in previous approaches.

We remain within the framework of standard DL, rather than building a scheme on top of DL, for several reasons. First, our approach can be immediately implemented by making use of existing DL theorem provers. Second, it is easier to compare differing types of preference within a single framework. Moreover, in "compiling" preferences into DL, and in using the standard machinery of default logic, we obtain insight into the notion of preference orderings. Thus for example we implicitly show that explicit priorities provide no real increase in the expressibility of default logic. In the next section, we briefly discuss the notion of "preference", and review default logic. The following section reviews our work on preferences in DL. In Section 4, we develop our approach, and the final section concludes with a brief discussion.

2 Background

2.1 Default Logic and Ordered Default Logic

Default logic [11] augments classical logic by *default rules* of the form $\frac{\alpha : \beta}{\gamma}$. A rule is *normal* if β is equivalent to γ; it is *semi-normal* if β implies γ. We sometimes denote the *prerequisite* α of a default δ by $Prereq(\delta)$, its *justification* β by $Justif(\delta)$ and its *consequent* γ by $Conseq(\delta)$. Empty components, such as no prerequisite or even no justifications, are assumed to be tautological. Defaults with unbound variables are taken to stand for all corresponding instances. A set of default rules D and a set of formulas W form a *default theory* (D, W) that may induce a single or multiple *extensions* in the following way.

Definition 1. *Let* (D, W) *be a default theory and let* E *be a set of formulas. Define* $E_0 = W$ *and for* $i \geq 0$:

$$\Gamma_i = \left\{ \frac{\alpha : \beta}{\gamma} \in D \,\middle|\, \alpha \in E_i, \neg\beta \notin E, \right\} \quad and \quad E_{i+1} = Th(E_i) \cup \{ Conseq(\delta) \mid \delta \in \Gamma_i \}$$

Then E *is an extension for* (D, W) *if* $E = \bigcup_{i=0}^{\infty} E_i$.

Any such extension represents a possible set of beliefs about the world at hand. The above procedure is not constructive since E appears in the specification of E_{i+1}. We define $\Gamma = \bigcup_{i=0}^{\infty} \Gamma_i$ as the set of default rules *generating* extension E.

2.2 Preference Orderings

For adding preferences among default rules, a default theory is usually extended with an ordering on the set of default rules. In analogy to [1,3], an *ordered default theory* $(D, W, <)$ is a finite set D of default rules, a set W of formulas, and a strict partial order $< \subseteq D \times D$ on the default rules. For simplicity, we assume the existence of a default $\delta_\top = \frac{\top : \top}{\top} \in D$ where for every rule $\delta_i \neq \delta_\top$ we have $\delta_i < \delta_\top$. This gives us a (trivial) maximally preferred default that is always applicable to "start things off".

Assume that we have an ordered default theory on individual default rules. Informally a higher-ranked default should be applied or considered before a lower-ranked default. As noted in [7], there is more than one way in which defaults may be applied, given an ordering. Consider where we have the defaults that "Canadians speak English by default", "Québecois speak French by default", "residents of the north of

Québec speak Cree by default": $\frac{Can:English}{English} < \frac{Que:French}{French} < \frac{NQue:Cree}{Cree}$. If a resi-
dent of the north of Québec didn't speak Cree, it would be reasonable to assume that
they spoke French, and if not French, then English. Basically, for a chain of defaults
$\delta_1 < \delta_2 < \ldots < \delta_m$ we apply δ_m if possible; then apply δ_{m-1} if possible; and continue in this fashion until no more than k (for fixed k where $1 \le k \le m$) defaults have
been applied. For implementing preferences, approaches such as [2, 3, 1] add explicit
preferences in default logic by modifying the definition of an extension.[1] In [7] we show
that this additional machinery is unnecessary, in that preferences can be "compiled" into
a standard default theory.

We consider here ordered default theories where the ordering is on *sets* of defaults.
[5] presents initial work with a similar goal, but no within the framework of *qualitative
value logic*. As before, we take an ordered theory and translate it into a standard default
theory. As an example, consider where in buying a car one ranks the price over safety
features over power, but safety features together with power is ranked over price. We
can write this as:

$$m_1:\left\{\tfrac{:P}{P}\right\} < m_2:\left\{\tfrac{:S}{S}\right\} < m_3:\left\{\tfrac{:E}{E}\right\} < m_{1,2}:\left\{\tfrac{:P}{P}, \tfrac{:S}{S}\right\} < m_\top:\{\delta_\top\}, \quad (1)$$

m_1, m_2, m_3, and $m_{1,2}$ are names of sets of defaults; we describe their use later. If we
were given only that not all desiderata can be satisfied (i.e. $W = \{\neg(P \wedge E \wedge S)\}$)
then we could apply the defaults in the set (named) $m_{1,2}$ and conclude that P and S can
be met. However, there is a problem with "side-effects" in the naive implementation
of this approach. For example, assume that P and S can't be jointly met (i.e. $W =
\{\neg(P \wedge S)\}$). We would expect that there just be a single extension containing E and
S. In a naive implementation, one would try to apply the defaults in $m_{1,2}$. On applying
the default $\frac{:P}{P}$ it would prove to be the case that $\frac{:S}{S}$ could not be applied. So we would
find that the topmost nontrivial set isn't applicable. However, in finding that defaults in
the set $m_{1,2}$ can't all be applied, we don't want to actually apply the default $\frac{:P}{P}$, since
if we did, we would then try to apply the default in the next set (viz. $\frac{:E}{E}$), which would
be successful, but then, given P we couldn't apply the default in m_2. The difficulty is
that, in determining that a default in the set named $m_{1,2}$ is inapplicable, we may obtain
a side-effect that another default in the preference ordering is blocked.

3 Preferences on Defaults

We show here how ordered default theories can be translated into standard default theories; this section reviews [7]. An *ordered default theory* $(D, W, <)$ is a finite set D of
default rules, a set W of formulas, and a strict partial order $< \subseteq D \times D$ on the default
rules. Our strategy is to introduce predicates in the default rules to enable the control
of rule application. We associate a unique name with each default rule. This is done by
extending the original language by a set of constants[2] N such that there is a bijective

---

[1] Other work, such as [12, 9, 6] have addressed the separate problem of adding specificity information in default logic. In this case one finds the most specific applicable default and, if
possible, applies it.

[2] This is done also in [4].

mapping $\eta : D \to N$. We write n_δ instead of $\eta(\delta)$ (and we often abbreviate n_{δ_i} by n_i to ease notation). For default rule δ along with its name n, we sometimes write $n : \delta$ to render naming explicit. To reflect the fact that we deal with a finite set of distinct default rules, we adopt a unique names assumption (UNA_N) and domain closure assumption (DCA_N) with respect to N. That is, for a name set $N = \{n_1, \ldots, n_m\}$, we add axioms $\forall x.\ name(x) \equiv (x = n_1 \vee \ldots \vee x = n_m)$ and $(n_i \neq n_j)$ for all $n_i, n_j \in N$ with $i \neq j$. For convenience, we write $\forall x \in N.\ P(x)$ instead of $\forall x.\ name(x) \supset P(x)$. The use of names allows the expression of preference relations between default rules in the object language. So $n_j : \frac{\omega : \phi}{\varphi}$ is preferred to $n_i : \frac{\alpha : \beta}{\gamma}$ is given by $n_i \prec n_j$, where $\prec$ is a new predicate in the object language.

If we are given $\delta_i < \delta_j$, then we want to ensure that before δ_i is applied, that δ_j be applied or found to be inapplicable. We do this by first translating a default rule $\delta = \frac{\alpha : \beta}{\gamma}$ to

$$\frac{\alpha \wedge \mathsf{ok}(n_\delta) : \beta}{\gamma \wedge \mathsf{ap}(n_\delta)}, \quad \frac{\mathsf{ok}(n_\delta) : \neg\alpha}{\mathsf{bl}(n_\delta)}, \quad \frac{\neg\beta \wedge \mathsf{ok}(n_\delta) :}{\mathsf{bl}(n_\delta)}. \tag{2}$$

Predicates $\mathsf{ok}(\cdot)$, $\mathsf{bl}(\cdot)$, and $\mathsf{ap}(\cdot)$ are special-purpose predicates introduced to control rule application. None of the rules in the translation can be applied unless $\mathsf{ok}(n_\delta)$ is true. Since $\mathsf{ok}(\cdot)$ is a new predicate symbol, it can be expressly made true in order to potentially enable the application of the three rules in the image of the translation. If $\mathsf{ok}(n_\delta)$ is true, the first rule of the translation may potentially be applied. If a rule has been applied, then this is "recorded" by assertion $\mathsf{ap}(n_\delta)$. The last two rules give conditions under which the original rule is inapplicable: either the negation of the original antecedent α is consistent (with the extension) or the justification β is known to be false; in either such case $\mathsf{bl}(n_\delta)$ is concluded.

For $\delta_i < \delta_j$ we can now fully control the order of rule application: if δ_j has been applied (and so $\mathsf{ap}(n_j)$ is true), or known to be inapplicable (and so $\mathsf{bl}(n_j)$ is true), then it's ok to apply δ_i. So we add to our world knowledge a formula

$$\forall x \in N.\ [\forall y \in N.\ (x \prec y) \supset (\mathsf{bl}(y) \vee \mathsf{ap}(y))] \supset \mathsf{ok}(x)$$

expressing that it is ok to apply a default if all higher-ranked defaults have been applied or are known to be blocked. We require other bookkeeping information. We have unique names and domain closure assumptions, as indicated above. As well we have a mapping of external preferences into an ordering on names expressed in our theory; that is to W we add $\{n_\delta \prec n_{\delta'} \mid (\delta, \delta') \in <\}$, along with an assertion (effectively) of complete knowledge on $\prec$, given by the additional default $\frac{: \neg(x \prec y)}{\neg(x \prec y)}$. This gives us a translation mapping ordered default theories onto standard default theories. Space considerations preclude a lengthy examination of the approach; see [7]. Suffice it to say that the approach is shown to have appropriate properties, for example that in an extension E of (the translation of) ordered default theory $(D, W, <)$, we have $\mathsf{ok}(n_\delta) \in E$ for every default δ; either $\mathsf{ap}(n_\delta) \in E$ or $\mathsf{bl}(n_\delta) \in E$; that defaults are applied in the appropriate order; and so on. The important overall consequence is that we have full control over default application.

As an example, consider the defaults:

$$n_1 : \frac{A_1 : B_1}{C_1}, \quad n_2 : \frac{A_2 : B_2}{C_2}, \quad n_3 : \frac{A_3 : B_3}{C_3}, \quad n_\top : \frac{\top : \top}{\top}.$$

We obtain for $i = 1, 2, 3$:

$$\frac{A_i \wedge \text{ok}(n_i) : B_i}{C_i \wedge \text{ap}(n_i)}, \qquad \frac{\text{ok}(n_i) : \neg A_i}{\text{bl}(n_i)}, \qquad \frac{\neg B_i \wedge \text{ok}(n_i) :}{\text{bl}(n_i)}$$

and analogously for $\delta_\top$ where A_i, B_i, C_i are $\top$. Given that $\delta_1 < \delta_2 < \delta_3$, we obtain $n_1 \prec n_2, n_2 \prec n_3, n_1 \prec n_3$ along with $n_k \prec n_\top$ for $k \in \{1, 2, 3\}$ as part of $W_\prec$. From $D_\prec$ we get $\neg(n_i \prec n_j)$ for all remaining combinations of $i, j \in \{1, 2, 3, \top\}$. We also obtain that $\text{ok}(n_3)$ and $(\text{ap}(n_3) \vee \text{bl}(n_3)) \supset \text{ok}(n_2)$, and $(\text{ap}(n_2) \vee \text{bl}(n_2)) \supset \text{ok}(n_1)$ are derivable; from this we get that n_3 must be applied first, followed by n_2 and then n_1.

4 Preferences on Sets of Defaults

We consider here ordered default theories where the ordering is on sets of defaults. As before, we take an ordered theory and translate it into a standard default theory. Consider a general assertion $D' < D''$ where $D', D'' \subseteq D$. Informally we prefer the application of the set D'' to that of D'. We can say that D'' is applicable if all its member defaults are, and inapplicable if one of its members is inapplicable. In our example (1), we satisfy our most preferred (non-trivial) criterion if we can conclude P, S; we cannot if we cannot conclude one of P, S. Consequently we consider D' after *all* defaults in D'' are found to be applicable, or *some* default in D'' is found to be inapplicable.

Our ordered default theories now apply to sets of rules:

Definition 2. *A set–ordered default theory is a triple $(D, W, <)$, where D is a finite set of default rules, W is a finite set of formulas, and $< \subseteq 2^D \times 2^D$ is a strict partial order.*

In order to refer to the sets involved in $<$, we define $2^D \big|_< = \{D', D'' \mid (D', D'') \in <\}$.

Since our focus lies now on sets rather than individual defaults, we must adapt our condition on the maximally preferred default $\delta_\top$:

$$\{\delta\} < \{\delta_\top\} \qquad \text{for } \delta \in D \text{ with } \delta \neq \delta_\top \tag{3}$$

Note that this implies that $\{\delta\} \in 2^D \big|_<$ for all $\delta \in D$. In addition, we stipulate that $m_\top : \{\delta_\top\}$ is also preferred over all (non singleton and thus substantial) sets involved in $<$:

$$D_i < \{\delta_\top\} \qquad \text{for } D_i \in 2^D \big|_< \text{ with } D_i \neq \{\delta_\top\} \tag{4}$$

Unless stated otherwise, we assume in what follows that any order $<$ on sets of defaults satisfies conditions (3) and (4).

Also, we extend our naming of individual defaults to naming sets of defaults. We have a bijective mapping $\eta : D \cup 2^D \to N \dot\cup M$ where $N \dot\cup M$ is a bipartite set of constants not appearing in the original theory, such that N and M are disjoint name sets for individual defaults and sets of defaults, respectively: $N = \{\eta(\delta) \mid \delta \in D\}$ and $M = \{\eta(D_i) \mid D_i \in 2^D \big|_<\}$. In order to ease notation, we denote individual defaults like δ_1 by n_1 instead of $\eta(\delta_1)$ and the name of sets like $\{\delta_1, \delta_2\}$ by $m_{1,2}$. Furthermore, we sometimes put a set $D_{1,2} = \{\delta_1, \delta_2\}$ in correspondence with its name by using the same indices, that is $\eta(D_{1,2}) = m_{1,2}$ or more generally $\eta(D_i) = m_i$. Finally, note the difference between names n_1 and m_1, induced by our notational convention.

A complicating factor is now that we do not only need to distinguish individual default rules but also different rule sets. So formally there may be $2^{|D|}$ different names for rule sets, along with $|D|$ constants for naming individual rules. However, our translation, below, is such that we do not need to mention sets of defaults not appearing explicitly in the preference ordering, and so we require names only for those sets explicitly used in the theory. As before we adopt a unique names assumption (UNA) and domain closure assumption (DCA) for our entire name set. Also, we must be able to relate names of rule sets with the names of their members. We introduce a binary predicate $in \subseteq N \times M$, where $in(x, y)$ is true just if the individual default named by x is a member of the set named by y. We do not need a full axiomatization of in, representing set membership, since we use it in a very restricted fashion.

So we can now express theories such as are given in (1). Consider how we would want to use this theory. If we had $W = \{\neg(P \wedge E \wedge S)\}$ then we could apply the defaults in the set (named) $m_{1,2}$ and conclude that P and S can be met. Since $m_{1,2}$ is most preferred after $m_\top$, we would assert that it is ok to consider $m_{1,2}$; from this one would conclude that it is ok to consider n_1 and n_2 (the corresponding individual defaults), and one would obtain P and S.

More precisely, for $D_i \subseteq D$ we assert $ok(m_i)$ (where $\eta(D_i) = m_i$) just if, for every D_j such that $D_i < D_j$, we have that every default in D_j is applied, or some default in D_j is blocked. If we have $ok(m_i)$ then we assert $ok(n_\delta)$ for every $\delta \in D_i$ *unless* we cannot jointly apply all $\delta \in D_i$. That is, before activating the constituent rules, we have to make sure that none of them will be blocked, because otherwise we risk of provoking side-effects by activating only a part of the set at hand. To see this, assume that in a particular case P and S can't be jointly met (i.e. $W = \{\neg(P \wedge S)\}$). In a naive extension of our approach, we conclude $ok(n_1)$ and $ok(n_2)$ from $ok(m_{1,2})$ as above. However, since both δ_1 and δ_2 have been flagged ok, but both can't be applied, one would obtain an extension containing P, E (since δ_1 can be applied), along with another extension containing S, E (since δ_2 can be applied). But this clearly violates our preference ordering where we would want a single extension with S, E. The difficulty is that, in determining that a default in the set named $m_{1,2}$ is inapplicable (say n_2), we may obtain a side-effect in that another default in $m_{1,2}$ (i.e. n_1), which appears elsewhere in the preference ordering, is flagged as being ok to consider.

So what we require for a set of defaults D_i in a preference ordering is the following: If D_i has been flagged as ok, and if all the defaults in D_i are applicable, then all the defaults should be applied, and D_i flagged as ap. However, if some default in D_i is inapplicable, then D_i must be withdrawn and flagged as ko (see below), and *there should be no other side effects*, in that no constituent default in the set should remain flagged ok, ap, or bl as a result. This in turn means that we need to be able to cancel simultaneously the consideration of all members of a set, once we detect that one of them is blocked. We accomplish this by introducing an additional predicate $ko(\cdot)$ and default rules of form

$$\frac{ok(m_i) \; : \; \neg ko(m_i)}{ok(n_1) \wedge \ldots \wedge ok(n_k)}$$

for every set $D_i = \{\delta_1, \ldots, \delta_k\}$ involved in the ordering. We block this rule (and with it the derivability of all $\text{ok}(n_i)$) when we detect that one of $\delta_1, \ldots, \delta_k$ is blocked. That is, $\text{ko}(m_i)$ will be an immediate consequence of $\text{bl}(m_i)$.

Now, for rule set D_i, we have that D_i is blocked ($\text{bl}(m_i)$) just if some rule in D_i is blocked. However, since we must control a whole set of default rules, we must check for the blockage of one of the constituent default rule in the context of all other rules in the set. As regards detecting the failure of consistency, we verify for a set $D_i = \left\{ \frac{\alpha_j : \beta_j}{\gamma_j} \mid j = 1..k \right\}$ and some set of formulas S, whether $S \cup \{\gamma_1, \ldots, \gamma_k\} \vdash \neg\beta_j$ rather than $S \vdash \neg\beta_j$ as in our original approach (cf. the third rule in (2)). This motivates for D_i and $j = 1..k$ the default rule

$$\frac{[(\gamma_1 \wedge \ldots \wedge \gamma_k) \supset \neg\beta_j] \wedge \text{ok}(m_i) :}{\text{bl}(m_i)} \tag{5}$$

This context, $(\gamma_1 \wedge \ldots \wedge \gamma_k)$, is not needed for detecting the failure of derivability, since this test is effectuated with respect to the final extension E via $\neg\alpha \notin E$. We thus also add

$$\frac{\text{ok}(m_i) : \neg\alpha_j}{\text{bl}(m_i)}$$

Finally, set of defaults D_i is applied ($\text{ap}(m_i)$) just if every rule in D_i is applied; importantly, it is only in this last case that the consequents of the constituent rules in D_i are asserted.

We obtain the following translation mapping set–ordered default theories in some language $\mathcal{L}$ onto standard default theories in the language $\mathcal{L}^+$ obtained by extending $\mathcal{L}$ by new predicates symbols $(\cdot \prec \cdot)$, $in(\cdot, \cdot)$, $\text{ok}(\cdot)$, $\text{ko}(\cdot)$, $\text{bl}(\cdot)$, and $\text{ap}(\cdot)$, and a set of associated names. (Following our notational convention, we simply write n_j (or n_{δ_j}) and m_i rather than $\eta(\delta_j)$ and $\eta(D_i)$, respectively.)

Definition 3. *Given a set–ordered default theory* $(D, W, <)$ *over* $\mathcal{L}$ *and its set of associated default names* $N \dot\cup M$, *define* $\mathcal{T}((D, W, <)) = (D', W')$ *over* $\mathcal{L}^+$ *by*

$$D' = D_N \cup D_M \cup D_\prec$$
$$W' = W \cup W_\prec \cup \{DCA_{N\dot\cup M}, UNA_{N\dot\cup M}\}$$

where

$$D_N = \left\{ \frac{\alpha \wedge \text{ok}(n) : \beta}{\gamma \wedge \text{ap}(n)} \;\middle|\; n : \frac{\alpha : \beta}{\gamma} \in D \right\}$$

$$D_M = \left\{ \frac{\text{ok}(m_i) : \neg\text{ko}(m_i)}{\text{ok}(n_1) \wedge \ldots \wedge \text{ok}(n_k)}, \; \frac{\text{ok}(m_i) : \neg\alpha_j}{\text{bl}(m_i)}, \; \frac{[(\gamma_1 \wedge \ldots \wedge \gamma_k) \supset \neg\beta_j] \wedge \text{ok}(m_i) :}{\text{bl}(m_i)} \;\middle|\; \right.$$
$$\left. j = 1..k \text{ and } m_i : D_i = \left\{ n_j : \frac{\alpha_j : \beta_j}{\gamma_j} \;\middle|\; j = 1..k \right\}, D_i \in 2^D \big|_< \right\}$$

$$D_\prec = \left\{ \frac{: \neg(x \prec y)}{\neg(x \prec y)}, \; \frac{: \neg in(x, y)}{\neg in(x, y)} \right\}$$

$$W_\prec = \{\text{ok}(m_\top)\}$$
$$\cup \{m_i \prec m_j \mid (D_i, D_j) \in <\}$$
$$\cup \{in(n_\delta, m_i) \mid \delta \in D_i, D_i \in 2^D \big|_<\}$$

$\cup \{\forall x \in M \left[\forall y \in M. (x \prec y) \supset (\mathsf{bl}(y) \vee \mathsf{ap}(y))\right] \supset \mathsf{ok}(x)\}$

$\cup \{\forall x \in M. [\mathsf{bl}(x) \supset \mathsf{ko}(x)]\}$

$\cup \{\forall y \in M \left[\forall x \in N. in(x,y) \supset \mathsf{ap}(x)\right] \supset \mathsf{ap}(y)\}$

For a set of defaults with name m, let δ_a^m, $\delta_{b_1}^m$, and $\delta_{b_2}^m$ be the corresponding default rules in D_M. And let δ_a^n denote the transform of the individual default named n in D_N. The sets D_N and D_M are justified above. $D_\prec$ says that those $\prec$- and in-instances that can't be shown to hold don't in fact hold, and so in an extension we have complete information about these predicates.

For $W_\prec$ the first term again says we have a trivial maximally preferred default set, while the second term translates our external order into an order on the set of names in our extended (object) language. Note that our predicate $\prec$ applies only to names for sets of defaults. The third term gives all positive instances of the in predicate for those sets taking part in the ordering $<$. The fourth term says that it is ok to consider a set of default rules just if all $\prec$-greater sets are blocked or applied. The fifth one allows us to conclude the ko of a rule set once we've detected its blockage.[3] The last term states that if all rules in a set apply then the set is applied.

Consider the defaults in our initial car example (1): In $W_\prec$, we have the preference propositions $m_1 \prec m_2$, $m_2 \prec m_3$, $m_3 \prec m_{1,2}$, $m_{1,2} \prec m_\top$ as well as transitivities in $\prec$.

For D_N and D_M, we obtain (after removing redundant defaults):

$$\frac{\mathsf{ok}(n_1):P}{P \wedge \mathsf{ap}(n_1)} \qquad \frac{\mathsf{ok}(n_2):S}{S \wedge \mathsf{ap}(n_2)} \qquad \frac{\mathsf{ok}(n_3):E}{E \wedge \mathsf{ap}(n_3)} \qquad\qquad \frac{\mathsf{ok}(n_\top):\top}{\mathsf{ap}(n_\top)}$$

$$\frac{\mathsf{ok}(m_1):\neg\mathsf{ko}(m_1)}{\mathsf{ok}(n_1)} \quad \frac{\mathsf{ok}(m_2):\neg\mathsf{ko}(m_2)}{\mathsf{ok}(n_2)} \quad \frac{\mathsf{ok}(m_3):\neg\mathsf{ko}(m_3)}{\mathsf{ok}(n_3)} \quad \frac{\mathsf{ok}(m_{1,2}):\neg\mathsf{ko}(m_{1,2})}{\mathsf{ok}(n_1)\wedge\mathsf{ok}(n_2)} \quad \frac{\mathsf{ok}(m_\top):\neg\mathsf{ko}(\top)}{\mathsf{ok}(n_\top)}$$

$$\frac{\neg P \wedge \mathsf{ok}(m_1):}{\mathsf{bl}(m_1)} \quad\; \frac{\neg S \wedge \mathsf{ok}(m_2):}{\mathsf{bl}(m_2)} \quad\; \frac{\neg E \wedge \mathsf{ok}(m_3):}{\mathsf{bl}(m_3)} \quad\; \frac{(\neg P \vee \neg Q) \wedge \mathsf{ok}(m_{1,2}):}{\mathsf{bl}(m_{1,2})}$$

The in predicate has positive instances:

$$in(n_1, m_1), \; in(n_2, m_2), \; in(n_3, m_3), \; in(n_\top, m_\top), \; in(n_1, m_{1,2}), \; in(n_2, m_{1,2}).$$

From $D_\prec$ we get $\neg in(x,y)$ for all remaining combinations of x and y; analogously for $\neg(x \prec y)$. Once we have derived $\mathsf{ap}(m_\top)$, the fourth term in $W_\prec$ allows us to deduce:

$$\mathsf{ok}(m_{1,2}),$$
$$[\mathsf{bl}(m_{1,2}) \vee \mathsf{ap}(m_{1,2})] \supset \mathsf{ok}(m_3),$$
$$([\mathsf{bl}(m_3) \vee \mathsf{ap}(m_3)] \wedge [\mathsf{bl}(m_{1,2}) \vee \mathsf{ap}(m_{1,2})]) \supset \mathsf{ok}(m_2),$$
$$([\mathsf{bl}(m_2) \vee \mathsf{ap}(m_2)] \wedge [\mathsf{bl}(m_3) \vee \mathsf{ap}(m_3)] \wedge [\mathsf{bl}(m_{1,2}) \vee \mathsf{ap}(m_{1,2})]) \supset \mathsf{ok}(m_1).$$

From the last term in $W_\prec$ we can deduce $[\mathsf{ap}(n_1) \wedge \mathsf{ap}(n_2)] \supset \mathsf{ap}(m_{1,2})$ along with $\mathsf{ap}(n_k) \supset \mathsf{ap}(m_k)$, for $k \in \{1, 2, 3, \top\}$.

Let $W = \{\neg(P \wedge E \wedge S)\}$, that is, not all desiderata can be satisfied. We obtain a single extension containing P and S. Informally we have initially $\mathsf{ok}(m_\top)$ and then

---

[3] This axiom is not necessary since we can replace negative occurrences of $\mathsf{ko}(m)$ by $\mathsf{bl}(m)$. We retain it for conceptual clarity.

also $\mathsf{ap}(m_\top)$, from which we derive $\mathsf{ok}(m_{1,2})$, and from which we obtain $\mathsf{ok}(n_1)$ and $\mathsf{ok}(n_2)$. If both δ_1 and δ_2 are applicable (which they are) then we conclude $P \wedge \mathsf{ap}(n_1)$ and $S \wedge \mathsf{ap}(n_1)$ as well as $\mathsf{ap}(m_{1,2})$. We then get $\mathsf{ok}(m_3)$, hence $\mathsf{ok}(n_3)$, hence (since we have $\neg E$) $\mathsf{bl}(m_3)$. To see that there are no other extensions, it suffices to observe that there is no way of deriving $\mathsf{ko}(m_{1,2})$ (and $\mathsf{bl}(m_{1,2})$).

Second, consider where $W = \{\neg(P \wedge S)\}$, and so we cannot satisfy our topmost (nontrivial) preference. From $\mathsf{ok}(m_\top)$ we derive $\mathsf{ok}(m_{1,2})$, from which we would obtain $\mathsf{ok}(n_1)$ and $\mathsf{ok}(n_2)$ provided that $\neg \mathsf{ko}(m_{1,2})$ was consistent. In view of $\{\neg(P \wedge S)\}$, we cannot have an extension in which both δ_1 and δ_2 apply, which is mirrored by the fact that we obtain $\mathsf{bl}(m_{1,2})$ and hence $\mathsf{ko}(m_{1,2})$ (while neither $\mathsf{ok}(n_1)$ nor $\mathsf{ok}(n_2)$ are derived). We subsequently obtain $\mathsf{ok}(m_3)$ from which we (eventually) get E and $\mathsf{ap}(m_3)$. From this we get $\mathsf{ok}(m_2)$, (eventually) S and $\mathsf{ap}(m_2)$. Finally we get $\mathsf{ok}(m_1)$, and eventually $\mathsf{bl}(m_1)$. We obtain a single extension, containing S, E, as desired.

The next example deals with the situation where defaults inside a set depend upon each other. We have $\{n_1 : \frac{:S}{S}, n_2 : \frac{:T}{T}, n_3 : \frac{:Q}{Q}, n_4 : \frac{Q:R}{R}\}$ with $\{\delta_1\} < \{\delta_2\} < \{\delta_3, \delta_4\}$. We get for D_N and the singleton sets $\{\delta_i\}$ the following rules.

$$\frac{\mathsf{ok}(n_1):S}{S \wedge \mathsf{ap}(n_1)} \qquad \frac{\mathsf{ok}(n_2):T}{T \wedge \mathsf{ap}(n_2)} \qquad \frac{\mathsf{ok}(n_3):Q}{Q \wedge \mathsf{ap}(n_3)} \qquad \frac{Q \wedge \mathsf{ok}(n_4):R}{R \wedge \mathsf{ap}(n_4)} \qquad \frac{\mathsf{ok}(n_\top):T}{\mathsf{ap}(n_\top)}$$

$$\frac{\mathsf{ok}(m_1):\neg \mathsf{ko}(m_1)}{\mathsf{ok}(n_1)} \quad \frac{\mathsf{ok}(m_2):\neg \mathsf{ko}(m_2)}{\mathsf{ok}(n_2)} \quad \frac{\mathsf{ok}(m_3):\neg \mathsf{ko}(m_3)}{\mathsf{ok}(n_3)} \quad \frac{\mathsf{ok}(m_4):\neg \mathsf{ko}(m_4)}{\mathsf{ok}(n_4)} \quad \frac{\mathsf{ok}(m_\top):\neg \mathsf{ko}(\top)}{\mathsf{ok}(n_\top)}$$

$$\frac{\neg S \wedge \mathsf{ok}(m_1):}{\mathsf{bl}(m_1)} \qquad \frac{\neg T \wedge \mathsf{ok}(m_2):}{\mathsf{bl}(m_2)} \qquad \frac{\neg Q \wedge \mathsf{ok}(m_3):}{\mathsf{bl}(m_3)} \qquad \frac{\neg R \wedge \mathsf{ok}(m_3):}{\mathsf{bl}(m_3)}$$

The set $\{\delta_1, \delta_2\}$ is captured via the following rules.

$$\frac{\mathsf{ok}(m_{1,2}):\neg \mathsf{ko}(m_{1,2})}{\mathsf{ok}(n_1) \wedge \mathsf{ok}(n_2)} \qquad \frac{\neg Q \wedge \mathsf{ok}(m_{1,2}):}{\mathsf{bl}(m_{1,2})} \qquad \text{and} \qquad \frac{(\neg Q \vee \neg R) \wedge \mathsf{ok}(m_{1,2}):}{\mathsf{bl}(m_{1,2})}$$

Assume that we have P and an assertion to the effect that no more than two of Q, R, S, T can hold. Having derived $\mathsf{ap}(m_\top)$, we obtain from $W_\prec$ that $\mathsf{ok}(m_3), \mathsf{ok}(m_4), \mathsf{ok}(m_{3,4})$ and $[\mathsf{bl}(m_{3,4}) \vee \mathsf{ap}(m_{3,4})] \supset \mathsf{ok}(m_2)$ and $([\mathsf{bl}(m_{3,4}) \vee \mathsf{ap}(m_{3,4})] \wedge [\mathsf{bl}(m_2) \vee \mathsf{ap}(m_2)]) \supset \mathsf{ok}(m_1)$ hold. We then obtain $\mathsf{ok}(n_3)$, and $\mathsf{ok}(n_4)$, which allow us to apply default δ_3, yielding in turn $Q \wedge \mathsf{ap}(n_3)$ and then $\mathsf{ap}(m_3)$. With Q at hand, we can now apply default δ_4, yielding $R \wedge \mathsf{ap}(n_4)$. This allows us to deduce $\mathsf{ap}(m_4)$ as well as $\mathsf{ap}(m_{3,4})$. Thus, we obtain an extension containing P, Q, R.

Problems may arise however if explicit preferences contradict the natural dependencies among defaults: For example, the image of the set–ordered default theory (under our translation)

$$\left(\{ \tfrac{A:B}{B}, \tfrac{B:C}{C} \}, \{A\}, \{ \{ \tfrac{A:B}{B} \} < \{ \tfrac{B:C}{C} \} \} \right) \tag{6}$$

has no extension. (This is also the case with our original approach [7].)

Interestingly, our approach allows to some extent for by-passing problematic sets of default rules causing the loss of extensions in standard default logic (provided that these sets have been identified in advance). This is because our approach provides us with control over default rules, once they are encapsulated in a set. Consider the set of default rules

$$n_1 : \tfrac{:A \wedge \neg B}{A}, \quad n_2 : \tfrac{:B \wedge \neg C}{B}, \quad n_3 : \tfrac{:C \wedge \neg A}{C},$$

along with $W = \emptyset$. This example was used in [8] to show that semi-normal default theories may lack extensions.

By Theorem 4 below, the translation of this theory in our approach, where there are no preferences except with respect to δ_T, also has no extension. However, consider where we encapsulate the three rules by putting them into one set: $\{\delta_1, \delta_2, \delta_3\} < \{\delta_T\}$ in order to obtain control over them. We then obtain in D_M three rules all of which reduce to $\frac{\text{ok}(m_{1,2,3}) :}{\text{bl}(m_{1,2,3})}$.

The following theorems summarize the major properties of our approach, and demonstrate that rules are applied in the desired order. Define $\overline{S} = \{\neg\alpha \mid \alpha \in S\}$.

Theorem 1. *Let E be an extension of $\mathcal{T}((D, W, <))$ for set–ordered default theory $(D, W, <)$. We have for all $\delta \in D$ and for all $D_1, D_2 \subseteq D$*

1. either $(m_1 \prec m_2) \in E$ or $\neg(m_1 \prec m_2) \in E$
2. either $in(n_\delta, m_1) \in E$ or $\neg in(n_\delta, m_1) \in E$
3. $\text{ok}(m_1) \in E$
4. either $\text{ap}(m_1) \in E$ or $\text{bl}(m_1) \in E$
5. $\text{ap}(m_1) \in E$ implies $Conseq(D_1) \subseteq E$
6. $\text{bl}(m_1) \in E$ implies $Conseq(D_1) \not\subseteq E$
7. $\text{ok}(n_\delta) \in E$ implies $\text{ap}(n_\delta) \in E$
8. $\text{ap}(n_\delta) \in E$ implies $(\text{ap}(m_3) \wedge in(n_\delta, m_3)) \in E$ for some $D_3 \in 2^D|_<$
9. $\text{ap}(n_{\delta'}) \in E$ for all $\delta' \in D_1$ implies $\underline{\text{ap}(m_1)} \in E$
10. $\text{ok}(m_1) \in E_i$ and $\underline{Prereq(D_1)} \subseteq E_j$ and $\overline{Justif(D_1)} \cap E = \emptyset$ implies $\text{ap}(m_1) \in E_{\max(i,j)+3}$
11. $\text{ok}(m_1) \in E_i$ and $\underline{Prereq(D_1)} \not\subseteq E$ implies $\text{bl}(m_1) \in E_{i+1}$
12. $\text{ok}(m_1) \in E_i$ and $\overline{Justif(D_1)} \cap E = \emptyset$ implies $\text{bl}(m_1) \in E_j$ for some $j > i$
13. $\text{ok}(m_1) \notin E_{i-1}$ and $\text{ok}(m_1) \in E_i$ implies $\text{ap}(m_1), \text{bl}(m_1) \notin E_j$ for $j \leq i$

Notably, Theorem 1.11 allows us to detect blockage due to non-derivability of the prerequisite immediately after having the ok for the default at hand. Another interesting property is expressed in Theorem 1.7: At first sight, one may wonder whether the defaults in D_N are superfluous, since $\text{ap}(n)$ is implied by $\text{ok}(n)$ anyway. In fact, the defaults in D_N are needed for guaranteeing (grounded) conclusions according to standard DL.

For an extension E and its generating default rules Γ, we trivially have $\delta_a^m \in \Gamma$ iff $\text{ap}(m) \in E$, and $\delta_{b_1}^m \in \Gamma$ or $\delta_{b_2}^m \in \Gamma$ iff $\text{bl}(m) \in E$.

Theorem 2. *Let E be an extension of $\mathcal{T}((D, W, <))$ for set–ordered default theory $(D, W, <)$ and Γ, Γ_i be defined wrt E. Then, we have for all sets of default rules $D_1 \subseteq D$*

14. $\delta_a^{m_1} \in \Gamma$ or $\delta_{b_1}^{m_1} \in \Gamma$ or $\delta_{b_2}^{m_1} \in \Gamma$
15. $\delta_a^{m_1} \in \Gamma$ iff $(\delta_{b_1}^{m_1} \notin \Gamma$ and $\delta_{b_2}^{m_1} \notin \Gamma)$

For all sets of default rules $D_1, D_2 \subseteq D$ such that $D_1 < D_2$ we have

17. $\delta_a^{m_2}, \delta_{b_1}^{m_2}, \delta_{b_2}^{m_2} \notin \Gamma_i$ implies $\delta_a^{m_1}, \delta_{b_1}^{m_1}, \delta_{b_2}^{m_1} \notin \Gamma_j$ for $j < i + 3$
18. $\delta_a^{m_2} \in \Gamma_i$ or $\delta_{b_1}^{m_2} \in \Gamma_i$ or $\delta_{b_2}^{m_2} \in \Gamma_i$ implies $\delta_a^{m_1} \in \Gamma_j$ or $\delta_{b_1}^{m_1} \in \Gamma_j$ or $\delta_{b_2}^{m_1} \in \Gamma_j$ for $j > i + 1$

19. $\delta_a^{m_1} \in \Gamma_i$ or $\delta_{b_1}^{m_1} \in \Gamma_i$ or $\delta_{b_2}^{m_1} \in \Gamma_i$ implies $\delta_a^{m_2} \in \Gamma_j$ or $\delta_{b_1}^{m_2} \in \Gamma_j$ or $\delta_{b_2}^{m_2} \in \Gamma_j$ for $j < i - 1$.

The minimum two-step delay between rules stemming from m_1 and those originated by m_2 is due to to the fact that in Definition 1 the deductive closure of E_i is determined at E_{i+1}. The important overall consequence of this series of propositions is that we have full control over default application.

Using these properties, we can show that whenever we deal with a semi-normal default theory whose ordering involves singleton sets of default rules only, we obtain extensions of standard default logic.

Theorem 3. *Let E be an extension of $\mathcal{T}((D, W, <))$ for set–ordered semi-normal default theory $(D, W, <)$ over $\mathcal{L}$, where $<$ satisfies (3) and $< \subseteq \{\{\delta\} \mid \delta \in D\} \times \{\{\delta\} \mid \delta \in D\}$. Then $E \cap \mathcal{L}$ is an extension of (D, W).*

Also, for semi-normal default theories, the approach is equivalent (modulo the original language) to standard default logic if there are no preferences:

Theorem 4. *For a semi-normal default theory (D, W) over $\mathcal{L}$ and a set of formulas E, we have that E is an extension of $\mathcal{T}((D, W, \emptyset))$ iff $E \cap \mathcal{L}$ is an extension of (D, W).*

Also, if preferences are expressed among sets with a single element only then the extended approach effectively reduces to the original. For this, let $\mathcal{S}$ be the translation of ordered default theories into standard default logic sketched in Section 3 and detailed in [7] and in the the full paper.

Theorem 5. *Let $(D, W, <)$ be an ordered semi-normal default theory over $\mathcal{L}$ and let $(D, W, <')$ be the set–ordered default theory, where $<' = \{ (\{\delta\}, \{\delta'\}) \mid (\delta, \delta') \in < \}$. Then $E \cap \mathcal{L}$ is an extension of $\mathcal{S}((D, W, <))$ iff $E \cap \mathcal{L}$ is an extension of $\mathcal{T}((D, W, <'))$.*

Notably, the previous restriction to semi-normal default theories does not limit the scope of the theorems, since it is well known that any default theory is expressible as a semi-normal default theory yielding the same extension, as shown in [10].

The reason why our approach has tight relationships to its predecessors in case of semi-normal default theories dealing with singleton sets only is that in this case annuls the contextual information in (5); see the full paper for details.

We conclude with the observation that our translation results in a manageable increase in the size of the default theory. For set–ordered theory $(D, W, <)$, the translation $\mathcal{T}((D, W, <))$ results in a theory a constant factor larger than the number of sets involved in $<$, namely, the size of $2^D\big|_<$.

5 Discussion and Related Work

We have presented an approach for representing and reasoning about preferences among sets of properties using default logic. In this approach one can assert for example that each of two outcomes are not individually preferred to a third, but together these two outcomes are preferred to the third. One begins with an ordered theory, consisting of a set of world knowledge, a set of defaults, and a set of preference relations among subsets of the defaults. This theory is translated into a second, standard default theory wherein the preferences are respected: sets of defaults are "applied" according to the given order; for a set of order-equivalent defaults, either all are applied, or none are.

Of other work in default logic treating preferences, we have argued in [7] that approaches such as [12, 9, 6] treat a separate problem, that of specificity orderings. [1] and [3] present prioritised variants of default logic in which the iterative specification of an extension is modified. None of these appraoches however deal with sets of preferences. In addition, we translate preferences into standard default theories. In a preliminary report, [5] consider sets of preferences, but not in default logic. The full paper fully compares approaches.

While the present approach is more general than previous work, the major point of contrast with previous work is that we remain within the framework of standard default logic (rather than building a scheme on top of default logic). This has several advantages. First, our approach can be immediately implemented by making use of existing DL theorem provers. Second, it is easier to compare differing approaches to handling such orderings, since we remain within the same "base" framework. Third, by "compiling" preferences into default logic, and in using the standard machinery of default logic, we obtain insight into the notion of preference orderings. Thus, and as a point of theoretical interest, we show that incorporating explicit priorities among sets of rules in default logic in fact provides no real increase in the expressibility of default logic.

References

1. F. Baader and B. Hollunder. How to prefer more specific defaults in terminological default logic. In *Proceedings Int'l Joint Conference on Artificial Intelligence*, 669–674, 1993.
2. C. Boutilier. What is a default priority? In *Canadian Conference on AI*, 140–147, 1992.
3. G. Brewka. Adding priorities and specificity to default logic. In L. Pereira and D. Pearce, editors, *European Workshop on Logics in Artificial Intelligence*, 247–260. Springer, 1994.
4. G. Brewka. Reasoning about priorities in default logic. In *Proceedings AAAI National Conference on Artificial Intelligence*, 940–945. AAAI Press/The MIT Press, 1994.
5. G. Brewka and T. Gordon. How to buy a porsche: An approach to defeasible decision making. In *AAAI-94 Workshop on Computational Dialectics*, Seattle, WA, July 1994.
6. J. Delgrande and T. Schaub. A general approach to specificity in default reasoning. In J. Doyle, P. Torasso, and E. Sandewall, editors, *Proceedings Fourth Int'l Conference on the Principles of Knowledge Representation and Reasoning*, 146–157. Morgan Kaufmann, 1994.
7. J.P. Delgrande and T. Schaub. Compiling reasoning with and about preferences into default logic. In *Proceedings Int'l Joint Conference on Artificial Intelligence*, 168–174, 1997.
8. D. Etherington. *Reasoning with Incomplete Information: Investigations of Non-Monotonic Reasoning*. PhD thesis, Dept. of Computer Science, University of British Columbia, 1986.
9. D.W. Etherington and R. Reiter. On inheritance hierarchies with exceptions. In *Proceedings AAAI National Conference on Artificial Intelligence*, 104–108, 1983.
10. W. Marek and M. Truszczyński. *Nonmonotonic logic: context-dependent reasoning*. Artifical Intelligence. Springer, 1993.
11. R. Reiter. A logic for default reasoning. *Artificial Intelligence*, 13:81–132, 1980.
12. R. Reiter and G. Criscuolo. On interacting defaults. In *Proceedings Int'l Joint Conference on Artificial Intelligence*, 270–276, 1981.

Frugality in Reasoning and the Role of Summary

Janet Aisbett and Greg Gibbon
Information Systems Group, School of Management,
University of Newcastle, Australia, 2308
{mgjea, mgggg}@cc.newcastle.edu.au

Abstract. This paper describes a system for problem-solving in complex, dynamic environments while adhering to the *principle of frugality*. Given a formulation of a problem as a set of hypotheses, any such system must be able to actively search for information to confirm or refute the hypotheses. However, rather than incorporate new information under a philosophy of minimal change, we argue the system should periodically *summarise* its working knowledge base and adjust the priority given to alternate hypotheses. Mechanisms for forming the summary are presented, adapting ideas used in text management. Demand forecasting in volatile environments is an important application for this type of "commonsense" system. An example is provided of the performance of such a system against a standard regression forecaster on a sales forecasting task with noisy data.

1 Introduction

Motivated by the apparent frugality of human reasoning [1, 2], this paper presents a commonsense reasoning system invoking summarisation. By summarisation we mean reduction of the size of a knowledge base (as measured, say, by the number of formula or the number of symbols) while conserving as much as possible of the information conveyed about the problem under consideration. We contend that summarisation is a key activity in reasoning, used to maintain a very small working memory in the face of continual acquisition of new information by the reasoner. This contrasts with the assumption of the objective of minimal change under revision commonly adopted by researchers in formal reasoning, eg. [3, 4].

The process of summarisation of an existing knowledge base, in conjunction with the active search for new information with which to appropriately extend that knowledge base, has the potential to allow complex problems to be solved with a dynamic working knowledge base which at any given time is very small. The use of summary and dynamic search seeks to capture the human ability to tackle complex problems with limited memory capacity, in line with the "less is better" principle recognised in the emerging area of relevance reasoning.

We are interested in the important application of demand forecasting which involves a mix of structured arithmetic-based decision making and heuristic decision making [5, 6]. Forecasting has received relatively little attention from the AI community, the notable exception being the expert system field. Rule based techniques have been incorporated alongside statistical methods in many commercial forecasting suites [7, 8], and tools support the acquisition of the rules behind human revision of statistical forecasts [9].

Given the well-documented limitations of human forecasting, eg [10-15], an argument needs to be mounted to justify our intention to mimic human approaches to forecasting. Section 2 attempts to do this, after a brief discussion of human forecasting illustrated with a case study to motivate examples used in the paper. Section 3 sketches the commonsense reasoning paradigm into which our summarisation strategy is to be incorporated. This paradigm, a version of which was presented in [16], alternates reasoning on the information to hand with search for more information upon which to reason. We allow for a special class of generic knowledge about processing, such as arithmetic knowledge.

Section 4 suggests possible summarisation schemes to apply with an acquisitive reasoning paradigm. It also discusses the role of *type* in restricting size. Section 5 illustrates our reasoning paradigm and the application of summarisation in the forecasting domain. It demonstrates a commonsense forecaster that outperforms a conventional auto-regressive forecaster in unstable conditions. Section 6 describes work in progress.

2 Forecasting and commonsense reasoning

All organisations and individuals, as consumers of goods and services, are involved in the activity of forecasting to determine how much to budget for an item, or how much to reorder. For stable line items, forecast decisions can be made routinely on the basis of historical data. However, in general forecasting is a mix of structured and unstructured decision making, in which the decision maker typically draws on experience and domain knowledge. Thus, in sales forecasting, the structured prediction processes associated with time series analyses are modified to allow for qualitative knowledge of the influence of new competitors, economic conditions, etc. [5].

2.1 Studies of human forecasting

Studies over many decades have suggested that humans modify statistical forecasts even when this intervention degrades the forecast performance [12-14]. Moreover, subjects avoid making accurate calculations even when tools to support this are available and even when there are rewards for accuracy [11]. Subjects focus on some, but not all, the available information [15].

Case study: These characteristics were demonstrated in a case study we reported in [18], which involved reorder decision making in a small wholesaler of floor coverings. Observations included a reorder session conducted between sales office staff for high value imported products that were significant income-producers for the company. The session was based around a table, handwritten onto a pre-printed paper proforma, containing the three fields: (1) *Stock Id*: a textual description of the manufacturer, the range and the colour and/or pattern of the product; (2) *Average Sales*: the average sales over the last six months, excluding anomalous large sales; and (3) *Forecast*: initially empty, to contain values computed in the session.

A notional "working knowledge base" of information deemed to be relevant to the decision was developed by the participants in the reorder decision making session. At first, this notional knowledge base was drawn from the data captured in the reorder sheet and in the previous month's reorder sheet, together with highly significant facts such as a manufacturer's promotion campaign for a product line. An initial demand forecast and associated reorder estimate were made after assessing the underlying sales trend using standard formulae [19].

If the participants in the session were not "comfortable" with the reorder quantity given the data to hand, they went back to check the identification of past sales with future sales, examining the information items in the working knowledge base which affected the setting of the demand forecast. Decision making was suspended to acquire more information, through the participants volunteering new information, such as their professional assessment of the fashionability of the colour of a product. The demand forecast was adjusted on the strength of this new information. If again the result was not felt to be satisfactory, the decision makers recalled more information such as adverse feedback from suppliers, or actively sought information from the finance manager, till they eventually recorded a final forecast and reorder quantity. The process was a mixture of information *acquisition* and information *processing*.

Observations of human decision making such as these, together with a wealth of experimental results, support the Heuristics and Biases School that argues that human decision making is adversely affected by failure to follow statistical and logical laws [20, 21]. Consequently, in some critical situations, 'irrational' human decision makers are prevented from over-riding their 'rational' advisory systems, eg. evidence based medicine systems may prevent doctors altering recommended treatment paths.

2.2 Limitations of such findings

It appears that in the simplified decision making environments of the psychology experiment, and in stable situations in which extensive domain knowledge is available to system designers, automatic systems can provide better advice than humans. However, in dynamic conditions in which the accuracy and validity of current data are uncertain, the assumptions behind statistical forecasting are violated, and the introduction of ad hoc rules to capture all the current exigencies may be infeasible. Simon's presentation of *satisficing* and *bounded rationality* emphasised that the reasoning style fitted the real world environment [22]. There are many observations of successful human managers making good "seat-of the pants" decisions, eg [23], in which they may overrule more analytically based advice and in which they do not use all available information.

It is generally accepted that humans have limited capacity for dealing simultaneously with different concepts, as vividly described in Miller's famous paper [2]. In order to explain why human reasoning is successful in conditions of uncertainty and incompleteness, Gigerenzer & Goldstein [1] investigated the performance of frugal problem-solving algorithms that attempt only a partial representation of the situation and use approximate data. On a simple classification problem, these authors showed that a classification algorithm that used only the most informative available attribute performed as well as standard multiple regression. In similar vein, but from the machine learning perspective, a classifier using only a relevant subset of attributes has out-performed one using all available data [24], and Sattar & Ghose perform frugal experiments in Belief Revision [36].

3. A paradigm and architecture for commonsense reasoning

This section outlines a common sense reasoning paradigm that operates within a standard Decision Support Systems architecture. We represent the decision under consideration as a set of hypotheses Φ, various subsets Φ_i of which could, if established, determine a decision. Each hypothesis is weighted to affect the priority that the decision maker gives to acquiring more information to try to establish it. Weights may be adjusted during the course of making a decision – this amounts to changing the *focus* of the reasoning, in a sense we describe below. This paradigm is applied to the demand forecasting application in the following sections.

The generic Decision Support Systems framework of Holsapple & Whinston (their Figure 6.2 in [25]) identifies an internal persistent knowledge base (represented as *KB* in Fig. 1), a problem-specific working knowledge base (*WKB* in Fig. 1) and a user (represented as *EKB1*). *WKB* may be augmented with knowledge obtained from the user through an *interface* (the language and presentation systems in the terminology of [25]). This basic architecture can be extended to allow dialogue with selected external information sources, depicted as *EKB2* in the figure. For example, there might be live Web links to stock exchange summaries, or links to customers' databases.

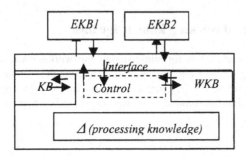

Fig. 1. Main data sources and flows in the Commonsense Reasoning system

The architecture needs to be extended to allow for the generic processing knowledge, labelled Δ in the figure. We reserve Δ for arithmetic knowledge and knowledge about data types. Dealing with arithmetic is always problematic in logical formalisations, because of the impracticality of expressing even fundamental concepts like integers. Typically, the infinite system needed to represent set theory and arithmetic will be adjoined to a finite domain theory, using a finite set of axioms to tie the two together, eg [26]. The same approach is used in modelling visual processing systems, eg [17], and is adopted here.

Under the reasoning paradigm we proposed in [16], problem solving proceeds via a heuristically-controlled switching between the activities of deduction on *WKB*, and searching for more information to potentially include in *WKB*. This continues until some resource bounded stopping criterion is attained. When the reasoning step has failed to provide a satisficing solution, the system must determine what information should be requested, and which source should be queried. (Some mechanisms for doing this were presented in [16].) When information on a requested topic is received in response to such a query, it is only included in *WKB* if it is sufficiently relevant to the facet of the problem under consideration.

In this paper, we contend that before a request for new information is formulated, *WKB* should be summarised, that is, reduced in size so that only the elements which carry most information about the hypotheses are retained. At the same time, the weights on the hypotheses are recalculated, so that the emphasis on the problem may change. The next section discusses ways of doing this

On a demand forecasting decision problem, a Commonsense Reasoning system obeying this paradigm might perform as follows. The initial focus is on a coarse set of hypotheses about the forecast (eg. *"Up from latest moving average"*, *"Down from latest moving average"*, *"Steady"*). The system seeks to validate these hypotheses, using data about previous sales in its persistent data store *KB,* or gathering data from external sources if necessary. When the trend is established, the hypotheses set being investigated changes, say, to a set of plausible numerical forecasts (*"Sales will be 150 units"*, *"Sales will be 160 units"* etc.) The system then seeks to determine support for each hypothesis, and may narrow the forecast by summarising and refocussing onto some of these hypotheses. The steps are repeated until a forecast is made.

4. Maintaining a small working knowledge base

This section investigates strategies for summarising the working knowledge base *WKB* and for refocussing the decision making through altering the weight function on elements of the hypotheses set Φ. In general, the refutation or confirmation of hypotheses will be included in the summary, and the corresponding hypotheses will be removed from Φ.

4.1 Summary

Summary is a fundamental tool of text management [27, 28]. The notion of the *importance* of a concept described in the text document is often used, but the importance ranking is usually subjectively assigned. While much of the work in document summarisation assumes the summary is being prepared for a generic reader, we have more context, in that we know the summary of *WKB* is being prepared as part of the task of establishing the truth values of a weighted set of hypotheses. Thus, importance of a logical formula γ could be defined in terms of the correspondence between the language used in the formula and that used in the hypotheses set.

Importance of γ could also be defined to be the relative value of the information brought by that formula, where information value is with respect to the set of hypotheses. A definition of the value of information is given in [29]. Let $I_\phi(\gamma)$ denote this information value (or the value computed using any preferred definition). Let $I(\gamma)$ denote the generic information content of a formula γ (that is, with respect to the null set) which will be associated to some probability function p through the standard formulae $I(\gamma) = -log(p(\gamma))$.

Under any reasonable definition of information, conjunction of formulae usually increases the generic information content over that conveyed by any of the constituent formula. However, it also increases the size of the formula. Thus, one way that summarisation could be approached would be to select for inclusion in the summary those formulae that convey most information about the problem, *relative to their generic information content*.

Because the problem is being represented in terms of sets of hypotheses which are assigned relative importance weightings, we need to take account of these relativities.

Guided by these considerations, the main text summarisation mechanisms can be adapted to provide alternative summarisation strategies for *WKB*. The following are adaptations from the Tipster project [30].

1. Extract formulae in *WKB* which contain the symbols which appear most frequently in *WKB*.
2. Use distinguished types to identify constants (e.g., person names, place names, company names, numeric data and temporal data) and summarise *WKB* as the set of formula that contain these constants. Distinguished types may be those that appear in the hypotheses set Φ.
3. Use distinguished types to identify constants and summarise using the set of consequences of *WKB* that contain the highest proportion of such constants.
4. Use types to identify distinguished constants, and summarise using these as symbols in the language describing an otherwise-empty *WKB*.
5. Extract formulae γ in *WKB* of high relative information value $u(\phi)I_\phi(\gamma)/I(\gamma)$ for some ϕ in Φ.
6. Extract formulae in *WKB* or which have been derived in the course of the processing in the current reasoning step so as to have the highest relative information values.
7. Extract from all the consequences γ of the formulae in *WKB* those with highest relative information value $u(\phi)I_\phi(\gamma)/I(\gamma)$
8. Take as summary the response to a complex query presented to *WKB*.

Strategy (8) may provide a good summary, but requires formulation of the "right" query. We recommended strategy (7) in [31] but this is clearly a computationally ambitious approach even if a very frual language is assumed. Restricting the definition to derived sentences rather than all consequences provides a workable compromise between (5) and (7). Strategies (2) – (4) have even lower workload, but (2) may not have sufficient summarisation power, and (4) may leave the working knowledge base too depleted.

4.2 Refocussing

We propose that the selected summarisation strategy is invoked at each stage at which the system is to request new information. Inconsistency between the new information and the old might also be reason for *WKB* to be summarised. In each case, the summarisation would be accompanied by a change in focus, in the sense of changing the problem specification through changing the weights on elements of Φ. We claim the reasoner will refocus on the subset of hypotheses that have the maximum joint probability given the summarised *WKB*. Specifically, if $\Phi(1)$, $\Phi(2)$, ... $\Phi(n)$ are a listing of all the minimal subsets of Φ from which a solution can be obtained, then assign to each of the hypotheses in $\Phi(i)$ a weighting that is a function of $p(\wedge_{\phi \in \Phi(i)} \phi | WKB)$. The form of the function will determine the degree of focus on a particularly promising solution path.

4.3 Typing

Our definition of the value of information in [29] drew on Lozinskii's definition of the logical probability and a model counting argument which could only be computationally feasible on very small languages. The "magic number 7" rule of [2] indicates that such restricted languages may reflect the human working memory. However, we argue that parsimony in real world problem-solving can only be implemented if the language is typed, and that it should be modelled outside *WKB*.

Unnecessary problems caused by under-utilising types have been previously experienced by the database community. The power of the relational model derived from its foundations on predicate logic, but typing was limited to the common built-in types inherited from programming languages. Codd admitted that typing should have been used more [33], and it has been finally recognised that objects in OO models are mapped onto the relational model through the typing of the domains of fields, not as generalisations of tables. Extensive typing is now supported in object-relational database management systems, led by the work of Stonebraker, for example, [34].

To illustrate typing, consider a sales demand forecasting decision problem, such as mentioned at the end of Section 3. In order to represent the concept *Forecast* it would usually be treated as a binary predicate with fields for the product identification (the primary key) and the forecast quantity, assigned string and integer types respectively. We claim that the natural domain of the first field is the set of products *being considered at that time*, and not all n-length strings, or even all the products in the world, or all the products that that company carries. The natural domain of the second field, the sales forecast quantity, is the plausible sales figures for the set of products under consideration, and is certainly not all integers, or even all positive integers representable by the systems. The granularity of the set of possible sales figures needs to be set appropriately. It may be that, as reasoning continues, the type definition of such a variable changes, as the decision maker "zooms in" to an increasingly accurate forecast.

One consequence of attention to typing is that the problem of recursive application of functions is usually eliminated. In formal languages, any function symbol brings an infinite number of terms to the language. In human language, functions are rarely recursive because they are typed differently to the type of their arguments. Recursive functions do exist, but are not held in memory in infinite recursion: try thinking of the concept of "father of".

5. An example of forecasting with a frugal algorithm

This section illustrates reduction of the size of a problem specific knowledge base through summarisation, using a forecasting scenario derived from that outlined in section 2. We compare the performance of a limited memory "commonsense" forecaster with a standard linear autoregression.

The hypotheses set Φ we consider is a set of atoms $\{Forecast(a): a \in F^*\}$ where F^* is a set of potentially valid forecast values, ranges and/or relative trends. The weight function u on Φ initially focusses attention on coarse forecasts, say on constants *up* and *down*. For simplicity, we use the summarisation scheme *(3)* from the previous section, in which formulae with types occurring in the hypotheses set are retained. This means that the summary of *WKB* will be the set of formulae in *WKB* in which the type of the domain of *Forecast* occurs proportionately most often. A refocus will be the set of hypotheses of the form *Forecast(a)* which are most probable, given the information in the summarised *WKB*.

In previous work we have shown how a problem base *WKB* can be built up in response to a problem represented by Φ by bringing in from *KB* or *EKB* the most relevant formulae to the problem [35]. We therefore start with a description of the initial *WKB* and relevant parts of the processing knowledge base Δ and the system knowledge base *KB*. We will not detail how new formulae are brought in (refer to [29]) and will consider just one consumer product.

Let $L(t)$ be the dynamic first order typed language describing *WKB* at time t, in which $\wedge$ denotes conjunction, $\vee$ disjunction and $\forall$ and $\exists$ denotes the usual quantifiers. A binary predicate $\in$ used to denote set membership is tied into *WKB* from Δ and defines type through domains likewise inherited from Δ. The set of symbols in the language can change with time. Assume that at any time t, $L(t)$ has enough symbols to express all the concepts required at that stage in the forecasting process, but is the smallest first order language sufficient to express the concepts required in *WKB*.

In *WKB*, *Forecast* has at time t a domain F which represents the set of plausible sales quantities for this period, which will be a subset of the values occurring in Φ. The cardinality of F is small; indeed, at the start of the forecasting process it may be empty, or may be coarse, say with two constants which are the range limits. Sales forecasts require a single value per period and hence a uniqueness constraint: $\forall y \in F$ $\forall z \in F\ Forecast(y) \wedge Forecast(z) \Rightarrow y == z$

Recall from the case study that the decision makers had last month's reorder sheet to hand, and the trend in sales figures was an issue. Represent *AverageSales* as a temporal function over a 2-valued domain T say $\{t^*, t^{**}\}$. The formal symbol *AverageSales(t*)* will later be assigned a numerical value, which we suppose to come from a set S of possible sales quantities for this product. Initially S may be empty. An assignment is represented using the binary predicate $=$ tied into *WKB* from Δ.

AverageSales is used to compute the trend, represented as a unary predicate *Trend* with domain *U*. *U* might eventually be populated with a qualitative set such as {*up, steady, down*}, but extension of the language to populate *U* need not occur till a later stage. Then, *Trend* may be computed using Δ. Formally,

$$\forall u \in U \; \forall x_{t^*} \in S \; \; Trend(u) \wedge_{t^* \in T} AverageSales(t^*) = x_{t^*} \Leftrightarrow u = g(x_1, x_2, \dots x_n). \quad (1)$$

Here *g* reflects a quantitative or qualitative relationship between the trend setting and the actual difference of the moving average sales figures over the times in *T*. Note again that the assignment = and *g* are derived from Δ.

As well, *Trend* must take at most one value in *U* so there is a uniqueness constraint.

The forecaster also has some "reality check" on the difference between the previous sales figures and the forecast. How close these figures are expected to be will depend on the trend. Model this through a ternary predicate *R* such that *R(x, y, u)* holds whenever *x* is a plausible sales figure given the latest average sales figure is *y* and the trend is *u*. Formally,

$$\forall u \in U \; \forall x \in F \; \forall y \in S \; R(x, y, u) \Rightarrow Trend(u) \wedge AverageSales(t^*) = y. \quad (2)$$

"Plausible" will be represented through a set of set-valued functions {h_u} relating allowable forecasts to last average sales, where the functions are indexed by the trend. Like the function *g*, these are assumed to be in Δ. Plausible values *x* must belong to *F*, the set of plausible sales figures determined in the absence of the latest sales figure. This is encapsulated in the definitional constraint:

$$\forall u \in U \; \forall x \in F \; \forall y \in S \; Trend(u) \wedge AverageSales(t^*) = y \wedge R(x, y, u) \Rightarrow x \in h_u(y). \quad (3)$$

To recapitulate: we are assuming at time $t = 0$ the language $L(t_0)$ has (at least) the constants t^{**} and t^*, has a function *AverageSales*, type predicates defined by domains *S, D, F, T* and *U*, typed unary predicates *Forecast* and *Trend*, and a typed ternary predicate *R*.

Suppose now that the decision maker acquires the average sales quantities for the product for the last two periods. The language has to be extended to represent these figures. The trend can now be computed, by appealing to (1) and possibly extending the language. Using (3) restricts the possible forecast to a range in *F* determined by the last average sales plus the trend. Summarising at this stage leaves a set of the form {*Forecast(a), Forecast(b), Forecast(c), ...*} since these are the only consequences of *WKB* which refer only to the type *F*. Refocusing occurs at this stage, giving non-zero weight only to hypotheses relating to the constants in this set. The focus has narrowed from the broad {*up, down*} to {*a, b, ...*}.

A search for new information in *KB* is next initiated, in which formulae which refer to predicates in the language $L(t_0)$ will be brought in [16]. Suppose there are two such formulae, concerning promotions and fashionability. Specifically, suppose that *KB* reflects the belief that a promotion will cause an increase in sales according to an arithmetic multiplier *k*, represented by the formula:

$$\forall u \in U \; \forall x \in F \; \forall y \in S \; Trend(u) \land AverageSales(t^*) \land Promo(on) \land R(x, y, u) \Rightarrow$$
$$k.x \in h_u(y) \qquad\qquad (4)$$

in which *Promo* takes the values *on* or *off* in the obvious fashion. *KB* also has a relationship of this form to adjust the reality check *R* for fashionability. Suppose that a fashionable (resp. unfashionable) product will have sales in the high (resp low) end of the usual range. Then the relationship is given by the formula

$$\forall u \in U \; \forall x \in F \; \forall y \in S \; Fashionability(good) \land R(x, y, u) \Rightarrow$$
$$(\forall z \in h_u(y)(z \geq l \land u \geq z) \land x \geq \tfrac{1}{2}(l + u)) \Rightarrow x \in f_u(y)) \qquad (5)$$

where $f_u(y)$ is the adjusted set of plausible values for forecasts, and l, u are abbreviations for the lower and upper-bounds of $h_u(y)$.

In the next round of information gathering, facts concerning *Promo* and *Fashionable* will be brought in to *WKB*. Suppose *KB* knows there is a promotion. Then the fact will be brought into *WKB* and (4) applied to adjust the forecast. Unfortunately, the formula about fashionability will be flushed out in the ensuing summary stage. However, it will be brought in again in the next information acquisition round, followed by a formula linking fashionability with colour and pattern supposing such a one exists in *KB*. The system will only then be in a position to apply (5) to adjust the forecast for fashionability.

To illustrate the performance of this "commonsense forecaster", we synthesised sales data according to the formula: $sales(t) = sales(t - 1) + trend + \Sigma_i P_i(t) + \Sigma_i H_i(t) + noise$. Here, *trend* is a constant or a step function, and *noise* is white noise which is set in the range. P_i is the impulse function over time period $[t_i, t_{i+3}]$ defined by $(+1, .05, -0.4, -0.6)$ which captures the initial surge, then fall off, in sales associated with promotions. H_i is an impulse function on the period $[t_i, t_{i+1}]$ of the form $(+a, -a)$ which captures fashion effects. Note that the data were not created to suit the commonsense reasoner, which incorrectly modelled the adjustment needed for both promotions and fashions. We set k in Eqn. (4) to be 1.1 if a promotion was initiated in that period, with a fall off of .95 in the next period, and no effect after that. We allowed the "commonsense" forecaster to correctly judge the direction of any fashionability effect, but used the inadequate modelling of Eqn. (5).

Linear regression forecasts for time t_i based on the data up to t_{i-1} were compared with the corresponding commonsense forecasts and forecasts made from the moving average data over multiple runs in which the noise, and trend line were varied. Example results over an 18 period run were, for a noise level around 5% and a broken trend line, a relative mean error of 4% with standard deviation 8% for the commonsense forecaster, as opposed to 6% and 9% respectively for the linear regression, and 5% and 9% for the moving average forecast. This pattern of results, in which the performance of the commonsense reasoner was slightly better than the other methods, was typical. Thus, on a noise level about 10%, we obtained a relative mean error of -1% with standard error 12% for the commonsense reasoner, as opposed to 12% and 13% respectively for the linear regression, and 3% and 12% for the moving average forecaster. The performance in steady trend conditions was comparable for all three forecasters.

6. Conclusion

This paper has covered a lot of ground in investigating a structure for a commonsense reasoning forecasting system to deal with a complex dynamic environment while maintaining a small working knowledge base. We started with a system described in [16] which alternates search with reasoning. We said this had to incorporate periodic summarisation of the working knowledge base, which we suggested could be approached through a variety of mechanisms adapted from the document management area. The task of summarisation was made easier, we claimed, by knowledge of the decision task being addressed by the system, in this case, the decision as to what forecast to make. We illustrated with a sales forecasting problem using the simple summarisation strategy of keeping those formulae which contained a high proportion of constants of a type contained in the problem description.

A thorough theoretical and comparative investigation of summarisation strategies is planned, with comprehensive trials. The development of a full Prolog -based system with Web and relational database-interfaces to support search for information is progressing. This will be tested on real forecasting data using "live" external knowledge bases that are human experts in the domain.

References

1. Gigerenzer, G. and Goldstein, D. Reasoning the fast and frugal way: Models of bounded rationality *Psychological Review,* 103, 4 (1996) 650-669.
2. Miller, G. The magical number seven plus or minus two: some limits on our capacity for processing information. *Psych Rev* 101 (1994) 343-352(reprinted from *Psychological Review,* 63 (1956) 81-97).
3. Alchouron, C.,Gardenfors, O. and Makinson, D. On the logic of theory change *J. Symbolic Logic,* 50 (1985)510-530.
4. Antoniou, G. *Nonmonotonic Reasoning: The Classical Approaches.* MIT Press (1997).
5. M. J. Lawrence and M. O'Connor, Can the use of a DSS improve decision making? *Proc. Pacific-Asia Conf. On IS* ISMRC/QUT (1997) 262-273
6. Dalrymple, D. J. Sales forecasting practices. *International Journal of Forecasting,* 3, (1987) 379-391.
7. Lee, J. K, Oh, S. B. and Shin, J. C. UNIK-FCST: Knowledge-Assisted Adjustment of Statistical Forecasts. *Expert Systems with Applications* 1(1) (1990) 39-50.
8. Ideal Stock Management Ltd, http://www.u-net.com/ism/demforc.htm, 1995
9. BIOSS (http://www.bioss.sari.ac.uk/BioSS/Computing/likely_2.html), Biomaths and Stats Scotland (1996).
10. Kahneman, D. and Tversky, A. On the psychology of prediction, *Psychological Review* (1973) 237-251.
11. Lawrence, M. An exploration of some practical issues in the use of quantitative forecasting models. *Journal of Forecasting,* 1 (1983) 169-179.
12. Kleindorfer, H. Kunreuther and P. Schoemaker, *Decision Sciences: An Integrative Perspective.* Cambridge University Press, (1993).
13. Davis, F., Lohse, G. and Kottemann, J. Harmful effects of seemingly helpful information on forecasts of stock earnings, *J. Economic Psychology,* 15 (1994) 253-267.
14. Remus, R., O'Connor, M.and Griggs, K. Does feedback improve the accuracy of recurrent judgmental forecasts? *Organizational behavior and Human Decision Processes,* 66 (1996) 22-30.

15. M. Handzic, Decision Performance as a function of information availability, *Proc. 2ⁿᵈ. SITIS Conference,* Uni. NSW (1997).
16. Gibbon G. and Aisbett J. Switching between reasoning and search, to appear, ed. M. Pagnucco, *Lecture Notes in AI,* Springer Verlag, (1998).
17. J. Aisbett and G. Gibbon (1997) A user dependent definition of the information in images and its use in information retrieval". *Journal of Visual Communication and Image Representation,* 8, 2, 97-106
18. Gibbon, G. and Aisbett, J. Common Sense, Artificial Intelligence and The Reorder Decision, *Proceedings of 1ˢᵗ Int. Conf. On Managing Enterprises ME-SELA'97,* Mechanical Engineering Publications, London, (1997) pp 541-546.
19. Starr, M. and Miller, D. Inventory Control: Theory and Practice. Prentice Hall, (1962).
20. Kahneman, D., Slovic, P. and Tversky, A. (ed) *Judgement under uncertainty: heuristics and biases* Cambridge University Press, (1982).
21. Heath, L et al *Applications of Heuristics and Biases to Social Issues* Plenum Press, (1994).
22. Simon, H., Rational choice and the structure of the environment, *Psch. Review* 63, (1956), 129-138.
23. Crainer, S. *Key management ideas,* Pitman Publishing (1996).
24. Kohavi, R and John, G. H. Wrappers for feature subset selection, *Artificial Intelligence,* 97 (1997) 273-324.
25. Holsapple, C. and Whinston A. *Decision Support Systems: A knowledge based approach.* West Publishing Co., (1996).
26. Gaifman, H. and Snir, M. Probabilities over rich languages, testing and randomness. J. Symbolic Logic, 47, 3, (1982) 495-548.
27. Hutchins, J. Summarization: Some problems and methods (abstracting), Meaning: The Frontier of Informatics - *Informatics* 9, (1987) 151-173
28. McKeown, K., Robin, J. and Kukich, K. Generating concise natural language summaries, *Information Processing and Management* 31(5):703-33, 1995.
29. Aisbett, J. and Gibbon, G. A practical measure of information, to appear *J. Exp. Theor.*
30. http://www.tipster.org/phaseiii.html, Phase III Overview TIPSTER Phase III Begins - A Four Part Program (1997)
31. Aisbett, J and Gibbon, G. Epistemic utility in commonsense reasoning, *3rd. International Conference on Information-Theoretic Approaches to Logic, Language, and Computation* (1998)(to appear)
32. E. Lozinskii, Resolving contradictions: a plausible semantics for inconsistent systems. *Journal of Automated Reasoning,* 12 (1994) 1-31.
33. Codd, E., *The relational model for database management: version 2* Addison-Wesley (1990)
34. Stonebraker, M., Olson, M. Large Object Support in POSTGRES. *ICDE* (1993) 355-362
35. Aisbett, J and Gibbon, G. Compiling a problem specific knowledge base, *Research and Development in Expert Systems XIV* ed. J. Hunt and R. Miles *Proceedings of ES97,* Cambridge (1997) 203-217.
36. Sattar, A. and Ghose, A. (1995) Experiments in Belief Revision, *Proc 8th Aust. Joint Conf. on AI,* AI'98, World Scientific, (1995), pp 515-522.

Data Mining for Risk Analysis and Targeted Marketing

G. Jha and S.C. Hui

School of Applied Science, Nanyang Technological University
Nanyang Avenue, Singapore 639798
{gunjan@booch.sas.ntu.ac.sg, asschui@ntu.edu.sg}

Abstract. Commercial databases often contain critical business information concerning past performance which could be used to predict the future. However, the huge amounts of data can make the extraction of this business information almost impossible by manual methods or standard software techniques. Data mining techniques can analyze, understand and visualize the huge amounts of stored data gathered from business applications and thus help companies stay competitive in today's marketplace. Currently, a number of data mining applications and prototypes have been developed for a variety of business domains. Most of these applications are targeted at predictive modeling that finds patterns of data to help predict the future trend and behaviors of some entities. Apart from predictive modeling, other data mining tasks such as summarization, association, classification and clustering could also be applied to business databases. In this paper, we will illustrate the different data mining tasks applied to a real-life business database for risk analysis and targeted marketing.

Keywords: Data mining, knowledge discovery in databases, data mining process, risk analysis, targeted marketing.

1. Introduction

Data mining or knowledge discovery in databases (KDD) [1,2,3] is a rapidly emerging field. This technology is motivated by the need of new techniques to help analyze, understand or even visualize the huge amounts of stored data gathered from business and scientific applications.

For the past few years, a number of data mining applications and prototypes have been developed for a variety of domains [4], including marketing, finance, banking, manufacturing, telecommunications and health care. In this paper, we will illustrate the different data mining tasks such as summarization, association, classification, prediction and clustering, applied to a real-life business database for risk analysis and targeted marketing. The paper is organized as follows. The paper starts by describing different data mining tasks that are currently supported by different data mining tools. Then, data mining techniques for each of these tasks are discussed. A case study is then given to show how data mining can be applied to a business database for risk analysis and targeted marketing using these tasks. Finally, the conclusion is given.

2. Data Mining Tasks

The two "high-level" primary goals as defined by Fayyad et al. [2] for data mining are prediction and description. Prediction involves using some variables or fields in the database to predict unknown or future values of other variables of interest. Description focuses on finding human-interpretable patterns describing the data. The goals of prediction and description are achieved by using the following data mining tasks.

- *Summarization*: it provides a description of a behavior from a subset of data. This often involves tools for query and reporting, multidimensional analysis and statistical analysis. Visualization techniques such as scatter plots and histograms are often used to allow viewing the results from different angles and perspectives. For example, weekly sales during the first quarter of 1996 and 1997 of a departmental store can be queried using a multidimensional database that organizes data along the predefined dimension on time and department.
- *Association*: it determines relations between fields in the database. This is useful to market basket analysis that identifies items commonly purchased with other items in supermarkets. During market basket analysis, association rules are generated. For example, people who buy cat food also buy kitty litter with probability P1 (say).
- *Classification*: it maps (or classifies) a data item into one of several predefined classes. The classification task uses database records that reflect historical data (information about past behaviour) to automatically generate a model that can be applied to unclassified data in order to classify it. For example in targeted marketing, classification uses data on past promotional mailings to identify the targets most likely to maximise return on investment in future mailings.
- *Prediction*: it is the same as classification except that the records are classified according to predefined future behaviour or estimated values. For example, to predict which telephone subscribers will order a value-added service such as voice mail or caller-id display.
- *Clustering*: it maps a data item into one of several categorical classes (or clusters) in which the cluster must be determined from the data. Clustering differs from classification in which the classes in classification are pre-defined. Clusters are defined by finding natural groupings of data items based on similarity metrics or probability density models. For example, to discover homogeneous sub-populations for consumer marketing databases. Clustering is often done as a prelude to some other form of data mining function. For example, one can divide a customer base into clusters of people with similar buying habits, and then ask what kind of promotion works best for each other.

3. Data Mining Techniques

There have been many data mining techniques for the various data mining tasks described in section 2. Some of the most commonly used techniques for each of these tasks are described as follows.

3.1 Summarization

Databases often contain information at primitive concept levels and one may need a summarization or a general description of the large set of attributes in the data, presented at a high concept level. The techniques for achieving this goal, also known as summarization or data generalization, include data cube approach and attribute-oriented induction approach.

Data cube approach [5] is to materialize frequent and expensive computations involving aggregate functions like count, sum, average, max, etc., and to store the materialized view in a multi-dimensional database (data cube) for decision support, knowledge discovery, and other applications. Aggregate functions are pre-computed according to the grouping of attribute into sets or subsets of attributes. Generalization can be performed on the data cube by mining multiple-level knowledge, which uses the techniques such as progressive generalization (roll-up) and progressive deepening (drill-down). Roll-up operation generalizes the data to higher abstraction level whereas drill-down does the reverse. Interactive roll-up and drill-down operation to desired conceptual level with different settings of thresholds and focuses can also be achieved using pre-computed aggregate functions.

Attribute-oriented induction approach is a technique for generalization of any subset of on-line data in a relational database and extraction of interesting knowledge from the generalized data. The generalized data may also be stored in a database, in the form of a generalized relation or a generalized cube, and can be updated incrementally upon database updates [6].

3.2 Association

This operation generates association rules of the form $X \Rightarrow Y$ (c, s) explained as "if a pattern X appears in a transaction, there is $c\%$ possibility (*confidence*) that the pattern Y holds in the same transaction and $s\%$ of total transactions contain (*support*) $X \cdot Y$". Related to association rules, many perspectives of work have been identified. Mining association rules is to discover strong association rules (rules with high support and confidence) in large databases; algorithms developed in this area include Apriori [7], DHP (Apriori + hashing) [8] and Partition [9]. Some other area of work in this direction include mining generalized and multi-level association rules by progressive deepening [10], meta-rule guided mining of association rules in relational databases [11] and interestingness measurement for association rules [10]. Techniques for improving the efficiency of mining association rules using database scan reduction [12], sampling (mining with adjustable accuracy) [10], incremental updating of discovered association rules [13] and parallel and distributed data mining [14] have also been studied.

3.3 Classification and Prediction

Both of these operations are similar in principle and hence use the same techniques for their specific tasks. Classification categorizes data based on a set of training objects and develops a model for each class. Predictive modeling consists of minimal generalization, attribute relevance analysis, generalized linear model construction and prediction. The techniques used include decision trees, example-based methods, neural networks, database techniques, genetic algorithms [15], statistics [16] and rough sets [17].

Decision trees are a powerful model produced by a class of techniques such as CART [18], ID3 [19] and C4.5 [20]. Example-based methods use known examples as a model to make predictions about unknown examples. The nearest-neighbour classification [21] and case-based reasoning [22] are the techniques used for example-based methods. Neural network approach for data mining is discussed in [23,24]. When applying neural network for data mining, the neural network acts as a non-linear predictive model that learns from a training set and then generalises classification patterns from it. Rule induction algorithms such as AQ [25] and CN2 [26] inductively learn a set of "if-then" rules from a set of training examples. To do this, it performs a general-to-specific beam search through rule-space for the "best" rule, removes training examples covered by that rule, then repeats until no more "good" rules can be found. As most of the decision tree techniques may encounter the problem of scalability and efficiency when they are applied to the mining of very large, real-world databases, database-oriented approaches, such as SLIQ [27], SPRINT [28] and generalization-based decision tree induction [29], have been proposed to tackle the problem. In addition to using decision tree induction, SLIQ and SPRINT propose pre-sorting techniques on disk-resident training data sets that are too large to fit in memory.

3.4 Clustering

Data Clustering (unsupervised learning) is to cluster objects into classes, based on their features, which maximize intraclass similarity and minimize interclass similarity. Clustering analysis can be divided into two basic approaches, probability based and distance based. Probability based clustering analysis algorithms include COBWEB (incremental concept formation) [30] and CLASSIT (COBWEB extended to real-valued data). Approaches for distance based clustering analysis are statistical approaches, CLARANS [31], BIRCH (balanced iterative reducing and clustering using hierarchies) [32] and a variation of CLARANS [33].

4. Case Study: Mining a Business Database

In this section, we describe a business application in which data mining techniques can be used for extracting the hidden information in business database and help predicting the future trends to stay competitive in the marketplace. The application is named as Credit Scoring Analysis that is an important area in banking. The application deals with credit scoring data from a multinational bank. The database contains data that represent positive and negative instances of people who were and were not granted credit. The data also contains the domain theory explaining the heuristic principles behind positive and negative scorings obtained directly from individuals working in the bank. Mining this data not only re-establishes most of the domain theory, it also helps extracting additional hidden information that may guide the bank in better credit scoring.

4.1 Data Mining Tool

DBMiner [34, 35] is a prototype data mining system developed by the DBMiner Research Group from the Database Systems Research Laboratory at Simon Fraser University, Canada. The system integrates data mining techniques with data warehousing technologies, and discovers various kinds of knowledge at multiple concepts from large relational databases. It was developed using the database-oriented approach. DBMiner supports both an SQL-like data mining query language, called DMQL, and a graphical user interface for interactive mining of multiple-level knowledge. The DBMiner system has been developed under both the PC (Windows-95, Windows/NT) and Unix platforms, it communicates with various commercial database systems using the ODBC technology.

Unlike most available data mining tools that support only predictive modeling technique, the DBMiner system provides a wide range of tools supporting different data mining tasks. The major data mining tasks supported include summarization, association, classification, prediction, clustering and time-series analysis. Therefore, the DBMiner system is chosen to mine the credit scoring data and to extract hidden information that can help identifying high-risk groups.

4.2 Data Mining Process

Fig. 1 shows the data mining process applied to the credit scoring analysis application. The process consists of the following steps:
1. Establish Mining Goals: The primary mining goals of the credit granting company are:
   (i) Risk Analysis: Identify the cluster of customers forming a risk group and thus optimize the credit scoring model by promoting customers not falling in the risk groups.
   (ii) Targeted Marketing: Mailing potential customers that are likely to respond to the campaign and at the same time can make it through the credit scoring system. This will result in a massive and high quality response.

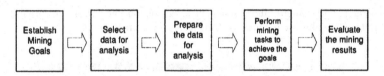

Fig. 1. Data mining process.

2. Select Data for Analysis: The business database contains particulars of all their customers. These include information on age, gender, marital status, employment status, location, amount of money on deposit in bank, item purchased through loan, loan payment amount per month, number of months to pay the loan, number of years working at current company and whether credit was granted or not. As the data is represented in various relational databases with different formats and possibly noisy and missing values. A *data warehouse* is used as a repository of information collected through multiple databases and stored under a unified schema at a single site. As DBMiner integrates the data mining and data warehousing technologies, the user is able to create and modify a data warehouse thus allowing for fast effective processing. By using the DBMiner's warehouse structure, all standard OLAP techniques including slicing, dicing, pivoting, filtering, drilling down and rolling up can be supported.

3. Prepare the data for analysis: After selecting the desired database tables and identifying the data to be mined, the data needs to be preprocessed for further analysis. The original data was transformed into SQL Server database format through which DBMiner can take input using ODBC connectivity. Also, the attribute "difference between deposit in bank and total loan amount to be paid" was added by using the available information on "loan payment amount per month" and "number of months to pay the loan". This surely gives better insight in risk analysis.

4. Perform data mining tasks: DBMiner is then used to perform data mining tasks on the credit screening data and assist the company achieve its goals. The following data mining tasks have been applied for the risk analysis of credit-scoring data:

Summarization: Given a huge database with large number of attributes, one needs to summarize the data using some characteristic rules that assist in constructing a model of the system and performing mining operations. DBMiner takes input as the specification of measurements that have to be analyzed and the dimensions against which to analyze them. The result of summarizing the dimensions age and item purchased is shown in Fig. 2. It can be seen that bike is purchased only by young people. Information on such trends helps in risk analysis.

Association: The most obvious application of association on the given data is market basket analysis. Association rules provide a good understanding of the model. Fig. 3 shows some the results of performing association on the attributes "number of years in current company", region and credit-grant using DBMiner. These rules provide a better insight in the model of the system and thus assist in risk analysis and targeted marketing. For example, those living in a bad region and having an unstable job record are less likely to get the credit and hence form a risk group.

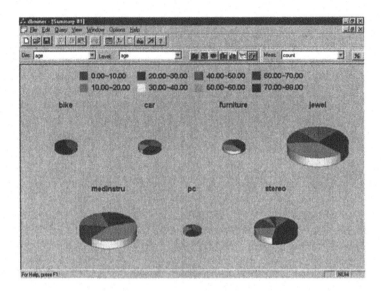

Fig. 2. Summarization in DBMiner.

Classification: The DBMiner classification method consists of four steps: partitioning of the data into training and testing data; analysis of the relevance of the attributes; construction of classification (decision) tree; and testing the effectiveness of classification using the test data set.

The result of analyzing the attribute credit-grant with respect to gender, marital status and item purchased by choosing training data to be 80% and classification threshold to be 85% is shown in Fig. 4. The classification tree thus generated shows many useful trends in the data. For example, female customers taking loan for purchasing bike are not granted credit, whereas married male customers purchasing bike are always granted credit. We classify a customer into pre-determined classes that determine the extent of risk associated with him. The influence of various combinations of the attributes associated with a customer and their corresponding values in a focused range was analyzed using the multi-level decision tree and it gives numerous trends under which the customer falls in a high or low risk group.

Clustering: We divide customers into clusters depending on similarities. It helps in targeted marketing and distinguishing loyal and rogue customers. The result of analyzing the dimensions employment status, location and probability of credit being granted is shown in Fig. 5. We can see a distinct cluster of customers who are employed, do not live in a bad region, belong to high age group, have higher deposit against loan and are stable in job. This information assists in target marketing.

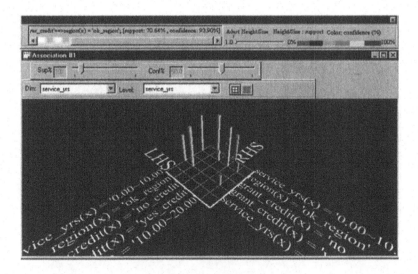

Fig. 3. Association in DBMiner.

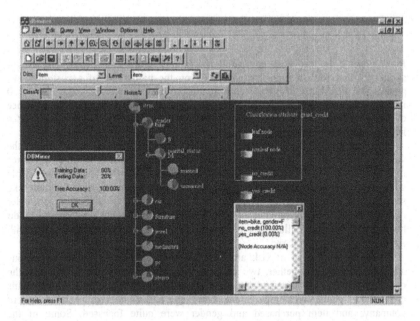

Fig. 4. Classification tree generated by DBMiner.

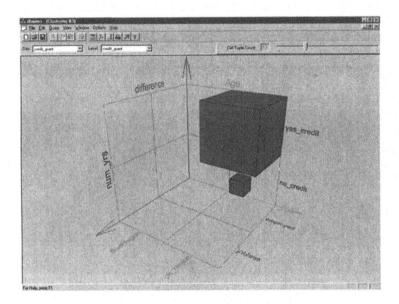

Fig. 5. Cluster Analysis in DBMiner.

Prediction: It is the most commonly performed task. It identifies clusters of applicants that form a high-risk group. Given the particulars of a customer, we predict the probability of credit being granted to the customer. A value close to 0 indicates the characteristics of the customer to determine a risk group. The influence of various attributes, individually or combined together, were examined to get a better picture of the risk groups.

In the first stage of the risk analysis using prediction technique, we predict the value of the attribute "credit granted" with respect to variations of other attributes individually. Not much clear trends could be obtained with this analysis but people with negative loan & deposit difference, jobless status and purchasing the item bike seemed to be in relatively high risk. On the other hand, people with stable job, older age and taking loan for purchasing a PC seemed to have better prospects of credit being granted. Fig. 6 illustrates the prediction of the attribute credit-grant with respect to the item purchased.

In the second stage of risk analysis, we evaluated the influence of various attributes combined together, two or more at a time. The results of some of the combinations like employment status and gender; marital status, employment status and gender; gender and employment status; age and number of years in current company; and item purchased and gender were quite focussed. Some of the combinations that indicated very high-risk groups were jobless males, jobless unmarried females, older people with unstable job and females purchasing bike. This shows that a risk group may be characterized by a specific combination of various features and discovering those features needs a good insight into the model of the system which is possible only through robust data mining techniques.

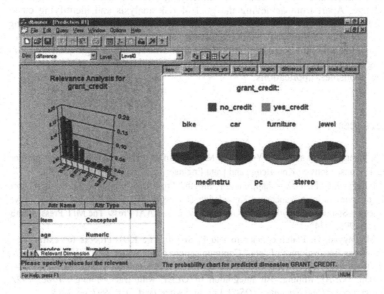

Fig. 6. Prediction in DBMiner.

5. Evaluate the mining results: The results obtained by mining the data are quite outstanding and provide a deep insight into the model constructed using the available data. DBMiner explores numerous hidden information from the data that helps in achieving the goals of risk analysis and targeted marketing. For risk analysis, characteristics of customers with a high probability of default when granted loan were identified. The characteristics of prospective customers who can make it through the company's credit-granting scheme were identified so as to assist the company in targeted marketing with high quality response. To help the company improve its policy and hence make its business more profitable, we also identified the characteristics of customers who could not make through the existing credit granting system but combined with some additional features, they prove to belong to low-risk groups. For example, customers purchasing the item bike seem to be in high-risk group but married male customers purchasing bike were identified to be loyal customers (see Fig. 4). This assisted the company in tuning its credit granting policy and approving credit to more customers without the usual risk increase.

5. Conclusion

In this paper, we have discussed different data mining tasks, including summarization, association, classification, prediction and clustering. Data mining techniques for these tasks have also been discussed. In addition, an application of the data mining process to a well-known business application, credit scoring in banking, using the data mining tool DBMiner is discussed to illustrate the different data mining tasks can be used together to analyze, understand and visualize the underlying business database to extract hidden knowledge. Apart from achieving the goal of risk analysis and identifying customers with a high probability of default when granted loan, the goal of targeted marketing was also achieved by identifying the characteristics of prospective customers who can make it through the company's credit-granting scheme. This results in high quality response in mailing campaigns. This paper has demonstrated considerable potential of applying data mining to business applications.

References

1. M.S. Chen, J. Han and P.S. Yu, "Data Mining: An overview from a database perspective," IEEE Transactions on Knowledge and Data Engineering, 8, 6 (Dec. 1996), 866-883.
2. U.M. Fayyad, G. Piatetsky-Shapiro and P. Smyth," From Data Mining to Knowledge Discovery: An overview," In Advances in Knowledge Discovery and Data Mining. U.M. Fayyad, G. Piatetsky-Shapiro P. Smyth and R. Uthurusamy, Eds. AAAI Press/ The MIT Press, Cambridge, Mass., 1996, 1-34.
3. U. M. Fayyad, G. Piatetsky-Shapiro and P. Smyth,"The KDD Process for extracting useful knowledge from volumes of data," Communications of the ACM, 39, 11 (Nov. 1996), 27-34.
4. R.J. Brachman et al., "Mining Business Databases", Communication of the ACM, pp. 42-48.
5. J. Han, "OLAP Mining: An Integration of OLAP with Data Mining", *Proc. 1997 IFIP Conference on Data Semantics (DS-7)*, Leysin, Switzerland, Oct. 1997, pp. 1-11.
6. J. Han, Y. Cai, N. cercone. Data-driven discovery of quantitative rules in relational databases. *IEEE Trans. Knowledge and Data Engineering*, 5:29-40, 1993.
7. R. Agrawal and R. Srikant. Fast Algorithms for mining association rules. In *Proc. 1994 Int.. Conf. Very Large Data Bases*, pp. 487-499, Santiago, Chile, September 1994.
8. J.S. Park, M.S. Chen, and P.S. Yu. An effective hash-based algorithm for mining association rules. In *Proc. 1995 ACM-SIGMOD Int. Conf. Management of Data*, pp. 175-186, San Jose, CA, May 1995.
9. A. Savasere, E. Omiecinski, and S. Navathe. An efficient algorithm for mining association rules in large databases. In *Proc. 1995 Int. Conf. Very Large Data Bases*, pp. 432-443, Zürich, Switzerland, Sept. 1995.
10. R. Srikant and R. Agrawal. Mining Generalized Association Rules. *Proceedings of the 21" International Conference on Very Large Data Bases*, pages 407-419, September 1995.
11. Y. Fu and J. Han. Meta-rule-guided mining of association rules in relational databases. In *Proc. 1" Int'l Workshop on Integration of Knowledge Discovery with Deductive and Object-Oriented Databases (KDOOD '95)*, pages 39-46, Singapore, Dec. 1995.
12. M.S. Chen, J.S. Park, and P.S. Yu. Data Mining for Path Traversal Patterns in a Web Environment. *Proceedings of the 16th International Conference on Distributed Computing Systems*, pages 385-392, May 27-30 1996.
13. D.W. Cheung, J, Han, V. Ng, and C.Y. Wong. Maintenance of discovered association rules in large databases: An incremental updating technique. In *Proc. 1996 Int'l Conf. On Data Engineering*, New Orleans, Louisiana, Feb. 1996.
14. J.S. Park, M.S. Chen, and P.S. Yu. Efficient parallel mining for association rules. In *Proc. 4th Int. Conf. On Information and Knowledge Management*, pp. 31-36, Baltimore, Maryland, Nov. 1995.

15. Z. Michalewicz, "Genetic Algorithms + Data Structures = Evolution Programs," Springer, 1996.

16. J. Elder IV and D. Pregibon, "A statistical perspective on knowledge discovery in databases," In Advances in Knowledge Discovery and Data Mining. U.M. Fayyad, G. Piatetsky-Shapiro P. Smyth and R. Uthurusamy, Eds. AAAI Press/ The MIT Press, Cambridge, Mass., 1996, pp. 83-115.

17. W. Ziarko, "Rough Sets, Fuzzy Sets and Knowledge Discovery," Springer-Verlag, 1994.

18. L. Breiman, J. Friedman, R. Olshen and C. Stone, "Classification of Regression Trees," Wadsworth, 1984.

19. J.R. Quinlan, "Induction of Decision Trees," Machine Learning, 1:81-106, 1986.

20. J.R. Quinlan, "C4.5: Programs for Machine Learning," Morgan Kaufmann, 1993.

21. B.V. Dasarathy, "Nearest Neighbour (NN) Norms: NN Pattern Classification Techniques," Los Alamitos, CA, IEEE Computer Society Press, 1991.

22. J. Kolodner, "Case-Based Reasoning," Morgan Kaufmann, 1993.

23. H. Lu, R. Setiono and H. Liu, "Effective Data Mining Using Neural Networks," IEEE Transactions on Knowledge and Data Engineering, Vol. 8, No. 6, Dec. 1996, pp 957-961.

24. J.P. Bigus, "Data Mining with Neural Networks: Solving Business Problems - From Application Development to Decision Support," New York: McGraw-Hill, 1996.

25. R.S. Michalski, "A theory and methodology of inductive learning," in Michalski et al. (editor), Machine Learning: An Artificial Intelligence Approach, Vol. 1, pp 83-134, Morgan Kaufmann, 1983.

26. P. Clark and T. Niblett, "The CN2 Induction Algorithm. Machine Learning," 3(4), pp 261-283, 1989.

27. M. Mehta, R. Agrawal, and J. Rissanen, "SLIQ: A fast scalable classifier for data mining," In Proc. 1996 International Conference on Extending Database Technology (EDBT '96), Avignon, France, March 1996.

28. J. Shafer, R. Agrawal and M. Mehta, "SPLINT: a scalable parallel classifier for data mining," inProc. 22nd Intl. Conf. Very Large Data Bases (VLDB), pp 544-555, India, 1996.

29. M. Kamber et. al, "Generalisation and Decision Tree Induction: Efficient Classification in Data Mining," Proc. of 1997 Intl Workshop on Research Issues on Data Engineering (RIDE '97), Birmingham, England, April 1997, pp. 111-120.

30. D. Fisher. Improving inference through conceptual clustering. In *Proc. 1987 AAAI Conf.*, pp. 461-465, Seattle, Washington, July 1987.

31. R. Ng and J. Han. Efficient and effective clustering method for spatial data mining. In *Proc. 1994 Int. Conf. Very Large Data Bases*, pp. 144-155, Santiago, Chile, September 1994.

32. T. Zhang, R. Ramakrishnan, and M. Livny. BIRCH: an efficient data clustering method for very large databases. In *Proc 1996 ACM-SIGMOD Int. Conf. Management of Data*, Montreal, Canada, June 1996.

33. M. Ester, H.P. Kriegel, and X. Xu. Knowledge discovery in large spatial databases: Focussing techniques for efficient class identification. In *Proc. 4th Int. Symp. On Large Spatial Databases (SSD '95)*, pp. 67-82, Portland, Maine, August 1995.

34. J. Han et al, "DBMiner: A System for Data Mining in Relational Databases and Data Warehouses," Proc CASCON '97 Meeting of Minds, Toronto, Canada, Nov 1997.

35. DBMiner System, Online document available at URL: http://db.cs.sfu.ca/DBMiner.

Applying Knowledge Discovery to Predict Infectious Disease Epidemics

Syed Sibte Raza Abidi and Alwyn Goh

School of Computer Sciences
Universiti Sains Malaysia
11800 Penang, Malaysia.
sraza@cs.usm.my, alwyn@cs.usm.my

Abstract. Predictive modelling, in a knowledge discovery context, is regarded as the problem of deriving predictive knowledge from historical/temporal data. Here we argue that neural networks, an established computational technology, can efficaciously be used to perform predictive modelling, i.e. to explore the intrinsic dynamics of temporal data. Infectious-disease epidemic risk management is a candidate area for exploiting the potential of neural network based predictive modelling—the idea is to model time series derived from bacteria-antibiotic sensitivity and resistivity patterns as it is believed that bacterial sensitivity and resistivity to any antibiotic tends to undergo temporal fluctuations. The objective of epidemic risk management is to obtain forecasted values for the bacteria-antibiotic sensitivity and resistivity profiles, which could then be used to guide physicians with regards to the choice of the most effective antibiotic to treat a particular bacterial infection. In this regard, we present a Web-based Infectious Disease Cycle Forecaster (IDCF), comprising a number of distinct neural networks, that have been trained on data obtained from long-term clinical observation of 89 types of bacterial infections, being treated using 36 different antibiotics. Preliminary results indicate that IDCF is capable of generating highly accurate forecasts given sufficient past data on bacteria-antibiotic interaction. IDCF features a client-server based WWW interface that allows for remote projections to be requested for and displayed over the Internet.

1   Introduction

Electronic data repositories are vastly expanding with an upward trend towards storing continuous historical data, such as stock markets, foreign exchange rates, weather patterns, medical monitoring and so on. Knowledge discovery or data mining then entails the detection of intrinsic recurring patterns from past temporal data, thereby rendering the opportunity to exploit the discovered knowledge to predict future behaviours of the system. Mathematically, any prediction system attempts to predict future values—x(t+Δt) = f(x(t), x(t-Δt), x(t-2Δt), ...) given sufficient data collected over some elapsed time period.

Predictive modelling based on temporal data (or in general time-series forecasting), in a knowledge discovery or data mining context, is regarded as the problem of deriving predictive knowledge from historical data—information about past behaviour is used to generate a model of the system that can be used to predict future behaviour[1], [2]. For example, a foreign exchange broker might want to predict the future currency exchange rates; a hospital administrator might want to predict the rate of patient admissions to the hospital; healthcare professionals might want to assess the future effects of certain drugs on particular infectious organisms; a marketing executive might want to predict whether a particular consumer will switch brands for a specific product and so on. In summary, time-series forecasting is widely employed for complex non-linear systems in areas ranging from financial markets to weather to medicine [3], [4], [5], [6].

Risk management is an innovative domain that can benefit from knowledge discovery activities. Modern risk management strategies advocate the use of large quantities of historical data (collected from the subject system) to build models that can assess future risk situations—to predict beforehand a possible disaster situation and to circumvent it by taking pre-emptive measures. In this paper, we apply predictive modelling techniques in the context of infectious-disease risk management. In a typical infectious-disease control scenario, the strategy is to eradicate the culprit bacteria before it has the chance to spread and infect a larger population. The most widely practised method to eradicate bacterial organisms is the use of stipulated antibiotics. Each infectious disease is propagated by a particular type of bacteria that is susceptible to only a few distinct antibiotics. Nevertheless, bacteria are quite resilient—they have the tendency to develop a temporary immunity towards a certain antibiotic, hence rendering it temporarily ineffective. Although, doctors know the bacterial origin of each infectious disease and the corresponding set of effective antibiotic drugs, yet they have no means of ascertaining the current effectiveness of an antibiotic towards the treatment of a certain bacteria. In practice, doctors choose an antibiotic from the set of effective antibiotics, in case the first choice antibiotic is ineffective then another antibiotic is prescribed with the hope of it being relatively more potent. In this scenario, prior knowledge of an antibiotic's effectiveness in treating a bacterial organism can potentially play a major role in controlling an infectious disease epidemic. Effective infectious-disease epidemic risk management then encompasses predictive modelling, based on past bacteria-antibiotic interactions, to determine the *future* effectiveness of candidate antibiotics towards a bacteria, and then choosing the most effective antibiotic to culminate the spread of the infectious disease.

The emergence of the artificial Neural Network (NN) paradigm has provided an innovative methodology for temporal data analysis, in that temporal data can be supplied as "training" input—so as to produce empirically correct relationships between past, present and predicted future values. This paper primarily introspects the possible efficacy of NNs towards knowledge discovery activities, in particular predictive modelling. The argument is extended further by demonstrating how NNs can be effectively used for predictive modelling—the problem domain addressed is epidemic risk management. In this regard this paper examines the temporal fluctuations in bacterial susceptibility towards a given antibiotic, which medical professionals have long suspected of possessing a recurrent pattern. Such recurrent patterns of a bacteria's susceptibility towards antibiotics are captured by a NN system that later provides a forecast of the behaviour of a bacteria towards various antibiotics [7]. It is argued that having a predictive model for bacteria-antibiotic interactions would be enormously useful, in that doctors usually have a choice of several antibiotics with which to treat a particular bacterial infection. Reliable "future" knowledge of how one antibiotic, amongst a possible choice of several antibiotics, can be used with optimal effect at a particular time can have significant implications towards the control of spread of infectious diseases. Finally, we present a web-based *Infectious Disease Cycle Forecaster* that allows for projections to be requested for by remote healthcare practitioners and displayed over the Internet.

2   The Essence of Predictive Modelling

Knowledge discovery manifests a synergy of a diverse set of computational technologies to address a central objective: to glean information that is buried in the enormous stocks of collected data and to develop and underpin strategies for improved decision making support. Of the many facets of data mining, we are particularly interested in predictive modelling—the analysis of historical data to discover predictive patterns [8] [9].

Typically, the exercise of mining useful information from data is predicated by the specification of the needs and goals. But, it is also true to state that the nature of the data circumscribes the nature of the knowledge that can be derived from it—the available data defines the scope of the problem, more so the data *defines* the problem and in turn the *extractable* knowledge [10]. Predictive modelling is characteristic of such *data-defined* problems as the mathematical model of the system generating the time-series data is not available, rather the phenomenon/functions realising the time-series data are concealed within the collected data. Predictive modelling encompasses the formation of a descriptive model of the system in question, either by inductive or deductive means, and then exploiting the model to predict future system behaviour. For that matter, within the knowledge discovery paradigm, predictive modelling can be regarded as a *discovery-driven* data-mining operation.

Mining predictive quality information is more an inductive problem—in the absence of both an abstract specification of the system generating the data and the non-linear and non-monotonic relationships between the data items in the data set, inductive learning techniques are more appropriate to produce a "generalisation" of the functions governing the system, i.e. a descriptive model of the system. The generalisation—perhaps provided by a trained NN—interpolates between and extrapolates beyond the data items used for its construction and hence can compute relations/values beyond those used to develop it. In a knowledge discovery context, predictive modelling of time-series data within an inductive learning paradigm can be understood as follows: The inductive learning system—a NN for that matter—is given a set of instances (derived from the data set) of the form (x, y), where y represents the variable that needs to be predicted by the system, and x is a vector of representative features deemed relevant to determining y. The inductive learning system is to induce a general mapping from x vectors to y values by way of building (or rather implicitly learning) a prediction model, $y = f(x)$ of the unknown/inherent function f, that allows the prediction of y values from unseen x vectors. For any prediction activity, knowledge about the current state of the system is essential as the predicted value is a function of the current state(s). In sum, the inductive learning system accounts for the *regularities* hidden within a seemingly arbitrary data set and uses the "learnt" generalisation to predict future values of some variables.

Given that predictive modelling involves inductive model-development activities, the computing literature offers a suite of inductive techniques that are candidates for performing predictive modelling—e.g. decision rule or decision tree induction, classifier rules, statistical linear discriminants, case based (nearest neighbour) methods, genetic algorithms and NNs [11]. Typically, predictive modelling is carried out using symbolic-induction techniques as the generated models are expressed as sets of if-then rules, and are therefore comprehensible and explainable. Yet, recently with the emergence of NNs as a powerful computational tool, with learning capabilities, there is a strong case for using NNs for predictive modelling.

3   The Efficacy of Neural Network for Effective Knowledge Discovery/Data Mining Activities

NNs have a natural propensity to learn—they learn how to solve problems from acquired/generated data (from the problem domain) as opposed to solving problems based on explicit problem specification. Furthermore, the learning characteristics of NN enable them to deal efficiently with noisy data—partial, incorrect and potentially conflicting data—and generalise well in situations not previously encountered. Hence, it can be argued that NN are well suited for data mining tasks, in particular to tackle *data defined problems* [12], [13].

Data mining literature does not seem to support the above conjecture. Despite the above-mentioned efficacy of NNs towards various knowledge discovery and data mining activities, predictive modelling being a prime candidate, NNs are not commonly used for data mining tasks. One explanation for this apparent lack of acceptance of NN by the data mining community is that *trained NNs are usually not comprehensible*—they are "black boxes" with no explanation on how they solved the problem. Below we will attempt to justify the efficacy of NNs for data mining, in particular predicative modelling, based entirely on accurate emprical comparisons.

Indeed, NNs when applied for predictive modelling applications do not render any symbolic rules or explanations towards the operational characteristics or phenomenon governing the system in question. It is not the case that NN do not possess such knowledge; on the contrary, the knowledge learnt from data by the NN—a model of the system—is sub-symbolic in nature and it is encoded using real-valued parameters (connection weights) and distributed representations within the NN.

From a pragmatic point of view, the goal of most time-series forecasting/predictive modelling applications is to predict the future values to be generated by the system (based on the present state of the system), as opposed to the understanding of the phenomenon that would lead to the generation of those values. Of course, symbolic rules and explanations may be desired to get a better understanding of the system itself, and for that matter current research efforts in NNs endeavour to generate the rules learnt by the NN from the training data [14], [15]. Not withstanding the fact that the availability of explicit "system defining" rules would make NNs more favourable for knowledge discovery/data mining activities, yet it may be noted that most of the rules currently derived from NNs are primarily geared towards classification and clustering problems [16]. As much as the rules generated from learnt NNs can identify salient/discriminant features (in the data set), responsible for eventual classifications of the data items, it is yet to be seen how well NNs being trained on temporal data can (a) explicate their knowledge of the complex system they are modelling and (b) why and what attributes are significant in determining the future values of the system. It can be argued that the richness and the temporal nature of time-series data used in predictive modelling renders difficulties in generating meaningful rules.

In conclusion, we argue that maybe it is not even useful to look for system-defining rules within a NN performing predictive modelling, rather a validation of the NN results based on collected data should be used as a benchmark to determine its efficacy towards forecasting future values. In relative terms, the efficacy of NN for predictive modelling is further validated by the fact that predictions performed by NN are derived from an inherently "learnt" mathematical model of the system. On the contrary, real-life explanations of temporal systems are at best speculative—experts within the area of investigation usually provide a subjective and speculative analysis of the causes for the temporal behaviours of the system—devoid of credible mathematical models of the system.

4   Neural Network Based Predictive Modelling

In general, real-life observational data is difficult to model using linear statistical models based on auto-regression or moving averages. NNs [17] have been shown to be able to decode non-linear time series data which adequately describes the characteristics of the time-series. Information contained in the NN's weighted synaptic connections—assuming a sufficiently rich architecture—enables the NN to calculate forecasted values that fit into the non-linear trend presumably present in the past values of the time-series.

NN is an information processing paradigm inspired by the architecture and distributed processing methodology of the biological nervous system. It is composed of a large number of functionally simple, but highly interconnected, processing units (neurons) which are normally organised into layers i.e. input, output and at least one hidden layer interposed between the input and output layers. The inter-neuron synaptic connections constitute a connection-weight matrix which can be modified during training so as to better reproduce the non-linear mappings between the input pattern and the corresponding desired output pattern. Training the NN requires that it be supplied with sufficient input-output vectors, from which it will hopefully "learn" the inherent behavioural patterns. NN systems are therefore extremely useful for data-defined problems, characterised by the abundant availability of empirical data for which an analytic rule-based description is difficult or non-existent.

Data mining, in particular predictive modelling, using NN need to be carried out according to five major steps. First, time-series data is collected. Second, the data is cleansed—the data is normalised and scaled in order to minimise noise. Third, an appropriate NN capable of capturing the hidden regularities within the time-series data is built by experimenting with various architectural and training parameters. Fourth, the NN is trained using the training data. Finally, the trained NN is extensively testing for accuracy using the validation and testing data. After the NN passes the validation criteria it can then be used for predictive modelling.

4.1 Data Collection and Pre-Processing

The bacterial sensitivity/resistivity data used in our research was provided by Universiti Sains Malaysia Hospital located in Kota Baharu, Malaysia. This data-set was compiled to observe the interactions of various microbiological organisms against several antibiotics prescribed as treatment. For each individual patient, sensitivity/resistivity variations in the infecting organism towards the antibiotic used were periodically recorded. In total, the original five-year (1993-97) study collected data on the sensitivity/resistivity of 89 organisms, for which 36 different antibiotics were prescribed. For our purposes, it was deemed appropriate to sum all occurrences of a particular bacteria-antibiotic interaction within a particular month. We tabulated monthly values for bacterial sensitivity (S), resistivity (R) and their difference (S-R); thereby producing a data-set with points at regular temporal intervals.

4.2 Data Cleansing

Data cleansing was performed in terms of normalising the data i.e. map the tabulated values onto the numerical range [0,1] prior to insertion into the input-layer of the forecaster. The numerical range [0,1] was important as the NN employed the binary sigmoidal function. Data normalisation was done firstly by calculating the differences between successive monthly values for a particular bacteria-antibiotic (BA) interaction ie $d_{BA}(t_i) = y_{BA}(t_i) - y_{BA}(t_{i-1})$ where $y(t_i)$ is the sensitivity/resistivity for the i-th month

Secondly, we performed linear normalisation with respect to the maximal and minimal values for the time-series of differential values i.e.

$$x_{BA}(t_i) = \frac{d_{BA}(t_i) - min_{BA}}{max_{BA} - min_{BA}} \qquad (1)$$

with $max/min_{BA} = max/min\{d_{BA}(t_i),$ for $\forall$ i in time-series$\}$.

This exercise resulted in normalised vector $x_{BA}(t_i)$ in N-space for i = -N+1, ...,-1,0.

Prior to embarking on any time-series forecasting exercise it is important to establish whether the time-series in question incorporates any sort of inherent trends, otherwise by definition forecasting would be impossible. For our case, the *Random Walk Hypothesis* testing determined that the time-series of interest (for most of the BA interactions) exhibited biased random walk behaviour with a "period" of 3 to 4 months. This observation implies that the "learnt" generalisations of the inherent trends within the time-series data can at best be used to <u>forecast no better than three months into the future</u>.

4.3   NN Forecaster System: Design and Training

NN, in particular backpropagation (BP) networks, can be used as effective non-linear general-purpose function approximators—the BP network is simply taught historical data of the time-series and the learnt BP network can be used to predict future outcomes.

We have used the Back-Propagation (BP) NN with sigmoidal Feed-Forward (FF) learning [18] as the basis for our forecaster. This NN model employs a supervised-learning algorithm requiring a sample time-series of form $x_i = x(t_i)$ where $t_i = t_0+i\Delta t$ in which N past values (including the present) are used as input towards the calculation of future values for the time-series. The limits imposed by the random-walk test require three past x_{BA} values (i = -3,-2,-1) and the present (i = 0) to generate three future x_{BA} value (i = 1,2,3). Generation of the training pattern for the subsequent computational cycle requires the shifting forward of the 4-month temporal "past" window (now i = -2,-1,0,1) in order to generate future x_{BA} values at i = 2,3,4. The observed cyclic parameter, based on a 4 month temporal window, discussed in the previous section allows for design of a NN to model the time-series $x_{BA}(t_i)$ for i = -3,-2,-1,0,1,2,3; with i = -3,-2,-1,0 as input and i = 1,2,3 as output. This coresponds to a NN with 4 input and 3 output units. Experiments subsequently determined the optimal network configuration to be one with 10 hidden units.

Intuitively, one expects the predicted accuracy to degrade with temporal distance, this will be demonstrated in the next section. Finally, we have considered $x_{BA}(t_i)$ and $x_{BA'}(t_i)$ to be independent time-series, essentially for simplicity. This means we do not take into account the effects of interaction BA on interaction BA', although work is currently in progress to quantify this assumption.

To develop the most efficacious NN model four different time-series representation schemes were studied, namely:-

1. (S – R) time-series data used to train a single NN
2. S and R data each used to train separate NNs
3. Differential (dS – dR) data used to train a single NN
4. dS and dR data each used to train separate NN

Option four realised the best NN model as it appeared that the difference between past values of R/S reflects the magnitude of fluctuations between the R/S values with time. For forecasting purposes this is a more important indicator of the behaviour of the system as opposed to the actual values of R/S. Also, it was observed that keeping the S and R values in separate networks yielded better forecasting results. This observation is in accordance with the fact that, in theory, the sensitivity and resistivity parameters are not reciprocal to each other. Hence, in practice, they are not supposed to influence each other and can thus be modelled by separate NNs.

4.4 Discussion of Experimental Results

The major problem encountered in our work was the occasional absence of documented data. The missing data value are inserted using linear interpolation so as to reconstruct the complete time series required for NN training. When uninterrupted data does exist, the performance of the NN forecaster tends to be reasonably accurate. Fig. 1 shows, monthly (actual and forecasted) occurrences of *Staphylococus Aureus* sensitivity towards *Cefuroxime* (Graph P) and *Acinetobacter* sensitivity towards *Amikacin* (Graph Q). As can be seen in Graphs P and Q (shown in Fig. 1), the time-series of 1-month forecasted data tends to "track" fairly well with the actual documented incidence of bacterial-antibiotic sensitivity. The 2-month and 3-month predicted time-series are successively less accurate.

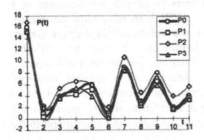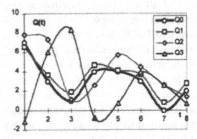

Fig. 1. Monthly actual and forecasted BA occurrences. In the legend, $(P/Q)_0$ = Actual recorded data; $(P/Q)_1$ = 1-mth; $(P/Q)_2$ = 2-mth and $(P/Q)_3$ = 3-mth predicted data

In order to ascertain the absolute accuracy of the system, we subtracted off the actual data values from each predicted time-series. Fig. 2 shows two graphs illustrating the differential comparison of monthly predictions against actual data for *Staphylococus Aureus* sensitivity towards *Cefuroxime* (Graph P) and *Acinetobacter* sensitivity towards *Amikacin* (Graph Q). From Fig. 2, we are thus able to conclude that the 1-month forecaster for both time-series produces output correct to within ±1 occurrences of sensitivity, with the 2-month and 3-month predictions being successively less accurate. Note that the discrepancy between predicted and recorded data tends to peak at the extremal points on the actual time-series, and that both predicted—especially the 1-month time-series—and recorded data tend to share similar minima and maxima. The system is hence able to predict reasonably well whether BA sensitivity is increasing or decreasing, information which is probably more important than a numerical forecast. Comparable levels of accuracy are typical for the BA interactions in our analysis, leading us to conclude that NN-based forecasting is indeed a reasonably accurate tool to counter bacterial infections.

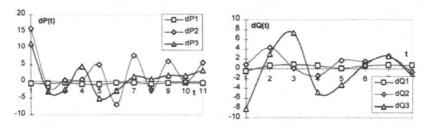

Fig. 2. Differential comparison of monthly predictions against actual data. In the legend, $d(P/Q)_1 = 1$-mth; $d(P/Q)_2 = 2$-mth; $d(P/Q)_3 = 3$-mth predicted differential

5 Infectious Disease Cycle Forecaster

The Infectious Disease Cycle Forecaster (IDCF) is the end-product of our research efforts. It allows remote health-care practitioners to forecast the behaviour of a bacteria/organism against one or more antibiotics. With increasing user-acceptance, we migrated IDCF from a stand-alone system to a web-based client-server system. The clients (remote healthcare professionals) run the user-interface front end using any Web browser to the IDCF server. Transactions between the client and server is via HTML pages—the client's web browser sends forecasting requests (names of bacterial organisms, antibiotics, duration of forecast and so on) and BA input values to the IDCF server, CGI programs initiate and co-ordinate all NN operations and calculations and finally results (i.e. forecast reports and graphs) are again sent to the client in the form of HTML pages.

The first panel in Fig. 3 shows the IDCF main input screen which requires specification of the organism, a list of interacting antibiotics, the nature of the forecast profile need to be generated, and the predictive time frame. The forecasted results are displayed on a dynamically generated Web-page (as shown in the second panel in Fig. 3), which illustrates the future S/R trends of the organism against the various selected antibiotics.

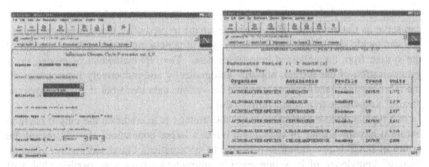

Fig. 3. The main screen of IDCF's web interface, followed by the forecast report for an exemplar bacteria-antibiotic interaction

The numerical data describing the future trend of certain bacteria-antibiotic interactions can be viewed as follows:-

- A single graph depicting either of the S or R profiles for one or more antibiotics (first panel of Fig. 4)
- A single graph showing both the S and R profiles for one antibiotic (second panel of Fig. 4)

with all graphs are generated dynamically from the NN output corresponding to one or more BA interactions.

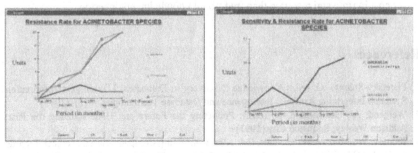

Fig. 4. Sample graphs illustrating the profiles of 3 different antibiotics against a common organism, and the S/R profile of a single antibiotic against a bacteria

6   Concluding Remarks

Typically, risk management—a scenario in a healthcare context being epidemic management—relies on human analysts to perform the necessary analysis of historical data and come up with a damage minimisation plan. However, with large databases storing continuous historical data, any attempt at real-life prediction involves the introspection of thousands of historical data items, while trying to deduce the inter-relations between the data items. Given this reality, we have argued that NN can serve as *normative decision-support systems* to predictive modelling problems—NN can tackle *data-defined* problems by way of generating a mathematical model of the system from the collected time-series data. The NN mathematical model, i.e. a generalisation of the system, not only automatically and inductively incorporates all the inherent inter-relationships between the various data items but it also exploits the "learnt" knowledge to predicts future values.

In a typical disease control scenario, the strategy is to eradicate the culprit bacteria before it has the chance to spread and infect a larger population. In this regard the utility of IDCF is paramount as it is able to systematically (and accurately) generate "future" knowledge of how one specific antibiotic—amongst a possible choice of several drugs—can be used with optimal effect at a particular time. Based on an IDCF-supplied prediction, informed decisions, such as discontinuation of less (or soon-to-be less) effective antibiotics in favour of more effective antibiotics, can subsequently be made by the respective agencies. Furthermore, major healthcare institutions will find it helpful to know ahead of time that they need to maintain sufficient quantities of the drugs projected to be most useful in dealing with certain infections, while perhaps reducing stockpiles for other less effective ones.

Finally, our results are significant because we have demonstrated that (a) NNs can offer a practical and automated solution to the problem of discovering knowledge from historical data to perform predictive modelling, and (b) NN-based learning techniques can provide "intelligent" predictive modelling systems at a significantly lower cost in time and resource than traditional knowledge engineering.

References

1. Piatetsky-Shapiro, G. (ed.): Knowledge Discovery in Databases. J. Intelligent Information Systems: Integrating Artificial Intelligence and Database Technologies. 4 (1). (1995)
2. Weigend, A., Gershenfeld, N. (eds.): Predicting the Future and Understanding the Past. Addison Wesley, Redwood City (1993)
3. Tierney, W., Murray, M., Gaskins, D.L., Zhou, X.: Using Computer-Based Medical Records to Predict Mortality Risk for Inner-City Patients with Reactive Airways Disease. J. American Medical Informatics Association, 4(4) (1997) 313-321
4. Jasic, T., Poh H.L.: Financial Time-Series Prediction using Neural Networks: A Case Study for the TOPIX Data. Proc. Sixth Australian Conf. Neural Networks. Sydney (1995)
5. Refenes, A.N., Zapranis, A., Francis, G.: Stock Performance Modelling using Neural Networks: A Comparative Study with Regression Models. Neural Network. 5 (1995)
6. Liu, J., Wong, L.: A Case Study for Hong Kong Weather Forecasting. Proc. Int. Conf. Neural Info. Processing. Hong Kong (1996)
7. Abidi, S. S. R., Goh, A.: Neural Network Based Forecasting of Bacteria-Antibiotic Interactions for Infectious Disease Control. Ninth World Congress on Medical Informatics. Seoul (1998)
8. Apte, C., Hong, S.J.: Predicting Equity Returns from Securities Data with Minimal Rule Generation. In: Fayyad, U.M., Shapiro, G.P., Smyth, P., Uthurusamy, R. (eds.): Advances in Knowledge Discovery and Data Mining. AAAI Press, California (1996)

9. Berndth, D.J., Clifford, J.: Finding Patterns in Time-Series: A Dynamic Programming Approach. In: Fayyad, U.M., Shapiro, G.P., Smyth, P., Uthurusamy, R. (eds.): Advances in Knowledge Discovery and Data Mining. AAAI Press, California (1996)

10. Partridge, D.: The Specification and Implementation of Data-Defined Problems. Proc. Data Mining. London (1996)

11. Shavlik, J., Mooney, R., Towell, G.: Symbolic and Neural Net Learning Algorithms: An Empirical Comparison. Machine Learning. 6 (1991) 111-143

12. Lu, H., Setiono, R., Liu, H.: Effective Data Mining using Neural Networks. IEEE Trans. Knowledge and Data Engineering. 8(6) (1996) 319-327

13. Lu, H., Setiono, R., Liu, H.: Neurorule: A Connectionist Approach to Data Mining. Proc. VLDB. (1995) 478-489

14. Towell, G. & Shavlik, J.: Extracting Refined Rules from Knowledge-Based Neural Networks. Machine Learning. 13(1) (1993) 71-101

15. Andrews, R., Diederich, J., Tickle, A.B.: A Survey and Critique of Techniques for Extracting Rules from Trained Artificial Neural Networks. Knowledge-Based Systems. 8(6) (1995)

16. Kaski, S., Kohonen, T.: Exploratory Data Analysis by the Self-Organising Map: Structures of Welfare and Poverty in the World. Proc. Third Int. Conf. Neural Networks in the Capital Markets. London (1995)

17. Haykin, S. Neural Networks. Macmillan, New York (1994)

18. Rumelhart, D., McClelland, J.: Parallel Distributed Processing: Explorations in the Macrostructure of Cognition. MIT Press, NewYork (1986)

Using Decision Tree Induction for Discovering Holes in Data

Bing Liu, Ke Wang, Lai-Fun Mun and Xin-Zhi Qi

School of Computing
National University of Singapore
Lower Kent Ridge Road, Singapore 119260

{liub, wangk}@comp.nus.edu.sg
http://www.comp.nus.edu.sg/{~liub, ~wangk}

Abstract. Existing research in machine learning and data mining has been focused on finding rules or regularities among the data cases. Recently, it was shown that those associations that are missing in data may also be interesting. These missing associations are the holes or empty regions. The existing algorithm for discovering holes has a number of shortcomings. It requires each hole to contain no data point, which is too restrictive for many real-life applications. It also has a very high complexity, and produces a huge number of holes. Additionally, the algorithm only works in a continuous space, and does not allow any discrete/nominal attribute. These drawbacks limit its applications. In this paper, we propose a novel approach to overcome these shortcomings. This approach transforms the holes-discovery problem into a supervised learning task, and then uses the decision tree induction technique for discovering holes in data.

1. Introduction

A company wants to profile its customers who use its two services, S_1 and S_2. It used a rule induction system for the purpose. One of the generated rules is:
If mthly_salary > 3000 **Then** S_1.
The rule says that if a person's monthly salary is more than \$3,000, he/she uses service S_1. The information contained in this rule is, however, rather incomplete and misleading. A close inspection of the database shows that very few professionals whose monthly salary is more than \$3,000 use the service, and there is no customer with a monthly income of over \$6,000 using S_1. These are "holes" in the data. Realizing these holes, the company can probe into the possibilities of improving its service or of doing more promotion in order to attract these potential customers. Clearly, only giving the above rule to the user does not provide him/her the complete knowledge.

A similar situation is that a company wants to launch a marketing campaign to enlarge its customer base. In order to be effective, it needs to have a good profile of those people who are not currently their customers. However, the company only has a database about its existing customers, but none on those non-customers (this is often the case in businesses). Then, the company cannot use an induction tool to profile non-customers because there is no data on them. This paper tries to solve this problem. It is essentially the problem of looking for holes in the database.

In general, each case in the database can be seen as a point in a multi-dimensional space. A hole is a region in the space that contains no or few data points. In a continuous space, there always exist a large number of holes. The existence of large holes is mainly due to the following two reasons: (1) insufficient data in certain areas; (2) certain attribute-value combinations are not possible or seldom occur. Clearly, not all holes are interesting. For example, holes that represent common knowledge in a domain are not interesting. However, those holes that we do not know before can be very important. For example, in a disease database we may unexpectedly find that certain symptoms and/or test values do not occur together, or when a certain medicine is used, some test values never go beyond certain range. Discovery of such information can be of great importance in medical domains because it could mean the discovery of a cure to a disease or some biological laws.

[7] first studied the problem of discovering holes. It proposed an algorithm for finding holes in a continuous space. The algorithm has a number of shortcomings:
1. A hole must be absolutely empty, i.e., containing no data point in it. This is too restrictive for most real-life applications because there are usually outliers.
2. The complexity of the algorithm is very high, which is $O(n^{2k-1}k^3(\log n)^2)$, where n is the number of data points and k is the number of dimensions. The number of holes produced is also very large.
3. It only works in a continuous space. It does not handle discrete attributes.

This paper proposes a novel approach to overcome these problems. The approach first transforms the holes-discovery problem into a supervised learning task, and then uses the decision tree technique to carve the space into filled and empty regions. The existing algorithm in [7] is also generalized so that it can take filled hyper-rectangles as input in addition to data points. It is used as a post-processing method in the proposed approach to produce maximal holes (which cannot be expanded further) based on the filled regions generated by the decision tree engine.

2. Problem Statement

Let D be a database of N cases, and let $A_1, ..., A_i, ..., A_m$ be the attributes. Some attributes take continuous values, and other attributes take discrete values. For a continuous attribute A_i, we use min_i and max_i to denote the bounding (minimum and maximum) values. For a discrete attribute A_i, we use a_i to denote its domain. min_i, max_i and a_i are provided by the user. The syntax of a hole has the following form:

$$<p_1, ..., p_i, ..., p_q>$$

where $1 \leq q \leq m$, and p_i is either
1. $(A_{i_j} = v_{i_j})$ with $v_{i_j} \in a_{i_j}$ if A_{i_j} is a discrete attribute, or
2. $(A_{i_j}, l_{i_j}, u_{i_j})$ with $min_{i_j} \leq l_{i_j} \leq u_{i_j} \leq max_{i_j}$ if A_{i_j} is a continuous attribute.

$A_{i_j} \in \{A_1, ..., A_i, ..., A_m\}$, and an attribute can only appear once in the expression.

Below we give the semantic definitions of a *hole* in three types of space.

Discrete attributes only: In this case, we call $<p_1, ..., p_i, ..., p_q>$, where p_i is only $(A_{i_j} = v_{i_j})$, a combination of attribute-value pairs. A *hole* is a combination of attribute-value pairs that has a *support* in D less than the user-specified *threshold*. A combination has a support s in D if $s\%$ of the data cases in D contain the combination. In this work we are interested in those holes that are maximal. A hole is *maximal* if any removal of attribute-value pair(s) will not result in a hole.

In the discrete case, the problem of discovering all the maximal holes can be solved by adapting an association rule discovery algorithm, e.g., the Apriori algorithm [1]. This algorithm generates all the itemsets (a set of items or attribute-value pairs) that satisfy the user-specified support threshold. In the process, it drops off those itemsets that do not meet the support requirement. The dropped-off itemsets are actually the maximal holes. Although useful in the discrete case, this method cannot be applied to continuous or mixed attribute cases.

Continuous attributes only: In this case, we define a *hole* as follows:

1. We first partition the whole continuous space into small hyper-rectangles, called *cells*. A cell is considered *filled* if its density is above a density *threshold*, otherwise it is considered *empty*.
2. A *hole* (or an *empty region*) is a sub-space in the space that consists of only connected empty cells, i.e., everywhere empty. Likewise, a *filled region* is a sub-space that consists of only connected filled cells.

The size of the cell and the choice of density threshold value depend on applications.

In this paper, we restrict the shape of a hole to hyper-rectangles. A hole is *maximal* if it is bounded on each side by some *filled* regions or a boundary of the original space.

In the continuous case, too small holes are not useful. We define a *sufficiently large* hole to be a hole that is larger than the user-specified *minimum size*. A simple way of measuring the size of a hole is by its length along each dimension.

A mixture of continuous and discrete attributes: Without loss of generality, we assume that the first k attributes are discrete attributes, $A_1, ..., A_k$, and the rest are continuous attributes, $A_{k+1}, ..., A_m$. A *cell* description is as follows:

$$(discr\text{-}cell, cont\text{-}cell)$$

where *discr-cell* is a cell in the discrete sub-space, which is $((A_1 = v_1), ..., (A_i = v_i), ..., (A_k = v_k))$ with $v_i \in a_i$, and *cont-cell* is a cell in the continuous sub-space for $A_{k+1}, .., A_m$. The meanings of *empty* and *filled* cells follow those in the continuous space respectively. A *hole* is represented with

$$(discr\text{-}region, cont\text{-}region)$$

which is a region consisting of a set of empty cells, where *discr-region* is a combination of attribute-value pairs, i.e.,

$$((A_{i_1} = v_{i_1}), ..., (A_{i_j} = v_{i_j}), ..., (A_{i_f} = v_{i_f})),$$

where $1 \le f \le k$, $A_{i_j} \in \{A_1, ..., A_i, ..., A_k\}$, and $v_{i_j} \in a_{i_j}$. When *discr-region* is fixed, *cont-region* is a set of connected empty cells in the continuous sub-space.

The definitions of a *maximal* hole and a *sufficiently large* hole are more complex in this case. We will not discuss them here. This paper focuses on the generation of *filled* and *empty* regions in a continuous space and a mixed space, and how to produce all the maximal holes in a continuous space.

3. The Proposed Approach

3.1 Overview of the Approach

Following our definition of a hole in a continuous space, our generalized hole discovery algorithm to be presented in Section 4 can already produce the complete set of sufficiently large maximal holes based on the filled cells. However, this solution may not be desirable for the same reasons as the existing algorithm in [7], i.e.,

1. It does not allow any filled cell to appear in a hole. This is too restrictive.
2. The running speed will be slow because of the high complexity of the algorithm and the large number of input cells. It also produces a huge number of holes.
3. It does not handle discrete attributes.

To address these issues, we transform the problem into a supervised learning task and use a decision tree engine to carve up the space into *filled* and *empty* regions. After obtaining the filled and empty regions (which are already holes, but may not be maximal) from the decision tree, we then use our generalized holes-discovery algorithm to produce all the maximal holes based on the filled regions.

This approach addresses the above problems as follows. Problem 1 is addressed because a decision tree engine allows errors, i.e., an empty region can contain some outliers (i.e., filled cells) and vice versa. Problem 2 is addressed because we go through two stages in producing maximal holes. First, the decision tree engine produces the filled and empty regions, which can be done very efficiently. Then, based on the filled regions we can use our generalized holes-discovery algorithm to produce all the maximal holes. Since the number of filled regions can be much smaller than the number of original filled cells, the algorithm will run much faster, and also produce fewer holes. The third problem is also addressed because a decision tree engine can work in a mixed space (with both continuous and discrete attributes).

3.2 The Details

Our approach consists of the following three steps:

Partition the space into cells: We first partition each continuous attribute into a number of equal-length intervals (or units). The lengths along different dimensions may be different. The discrete attributes do not need to be partitioned. After partitioning, we can regard the space as consisting of hyper-rectangular cells. Those cells that have a density greater than the user-specified *threshold* (which is normally 0) are considered *filled*, otherwise, they are considered *empty*.

To partition the space, we need to know the cell size (for continuous attributes). This is computed using the user-specified minimum size of a *sufficiently large* hole. For continuous attributes, the user needs to provide the minimum length of the hole for each attribute. This is reasonable because in real applications, too small a hole is not meaningful. Assume our space has k continuous dimensions, and $l_1, ..., l_i, ...l_k$ are the user-specified minimum length of the hole along the dimensions. Then, the cell size along each dimension i will be $l_i/2$. The reason for choosing $l_i/2$ to partition the space is that when the cell is too small, we will find too many small holes, and this wastes computation. If the cell is too large, a filled region may contain sufficiently large holes. See Figure 1 below (the dashed box represents a sufficiently large hole, and the solid lines form the cells). In Figure 1(a), we see that each side of the cell is less than $l_i/2$. The area surrounded by the 4 points has some empty cells in it, which may form some leaf nodes (labeled *empty*) in the decision tree. But none of them is large enough. The cells in Figure 1(b) are too large. Although the 4 cells are all filled, there is an empty region among them that is sufficiently large. Figure 1(c) is the suitable size (= $l_i/2$) (i.e., the minimum sufficiently large hole in the figure is the size of the 4 cells combined). The 4 filled cells cannot contain a sufficiently large hole in it.

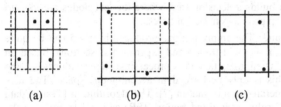

(a) (b) (c)

Figure 1. Selecting the cell size

Classifying the empty and filled regions: We use the decision tree engine in C4.5

[11] to carve the space into filled and empty regions. To apply C4.5 directly to the problem is not possible because those empty cells are not represented in the database. One solution is to add the points representing the empty cells into the original database. However, this may drastically increase the size of the database. We have modified C4.5 so that it can compute the required information regarding the empty cells when needed (see below). After the decision tree is constructed, the tree leaves labeled *empty* represent the empty regions, and the rest the filled regions.

The main modification to C4.5 is as follows. C4.5 uses information gain ratio in its computation to decide where to split the space. For this computation it only needs the frequency or the number of data points (in our case, cells) of each individual class on each side of a possible split. Since we do not have the points representing the empty cells, we have to compute it. This computation is quite simple. For a split in a subspace, the total number of cells on each side of the split is just the product of the number of units in each dimension. A unit along each continuous dimension i is $l/2$, and a unit along each discrete dimension is an individual value. Since we know the number of filled cells, we can easily compute the number of empty ones. Let us see an example. Figure 2 shows a continuous space.

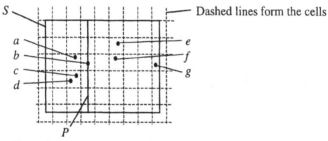

Figure 2. Computing the number of filled or empty cells

Assume the system is computing the information gain ratio at a possible split P. Note that splits are at data points as in C4.5 rather than along the borders of the cells. Let us compute the number of filled and empty cells. Assume a cell with one or more point is considered *filled*. On the left-hand-side of P, there are 16.5 cells altogether (partial cells are counted proportionally). 2.5 of them are filled cells. Note that point c and d are in the same cell and thus counted as representing one filled cell. Point b is in a partial cell on the left-hand-side. Assume it is half the size of a cell. Then the number of empty cells on the left-hand-side is 16.5 - 2.5 = 14. Likewise, the total number of cells on the right-hand-side of P is 27.5, and the number of filled cells is 2.5. Then the number of empty cells is 27.5 - 2.5 = 25.

With these numbers, C4.5 will be able to compute the information gain ratio to decide the best split. Finally, it builds a decision tree, where the leaf nodes are labeled either *filled* or *empty*. Next step produces maximal holes.

Produce all the maximal holes: The empty regions produced by C4.5 can be quite fragmented (see the example in the "illustration and experiments" section). Based on the filled regions in the decision tree, this post-processing step produces all the maximal holes. Currently, this is only performed in a continuous space. The new algorithm (Section 4) is a generalization of that in [7]. The algorithm in [7] uses data points as input. The new algorithm uses *filled regions* (FR) as input to produce the maximal holes. The algorithm in [7] is only a special case as a point is a special FR.

4. Producing All the Maximal Holes

After the space has been carved up, we use the *filled* regions (FR) to produce all the maximal holes. Since we only want those holes that are *maximal* and *sufficiently large*, our objective is to find all the holes in the k-dimensional space that satisfy the user-specified sufficiently large criterion and to rank them according to their sizes. Note that all the regions generated in the decision tree are hyper-rectangles [11].

Definition 1: Given a k-dimensional continuous space S bounded in each dimension i ($1 \leq i \leq k$) by a minimum and a maximum value (denoted by min_i and max_i), a hyper-rectangle (or HR in short), H, in S is defined as the region that is bounded on each dimension i by a minimum and a maximum value, denoted by $L_i(H)$ and $U_i(H)$ respectively, where $L_i(H) \geq min_i$ and $U_i(H) \leq max_i$. A HR has $2k$ bounding surfaces, 2 on each dimension. The two bounding surfaces on dimension i are parallel to axis i and orthogonal to all others.

In this paper, we are interested in the so-called *maximal hyper-rectangles* (*MHR*), which are our maximal holes.

Definition 2: Given a k-dimensional continuous space S and n FRs in S, a *maximal hyper-rectangle* (MHR) in S is an empty HR that does not intersect (in a normal sense) with any FR, and has at least one FR lying on each of its $2k$ bounding surfaces. We call these FRs the *bounding* FRs of the MHR.

Definition 3: A HR, H_1, *lies* on the lower (or upper) bounding surface in the ith dimension of another HR, H_2, if H_1 touches that bounding surface of H_2 in the ith dimension, and H_1 does not intersect with H_2.

4.1 Basic Idea of the Algorithm

The basic idea of the algorithm is as follows. Given a k-dimensional continuous space S, and n FRs (which may intersect with one another) in S, we first start with one MHR, which occupies the entire space S. Then each FR is incrementally added to S. At each insertion, we update the set of MHRs that have been found this far. The update is done as follows. When a new FR is added, we identify all the existing MHRs that intersect with this FR. These hyper-rectangles are no longer MHRs since they now contain part of the FR within their interiors. They are then removed from the set of existing MHRs. Using the newly added FR as reference, a new lower and upper bound for each dimension are formed to result in 2 new hyper-rectangles along that dimension. If these new hyper-rectangles are found to be MHRs and sufficiently large, they are inserted into the list of existing MHRs, otherwise they are discarded. The main difference between this algorithm and that in [7] is that we tests for intersection of hyper-rectangles, while the algorithm in [7] tests for containment of a point in a hyper-rectangle.

4.2 The Detailed Algorithm

Before presenting the algorithm, let us define the main representations and functions used. A *filled HR* (FR), H, is denoted by:

$$H = ((L_1(H), U_1(H)), ..., (L_i(H), U_i(H)), ..., (L_k(H), U_k(H)))$$

where $L_i(H)$ and $U_i(H)$ are respectively the lower and upper *bounding values* of H along the ith dimension. A MHR, M, is denoted by:

$$M = ((Sl_1, Su_1), ..., (Sl_i, Su_i), ..., (Sl_k, Su_k))$$

where Sl_i and Su_i are respectively the sets of lower and upper bounding FRs of M along the ith dimension.

```
1  Algorithm FindMHR
2    Insert(T, (({bl_1},{bu_1}), ..., ({bl_i},{bu_i}), ..., ({bl_k},{bu_k})));
3    for each FR H in the decision tree do
4      RL = IntersectionSearch(T, H);
5      for each M = ((Sl_1,Su_1), ..., (Sl_i,Su_i), ..., (Sl_k,Su_k)) in RL do
6        if H is on a surface of M then   insert H into the set of bounding FRs in that surface
7        else  Delete(T, M);
8             for each dimension i do
9               if L_i(H) > U_i(l) for l ∈ Sl_i then
10                for each j ≠ i do
11                   Sl'_j = {l ∈ Sl_j | L_i(l) < L_i(H)};
12                   Su'_j = {u ∈ Su_j | L_i(u) < L_i(H)};
13                endfor;
14                if Sl'_j and Su'_j not empty for all j ≠ i and
                     BigEnough(M' = ((Sl'_1, Su'_1), ..., (Sl_i, {H}), ..., (Sl'_k, Su'_k)) then
15                   Insert(T, M')
16                endif;
17              endif;
18              if U_i(H) < L_i(u) for u ∈ Su_i then
19                for each j ≠ i do
20                   Sl''_j = {l ∈ Sl_j | U_i(l) > U_i(H)};
21                   Su''_j = {u ∈ Su_j | U_i(u) > U_i(H)}
22                endfor;
23                if Sl''_j and Su''_j not empty for all j ≠ i and
                     BigEnough(M'' = ((Sl''_1, Su''_1), ..., ({H},Su_i), ..., (Sl''_k, Su''_k)) then
24                   Insert(T, M'')
25                endif
26              endif
27            endfor
28       endif
29     endfor
30   endfor
31   Sort and report all the MHRs in T according to their sizes;
```

Figure 3. The Holes Discovery Algorithm

Note that the lower (or the upper) bound of a MHR is bounded by a set of lower (or upper) bounding FRs, rather than a single bounding value as used in a FR. The upper bounds of all the FRs in Sl_i along the ith dimension are the same, and the lower bounds of all the FRs in Su_i along the ith dimension are also the same. That is,

$U_i(H_a) = U_i(H_b)$ for all $H_a, H_b \in Sl_i$, and

$L_i(H_a) = L_i(H_b)$ for all $H_a, H_b \in Su_i$.

For simplicity of notation, we let bl_i and bu_i to be the lower and upper bounding FRs (in each dimension i) of the initial space, S, where $L_i(bl_i) = U_i(bl_i) = min_i$ and $L_i(bu_i) = U_i(bu_i) = max_i$, and $L_j(bl_i) = U_j(bl_i) =$ undefined for $i \neq j$. Any comparison with $L_j(bl_i)$ or $U_j(bl_i)$ (where $i \neq j$) is always true. Hence, bl_i and bu_i serve as the lower and upper *bounding planes* along the ith dimension respectively.

Next, we define the functions used in the algorithm. Let T be a data structure that stores a collection of sufficiently large MHRs. T supports the following functions:

(1) *Insert(T, M)*: it inserts the MHR M into T.

(2) *Delete(T, M)*: it deletes the MHR M from T.

(3) *IntersectionSearch(T, H)*: it returns a list of MHRs *(RL)* from T, where each $M \in$ *RL* either intersects with the FR H or H lies on a surface of M.

Lastly, we define a function *BigEnough(M)* which returns TRUE if the MHR M is considered to be sufficiently large. Note that if *BigEnough(M')* is true, then *BigEnough(M)* must be true for all M that contain M'. The algorithm is shown in Figure 3.

The worse case time complexity of the algorithm is the same as the algorithm in [7]. However, the new algorithm is more practical because it takes FRs rather than data points as input. The number of FRs produced in a decision tree is normally small. The correctness of the algorithm can be similarly proved as the algorithm in [7]. See [9] for the detailed proof and complexity analysis.

4.3   An Example

We now use an example to illustrate the working of the algorithm. Suppose we have a 2-dimensional space S (ABCD) as shown in Figure 4. The first MHR is the whole space, ABCD, which is described with:

$$M = ((\{bl_1\}, \{bu_1\}), (\{bl_2\}, \{bu_2\})))$$

Line 3.   We add the first FR H_1 to the inside of ABCD (see Figure 5).

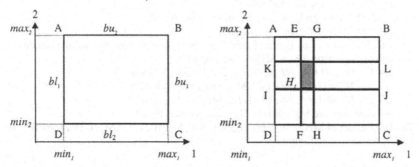

Figure 4: The initial space S or the initial MHR   Figure 5. Splitting ABCD

Line 4. Since in this case there is only one MHR (the original space ABCD) intersecting H_1 in T, thus

$$RL = \{((\{bl_1\}, \{bu_1\}), (\{bl_2\}, \{bu_2\})))\}.$$

Line 5. The first MHR to be considered is

$M = ((\{bl_1\}, \{bu_1\}), (\{bl_2\}, \{bu_2\}))$, i.e., ABCD.

Line 6. Since H_1 (Figure 5) is not on a surface of M, we proceed to Line 7.

Line 7. M is deleted since it is no longer a MHR.

Line 8. We split M along each dimension. D-1 is considered first.

Line 9-17. This part forms the new MHR to the left side of H_1. Sl'_2 and Su'_2 are the sets of lower and upper bounding FRs for the new MHR. We obtain:

$Sl'_2 = \{bl_2\}$ and $Su'_2 = \{bu_2\}$.

The new MHR is thus: $M' = ((\{bl_1\}, \{H_1\}), (\{bl_2\}, \{bu_2\}))$, i.e., AEFD,

Line 18-26. This part forms the new MHR to the right side of H_1. Sl''_2 and Su''_2 are the sets of lower and upper bounding FRs for the new MHR along dimension 2. We obtain: $Sl''_2 = \{bl_2\}$ and $Su''_2 = \{bu_2\}$.

The new MHR is thus: $M'' = ((\{H_1\}, \{bu_1\}), (\{bl_2\}, \{bu_2\}))$, i.e., GBCH.

After considering D-2, we form 2 more MHRs:

$M' = (((\{bl_1\}, \{bu_1\}), (\{bl_2\}, \{H_1\}))$, i.e., IJCD.

$M'' = (((\{bl_1\}, \{bu_1\}), (\{H_1\}, \{bu_2\})))$, i.e., ABLK.

Assume the 4 new MHRs are big enough and are inserted into T. Adding the first FR is completed. Let us now add another FR, H_2 (see its location in Figure 6).

Line 4. The set of MHRs in T intersecting H_2 is:

$$RL = \{(((\{bl_1\}, \{bu_1\}), (\{bl_2\}, \{H_1\}))),$$
$$((\{H_1\}, \{bu_1\}), (\{bl_2\}, \{bu_2\})))$$

They are IJCD and GBCH respectively in Figure 5.

Line 5-7. We consider the first MHR, $M = (((\{bl_1\}, \{bu_1\}), (\{bl_2\}, \{H_1\})))$,

which is IJCD in Figure 5 and 6. Since H_2 is not on a surface of M, M is deleted.

Line 8-27. After considering all the dimensions, we obtain the following two new MHRs (see Figure 6):

D-1: $M' = (((\{bl_1\}, \{H_2\}), (\{bl_2\}, \{H_1\})))$, i.e., IMND.

D-2: $M' = (((\{bl_1\}, \{bu_1\}), (\{bl_2\}, \{H_2\})))$, i.e., OPCD.

There is no M'' in D-1 because $Su'_2 = \{\}$. M'' should be (if it exists) VJCS in Figure 6, but VJCS is not a MHR because there is no bounding FR on VJ. Its space will be occupied later by another MHR. There is also no M'' in D-2 because the condition in line 18 is not satisfied. Assume the above two MHRs are big enough. They are inserted into T.

Line 5-29. We now go back to work on the other MHR,

$$M = \{(((\{H_1\}, \{bu_1\}), (\{bl_2\}, \{bu_2\})))$$,

which is GBCH in Figure 5 and 6. After going though the similar process as above, we obtain 3 new MHRs (see Figure 6),

D-1: $M' = ((\{H_1\}, \{H_2\}), (\{bl_2\}, \{bu_2\}))$, i.e., GQNH.

$M'' = (((\{H_2\}, \{bu_1\}), (\{bl_2\}, \{bu_2\})))$, i.e., RBCS.

D-2: $M'' = (((\{H_1\}, \{bu_1\}), (\{H_2\}, \{bu_2\})))$, i.e., GBUT.

Assume they are big enough. They are inserted into T.

The final of set of MHRs in T are GQNH, RBCS, GBUT, IMND, OPCD, AEFD, and ABLK respectively (Figure 6).

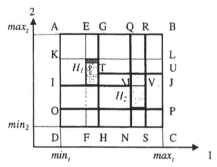

Figure 6. Forming MHRs after H_2 is inserted

5. Illustration and Experiments

A system has been implemented in C, which consists of two parts. The first part, which builds the decision tree, is modified from C4.5 [11]. The second part implements our generalized MHR discovering algorithm. So far we have carried out many experiments. Since there is no existing system to compare with, this section first gives an example to show the working of the system, and then presents some experiment results of the generalized MHR discovering algorithm. It is not appropriate to compare the holes discovered by our system with the holes produced by the algorithm in [7] because the algorithm in [7] does not allow any point in its MHRs.

Our example uses the Iris data from UCI machine learning repository [8], which has 150 cases and 4 continuous attributes. Only two attributes are used here. The class information in the data is not needed. Figure 7 shows the splits produced by our modified C4.5, which form many filled and empty rectangles. The minimal size of the hole we use is 0.6×0.6. The shaded rectangles are the filled regions, and the rest are the empty regions (which also contain some data points). From the figure, we see that the empty regions are fragmented. Figure 8 shows the final results after running our generalized MHR discovering algorithm. There are 7 MHRs discovered (numbered in the two opposite corners of each MHR). Clearly, these MHRs are better than the empty regions in Figure 7. The algorithm in [7] actually finds 22 MHRs, which are different from ours as they contain no data points.

Next, we show the performances of our generalized MHR discovery algorithm. All the data sets are randomly generated. We present the results from our experiments in 2-D, 3-D, 4-D, 5-D and 6-D spaces. Holes with more than 4-D are quite hard to understand. For each number of dimensions, we generated 6 data sets with, 50, 100, ..., and 500 FRs respectively. We did not use more FRs in our experiments because a decision tree does not normally produce a large number of FRs. In data generation, as the number of FRs increases, we also increase the size of the space proportionally. We used two minimum hole sizes in our *BigEnough* function. The first one (min. size 1) is 40.00 in each dimension, and the second (min. size 2) is 50.00 in each dimension. Table 1 shows the number of MHRs found in each experiment. Table 2 summarizes the running times (512MB Sparc Ultra-2).

From the tables, we see that when the minimum size of the MHR decreases, the time taken to find all the sufficiently large MHRs increases. As the number of FRs increases, the time taken to find all the large MHRs also increases. However, in general, the relationship between the number of FRs and the time taken to find all the large MHRs is complex because there are other factors that also need to be considered, e.g., the distribution of the FRs, and the size of the initial space.

In all experiments, the running times are reasonable. Although there can be many MHRs produced, the user does not have to see all of them at one time. A query system can be implemented to allow the user to specify what he/she is interested in seeing. It is also possible that the user simply takes those large empty regions produced in the decision tree as the final holes without generating all the maximal ones.

6. Related Work

Current research in machine learning and data mining focuses on finding rules that exist in data. Our work is different from rule induction (e.g., [11]) and conceptual clustering (e.g., [5]) because they are only concern with what is in the data, while we are concerned with both what is in the data and what is missing from the data.

Scientific discovery systems such as Abacus [3], and Bacon [6] typically discover mathematical formulas in data. With the formulas, we know exactly where the data points are and where there should be no point. However, in most business databases such formulas rarely exist.

[7] first studied the problem of discovering holes in data. An algorithm was pro-

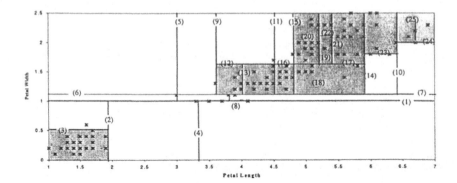

Figure 7: Splits produced by the decision tree

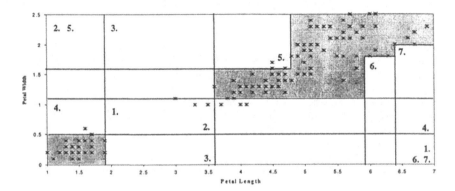

Figure 8: Resulting MHRs

No. of	Min.	Dimensions				
FRs	Size	2-D	3-D	4-D	5-D	6-D
	1	10	76	295	817	3783
50	2	4	20	81	294	1016
	1	17	106	484	2372	11733
100	2	6	29	179	569	1448
	1	36	249	1597	5187	28036
200	2	6	73	464	1626	5589
	1	75	450	1827	8268	34139
300	2	22	179	589	2311	7027
	1	94	545	3038	13546	55033
400	2	28	137	1002	4276	10144
	1	89	755	3471	16577	68530
500	2	27	239	1179	5041	15347

Table 1. Number of MHRs found

No. of	Min.	Dimensions				
FRs	Size	2-D	3-D	4-D	5-D	6-D
	1	0.00	0.04	0.12	0.26	1.24
50	2	0.00	0.02	0.05	0.12	0.37
	1	0.01	0.06	0.17	1.02	4.87
100	2	0.01	0.03	0.08	0.27	0.74
	1	0.02	0.12	0.64	2.37	14.25
200	2	0.01	0.07	0.23	0.71	3.18
	1	0.04	0.22	0.93	4.90	22.13
300	2	0.02	0.11	0.39	1.33	5.49
	1	0.06	0.31	1.74	9.00	42.39
400	2	0.03	0.12	0.69	2.65	8.12
	1	0.07	0.46	2.05	12.74	58.16
500	2	0.04	0.20	0.81	3.74	13.64

Table 2: Run time results (in sec.)

posed to discover holes by taking data points as input. Our generalized algorithm can take either FRs or data points (as input). We have discussed the shortcomings of that algorithm throughout the paper. This research helps to overcome its major problems.

In geometric algorithms research, there are algorithms [2, 10] that can find empty rectangles in the 2-D space, these algorithms cannot be extended to the multi-dimensional space. They also do not allow any point in each empty rectangle.

Our work is also related to density estimation in statistics research [12]. Density estimation is the construction of an estimate of a density function from the given data. It does not provide descriptions of empty regions (for which further processing is needed), and it also does not handle discrete attributes. The proposed technique deals with both. Our technique for finding holes is also quite different from the density estimation method as we use information theory and a geometric algorithm.

7. Conclusion

Although discovering the associative relations that exist in data is important, in many situations, discovering of large holes in the database is also significant and interesting. This paper presented a new approach for discovering holes. It first transforms the problem into a supervised learning task and uses a decision tree induction engine to divide the space into filled and empty regions. It then produces maximal holes using the filled regions generated in the decision tree. This new approach overcomes three major shortcomings of the existing method in [7].

References

1. Agrawal, R., and Srikant R. 1994. Fast algorithms for mining association rules. *VLDB-94*, 1994.
2. Chazelle, B., Drysdale, R. L., and Lee, D. T. 1986. Computing the largest empty rectangle. *SIAM Journal of Computing*, 15(1) 300-315.
3. Falkenhainer, F., and Michalski, R. 1986. Integrating quantitative and qualitative discovery: the ABACUS system. *Machine Learning*, 1(4):367-401.
4. Fayyad, U., Piatesky-Shapiro, G., and Smyth, P. 1996. From data mining to knowledge discovery in databases. *AI Magazine* 37-54.
5. Fisher, D. 1987. Knowledge acquisition via incremental conceptual clustering. *Machine Learning*, 2:139-172.
6. Langley, P., Simon, H., Bradshaw, G., and Zytkow, Jan. 1987. *Scientific discovery: computational explorations of the creative process*, The MIT press.
7. Liu, B., Ku, L. P., and Hsu, W. 1997. Discovering Interesting Holes in Data. *IJCAI-97*, 930-935.
8. Merz, C. J, and Murphy, P. 1996. UCI repository of machine learning database [http://www.cs.uci.edu/~mlearn/MLRepository.html].
9. Mun, L. F. 1998. *Discovering missing and understandable patterns in databases*. MSc thesis, National University of Singapore.
10. Orlowski, M. 1990. A new algorithm for the largest empty rectangle problem. *Algorithmica*, 5:65-73.
11. Quinlan, J. R. 1992. *C4.5: program for machine learning*. Morgan Kaufmann.
12. Silverman, B. W. 1986. Density Estimation for Statistics and Data Analysis. Chapman and Hall.

DODDLE : A Domain Ontology Rapid Development Environment

Rieko Sekiuchi, Chizuru Aoki, Masaki Kurematsu
and Takahira Yamaguchi
School of Information, Shizuoka University,
3-5-1 Jouhoku Hamamatsu, 432-8011 JAPAN
Phone: +81-53-478-1473
FAX: +81-53-473-6421
E-mail Address :{s3026, yamaguti}@cs.inf.shizuoka.ac.jp

Abstract. This paper focuses on how to construct domain ontologies, in particular, a hierarchically structured set of domain concepts without concept definitions, reusing a machine readable dictionary (MRD) and making it adjusted to specific domains. In doing so, we must deal with concept drift, which means that the senses of concepts change depending on application domains. So here are presented the following two strategies : match result analysis and trimmed result analysis. The strategies try to identify which part may stay or should be moved, analyzing spell match results between given input domain terms and a MRD. We have done case studies in the filed of some law. The empirical results show us that our system can support a user in constructing a domain ontology.

1 Introduction

The work in the field of knowledge engineering moves from interview systems such as MORE[13] to modeling domains and tasks (problem solving methods) at knowledge levels. Subsequently, ontologies engineering has been emerging as a new field in the nineties. In the new field, much attention has first been paid to representation issues for ontologies, such as KIF[9] and Ontolingua[6]. Recently the attention seems to shift from representation to contents or the methodology of constructing ontologies. According to [8], there are several distinguished ontologies, such as generic ontologies for conceptualizations across many domains, domain ontologies to put constraints on the structure and contents of domain knowledge in a particular-field and task ontologies for describing problem-solving methods. Several natural language ontologies (including generic ontologies) have already been developed as MRDs (machine-readable dictionaries), such as CYC[10], WordNet[12] and EDR[5]. Task ontologies have also been developed from abstract models of methods, such as Generic Tasks[4], PROTEGE-II[15] and CommonKADS[3]. Because domain ontologies have large number of specified concepts, they make less progress than generic ontologies and task ontologies that have just a few specified concepts. Thus this paper focuses on how to construct domain ontologies, in particular, a hierarchically structured set of domain concepts without concept definitions, reusing existing MRDs and making them adjusted to specific domains. Actually, from the same motivation, we have already presented a domain ontology refinement support environment called LODE[1] . A user gives an initial domain ontology with a hierarchically structured set of domain concepts and the relationships between them to LODE. LODE does match between the initial domain ontology and EDR. The match results have been analyzed from several syntactical features in order to refine the initial domain ontology into better one. Applying LODE to the field of particular law, we find that LODE can support a legal expert in refining an initial legal ontology into better one. However, it took costs to prepare an initial legal ontology and legal experts did not like it. We must reduce the costs to set up the input to LODE. To do so, the technical issue of "concept drift" comes up to us. Because the senses of concepts in a MRD come from a common domain and so not good for some specific domain, we must deal with the change of concept's senses caused by the change of domains, called concept drift. Our domain ontology rapid development environment (called DODDLE) tries to manage concept drift, analyzing match results by several strategies for concept drift. In order to evaluate DODDLE, case studies have been done in the particular law called Contracts for the International Sale of Goods (CISG). The empirical results have shown us that DODDLE can support a user in constructing a domain ontology.

2 Ontology Capture

Various approaches of ontology design have been proposed by many researchers. According to [7],ontology capture consists of identifying and defining the important concepts and terms. They propose the following approach to capture ontologies; 1) Have a brainstorming session to produce all potentially relevant terms and phrases. 2) Structure the terms loosely into categories corresponding to naturally arising sub-groups. 3) Commit to the basic terms that will be used to specify the ontology. 4) Address each category in tern and define each term in the category. 5) Commit to the ontology.

In using DODDLE, domain terms are supposed to be already identified and given to DODDLE. Since DODDLE just generates a hierarchically structured set of domain terms, it support a user in structuring terms into categories and giving names to the categories in the second phase in the above-mentioned ontology design. Furthermore, DODDLE may contribute to identifying basic terms and defining each term in the third and fourth phases, through the process of adjusting concept hierarchies from DODDLE to specific domains.

3 Ontological Bugs and Concept Drift

Suppose that we could extract information relevant to given input domain terms from a MRD. We call it an initial model in this paper. The initial model is not sufficient for a domain ontology. It might have bugs such that some important domain-specific concepts are missing and/or the concept hierarchy has flawed part from the point of domain specificity. Which type of bug could emerge in the initial model ? The following typical bugs could appear: missing concepts, existing unnecessary concepts, flawed hierarchical relationships such as confusion of super-sub relationship and parent-child relationship, missing concept definitions and existing unnecessary concept definitions.

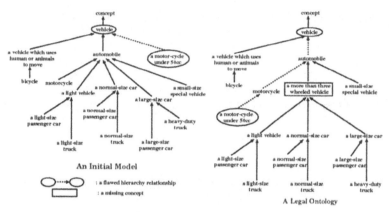

Fig. 1. Ontological Bugs

Figure 1 shows an example of an initial model and a legal ontology (a hierarchically structured set of legal concepts without the relationships between them). There are two types of bugs in Figure 1. "A more than three wheeled vehicle" marked with a rectangle in the legal ontology is an example of missing concepts. The other bug is an example of a flawed hierarchical relationship, the parent-child relationship of "vehicle" and "a motor-cycle under 50cc" in an initial model. It should be corrected into the ancestor-child relationship, illustrated by a dotted line in the legal ontology. Judging from the field of Traffic Law, it is better to correct these bugs as described above.

When we change an initial model into a domain ontology, the part infected with domain specificity is regarded as ontological bugs in the initial model. Because DODDLE just constructs a hierarchically structured set of domain concepts without concept definitions, flawed hierarchical structures and existing unnecessary concepts seem to come up frequently as the part drifted by domain specificity. DODDLE takes the strategies based on match result analysis and trim result analysis to do so, as described in section 4.3.

4 DODDLE Design

After giving an overview of DODDLE, we present detailed descriptions about WordNet taken as a MRD and strategies for concept drift.

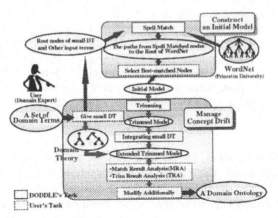

Fig. 2. DODDLE Overview

4.1 An Overview of DODDLE

Figure 2 shows an overview of DODDLE. In order to analyze concept drift between a MRD and a domain ontology (a hierarchically structured set of domain concepts), here are two basic activities: constructing an initial model from a MRD (extracting information relevant to given domain terms from a MRD) and managing concept drift (making an initial model adjusted to the domain).

A user gives a (not structured) set of domain terms to DODDLE. The user can also give small size of trees including domain concepts, which are called small DT (Domain Theory) later. Because the input terms in small DT have already been structured, it is no necessary to do spell match between them and a MRD. However, in order to integrate small DT into a trimmed model, spell match must be done between just root nodes of small DT and a MRD. So DODDLE do spell match between other all input terms except inner and leaf nodes of small DT and a MRD. These terms are linked to a MRD by the spell match. The spell match results are a hierarchically structured set of all the nodes on the path from these terms to the root of a MRD. Because a matched node (concept) from a MRD sometimes has one or more senses, it must be selected which sense is best. DODDLE supports the user in doing the selection by showing the user the following information: detailed descriptions on each sense and where each sense is put in the concept hierarchy structure from a MRD. We call the selected nodes "best-matched nodes" and the hierarchy structure composed of paths from best-matched nodes to the root in a MRD "an initial model".

Because an initial model has been extracted from a MRD, DODDLE tries to manage the infection (concept drift), analyzing match results by several strategies for concept drift. Here are three basic processes to do so: removing unnecessary internal terms in the initial model (called 'a trimmed model' later), integrating small DT into the trimmed model and finding out which part should

Table 1. WordNet

Dictionary Name	word synsets	word senses
Noun dictionary	60557	107424
Verb dictionary	11363	25761
Adjective dictionary	16328	28749
Adverb dictionary	3243	6201
Index dictionary	91519	119217

be drifted in the trimmed model. the latter process has the following two strategies: match result analysis and trimmed result analysis. After moving the part infected with domain specificity and doing additional modifications, the user finally gets a hierarchically structured set of domain concepts as a domain ontology.

4.2 WordNet

DODDLE takes WordNet[12] as a MRD. WordNet is an on-line lexical reference system and is developed by a group of psychologists and linguists at Princeton University. WordNet contains English nouns, verbs, adjectives and adverbs. Table 1 shows WordNet specification. We use a noun dictionary and an index dictionary for DODDLE.

4.3 Managing Concept Drift

In order to remove unnecessary internal nodes in an initial model based on match result analysis, internal nodes are divided into important internal nodes called SINs (Salient Internal Nodes) and other internal nodes. If internal nodes branch subordinate best-matched nodes, they work for keeping structural relationships among best-matched nodes, such as parent-child relationship and sibling relationship. So SINs are regarded as internal nodes that branch sub-ordinate best-matched nodes and other SINs. Thus DODDLE leaves a root, best-matched nodes and SINs in an initial model. The process looks like a trimming. Thus DODDLE gets a trimmed model.

Figure 3 illustrates the trimming process. Because the structural relationships among best-matched nodes are kept even by removing white nodes, the original tree is reduced. Because the cross-hatched nodes work for branching best-matched nodes, they become SINs. Thus DODDLE gets a trimmed model that includes only best-matched nodes and SINs.

Because the nodes on lower part have much domain specificity, it may be a better way for a user to give another structure to them. It comes from DT given by a user. So then it can be integrated into trimmed models.

Figure 4 illustrates extending a trimmed model. After matching the root node of small DT with a trimmed model, matched part in the trimmed model

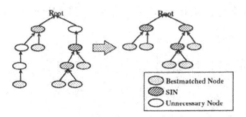

Fig. 3. Trimming Process

is replaced with the small DT. After the sub nodes the replaced part are reconfigurated by the user. DODDLE gets an extended trimmed model.

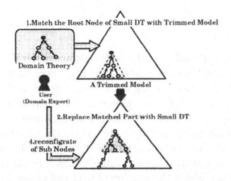

Fig. 4. Integrating Small DT into a Trimmed Model

Here are two strategies for managing concept drift.

Strategy1:Match Result Analysis for Concept Drift In order to find out which part should be drifted in the trimmed model, DODDLE takes a look at the distribution of best-matched results. Thus the following strategies come to DODDLE: A trimmed model is divided between a PAB (PAth including only Best-matched nodes) and a STM (SubTree Moved) based on the distribution of best-matched nodes. On one hand, a PAB is a path that include only best-matched nodes that have the senses good for given domain specificity. Because all nodes have already been adjusted to the domain in PABs, PABs can stay there in the trimmed model. On the other hand, STM is such a subtree that a SIN is a root and the subordinates are only best-matched nodes. Because SINs have not been confirmed to have the senses good for a given domain and so STMs can be infected with domain specificity, STMs can be moved somewhere in the trimmed model. Thus DODDLE identifies PABs and STMs in the trimmed model automatically and then supports a user in constructing a domain ontology by moving STMs. Figure 5 illustrates examples of PABs and STMs in a trimmed model.

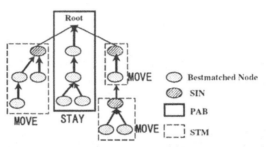

Fig. 5. PABs and STMs

Strategy2:Trimmed Result Analysis for Concept Drift In order to manage concept drift in the trimmed model, DODDLE uses trim result analysis as well as match result analysis. Taking some sibling nodes with the same parent node, there may be many difference about the number of trimmed nodes between them and the parent node. When such a big differences comes up on a subtree in the trimmed model, it may be to change the structure of the subtree. DODDLE suggests the user in changing the structure of the subtree. Based on empirical analysis, DODDLE takes reconstructed part as the subtree which has two and more difference about the number of trimmed nodes. Figure 6 illustrates examples of reconstructing a subtree in a trimmed model.

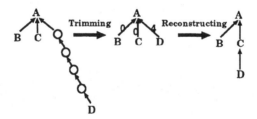

Fig. 6. Reconstructing a Subtree in a Trimmed Model

After managing concept drift with two strategies, the user do additionally modification just node by node without support from DODDLE. Finally, the user gets a hierarchically structured set of domain concepts as a domain ontology.

Based on the above-mentioned design, DODDLE has been implemented by Perl language and Tcl-tk on UNIX platforms. Table 2 shows the specification of DODDLE. Figure 7 shows a typical screen of DODDLE.

Table 2. DODDLE Specifications

Module	Language	Size(KB)
Construct an Initial Model	Perl&Tcl-Tk	62.5
Manage Concept Drift	Perl&Tcl-Tk	86.2
GUI	Tcl-Tk	46.5

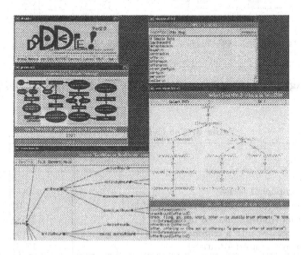

Fig. 7. DODDLE Browser

5 Case Studies in a Legal Domain

In order to evaluate how DODDLE is doing in practical fields, case studies have been done in a particular law called Contracts for the International Sale of Goods (CISG). Two lawyers joined the case studies. In the first case study, input terms are 46 legal terms from CISG Part-II. In the second case study, they are 103 terms including general terms in an example case and legal terms from CISG articles related with the case. One lawyer did the first case study and the other lawyer did the second.

Table 3 shows the case studies results. Figure 8 shows how much is included in final domain ontology the intermediate products at each DODDLE activity.

Generally speaking, in constructing legal ontlogies, 70 % or more support comes from DODDLE. About half part of the final legal ontology results in the information extracted form WordNet. Because the two strategies just imply the part where concept drift may come up, the part generated by them has just low component rates and about 30 % hit rates . So one out of three indication based on the two strategies work well in order to manage concept drift. Because the two strategies use just such syntactical feature as matched and trimmed results, the hit rates are not so bad. In order to manage concept drift smartly, we maybe

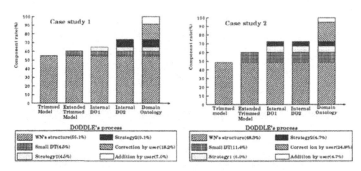

Fig. 8. The Component Rate of the Final Domain Ontology

Table 3. The Case Studies Results

The number of X	The first case study	The second case study
Input terms	46	103
Small DT(Component terms)	2(6)	6(25)
Nodes matched with WordNet(Unmatched)*	42(0)	71(4)
Salient Internal Nodes(Trimmed nodes)	13(58)	27(83)
Small DT integrated into a trimmed model(Unintegrated)	2(0)	5(1)
Modification by the user(Addition)	17(5)	44(7)
Evaluation of strategy1**	4/16(25.0%)	9/29(31.0%)
Evaluation of strategy2**	3/10(30.0%)	4/12(33.3%)

* "Nodes matched with WordNet" is the number of input terms which have be selected proper senses in WordNet and "Unmatched" is not the case.
** The number of suggestions accepted by a user/The number of suggestions generated by DODDLE

need the strategies using more semantic information that is not easy to come up in advance.

6 Related Work

Because domain ontologies have large number of specified concepts, we need existing useful information resources in designing domain ontology environments. Here are two information resources for the purpose: existing similar domain ontologies and natural language ontologies such as MRDs.

On one hand, Gertjan van Heijst et. al. try to reuse existing a similar medical domain ontologies, extending it with domain specificity and method specificity [8]. When similar domain ontologies are missing in constructing a new domain ontology, it is hard to construct it.

On the other hand, Ontosaurus [18] has points similar to DODDLE. Ontosaurus constructs a domain ontology using SENSUS [11] as a MRD semi-automatically. A user has only to input some "seed" terms that (s)he identified. However, Ontosaurus supports a user in constructing a domain ontology just by giving spell match results between seed terms and SENSUS. The idea of managing concept drift in DODDLE is missing in Ontosaurus. Furthermore, LODE [1] already came up as our first approach. However, it took costs for a user to give an initial domain ontology with a hierarchically structured set of domain concepts and concept definitions. Although it is hard to scale up the approach, the integration of LODE and DODDLE is pro-missing.

From the point of knowledge representation, the KL-ONE family, such as CLASSIC [2] and LOOM[14], is good for representing conceptual definitions and hierarchies. If DODDLE would be re-implemented by he KL-ONE family, DODDLE could get the facilities for property inheritance and subsumption of two descriptions and so on.

7 Conclusions and Future Work

This paper discusses how to construct a domain ontology using existing MRDs. T o do so, concept drift came up as an important technical issue. In order to m ake concept drift operational, two strategies have been proposed and empirical results show us that they work well. However, we have just syntactical strategies to identify concept drift. In order to manage concept drift so well , we need to operationalize semantic strategies using more information with domain specificity. Furthermore, we need to extend DODDLE into getting more facilities such as learning from case data and referring to other ontology descriptions, in order to facilitate DODDEL in large scale application domains.

Acknowledgments

We would like to express our thanks to Professor H.Yoshino, Professor S.Kagayama and the members in the study of legal expert systems development.

References

1. C.Aoki, M.Kurematsu and T.Yamaguchi(1996). LODE:A Legal Ontology Development Environment : Proc. PKAW'96, pp.190-209.
2. R.J.Brachman, A.Borgida, D.L.McGuinness, P.F.Patel-Schneider, and L.A.Resnick. The CLASSIC knowledge representation system, or, KL-ONE, the next generation : Proc. the International Conference on Fifth Generation Systems, pp.1036-1043, Tokyo, June 1992.
3. J.Breuker and W.Van de Velde. Common KADS Library for Expertise Modeling : IOS Press.

4. Bylander,T. & Chandrasekaran,B. (1988). Generic Tasks in Knowledge-based Reasoning: The "Right" Level of Abstraction for Knowledge Acquisition. In *Knowledge Acquisition for Knowledge Based Systems Vol.1*, ed. B.Gaines & J. Boose, 65-77. London : Academic Press.

5. Japan Electronic Dictionary Research Institute LTD.(1993). EDR Electronic Dictionary Technical Guide : Japan Electronic Dictionary Research Institute LTD.

6. Gruber, T.R.(1992). Ontolingua: A Mechanism to Support Portable Ontologies : Technical Report, KSL 91-66, Computer Science Department, Stanford University, San Francisco, CA.

7. M.Uschold and M.Gruninger(1996). Ontologies: Principles, Methods and Applications: AAAI-96 tutorial syllabus. SA1, 1996.

8. Heijst,G.(1995). The Role of Ontologies in Knowledge Engineering : Ph.D. diss., University of Amsterdam.

9. Genesereth,M.R. and Fikes, R.(1992). Knowledge Interchange Format Version 3.0 Reference Manual : Technical Report, Logic-92-1, Computer Science Department, Stanford University, San Francisco, CA.

10. R.V.Guha and D.B.Lenat(1990). Cyc : A Mid-term Report : AI Magazine, Vol.11,No.3,pp.32-59.

11. K.Knight, S. Luk (1994). Building a Large Knowledge Base for Machine Translation : Proc. AAAI-94. Seattle, WA. 1994.

12. Miller,G.(1990). WordNet An on-line lexical database : International Journal of Lexicographer 3(4) (Special Issue).

13. Kahn,G., Nowlan,S. & McDermott,J.(1985). MORE: An Intelligent Knowledge Acquisition Tool : Proc. the 9th International Joint Conference on Artificial Intelligence, 581-584. LosAngeles:Morgan Kaufmann.

14. Robert M.MacGregor(1991). The evolving technology of classification - based knowledge representation systems : Principles of semantic networks: explorations in the representation of knowledge, John F. Sowa, ed., The Morgan Kaufmann series in representation and reasoning, Morgan Kaufmann Publishers, Inc., San Mateo, CA, 385-400

15. Musen,M.A., Gennari,J.H., Eriksson,H., Tu,S.W., and Puerta,A.R. (1994). PROTÉGÉ-II: Computer Support For Development Of Intelligent Systems. Genesereth,M.R. & Fikes, R. 1992. Knowledge Interchange Format Version 3.0 Reference Manual : Technical Report. KSL-94-60, Computer Science Department, Stanford University, San Francisco, CA.

16. Peiwei Mi and Walt Scacchi. A Knowledge-Based Environment for Modeling and Simulating Software Engineering Processes : IEEE Transactions on Knowledge and Data Engineering,Vol.2,No.3:283-294 (1990)

17. K.Sono and M.Yamate (1993). United Nations Convention on Contracts for The International Sales of Goods : Seirin Shoin.

18. Bill Swartout, Ramesh Patil, Kevin Knight and Tom Russ (1996). Toward Distributed Use of Large-Scale Ontologies : Proc. of the 10th Knowledge Acquisition Workshop (KAW'96).

CAMLET: A Platform for Automatic Composition of Inductive Learning Systems Using Ontologies

Akihiro SUYAMA, Naoya NEGISHI, and Takahira YAMAGUCHI

School of Information, Shizuoka University
3-5-1 Johoku Hamamatsu Shizuoka, 432-8011 JAPAN

E-mail:{suyama,s4029,yamaguti}@cs.inf.shizuoka.ac.jp
Phone:+81-53-478-1473
Fax   :+81-53-473-6421

Abstract. Here is presented a platform for automatic composition of inductive learning systems using ontologies called CAMLET, based on knowledge modeling and ontologies engineering technique. CAMLET constructs an inductive applications with better competence to a given data set, using process and object ontologies. Afterwards, CAMLET instantiates and refines a constructed system based on the following refinement strategies: greedy alteration, random generation and heuristic alteration. Using the UCI repository of ML databases and domain theories, experimental results have shown us that CAMLET supports a user in constructing a inductive applications with best competence.

1 Introduction

During the last ten years, knowledge-based systems (KBSs) have been developed using knowledge modeling techniques. In particular, in order to exploit reusable knowledge components, extensive research effort has been placed on exploiting problem solving methods (PSMs) at high levels of abstraction, such as Generic Tasks [3], PROTEGE-II [12] and Common-KADS [2]. PSMs are high-level languages specify problem solving processes independent of implementation details. Now the research effort moves into ontologies engineering, together with PSMs. An ontology is an explicit specification of a conceptualization [4]. According to [5], there are several distinguished ontologies, such as generic ontologies for conceptualizations across many domains, domain ontologies to put constraints on the structure and contents of domain knowledge in a particular-field, and PSMs (some researchers call them task ontologies recently).

On the other hand, during the last twenty years, many inductive learning systems, such as ID3 [13], GA based classifier systems [6] and data mining systems, have been developed, exploiting many inductive learning algorithms. However, the competence with inductive learning systems changes, depending on the characteristics of given data sets. So far we have no powerful inductive learning systems that always work well to any data set.

From the above background, it is time to decompose inductive learning algorithms and organize inductive learning methods (ILMs) for reconstructing inductive learning systems. Given such ILMs, we may construct a new inductive learning system that works well to a given data set by re-interconnecting ILMs. The issue is to learn (or search) a inductive learning system good for a given data set. Thus this paper focuses on specifying ILMs into an ontology for objects manipulated by learning processes (called a process ontology here) and also an object ontology for objects manipulated by learning processes. After constructing two ontologies, we design a computer aided machine (inductive) learning environment called CAMLET and evaluates the competence of CAMLET using several case studies from UCI Machine Learning Repository.

2 Ontologies for Inductive Learning

Before specifying ontologies for inductive learning processes, we have analyzed popular inductive learning systems, such as ID3 [13], GA based classifier systems [6] and data mining systems. A process ontology is for ILMs that compose inductive learning systems. An object ontology is for objects manipulated by ILMs from the process ontology. In order to specify process and object ontologies, we need to specify conceptual hierarchies and conceptual schemes (definitions) on two ontologies.

2.1 Process Ontology

In order to specify the conceptual hierarchy of a process ontology, it is important to identify how to branch down processes. Because the upper part is related with general processes and the lower part with specific processes, it is necessary to set up different ways to branch the hierarchy down, depending on the levels of hierarchy.

In specifying the upper part of the hierarchy, we have analyzed popular inductive learning systems and then identified the following five popular and abstract components : "generating training and test data sets", "generating a classifier set", "evaluating data and classifier sets", "modifying a training data set" and "modifying a classifier set", with the top-level control structure as shown in Figure 1. Although we can place finer components on the upper part, they seem to make up many redundant composition of inductive learning systems. Thus these five processes have been placed on upper part in the conceptual hierarchy of the process ontology, as shown in Figure 2.

In specifying the lower part of the hierarchy, the above abstract component has been divided down using characteristics specific to each. For example "generating a classifier set" has been divided into "(generating a classifier set) dependent on training sets" and "(generating a classifier set) independent of training sets" from the point of the dependency on training sets. Thus we have constructed the conceptual hierarchy of the process ontology, as shown in Figure

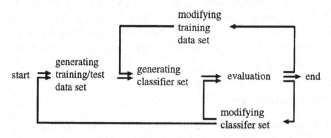

Fig. 1. Top-level Control Structure

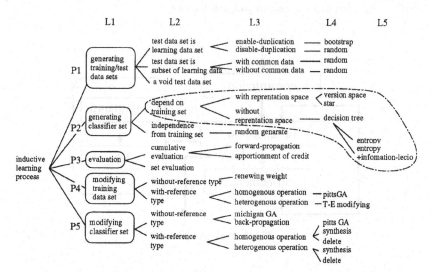

Fig. 2. Hierarchy of process ontology

2. In Figure 2, leaf nodes correspond to the library of executable program codes that have been manually developed by C language.

On the other hand, in order to specify the conceptual scheme of the process ontology, we have identified the learning process scheme including the following roles: "input", "output" and "reference" from the point of objects manipulated by the process, and then "pre-process" just before the defined process and "post-process" just after the defined process from the point of processes relevant to the defined process.

2.2 Object Ontology

In order to specify the conceptual hierarchy of the object ontology, we use the way to branch down the data structures manipulated by learning processes, such as sets and strings. Because objects contribute less to construct inductive learning systems than processes, object scheme has less information than process. So it has just one role "process-list" that is a list of processes manipulating the object.

3 Basic Design of CAMLET

Figure 3 shows the basic activities for knowledge systems construction using PSMs [5]. In this section, we apply the basic activities to constructing inductive application using process and object ontologies.

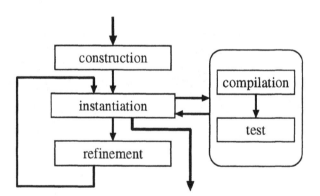

Fig. 3. Basic Activities

The construction activity constructs an initial specification for an inductive applications. CAMLET selects a top-level control structure for an inductive learning system by selecting any path from "start" to "end" in Figure 1. Afterwards CAMLET retrieves leaf-level processes subsumed in the selected top-level processes, checking the interconnection from the roles of pre-process and post-process from the selected leaf-level processes. Thus CAMLET constructs an initial specification for an inductive application, described by leaf-level processes in process ontology. In order to reconstruct the specification later, the selected leaf-level processes have been pushed down into a process stack.

The instantiation activity fills in input and output roles of leaf-level processes from the initial specification, using data types from a given data set. The values of other roles, such as reference, pre-process and post-process, have not been instantiated but come directly from process schemes. Thus an instantiated specification comes up. Additionally, the leaf-level processes have been filled in the process-list roles of the objects identified by the data types.

The compilation activity transforms the instantiated specification into executable codes using library for ILMs. When the process is connected to another process at implementation details, the specification for I/O data types must be unified. To do so, this activity has such a data conversion facility that converts a decision tree into classifier.

The test activity tests if the executable codes for the instantiated specification goes well or not, checking the requirement (accuracy) from the user. The evaluation will come up to do a refinement activity efficiently, which is explained later. This activity evaluates how are good a top-level control structure in Figure 1 and four sub-control structures in Figure 4.

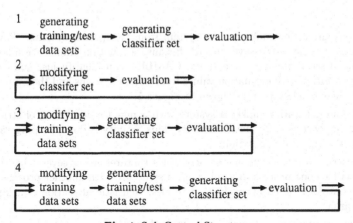

Fig. 4. Sub-Control Structures

When the executable codes do not go well, the refinement activity comes up in order to refine or reconstruct the initial specification and get a refined specification back to the instantiation activity. The refinement activity is a kind of search task for finding out the system (or control structure) satisfied with a goal of accuracy. Although several search algorithms have been proposed, genetic programming (GP) is popular for composing programs automatically. GP goes well for global search but no so well for local search. So, in order to solve this problem, here is presented the hybrid search that combines GP with a local search with several heuristics based on empirical analysis. This activity has been done with the following three strategies: greedy alteration, random generation and heuristic alteration.

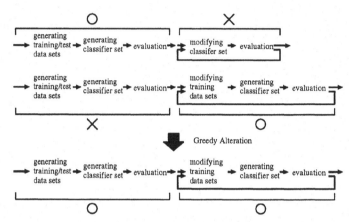

Fig. 5. Greedy Alteration

Greedy alteration makes a new system from two parent systems. This operation works like G-crossover in GP. Because evaluation values are added to sub-control structures at test activity, CAMLET can identify just sub-control structures with better evaluation values from parent systems and then put them into one new child system, as shown in Figure 5.

Random generation makes a system with a new top-level control structure in the same way as construction activity. This activity is done, keeping various control structures in population.

Heuristic alteration change sub-control structures using several heuristics, which replace one process in a sub-control structure with another process from process ontology based on evaluation results. Heuristic alteration is a kind of local search.

Figure 6 summarizes the above-mentioned activities. A user gives a data set and a goal of accuracy to CAMLET. CAMLET constructs the specification for an inductive application, using process and object ontologies. When the specification does not go well, it is refined into another one with better performance by greedy alteration, random generation and heuristic alteration. To be more operational, in the case of a system's performance being higher than $\delta(= 0.7*$ goal accuracy), the heuristic alteration comes up. If not so, in the case of that system population size is equal or larger than some threshold ($N \geq \tau = 4$), CAMLET executes greedy alteration, otherwise, executes random generation. All the system refined by three strategies get into a system population. As a result, CAMLET may (or may not) generate an inductive application satisfied with the accuracy from the user. When it goes well, the inductive application can learn a set of rules that work well to the given data set.

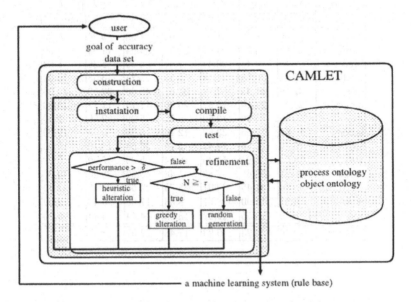

Fig. 6. An Overview of CAMLET

4 Case Studies and Discussions

Based on the basic design, we have implemented CAMLET on UNIX platforms with C language, including the implementations of fifteen components in the process ontology with C language. We did case studies of constructing inductive applications for the fourteen different data sets from the UCI Machine Learning Repository. Five complete 5-fold cross-validations were carried out with each data set.

The results of these trials appear in Table 1. For each data set, the second to sixth column show mean error rates over the five cross-validations of popular inductive learning systems, such as ID3, Classifier Systems, Bagged C4.5 an Neural Network. The seventh column contains similar results for inductive applications constructed by CAMLET. The final column shows error rates given as goal accuracy. Table 1 says CAMLET constructs inductive applications with best competence. In detail, the competence of CAMLET is better than that of Neural Network on the average, except the following three data sets: annealing, breast-w and waveform.

Although the processes from Neural Network have been implemented in th e process ontology, CAMLET still has some problem on converting neural net-

Table 1. Comparison of CAMLET and Popular Inductive Learning Systems

Data	C4.5	ID3	CS	B_C4.5	NN	CAMLET	
	err (%)	err (%)	err (%)	err (%)	err (%)	err (%)	goal (%)
annealing	9.00	18.00	21.00	11.00	1.00	9.00	10.00
audiology	26.92	15.38	84.62	11.54	84.64	11.54	12.00
breast-w	7.18	7.46	20.44	7.46	4.42	5.36	8.00
credit-s	18.48	20.38	24.18	16.85	22.24	13.53	15.00
glass	32.69	41.35	80.77	33.65	48.08	32.69	33.00
hepatitis	24.29	27.14	18.57	20.00	17.14	11.72	15.00
iris	5.00	5.00	12.50	7.50	5.00	2.50	5.00
labor	17.65	17.65	23.53	12.76	5.88	5.88	12.00
soybean	16.76	26.33	74.47	15.16	35.64	15.16	16.00
vote	5.09	6.94	14.35	6.94	5.09	2.59	5.00
water	60.28	38.65	57.80	41.48	43.97	38.65	39.00
waveform	45.84	31.45	34.01	38.76	20.66	31.45	32.00
wine	8.33	11.90	28.57	8.33	17.86	5.47	9.00
zoo	8.89	15.56	22.22	13.33	4.44	4.44	5.00
average	20.46	20.23	36.93	17.48	22.57	13.57	

work s into other data types, such as classifiers and decision trees. Because neural networks keep many weights between nodes (concepts), they are missing in converting into other data types. So CAMLET does not use the processes from Neural Network in constructing inductive applications in these case studies.

The inductive applications constructed by CAMLET are specified in Table 2. It show us that the error rates of the inductive applications constructed by CAMLET are almost over those of popular inductive learning systems. Table 2 shows us the rough specifications o f all the inductive applications constructed by CAMLET. They include five kind s of new inductive applications , which are different from popular inductive learning systems. One new inductive application is specified by Figure 7. It consists of bootstrap, star algorithm, apportionment of credit, and T-E modifying. Because the star algorithm process generates jus t rules covering positive instances and not covering all negative instances, i t tends to have overfitting to a given training data set. In order to reduce the overfitting, the training data set has a bootstrap process and is polished T-E modifying process. In these case studies, this specification has been genera ted seven times to the following two data sets: labor and zoo. Maybe it is a n ew fact that the combination of star algorithm, bootstrap and T-E modifying is a promising pattern to design inductive applications. We might get more design patterns for constructing inductive applications through more case studies. Thus it is all right to say that CAMLET works well as a platform of constructing inductive applications.

Table 2. Inductive Applications Constructed by CAMLET

Data	System				
	1	2	3	4	5
annealing	C4.5	C4.5	C4.5	C4.5(w)[1]	C4.5
audiology	B_C4.5	B_C4.5	B_C4.5	B_C4.5	B_C4.5
breast-w	AQ15	C4.5	New(1)[1]	AQ15	vs[1]
credit-s	ID3	C4.5	New(2)	New(3)	ID3
glass	C4.5	C4.5	C4.5	C4.5	C4.5
hepatitis	C4.5	New(4)	C4.5	New(3)	ID3
iris	C4.5(w)	C4.5(w)	C4.5(w)	C4.5(w)	ID3
labor	ID3	New(5)	New(5)	New(5)	C4.5
soybean	B_C4.5	C4.5(w)	B_C4.5	B_C4.5	B_C4.5
vote	New(4)	B_VS	New(4)	C4.5	vs
water	B_ID3	B_C4.5	ID3	ID3	ID3
waveform	CS	ID3	ID3	ID3	ID3
wine	B_ID3	C4.5	C4.5(w)	ID3	ID3
zoo	New(5)	New(5)	New(5)	C4.5	New(5)

5 Related Work

Although basic activities based on PSMs have usually been done by hands in constructing knowledge systems, CAMLET tries to automate the basic activities at the level of specifications (not yet at the level of codes).

Besides PSMs, there are several ontologies specific to processes, such as Gruninger's enterprise ontologies specific to business processes and PIF [9] and software process ontologies. Although our learning process ontology has some similarities to PSMs and other process ontologies about how to decompose processes, it decomposes processes, using more information specific in the field of task-domain (learning in our case).

From the field of inductive learning, CAMLET has some similarities to MSL [7]. MSL tries to put two or more machine learning systems together into an unified machine learning system with better competence. MSL does not decompose machine learning systems (the adaptation of machine learning systems sometimes comes up for interconnection). So the grain size of the components in CAMLET is much finer than the grain size of ones in MSL. Furthermore, MSL has no competence to invent a new machine learning system like CAMLET.

MLC++ [8] is a platform for constructing inductive learning systems. However, MLC++ has no facility for automatic composition of inductive learning systems like CAMLET.

---

[1] C4.5(w):C4.5 with windowling strategy, VS: Version Space, New(x): new systems different from popular systems

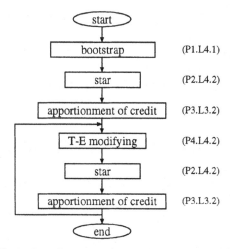

Fig. 7. Specification of A New System – New (5) –

6 Conclusions and Future Work

This work comes from inter-discipline between machine learning and ontologies engineering. We put recent efforts on specifications and codes for ontologies and less on efficient search mechanisms to generate inductive learning systems with best performance. We need to make the refinement activity more intelligent and efficient with failure analysis and parallel processing. The refinement activity should move into an invention activity to invent new learning processes and new objects manipulated by learning processes.

References

1. Leo Breiman: Bagging predictors, *Machine Learning*, Volume 24, Number 2, pp.123-140, August 1996.
2. J.Breuker and W.Van de Velde: Common CADS Library for Expertise Modeling, IOS Press, 1994.
3. T. Bylander and B. Chandrasekaran: Generic Tasks for Knowledge-Based Reasoning: The "Right" Level of Abstraction for Knowledge Acquisition, *IJMMS; International Journal of Man-Machine Studies*, Volume 26, pp.231-243, 1987.
4. Gruber,T.R.: Ontolingua: A Mechanism to Support Portable Ontologies, Technical Report, KSL 91-166, Computer Science Department, Standford University, San Francisco, CA, 1992.
5. Gertjan van Heijst: The Role of Ontologies in Knowledge Engineering, Dr Thesis, University of Amsterdam, 1995.
6. L.B.Booker, D.E.Goldberg, J.H.Holland: Classifier Systems and Genetic Algorithms, *Artificial Intelligence 40*, pp.235-282, 1989.
7. Raymond J.Mooney, Dirk Ourston: A Multistrategy Approach to Theory Refinement, *Machine Learning: A Multistrategy Approach*, Volume 4, pp.141-164, 1994.

8. Kohavi,R. and Sommerfield, D: Data Mining using MLC++ - A Machine Learning Library in C++, Proc. 8th International Conference on Tools with Artificial Intelligence, pp.234-245, 1996.

9. Lee,J.G., Yost, and the PIF Working Group: The PIF Process Interchange Format and Framework, MIS CCS Working Report#180, 1994.

10. Michalski,R.S., Carbonell,J.G., Mitchell,J.M.(eds.): Machine learning: An artificial intelligence approach, Morgan Kaufmann, Los Altos, CA, 1983.

11. M.Shaw and D.Garian: Software Architecture: Perspective on an Emerging Discipline, Prentice Hall, 1996.

12. Musen M.A. et al.: Overcoming the limitations of role-limiting methods, editorial special issue, Knowledge Acquisition, 4(1):162-168, 1992.

13. J.R.,Quinlan: Induction of Decision Tree, *Machine Learning*, 1, pp.81–106 (1986).

14. J.R.,Quinlan: C4.5 : Programs for Machine Learning, Morgan Kaufmann, 1992

15. J.R.,Quinlan: Bagging, Boosting and C4.5, *AAAI*, 1996.

Management of Worker's Experiences:
A Knowledge-Based Approach

Leila Alem[1], Pierre Marcenac[2]

(1) CSIRO Mathematical and Information Science, Locked bag 17,
North Ryde NSW 2113 - Australia.
leila.alem@cmis.csiro.au

(2) IREMIA, University of La Réunion,
BP 7151, 97715 St Denis Messag. Cedex 9, La Réunion, France
marcenac@univ-reunion.fr

Abstract. In this paper we present the key concepts of an experiences based management system that assists the transformation of individual experiences into usefull knowledge. Such a framework is designed around the notion of capturing and delivering experiences for improving worker's practices and tasks. The study has been done in the area of customer relationships. In this paper we present our approach to modelling and representing individual experiences, as well as our approach to dynamically generating collective experiences, on user request, in order to assist workers in making the best use of existing experiences. The research framework called L2Corp is described in term of its various knowledge components and its associated functional processes for assisting users in authoring the knowledge as well as assisting them in the producing value added knowledge. In this framework, collective knowledge is dynamically generated using broadcasting and self-organisation mechanisms, initally developed in multiagent systems. This approach is at the feasability stage, it is promising as it constitutes a first step towards the formalisation of the know-how using AI techniques. Such know-how is the missing element in existing experiences based management systems, and is what will allow to move from passive systems illustrating the know-how to more active systems which assist its production.

1. Introduction

Few organisations have recognised that a great portion of their everyday activities generates information that, when recognised for its potential usefulness, can be captured, stored for future use and made available to decisions makers when needed. Such organisations have attempted to capture their experiences in ways that effectively transform them into available knowledge [Van Heijst and al. 96]. These efforts have led to the development of a number of experiences based management systems such as: REX-SPX, CAUSE, ELODIE, DIESEL, etc. [Malvache and Prieur 93]. These initiatives have been taken mostly in defence and service industry sectors.

Such systems are adopting a documentation approach to capturing experiences using database techniques (relational objects, SGML document, hyper document for modelling, and indexing and retrieval for delivery). Their focus has been on organisational documents, technical notes, design document etc., all of which capture in writing some form of implicit or explicit knowledge. The knowledge captured in such systems relates to knowledge accumulated during the activity of the worker such as most often-repeated mistakes, problems, worst practice, recommendations etc. The representation and delivery of such knowledge is mostly passive, it can only illustrate the know-how. Such knowledge when delivered is difficult to put into action.

What is missing is the knowledge related to the experience that a worker has used and demonstrated as well as the underlying practice. This corresponds to the worker's method, practice or way of doing things. There is therefore a need for a knowledge-based approach to complement this document-based approach taken by such systems, in order to operationalism workers' experiences. In our view, access to such knowledge not only will assist workers in their activity by providing them with the capacity for effective action, but can also assist organisations in their effort in improving their practice. Beyond this consideration, if technology has played a leading role in storing, distributing and collating such knowledge, emphasis today is shifting to "the transformation of that experience into knowledge accessible to the whole organisation and relevant to its core purpose" [Senge 90]. These considerations translates into the following research questions:

1. How to model and represent the dynamic aspects of knowledge in individual experiences?
2. What type of new knowledge should be created that will help the worker in building his capacity for effective action?
3. What sort of intelligent function should be defined and designed to assist the production of such knowledge?

This paper proposes partial solutions to these research questions. The study has been made in the context of the design of a research framework, called L2Corp (Lessons Learned Based Corporate Memory) initially specified in [Alem 98]. The paper is organised as follows: section 2 presents the framework and its knowledge components as well as functional processes, section 3 focuses on the knowledge representation model, and section 4 presents the tool designed for assisting the worker in making a more effective use of peers experiences. Finally section 5 concludes by pointing out the benefits of the approach as well as further investigations.

2. The framework

L2Corp is described in Figure 1, its key features are:
- An explicit representation of the organisational business processes,
- A representation of individual experiences and their link to business processes,

- A tool to support the authoring of experiences in a way that promotes reflection and assessment of individual experience,
- A tool that generates useful knowledge, ie collective knowledge in order to assist users in making the best use of individual experiences.

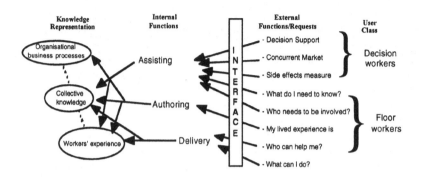

Fig. 1: Overview of the L2Corp framework

L2Corp framework has been designed for two types of end-users:
- Decision-makers, who are looking inward into the organisation in order to assess organisational training needs, current practices, current bottlenecks etc.
- Floor workers, looking for help on what and who can help them in their activity, who can help them in describing their own experience, their lessons learned, etc.

This paper focuses on the second type of end-users, and presents outcome of investigations with regard to the knowledge modelling and representation problem (section three) as well as the tool designed to assist turning experiences into collective knowledge (section four). Both sections are described using examples taken from an application of L2Corp in the area of commercial customer relations.

3. Knowledge modelling and representation

L2Corp includes a model of business processes describing the different activities the organisation is concerned with. Workers' experiences, reflecting the dynamic aspects of their practice are represented in term of lessons learned. Next sections describe both the model of business process and the model of lesson learned.

3.1. Business process model

An organisation is described by its activities and related core business processes. For example, in the application in commercial customers, one activity is developing commercial projects with clients. The activity will be composed of a number of core businesses including: establishing the client interest, producing a proposal for discussion, determining the commercial contract, managing the project... Each of these business processes is represented in the form of an object of the generic class *business process*.

The business process class is described as:

1. activities, type list of instances of the *activity* class,
2. business process title, type text,
3. lessons learned, type list of instances of the *lesson learned* class (see 3.2),
4. documents, type list of documents,
5. factors, type list of variables.

The last attribute *factors* contains the list of factors the business process is associated with. An example of such factors related to establishing the client interest could include re-working (RW) to indicate the number of time the company has been working with this specific client.

The attribute *documents* contains the documents that have been produced in the course of action of the business process. These documents are proposals, letters to client, recommendations reports etc. The idea here is provide workers with such documents as positive examples for reuse, or negative examples for demonstrating things to avoid doing.

3.2. Lesson learned model

Each instance of business process is associated with a collection of lessons learned describing workers' experiences. A Lesson Learned (LL) is an instance of the *lesson-learned* class.

In L2Corp, the lesson-learned class is described as:

1. author of the lesson learned and contact,
2. the business process related to,
3. a general description: actors, date and place,
4. the initial situation,
5. the action taken and its objective, and the barriers and/or enabling factors (see 3.3),
6. the resulting situation,
7. versions (list of instances of lesson learned),
8. usage counter,
9. type of the lesson.

An instance of lesson learned could be of three types: it could be a positive lesson (LL+), a negative lesson (LL-), or a neutral lesson (LLo). A positive lesson learned is one in which the objective of the action is met or partially met. A negative lesson learned is one in which the objective of the action has not been met, leading to a resulting situation that is worst than the initial situation. A neutral lesson learned (LLo) is one in which the resulting situation can not be assessed as being better or worst than the initial one.

The class lesson learned has a set of methods, such methods are presented in the context of their use in the sub section 4.1.

3.3. Authoring lessons learned

The purpose here is to engage the users in a process of reflection on their experience. The users are not asked to report on an activity but to think critically about what went well and what did not. One of our basis hypotheses is that users will describe their experience for both reflecting on it and articulating its content in a way that their peers can make use of it. When authoring a lesson the user needs first to provide the general context of the lesson, selecting a business process from an existing list does this. Such a list includes all possible business processes related to the activity for which the system is designed. This selection automatically creates an instance of the business process selected. Such instance inherits from its class the default value of its attributes (if there is any).

As specified above, a lesson learned is centred on the action made by the author. The end-user then needs to specify/evaluate the situation at hand; scoring the factors related to the business process does this. Some of these factors directly relate to the key success factors of the organisation. The scoring of these factors forces discrimination and helps focusing the interaction with the system. The objective of the action undertaken by the user is expressed in terms of increasing or decreasing the scores of one or more key factor(s).

In the previous example, factors and scores could include:
1. Re-working (RW: score 1 to 3, 1 being first time and 3 being more than twice), this factor being also a key success factor for the organisation,
2. Alignment with business strategy (ABS: score from 1 to 5),
3. Match of interest (MI: score from 1 to 5, 1 being poor match).

A situation, in this example, can be described as RW= 1, ABS= 3 and MI= 1. The user is then requested to evaluate the action, this is done by identifying the enabling factors or the barriers relative to the action. In the customer example, an enabling factor could be a time factor, a friendly contact, and barriers could be wrong timing, the contact in the client side is not the champion, etc.

So, lets' say that, when establishing the client interest with client X the organisation of a workshop in order to look for a better match of interest had worked and the presence of Peter had helped. This piece of knowledge is represented as:

Author: Leila (3151).

Core business process = establishing the client interest.

Actors = JohnF from end-user group and PierreB from management,

Date=28/02/98,

Place: Client X.

Initial Situation: RW=1, ABS=3, MI=1.

Action: organise a workshop with client, objective: increase the match of interest.

Enabling factor: Peter, Peter is my champion.

Barriers: Timing of the action, it was prior to project evaluation.

Resulting Situation: RW =1, ABS =3, MI =2.

Versions: (LL31, LL32).

Usage counter = 3.

Type of the lesson: (LL+).

This approach adds value to the traditional document experiences based systems described above, by assisting the workers in reflecting in their own experience in order to gain insight and understanding from experience through reflection, assessment of own experience in light of both successes and failures. The main conceptual differences are:

- An explicit representation of the assessment of the worker's owns experiences in term of the impact of their action, the outcomes reached.
- An explicit representation of the workers reflection on what are the elements of the situation that have contributed to a success or a failure of the actions taken, ie what had helped (enabling factors) and/or what were the barriers.

These conceptual differences enable the articulation of the workers know-how used in their experience. As specified in [Malhotra 96], this approach implies that the ability of the worker is not only reflected by what he knows, but also by how he learns.Figure 2 below illustrates the knowledge representation model (excluding collective knowledge described in section 4) which has been designed using UML [Rational 97].

We have described our model of business processes and individual lessons learned. Next section describes our approach to generating collective knowledge in order to assist the worker in assimilating different experiences and deriving their own one based on this knowledge.

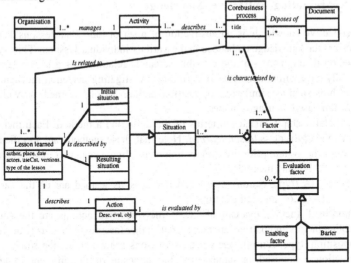

Fig. 2: L2Corp Classes diagram

4. Assisting the more effective use of experiences

Our purpose here is to design a tool that will assist the worker in improving their approach to problem solving based on peers' experiences. Such assistance can be based on a judicious combination of existing experiences. A simple approach to this combination problem is based on a single interpretation of the similarity between experiences [Malhotra 96]. This approach does not allow for multiple interpretations and therefore limits the full exploitation of the available knowledge. We propose to base the combination on the multiple points of view expressed in the various lessons learned, in order to generate richer knowledge and fully capitalise on the available knowledge.

This section proposes to constitute the notion of collective knowledge that embeds the potential multiple viewpoints related to existing experiences. We propose to generate collective knowledge as a mean for assisting him/her in making the best use of the experiences knowledge base. Two issues characterise this problem. The first one is a modelling and representation problem, how such knowledge should be represented? The second is that if such knowledge was to be generated, how can it be effective, how can it reflect the changes in the knowledge base, and how can it be maintained?

Section 4.1 presents how such knowledge has been modelled. Section 4.2 presents the generation on demand of the collective knowledge, using self-organisation mechanisms.

4.1. Representing collective knowledge

A collective knowledge is an abstraction of a set of individual lessons learned. It synthesizes the knowledge embedded in the various individual lessons. This synthesis is based on determination of the possible semantic relationships a lesson learned can potentially have with others. We are currently investigating detection mechanisms for relationships such as similarity, opposition among lessons learned, as well as the comparison based on usage counter.

Each relationship translates in terms of the definition a method. Each method is a class method of the class *lesson-learned*. Note that these methods are specified by the designer of the system prior the exploitation phase. In the customer example, we have defined the following methods:

- Similarity-A (type, action): true when two lessons learned are of the same type (LL+, LL-, LLo), and same action.
- Similarity-F (action, evaluationFactor): true when two actions are the same, and enabling factors and barriers are recognized similar (according to a fuzzy degree).
- Opposition (type, action): true when two lessons learned are of the same type, but the action is opposed, or same action but opposite result (different value of the lesson type).
- Opposition (initial Situation, action, type): true when two lessons learned have similar situation and different actions, and opposed outcomes.
- More-Often-used: simple comparison assessing the most used lesson based on usage counters.

Collective knowledge is represented as a graph, where the nodes correspond to various pieces of lessons learned (such as actions, situations related to...), and the links correspond to the relationships between them (see figure 3 below).

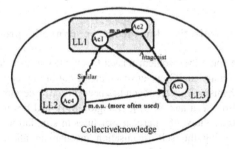

Fig. 3: Collective knowledge representation in L2Corp

In the customer example, suppose we have three lessons in the business process establishing the client interest (the examples are here simplified):

LL1	LL2	LL3
Paul (3151)	Pierre (3147)	Jacques (3200)
establishing client interest with Client X	establishing interest with Client Y	establishing client interest with Client Z
action: Workshop enabling factor: involvement of the champion	action: Focus group enabling factors: good timing, repeated business, CMIS good reputation	action: Focus group enabling factor: contact interested had responded quickly
barriers: wrong timing, prior to project evaluation	barriers: personal agenda of the contact (he is planning to start up his own project)	barriers: changes in management, contact had no influence
task duration: 2 months between first contact and follow up	task duration: 2 weeks	task duration: since Jan 98 till ?
LL-	LL+	LL-
UsageCnt = 17	UsageCnt = 3	UsageCnt = 1

These three lessons learned will be aggregated in the form of collective knowledge which highlights the following: Paul and Jacques have used different strategies (actions) to establish the client interest, and both have failed (opposition); Pierre and Jacques have used the same strategy, but with opposite results (one is LL+, the other is LL-); Paul's lesson is the most often used one (meaning that Paul's experience was revealed better than peers ones, or is the oldest).

In our approach, the collective knowledge is generated using a broadcasting technique and a self-organisation mechanism. The next section describes the dynamic generation of the collective knowledge.

4.2. Generating collective knowledge: a dynamic process

In order to overcome the problem related to maintenance of the knowledge created dynamically [Gasser and al. 93] we have adopted a bottom-up approach using the self-organisation mechanism. This approach has been initially developed in Artificial Life techniques (see [Bonabeau and al. 95], [Langton 89]), and has recently proved to be very effective in the context of emergent structures in simulation of complex systems [Marcenac 98b]. Using the self-organisation mechanism allows the generation of collective knowledge on demand (based on user's request and the current state of the lessons learned). As a result, the collective knowledge dynamically generated is up to date and therefore does not need to be maintained by a complex and labor-intensive process.

The mechanisms by which relationships are detected by the system are based on local interactions between lessons learned. Each lesson learned interacts with a limited number of others lessons learned in order to detect potential relationships. This is done using a broadcasting technique, described in more detailed in [Marcenac 98a]. The detection consists in looking for relationships, by broadcasting the message to all lessons learned in the knowledge base. This mechanism avoids the cycling problem, and allows the emergence of a new structure in the knowledge base.

The overall process consists of (1) the identification of the relationships among existing lessons learned by using broadcasting, (2) the generation of collective knowledge by self-organisation. Figure 4 below illustrates the overall process. The user's query being what do I need to know for this task?

1. Upon the worker's query, the system selects the lesson learned in the knowledge base, which best matches the query.
2. The detection mechanism is activated within each lesson learned by broadcasting. The result of this activation consists in determining the various relationships among lessons learned, such as similarity, opposition and usage ratio.
3. After completion of the detection process, the system generates a graph that represents the collective knowledge. Such a graph is composed of the relationships that have been identified in step 2.
4. Such collective knowledge is then presented to the worker.
5. The worker can then use this knowledge for assisting his own interpretation of the potential approaches, potential bottlenecks etc. This knowledge will help increase the level of awareness of the worker, which hopefully can be reflected in the approach/action adopted by him/her in the specific business process of interest. After achieving his task, the worker is asked to input his own lesson learned in the context of the collective knowledge generated for him/her.

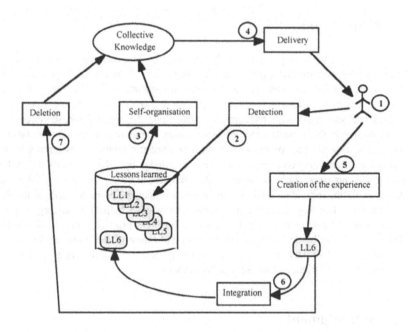

Fig. 4: Generation of collective knowledge based on a self-organisation approach

6. The new lesson learned is integrated in the knowledge base. This lesson learned is an adding value to the existing knowledge, as it is based on the interpretation of the advice reflected in collective knowledge.
7. The collective knowledge is deleted from the system, and the use counter of the individual lessons that have participated to the creation of the collective knowledge are updated.

The self-organisation mechanism is an interesting mean for dynamically generating knowledge "just in time" and in doing so, overcomes the maintenance problem. The benefit of our approach is not in getting richer solutions to a problem, but more to draw the attention of the worker to a number of issues that have been identified by peer workers in their experiences. This assists the worker in both improving their practice as well as the quality of the resulting lesson learned (LL6 in figure 4).

The self-organisation mechanism referred in this framework has already been designed and implemented (in Java) in the generic multi agent architecture called GEAMAS [Marcenac 98a]. Such architecture has been used to develop simulation applications of natural phenomena [Marcenac and Giroux 98]. We are planning to reuse the software component to implement this aspect of L2Corp.

5. Conclusions

In this paper we have presented the key concept of an experiences based knowledge management system that assists the transformation of individual experiences into useful knowledge, as well as the research framework called L2Corp. We have emphasized the use of AI techniques to represent and process the dynamic aspect of the experience; such aspects are not captured in traditional document database systems. We have presented the models used for representing the experiences and the business processes, as well as the processes for detecting semantic relationships among lessons learned and generating on demand collective knowledge by self-organisation. We have illustrated our paper with examples in the commercial customers activity. We argue that articulating individual lessons learned helps reflection, promotes critical thinking and therefore learning. Generating collective knowledge helps formalizing corporate know-how and assists in improving worker's business practice. This work suggests that AI tools can be designed to assist the formalization of the corporate know-how, the later, once stabilized, can assist in improving decision making, responsiveness to customers and efficiency of workers and operations.

Acknowledgment

The work described in this paper was completed during Pierre Marcenac's visit at the CSIRO Mathematical and Information Science (CMIS), Macquarie University, Sydney. The contribution to this work by the members of that Centre is gratefully acknowledged.

References

[Alem 97]: "Knowledge Management and organisational memory : preliminary investigations", June 1997, CMIS internal document.

[Alem 98]: L. Alem, "Learning in the workplace: initial requirements of a lessons learned centered corporate memory", to be printed in Proceedings of ITS'98, Austin, TX, Springer-Verlag, July 1998.

[Bonabeau and al. 95]: E. Bonabeau, J.L. Dessalles, A. Grumbach, "Characterizing emergent phenomena (1) and (2): A critical review", in Revue Internationale de Systémique, Hermes, Vol. 9 (3), Pages 327-346 and Pages 347-371, 1995.

[Damiani and al. 93]: M. Damiani, P. Randi, E Bertino and L. Spampinato, "The AIMS project: an information server architecture integrating data, knowledge and multimedia information",. in Enterprise Integration modelling-proceedings of the first International conference, 1993.

[Gasser and al. 93]: L. Gasser, I. Hulthage, B. Leverich, J. Lieb and A. Majchrzak, "Organisations as complex, dynamic design problems", in proceeding of the 6th Portuguese conference on AI, October 1993.

[Godbout 97]: A.J. Godbout, "Integrated approach to knowledge modelling", http://infoweb.magi.com /~godbout/Kbase/dt9720.htm, 1997.

[Langton 89]: C.B. Langton, "Artificial Life", in Artificial Life, Santa Fe Institute Studies in the Sciences of Complexity, Vol. VI, Addison-Wesley publishers, pp. 1-48, 1989.

[Malhotra 96]: Y. Malhotra, "Organizational learning and learning organizations: an overview", http://www.brint.com/papers/orglrng.htm, 1996.

[Malvache and Prieur 93]: P. Malvache and P. Prieur, "Mastering corporate experience with the REX method", in Proceedings of ISMICK-93, Management of Industrial and Corporate Knowledge, Compiegne, France, October 1993, pp. 33-41.

[Marcenac and Giroux. 98]: P. Marcenac, S. Giroux, "GEAMAS: A Generic Architecture for Agent-Oriented Simulations of Complex Processes", International Journal of Applied Intelligence, Neural Networks, and Complex Problem-Solving Technologies, Kluwer Academic Publishers, Vol. 8, N°3, May/June 1998.

[Marcenac 98a]: P. Marcenac, "Towards an emergence machine for complex systems simulations", IEA-98-AIE International Conference, Spain, to be printed in Springer-Verlag LNCS, April 1998.

[Marcenac 98b]: P. Marcenac, "Modeling MultiAgent Systems as Self-Organized Critical Systems", 31st Hawaii International Conference on System Sciences, HICSS-31, IEEE Computer Society Press, Vol. 5, Dan Dolk eds, Pages 86-95, 1998.

[Maret & Pinon 97]: P.Maret, J.M Pinon, "Ingénierie des savoir-faire, compétences individuelles et mémoire collective", Editions HERMES, ISBN 2-86601-620-3. Paris, 1997.

[Rational 97]: Rational Software Corporation, "Unified Modeling language", Notation Guide, 1.0, March 1997.

[Senge 90]: P. Senge, "Fifth Discipline: Theory and Practice of the Learning Organisation", Doubleday, New York, 1990.

[Van Heijst and al. 96]: G. van Heijst, R. Van der Spek and E. Kruizinga, "Organizing Corporate Memory", in Proceedings of the 10th Banff Knowledge Acquisition for knowledge based systems workshop, Banff, Alberta, Canada, Nov 9-14, 1996.

The Minimum Description Length Based Decision Tree Pruning

Igor Kononenko

University of Ljubljana, Faculty of Computer and Inf. Sc.
Tržaška 25, SI-1001 Ljubljana, Slovenia
e-mail: igor.kononenko@fri.uni-lj.si

Abstract. We describe the Minimum Description Length (MDL) based decision tree pruning. A subtree is considered unreliable and therefore is pruned if the description length of the classification of the corresponding subsets of training instances together with the description lengths of each path in the subtree is greater than the description length of the classification of the whole subset of training instances in the current node. We compare the perfomance of our simple, parameterless, and well-founded MDL method with some other methods on 18 datasets. The classification accuracy using the MDL pruning is comparable to other approaches and the decision trees are nearly optimally pruned which makes our method an attractive tool for obtaining a first approximation of the target decision tree during the knowledge discovery process.

Keywords: machine learning, decision trees, MDL principle

1 Introduction

In top down induction of decision trees various pruning techniques are used to overcome the overfitting of training instances: the chi-square pruning (Quinlan, 1982) the minimal cost-complexity pruning (Breiman et al., 1984), prepruning with some (ad-hoc) parameters (Kononenko et al., 1984), lookahead with resampling (Bratko and Kononenko, 1987), reduced error pruning (Quinlan, 1987), postpruning using the probability estimates based on the Laplace's law of succession (Niblett and Bratko, 1986), postpruning with the m-estimate of probabilities (Cestnik and Bratko, 1991), and pessimistic pruning (Quinlan, 1993). Experimental comparisons (Mingers, 1989; Esposito et al., 1995) show that, typically, various methods are comparable with respect to classification accuracy and with respect to the size of decision trees although some differences can be detected.

The intuition behind all above methods is that with smaller number of training instances the selection of the attributes in the decision tree becomes unreliable. The problem is to determine the right measure for the unreliability of the decision subtree and, what is even more difficult, to select the appropriate point (threshold) that determines when to prune the subtree. All the above methods are either ad-hoc and/or need parameter tuning. The parameter tuning is done with cross-validation by using, besides a training set, also an additional "pruning" subset of instances. The parameter tuning makes pruning a time consuming process.

The minimum description length (MDL) principle (Rissanen, 1984; Li and Vitanyi, 1993) seems to be a natural non-ad-hoc approach to avoiding the overfitting in general. The basic idea of the MDL-based approach to pruning is that a subtree should be pruned if the description length of classification of training instances given the (whole) tree plus the description length of the (whole) tree is greater than if the subtree is pruned. Various implementations of this idea are possible. Recently Kovacic (1995) developed a MDL-based decision tree pruning algorithm. However, the algorithm has serious disadvanatges as discussed below.

The next section discusses the disadvantages of the existing approaches to decision tree pruning. In Section 3 we propose a simple, parameterless, and well-founded MDL-based method for decision tree pruning. Empirical results in Section 4 confirm that the proposed method is an attractive way to obtain a first approximation of the target decision tree.

2 Disadvantages of existing pruning methods

Chi-square pruning: Quinlan (1982) used a chi-square test to determine whether the best attribute is relevant or not for generating a subtree of the current node. The problem with the chi-square test is that it becomes highly unreliable with small number of instances which is in direct contradiction with the aim of pruning.

Minimal cost-complexity: The idea introduced by Breiman et al. (1984) is to find a series of trees that minimize an (ad-hoc) function that linearly combines the classifications error and the number of leaves in the tree using a parameter α. For different values of α different trees are generated. Cross-validation is used to select the best tree by using additional 1SE (standard error) bias towards smaller trees. Besides the ad-hoc formula for combining the classification error with the number of leaves, a disadvantage of the approach is the computational cost (due to cross-validation).

Prepruning in Assistant: Kononenko et al. (1984; Cestnik et al., 1987) used various ad-hoc parameters with empiricaly selected thresholds to stop the building of a subtree if either the number of instances or the estimate of the quality of the best attribute or the classification error on training instances in the current node becomes small enough. Ad-hoc parameters have to be appropriately tuned which is an obvious disadvantage of the approach.

Lookahead with resampling: The idea introduced by Bratko and Kononenko (1987) is to use resampling in order to several times split the instances in the current node into training and testing subsets and to build a one-level subtree for each split. If the average classification error of the one-level subtrees is greater than the classification error in the current node, the building of the subtree is terminated and the current node becomes a leaf. The method is impractical due to computational complexity, which can be partially overcome with (ad-hoc) heuristics.

Reduced error pruning: Quinlan (1987) uses a distinct pruning set of instances that are not used for building the decision tree. The obvious disadvantage of the approach is that the detection of uncertain parts of the tree (that are built from too small number of training instances) requires an additional reduction of the number of training instances.

Postpruning with the Laplace's law: The idea by Niblett and Bratko (1986) is to use the generalized Laplace's law of succession for estimating the majority class probabilities in the nodes:

$$P(C_i|node) = \frac{N(C_i \& node) + 1}{N(node) + \#classes}$$

$N(node)$ is the number of all instances in the current node and $N(C_i \& node)$ is the number of instances from class C_i. The subtree is pruned if the estimated error of the current node is smaller than the estimated error of the subtree. The problem of this approach is two-fold. The proposed use of the Laplace's law of succession does not satisfy the law of the decrease of the entropy, i.e. for an attribute with values $V_1..V_k$ it should hold:

$$H(C) \geq \sum_{i=1}^{k} P(V_i)H(C|V_i)$$

where C is the class variable and $H(X)$ is the entropy of variable X. The second disadvantage is that the basic assumption of the law of succession is the uniform prior probability distribution, which is in practice most often violated.

Postpruning with the m-estimate: Cestnik and Bratko (1991) overcome the latter disadvantage of the Laplace's law by using the m-estimate of probabilities (Cestnik, 1990) instead:

$$P(C_i|node) = \frac{N(C_i \& node) + mP(C_i)}{N(node) + m}$$

where m is the parameter of the estimate and $P(C_i)$ is the prior probability of class C_i estimated from the whole training set. However, when pruning with the m-estimate the former disadvantage of the Laplace's law (the violation of the law of the entropy decrease) remains and, in addition, a paramater is introduced (m) that needs to be tuned.

Pessimistic pruning: Quinlan (1993) introduces the use of the confidence limits for the binomial distribution when estimating the upper bound of the error in the current node. Besides violating the statistical notions of sampling and confidence limits, the approach introduces a paramater, the confidence level, that has to be appropriately tuned.

Kovacic's MDL pruning: Kovacic (1995) uses a (rather complicated) coding scheme to encode the entire tree together with the classification of all training instances. Kovacic searches the space of all compressive trees. A tree is said to be compressive if the encoding length of the tree plus the encoding length of the classification of all instances given the tree is shorter than the description length of the classification of instances without the tree. From all compressive trees one with the minimal classification error on the training set is selected (Kovacic, 1995).

Besides the complexity of the encoding scheme, a problem with the approach is that the description length of the whole tree is nonlocally affected with the removal of the subtree. The proposed scheme is of course not optimal, as optimal coding is not computable (Li and Vitanyi, 1993). The removal of the subtree non-locally affects the encoding of the whole tree which in turn makes the coding scheme even less optimal. Besides, the criterion of the best classification accuracy on the training set is questionable as it favorizes the theories that (over)fit the training data. The experimental results of Kovacic (1995) are mixed which confirms the non-optimality of the approach.

3   A simple MDL-based pruning

We shall use the following scenario: given the description of the complete decision tree and the description of all training instances in terms of values for all attributes and the class label, find the pruned tree which minimizes the description length of the remaining structure of the tree plus the description length of the classification of all instances given the pruned tree. This problem can be solved with the solution of the following subproblem: for the given node and the corresponding subtree decide whether to prune the subtree or not by the MDL criterion. The decision is based on the difference between the decription length of the classification of instances that fall into the given node (treated as a leaf) and the description length of the structure of the subtree plus the description lengths of the classifications of the subsets of instances in all the leaves of the subtree. If the difference is negative (or equal zero), the subtree should be pruned. Note that by this scenario one need only the local measures of the description lengths and can ignore the other parts of the tree.

Recently Kononenko (1995) developed a MDL-measure for estimating the quality of attributes. The idea of the MDL-measure is to use an impurity measure equal to the encoding length of the classification of n instances into c classes:

$$Prior\_MDL(node) = \log \binom{n}{n_1, ..., n_c} + \log \binom{n + c - 1}{c - 1}$$

where n_i is the number of instances from the i-th class. The first term represents the encoding length of classes of n instances and the second term represents the encoding length of the class frequency distribution. Kononenko defined the quality of an attribute A with values $V_1..V_k$ as the compression, i.e. the difference between the encoding length of the node and the sum of encoding lengths of a successor for each value of the attribute:

$$MDL(A) = Prior\_MDL(node) - Post\_MDL(A, node)$$
$$= Prior\_MDL(node)$$

$$- \sum_{i=1}^{k} Prior\_MDL(child(V_i, node)) - \log \#attributes$$

The last term ($\log \#attributes$) is needed to encode the selected attribute in the current node which is, for the attribute selection problem, constant and can be ignored. Note that this measure estimates the compressiveness of an attribute when used as the root of a one-level subtree. For the above measure Kononenko (1995) empirically showed the most acceptable bias, among a series of different measures, when estimating the multivalued attributes.

We can straightforwardly generalize the above measure to estimate the compressiveness of the decision subtree. The generalized estimate can then be used for decision tree pruning. The subtree should be pruned if its compressiveness is negative or zero.

The *Prior_MDL* itself suffices for the estimation of the description length of the classification in one node (treated as a leaf). However, for the subtree we need to encode also the structure of the tree. By the above scenario the structure of the full tree is known in advance. Therefore, we need to encode only the label "not-prune" and need not to encode the actual attributes in the nodes. This label brings one additional bit for each internal node of the subtree. The formula is therefore as follows. For the node we have *Prior_MDL(node)* and for the subtree of the node we have:

$$Post\_MDL(subtree(node)) =$$

$$1 + \sum_{i=1}^{k} Post\_MDL(subtree(child(V_i, node)))$$

where $Post\_MDL(leaf) = Prior\_MDL(leaf)$.

The subtree is pruned if

$$Prior\_MDL(node) - Post\_MDL(subtree(node)) =$$

$$= MDL(node) \leq 0$$

The complete algorithm follows that of Cestnik and Bratko (1991) for post-pruning with the m-estimate of probabilities. The algorithm proceeds bottom-up from leaves towards the root of the complete tree and for each internal node makes a decision whether to prune the subtree or not by the $MDL(node) \leq 0$ criterion.

4 Empirical results

To verify the effectiveness of the proposed MDL measure we performed a series of experiments with 6 artificial datasets and 12 real-world data sets. Table 1 contains the basic description of datasets, most of which are available at Irvine database (Murphy and Aha, 1991).

We used three variants of algorithms for generating decision trees: one that uses the ReliefF algorithm for estimating the quality of attributes, one that uses information-gain, and one that uses ReliefF and generates one decision tree for each class. Kononenko and Simec (1995) developed ReliefF and used it for estimating the quality of the attributes when building decision trees. ReliefF is an extention of RELIEF, developed by Kira and Rendell (1992). In the following, for brevity, we give only the results of the first algorithm that uses ReliefF. The relative performance of different pruning algorithms is very similar for all three variants.

Table 1 Basic description of data sets

domain	#class	#atts.	#val/att.	# instances	maj.class (%)	entropy(bit)
BAYS	2	10	2.0	200	56	0.99
TREE	2	11	2.0	200	57	0.99
PAR2	2	12	2.0	200	54	0.99
PAR3	2	13	2.0	200	54	0.99
PAR4	2	14	2.0	400	50	1.00
BOOL	2	6	2.0	640	67	0.91
PRIM	22	17	2.2	339	25	3.89
BREA	2	10	2.7	288	80	0.73
LYMP	4	18	3.3	148	55	1.28
RHEU	6	32	9.1	355	66	1.73
HEPA	2	19	3.8	155	79	0.74
DIAB	2	8	8.8	768	65	0.93
HEART	2	13	5.0	270	56	0.99
SOYB	15	35	2.9	630	15	3.62
IRIS	3	4	6.0	150	33	1.59
ELPI	2	18	16.6	500	50	1.00
SEGM	7	19	8.3	2310	14	2.81
VOTE	2	16	2.0	435	61	0.96

We compared the performance of our MDL pruning with postpruning using the m-estimate of probabilities, which has been shown to perform comparably to existing methods (Cestnik and Bratko, 1991; Esposito et al., 1995). We show the results with the default value of parameter $m = 2$ (which is comparable with our parameterless method) and the best results with respect to the classification accuracy among different values of
$m \in \{0.0, 0.01, 0.1, 1.0, 2.0, 5.0, 10, 20, 50, 100\}$. Note that the latter results are an upper bound for the m-estimate as the parameter m is selected when the results on testing sets are already known.

In each domain we used 10 random splits of available data on 70% of instances for training and 30% for testing. A complete tree for each split was build and then pruned with different methods. The results in tables are the averages of ten runs. We measured the classification accuracy (see Table 2), information score (Kononenko and Bratko, 1991), and the number of leaves in the pruned tree (see Table 3). For brevity, we ommit the information score from the tables. The relative results are practically the same as that of classification accuracy. In tables 2 and 3 we provide also the standard deviations.

Table 2 Classification accuracy (%) achieved by different pruning methods

domain	no pruning	$m = 2$	best acc.	best m	MDL
BAYS	65.9 ± 5.6	69.8 ± 2.9	72.6 ±3.0	10	72.1 ± 3.1
TREE	76.1 ± 7.7	78.0 ± 7.8	81.3±6.1	20	80.1 ± 6.9
PAR2	94.1 ± 2.1	94.6 ± 2.7	95.6±2.2	100	95.6 ± 2.2
PAR3	91.5 ± 2.9	94.6 ± 3.0	96.4±2.8	20	95.8 ± 3.3
PAR4	91.3 ± 1.6	94.3 ± 0.9	95.0±1.4	20	94.4 ± 1.6
BOOL	90.5 ± 0.8	90.5 ± 0.8	90.5±0.8	2	90.5 ± 0.8
PRIM	39.5 ± 5.9	40.1 ± 5.8	40.1±5.8	2	41.1 ± 6.1
BREA	78.6 ± 4.6	78.5 ± 4.5	78.6±4.0	50	78.6 ± 4.0
LYMP	75.8 ± 5.3	75.8 ± 5.3	75.8±5.3	2	74.7 ± 3.9
RHEU	66.2 ± 4.3	66.2 ± 4.7	68.0±3.6	100	67.6 ± 4.3
HEPA	83.2 ± 3.8	83.0 ± 3.5	83.2±3.8	0	78.4 ± 4.7
DIAB	70.6 ± 3.1	70.9 ± 2.2	74.4±2.4	20	73.4 ± 2.2
HEART	76.8 ± 2.5	77.9 ± 2.9	79.7±4.0	10	79.3 ± 3.3
SOYB	87.5 ± 1.9	87.0 ± 2.8	87.5±1.9	0	86.2 ± 3.7
IRIS	95.2 ± 3.0	95.4 ± 2.6	96.1±3.3	100	95.6 ± 2.7
ELPI	81.1 ± 2.0	81.2 ± 2.1	81.6±1.9	10	82.1 ± 1.9
SEGM	89.5 ± 1.5	89.3 ± 1.6	89.5±1.5	0	86.9 ± 1.7
VOTE	95.1 ± 1.2	95.3 ± 1.3	95.4±1.0	100	95.0 ± 1.2

The classification accuracy achieved using the MDL-pruning and pruning using the m-estimate are practically the same in most of the domains and indeed in neither of the data sets there is any significant difference in the accuracy (with the confidence level 0.05) and in the information score. However, the numbers of leaves in Table 3 show that the trees generated by the MDL-pruning are significantly smaller when compared to $m = 2$ pruning and have comparable sizes with the trees generated by the "best m" pruning. In Table 2 we give also the actual value of m that gives the best classification accuracy. Note the high variation of the value of the best m in different domains. This suggests that, indeed, the parameter m has to be tuned and the user cannot rely on any default value of m.

The results on parity data sets of order 2 (PAR2), 3 (PAR3) and 4 (PAR4) suggest that the MDL criterion and the "best m" method are able to almost optimally prune the trees. These data sets contain 5% of class noise and the optimal trees contain 4, 8, and 16 leaves, respectively.

Table 3 The average number of leaves generated by different pruning methods

domain	no pruning	$m = 2$	"best m" size	MDL
BAYS	37.9 ± 4.5	20.2 ± 5.0	8.5±1.3	7.9 ± 1.1
TREE	31.2 ± 3.0	20.5 ± 2.4	7.1±2.0	10.2 ± 2.3
PAR2	7.8 ± 3.5	4.6 ± 1.3	4.0±0.0	4.0 ± 0.0
PAR3	14.0 ± 3.7	9.2 ± 1.3	8.0±0.0	8.3 ± 0.7
PAR4	28.1 ± 4.8	19.8 ± 1.4	16.3±0.7	17.6 ± 1.4
BOOL	54.0 ± 3.6	15.0 ± 0.0	15.0±0.0	15.0 ± 0.0
PRIM	44.4 ± 6.8	35.8 ± 7.3	35.8±7.3	26.0 ± 4.5
BREA	40.5 ± 5.0	27.5 ± 5.1	6.0±2.8	5.4 ± 3.1
LYMP	17.5 ± 1.3	17.0 ± 1.4	17.5±1.3	7.9 ± 2.1
RHEU	60.2 ± 7.3	54.1 ± 6.1	6.5±2.9	11.1 ± 2.9
HEPA	11.1 ± 4.0	9.8 ± 3.2	11.1±4.0	2.7 ± 2.0
DIAB	97.4 ± 6.5	62.4 ± 4.8	14.5±4.0	22.0 ± 6.9
HEART	39.8 ± 4.3	27.0 ± 5.2	14.2±2.2	12.7 ± 3.5
SOYB	40.6 ± 3.7	32.6 ± 2.3	40.6±3.7	22.6 ± 2.2
IRIS	7.3 ± 1.0	4.8 ± 1.6	3.0±0.0	3.5 ± 1.1
ELPI	47.8 ± 11.1	35.3 ± 5.5	13.4±3.5	21.5 ± 3.4
SEGM	56.9 ± 6.1	37.0 ± 7.8	56.9±6.1	21.9 ± 5.5
VOTE	7.8 ± 2.1	6.0 ± 1.6	2.0±0.0	5.6 ± 1.4

5 Conclusion

A natural and intuitive approach to the problem of decision tree pruning is to use the minimum description length principle. The proposed MDL criterion is simple, well founded and straightforward to implement. It doesn't require any parameter tuning and doesn't require a separate pruning set of instances. The empirical results suggest that it achieves the classification accuracy that is comparable to existing pruning methods and the resulting decision trees are almost optimally pruned.

During the beginning of the data analysis it is important to get an impression, what classification accuracy can be achieved with decision trees, and to get a feedback of which are important attributes and what relations do hold between the attributes and the class. Smaller decision trees are more simple and more readable and can provide more transparent insight into the classification problem at hand. For that reason, the analyst needs a prompt support from the induction algorithm, that must be able to quickly produce a small and accurate decision tree. The MDL-pruning is simple, well-founded, efficient, parameterless, and produces small and accurate decision trees. All these features makes it an attractive tool that can serve for efficiently generating a first approximation of the target decision tree in the knowledge discovery process. However, in the continuation of the data mining process the analyst may need more flexibility. This can be obtained by adding a parameter to the MDL criterion or by switching to other pruning methods, such as the m-estimate pruning.

Acknowledgments

I thank Matevž Kovačič and Uroš Pompe for discussions on the MDL principle and Janko Kampuš, Aljoša Počič, and Janez Resnik for their help in experiments. This work was supported by The Slovenian Ministry of Science and Technology.

References

1. I.Bratko, I.Kononenko. Learning diagnostic rules from incomplete and noisy data. In: B. Phelps (ed.) *Interactions in Artificial Intelligence and Statistical Methods*, Technical Press.
2. L. Breiman, J.H. Friedman, R.A. Olshen, and C.J. Stone. *Classification and Regression Trees*. Wadsworth International Group, 1984.
3. B. Cestnik. Estimating probabilities: A crucial task in machine learning. *Proc. European Conference on Artificial Intelligence ECAI-90*, Stockholm, August 1990, pp.147-149.
4. B. Cestnik and I. Bratko. On estimating probabilities in tree pruning. *Proc. European Working Session on Learning*, (Porto, March 1991), Y.Kodratoff (ed.), Springer Verlag. pp.138-150.
5. B. Cestnik, I. Kononenko, and I. Bratko. ASSISTANT 86 : A knowledge elicitation tool for sophisticated users. In: I. Bratko and N. Lavrac (eds.), *Progress in Machine Learning*. Wilmslow, England: Sigma Press.
6. F. Esposito, D. Malerba, and G. Semeraro. Simplifying decision trees by pruning and grafting: new results. *Proc. Europ. Conf. on Machine Learning ECML-95* (N. Lavrac and S. Wrobel, eds.), Springer Verlag, pp.287-290.
7. K. Kira and L. Rendell. A practical approach to feature selection. *Proc. Intern. Conf. on Machine Learning ICML-92* (Aberdeen, July 1992) D.Sleeman & P.Edwards (eds.), Morgan Kaufmann, pp.249-256.
8. I. Kononenko. On biases in estimating multivalued attributes. *Proc. Int. Joint Conf. on Artificial Intelligence IJCAI-95*, Montreal, August 20-25 1995, pp. 1034-1040.
9. I. Kononenko and I. Bratko. Information based evaluation criterion for classifier's performance. *Machine Learning*, 6:67-80.
10. I. Kononenko, I. Bratko, E. Roskar. Experiments in automatic learning of medical diagnostic rules. International School for the Synthesis of Expert's Knowledge Workshop ISSEK-84, Bled, Slovenia, August 1984.
11. I.Kononenko, E.Simec Induction of decision trees using ReliefF. In: G.Della Riccia, R.Kruse, and R.Viertl (eds.). *Mathematical and Statistical Methods in Artificial Intelligence*, Springer Verlag.
12. M. Kovacic. Stochastic Inductive Logic Programming. Ph.D. Thesis, University of Ljubljana, March 1995, (available at: http://ai.fri.uni-lj.si/papers/index.html).
13. M. Li and P. Vitanyi. *An introduction to Kolmogorov Complexity and its applications*, Springer Verlag, 1993.
14. J.Mingers. An empirical comparison of selection measures for decision tree induction. *Machine Learning*, 4:227-243.
15. P.M. Murphy and D.W. Aha. *UCI Repository of machine learning databases* [Machine-readable data repository]. Irvine, CA: University of California, Department of Information and Computer Science.

16. T. Niblett and I. Bratko. Learning decision rules in noisy domains. *Proc. Expert Systems 86*, Brighton, UK, December 1986.

17. J.R. Quinlan. Semi-autonomous acquisition of pattern-based knowledge. *Machine Intelligence 10* (J. Hayes, D. Michie, and J.H. Pao, eds.), Horwood & Wiley.

18. J.R. Quinlan. Simplifying decision trees. *Int. J. of Man-Machine Studies*, 27:221-234.

19. J.R. Quinlan. *C4.5 programs for machine learning*, Morgan Kaufmann.

20. J. Rissanen. Universal coding, information, prediction, and estimation. *IEEE Trans. on Information Theory*, 30(4):629-636.

Hybrid Search of Feature Subsets

Manoranjan Dash[1] and Huan Liu[2]

[1] BioInformatics Centre, National University of Singapore, Singapore 119074.
[2] School of Computing, National University of Singapore, Singapore 119260.

Abstract. Feature selection is a search problem for an "optimal" subset of features. The class separability is normally used as one of the basic feature selection criteria. Instead of maximizing the class separability as in the literature, this work adopts a criterion aiming to maintain the discriminating power of the data. After examining the pros and cons of two existing algorithms for feature selection, we propose a hybrid algorithm of probabilistic and complete search that can take advantage of both algorithms. It begins by running LVF (probabilistic search) to reduce the number of features; then it runs "Automatic Branch & Bound (ABB)" (complete search). By imposing a limit on the amount of time this algorithm can run, we obtain an approximation algorithm. The empirical study suggests that dividing the time equally between the two phases yields nearly the best performance, and that the hybrid search algorithm substantially outperforms earlier methods in general.

1 Introduction

The basic problem of classification is to classify a given pattern (example) to one of m known classes. A pattern of features presumably contains enough information to distinguish among the classes. When a classification problem is defined by features, the number of features (N) can be quite large. Pattern classification is inherently connected to information reduction. Features can be redundant or irrelevant. An irrelevant feature does not affect the underlying structure of the data in any way. A redundant feature does not provide anything new in describing the underlying structure. Because redundant and irrelevant information is cached inside the totality of the features, a classifier that uses all features will perform worse than a classifier that uses relevant features that maximize interclass differences and minimize intraclass differences [2]. Feature selection is a task of searching for "optimal" subset of features from all available features [4]. Its motivation is three-fold: *Simplifying the classifier; Improving the accuracy of the classifier; and Reducing data dimensionality for the classifier*. The last point is particularly relevant when a classifier is unable to handle large volume of data. The fundamental function of a feature selector is to extract, with appropriate tools, the most useful information from the representation vector (feature values), and present it in the form of a pattern vector of a lower dimensionality whose elements represent only the most significant aspects of the input data [5, 11].

In order to measure the usefulness (or optimality) of selected features, we need selection criteria to measure feature goodness. The class separability is often used as one of the basic selection criteria. When a set of features maximizes the class separability, it is considered to be well suited for classification [17]. From a statistics viewpoint, five different measurements for class separability are analyzed in [5]: error probability, interclass distance, probabilistic distance, probabilistic dependence and entropy. Information-theoretic considerations [20] suggested something similar: using a good feature of discrimination provides compact descriptions of each of the two classes, and these descriptions are maximally distinct. Geometrically, this constraint can be interpreted to mean that (i) such a feature takes on nearly identical values for all examples of the same class, and (ii) it takes on some different values for all examples of the other class. In this work, we use a selection criterion that does not try to maximize the class separability but tries to retain the discriminating power of the data defined by original features. That is, feature selection is formalized as finding the smallest set of features that is "consistent" in describing classes with the full set, where a set S of features is consistent if no two examples with the same values on S have different class labels [1]. Applying this criterion does make feature selection simpler and the class separability of the original data can be retained.

This aspect of feature selection is related to the study of search strategies. Extensive research effort has been devoted to this study [19, 18, 10]. Examples are Branch & Bound [15, 18], Relief [6, 9], Wrapper methods [7], Approximate Markov Blanket [8], and LVF [13]. The search process starts with either an empty set or a full set. For the former, it expands the search space by adding one feature at a time (Step-wise Forward Selection) - an example is Focus [1]; for the latter, it expands the search space by deleting one feature at a time (Step-wise Backward Selection) - an example is 'Branch & Bound' [15]. If the size of the smallest consistent feature set is even moderately large, Focus will take a long time. Similarly, if there are a moderate number of irrelevant features, 'Branch and Bound' will take a long time. A third, more robust, option is to start with a random feature set and expand the search space by randomly generating new subsets (e.g., LVF [13]). In the rest of the paper P is the number of patterns, N is the number of features, and M is the minimal size of features.

The above three representative methods are designed for different situations. When the minimal size (M) is small, it is sensible to apply Focus since 2^M is not large; when M is large, that is, most features are relevant, it is reasonable to apply 'Branch & Bound' assuming there exists a monotonic measure; and when M is neither large nor small, it is suitable to apply LVF. This work aims at a hybrid algorithm that takes advantage of these three algorithms.

The contributions of this paper are: adopting a selection criterion to be used by all three algorithms; and proposing and implementing a hybrid search algorithm for feature selection which is better than any of the non-hybrid algorithms in terms of time and accuracy of a classifer. In Section 2, we briefly review LVF and ABB [12] and perform experiments and analysis to investigatetheir strengths and weaknesses. In Section 3, we propose to combine LVF and ABB based on the results in Section 2, and consider when such a hybrid algorithm should be switched from LVF to ABB, given a certain amount of time, in order to achieve the best performance. In Section 4, we compare the algorithms on several datasets and evaluate the benefits of the hybrid search. The paper concludes in Section 5 with guidelines on applying FocusM, ABB and the hybrid (QBB).

2 Probabilistic Search and 'Branch & Bound'

We review two algorithms, LVF (probabilistic) [13] and ABB (complete) [12] and explore their advantages and disadvantages. Both methods use an *inconsistency rate* as the feature goodness measure (U). In [12], it is shown that U is a monotonic measure. For detailed accounts, refer to [11]. In all the algorithms S is the original feature set and D is the dataset.

2.1 LVF

This is a Las Vegas algorithm [3] for feature subset selection which makes probabilistic choices of subsets in search of an optimal set. LVF keeps the smallest subset of features randomly generated so far that satisfies a threshold (by default it is the inconsistency rate of the data with all features). It is fast in reducing number of features and can produce optimal solutions if computing resources permit. In the algorithm *inConCal* is a function that calculates the inconsistency of a feature set and returns the inconsistency rate and 'yet another solution' means a solution of the same size as the last found solution.

$\delta = inConCal(S, D)$;
$T = S$;
LVF(S, $MaxTries$, D) {
   for j=1 to $MaxTries$ {
      randomly choose a subset of features, S_j;
      if $card(S_j) \leq card(T)$
         if $inConCal(S_j, D) \leq \delta$
            if $card(S_j) < card(T)$
               $T = S_j$;
               output S_j;
            else
               append S_j to T;
               output S_j as 'yet another solution'; }
   return T; }

Experiments and Analysis

We have conducted experiments to observe how the number of valid features (M') drops as the number of randomly generated feature sets increases. A total of 10 datasets, both artificial and real, are chosen for the experiments from the UC Irvine data repository [14] (Table 1). Two typical graphs are shown in Figure 1.

Data	LED24	Lung	Lymph	Mush	Par	Promo	Soy	Splice	Vote	Zoo
N	24	56	18	22	12	57	35	60	16	16
$M'(M)$	12(5)	19(4)	8(6)	8(4)	5(3)	15(4)	12(2)	19(9)	13(8)	9(5)
#Eval	230	155	215	22	25	187	42	284	215	25
#Max	2^{24}	2^{56}	2^{18}	2^{22}	2^{12}	2^{57}	2^{35}	2^{60}	2^{16}	2^{16}

Table 1. The number of valid features drops sharply in the first few hundred runs for all the datasets. N and M are defined earlier. #Eval is number of subsets generated and evaluated. #Max is maximum possible subsets.

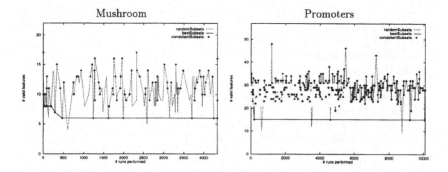

Fig. 1. The typical trends of the decreasing number of valid features versus the number of runs performed.

The *trend* found in all the experiments is that M' drops sharply from N in the first few hundred runs (one run means one feature set is randomly generated and evaluated). Afterwards, it takes quite a long time to further decrease M'. Some analysis would confirm this finding. A particular set has a probability of $1/2^N$ to be generated. At the beginning, the full set is a valid one. Many subsets can satisfy the inconsistency criterion. As M' decreases from N to M, fewer and fewer subsets can satisfy the criterion. However, the probability of a distinct set being generated is still $1/2^N$. That explains why the curves have a sharp drop in the beginning and then become flat.

2.2 ABB

Branch & Bound for feature selection was first proposed in [15]. It starts with a full set of features, removes one feature at a time. If the full set contains three features, the root is (1 1 1). Its child nodes are (1 1 0), (1 0 1), and (0 1 1), etc. When there is no restriction on expanding nodes in the search space, this could lead to an exhaustive search. However, if each node is evaluated by a measure U and an upper limit is set for the acceptable values of U, then Branch & Bound backtracks whenever an infeasible node is discovered. If U is monotonic, no feasible node is omitted as a result of early backtracking and, therefore, gained savings of search time do not violate the optimality of the selected subset. As was pointed out in [19], the measures used in [15] have disadvantages (non-monotonicity is one); the authors of [19] proposed approximate monotonicity.

ABB is a Branch & Bound algorithm where the bound is the inconsistency rate of the dataset with the full set of features. It starts with the full set of features S^0, removes one feature from S_j^{l-1} in turn to generate subsets S_j^l where l is the current level and j specifies different subsets at the lth level. If $U(S_j^l) > U(S_j^{l-1})$, S_j^l stops growing (its branch is pruned), otherwise, it grows to level $l + 1$, in other words, one more feature will be removed.

```
δ = inConCal(S, D);
ABB (S, D) {
    /* subset generation */
    For all feature f in S {
        S₁ = S − f; /* remove one feature at a time */
        enQueue(Q, S₁);} /* add at the end */
    while notEmpty(Q) {
        S₂ = deQueue(Q); /* remove at the start */
        if (S₂ is legitimate ∧ inConCal(S₂, D) ≤ δ )
            /* recursion */
            ABB (S₂, D); }}
```

The legitimacy test is to test whether a node (subset) is a child node of a pruned node. A node is illegitimate if it is a child node of a pruned one. Each node is represented by a binary vector where 1's stand for presence of a particular feature in that subset and 0's for its absence. The test is done by checking the Hamming distance between the child node under consideration and pruned nodes. If the Hamming distance with any pruned node is 1 (i.e., the difference of the two representative binary vectors is 1), the child node is the pruned node's child. Thus found all illegitimate nodes at a level.

ABB guarantees an optimal solution. However, a brief analysis can tell us that ABB's time performance can deteriorate if M is not large with respect to N. This issue is directly related to the size of the search space, or, how many nodes (subsets) have been generated. The other factors about time complexity of ABB are (1) time complexity of inconsistency checking, which is $O(P)$; and (2) time complexity of legitimacy test, which is $O(N)$. As they are relatively the same for each node, so the key factor is the search space. The search space of ABB is closely related to the number of relevant features. In general, the more the number of relevant features, the smaller the search space due to the early pruning of the illegitimate nodes.

In summary, our findings are: (1) LVF reduces the number of features quickly during the initial stage; but searches in the same way (i.e., blindly) after that, wasting the computing resource on generating subsets that are obviously illegitimate; and (2) on the other hand, ABB expands the search space quickly but is inefficient in reducing the search space although it guarantees optimal results.

3 Hybrid Search

The combination of LVF and ABB brings about a hybrid algorithm QBB. It runs LVF in the first phase and records all the subsets output by it. Next it runs ABB over each subset output by LVF. ABB, instead of starting from the complete feature set, now initializes the starting set by the subsets output by LVF, and keeps the minimum sized subsets so that ABB is more focused. In this way, LVF and ABB complement each other.

```
δ = inConCal(S, D); T = S;
QBB (S, D) {
    S' = LVF(S, MaxTries, D);
    /* All legitimate subsets from LVF are in S' */
    MinSize = card(S);
    for all S_j in S' {
        T' = ABB(S_j, D);
        if MinSize > card(T') {
            MinSize = card(T');
            T = S_j; }}
    return T; }
```

There are two major issues affecting the efficacy of QBB: 1. when one should choose QBB over ABB, and 2. the crossing point at which ABB takes over from LVF. ABB may not terminate in a realistic time (a few hours) for datasets having large N but not so large M. So we restrict the size of N (say $N \leq 9$), no matter what the size of M is, ABB can stop in a reasonable time (more in Conclusion). The second issue is regarding the point where ABB takes over from LVF. If we allow only a certain amount of time to run QBB, the point at which ABB takes over from LVF is crucial for the efficiency of QBB. We conducted a number of experiments to determine a robust crossing point. Ten datasets (summarized in Table 2) with both P and N varying substantially are taken. We set five different total numbers of runs[1] (*TotalRuns* = 1K, 2K, 3K, 4K, and 5K) for LVF and ABB together. For each experiment 9 crossing points were set at every tenth of *TotalRuns*. Each of these experiments was conducted 50 times to average out the probabilistic nature of LVF in QBB. Hence, a total of 10*5*9*50 = 22500 experiments were conducted. In Figure 2, we show three graphs with different levels of details. Figure 2(a) displays the results for all the datasets when the *TotalRuns* is 3000; Figure 2(b) shows the average results over all the datasets for different *TotalRuns*; and Figure 2(c) is the average over all datasets and *TotalRuns*. These graphs show that results are better when the crossing point is around the middle of *TotalRuns* (i.e., 0.5*TotalRuns*) than when it is near the beginning or the end. The conclusion is that dividing the total time equally between LVF and ABB is a robust solution and is more likely to yield the best results. A simple analysis of this result would show that if the crossing point is quite early, then LVF might not have reduced the valid subset

---

[1] Here one run means generating and evaluating a subset of features.

size substantially for ABB to perform well[2], and if the crossing point is quite late, then the small sized subsets generated by LVF at the crossing point might not contain any minimal size subset.

	LED24	Lung	Lymph	Mush	Par	Promo	Soy	Splice	Vote	Zoo
D_{Tr}	800	21	100	4750	42	71	30	2126	300	50
D_{To}	1200	32	148	7125	64	106	47	3190	435	74
M	5	4	6	4	3	4	2	9	8	5
M_{QBB}	5.0	6.36	6.54	4.24	3.0	5.6	2.38	9.0	8.0	5.0

Table 2. QBB does well for most of the datasets. D_{Tr} - training data size for feature selection, D_{To} - total data size, M - minimal size, and M_{Avg} - average size by QBB.

4 Futher Experiments

We want to verify that (1) QBB can find minimal size feature subsets most of the time; (2) it is faster than LVF, ABB, and FocusM in general; (3) Subsets chosen by QBB achieve nearly equal or better accuracy for two different kinds of classifiers (decision tree and neural networks) than the full feature sets do; and (4) QBB is particularly suitable for huge datasets. The experimental procedure is: (1) choose the datasets frequently used by the community; (2) run ABB to get the minimal size as reference; (3) compare the performance (average time and number of selected features) of QBB with that of LVF, FocusM and ABB; and (4) compare the accuracy of two different classifiers (C4.5 [16] and Back-propagation neural network [21]) over datasets before and after feature selection.

A total of 10 datasets, both artificial and real, are chosen for the experiments from the UC Irvine data repository [14]. The Par3+3 dataset is a modified version of the original Parity3 dataset. The target concept is the parity of three bits. It contains 12 features: 3 relevant, 3 redundant, others irrelevant.

Table 2 shows the results of QBB over the 10 datasets. To average out the probabilistic nature of LVF in QBB, each experiment is conducted 50 times. In each experiment *TotalRuns* is set to 5K and crossing point is 0.5 as per our previous finding. The experiments show that $M_{QBB} = M$ all the time for many datasets (e.g., LED-24, Par3+3, Vote), whereas for others M_{QBB} exceeds M by a small margin.

Figure 3 shows *a comparison of the performance (both average time and number of selected features) of QBB with that of LVF, FocusM, and ABB*. First ABB

---

[2] For some datasets, ABB by itself only does not terminate in realistic time (a few hours) as M is very small compared to N for these datasets.

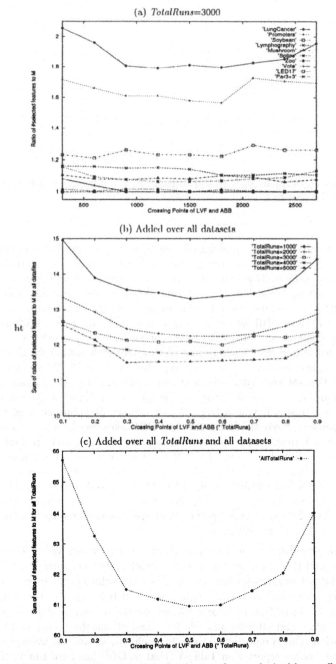

Fig. 2. Experimental results show that best results are obtained by equally dividing the time between LVF and ABB.

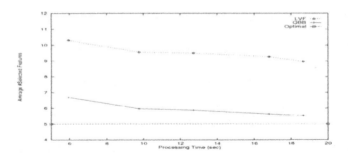

Fig. 3. Experimental results show that QBB performs well in comparison to FocusM, LVF, and ABB in general.

is run over the 10 datasets to find the M (minimal size) values. For comparison purpose we have calculated the average minimal value, M_{Avg}, over all datasets which is found to be 5. This value is used as a reference line in Figure 3. Out of the 4 competing algorithms, FocusM and ABB are deterministic, whereas LVF and QBB are non-deterministic due to their probabilistic nature. Hence, to compare LVF and QBB we chose 5 different sets of runs (i.e., *TotalRuns* = 1K, ... , 5K). QBB spends half of the time running LVF and the other half running ABB.Each experiment was repeated 50 times for each dataset for LVF and QBB, and the average size and time are reported in Figure 3. Notice that the outcomes of FocusM and ABB are not shown in the graph as the average time taken by them falls outside the range of the 'processing time' in the x-axis of the graph.For datasets having a large N and a small M values such as Lung Cancer, Promoters, Soybean, Splice datasets ABB takes very long time (a number of hours) to terminate. For datasets having large N value and substantially big M value such as Splice dataset FocusM takes many hours to terminate. The comparison in Figure 3 shows that QBB is more efficient both in average time and number of selected features compared to LVF, FocusM, and ABB. The average size of the subsets produced by QBB is close to M_{Avg} and it approaches to M_{Avg} with time. LVF is poor in finding small sized consistent subsets although it reaches a mediocre size very soon.

The error probability is often used as a validation criterion. We choose C4.5 decision tree and Back-propagation neural network as two classifiers for validation. Each dataset was divided into a training set (two-third of the original size) and a testing set (one-third of the original size). QBB is run over the training set to find a subset of features. For C4.5, we use the default settings, apply it to datasets before and after feature selection, and obtain the results of 10-fold cross-validation. This is repeated 10 times for each dataset and the average error rate and tree size are reported in Table 3. That is, QBB has been run 10 times and C4.5 100 times. It shows improvement for most of the datasets (9 out of 10) in C4.5's accuracy after feature selection.

| Data | C4.5 | | | | Back-Propagation | | | |
| | Tree Size | | Error Rate | | | | Error Rate | |
	Bef	Aft	Bef	Aft	Cycles	#HU	Bef	Aft
LED-24	19.0	19.0	0.0	0.0	1000	12	0.06	0.0
Lung	19.0	10.9	50.0	41.8	1000	28	75.0	75.0
Lymphography	26.9	22.1	21.8	21.4	7000	9	25.0	25.0
Mushroom	36.3	34.2	0.0	0.0	5000	11	0.0	0.0
Par3+3	12.0	15.0	41.9	0.0	1000	6	22.2	0.0
Promoters	21.4	8.2	26.3	22.1	2000	29	46.8	25.0
Soybean	7.1	9.4	2.5	2.0	1000	18	10.0	0.0
Splice	173.0	187.0	5.9	14.0	6000	30	25.64	42.33
Vote	14.5	14.2	5.3	5.3	4000	8	6.7	4.0
Zoo	17.8	17.7	7.8	6.6	4000	8	10.3	3.4

Table 3. Classifier results. #HU is number of Hidden Units.

Running Back-propagation involves the setting of some parameters, such as the network structure (number of layers, number of hidden units), learning rate, momentum, number of CYCLES (epochs), etc. In order to focus our attention on the effect of feature selection by QBB, we try to minimize the tuning of the parameters for each dataset. We fix the learning rate as 0.1, the momentum as 0.5, one hidden layer, the number of hidden units as half of the original input units for all datasets. The experiment is carried out in two steps: (1) a trial run to find a proper number of CYCLES for each dataset which is determined by a sustained trend of no decrease of error; and (2) two runs on datasets with and without feature selection respectively using the number of CYCLES found in step 1. Other parameters remain fixed for the two runs in step 2. The results are shown in Table 3. In most cases, error rate decreases (6 out of 10) or does not change (3 out of 10) after feature selection.

The fact that the consistency criterion does not incorporate any bias relating to a particular classifier enables it to be used with a variety of different learning algorithms. As shown above, for the two different types of classifiers, selected features improve the performance in terms of lower error rates in most cases. On the other hand, since a set of features is deemed consistent if *any* function maps from the values of the features to the class labels, any algorithm optimizing this criterion may choose a small set of features that has a complicated function, while overlooking larger sets of features admitting simple rules. Although intuitively this should be relatively rare, it can happen in practice, as apparently was the case for the Splice dataset where both C4.5 and Back-propagation's performance deteriorate after feature selection.

QBB is quite helpful for datasets of huge N. For such datasets both Focus-M and ABB are inefficient because of their complete search from the empty set (as in Focus-M) or from the complete set (as in ABB). LVF also is not helpful because the hugeness of the dataset reduces the efficiency of a pure probabilistic search. To prove this point we ran LVF, QBB, ABB, and Focus-M on the Letter dataset with 20,000 patterns. LVF was not able to reduce the size in any of its run. Focus-M took more than 2 days to finish and produce an minimal size feature set of 11 features. ABB took more than 7 hours to produce the minimal size feature set. For QBB in all its run with totalRuns set to 5000, it produced the minimal size feature sets in less than 2 hours.

5 Concluding Remarks

We have proposed a hybrid algorithm (QBB) for feature selection which tries to maximize the use of both probabilistic and exhaustive search. The hybrid algorithm is shown to be robust, probabilistic, and approaches an optimal solution faster than previously proposed methods such as FocusM, LVF and ABB in a general setting. Two different types of classifiers (C4.5, Back-propagation) are employed to verify whether features of various datasets selected by QBB can pass the ultimate error probability criterion.

In this work, we have investigated several feature selection algorithms (FocusM, LVF, ABB). The guideline of taking maximum advantages of these different algorithms can be summarized into a simple procedure as follows:

If M is known as SMALL

    Apply **FocusM**

Else If $N \leq 9$

    Apply **ABB**

Else

    Apply **QBB**

SMALL is a floating concept which depends on the time available. Furthermore, M is usually not known *a priori*, though sometimes, we can pre-specify a number in some applications (e.g., visualization). So, without any knowledge about M, we often end up making a choice between **ABB** and **QBB**.

Acknowledgement

The authors wish to thank P. M. Long for his insightful comments.

References

1. H. Almuallim and T.G. Dietterich. Learning with many irrelevant features. In *Proceedings of the Ninth National Conference on Artificial Intelligence*, pages 547–552, Anaheim, California, 1991. AAAI Press/The MIT Press, Menlo Park, California.
2. A.L. Blumer, A. Ehrenfeucht, D. Haussler, and M.K. Warmuth. Occam's razor. In J.W. Shavlik and T.G. Dietterich, editors, *Readings in Machine Learning*, pages 201–204. Morgan Kaufmann, 1990.
3. G. Brassard and P. Bratley. *Fundamentals of Algorithms*. Prentice Hall, New Jersey, 1996.

4. M. Dash and H. Liu. Feature selection methods for classifications. *Intelligent Data Analysis: An International Journal*, 1(3), 1997. http://www-east.elsevier.com/ida/free.htm.

5. P.A. Devijver and J. Kittler. *Pattern Recognition: A Statistical Approach*. Prentice Hall International, 1982.

6. K. Kira and L.A. Rendell. The feature selection problem: Traditional methods and a new algorithm. In *Proceedings of the Tenth National Conference on Artificial Intelligence*, pages 129–134. Menlo Park: AAAI Press/The MIT Press, 1992.

7. R. Kohavi. *Wrappers for performance enhancement and oblivious decision graphs*. PhD thesis, Department of Computer Science, Standford University, Stanford, CA, 1995.

8. D. Koller and M. Sahami. Toward optimal feature selection. In L. Saitta, editor, *Machine Learning: Proceedings of the Thirteenth International Conference (ICML-96), July 3-6, 1996*, pages 284–292, Bari, Italy, 1996. San Francisco: Morgan Kaufmann Publishers.

9. I. Kononenko. Estimating attributes : Analysis and extension of RELIEF. In F. Bergadano and L. De Raedt, editors, *Proceedings of the European Conference on Machine Learning, April 6-8*, pages 171–182, Catania, Italy, 1994. Berlin: Springer-Verlag.

10. P. Langley. Selection of relevant features in machine learning. In *Proceedings of the AAAI Fall Symposium on Relevance*. AAAI Press, 1994.

11. H. Liu and H. Motoda. *Feature Selection for Knowledge Discovery Data Mining*. Boston: Kluwer Academic Publishers, 1998.

12. H. Liu, H. Motoda, and M. Dash. A monotonic measure for optmial feature selection. In C. Nedellec and C. Rouveirol, editors, *Machine Learning: ECML-98, April 21 - 23, 1998*, pages 101–106, Chemnitz, Germany, April 1998. Berlin Heidelberg: Springer-Verlag.

13. H. Liu and R. Setiono. A probabilistic approach to feature selection - a filter solution. In L. Saitta, editor, *Proceedings of International Conference on Machine Learning (ICML-96), July 3-6, 1996*, pages 319–327, Bari, Italy, 1996. San Francisco: Morgan Kaufmann Publishers, CA.

14. C.J. Merz and P.M. Murphy. UCI repository of machine learning databases. http://www.ics.uci.edu/~mlearn/MLRepository.html. Irvine, CA: University of California, Department of Information and Computer Science, 1996.

15. P.M. Narendra and K. Fukunaga. A branch and bound algorithm for feature subset selection. *IEEE Trans. on Computer*, C-26(9):917–922, September 1977.

16. J.R. Quinlan. *C4.5: Programs for Machine Learning*. Morgan Kaufmann, 1993.

17. T.W. Rauber. *Inductive Pattern Classification Methods - Features - Sensors*. PhD thesis, Dept. of Electrical Engineering, Universidade Nova de Lisboa, Lisboa, 1994.

18. J. C. Schlimmer. Efficiently inducing determinations : a complete and systematic search algorithm that uses optimal pruning. In *Proceedings of the Tenth International Conference on Machine Learning*, pages 284–290, 1993.

19. W. Siedlecki and J. Sklansky. On automatic feature selection. *International Journal of Pattern Recognition and Artificial Intelligence*, 2:197–220, 1988.

20. S. Watanabe. *Pattern Recognition: Human and Mechanical*. Wiley Interscience, 1985.

21. A. Zell and et al. Stuttgart neural network simulator (SNNS), user manual, version 4.1. Technical Report 6/95, Institute for Parallel and Distributed High Performance Systems (IPVR), University of Stuttgart, FTP: ftp.informatik.uni-stuttgart.de/pub/SNNS, 1995.

Concurrent Discretization of Multiple Attributes

Ke Wang and Bing Liu

School of Computing Science
National University of Singapore
{wangk,liub}@comp.nus.edu.sg

Abstract. Better decision trees can be learnt by merging continuous values into intervals. Merging of values, however, could introduce inconsistencies to the data, or information loss. When it is desired to maintain a certain consistency, interval mergings in one attribute could disable those in another attribute. This interaction raises the issue of determining the order of mergings. We consider a globally greedy heuristic that selects the "best" merging from *all* continuous attributes at each step. We present an implementation of the heuristic in which the best merging is determined in a time independent of the number of possible mergings. Experiments show that intervals produced by the heuristic lead to improved decision trees.

1 Introduction

1.1 Motivation

Continuous values, mainly reals and integers, are linearly ordered. Unlike discrete values, there could be many continuous values and each appears only a few times in the data. Directly applying induction algorithms designed for discrete values to continuous values will generate too many rules with poor predictive power. A common technique for handling continuous values is *discretization*, that is, merging adjacent values into intervals if their distinction contributes little to the structure of the problem. However, such mergings could introduce inconsistencies to the data where two examples with the same attribute values have conflicting classes, consequently, leaves little room for an induction algorithm to do its job. On the other hand, when the inconsistency level is constrained, interval mergings in different attributes are no longer independent of each other. Let us explain using an example.

Example 1. Consider the data in Table 1(A) where the underlying concept for Class star is

$$Age \leq 40 \land Salary \geq 50K \rightarrow Class = star.$$

ChiMerge [2] starts with one interval per continuous value and repeatedly merges two adjacent intervals that are most similar in the attribute being considered, measured by the smallest χ^2 value of two adjacent intervals. The merging process is stopped by a threshold on the χ^2 value. If the threshold is too small, similar intervals cannot be merged. If the threshold is too large, an attribute, say Age, may be over-merged, which prevents other attributes, say Salary, from being merged due to a consistency requirement. In particular, if all ages were merged into one interval, to keep the data consistent, the intervals in Salary at the best can be S1=[40K], S2=[50K], S3=[54K], S4=[57K,59K], as in Table 1(B). [1] These intervals give rise to the rules

$$Salary \in S2 \rightarrow Class = star$$
$$Salary \in S4 \rightarrow Class = star,$$

which clearly do not capture the underlying concept. A similar argument applies if Salary is merged into one interval first.

A

Age	Salary	Class
33	50K	star
39	57K	star
40	59K	star
45	54K	non-star
35	40K	non-star

B

Age	Salary	Class
A_1	S_2	star
A_1	S_4	star
A_1	S_4	star
A_1	S_3	non-star
A_1	S_1	non-star

C

Age	Salary	Class
A_2	S_2	star
A_2	S_2	star
A_2	S_2	star
A_1	S_2	non-star
A_2	S_1	non-star

Table 1. A motivating example

Suppose we always merge the two adjacent intervals that have the smallest χ^2 value in the two attributes (rather than in the attribute being considered), the following sequence of mergings can be produced:

step 1. Salary: $[40K] \overset{2.0}{\rightarrow} [50K] \overset{0.0}{\rightarrow} [57K] \overset{0.0}{\rightarrow} [59K]$

step 2. Age: $[33] \overset{2.0}{\rightarrow} [35] \overset{2.0}{\rightarrow} [39] \overset{0.0}{\rightarrow} [40] \overset{2.0}{\rightarrow} [45]$

step 3. Salary: $[40K] \overset{3.0}{\rightarrow} [50K, 57K] \overset{0.0}{\rightarrow} [59K]$

step 4. Salary: $[40K] \overset{4.0}{\rightarrow} [50K, 59K]$

step 5. Age: $[33] \overset{2.0}{\rightarrow} [35] \overset{3.0}{\rightarrow} [39, 40] \overset{3.0}{\rightarrow} [45]$

step 6. Age: $[33, 35] \overset{4.0}{\rightarrow} [39, 40] \overset{3.0}{\rightarrow} [45]$

step 7. Age: $[33, 40] \overset{1.33}{\rightarrow} [45]$

where "$\rightarrow$" links all adjacent intervals, and the χ^2 value for two adjacent intervals is written between them. For example, at step 3 intervals [50K] and [57K] are merged into [50K,57K], at step 4 intervals [50K,57K] and [59K] are merged into [50K,59K], etc. Steps 4 and 7 give the final intervals for Salary and Age because further mergings make the data inconsistent. Table 1(C) shows the data

---

[1] Note that we simplify the presentation by considering only observed values for the boundary of an interval.

discretized by these final intervals, from which we can easily induce the correct rules

$$Age \in A_2 \wedge Salary \in S_2 \rightarrow Class = star.$$

This example shows that at each step merging the best pair of adjacent intervals, whatever attributes they come from, leads to better rules.

1.2 Main results

Given an inconsistency threshold, mergings of intervals are no longer independent of each other. We propose a globally greedy heuristic that at each step merges the "best" pair of intervals chosen from *all* continuous attributes, rather than the attribute being considered. The idea is simple: given the limited tolerance of inconsistency, the best merging in all continuous attributes should be considered first. We consider two goodness measures of mergings, the χ^2 value and the change in entropy. A distinctive feature of the global greediness is that mergings in several attributes are *concurrent*, in the sense that mergings in attribute A can be performed without completing all mergings in attribute B.

Two questions need to be answered. First, is it really a good idea to be globally greedy when the goodness of mergings itself is only a heuristic. In other words, can the quality of rules learnt really be improved by being globally greedy. We conducted several experiments to answer this question.

The second question is: can the globally greedy heuristic be implemented efficiently, especially for large datasets. At each step, a critical operation is to find the best merging across all continuous attributes. It does not work to sort all possible mergings by their goodness and perform mergings in the sorted order because early mergings will affect the goodness of later ones. Scanning all pairs of adjacent intervals for each merge is not acceptable because the merging is performed frequently, in the worst case, equal to the number of distinct values. We propose the *Merge-tree* to find the best merging in a time independent of the number of intervals.

2 ConMerge Algorithm

The proposed algorithm, called *ConMerge* (for Concurrent Merger), consists of an initialization step and a bottom-up merging process. In the initialization step, we put each continuous value into its own interval. In the merging process, we repeatedly select the best pair of adjacent intervals from *all* continuous attributes according to a goodness criterion. The selected pair are merged if doing so does not exceed a user-specified inconsistency threshold. (By default, the inconsistency in the original data is used, but can be overridden by a larger value.) If the pair are not merged, the merging of this pair is excluded from further consideration. The merging process is repeated until no more merging is possible. This is described below.

Conceptual **ConMerge**:
Initialization:
    sort observed values for each continuous attribute;
    put each continuous value into its own interval;
Merging process:
    while there are interval pairs to merge **do**
        select the best interval pair from all continuous attributes;
        if merging the pair does not exceed the inconsistency threshold
            then merge the pair into one interval
            else exclude the pair from further merging;

Several questions remain to be answered: (a) how is the inconsistency formally defined, (b) what is a goodness criterion of mergings, (c) how is the above algorithm implemented efficiently, (d) does it produce good intervals. We answer (a) and (b) in the rest of this section. (c) and (d) will be addressed in sections on Implementation and Empirical Evaluation, respectively.

2.1 Inconsistency rate

Inconsistency refers to conflicting class information for examples that agree on all attributes. For a set of examples agreeing on all attributes, called a *matching pattern*, the *inconsistency count* is the number of examples in the set minus the number of examples belonging to a majority class in the set. For example, suppose that, for a set of n examples having the same matching pattern, c_1, c_2, c_3 are the numbers of examples for class 1, 2, and 3, where $c_1 + c_2 + c_3 = n$. If c_1 is the largest, the inconsistency count for the matching pattern is $c_2 + c_3$. The *inconsistency rate* is the sum of all inconsistency counts (for all matching patterns) divided by the total number of examples. The following monotonicity of inconsistency rate implies that if two adjacent intervals cannot be merged because of execeding the inconsistency threshold, they cannot be merged later. (The proof is straightforward, so omitted.)

Theorem 1. *Merging two adjacent intervals does not decrease the inconsistency rate of the data.*

To check the inconsistency threshold, in the merging process we can keep track of inconsistency counts for each interval. Each time two intervals I_1 and I_2 are merged, we find inconsistency counts for the merged interval $I_1 \cup I_2$ by sorting examples in $I_1 \cup I_2$ on all attribute values. If the sorting was kept for each of I_1 and I_2, the sorting for $I_1 \cup I_2$ can be obtained by merging the sorted lists for I_1 and I_2. Therefore, for each merging operation the inconsistency threshold can be checked by a linear scan of examples in the two intervals merged.

In the presence of unknown values, the inconsistency count is defined as follows. If example e has known values on attributes $A_1, \ldots, A_p$, e will match the pattern that agrees with e on $A_1, \ldots, A_p$ and has the largest number of examples. The inconsistency rate is defined as before.

2.2 Merging criteria

We consider two goodness criteria for the merging of two intervals.

The χ^2 value. The χ^2 value of two adjacent intervals, first used in [2], is a statistic measure about how the class is independent of the choice of the two intervals. A smaller χ^2 value implies more independence, or equivalently, less significance in distinguishing the two intervals. Therefore, the smaller the χ^2 value, the more similar the two intervals. The χ^2 value of two adjacent intervals is computed by

$$\chi^2 = \Sigma_{i=1}^m \Sigma_{j=1}^k \frac{(C_{ij}-E_{ij})^2}{E_{ij}}, \text{ where}$$

$m = 2$ (the 2 intervals being compared)
$k =$ number of classes
$C_{ij} =$ number of examples in ith interval, jth class
$R_i =$ number of examples in ith interval $= \Sigma_{j=1}^k A_{ij}$
$C_j =$ number of examples in jth class $= \Sigma_{i=1}^m C_{ij}$
$N =$ total number of examples $= \Sigma_{j=1}^k C_j$
$E_{ij} =$ expected frequency of $C_{ij} = \frac{R_i * C_j}{N}$

The change in entropy. The entropy for the ith interval I_i is defined as

$$ent(I_i) = -\Sigma_j \frac{C_{ij}}{R_i} log_2 \frac{C_{ij}}{R_i},$$

where C_{ij} and and R_i are as before. The more mixed the classes in interval I_i, the larger $ent(I_i)$. Let $I_1 \cup I_2$ denote the merged interval of I_1 and I_2. The change of the entropy after merging I_1 and I_2 is given by

$$\Delta = ent(I_1 \cup I_2) - \frac{R_1}{R_1+R_2}ent(I_1) - \frac{R_2}{R_1+R_2}ent(I_2).$$

(Note that Δ is non-negative [4].) Δ is the information gain by splitting the merged interval into the two original intervals, or equivalently, the information loss by merging the two intervals. Therefore, merging the two intervals with the minimum Δ minimizes the information loss or maximize the pureness of classes. In the literature, entropy has only been used in the top-down splitting approach.

Suppose that I_0, I_1, I_2, I_3 are 4 adjacent intervals and that I_1 and I_2 are merged into a single interval. The count information C_{ij}, C_j, R_i for the new interval $I_1 \cup I_2$ can be computed from those for I_1 and I_2. Therefore, the χ^2 value or Δ for the affected pairs $(I_0, I_1 \cup I_2)$ and $(I_1 \cup I_2, I_3)$ can be computed efficiently. In the rest of the paper, the χ^2 value and Δ are called *goodness values*.

3 Implementation

At each merging, a critical operation is finding the best pair of adjacent intervals from all continuous attributes. The implementation will affect the efficiency of the algorithm significantly. For large datasets, scanning all pairs of adjacent intervals for each merging operation adds one more order to the complexity. A

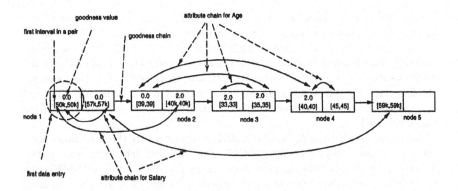

Fig. 1. The leaf level of the Merge-tree

minimum requirement is that the best pair be found in a time independent of the number of intervals. We propose a *Merge-tree* structure, a modified B-tree, to achieve this goal. This is not "just an implementation issue", but an issue that determines how useful the method is in real-world applications.

The Merge-tree. We modify the B-tree into a structure, called the *Merge-tree*, for finding the best merging at the cost of B-tree operations. Each data entry represents a potential merging of two adjacent intervals. (I_1, I_2) denotes the data entry for the potential merging of I_1 and I_2. The search key value for (I_1, I_2) is the goodness value (either χ^2 value or Δ of entropy) of merging I_1 and I_2. As in the B-tree, all leaf nodes are chained in the ascending order of the goodness value, called the *goodness chain*. The best merging is thus represented by the first data entry on the goodness chain.

There are two differences from the B-tree. The first difference is that all data entries for the same continuous attribute are doubly chained according to the adjacency of intervals. This chain is called an *attribute chain*. After merging intervals I_1 and I_2 into a larger interval $I_1 \cup I_2$, by following the two attribute chain pointers in (I_1, I_2), we can find the two affected data entries of the form (I_0, I_1) and (I_2, I_3), which must be replaced with new data entries $(I_0, I_1 \cup I_2)$ and $(I_1 \cup I_2, I_3)$ because I_1 and I_2 were replaced with the new $I_1 \cup I_2$. The second difference is that there are two kinds of data entries in the Merge-tree. Initially, all data entries are *unexamined*. When a pair of adjacent intervals is examined and no merging can be done (because of the inconsistency threshold), the corresponding data entry becomes *non-mergeable*. Since there is no need to search non-mergeable data entries, they will be deleted from the goodness chain. However, a non-mergeable data entry (I_1, I_2) is still kept on the attribute chain. This is because the boundary of I_1 (or I_2) needs to be updated if a merging of the form (I_0, I_1) (or (I_2, I_3)) is performed.

Let us look at one example. Figure 1 shows leaf nodes for attributes Age and Salary in Example 1 before any merging. (Non-leaf nodes are omitted for simplicity.) Each node contains 2 data entries, though typically much more. Each interval, except the first and last for an attribute, is involved in two data entries, one for "left-merging" and one for "right-merging". Instead of storing each interval twice, only the first interval I_1 is stored at data entry (I_1, I_2); I_2 can be found at data entry (I_2, I_3) by following the attribute chain in (I_1, I_2). For example, the first data entry represents the potential merging of intervals [50K,50K] and [57K,57K], the second represents the potential merging of intervals [57K,57K] and [59K,59K], etc.

Suppose that [50K,50K] and [57K,57K] (represented by the first data entry) are merged into [50K,57K]. We need to delete the first data entry and update affected data entries. The affected data entries are ([40K,40K],[50K,50K]) and ([57K,57K],[59K,59K]) because intervals [50K,50K] and [57K,57K] are replaced with the new interval [50K,57K]. By following the attribute chain in the first data entry, we find these affected data entries, delete them, and insert new data entries ([40K,40K],[50K,57K]) and ([50K,57K],[59K,59K]). The insertions are guided by the new goodness values, thus, not necessarily going back to the old places. Since deletion and insertion are standard B-tree operations, we omit the detailed description.

The merging process stops when the Merge-tree becomes empty, at which time all data entries are non-mergeable and are linked by attribute chains. Non-mergeable entries contain the boundary information of all final intervals, which will be used to discretize the testing data. The time for the merging process is $\Sigma_i(c + n_i)$, where c is the constant time for updating the Merge-tree for each merging, as discussed above, and n_i is the number of examples in the two intervals for the ith merging.

4 Empirical Evaluation

To evaluate the effectiveness of the proposed algorithm, we compare three methods: (a) Release 8 of C4.5, denoted C4.5(R8), (b) ConMerge using χ^2, denoted ConMerge(χ^2), and (c) ConMerge using the change of entropy, denoted ConMerge(Δ). Unlike all previous releases, C4.5(R8) improves the performance on continuous values by employing an MDL-inspired penalty to adjust the gain of a binary split of continuous values. [5] shows that C4.5(R8) compares favorably with other discretization methods. Therefore, we choose C4.5(R8) as a benchmark.

The three methods are applied to 15 datasets chosen from the UCI repository [3] based on the variety of involvement of continuous attributes. For ConMerge, the procedure is as follows. We partition a dataset into 10 runs using 10-fold cross validation. For each run, ConMerge is applied to the training set to produce intervals, C4.5 is applied to the discretized training set to produce the (pruned) decision tree, and the error rate is collected for the testing set and averaged over 10 runs. In all cases C4.5 was run using the default setting. The default inconsistency threshold is 0% because all original datasets are consistent. The result is shown in Table 2. The numbers following $\pm$ are standard errors.

Dataset	C4.5(R8)		ConMerge(χ^2)		ConMerge(Δ)	
	size	error (%)	size	error (%)	size	error (%)
Anneal	66.8±2.3	7.5±0.5	**46.6± 3.7**	12.2±0.6	**66.3±2.0**	9.5±0.8
Australian	35.7±3.5	14.8±1.1	**29.9±4.3**	15.9±1.2	39.6±3.2	15.5±1.3
Breast-c	28.2±1.7	5.6±0.8	**18.5±1.3**	**5.3±0.6**	**22.2±1.2**	**4.4±0.6**
Bupa	43.8±4.0	34.8±1.5	**41.7± 2.2**	39.1±2.5	48.0±2.7	35.6±1.9
Cleve	77.9±3.8	47.2±2.0	**62.3±3.7**	48.2±2.2	**68.7±5.6**	47.9±2.0
Crx	32.1±4.2	15.0±1.2	39.2±3.6	**13.6±1.5**	**27.4±1.9**	**14.0±1.5**
Diabetes	46.6±4.4	26.1±1.5	**22.7± 1.4**	24.2±1.4	**37.8±1.8**	**24.0±1.3**
German	142.8±6.3	26.2±0.7	**90.2± 3.6**	24.4±0.6	**122.0±7.5**	28.8±1.6
Heart	36.4±1.8	21.8±1.6	**15.9± 1.1**	**18.1±2.1**	**20.1±6.7**	**16.3±2.2**
Hepatitis	18.2±1.7	18.2±2.0	**5.4±0.5**	16.9±2.1	**8.6±2.2**	17.6±2.1
Iris	8.8±0.7	4.7±2.0	**6.4±0.4**	4.7±1.7	10.0±0.0	5.3±2.4
Labor	5.9±0.9	22.3±5.5	**3.0±0.0**	**12.5±4.2**	**5.1±0.3**	25.0±9.1
Sick-euthyroid	24.1±1.7	2.4±0.3	60.8±1.8	2.6±0.3	**21.1±2.3**	3.8±0.3
Glass	11.0±0.0	2.8±1.0	**9.0±0.0**	**0.5±0.5**	23.1±4.8	8.9±1.6
Wine	9.2±0.2	7.3±2.9	11.2±0.2	**2.2±0.9**	10.2±0.3	**6.2±1.8**
Average	39.2	17.1	**30.9**	**16.0**	**35.3**	17.5

Table 2. Tree size and error rate at default (0%) inconsistency threshold

Tree size. ConMerge(χ^2) and ConMerge(Δ) win over C4.5 12 and 10 out of the 15 cases, respectively, as in bold face. For Hepatitis, Heart, Diabetes, Labor, German, the size produced by ConMerge(χ^2) is only 29%, 44%, 48%, 51%, 63% of the size produced by C4.5. On the other hand, for Sick-euthyroid, the size produced by ConMerge(χ^2) is much larger. This is mainly due to the 0% inconsistency threshold. We will discuss the effect of the threshold below.

Error rate. On the error rate, ConMerge(χ^2) wins over C4.5 10 out of the 15 cases, with the biggest wins for Labor, Glass, and Wine. ConMerge(Δ) wins only 6 out of the 15 cases, therefore, is not more accurate than C4.5.

Effect of inconsistency thresholds. Tables 3 (a) and (b) show tree size and error rate for inconsistency thresholds between 2% and 10%. In general, for both ConMerge algorithms, as the inconsistency threshold is increased, the tree size is reduced and the error rate is increased, as shown by Average in the two tables, because fewer intervals and more inconsistencies are produced. Interestingly, ConMerge(χ^2) performs better at 0% threshold than at 2% threshold, on both error rate and tree size. Compared to C4.5, ConMerge(χ^2) at 2% threshold wins 13 out of 15 cases on tree size, and wins or ties 11 cases out of 15 on error rate.

Dataset	C4.5(R8)	ConMerge(χ^2)					ConMerge(Δ)				
		2%	4%	6%	8%	10%	2%	4%	6%	8%	10%
Anneal	66.8	54.2	18.0	18.0	17.6	17.6	82.4	62.4	62.6	55.0	17.6
Australian	35.7	23.9	43.3	34.2	34.2	34.2	36.0	40.3	34.2	34.2	34.2
Breast-c	28.2	21.2	17.2	7.4	5.0	3.0	23.8	10.0	13.2	5.0	4.8
Bupa	43.8	42.5	37.3	29.3	45.9	35.6	38.7	32.8	27.9	31.9	29.2
Cleve	77.9	63.8	52.5	49.2	50.0	50.4	61.4	60.3	49.5	51.6	50.1
Crx	32.1	33.7	33.7	33.7	33.7	33.7	33.7	33.7	33.7	33.7	33.7
Diabetes	46.6	65.0	66.3	48.1	46.0	33.3	40.0	41.1	28.1	35.6	25.6
German	142.8	73.4	64.1	54.0	49.8	40.6	107.2	103.2	93.6	88.4	76.4
Heart	36.4	22.8	28.2	19.4	22.2	15.4	21.8	21.8	15.8	20.4	16.0
Hepatitis	18.2	3.4	3.4	3.4	3.4	3.4	4.8	3.4	3.4	3.4	3.4
Iris	8.8	6.4	5.0	5.0	5.0	5.0	18.2	13.3	8.4	13.5	12.0
Labor	5.9	3.0	4.4	4.4	4.4	4.4	5.1	4.4	4.4	4.4	4.4
Sick-euthyroid	24.1	11.1	15.4	12.0	12.0	12.0	52.0	16.1	8.8	12.0	12.0
Glass	11.0	10.0	10.0	8.6	8.0	8.0	24.0	24.8	38.2	34.5	32.8
Wine	9.2	11.0	8.4	8.0	8.8	8.8	11.0	10.4	9.2	9.0	7.0
Average	41.4	29.7	27.1	22.3	23.1	20.4	35.3	25.0	26.4	28.8	26.6

(a) Tree size

Dataset	C4.5(R8)	ConMerge(χ^2)					ConMerge(Δ)				
		2%	4%	6%	8%	10%	2%	4%	6%	8%	10%
Anneal	7.5	11.7	19.1	19.1	21.5	21.5	13.4	16.7	16.1	16.3	21.5
Australian	14.8	12.9	17.9	15.5	15.5	15.5	14.6	14.9	15.5	15.5	15.5
Breast-c	5.6	4.6	4.9	6.4	7.4	9.3	4.7	5.1	5.3	7.0	10.3
Bupa	34.8	34.2	35.0	39.1	35.1	33.9	32.1	39.4	31.6	34.8	33.0
Cleve	47.2	49.2	48.1	45.2	46.2	46.8	48.5	47.8	48.5	45.2	45.2
Crx	15.0	14.3	14.3	14.3	14.3	14.3	14.3	14.3	14.3	14.3	14.3
Diabetes	26.1	23.6	21.8	22.8	22.3	23.5	24.5	25.7	25.9	25.1	26.3
German	26.2	27.9	27.3	27.1	26.6	27.2	29.3	30.0	28.2	27.9	27.7
Heart	21.8	17.4	17.4	18.1	18.9	18.1	17.4	16.6	15.9	19.2	19.2
Hepatitis	18.2	16.9	16.9	16.9	16.9	16.9	16.9	16.9	16.9	16.9	16.9
Iris	4.7	4.0	4.0	4.0	4.0	4.0	6.0	9.3	8.0	13.3	17.3
Labor	22.3	12.5	27.5	27.5	27.5	27.5	25.0	27.5	28.5	27.5	27.5
Sick-euthyroid	2.4	2.7	4.7	5.6	5.6	9.3	8.0	8.9	35.0	9.3	9.3
Glass	2.8	2.8	2.8	8.8	7.0	7.0	9.8	9.3	24.3	22.9	22.8
Wine	7.3	2.2	3.4	7.3	6.8	9.6	8.4	8.9	7.3	6.7	9.5
Average	17.1	15.8	17.7	18.5	18.4	19.0	18.2	19.4	21.4	20.1	21.1

(b) Error rate

Table 3. Comparison for different inconsistency thresholds

5 Related Work

Existing interval mergings methods include ChiMerge [2] and StatDisc [6]. ChiMerge merges two adjacent intervals at a time whereas StatDisc merges several. Both algorithms merge intervals for one attribute at a time. The merging for the current attribute is stopped when the similarity of every two adjacent intervals for the attribute drops below a threshold. The similarity measure depends only on the current attribute and the class attribute, thus, the mergings in one attribute do not affect mergings in other attributes. One problem with these methods is that the user has no control over the inconsistency in the discretized data, and a poorly chosen similarity threshold could either under-discretize the data, where intervals are not merged enough, or over-discretize the data, where the data becomes highly inconsistent. Other works on discretization, e.g., those in [1], are less related to our work.

6 Summary

The main contribution in this paper is (a) the establishment of an inconsistency threshold as a quality control factor for discretizing continuous data and (b) a discretization method that handles the attribute interaction raised by the inconsistency threshold. Our method selects the best merging of intervals from all continuous attributes, rather than from the one being considered. We proposed an implementation that finds the best merging in a constant time, thus scales up well in large datasets. Experiments show that by constraining the inconsistency and merging the overall best pair of intervals at each step, the discretized data does produce better decision trees, compared to the latest release of C4.5 improved for handling continuous attributes.

References

1. J. Dougherty, R. Kohavi, M. Sahami. Supervised and Unsupervised Discretization of Continuous Features. In *the 12th International Conference on Machine Learning*, 1995.
2. R. Kerber. ChiMerge: Discretization of Numeric Attributes. In *Ninth National Conference on Artificial Intelligence*, 1992, 123-128.
3. C.J. Merz, P.M. Murphy. UCI Repository of machine learning databases [http://www.ics.uci.edu/ mlearn/MLRepository.html].
4. J.R. Quinlan. *C4.5: Programs for Machine Learning.* Los Altos, CA: Morgan Kaufmann, 1993.
5. J.R. Quinlan. Improved Use of Continuous Attributes in C4.5. In *Journal of Artificial Intelligence Research 4*, 1996, 77-90
6. M. Richeldi and M. Rossotto. Class-driven Statistical Discretization of Continuous Attributes. In *Proc. of European Conference on Machine Learning* 1995, Springer Verlag, 335-338

The Integration of Machine and Human Knowledge by Fuzzy Logic for the Prediction of Stock Price Index

Myoung-Jong Kim[1], Ingoo Han[2], and Kunchang Lee[3]

[1]Graduate School of Management, Korea Advanced Institute of Science & Technology,
P.O.Box 201, Cheongryang, Seoul, 130-650, Korea
[2]Graduate School of Management, Korea Advanced Institute of Science & Technology,
P.O.Box 201, Cheongryang, Seoul, 130-650, Korea
ingoohan@msd.kaist.ac.kr
[3]School of Business Administration, Sung Kyun Kwan University, Seoul 110-745, Korea

Abstract. Integration of machine and human knowledge is more effective rather than a single kind of knowledge in solving unstructured problems. This paper proposes the knowledge integration of machine and human knowledge to achieve a better reasoning performance in the stock price index prediction problem. Causal model and the evaluation by experts generate the machine and human knowledge about the stock price index of next month, respectively. The machine and human knowledge are integrated by fuzzy logic-driven framework to generate the integrated knowledge. The conflicts among the integrated knowledge are solved by fuzzy rule base. The experimental results show that the proposed knowledge integration significantly improves the reasoning performance.

1. Introduction

One of the major issues in artificial intelligence is the management of uncertain knowledge. A various methods for dealing with uncertainty have been proposed. They are certainty factor model [3], theory of evidence [22], Bayesian probability theory [8], non monotonic logic [2], [18], endorsement theory [6], [7], and fuzzy theory [11], [17], [21], [24], [25], [26].

Fuzzy theory has been considered a generalization of classical set theory. Fuzzy theory has been applied to various fields of artificial intelligence so that the systems based on fuzzy theory such as fuzzy neural network, fuzzy genetic algorithms, and fuzzy mathematical programming have been proposed. Fuzzification provides an enhanced generality and expression capability to model real-world problems and a methodology for exploiting the tolerance for imprecision [18]. Fuzzy theory has also been used in integration of multiple sources of knowledge as well as in solving the conflicts among knowledge [15], [23].

The decision support literatures have long recognized that multiple sources of knowledge is more effective rather than a single kind of model in solving unstructured problems [1], [20]. This implies that knowledge integration can improve the reasoning performance in unstructured problems.

This paper proposes the knowledge integration of the machine and human knowledge in the purpose of achieving a better reasoning performance in the stock price index prediction problem. The knowledge integration is applied to the stock price index prediction problem using Korea Stock Price Index (KOSPI), which is one of unstructured and complex problems. Causal model and the evaluation by experts generate the machine and human knowledge about the stock price index of next month, respectively. The machine and human knowledge are combined to derive the integrated knowledge. Fuzzy rule base resolves the conflicts among the integrated knowledge. The experimental results show that the proposed knowledge integration produces an enhanced reasoning performance and understanding on the stock price index prediction problem. This implies that the knowledge integration is useful tool for dealing with the unstructured and complex stock price index prediction problem.

The organization of this paper is as follows. Section 2 reviews research background. The models used in the knowledge integration are explained in section 3. The empirical test and results are shown in section 4. Finally, some concluding remarks are described in section 5.

2. Research Background

Machine and human knowledge are complementary in real world. In general, human knowledge (or expert knowledge) is subjective and adaptive in nature. Experts have highly organized and domain-specific knowledge and perform reasoning using their experiences and knowledge [4], [14], [16]. The cognitive science literatures have been suggested that expert knowledge is especially better at diagnosis than at predicting [9], [10], [12]. Meanwhile, machine knowledge is the objective because it is derived from historical instances that possess the regularities useful for interpreting some part of phenomena in a specific domain. The most significant difference between machine and human knowledge is that the former relies on the objective method and the latter on human expertise. Each knowledge has unique and to a large extent complementary features. This implies that these two kinds of knowledge can be cooperatively used in solving the stock price index prediction problem.

The human knowledge discussed here is the judgmental knowledge of experts about various factors that might affect stock market. In a research of [13], the following four factors are obtained from the survey analysis; macroeconomics prospects, internal situation of stock market, foreign economic trend, and political situation. These factors are used to generate the human knowledge in this study. Each factor includes a wide variety of the economic and the stock market-related features. These factors and the corresponding features are described in Table 1.

Causal model is used to derive the machine knowledge. Causal model represents the knowledge by a path diagram. The arrows of the path diagram indicate the direction of causality while the value on each arrow means the strength of its direct effect of one factor on another linked factor.

Table 1. The Factors and The Corresponding Features

Factors	Features
Macro Economics Prospects	GNP
	Money Supply
	Foreign Trade
	Business Indicators
	Price Index
	Interest Rate
	Exchange Rate
	Economic Policy
Internal Situation of Stock Market	Balance of Customer's Deposit
	Credit Balance in Margin Transaction
	Trading Volume of Stocks
	Trading Value of Stocks,
	Total of Institutional Investors
	Corporate Funds Raised through Stock Market
	Securities Market Policy
Foreign Economic Trend	Overseas Economy Trend
	Overseas Stock Market
	International Exchange Rate
	World commodity Prices
Political Situation	South-North Korea Relations
	Labor Problems
	Domestic Policy Situation

3. The models in the Knowledge Integration

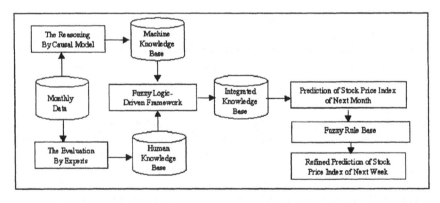

Fig. 1. The Framework of the Knowledge Integration

The proposed knowledge integration is shown in Figure 1. Causal model manages quantitative information and generates the machine knowledge while the evaluation by experts deals with qualitative information to derive the human knowledge. The knowledge integration of machine and human knowledge is achieved by fuzzy logic-driven framework to generate the integrated knowledge. Fuzzy rule base resolves the conflicts among the integrated knowledge. The models used in the knowledge integration are causal model, fuzzy logic-driven framework, and fuzz rule base.

3.1 Causal Model

The purpose of causal model is to explain and predict the phenomena based on causal notions embedded in a model. Propagating changes through cause-effect relations associated with domain knowledge is an intuitive and natural way to realize explanations and predictions of model structure and behavior. In causal model, a particular variable has a direct and/or an indirect effect. A direct effect indicates that a particular independent variable affects a dependent variable directly while an indirect effect means that a particular independent variable affects a dependent variable via mediating variables. The argument suggested by [5] is that regression and neural network may lose external validity due to their ignorance of the indirect effect. Thereby causal model has been recognized as one of the approaches that are capable of enhancing external validity.

A path diagram is served as a useful tool in presenting and discussing a causal model. The factors that affect stock market are used as notions for causal model. The direction of causality among such factors is acquired from stock market analysts. The coefficients of effects are acquired from the past data because they are difficult for experts to derive. As a result, the causal knowledge is expressed as the direction of causality and the effects of factors on the stock price index depicted in the corresponding path diagram.

Seven factors are selected to generate the causal knowledge from a set of procedure as follows. First, we collect a total of 12 factors composed of 7 groups as described in table 2. The data for economic and internal factors of stock market are respectively collected from the monthly data set of the Bank of Korea and KOSPI. The feature values are converted into monthly-change rate and annual-change rate which represent the monthly change and annual change of feature values, respectively. We apply the following sigmoid function to variables for normalization.

$$Y = 1/(1 + e^{-(X - \mu)/\sigma})$$ (1)

where, Y, X, μ, and σ denote normalized value, value, mean, and standard deviations, respectively. Finally, Seven factors, which have the highest correlation coefficient with the trend of stock price index in each group, are obtained from correlation analysis. The type of annual-change rate is selected for the leading index as one of the composite business indicator (LI), exchange rate of Won to U.S. dollar (WD), and M2 average (M2) while the type of monthly-change rate is selected for balance of current account (BCA), trading value of stocks (TV), corporate bond yields (CBY), and trading volume of stocks (TO). The results of the above procedure are listed in Table 2.

Table 2. The Results of Correlation Analysis (selected variables are marked as *)

Group	Factor	Correlation Analysis	
		Annual-Change Rate	Monthly-Change Rate
Money Supply	M2 Average	-.0360(.668)*	-.0020(.981)
	M3 Average	.0115(.892)	.0353(.675)
Foreign Trade	Balance of Trade	-.0359(.669)	.0809(.335)
	Balance of current account	.0290(.730)	.1228(.143)*
Business Indicator	Leading Index	.2533(.002)*	.2228(.007)
	Coincident Index	.1696(.042)	.1362(.104)
Interest Rate	Corporate Bonds Yields	-.1538(.066)	-.1722(.039)*
	Government Bonds Yields	-.1640(.050)	-.0488(.561)
Exchange Rate	Won to U.S. Dollar	-.2687(.001)*	-.1624(.052)
	Won to Yen	.2316(.007)	.0427(.611)
Trading Value	Trading Value of stocks	.0950(.257)	.1499(.073)*
Trading Volume	Trading Volume of stocks	.1264(.131)	.2156(.009)*

The dependent variable is the trend of the stock price index of next month. We classify it into the following four categories: Bear (1), Edged-Down (2), Edged-Up (3), Bull (4). A criterion that has been used by stock market analysts, (-3%, 0%, +3%) is used for determining category. If a return of the next month is greater than 3%, the corresponding stock market stage is regarded as Bull. Similarly, Edged-Up, Edged-Down, and Bear when the KOSPI return is between 0% and 3%, between -3% and 0%, and less than -3%, respectively.

3.2 Fuzzy Logic-Driven Framework

Fuzzy logic-driven framework is the logic to integrate different kinds of knowledge [15]. Fuzzy logic-driven framework consists of three phases: (1) machine knowledge-based inference phase, (2) human knowledge-based inference phase, and (3) combining phase. We will explain it with an example.

Machine Knowledge-based Inference Phase

We can define a fuzzy prediction vector (FPV) to convert machine knowledge (MK)-based result into fuzzy membership function as follows:

$$FPV_{MK}=(\mu_{MK}(Bear), \mu_{MK}(Edged\text{-}Down), \mu_{MK}(Edged\text{-}Up), \mu_{MK}(Bull))$$

We use a triangular-typed fuzzy function with a center value c and a width w. The center value indicates the most probable value and the width means a level of expertise. It is assumed in fuzzy logic-driven framework that the width of fuzzy membership function is 2.

Supposed that we obtain a particular result of causal model indicating that the stock price index of next month is regarded as Bull. Therefore, MK-based fuzzy membership function for the above case is as follows: $FPV_{MK}= (0,0,0.5,1.0)$.

Human Knowledge-based Inference Phase

The human knowledge (HK) consists of the experts' evaluations of the factors that affect stock market. The human knowledge is represented as one of five evaluation alternatives: very bad (0), bad (1), not bad or not good (2), good (3), and very good (4). Let FEV^i_{HK} denote fuzzy evaluation vector to convert HK-based evaluation of ith factor into fuzzy membership function, $\mu^i_{HK}(x)$, as follows:

$$FEV^i_{HK}=(\mu^i_{HK}(\text{very bad}), \mu^i_{HK}(\text{bad}), \mu^i_{HK}(\text{not bad}), \quad (2)$$
$$\mu^i_{HK}(\text{good}), \mu^i_{HK}(\text{very good}))$$

Let FEM_{HK} denote HK-based fuzzy evaluation matrix considering all four factors as follows; $FEM_{HK}=[FEV^i_{HK}]$, I=1,2,3,4. Suppose that HK-based evaluation is bad for macroeconomics prospects, not good for internal situation of stock market, good for foreign economic trend, and very good for political situation. Then, we can obtain FEM_{HK} as follows:

$$FEM_{HK}=\begin{vmatrix} 0.5 & 1.0 & 0.5 & 0.0 & 0.0 \\ 0.0 & 0.5 & 1.0 & 0.5 & 0.0 \\ 0.0 & 0.0 & 0.5 & 1.0 & 0.5 \\ 0.0 & 0.0 & 0.0 & 0.5 & 1.0 \end{vmatrix}$$

Let us define the weight vector to consider the effect of each factor on five evaluation alternatives as $W=(W_1, ..., W_m)$, $0<w<1$ for m factors where the sum of weights should be equal to 1. In our case, we assumed that W is (.25 .25 .25 .25). By multiplying W with the FEM_{HK}, HK-based unified fuzzy evaluation vector ($UFEM_{HK}$) can be calculated as follows: $UFEM_{HK} =W\times UFEM_{HK} =(0.125, 0.375, 0.5, 0.5, 0.375)$. Finally, consider the following 5 by 4 conversion matrix (CM) to transform five evaluation alternatives of $UFEV_{HK}$ into four alternatives of stock price index:

$$CM=\begin{vmatrix} 0.5 & 0.0 & 0.0 & 0.0 \\ 0.5 & 0.5 & 0.0 & 0.0 \\ 0.0 & 0.5 & 0.5 & 0.0 \\ 0.0 & 0.0 & 0.5 & 0.5 \\ 0.0 & 0.0 & 0.0 & 0.5 \end{vmatrix}$$

We can obtain a Fuzzy Prediction Vector (FPV) to determine a final result of the next month by multiplying $UFEV_{HK}$ with CM as follows:

$$FEV_{HK}=(\mu_{HK}(\text{Bear}), \mu^i_{HK}(\text{Edged-Down}), \mu^i_{HK}(\text{Edged-Up}), \mu^i_{HK}(\text{Bull})$$
$$=(0.25, 0.4375, 0.5, 0.4375).$$

Therefore, the fuzzy value for Edged-UP is the highest so that HK-based result is regarded as Edged-Up.

Combining Phase

We obtained FPV_{HK} and FPV_{MK} from machine knowledge-based inference phase and human knowledge-based inference phase, respectively. Then we use min operator ($\wedge$) for combining FPV_{HK} with FPV_{MK} and generating the integrated knowledge(IK) as follows; $FPV_{IK} = FPV_{HK} \wedge FPV_{MK} = (0, 0, 0.5, 0.4375)$. The stock price index of next month is predicted as Edged-Up with a fuzzy value 0.5.

3.3 Fuzzy Rule Base

The refined prediction of stock price index is obtained from the following steps.

Step 1: Generate the fuzzy rules from input-output data pairs
The above case consists of two input signals (the results of MK and HK) and one output signal (IK). We can define one rule from the above case as follows:
Rule 1: (MK, HK; IK) ⇒(Edged-Down, Edged-Up; Edged-Up)
IF MK is Edged-Down and HK is Edged-Up, THEN IK is Edged-Up.

Step 2: Resolve the conflict among rules.
There are a lot of rules because each data pair of two input signals and one output signal generates a correspondent rule. Therefore the conflicts among rules may occur if the different rules which contain the same IF parts have different THEN parts. Fuzzy principle rules are used to solve such a problem. Fuzzy principle rules are determined by the occurrence frequency. For example, consider Rule 1: (Edged-Down, Edged-Up; Edged-Up) and Rule 2: (Edged-Down, Edged-Up; Edged-Down). These two rules have the same IF parts, but different THEN parts. In such a case, Rule 1 is counted as the principle rule if Rule 1 occurs more frequently than Rule 2.

Step 3: Create a combined fuzzy rule base
The principle rules are represented in fuzzy rule base. The alternatives of MK and HK are respectively listed in the column and row of fuzzy rule base and IK is filled in the boxes.

4. Empirical Tests

Total samples are collected from January 1984 to December 1995. The training samples are obtained from January 1984 to December 1992 composed of 108 months (34 bear-phase months, 31 Edged-Up-phase months, 23 Edged-Down-phase months, and 50 Bull-phase months). The hold-out samples cover the period from January 1993 to December 1995 composed of 36 months (12 bear-phase months, 6 Edged-Up-phase months, 6 Edged-Down-phase months, and 12 Bull-phase months). Qualitative data are obtained from January 1993 to December 1995.

Figure 2 shows the path diagram with direct effects. The effects including direct effect, indirect effects, total effects and the goodness of fit of causal model are summarized in Table 3. The overall fit measures indicate that causal model fits the data well.

Stock price index is classified into four categories: Bear (1), Edged-Down (2), Edged-Up (3) and Bull (4). Numeric values are assigned to each of four categories; 1, 2, 3 and 4 for Bear, Edged-Down, Edged-Up and Bull. The midpoints, (1.5, 2.5, 3.5) are used for determining the stock price index of MK-based results. If MK-based result of the next month is less than 1.5, the corresponding stock price index is regarded as Bear. Similarly, Edged-Down, Edged-Up, and Bull when each result is between 1.5 and 2.5, between 2.5 and 3.5, and greater than 3.5, respectively.

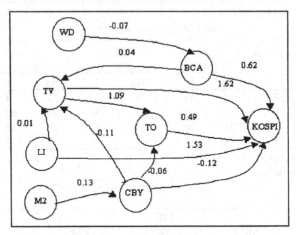

Fig. 2. The Path Diagram

Table 3. The Effects of the Factors and The Assessment of Fit

Factors	Direct Effects	Indirect Effects	Total Effects
WD	-	-0.05	-0.05
BI	1.53	0.03	1.56
MS	-	-0.05	-0.05
BT	0.62	0.08	0.70
IR	-0.12	-0.26	-0.38
TV	1.62	0.54	2.18
TO	0.49	-	0.49
Sum of Total Effects			4.45

(a) The Effects of the Factors

Measure of Fit	Value
χ^2	0.57
NNFI	1.01
NFI	0.94
GFI	0.97
AGFI	0.93

(b) The Overall Fit Measures of Causal Model

Neural network (NN) and multivariate discriminant analysis (MDA) are used as the benchmark of causal model in the comparison of reasoning performance. Table 4 summarizes the empirical results. The deviation column indicates the difference between the actual status and the predicted status. Table 4(a) shows the reasoning performance of machine knowledge such as MDA, NN, and causal model (CM) in the training samples. Table 4(b) shows the reasoning performance of all 3 kinds of the machine knowledge and the integrated knowledge (IK) in the hold-out samples.

Table 4. The Reasoning Performance

Deviation	MK							
	MDA		NN		CM			
	No.	%	No.	%	No.	%		
0	55	51	39	36	26	24		
1	23	21	54	50	60	55		
2	21	20	14	13	19	18		
3	9	8	1	1	3	3		
Average Deviation	0.85		0.78		1.06			

(a) The Training Samples (n=108)

Deviation	MK						IK	
	MDA		NN		CM			
	No.	%	No.	%	No.	%	No.	%
0	9	25	6	17	6	17	14	39
1	11	30	17	47	22	61	22	61
2	10	28	8	22	8	22	0	0
3	9	8	1	1	3	3	0	0
Average Deviation	1.36		1.33		1.06		0.61	

(b) The Hold-Out Samples (n=36)

In the case of MDA and NN, the performances between the training and hold out samples are significantly different at 5% and 1% level respectively while it is indifferent in the case of causal model as shown in Table 5. These results show that causal model has more consistent external validity than MDA and NN whose knowledge is driven by past data.

Table 5. The Difference of Performance between the Training and Hold-Out Samples

T-Test	MDA	NN	CM
T-Value	0.55	2.73	0.51
Significance	0.013	0.0000	not significant

Table 6 describes that IK shows the better performance than any other types of MK-based performance in the hold-out samples. The performance between all types of MK and IK is significantly different at 1% level. This result indicates that performance differs significantly according to knowledge types and the knowledge integration is effective in solving the unstructured stock price index prediction problem.

Table 6. The Difference of Performance in the Hold-Out Samples

T-Test	MDA	NN	CM
T-Value	5.29	3.73	3.60
Significance	0.000	0.000	0.001

The fuzzy rule base is shown in Table 7. FRB consists of 9 rules. 7 blank boxes mean that there are no generated rules, however, 9 fuzzy rules are sufficient for controlling all the input-output data pairs.

Table 7. The Principle rules of Fuzzy Rule Base

HK / MK	Bear	Edged-Down	Edged-Up	Bull
Bear	Bear			
Edged-Down	Bear	Edged-Down	Edged-Up	Bull
Edged-Up		Edged-Down	Edged-Up	Bull
Bull				Bull

The result of fuzzy rule base is shown in Table 8. When compared with the result of IK in Table 4(b), this result indicates that the synergistic combination can achieve a bette000000r performance and understanding on the stock price index prediction problem. T-test of Table 9 shows that the reasoning performance of fuzzy rule base (FRB) is significantly better than that of IK at 5% level.

Table 8. The Reasoning Performance

Deviation	FRB	
	No.	%
0	21	58
1	14	39
2	1	3
3	0	0
Average Deviation	0.42	

Table 9. The Difference of Performance between the IK and FRB

T-Test	IK	
	T-Value	Significance
	2.24	0.032

5. Concluding Remarks

This paper proposes the knowledge integration in the purpose of achieving a better reasoning performance and understanding on the unstructured and complex stock price index prediction problem. The machine and human knowledge are derived from quantitative and qualitative information. The knowledge integration is achieved by fuzzy logic-driven framework to generate the integrated knowledge. Finally, fuzzy rule base resolves the conflicts among the integrated knowledge.

The experimental results show that the integration of machine and human knowledge rather than a single kind of knowledge can improve reasoning performance in the unstructured stock price index prediction problem so that it can provide a better reasoning performance and understanding on the stock price index prediction problem.

This study has the twofold contribution. One is that stock market analysts have complementary used machine and human knowledge in their problems such as the prediction of stock price index and portfolio selection. However, it is a difficult work to integrate deterministic machine knowledge and subjective human knowledge. The knowledge integration of this study can be a useful tool to support them and generates a more robust knowledge so that it can improve the reasoning performance and the explanatory capability in the stock price index prediction problem. The other is that this study proposes a more rigorous application of fuzzy theory. Fuzzy theory plays an important role in generating of knowledge, the integration of multiple kinds of knowledge and the synergistic combination. Such fuzzification provides the enhanced ability to deal with the fuzziness in information and knowledge of stock market.

The further research issues still remain as follows:

1) There exist several methods for determining fuzzy membership functions such as singleton-typed, triangular-typed, and bell-typed fuzzy membership functions, but the selection criterion for appropriate fuzzy membership function is subjective to researchers. Thus, the more refined and objective methods for determining fuzzy membership functions are required.

2) The fuzzy rules obtained from fuzzy rule base can be converted into fuzzy expert systems. This conversion provides the better understanding and more effective inference.

References

1. Bonczek, R. H., Holsaplle, C. W., & Whinston, A. B. (1981). *Foundations of decision support Systems*. New York: Academic Press
2. Bossu, G., & Siegel, P. Saturation. (1984). Nonmonotonic reasoning and the closed world assumption. *Artificial Intelligence* 25, 13-64.
3. Buchanan, B.G., & Shortliffe, S.H. (1984). *Rule-based expert systems*. Addison-Wesley.
4. Chi, M. T. H., Glaser, R., & Rees, E. (1981). *Expertise in problem-solving*. In R. J. Sternberg (Ed.), Advances in the Psychology of Intelligence, Erbaum, Hilldale, NJ.

5. Cohen, J., & Cohen. P. (1983). *Applied Multiple Regression Correlation Analysis for the Behavioral Science* (2nd ed.). Hillsdale, New Jersey: Lawrence Erlbaum Associates.

6. Cohen, P. R. (1985). *Heuristic reasoning about uncertainty: an AI approach*. Pitman, Boston, Mass.

7. Cohen, P.R. (1987). The control of reasoning under uncertainty: A discussion of some programs. *Knowledge Engineering Review* 2, 5-26.

8. Duda, R.O., Hart, P.E., & Nilsson, N.L. (1976). Subjective Bayesian methods for a rule-based inference system. *Proceedings of National Computer Conference* 45, 1075-1082.

9. Einhorn, H.J. (1974). Cue definition and residual judgment. *Organizational Behavior and Human Performance* 12, 30-49.

10. Goldberg, L. (1959). The effectiveness of clinician's judgments: the diagnosis of organic brain damage from the Bender-Gestalt test. *Journal of Consulting Psychology* 23, 25-33.

11. Graham, I. (1991) Fuzzy logic in commercial expert systems- result and prospects. *Fuzzy Sets and Systems* 40, 451-472.

12. Hoch, S.J. (1987). Perceived consensus and predictive accuracy: the pros and cons of projection. *Journal of Personality and Social Psychology* 53, 221-234.

13. Kim, S. K., & Park, J. (1995). A structural equation modeling approach to generate explanations for rules induced, *proceedings of '95 Korea Conference on Expert Systems*, Korea Expert Systems Society, 315-328.

14. Larkin, J., McDermott, J., Simon, D.P., & Simon, H.A. (1980). Expert and novice performance in solving physics problems. *Science* 208 (June), 1335-1342.

15. Lee, K. C., Han, J. H., & Song, Y. U. (1998). A fuzzy logic-driven multiple knowledge integration framework for improving the performance of expert systems, forthcoming in *Intelligent Systems in Accounting, Finance and Management*.

16. Lesgold, A., Rubinson, H., Feltovich, P., Glaser, R., & Klopfer, D. (1988). *Expertise in complex skills: diagnosing X-ray pictures*. in M.T.H. Chi, R. Glaser, and M.J. Farr (Eds.), The Nature of Expertise, Erlbaum, Hilssdale, NJ.

17. Leung, K. s., Wong, W. S. F., & Lam, W. (1989). Applications of a novel fuzzy expert system shell, *Expert Systems* 6, 2-10.

18. Lin, C. T., & Lee, C. S. G. (1992). *Neural Fuzzy Systems*, Prentice Hall, NJ.

19. McDermott, D., & Doyle, J. (1980). Non-monotonic logic I. *Artificial Intelligence* 13, 41-72.

20. Mitra, S. & Dutta, A. (1994). Integrating optimization models and human expertise in decision support tools. *Expert Systems with Application* 7, 93-107

21. Negoita, C. V. (1985). *Expert systems and fuzzy systems*. The Benjamin/Cummings Publishing Company.

22. Shafer, G. (1976). *A mathematical theory of evidence*. Princeton University Press, Princeton, NJ.

23. Wang, L. X., & Mendel, J. M. (1992) Generating fuzzy rules by Learning from Examples. *IEEE Transactions on Systems, Man, And Cybernetics* 22(6), 1414-1427.

24. Zadeh, L. A.. (1965). Fuzzy sets. *Information and Control* 8(3), 338-353.

25. Zadeh, L. A.. (1973). Outline of a new approach to the analysis of complex systems and decision processes. *IEEE Transactions on Systems, Man, and Cybernetics* 3, 20-44.

26. Zadeh, L. A. (1983). The role of fuzzy logic in the management of uncertainty in expert systems. *Fuzzy Sets and Systems* 11, 199-227.

Computational Intelligence Techniques for Short Term Generation Scheduling in a Hybrid Energy System

C.C. Fung, V. Iyer and C. Maynard

School of Electrical and Computer Engineering
Curtin University of Technology,
GPO Box U1987, Perth 6845,
Western Australia
Tfungcc@cc.curtin.edu.au

Abstract. An application of computational intelligence techniques to the optimisation of a hybrid energy system operational cost is reported in this paper. The hybrid energy system is an example of the Remote Area Power Supply (RAPS) systems used in many countries in the Pacific Rim. A hybrid energy system typically comprises of a diesel generator, solar panels and a battery bank. It is used in areas where the main electricity supply grids are unavailable. In this study, a fuzzy logic algorithm is used to determine the initial generator operational schedule and the battery discharge-charge schedules for the next 24-hour period. A genetic algorithm is then used to find an optimum solution with minimal generation cost. Simulation of the algorithm has been carried on a system operating at a remote site in the Northern Territory, Australia. An average saving of 10% in fuel cost was demonstrated in the case study.

1   Introduction

In the past decades, many countries in the Pacific Rim have experienced great changes in their social, economic and industrial environments. One common thread found among all these changes is the increasing dependency on electricity supply. While the majority of the population living in metropolitan areas have taken the utility for granted, there are many communities having to pay a high price for such privilege. Take Australia as an example, due to the size of the continent, many communities and homesteads in the outback are left out of the main electricity supply systems. Other examples are communities living on the Asian-Pacific islands. Depending on the population size and the load demands, the daily power consumption may vary between a few kWh to tens or hundreds of kWh within the 24-hour period. To meet the demands, stand-alone power systems based on diesel generators are normally used.

In recent years, more and more hybrid energy systems and photovoltaic systems have been used instead of the traditional diesel generators. In particular, many countries in the Pacific Rim such as India, Indonesia and Australia have installed hybrid power systems. Although diesel generators have low initial costs, due to the fluctuating nature of the load demands, the generator will not be operating constantly in its most efficient setting. This leads to poor operation efficiency and results in high overall generation costs. Stand-alone photovoltaic systems on the other hand are simple to install, but they are characterised by high initial costs and limited power capacity. A typical hybrid energy system utilises energy from multiple sources. In conjunction with the diesel generators, solar cells and storage batteries are incorporated. The storage batteries are used to store the excess power from the diesel generators and the solar cells if the load demand is low. When demand exceeds the capacity of the generators, the batteries will supplement the supply together with the output from the solar cells. In order to operate the hybrid energy system in the most efficient manner, operation of the batteries and solar cells must be scheduled in accordance with the forecast load demand and solar radiation.

In the area of hybrid energy system research, world-wide focus is on the optimisation of the dispatch strategy and the component sizing of these systems. Some of the techniques used previously are linear programming and dynamic programming [1, 2, 10]. Other methods used are fuzzy logic and simulated annealing [4, 11]. In this paper, a fuzzy logic algorithm has been developed based on heuristic knowledge of the system. It is initially used to schedule the diesel generator operation for the next 24-hour period. The scheduling result from this method is then further optimised by means of a Genetic Algorithm (GA) technique. The proposed algorithm have been implemented and applied to a remote site in the Northern Territory of Australia. A saving of approximately 10% is demonstrated from the simulation case study.

2   System description and problem formulation

The characteristics of the hybrid energy system under investigation is based on a real-life system operating at a remote site called Epenarra in the Northern Territory, Australia. The hybrid energy system in the Epenarra power station comprises of two diesel generators, a battery bank and a small PV array. Power ratings of the two diesel generators are 52 kW and 80 kW respectively. The solar PV power is relatively small at 1 kW. In practice, the contribution by the solar panel in this case is insignificant. The storage capacity of the battery bank is 100 kWh and it plays an important role in the optimisation of the system efficiency. The Epenarra power station uses a control system that senses both the three-phase and the single phase site loads and arranges the diesel generator dispatch strategy accordingly. The 52kW generator has been used alone in the majority of the days to meet the load demands. A schematic diagram of the system is given in Figure 1.

Data from the Epenarra station has shown that the maximum load demand recorded during the period under study was 40 kW. This is relatively low as compared to the total capacity of the entire system. It is understandable as extra reserves are normally planned in order to meet future expansion and any unexpected demands. As the actual load demand can be sufficiently met by a single generator, only one diesel generator with a battery bank of 100 kWh capacity is considered in the simulation study. It is assumed that the scheduling of the system operation is performed at the beginning of a 24-hour period and the solutions to be determined are:

(a) the optimal diesel generator loading for the next 24-hour period, and,
(b) the optimal battery discharge-charge strategy.

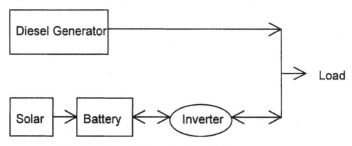

Fig. 1. Schematic diagram of a hybrid energy system

The problem to solve in this scheduling problem is the minimisation of the generation cost over the scheduling horizon, subject to the satisfaction of the system constraints. The constraints are:

(a) the diesel generator must be operated within the minimum and maximum allowable rating,
(b) the total power generated by the diesel generator and the battery must meet the load demand,
(c) the battery should not be excessively charged or discharged as there are limitations on the battery storage, and,
(d) the battery must be charged to the maximum level at the end of the day so as to avoid using the diesel generator in the night.

In terms of the cost of operating a hybrid energy system, it is made up of fuel cost, start-up cost, shut-down cost and battery cost. The fuel cost is the main component of the hybrid energy system's life cycle cost, minimisation of fuel consumption cost is therefore considered as the prime objective in the present study. The start-up and shut-down costs are related to the ON/OFF cycle of the diesel generator. The figures will be related to the overall maintenance cost. Hence, the ON/OFF cycle should be reduced as much as possible. The battery cost depends on the operation of the battery. As the battery life is governed by the depth of discharge (DOD) of the battery in each cycle of its operation, the charge/discharge cycle should also be minimised.

3 Fuzzy Logic and Genetic Algorithm

In hybrid energy system research, the use of fuzzy logic and Genetic Algorithms (GA) for operation optimisation is relatively new. Fuzzy logic is emerging as a powerful tool which can be used to deal with systems which are characterised by uncertainty, random disturbances and an ill defined problem domain. In particular, this technique has been found to be suitable for applications involving dynamic, time-varying and non-linear systems. Fuzzy logic systems are characterised by the use of linguistic fuzzy rules to represent the knowledge about a system and the use of fuzzy variables in the inference process. Through a procedure of *Fuzzification, Fuzzy Inference* and *De-fuzzifcation*, a fuzzy logic system can be used to provide a solution based on a set of inputs and the fuzzy knowledge of the system. In this study, this approach is used to determine an initial schedule for the generator settings.

On the other hand, GA's are used to solve optimisation problems using an approach inspired by the phenomenon of natural evolution. The process is based on the survival of the fittest. It works on the theory that a population of a certain species, after many generations, adapts to live better in its environment. Although genetic algorithms have been used to solve the problem of unit commitment in power system engineering [3,6,8], the method is rarely attempted for the hybrid energy systems. When implemented, GA can be executed as a parallel mathematical algorithm that transforms a set (population) of individual mathematical objects (fixed length character strings) into a new population of individuals. In GA terminology, each individual is called a *chromosome string*. This in effect is a solution vector in the problem domain. The transformation of the chromosomes is achieved by operations based on the Darwinian principle of reproduction and survival of the fittest, and, natural genetic operations. The genetic operators most commonly used to produce new chromosomes are crossover and mutation. As each chromosome string is associated with a fitness value, or cost, this provides a measure of the "goodness" of the solution. Compared to other optimisation techniques, GA is distinguished by the feature that the search towards the optimum solution is proceeded by incremental changes to a population of solutions rather than changes on a single solution. This approach is therefore adopted in the present problem to obtain the "best" generation schedule while taking into account the system constraints.

4 Combined fuzzy logic and genetic algorithm for generation scheduling

In this paper, a fuzzy logic algorithm based on the heuristic knowledge about the hybrid energy system is developed. It is used initially to calculate the preliminary diesel generator schedule and the battery charge/discharge strategy. The fuzzy logic algorithm has three main modules. The first module is the *Fuzzification unit*. It is used to translate the inputs from discrete values into fuzzy terms. In the present study, three input parameters are used. They are the *load demand, time-of-day* and *the battery state-of-charge*. Each of these parameters is fuzzified into different levels, with linguistic variables used to describe each level. Triangular functions are used to define the fuzzy memberships for each linguistic variable. The process of fuzzification involves the division of each input variable's universe of discourse into ranges of fuzzy sets. A mathematical function applied across each range will determine the membership of the variable's current value in the fuzzy sets. The value at which the membership is at its maximum is called the *peak value*. The *width* of a fuzzy set is determined by the distance from the peak value to the point where the membership value becomes zero. The second module is the *Rule-Base* that consists of linguistic rules expressing the explicit relationships between the input and the output variables. All the possible combinations of the inputs have been considered for the establishment of the rules. Eighty rules have been derived in this case study. System constraints described in the previous section have been taken into consideration during the development of the rule base. The heuristic knowledge used to construct the rule base is described as follows:

(a) the diesel generator is inefficient at low power output settings,
(b) the diesel generator should be turned off at lower load levels,
(c) the battery should not be discharged below 20% of its maximum capacity,
(d) at the end of the day, battery should be charged to nearly 90% of its full capacity,
(e) the probability of losing supply to load should be avoided, and,
(f) the load is anticipated to increase after midday.

Fine-tuning of the rule-base was done by running a number of simulations of the algorithm using the actual load data from the test site. These rules are in the form of IF-THEN conditional statements as shown below.

IF *load* is low and *time* is morning and the *battery* is xhigh THEN the *Gen* is off.
IF *load* is low and *time* is night and the *battery* is low THEN the *Gen* is optimum.

where low, xhigh, off and optimum are some of the linguistic terms used to describe the input and output variables.

During execution, the inference process determines the rules that are fired and the resultant fuzzy set for the output variable. In this case, the output variable is the power level of the diesel generator that should be set at the current simulation time interval. Finally, the *De-fuzzification unit* uses the output of the inference process to derive a single crisp output value. The center-of-area method is used in this case study to obtain a singleton, which is a representative point for the resulting fuzzy set of the output. The *rule base* used to derive the generator outputs is given in Table 1.

	Battery	Vlow	Low	High	vhigh	xhigh
Load	**Time**	**Generator output**				
Vlow	**morn**	Med	Off	Off	off	off
	anoon	Med	Off	Off	off	off
	eve	Med	Med	Off	off	off
	night	Med	Off	Off	off	off
Low	**morn**	Med	Off	Off	off	off
	anoon	Med	Off	Off	off	off
	eve	Hi	Med	Med	med	med
	night	Opt	Hi	Hi	med	med
High	**morn**	Med	Off	Off	off	off
	anoon	Med	Off	Off	off	off
	eve	Opt	Hi	Med	med	med
	night	Vhi	Opt	Hi	med	med
vhigh	**morn**	Opt	Hi	Hi	med	med
	anoon	Opt	Hi	Hi	med	med
	Eve	Opt	Opt	Hi	hi	med
	Night	Vhi	Opt	Opt	hi	med

Table 1.   Rule-base of the fuzzy logic algorithm

Once an initial schedule for the generator settings is established, a GA is used to operate on the rule base of the fuzzy algorithm in order to find an optimal solution. The chromosome string is made up of 24 genes each representing one of the generator output settings in fuzzy terms. The fuzzy terms are off, med, hi, vhi, opt, med, vhi and a combination of these terms. A total of thirty-one combinations were used and they are given in Table 2. A typical chromosome used to determine the generator setting is given in Table 3.

As an example, consider one hour of the 24-hour period to illustrate how the generator output is determined. The time of the day is 3 o'clock in the afternoon, when the load value is 19.9 kW and battery charge is 58.7 kWh. The input terms *time, load* and *battery state-of charge* are fuzzified into fuzzy values with associated their fuzzy terms (*time-* anoon, eve; *load-* low, high; and *battery-* low, high*)*. The inference engine determines the rules fired with this combination as shown in Table 4. The GA algorithm works on this set of rules and gives the best membership function of the generator output, as the *med+hi* combination. Then the *centre of area* method is used on this membership function to translate it to a non-fuzzy crisp value of the generator output as 21 kW.

Genes and Generator Settings used in Chromosome Strings					
1	Off	11	off+med+opt	21	off+hi+vhi
2	Med	12	hi+opt	22	med+hi+vhi
3	off+med	13	off+hi+opt	23	off+med+hi+vhi
4	Hi	14	med+hi+opt	24	opt+vhi
5	off+hi	15	off+med+hi+opt	25	off+opt+vhi
6	med+hi	16	vhi	26	med+opt+vhi
7	off+med+hi	17	off+vhi	27	off+med+opt+vhi
8	Opt	18	med+vhi	28	hi+opt+vhi
9	off+opt	19	off+med+vhi	29	off+hi+opt+vhi
10	med+opt	20	hi+vhi	30	med+hi+opt+vhi
				31	off+med+hi+opt+vhi

Table 2.   Range of values of genes used in GA

Time Interval (Hr)	1	2	3	4	5	6	7	8	9	10	11	12
Gene Value	3	3	3	28	3	27	3	3	3	3	3	3
Time Interval (Hr)	13	14	15	16	17	18	19	20	21	22	23	24
Gene Value	3	3	3	27	3	28	27	27	28	3	27	3

Table 3.   Example of a Typical Chromosome string

		Generator output	
Load	**Time**	**Battery Low**	**Battery High**
Low	anoon	off	off
Low	eve	med	Med
High	anoon	Off	Off
High	eve	Hi	med

Table 4.   Example of rules fired for a single time period

5   Simulation Results

Actual load profiles and component characteristics from the test site have been used for the simulation study. The battery state-of-charge is calculated by assuming a battery model with constant charge and discharge efficiency parameters. As the optimisation of the hybrid energy system operational cost is the primary objective of the present research, the detailed model analysis of the components are not provided in this paper. Data from the site were recorded at 15-minute intervals but for simulation purpose, one-hour time intervals were considered. For each time interval the generator ON/OFF state, the expected power generation, the battery discharge/charge status and battery's state of charge are determined. The fuel consumption of the generator for each time interval is then calculated and used as a comparison with the actual test site operational data. The fuel consumption model based on Reference [6] is given in equation (1) as shown below.

$$FC = 0.246*Popr+0.08415*Pr \qquad l/hr \qquad (1)$$

where FC is the fuel consumption
$Popr$ is the operating power of the generator
Pr is the rated power of the generator, which is 40 kW for the simulation
l/hr is the units in litres/hour.

The fuel cost per hour is given as

$$C= FC * Cf \qquad (2)$$

where C is the fuel cost per hour
Cf is the cost of fuel per litre

The parameters used in the GA process are:

(a)   Population size   100
(b)   Crossover rate   0.9
(c)   Mutation   0.1
(d)   Range of values for chromosome string   1-31

The site operation indicates that the solar power has not been used, so the simulation study also ignored the solar input. Simulation study has been applied to a number of days and the results were compared with those from the actual operation. A comparison completed for three typical days is given in Table 4. The results indicated that the operation scheduling using the fuzzy method is more efficient than the existing operation method.

	Day-1 Result		Day-2 Result		Day-3 Result	
Schedule Algorithm :	GA	Site	GA	Site	GA	Site
Load energy (kWh)	411.4	411.4	553.9	553.9	468.6	468.6
Average power (kW)	17.1	17.1	23.1	23.1	19.5	19.5
Maximum power (kW)	31.4	31.4	31.7	31.7	25.7	25.7
Minimum power (kW)	4.2	4.2	13.3	13.3	15.7	15.7
Diesel generator size (kW)	40	52	40	52	40	52
Battery size (kWh)	100	100	100	100	100	100
Battery starting state (kWh)	90	90	90	90	91.6	91.6
Battery state at the end (kWh)	92.4	82.8	91.3	79.3	92	83
Load provided by diesel (kWh)	358.5	338.3	515.4	494.2	442.3	437.8
Load provided by battery (kWh)	52.9	73.1	38.5	59.6	26.3	30.8
Diesel output energy (kWh)	444.2	443.6	577.1	574	484	475.2
Diesel Run Hours	20.0	17.0	22.0	20.0	23.0	23.0
Fuel consumed (lts)	190	214	222.8	246.2	199.8	221.9
Percentage Saving (%)	11.2%		9.5%		10%	

Table 5. Results of comparison

In general, results from the simulation study have shown an average fuel saving of 10%. The results are also consistent with other findings that were not included in this paper. In addition to the saving in fuel consumption, the battery states-of-charge at the end of the three days was above 90%. As compared to the data from the actual site operations, the charge of the battery in those days was dropped to around 80%. This indicates that the GA approach has ensured that the batteries were fully charged at the end of the scheduling period in accordance to the system constraints. In terms of meeting the load demands, the diesel generator has delivered more power to meet the load in the case of the GA solution. This effectively reduces the battery charge/discharge cycles and extends the life of battery. It also means that the battery cost will be reduced in the long run. From Table 5, although the diesel generator running hours has shown to be higher as compared to the actual site operation, it simply means that the generators are operating much longer at the optimal region. This has the effect of reducing the start-up and shut-down cost. Finally, the simulation study has been based on a 40 kW diesel as it demonstrated that the load can be sufficiently met by a smaller generator. This implies that the initial cost of the system can be reduced even further by incorporating a smaller diesel generator.

6 Conclusions

An application of the fuzzy logic and genetic algorithm to the optimisation of a hybrid energy system operational cost is reported in this paper. These two techniques are used extensively in the broad discipline of computational intelligence. The proposed techniques can be applied to improve the operation efficiency of hybrid energy systems used in many countries in the Pacific Rim. In this study, the fuzzy logic algorithm is initially used to determine the diesel generator's operation schedule and the battery discharge-charge strategy. A genetic algorithm is then used to find an optimum solution with an aim to minimise the total generation cost. Simulation studies of the algorithm have been carried on a system operating at a remote site in the Northern Territory, Australia. An average saving of 10% in fuel cost was demonstrated in the case study. Other costs such as start-up, shut-down and battery costs are also expected to be reduced due to a more efficient operation of the diesel generator. Implementation of the proposed algorithm to an existing hybrid energy system is currently under investigation.

Acknowledgment

The work reported in this paper was supported by an Australian Research Council Small Grant. In addition, Vanaja Iyer is a recipient of the Alternative Energy Development Board (AEDB) scholarship. The authors are grateful for the support given to this study.

References

1. Bakirtzis, A.G., Dokopoulos, P.S., 'Short term generation scheduling in a small autonomous system with unconventional energy sources' *IEEE Transactions on power systems* 3(3) (1988) pp.1230-1236.
2. Bakirtzis, A.G., Gavanidou, E.S., ' Optimum operation of a small autonomous system with unconventional energy sources' *Electric power systems research* 23(2) (1992) pp.93-102.
3. Dasgupta, D., McGregor, D.R., 'Short term unit-commitment using genetic algorithms' *Proc. Of the IEEE, International conference on tools of AI,*(1993) pp.240-247.
4. Fung, C.C., Ho, S.C.Y., Nayar, C.V., 'Optimisation of a hybrid energy system using simulated annealing technique' *IEEE TENCON 1993*, (1993) pp.235-238.
5. Hunter, R., Elliot, G. *Wind- Diesel Systems* Cambridge (UK) : Cambridge univ. press. (1994).
6. Kazzrlis, S.A., Bakirtzis, A.G., Petridis, V., 'A genetic algorithm solution to the unit commitment problem' *IEEE Trans. on Power Systems,* Vol. 11, No. 1, (1996) pp. 83-90.
7. Li, H., Gupta, M., *Fuzzy logic and Intelligent systems* Kluwer Academic publications, 1995.
8. Oreo S.O., M.R. Irving, M.R., 'A genetic algorithm for generator scheduling in power systems' *Electrical Power & Energy Systems* Vol. 18, No.1, (1996) pp. 19-26.
9. Skarstein, O., Uhlen, K., 'Design considerations with respect to long-term diesel saving in wind/diesel plants' *Wind engineering*, Vol.13, No.2, (1989) pp.72 -87.
10. Swaminathan, S., Kottathra, K., Phillips, S., Teh, K., 'A MNLP Formulation for Power System Scheduling' *Solar 93 conference proceedings* Vol.2 (1993) pp.446-451.
11. Wong, K.P., Fung, C.C., Eskamp, T., 'Development of a fuzzy-logic-based control algorithm for the commitment of energy sources in an integrated energy system' *Proc. ANZIIS-93*, (1993)
12. Yager, R.R., Zadeh, L.A., An introduction to fuzzy logic applications in intelligent systems, Kluwer Academic Publishers, Boston (1992).

Fuzzy Rules Extraction Based-Integration of Linguistic and Numerical Information for Hybrid Intelligent Systems

Changjiu Zhou, Qingchun Meng

Department of Electronics & Communication Engineering
Singapore Polytechnic, 500 Dover Road, Singapore 139651
ZhouCJ@sp.edu.sg

Abstract: A fuzzy rules extraction based-integration (FREI) method is proposed to integrate numerical data from measuring instruments and linguistic rules from human experts. At first, the fuzzy IF-THEN rules are extracted from numerical data and acquired from experts individually. Based on a simple and intuitive integration scheme, a uniform fuzzy rules base is constructed through integrating above two kinds of information. The integrated information can be used for hybrid intelligent systems (HIS) design. With inverse learning, the proposed FREI method is able to integrate linguistic and numerical information with various forms, such as direct and indirect, and thus improve the performance of HIS using a priori knowledge where it is available. The validity of the proposed methods are verified through the fuzzy rules extraction-based hybrid intelligent control of a biped walking robot.

1 Introduction

When the complexity of a problem or the uncertainty prevents a priori specification of a satisfactory solution, intelligent systems must learn to improve its performance using information accumulated from the interacting environment. This should be achieved preferably without relying on an accurate model of the plant, but *any a priori knowledge* should be used where it is available.

For complex engineering systems, two kinds of information are available. One is numerical information from measuring instruments, and the other is linguistic information from human experts. However, each of the two kinds of information alone is usually incomplete. Linguistic rules alone are usually not enough for system design since either it is difficult to built a complete knowledge base or some useful information will be lost when experts express the knowledge by linguistic rules. On the other hand, the numerical information from input-output data pairs usually cannot cover all situations the system will face. Furthermore, most of information available obtained are usually hybrid, that is, their components are not homogeneous but a blend of linguistic rules and numerical data with various form. As an example, for control system design, only *direct* information (control knowledge) can be directly used to design controller, while *indirect* information is used to describe the behavior of the plant not the controller itself. Therefore, there is a need to develop a method to integrate linguistic rules and numerical data with different forms, such as direct and indirect.

Fuzzy logic (FL) and artificial intelligence (AI) are appropriate if sufficient linguistic knowledge is available, while neural networks (NN) and conventional system theory are useful if sufficient numerical data is available or measurable. The finding suitable intelligent techniques to integrate various forms of linguistic-numerical integrated information (direct/indirect) is still an open problem. Therefore, we need to study how to process above hybrid information using the hybrid intelligent systems (HIS) which integrate FL, NN, genetic algorithms (GA) and some other intelligent techniques [6,11].

This paper is organized as follows: Section 2 gives a brief review on various forms of linguistic and numerical information for HIS design. Section 3 provides a representation method of linguistic and numerical information in this paper. Section 4 introduces the general methods on the fuzzy if-then rules extraction from numerical data. In section 5, based on fuzzy rules extraction and inverse learning, a simple and intuitive integration method is proposed to integrate linguistic and numerical information with direct and indirect forms. Section 6 verifies the effectiveness of the proposed methods through the fuzzy rules extraction-based hybrid intelligent control of the biped walking robot.

2 Linguistic and Numerical Information in Hybrid Intelligent Systems (HIS)

FL, NN, GA and symbolic AI are complementary rather than competitive[11]. Each intelligent technique has particular computational properties (e.g. ability to learn) that make them suited for particular problems and not for others. These limitations have been a central driving force behind the creation of HIS where two or more techniques are combined in a manner that overcomes the limitations of individual techniques. HIS are also important when considering the varied nature of application domains.

FL has been proven effective for complex, nonlinear and imprecisely define process, however, it needs to be augmented with a learning capability to increase its robustness and adaptability, and in this regard, NN and GA have been suggested as a suitable learning medium. The choice of learning method, however, is dictated by the nature of the task domain and the available information. For NN learning, it needs sufficient data representing the input-output mapping of the system to be modeled, while in a situation where such data cannot be obtained an alternative approach, such as GA, would be necessary [5].

There are several models for HIS, such as stand-alone, transformations, loose coupling, tight coupling, and full integration, and each having their advantages and disadvantages [6].

In this paper, we will study how to integrate various forms of linguistic and numerical data for HIS design and learning rather than how to design HIS for various application domains. As an example, for a control system, from a high-level conceptual point of view, any control system consists of at least a plant and a controller. For controller design, there are two types of expert knowledge. One is the *plant knowledge* which describe the behavior of the unknown plant; Another is *control knowledge* which can be described as fuzzy rules that state in which situations what control actions should be taken. The control knowledge can be *directly* used to design the controller, while the plant knowledge must be used in an *indirect* way. The control knowledge may also be classified into two categories: *conscious* knowledge and *subconscious* knowledge. By conscious knowledge we mean the knowledge that can be explicitly expressed in words, therefore, we can simply ask the human experts to express it in terms of fuzzy IF-THEN rules. By subconscious knowledge we refer to the situations where the human experts know what to do but cannot express exactly in words how to do it, what we can do is to ask the human experts to demonstrate, and collect a set of input-output *numerical* data pairs. Therefore, the knowledge available for HIS design and learning can be classified in five categories as shown in Fig. 1.

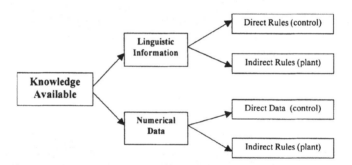

Fig. 1 The various forms of linguistic and numerical information

3 Representation of Linguistic and Numerical Information

When constructing information processing systems, two kinds of information are available. One is numerical information from measuring instruments and the other is linguistic information form human experts. The numerical information can be naturally represented using real numbers. It has been popular for using fuzzy sets to represent linguistic information.

In this paper, we consider a single-output fuzzy rule-based system in the n-dimensional input space $[0,1]^n$. Let us assume that the following fuzzy IF-THEN rules are given by human experts:

$$R^{(l)}: \quad IF \quad x_1 \quad is \quad F_1^l \quad and...and \quad x_n \quad is \quad F_n^l \qquad THEN \quad y \quad is \quad G^l \tag{1}$$

where F_i^l and G^l are fuzzy sets, $X = (x_1, ... x_n)^T \in U \subset R^n$ and $y \in V \subset R$ are input and output linguistic variables, respectively, $l = 1, 2, ... M$, and M is the number of rules in the fuzzy rule base.

We also assume that the following input-output pairs are given as numerical data from measuring instruments:

$$(X^p ; y^p \mid p = 1, 2, \cdots, P) \tag{2}$$

where $X_p = (x_1^p, x_2^p, ..., x_n^p)$ is the input vector of the pth input-output pair and y_p is the corresponding output.

The hybrid information in HIS usually has different forms, linguistic and numerical, direct and indirect as shown in Fig. 1. As an example, we consider the above various information representation in a control system. For simplicity, we assume that the plant has only one state $x(k)$ and one input $u(k)$, the control objective is to design a controller such that the plant state $x(k)$ can follow a desired trajectory $x_d(k)$ as closely as possible. The different kinds of information obtained for controller design can be reprsented as follows.

- Direct Rules (DR): $IF \quad x(k) \quad AND \quad x(k+1) \quad THEN \quad u(k)$ (3)

- Direct Data (DD): $(x(k), x(k+1); u(k))$ (4)

- Indirect Rules (IR): $IF \quad x(k) \quad AND \quad u(k) \quad THEN \quad x(k+1)$ (5)

- Indirect Data (ID): $(x(k), u(k); x(k+1))$ (6)

4 Fuzzy IF-THEN Rules Extraction From Numerical Data

In many applications of fuzzy rule-based systems, fuzzy IF-THEN rules are obtained from human experts. Recently, Several different methods for extracting fuzzy IF-THEN rules from numerical data have been developed. Most of these methods have involved iterative learning procedures or complicated rule generation mechanisms such as gradient decent learning method, least-squares method, fuzzy c-means method, NN based method, GA based method, fuzzy NN method and heuristic method[8].

Fuzzy rules are defined for multiple subspaces obtained by directly partitioning the input space. For application with high-dimensional input space, the above methods usually need a long ruls requisition (RA) time. The major restriction of the NN based method is that the number of rules must be defined before training[3]. The *cluserting* based method, such as fuzzy rules extraction based on hyperboxes[1], can group the input-output pairs into clusters and use one rule for one cluster, that is, the number of rules equals the number of clusters, and thereby the number of fuzzy rules is not fixed before learning. In Wang and Mendel method[9], an efficient rule generation method with no iterative procedure was proposed and its high performace was demonstrated. This is a one-pass build-up procedure that avoids time consuming training, the approach is very straightforward, however, again the input space must be divided in advance. In this section, we extend Wang and Mendel method[9] to extract fuzzy IF-THEN rules from numerical data (2). It divides the input space according to the partition of the training data.

Construction of fuzzy logic rules from numerical data for control consists of two phases: fuzzy partitioning of the input space and identification of a fuzzy logic rule for each fuzzy subspace. If the fuzzy logic rules to be found consists of fuzzy consequent parts, we further need to consider the fuzzy partitioning of the output space. The fuzzy rules extraction used in this paper can be described as follows.

Step 1. Partition the training data (2). To avoid under-fitting or over-fitting of the training data, we partition the training data using a heuristic method. The partition process will be terminated before over-fitting.

Step 2. Divide the input and output spaces into fuzzy regions according to the data partition results. The domain intervals of $x_1, x_2, \cdots, x_n$ and y are $[x_1^-, x_1^+]$, $[x_2^-, x_2^+]$, ... , $[x_n^-, x_n^+]$ and $[y^-, y^+]$ respectively. Fig. 2 shows an example how to divide fuzzy regions and assign fuzzy membership function according to the data partition.

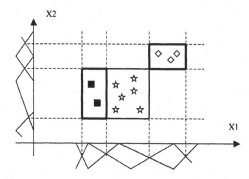

Fig. 2 An example of dividing input space into fuzzy regions and assigning the corresponding membership functions according to the partition of the training data.

Step 3. Generate fuzzy rules from numerical data pairs (2).

Step 4. Assign a truth degree to each rule. The following product and maxium strategies are used to assign a truth degree to the rule: " IF x_1 is A_1 and x_2 is A_2 and ... and x_n is A_n THEN y is B ".

• Product strategy

$$w^N = \mu_{A_1}(x_1)\mu_{A_2}(x_2)\cdots\mu_{A_n}(x_n)\mu_B(y) \tag{7}$$

• Maximum strategy

$$w^N = Max\{\mu_{A_1}(x_1), \mu_{A_2}(x_2), \cdots, \mu_{A_n}(x_n), \mu_B(y)\} \tag{8}$$

Note that if two or more generated fuzzy IF-THEN rules have the same IF and THEN parts, use the rule that has maximum truth degree.

5 Fuzzy Rules Extraction Based-Integration (FREI)

There are several approaches[15] to integrate the above linguistic rules (1) and numerical data (2) into a HIS. In the first approach, a neural network based fuzzy system is constructed from a fuzzy rule base, and then its parameters are fine-tuned by the numerical data base. This is a most common method used for neurofuzzy systems. In the second approach, we can develop a neurofuzzy system with fuzzy learning to process the hybrid of numerical and fuzzy information [3,4]. In order to handle linguistic information in NN, the fuzzy data are viewed as convex and normal fuzzy sets represented by α-level sets. Since the α-level sets of fuzzy numbers are intervals, the operations of real number in the traditional NN are extended to closed intervals. A notable deficiency in this approach is that the computations become complex (e.g. multiplication of interval) and time-consuming.

In this section, we will propose a new method to integrate linguistic and numerical information, Fuzzy Rules Extraction based-Integration (FREI). It can extract fuzzy rules, that is, numeric based fuzzy rules (NFR), from numerical data, and then integrate them with experts linguistic knowledge based fuzzy rules (EFR). The final uniform fuzzy rules (UFR) include both linguistic information from experts and numerical information from measuring instruments. The HIS can be interpreted as fuzzy system, and the UFR thus can be used to design HIS directly.

5.1 FREI of Linguistic and Numerical Information

The proposed FREI, which use numerical and linguistic integrated information, can be summarized as follows.

Step 1. Define the final uniform fuzzy system UFR structure in advance. The input and output space are divided into fuzzy regions, and assign each region a fuzzy membership function according to expert knowledge. This prescribed fuzzy system structure will be used for both fuzzy rules extraction from numerical data and fuzzy rules acquisition from experts. In this way, we design a fuzzy rule base formed as a look-up table for next two steps.

Step 2. Extract fuzzy rules NFR from numerical data and construct NFR base (NFRB).

Step 3. Acquire fuzzy rules EFR from experts. The truth degree to each rule can be given by experts, and thus we obtain a EFR base (EFRB).

Step 4. Construct a UFR base (UFRB) through integrating NFRB with EFRB. Because EFRB, NFRB and UFRB have the same structure, we only consider the rules with same IF part for combination (see Fig. 3). A simple and intuitive integration method will be given in section 5.2.

Step 5. Design the HIS using UFRB.

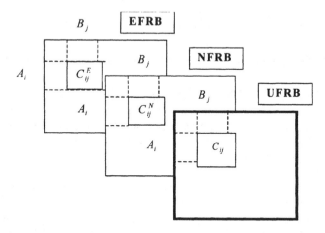

Fig. 3 Construction of the final uniform fuzzy rule base (UFRB) by integrating expert knowledge based fuzzy rule base (EFRB) and numerical data based fuzzy rule base (NFRB)

5.2 The Integration of Fuzzy Rule Base EFRB and NFRB

The topic of integrate multi-source information and expert opinions has recently gained a lot of attention [2]. Integration techniques are typically based on weighting schemes in which each source is weighted according to its importance, relevance, or reliability, and then the weighted sources are combined. When pieces of information issued from several sources have to be integrated, each of them represented as a degree of belief in a given event, these degrees are combined in the form $F(x_1, x_2, \cdots, x_n)$, where x_i denotes the representation of information issued from sensor i. A large variety of information combination operators F for data fusion have been proposed [2].

In this section, a simple and intuitive information combination operator is proposed for linguistic and numerical data integration.

Let us suppose the fuzzy rules in EFRB, NFRB, and UFRB have the following forms:

$$\text{EFRB: } R_{ij}^E: \quad IF \quad A_i \quad AND \quad B_j \quad THEN \quad C_{ij}^E \quad (w_{ij}^E) \tag{9}$$

$$\text{NFRB: } R_{ij}^N: \quad IF \quad A_i \quad AND \quad B_j \quad THEN \quad C_{ij}^N \quad (w_{ij}^N) \tag{10}$$

$$\text{UFRB: } R_{ij}: \quad IF \quad A_i \quad AND \quad B_j \quad THEN \quad C_{ij} \quad (w_{ij}) \tag{11}$$

where w_{ij}^E, w_{ij}^N, and w_{ij} are truth degree for each fuzzy rule, A_i, B_j, and C_{ij} are fuzzy sets.

The fuzzy rules integration method we proposed in this paper can be described as follows.

Step 1. Convert the EFRB and NFRB into the complete fuzzy rule base

If there are no rules in some of the fuzzy grids, we will take the fuzzy rules with same IF parts from another fuzzy rule base, and then zero truth degree will be given. As an example, if there is no rule in " *IF* A_i *and* B_i " grid for NRRB, then we can "borrow" a rule from EFRB.

$$\begin{cases} C_{ij}^N = C_{ij}^E \\ w_{ij}^N = 0 \end{cases} \tag{12}$$

Step 2. Choose rules with maximum truth degree if conflict

If there are conflicting rules in EFRB and NFRB, that is, rules with the same IF parts but different THEN parts ($C_{ij}^E \ne C_{ij}^N$), we can choose the rule that has maximum degree.

$$C_{ij} = \begin{cases} C_{ij}^E & if \quad w_{ij}^E > w_{ij}^N \\ C_{ij}^N & otherwise \end{cases} \tag{13}$$

$$w_{ij} = \max(w_{ij}^E, w_{ij}^N) \tag{14}$$

Step3. Calculate the truth degree for UFRB

Through the above processing, the numerical data based fuzzy rule base NFRB and experts linguistic knowledge based fuzzy rule base EFRB can be integrated as one uniform fuzzy rule base UFRB. If the fuzzy rules are consistent, that is, the THEN parts are same for the same IF condition, set $C_{ij} = C_{ij}^E$ or C_{ij}^N. The truth degree of UFRB can be calculated by different ways. Here, we proposed two simple methods.

•Maximum truth degree method

$$\begin{cases} C_{ij} = C_{ij}^E \text{ or } C_{ij}^N \\ w_{ij} = \max\left(w_{ij}^E, w_{ij}^N\right) \end{cases} \tag{15}$$

• Weighted average method

$$\begin{cases} C_{ij} = C_{ij}^E \text{ or } C_{ij}^N \\ w_{ij} = \alpha w_{ij}^E + (1-\alpha)w_{ij}^N \end{cases} \tag{16}$$

where α is a weighted factor. If experts knowledge play an important role in the integrated information, we can choose a big α, otherwise, choose a small one. As an example, if only numerical information from measuring instruments is used to design HIS, set $\alpha = 0$, otherwise, if only use linguistic rules obtained from experts, let $\alpha = 1$. We can set $\alpha = 0.5$ for processing linguistic-numerical integrated information if the experts knowledge is as important as measuring numerical data.

5.3 Inverse Learning Based-Integration of Direct and Indirect Information

The above proposed FREI method can only integrate direct data (DD) and direct rules (DR), or indirect data (ID) and indirect rules (IR). However, in practical application, most of numerical data are obtained from plant measurement instruments, i.e., the indirect data (ID), and most of linguistic rules acquired from human control experts are direct rules (DR). In order to integrate both direct and indirect information for HIS design, an inverse learning based-integration method is proposed in this section. As an example, we only consider DR and ID integration.

Step 1. Get the ID from measurement instruments.

Step 2. Apply inverse learning to convert ID into direct information.

Step 3. Extract fuzzy rule from direct data which is converted from ID using inverse learning. Construct numerical data based-fuzzy rules base NFRB.

Step 4. Acquire fuzzy rules from human experts. Construct experts knowledge based-fuzzy rules base EFRB.

Step 5. Construct uniform fuzzy rules base by integrating NFRB and EFRB.

Step 6. Choose the structure and set the initial parameters for a selected HIS. (using UFRB).

Step 7. Tune the fuzzy partition of the input and output spaces for HIS (structure learning).

Step 8. On-line tune the HIS parameters (parameter tuning).

6 Case Study: Fuzzy Rules Extraction Based-Hybrid Intelligent Control of the Biped Walking Robot

The biped robot control is a challenging problem due to its high order nonlinear dynamics and uncertainty. In this section, we verify the effectiveness of the proposed fuzzy rules extraction based-hybrid intelligent control strategy through a 5-link biped robot simulation.

The hierarchical control structure of the biped robot consists of walking plan, gait synthesis and joint control levels[14]. In the organization (walking plan) level, the system reasons symbolically for strategic plans or schedules of biped motion using the knowledge base. This level should also include common sense knowledge for biped motion. This knowledge at organization level is mainly given by human operator in top-down manner. There are three kinds of information available for gait synthesis level: (1) the sampled biped robot experimental data (numerical); (2) the intuitive walking knowledge (linguistic); (3) the walking knowledge which has been obtained from biomechanical studies of human being walking (linguistic). For joint control level, the information is mainly given by measuring instruments in bottom-up manner (numerical). Moreover, the servo control knowledge (linguistic) is also useful for joint controller design and tuning. How to integrate linguistic knowledge and numerical data in different levels for the biped walking robot is still an open problem[12,13,14].

The 5-link biped robot can be described by the following model [7].

$$J(\theta)\ddot{\theta} + X(\theta)\dot{\theta}\dot{\theta} + Y(\theta)\dot{\theta} + Z(\theta) = E\tau \qquad (17)$$

where $\theta = (\theta_1, \theta_2, \theta_3, \theta_4, \theta_5)^T$, θ_i is the absolute angle of ith link measured from the vertical. $J(\theta)$ is the inertia matrix of the biped robot. $X(\theta)$, $Y(\theta)$ and $Z(\theta)$ are terms due to centripetal, Coriolis and gravitational forces. These terms are strongly nonlinear and their effect increases drastically as the velocities of the biped's joints increase. $\tau = (\tau_1, \tau_2, \tau_3, \tau_4)^T$ is the vector of the driving torque.

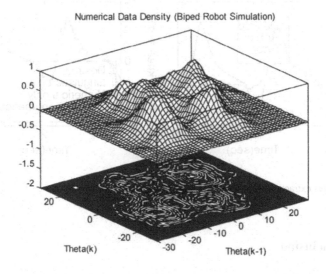

Fig. 4 Data density and density contours of the training data (numerical) for biped robot

The direct rules (DR) for joint control are obtained from control experts. The indirect data (ID) is collected from biped dynamic model (17). The data density and density contours are shown in Fig. 4. From Fig. 5, we can find that both expert rules based HIS controller (using EFRB) and numerical data based HIS controller (using NFRB) can only roughly track the desired trajectory, while the biped joint control performance can be significantly improved by the rules extraction based HIS which use linguistic-numerical integrated information (UERB).

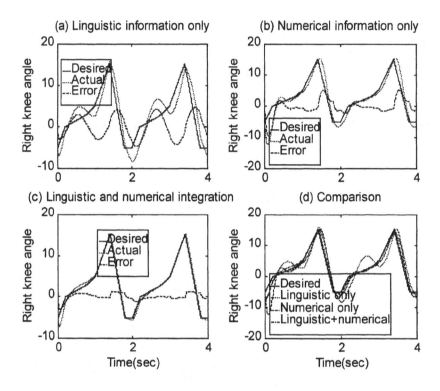

Fig. 5 Rules extraction based HIS for the biped joint control

7 Conclusion

The proposed FERI method can integrate the numerical data and linguistic rules with both direct and indirect forms. The numerical-linguistic integrated information can be used to improve the performance of HIS. The application to the biped walking robot shows that the both biped gait and joint control performance can be significantly improved by the fuzzy rules extraction-based HIS which use linguistic-numerical integrated information.

The fuzzy rules extraction-based HIS proposed in this paper use inverse learning. However, the existence of the inverse of the plant or controller is not valid in general. Some results from adaptive inverse control [10] should be useful for the general HIS development.

The hybrid information for complex systems learning and control usually has different forms, symbolic and numerical, precise and fuzzy, direct and indirect, and etc., however, the proposed method can only process a few simple forms of hybrid information. The use of HIS techniques to process some of complicated forms of hybrid information, such as the hybrid of direct rules, indirect rules, direct data, and indirect data, are still an open problem. We are currently extending the FREI scheme proposed in this paper to the data fusion with the expectation that to develop HIS based heterogeneous fuzzy data fusion scheme.

Acknowledgment

We would like to thank Prof. Shaolu Zhu of Dalian Maritime University and Dr. K. Jagannathan of Singapore Polytechnic for their assistance.

References

1. Abe, S., Lan, M.S.: Fuzzy rules extraction directly from numerical data for function approximation. IEEE Trans. on Systems, Man, and Cybernetics. 1(1995) 119-129.
2. Bolch, I.: Information combination operators for data fusion: a comparative review with classification. IEEE Trans. On Systems, Man, and Cybernetics. 1(1996) 52-67.
3. Ishibuchi, H., Fujioka, H., Tanaka, H.: Neural networks that learn from fuzzy if-then rules. IEEE Trans. Fuzzy Syst. 1(1993) 85-97.
4. Lin, C. T., Lu, Y. C.: A neural fuzzy system with fuzzy supervised learning. IEEE Trans. Systems, Man, and Cybern. 5(1996) 744-763.
5. Linkens, D. A., Nyongesa, H. O.: Learning systems in intelligent control: an appraisal of fuzzy, neural and genetic algorithm control applications. IEE Proc.- Control Theory Appl. 143(1996) 367-386.
6. Medsker, L. R.: Hybrid Intelligent Systems. Kluwer Academic Publisher (1995).
7. Mita, T., et al.: Realization of a high speed biped using modern control theory. Int. J. Control , 1(1984) 107-119.
8. Nozaki, K., Ishibuchi, H., Tanaka, H.: A simple but powerful heuristic method for generating fuzzy rules from numerical data. Fuzzy Sets and Systems. 86(1997) 251-270.
9. Wang, L.X., Mendel, J.M. (1992): Generating fuzzy rules by learning from examples. IEEE Trans. Systems, Man, and Cybern. 22(1992) 1414-1427.
10. Widraw, B. and Walach, E.: Adaptive Inverse Control. Prentice-Hall, Englewood Cliffs, NJ(1996).
11. Zadeh, L.A.: Fuzzy logic, neural networks and soft computing. Communications of the ACM. 37(1994) 77-84.
12. Zhou, C., Jagannathan, K., Messom, C.: Neurofuzzy gait synthesis for a biped robot. Proc. 4th Int. Conf. on Control, Automation, Robotics and Vision. Singapore. 211-215(1996).
13. Zhou, C., Jagannathan, K.: Neurofuzzy control of a biped robot using genetic algorithm. Proc. Joint Pacific Asian Conf. on Expert Syst./Singapore Int. Conf. on Intelligent Syst. Singapore. 559-606(1997).
14. Zhou, C., Jagannathan, K., Messom, C.H.: Hierarchical neural fuzzy control of a biped walking robot. Proc. Of 7th World Congress of IFSA. Prague, Czech. 4(137-142) 1997.
15. Zhou, C., Ruan, D., Zhu, S.: Hybrid intelligent fuzzy control for nonlinear systems. J. of Communication and Cognition-Artificial Intelligence (CCAI). 14(163-189) 1997.

Reasoning about Continuous Change

Tyrone O'Neill and Norman Foo

Knowledge Systems Group
Department of Artificial Intelligence
School of Computer Science and Engineering
University of New South Wales, Australia
tyroneo|norman@cse.unsw.edu.au

Abstract. The problem of formalising continuous change within reasoning about action systems such as the situation calculus has recently been receiving increasing attention ([Rei96], [MS96]). In this paper we show that a long-existing systems theoretic reasoning methodology, that of Zeigler's DEVS (discrete event system specification), not only subsumes the standard situation calculus but is able to elegantly describe continuous change within a discrete description structure. We demonstrate that on the semantic level both Reiter's recent formalisation of continuous change within the situation calculus, and Miller and Shanahan's formalisation of continuous change within the event calculus fit neatly into a DEVS framework. Our results not only evince a significant connection between logic-based action formalisms and the algebraic formalism of systems theory, and between reasoning about action and discrete event simulation, but also provides support for using DEVS—a well-studied and rigorously implemented framework—as an underlying semantic framework for reasoning about action formalisms.

1 Introduction

One of the primary difficulties in the research area of reasoning about action is, as has been often identified, the lack of a common framework by which to compare what should be comparable systems. The situation calculus ([MH69]) is a framework which serves in some respects as a benchmark, but its peculiarities have led many to prefer other formalisms. Closer to the goal are the A languages ([GL92]), which are intended to serve as high-level description languages, into and from which other languages can be translated - and so compared. The A languages serve their function usefully, but they are essentially syntactic. Sandewall ([San94]) has proposed an important semantic characterisation of formalisms, but his framework, while very comprehensive in scope, seems useful mainly as a theoretical tool for assessing reasoning formalisms.

This paper proposes another framework for comprehension of reasoning about action formalisms. Our framework is predominantly semantic and, moreover, is specially designed to accommodate continuous change. Furthermore, because our proposed framework is based on an implemented and rigorously engineered system, demonstrating its connection to reasoning about action formalisms provides a further prospect of practical utilisation of such formalisms.

We are not the authors of this proposed framework, merely its advocates. The framework is the DEVS (discrete event system specification) modelling and simulation methodology, first proposed by Zeigler ([Zei76],[Zei90]) more than twenty years ago, and since developed extensively in theory and implementation. DEVS arises from a systems theoretic framework, and implemented systems employ object-oriented techniques to represent and compute with modular, hierarchical models.

In this paper we demonstrate that DEVS, despite having been developed for modelling and simulation, seems as if it could have been custom-designed to act as a semantic foundation for comparing formalisations of continuous change within a discrete description ontology. It elegantly incorporates natural actions and parameterised continuous change, yet provides for a specification of system dynamics separate from the syntactic expression of a system. In presenting a translation between DEVS and two well known formalisations of continuous change - Reiter and Pinto's situation calculus formalisation, and Miller and Shanahan's event calculus formalisation - we demonstrate that DEVS is able to act as a common framework for system comparison.

Furthermore, our adducement of a strong relationship between DEVS and reasoning about action formalisms not only provides a better understanding of how systems theory bears upon logic-based action formalisms, it also presents an opportunity to interface the action formalisms with discrete event simulation.

We now outline the DEVS methodology.

2 Discrete Event Systems

In his classic text on discrete event systems, Zeigler ([Zei76]) contrasts discrete event systems with both differential equation systems, in which system changes occur continuously and are specified by differential equations, and discrete time systems, in which system changes occur only at fixed time points (such as at the beginning or end of regular intervals of a given duration). Discrete event systems change in state only through the occurrence of some discrete event; that these events are discrete rather than continuous means that events occur, or at least begin occurring, at specifiable time points when the system changes in quantum-like 'leaps'. However discrete event systems also provide for representation of continuous change, because changes of system values can occur *within system states*. This apparent contradiction is seen to resolve itself with the observation that in DEVS there are two types of states - *sequential states*, which can change only discretely, and *total states* which allow for variation of real-valued continuous parameters. Total states correspond most closely to the traditional notion of a state.

Such systems are described in a discrete event system specification (DEVS), a seven-tuple of the form $<X, Y, States, ta, \delta_{int}, \delta_{ext}, \lambda>$:

X is a set of external input types

Y is a set of external output types

States is a set of sequential system states

ta: States↦ $\Re^+$, specifies the duration of state $s \in States$

δ_{int}: States↦States, specifies the internal transition function

δ_{ext}: Q×X↦States, specifies the external transition function

$\lambda : Q \mapsto Y$, specifies the (observable) output function

where $Q = \{(s,t) | s \in States \text{ and } 0 \le t \le ta(s)\}$ specifies the set of total system states.

The system's dynamism is specified in the two transition functions, δ_{int} and δ_{ext}, the first of which specifies changes of a continuous (non discrete) kind which occur within a particular discrete state, and the second of which is the state transition function for discrete changes in the system. The external transition is used to calculate the effect of *external events*—those which are imposed upon the system from outside. Obviously the corresponding notion for the internal transition function is the *internal event*. Internal events are those which are constituted as discrete changes in the system caused by continous change over a period. For example, suppose we have a system in which a cup is being held over a floor. Let's suppose the system is intially static (no continous change occurring). Then an external event, *drop* occurs, changing the system state; as the cup falls (it's location at any time can be identified using the output function λ) its height above the ground reduces, and when it reaches the ground the internal event *hits-ground* occurs. Internal events occur through a natural evolution of the system, and thus can be described as 'natural' events.

DEVS in its purest form (as presented above) when applied to reasoning about action assumes that the frame problem, the qualification problem, the ramification problem, and all other traditional dilemmas of reasoning about action are solved. The two transition functions are assumed to embed the 'correct' transition operation, with ramifications and so on included. It is for this reason that we are proposing DEVS as a semantic framework for comparison between alternative formalisations of continuous change in discrete description domains. This paper provides support for a proposal to use DEVS as a device characterising the compass of currently used non-monotonic and monotonic inference mechanisms. The difference between non-monotonic and monotonic formalisms is present at the level of specification; DEVS is silent on how systems should be specified—it embodies only the actual system dynamics.

2.1 A Retail Check-out System

In illustration of a DEVS, suppose we are modelling the dynamics of a proposed check-out/purchasing system in a retail store (say for the purpose of acertaining its viability compared with the current check-out arrangement). Our model will be simple.

Let the shop—which we will understand as a system–consist only of (a) a browsing area, (b) a checkout queue, and (c) customers. At any time there are a known number of customers in the shop, either browsing or queueing/purchasing. The dynamics of the system consists of customers *entering* the shop, spending a randomly assigned amount of time browsing, then entering the check-out queue.

We assume that the processing time for each customer's purchases is constant for all customers.

In the system the only external event is $enter(c_i)$ (customer i enters the store). We assume that each c_i is assigned a random number ($\in \Re$) representing the duration of their browsing; this is one of the output types, the other three denote the set of customers currently browsing, the amount of browsing time ($\in \Re$) remaining for a customer at any particular system time, the length ($\in N$) of the checkout queue, and the purchasing time remaining ($\in \Re$) for the customer at the front of the queue.

$X = \{enter(c_i)\}$

$Y = \{total\text{-}browsing\text{-}time(c_i), \ customers\text{-}browsing(t),$
$\quad remaining\text{-}browsing\text{-}time(c_i,t), \ length\text{-}of\text{-}queue(t),$
$\quad remaining\text{-}current\text{-}purchase\text{-}time(t)\}$

The real-valued output types (*remaining-browsing-time* and *remaining-current-purchase-time*) are parameterised by time, and their values can be calculated using a system clock.

The external transition function—which, since there is only one external event, *enter*, always applies the same transformation—acts by increasing *customers-browsing(t)* by one, and assigning a value of *total-browsing-time* and *remaining-browsing-time* for the new customer c_i.

An internal transition occurs when either *remaining-browsing-time* for some c_i becomes equal to zero or *remaining-current-purchase-time* becomes equal to zero. In the first case, the relevant entry in *customers-browsing* is deleted and *length-of-queue* is incremented; in the second case *length-of-queue* is decremented.

We have not provided a formal specification of the model used, because the provision of a specification of the kind typically used to illustrate logic-based formalisms is not applicable to DEVS. In logical formalisms such as the situation or event calculi, domains are typically illustrated by sentential specification of system dynamics coupled with a inference scheme. DEVS, however, is not a logic-based framework. It allows specification of system dynamics with respect to what, in the vocabulary of logic-based formalisms, would be considered semantics. However, the algebraic formalism of DEVS is not framed within the logic-based dichotomy between syntax and semantics; the DEVS symbolism is not a syntactic formalism with a corresponding semantic model, it is simply a symbolic specification of system semantics. The complete, syntactic specification of a DEVS is normally its implementation; as we have chosen not to go into the details of implementation in this paper, we will leave the DEVS illustration imprecise, as it is.

DEVS is a very powerful formalism which has been used to impressive effect in practical domains of significant complexity. As DEVS was first developed for use in modelling and simulation, its application to the domains such as the above is obvious. However it can also be used for more AI-typical reasoning about action.

3 Continuous Change in Discretely Described Systems

Reasoning about action has traditionally taken as a paradigm systems whose states and transition functions can be described discretely, using discrete language components (fluents, predicates) and discrete actions or events. Sandewall was perhaps the first in the area of reasoning about action to consider the subject of continuous change ([San89]). However following a several year hiatus since the publication of Sandewall's paper, there has recently arisen considerable interest in formalising continuous change within logic-based discrete event formalisms such as the situation calculus ([GLR91], [PR95], [Rei96] within the situation calculus; [MS94] within the event calculus).

The principal result of this paper is that at the semantic level DEVS subsumes a number of the recently advanced proposals for incorporating continuous change into formalisms for reasoning about discrete actions. We demonstrate in what follows a correspondence between DEVS and two representative formalisms of continuous change: Reiter and Pinto's (within the situation calculus); and Miller and Shanahan's (within the event calculus).

Although we have omitted formal proofs of these correspondences, the key idea of the proofs is simple to outline: first, initial states in the AI-formalism and the DEVS formalism are shown to correspond; subsequently, an induction on events is shown to preserve the correspondence.

3.1 The Reiter/Pinto Formalisation of Continuous Change

When dealing with continuous change in a non-concurrent system, Reiter ([Rei96]) construes the situation calculus as a many-sorted, second-order language comprised of the following components[1]:

a sort act, of actions

a sort sit, ranging over sequences of actions

a sort $time$, ranging over the reals

a function symbol $time{:}act{\mapsto}\Re$, start time of action a

a function symbol $start{:}sit{\mapsto}\Re$, start time of situation s

a function symbol $do{:}act \times sit \mapsto sit$

a constant S_0, denoting the initial situation

the distinguished predicate symbol $Poss(c,s)$, interpreted to mean that action a can be performed in situation s

the distinguished predicate symbol $< (s, s')$, interpreted to mean that one can get from situation s to situation s' by a sequence of executable actions

distinguished predicate symbols DP - $natural$, $coherent$, $legal$, and $lntp$

a set $Fluents$ of other predicate symbols

Foundational axioms chosen by Reiter are consistent with the identification of situations with sequences of actions: the space of situations takes a tree shape

---

[1] We are not presently interested in the phenomenon of concurrent actions, however it appears to us that Reiter's approach to concurrency could be carried across in an extended translation to DEVS.

rooted at the initial situation. Domain constraints, observation sentences, and effect axioms are specified in the normal way using proper axioms comprised of the aforementioned terms of the language. Reiter uses his own successor-state axioms to deal with the frame problem, thus achieving a monotonic solution to the frame problem.

The main feature of Reiter's framework is its ability to handle continuous change and, in particular, natural actions. Natural actions are those which, as indicated in the previous section, are essentially a 'breakpoint' reached after gradual, continual change of a system, such as the overflow of a filling cup, or the landing of a falling ball. Natural actions, which are identified as such using the distinguished predicated $natural(a)$, cause a transition to a new situation, as determined by the (specified) dynamics of the system. In any situation the time of the next natural action—given no occurrence of non-natural events—is specified in the $lntp(t)$ ('least natural time point') predicate.

We will present a formal relationship between Reiter's framework and DEVS. Since we are proposing DEVS as a semantic framework for describing dynamic systems, we are looking to translate the semantic structure generated by Reiter's representational formalism into DEVS.

A situation calculus theory corresponds to a set of models (interpretations); if the theory is complete the corresponding set of models is a singleton, but we assume without loss of generality that whether it is complete or incomplete a situation calculus theory corresponds to a set of models. So we want, first, to show that any situation calculus model can be translated to a DEVS (we will then consider set of models). We do this by adducing a component-wise translation.

Consider any situation calculus interpretation $I =$
$$< act, sit, \Re, time, start, do, S_0, DP, Fluents >$$
The corresponding DEVS $\Gamma = <X, Y, States, ta, \delta_{int}, \delta_{ext}, \lambda >$ is determined by a translation which we shall denote Ψ. I.e., $\Gamma = \Psi(I)$. For an arbitrary model I, the components of $\Psi(I)$ are defined thus:

$X = \{a \mid a \in act \land \neg natural(a)\}$
$Y = Fluents$
$States = sit$

We see that the DEVS external actions are analagous to the non-natural actions of the situation calculus interpretation. Recall that natural actions are those which occur through a 'natural' evolution of the world—an evolution/change which does not include the intervention or action of any agent. DEVS output types coincide with the situation calculus fluents, and system states coincide with situations.

Let a member-level translation θ exist for each of the members of A, Y, and States; i.e.,

$X = \{\theta(a) \mid a \in act \land \neg natural(a)\}$
$Y = \{\theta(f) \mid f \in Fluents)\}$
$States = \{\theta(s) \mid s \in sit\}$

The rest of the components of the DEVS can now be defined:

$ta(s_{DEVS})=(t - start(s))$, *such that Intp(t,s)*

The time advance function is defined to equal the least natural time point—the time at which, given no other events, a 'natural' action would next occur.

$\delta_{ext}(s_{DEVS},t,x) = \{do(a,s_{SC}) \mid \neg natural(a) \wedge \theta(s_{SC})=s_{DEVS} \wedge \theta(a)=x)\}$

External actions correspond closely to the 'regular' situation calculus actions, initiated by an agent—actions as they would normally be understood in the sequential, non-continuous situation calculus, such as *pickup, move* and *serve-coffee.*

$\delta_{int}(s_{DEVS}) = \{do(a,s_{SC}) \mid natural(a) \wedge legal(do(a,s_{SC})\}$

The internal actions are those which occur naturally (a glass *overflowing* after being filled, or *shattering* after being dropped); the requirement that the corresponding situation calculus actions be 'legal' prevents anomalous natural actions.

$\lambda(s_{DEVS},t)=\{y \mid (\exists t)(\theta(s_{SC})=s_{DEVS} \wedge 0 \leq t \leq t' \wedge Intp(t',s) \wedge y = \theta(f))\}$

This translation assumes, consistent with Reiter, that change in real-valued parameters directed towards the occurrence of some natural action which is interrupted by the performing of an external action is lost. (E.g., a ball which, half-way to the ground is interrupted by a 'catch' action, is considered to be in the same position as it was before it was dropped) As we saw in the illustration of section 2, DEVS is able to change states preserving such parameter change (as also indicated in the discussion of Miller and Shanahan's formalism, below), thus overcoming this drawback.

The above translation takes a single situation calculus model and produces a single corresponding DEVS, but we need to provide a translation from situation calculus theories (or sets of models) to sets of DEVS.

A simple translation would be as follows: a situation calculus theory T is modelled by the interpretations $M_1, M_2, \ldots, M_n$ (the models need not be finite, but here we shall assume that they are); since Γ translated a single situation calculus model to an equivalent DEVS, then T is equivalent to the set of DEVS $\{\Gamma(M_1), \Gamma(M_2), \ldots, \Gamma(M_n)\}$.

In Section 4 we shall see that such a correspondence is exactly what we are looking for: if we are using DEVS to perform stochastic modelling of discrete, dynamic systems, and if do not assume complete system knowledge—precisely the situation we are in—we want a multiplicity of DEVS.

3.2 Miller and Shanahan's Formalisation of Continuous Change within the Event Calculus

The event calculus is a formalism first developed by Kowalski and Sergot ([KS86]) for use in logic programming. In the hands of Miller and Shanahan it has recently been demonstrated to be a useful framework for formalising reasoning about action, and has attracted considerable interest. It's main point of departure from the situation calculus is that it is a *narrative* based formalism. In contrast to the hypothetical reasoning of the situation calculus—where no particular events are held to occur, but reasoning proceeds on the supposition that certain events do occur—in narrative-based reasoning particular events are specified to occur, thereby generating a particular sequence of actual events, a narrative.

The event calculus is a sorted predicate calculus, with the following sorts:

Actions (*A*)

Fluents (*F*), used for discrete description

Parameters (*P*), expresses the value of continuous variables

Domain objects (*D*), used in specifying fluents and parameter values

Time (*T*), assumed to range over the non-negative reals

Reals (*R*)

Three important function symbols are used:

Value:$P \times T \mapsto R$, the numerical value of *P*

δ:$P \mapsto P$, the first derivative of *P*

Next:$T \mapsto T$, the time of the next state change

Predicate symbols:

Happens(a,t)

HoldsAt(f,t)

HoldsAt(f,t) is the key predicate for system description: it specifies which fluents hold true at any time. *Happens(a,t)* is true when action *a* occurs at time *t*. A number of other predicate symbols are used as part of Miller and Shanahan's circumscriptive technique for achieving a correct temporal reasoning result; with the exception of the predicates which specify fluents which are initially true or false—all the other predicates are used solely for purposes of achieving a correct circumscription and for determining the value of *HoldsAt*; thus we will refer to them collectively as InfP (inference predicates). As we are not dealing in this paper with inference techniques, we will not discuss their technique (we refer readers to [MS96] and [Sha97]). What we are interested in is the semantics of their framework. We represent a model of an event calculus as the tuple <A,F,P,D,T,Happens,HoldsAt,Next,InfP>.

We define a translation Υ from event calculus models to DEVS. For an arbitrary model *I*, the corresponding DEVS Υ(I) <X,Y,States,ta,δ_{int},δ_{ext},λ > is defined thus:

$X = \{a \mid a \in A\}$

$Y = F \cup P$

States correspond to the sequences of actual events, and are defined inductively beginning with an introduced constant *InitState*; each is associated with a time, denoting the start time of the state.

$S_0 = < \{InitState\}, 0 >$

$S_{i+1} = \{< InitState : a, t' > \mid S_i = < s, t > \wedge t' = Next(t) \wedge Happens(a, t)\}$

$States = \bigcup_{i=0}^{\infty} S_i$

Let a member-level translation θ exist for the members of A and Y, i.e.,

$A = \{\theta(a) \mid a \in A\}$

$Y = \{\theta(b) \mid b \in F \vee b \in P\}$

The crucial difference between this translation and that used in the case of Reiter's situation calculus is that in a DEVS translated from an event calculus specification, *there is no external transition function*. This difference arises because the event calculus is a narrative-based formalism; consequently, all events which occur in a system must be specified when the rest of the system is specified - no other (external) events can occur.

This difference requires elaboration. Only through syntax can any distinction in the event calculus be made between events which are 'imposed' and events which occur 'naturally'. When the system is initially specified, some events are unconditionally asserted using a statement of the form *Happens(a,t)*; these are essentially the 'imposed' events. However, the other way in which events can occur is through specifying conditional change - via conditional sentences whose consequent is of the form *Happens(a,t)*; the antecedent of these conditional sentences normally contains a parameterised value, which changes continuously. For example, the antecedent may become true after the a parameter such as 'water-level' reaches a certain point; in this case, the consequent could be 'overflow'.

As a DEVS translated from the event calculus changes only through internal transitions, its changes correspond exactly to the changes required by the *Happens* predicate. The extensions of *Happens* and *HoldsAt* encapsulates the circumscriptive machinery implicit in the event calculus framework, and it is upon these two predicates that the internal transition function and the output function rely.

$$\delta_{int}(s) = \{< aseq', t' >| (< aseq, t >= s\}) \wedge t' = Next(t) \wedge$$
$$Happens(a', t') \wedge (aseq' = aseq : a)\}$$
$$ta(s) = Next(t) - t, \text{ where } s =< aseq, t >$$
$$\lambda(s,t) = <\{f|HoldsAt(f,t)\}, \{p| Value(p,t)\}>$$

The above translation will transform any event calculus model into a DEVS; along with the situation calculus translation, this is the primary technical result of this paper. However it is sets of models which correspond to predicate calculus theories such as those of the situation or event calculi; so it is to sets of models that we now turn.

4   Discrete Event Systems, Modelling, and Simulation

Simulation is unquestionably an area of considerable importance in computer science. Yet despite an apparently considerable amount of value in applying simulation techniques to reasoning about action (or vice versa), simulation seems not to have been the subject of much attention in AI. The results of the previous sections will hopefully assist in the improvement of relations.

Suppose we are hoping to simulate a dynamic system about which we have incomplete information. Were we to have complete knowledge of the system dynamics the simulation would be straightforward: we would perform only one 'run' of the simulated system; any further runs would achieve the same result. But we have supposed that we have incomplete knowledge. Consequently, the result of an accurate simulation run would not be deterministic—different runs might produce different results. Obviously, then, to be able to ascertain the behaviour of the system we will need to repeat runs of the simulated systems to gain an indication of the possible outcomes. This is *stochastic* simulation, and is precisely the kind which, were we to use simulation, would be applicable to problems of reasoning about action.

Simulation of stochastic models is non-deterministic—the behaviour of two distinct runs of the same simulation may differ. We are aware that non-determinism can be modelled as a 'hidden variable' phenomena: were the value of the (perhaps very complex) hidden variable known, the system would be understood as deterministic. Essentially this view of nondeterminism grounds the implementation of stochastic simulation: each run of a simulation is provided with an input value (often with numerous components) which makes the simulation deterministic. Results of the simulation are calculated by probabilistic means, correlating the behaviours of the system with the range of inputs.

Further implementation will be required to confirm the apparent viability of simulating tradition AI domains of temporal reasoning. In particular, we anticipate reviewing the relationship between reasoning about action, simulation, and the very important neighbouring field of qualitative simulation.

5 Conclusion

DEVS is an engineering methodology. It was designed to assist in the development of implemented modelling and simulation environments and has been used in a wide range of applications. Recent implementations have been founded on techniques of object-oriented modelling, thus providing even greater flexibility in the application of DEVS ([Zei90]).

The field of reasoning about action needs to make better connections with adjacent fields of research. In this paper we have indicated the first stage of a route to bridging between reasoning about action and discrete event simulation. Furthermore, the proposal to use DEVS as a framework for comparison of systems is of use even in itself. We have seen that continuous change with a discrete system is neatly described in DEVS, as is the distinction between narrative and hypothetical reasoning about action formalisms (narrative formalisms correspond to systems without external inputs). Moreover, it would seem that DEVS provides promise as a framework for general expression of the dynamics of action-oriented systems.

References

[GL92]   M Gelfond and V Lifshitz. Representing actions in extended logic programs. In *Joint International Conference and Symposium on Logic Programming*, 1992.

[GLR91] Michael Gelfond, Vladimir Lifshitz, and A. Rabinov. What are the limitations of the situation calculus? In R. Boyer, editor, *Essays in honour of Woody Bledsoe*. Kluwer, 1991.

[KS86]   R. A. Kowalski and M. J. Sergot. A logic-based calculus of events. *New Generation Computing*, 4:67–95, 1986.

[MH69]   John McCarthy and Patrick J. Hayes. Some philosophical problems from the standpoint of artificial int elligence. *Machine Intelligence*, 4:463–502, 1969.

[MS94]   Rob Miller and Murray Shanahan. Narratives in the situation calculus. *Journal of Logic & Computation*, 4(5):513–530, October 1994.

[MS96]   Rob Miller and Murray Shanahan. Reasoning about discontinuities in the event calculus. In *KR '96*. Morgan Kaufmann, 1996.

[PR95]   Javier Pinto and Raymond Reiter. Reasoning about time in the situation calculus. *Annals of Mathematical and Artifical Intelligence*, 14:251–268, September 1995.

[Rei96]   Raymond Reiter. Natural actions, concurrency and continous time in the situation calculus. In *KR '96*, 1996.

[San89]   Erik Sandewall. Filter preferential entailmentfor the logic of action in almost con tinuous worlds. In *Proceedings of IJCAI '89*. Morgan Kaufmann, 1989.

[San94]   Erik Sandewall. *Features and Fluents*. Oxford University Press, 1994.

[Sha97]   Murray Shanahan. *Solving the Frame Problem*. MIT Press, 1997.

[Zei76]   Bernard P. Zeigler. *Theory of Modelling and Simulation*. Wiley, New York, 1976.

[Zei90]   Bernard P. Zeigler. *Object-oriented simulation with hierarchical, modular models: intelligent agents and endomorphic systems*. Academic Press, Boston, 1990.

Point-Based Approaches to Qualitative Temporal Reasoning

T. Van Allen, J. Delgrande, A. Gupta *

School of Computing Science,
Simon Fraser University,
Burnaby, B.C., Canada, V5A 1S6.
E-mail: {vanalle, jim, arvind}@cs.sfu.ca

Abstract. We are interested in the problem of qualitative, point-based temporal reasoning. That is, given a set of assertions concerning the relative positions of points in time, we are interested in compiling the assertions into a representation that supports efficient reasoning, determining consistency, computing the strongest entailed relation between any two points and updating the set of assertions. We begin by considering a general set of operations and their corresponding algorithms, applicable to general point-based temporal domains. We also consider special-purpose reasoners, which may be expected to perform well in an application domain with a restricted structure. Lastly we consider reasoners which incorporate restricted structures into a more general reasoning framework. Finally, we present instances of each such approach and give a comparison of their performance on random data sets.

1 Introduction

Temporal reasoning is essential in many areas of Artificial Intelligence, including planning, reasoning about action and causality, and natural language understanding. There is a fundamental choice between time points and time intervals as temporal primitives. Time intervals are more expressive, but more efficient algorithms exist for point-based reasoners [VK86,VKvB90]. Moreover many important and interesting problems are expressible in terms of assertions about time points. In this paper, we are interested in the general problem of qualitative, point-based temporal reasoning.

A significant problem, even in point-based approaches, is that of *scalability*. Even if an algorithm has good complexity bounds requiring, say, $O(n^2)$ time, such a bound is unacceptable for a large database, particularly if frequent use is to be made of such an algorithm. Matrix based deductive closure techniques are known for qualitative point based reasoning [VKvB90], but require $O(n^2)$ space

---

* We thank Tom Shermer for an observation simplifying our description of determining < relations in series parallel graphs. This work was supported by the Natural Sciences and Engineering Research Council of Canada. The third author also acknowledges the support of the British Columbia Advanced Systems Institute.

and $O(n^4)$ time for a set of assertions between n points. We are interested in methods that are appropriate when the number of assertions is roughly linear on the number of points. We present a simple dynamic reasoner for such applications, which performs all operations in time and space linear on the data set.

Another consideration is the nature of the application domain. Even though a problem may not admit a general efficient solution, certain restrictions of the problem may. Consequently, we investigate restrictions of temporal reasoning problems and corresponding special-purpose reasoners for which efficient algorithms exist. We present an efficient solution to the point based reasoning problem on *series parallel graphs*. From this we investigate general reasoners that make use of such special-purpose reasoners. In this situation, a desideratum is that such an approach degrade gracefully, in that as one moves from restricted cases to general cases, the time required will increase "proportionally". We show how our series parallel graph algorithms can be incorporated into a reasoner for general domains. This work is in the spirit of [GS95], who present a general reasoner based on the analysis of the problem domain into *time chains*. Lastly, we compare the performance of these approaches on randomly generated data sets.

This paper is an abridged version of a longer paper, consequently algorithms and proofs are represented by thumbnail sketches. They can be found in their entirety in the full paper, which is available by request from the authors.

2 Related Work

Allen [All83] proposed the *interval algebra* (IA) of temporal relations wherein time intervals are taken as primitive. Reasoning within this algebra (that is, reasoning about implied interval relations or determining the consistency of a set of assertions) is NP-complete [VK86]. The *point algebra* (PA), introduced in [VK86,VKvB90], is based on time points as primitives. The subset of the IA that can be translated into the PA is called the *pointisable interval algebra* (SIA) [vB90]. [GS93] consider complexity characteristics of various restrictions of the IA.

Some approaches to point based reasoning are designed for special domains. In the work of Schubert and collaborators [MS90,GS95] temporal reasoning is centred on *chains* of events. Reasoning within a chain takes constant time; reasoning between chains is less efficient, but is determined by a graph significantly smaller than the original (assuming the original graph is dominated by chains). In the worst case, however, their approach takes time and space squared on the number of assertions. [DG96] addresses reasoning in a restricted class of graphs, that of series-parallel graphs. Notably, for series parallel graphs with edge labels from $\{<=, <\}$, there is a linear time closure operation. Here we generalize the results of [DG96], by improving on their closure algorithm. We also develop the notion of a *metagraph* and describe an algorithm for analysing a graph into maximal series parallel components. The results here then generalise those of [GS95] as well as the related approach of [GM89].

3 Preliminaries

Notational Issues: Our results will rely substantially on graph theoretic concepts. The graphs that we use are simple, finite and directed. For a graph G, we denote the vertex and edge sets of G by $V(G)$ and $E(G)$ respectively. We refer the reader to [BM76] for terms not defined here. For complexity measures, we will use n to denote the number of nodes in a graph or the number of points in a database of point relational constraints (since we represent sets of constraints as graphs), and likewise e will denote the number of edges in a graph or the number of constraints in such a database. We represent an unlabeled edge (or an edge where the label is implicit) as (u, v) where u and v are nodes, and a labeled edge as (u, m, v), where m is a label. We assume that edge labels support the standard operations of composition and summation, which we denote $\odot$ and $\oplus$ respectively (see [CLR90] for more details). Via these operations we extend the notion of edge labels to path labels. We use the notation $u \rightsquigarrow v$ to indicate that there is a path from u to v, where a path may be of zero length. A subscript will denote a path label: $u \rightsquigarrow_r v$.

Models of Computation: We assume throughout that basic operations on small integers (of size $\log n$) can be performed in constant time and that such numbers take unit space for storage. This is a standard complexity-theoretic assumption – for example, in sorting algorithms, it is assumed that a comparison of two numbers is performed in constant time. This approach also consistent with other work in temporal reasoning. If a log-cost RAM model of computation is used, the complexity of our algorithms is increased by a factor of $\log \log n$.

4 Point Relations

Points are primitive. Although intuitively we can think of them as "points in time" or points on the real number line, we make no particular demands on them. We will denote the infinite set of all points as P, and generally refer to individual points as $s, t, u, v, w \ldots$

The point relations are: $\{\emptyset, <, >, =, <>, <=, >=, <=>\}$. We will call this set R. Each relation corresponds to an element of the powerset of $\{<, =, >\}$, the primitive point relations. Each complex relation is a disjunction of the primitive relations that make it up; thus $\emptyset$ is the relation that never holds between two points, and $<=>$ is the relation that always holds. We will call one relation "stronger" than another iff the first is a subset of the second. The standard set operations: union, intersection, set-equality, etc, are defined over the point relations, with obvious interpretations. As well, we have the following two functions:

1. *sequence* : $R \times R \rightarrow R$

2. $inverse : R \to R$

Sequence represents the transitive relation entailed by a sequence of two point relations. It is the composition operation for edge labels taken from R. Intersection, by contrast, gives the relation entailed by two relations that hold in parallel. Inverse maps a single relation onto the relation that holds in the opposite direction.

We implement the point relations as the numbers $0, 1, 2 \ldots 7$. We implement all set operations as bit level logical operations, sequence as lookup in an 8×8 matrix and inverse as lookup in an 8 element vector. All operations take $O(1)$ time.

Constraints: We define the language C as the set of all sentences $S ::= P\,R\,P$. That is, a constraint is a point followed by a point relation followed by a point. Sometimes we will use the term "assertion" instead of "constraint". Entailment in C can be axiomatized as follows:

1. $\{\} \models x = x$, for all $x \in P$
2. $\{\} \models x <=> y$, for all $x, y \in P$
3. $\{x\,r\,y\} \models y\,inverse(r)\,x$
4. $\{x\,r_1\,y\} \models x\,r_1 \cup r_2\,y$, for all $r_2 \in R$
5. $\{x\,r_1\,y,\ y\,r_2\,z\} \models x\,sequence(r_1, r_2)\,z$
6. $\{x\,r_1\,y,\ x\,r_2\,y\} \models x\,r_1 \cap r_2 y$
7. $\{x <= v,\ x <= w,\ v <> w,\ v <= y,\ w <= y\} \models x < y$

In Axiom 7, if $a <> b$ then either $a < b$ or $b < a$. But then, if $x <= a$ and $x <= b$, then either $x < a$ or $x < b$. This is a valid entailment in propositional logic but one we cannot express in C. However, since $a <= y$ and $b <= y$, it follows that $x < y$. Where the paths converge, so do the implications of the disjunction. [GS95] prove completeness for this formulation. We will call inconsistent any set of assertions which entails $x\,\emptyset\,y$ for any $x, y \in P$.

Operations on Constraint Sets: We are interested in the general problem of computing the entailments of a given set of point relational constraints. To compute all entailments, one could define a deductive closure operation on constraint sets. Such a closure operation, however, might be (in fact, is) computationally expensive, and so it is of interest to look at the problem of finding the strongest relation between only two points, where this can be done more expeditiously. We are interested in this problem, and in representation schemes which allow us to quickly find the relation between two points. Generally, the problem breaks down into two subproblems:

1. Compilation: compiling a set of constraints in the language C into some representation that allows efficient reasoning.
2. Querying: computing the strongest relation between two points, given such a representation.

We also look, in passing, at the problem of updating the representation by adding a new constraint.

5 Temporally Labeled Graphs

Temporally labeled graphs [GS95] are a means of representing consistent sets of point relations. Each node in a temporally labeled graph represents some set of nodes which are all $=$ to one another; edges are either directed and labeled $<$ or $<=$, or undirected and labeled $<>$. Partitioning the edge sets on their labels, we have $E_<$, $E_{<=}$, $E_{<>}$. The graph composed of only edges from $E_< \cup E_{<=}$ we refer to as the $(<, <=)$ subgraph. Note that any set of constraints from C can be translated into a set of constraints using only the relations $\{<, <>, <=\}$. The edge set of a temporally labeled graph corresponds exactly to some such set of constraints, and we will say that the graph entails a relation when the relation is entailed by this set of constraints. Algorithms for compiling a set of assertions into such a graph and testing it for consistency are given in [GS95] and [vB92] so we do not go into these areas further. We give an outline of an algorithm to find the strongest relation between two points in such a graph, and an algorithm to update the graph when a constraint is added. Both algorithms run in $O(e)$ time.

We want to compute the strongest relation between v and w. Consider the subproblem of finding only the strongest relation in one "direction", that is, finding the strongest temporal "path" from v to w. If we can solve this subproblem, then we can trivially solve the problem by finding the relation from v to w, then the relation from w to v, and combining the results. We can solve the subproblem for v and w as follows:

Definition: For nodes v, w in a temporally labeled graph, $LEQ(v, w) = \{x : v \leadsto_{<=} x, x \leadsto_{<=} w\}$.

By traversing all paths from v to w and taking their intersection, we can compute the strongest path from v to w. This is easily done with a single depth first search of the $(<, <=)$ subgraph. We can compute the LEQ set for v and w at the same time. If the strongest path is labeled $<$ or $=$ then the problem is solved. If the strongest path is labeled $<=>$ then the result is $<>$ or $<=>$, depending on whether or not $(v, <>, w)$ is an edge. Otherwise, the strongest path is labeled $<=$, and then the result is $<=$ or $<$ depending on whether or not there is an edge $(x, <>, y)$ such that $x, y \in LEQ(v, w)$. This algorithm visits each edge at most once and does a constant amount of work at each one, and thus is linear on the number of edges.

As for updates, we can add an assertion $x\, r_1\, y$ by first computing the strongest relation, r_0, between v, the node x maps onto, and w, the node y maps onto. If r_0 is inconsistent with r_1 then the update fails. Otherwise, the update goes ahead; if the update introduces a cycle, however, we have to "collapse" the set $LEQ(v, w)$ into a single node. If no cycle is created, we can simply add an edge.

Ranking: We can speed up multiple searches in a directed acyclic graph (DAG) by bounding search depth. We assign each node an index called its *rank*, so that every edge points from a lower ranked node to a higher. To search all paths between two nodes we can confine our search to those nodes with intermediate ranks. Note that the smaller the set of indices used, the better the expected performance. There is a drawback to ranking, however, in that it may have to be recomputed in order to update the graph.

6 Series Parallel Graphs

The point algebra provides us with a very general framework for reasoning. It can be used in any domain that we model as points on a line. Although this generality is a nice feature, certain restricted domains lend themselves to more efficient reasoning strategies. Here we examine one such domain.

People use hierarchical structures to manage complex information. We organize temporal information into units based on natural cycles such as the year, the lunar month, and the day. We also organize events into subevents according to their causal dependencies and interrelations. Allen [All83] introduced the notion of a reference interval which acts as an interface through which a cluster of intervals would relate to intervals outside the cluster. In Allen's framework an interval could have more than one reference interval, but he noted that more treelike frameworks of reference intervals would lead to better reasoning times.

Suppose we have a domain where events are constructed from elemental events according to some simple operations. For example, we might "concatenate" two events that are temporally adjacent, or "overlay" two events that occur during the same time frame. If we restrict ourselves to events constructed recursively by these two operations, we can reason more efficiently about their internal structure than we could with the point algebra.

First we define the notion of a series parallel tree, then we define series parallel graphs in terms of series parallel trees. A series parallel tree represents one possible derivation/parse of a series parallel graph.

Definition: A sp-tree T with its associated properties $source(T)$, $sink(T)$, $label(T)$, $nodeset(T)$, $edgeset(T)$, is given by one of the following:

1. (Base case) $T = edge(v, r, w)$, where:
   (a) $source(T) = v$
   (b) $sink(T) = w$
   (c) $label(T) = r$
   (d) $nodeset(T) = \{v, w\}$
   (e) $edgeset(T) = \{(v, r, w)\}$
2. (Inductive case) $T = series(T_1, T_2)$ where:
   (a) T_1 and T_2 are sp-trees
   (b) $source(T) = source(T_1)$
   (c) $sink(T) = sink(T_2)$
   (d) $label(T) = label(T_1) \odot label(T_2)$
   (e) $nodeset(T) = nodeset(T_1) \cup nodeset(T_2)$
   (f) $edgeset(T) = edgeset(T_1) \cup edgeset(T_2)$
   (g) $nodeset(T_1) \cap nodeset(T_2) = \{sink(T_1)\} = \{source(T_2)\}$
   (h) $edgeset(T_1) \cap edgeset(T_2) = \{\}$

3. (Inductive case) $T = parallel(T_1, T_2)$ where:
    (a) T_1 and T_2 are sp-trees
    (b) $source(T) = source(T_1) = source(T_2)$
    (c) $sink(T) = sink(T_1) = sink(T_2)$
    (d) $label(T) = label(T_1) \oplus label(T_2)$
    (e) $nodeset(T) = nodeset(T_1) \cup nodeset(T_2)$
    (f) $edgeset(T) = edgeset(T_1) \cup edgeset(T_2)$
    (g) $nodeset(T_1) \cap nodeset(T_2) = \{source(T_1), sink(T_1)\}$
    (h) $edgeset(T_1) \cap edgeset(T_2) = \{\}$

Definition: We define series parallel graphs in terms of sp-trees as follows: G is a series parallel graph iff there exists a sp-tree, T such that $V(G) = nodeset(T)$, $E(G) = edgeset(T)$.

Note that series parallel graphs are thus necessarily single source, single sink graphs, and that the label of a sp-tree summarizes all paths from source to sink in its associated graph. We say that $source(G) = source(T)$ and $sink(G) = sink(T)$. Note also that there may be several sp-trees corresponding to any given series parallel graph, but only one series parallel graph for any given sp-tree. Where a sp-tree T has an associated series parallel graph G we say that $spg(T) = G$. Conventionally, the definitions are given in the reverse order; the tree structure is defined in terms of the graph. We find this order more convenient because the graphs must be defined inductively and the tree represents the composition of the graph from subgraphs.

6.1 Transitive Closure on Series Parallel Graphs

We can compute transitive closure for series parallel graphs in $O(n^2)$ time and space for arbitrary edge labels (that support $O(1)$ operations of composition and intersection). Given the special structure of series parallel graphs, however, we can define more efficient algorithms for special cases. For example, we can compute simple path closure (is there a path between two nodes?) in $O(n)$ time and we can store this information in $O(n)$ space. We do this by embedding the graph in the Cartesian plane and storing the coördinates of each vertex. We embed the graph so that there is a path from v to w iff the x and y coördinates of v are less than, respectively, the x and y coördinates of w. Details of this technique can be found in [DG96]. Given path closure, we can also compute the closure of $<, <=$ labels on the edges of a series parallel graph, and again, we can do this in $O(n)$ time and space.

Definition: For a node v in a series parallel graph G: $s(v)$ is the maximum number of $<$ edges on any path from $source(G)$ to v. This can be computed for all nodes in $O(n)$ time.

Definition: $a(v)$ is given by the following: if $v = sink(G)$ or $(v, <, w) \in E(G)$ for some w, then $a(v) = s(v)$, otherwise, $a(v) = \min\{a(w) : (v, <=, w) \in E(G)\}$

Theorem: For any two nodes v, w such that $v \rightsquigarrow w$ in a series parallel graph G, $a(v) < s(w)$ iff $v \rightsquigarrow_< w$.

The proof is difficult and may be found in the full paper. The intuition, however, is that every node v in a series parallel graph is in some *maximal* series parallel subgraph S such that not $v \rightsquigarrow_< sink(S)$. Note that every node w such that $v \rightsquigarrow w$ is either in this subgraph or is reachable from its sink. In the first case, $s(w) \leq s(sink(S))$ and not $v \rightsquigarrow_< w$, wheras, in the former, $s(w) > s(sink(S))$ iff $sink(S) \rightsquigarrow_< w$. This is less obvious, but it follows from S being maximal.

We can compute the s-label for all nodes using depth first search of the series parallel graph or a left to right, depth first traversal of the sp-tree. Likewise, given the s-labeling, we can compute the a-labels with a right to left, depth first traversal of the sp-tree, or a corresponding depth first search on the transpose of the graph.

This technique improves on [DG96] in that their closure algorithm requires real numbers of arbitrary precision, whereas ours uses only integers in $[0, n]$.

7 Metagraphs

In this section, we borrow the terms "metagraph", "metaedge" and "metanode" from [GS95] and generalize the notion somewhat.

Definition (partial): A graph (V', E') is a metagraph of a directed acyclic graph (V, E) if V contains V' and there is an onto function $m : E \rightarrow E'$ such that, for all $(x, y) \in E$ where $m((x, y)) = (u, v)$:

1. Either $x = u$ or both of the following:
   (a) There is an edge (w, x) in E such that $m((w, x)) = (u, v)$.
   (b) For all edges $(w, x) \in E$, $m((w, x)) = (u, v)$.
2. Either $y = v$ or both of the following:
   (a) There is an edge $(y, w) \in E$ such that $m((y, w)) = (u, v)$.
   (b) For all edges $(y, w) \in E$, $m((y, w)) = (u, v)$.

We call elements of V' metanodes and elements of E' metaedges. Metaedges correspond to (edge disjoint) single source, single sink components of the "base" graph. We can extend our definition to include edge labels, and then define the label of a metaedge (u, v) to be the intersection of the labels of all paths from u to v in the base graph.

The purpose of the metagraph construct is that it allows us to encapsulate subgraphs "behind" a convenient interface. All relations between nodes strictly internal to a metaedge (nodes that are part of the corresponding component but not metanodes) are determined entirely by the subgraph that corresponds to that metaedge; relations between metanodes are determined entirely by the metagraph; relations between nodes internal to different metaedges are determined by their internal relations to the sources and sinks of their metaedges, and by the relations between those source/sink metanodes.

The metagraph notion is useful for representing domains where relational data is composed of many "self-contained" units connected to each other only through common sources and sinks, especially when such units may be entered whole by a user. Using a metagraph may improve efficiency where graphs are largely composed of substructures that lend themselves to more efficient implementation of basic operations (search, closure, updates, etc.).

7.1 Series Parallel Metaedges

Here we present a method for partitioning the edge set of a graph into maximal series parallel metaedges. We start with a very high level algorithm that collapses all series parallel components into single edges.

Let G be a directed acyclic metagraph.

Rule A: If there is a vertex $v \in V(G)$ such that v has only one incoming edge (u, m, v) and only one outgoing edge (v, n, w) then remove these edges and add the edge $(u, m \odot n, v)$.

Rule B: If there are two edges (u, m, v) and (u, n, v) in G then remove these edges and add the edge $(u, m \oplus n, v)$.

These rules are applied iteratively to G until no new rules can be fired. The result is a metagraph where each metaedge represents an edge disjoint, maximal series parallel component of the original graph. We see that this algorithm correctly reduces the graph to its maximal series parallel components, in that, if it did not, then there would be two metaedges left in series or in parallel. But all metaedges are expanded: the initial edges are all expanded and all created edges are expanded. But then one of the two edges must have been expanded last. But then it was in series or parallel with the other, and they would have been collapsed. Note that we can label metaedges with sp-trees and define $\odot$ as a series composition step; $\oplus$ as a parallel step.

How can we refine our algorithm to be more efficient? Rules A and B are in a "feeding" relationship with each other: the output of each may create the firing conditions for the other. By recursively applying the rules to their own output, we can define a linear time algorithm; we simply need to test each output edge from a rule for local conditions that would fire a rule, and if those conditions exist, fire the rule. Thus we iterate over the graph only once. Under the assumption that we can find parallel edges in constant time, and insert and remove edges in constant time, this algorithm runs in linear time (on the edges of the graph), since we make a recursive call only when an edge has been deleted from the graph by the application of some rule. We can use a lookup table to store the edges, indexed by node pairs, and another table, indexed by nodes, to store indegrees and outdegrees.

The implementation of the edge table is an issue. Using a matrix gives us $O(1)$ lookup, but forces us to relax our space requirements to allow $O(n^2)$ space usage. Alternatively, since the table will (hopefully) be quite sparse, we could use a hashing scheme, and expect minimal added cost on average. In fact, by slightly modifying our algorithm, we can use a stack to store metaedges as we create them; by expanding the edges in a more specific order, we can ensure that metaedges in parallel are never separated in this stack by other metaedges unless those metaedges are maximal (and so can be popped). Thus the algorithm can be enhanced to use only linear space as well as time. This enhancement is somewhat more complicated, and probably unnecessary in most cases. Therefore it isn't given in further detail here.

7.2 Temporal Reasoning Revisited

Given our point algebra reasoner, closure algorithms for series parallel graphs, and our algorithm to analyse a graph into series parallel metaedges, it seems natural to combine them in the field of temporal reasoning. Given that we have linear time algorithms for all of the above subproblems, we can design a linear time approach to temporal reasoning that takes advantage of domain structure, yet degrades gracefully. When the domain does not live up to our expectations we will do worse than the simplest approach by only a constant factor. The hybrid scheme proposed is to first construct an temporally labeled graph, then analyse it into maximal series parallel metaedges (where each <> edge corresponds to a single metaedge). We then compute the internal closure of these metaedges. We can now answer queries using lookup for two points in the same metaedge; for points not in the same metaedge we need only search the graph made up of the metaedges. Updating and revision would follow a similar pattern. We believe that such an approach will be of use in domains where temporal information tends to be hierarchically structured, and when queries of that information tend to reflect that structure. We believe that this is the case in several domains of interest, for example, in modelling process execution.

8   Implementation and Testing

We have implemented the following:

1. The dynamic graph-based approach in its simplest form.
2. The dynamic graph-based approach using ranking to speed up search.
3. Decomposing a DAG into series parallel components, computing closure for these, and combining lookup with rank-bounded metagraph search to answer queries.

Common Lisp was the language used, and data structures were kept consistent between the approaches. The implementations could probably be tuned to a much higher performance; however, we were interested more in their relative, as opposed to absolute, performance. We have tested our implementations for correctness quite extensively. We also carried out tests of efficiency on random data sets; the results of which are summarised below.

8.1   Random Graphs

In order to compare our approaches, we generated random sets of constraints and compared compile times and query times. Since we represent sets of constraints as graphs, we generated sets of constraints by generating random graphs. In fact, we generated only directed, acyclic graphs, since the algorithms of interest to us: path queries, metagraph compilation, act on graphs of this type. To generate a DAG over the nodes $v_1, v_2, \ldots v_n$, we let the ordering define a topological sort of the intended graph, and define the graph by enumerating the forward edges and deciding to add each one based on some probability. For the purpose of testing the approaches presented in this paper, we were interested only in sparse graphs, that is, when e is $O(n)$. To produce sparse graphs we choose to add an edge with a probability of approximately k/n, for $0 \leq k < n$. Then we randomly assign labels from $\{<, <=, <>\}$ to the edges. This set of edges corresponds to a set of assertions.

We experimented with various modifications to this basic scheme, since we are interested in special domains. We investigated domains where most constraints were non-redundant, domains based on a series parallel graph with a certain amount of "noise" (random edges) introduced, and domains based on chains where, again, a certain amount of noise was added. Here, for reasons of brevity, we present test results for data sets generated using the basic scheme only.

8.2 Test Results

Thirty sparse graphs were generated for each value of n, where edge labels $<$, $<=$ and $<>$ were equiprobable. The average number of edges per graph, the average time to compile and the average time to answer 100 queries are all given below. The approaches are numbered as enumerated above. Times are given in milliseconds and the tests were run on a Sun Microsystems UltraSparc 1 workstation.

Nodes	Edges	Compile Time			Query Time		
Approach:		1	2	3	1	2	3
100	503	5	4	69	38	19	18
200	1000	9	10	138	56	25	25
300	1496	13	16	207	69	28	30
400	2024	17	21	286	78	31	33
500	2494	22	27	354	91	35	35

The results indicate that the simple approaches are superior on generic, sparse data sets. The use of ranking to bound search depth considerably reduced average query time. Comparing compilation times, the simple approaches were about 5 times faster than the series parallel metagraph approach. On chain based and series parallel based data sets, the series parallel metagraph approach began to diverge from the simple ranked approach; these results are given in the full paper.

9 Conclusions and Extensions

We believe that the simple approach presented in this paper is useful because it is easy to implement and allows for quick compilation and updates. It is well-suited to form the backbone of a more powerful reasoner, one for SIA constraints, for instance. It provides a benchmark against which to measure the performance of other approaches, and we are interested in comparing it to the approach of [GS95]. The series parallel metagraph approach, on the other hand, is appropriate in certain domains, but does not give significant benefits in the general case. Series parallel graphs provide a temporal reasoning paradigm for certain domains and are of independent interest, therefore we continue to study series parallel graphs. The metagraph concept and formalization may be useful in other domains; particularly those involving a sparse graph and a complexity that is exponential or higher degree polynomial on the graph size. We are interested in applying the methods developed here to such domains.

References

[All83]   James Allen. Maintaining knowledge about temporal intervals. *Communications of the ACM*, 26(1):832–843, 1983.

[BM76]   J. Bondy and U.S.R. Murty. *Graph Theory with Applications*. North-Holland, 1976.

[CLR90]   T.H. Cormen, C.E. Leiserson, and R.L. Rivest. *Introduction to Algorithms*. The MIT Press, Cambridge, 1990.

[DG96]   J.P. Delgrande and A. Gupta. A representation for efficient temporal reasoning. In *Proceedings of the AAAI National Conference on Artificial Intelligence*, pages 381–388, Portland, Oregon, August 1996.

[GM89]   Malik Ghallab and Amine Mounir Alaoui. Managing efficiently temporal relations through indexed spanning trees. In *Proceedings of the International Joint Conference on Artificial Intelligence*, pages 1297–1303, Detroit, 1989.

[GS93]   M. Golumbic and R. Shamir. Complexity and algorithms for reasoning about time: A graph-theoretic approach. *JACM*, 40(5):1108–1133, 1993.

[GS95]   Alfonso Gerevini and Lenhart Schubert. Efficient algorithms for qualitative reasoning about time. *Artificial Intelligence*, 74(2):207–248, April 1995.

[MS90]   S.A. Miller and L.K. Schubert. Time revisited. *Computational Intelligence*, 6:108–118, 1990.

[vB90]   Peter van Beek. Reasoning about qualitative temporal information. In *Proceedings of the AAAI National Conference on Artificial Intelligence*, pages 728–734, 1990.

[vB92]   Peter van Beek. Reasoning about qualitative temporal information. *Artificial Intelligence*, 58(1-3):297–326, 1992.

[VK86]   Marc Vilain and Henry Kautz. Constraint propagation algorithms for temporal reasoning. In *Proceedings of the AAAI National Conference on Artificial Intelligence*, pages 377–382, Philadelphia, PA, 1986. temporal reasoning.

[VKvB90]   Marc Vilain, Henry Kautz, and Peter van Beek. Constraint propagation algorithms for temporal reasoning: A revised report. In *Readings in Qualitative Reasoning about Physical Systems*, pages 373–381. Morgan Kaufmann Publishers, Inc., Los Altos, CA, 1990.

An Experimental Study of
Reasoning with Sequences of Point Events

R. Wetprasit, A. Sattar and M. Beaumont

Knowledge Representation and Reasoning Unit
School of Computing and Information Technology, Griffith University,
NATHAN, Brisbane, 4111 AUSTRALIA
{rattana, sattar, mbeaumon}@cit.gu.edu.au

Abstract. Interval and point algebras are two influential frameworks to model an interval and point based temporal entities. However, in many real world situations we often encounter recurring events that include multiple points, multiple intervals or combinations of points and intervals. Recently, point-based frameworks (MPE [9] and GMPE [10]) for representing and reasoning with sequences of point events have been proposed. These frameworks include new algorithms for solving reasoning tasks with an improved complexity. However, no empirical investigation has been made yet. This paper presents an experimental study of these two frameworks. In this study, we present the design of experiments, implementation of the algorithms, and an empirical performance analysis. Our results indicate that the MPE and GMPE frameworks are not only expressively richer, but also perform better than the traditional approaches to temporal reasoning.

1 Introduction

Two classical frameworks to model temporal information are: *interval algebra* (IA) [1] and *point algebra* (PA) [8]. While interval algebra considers an event as a continuous phenomena on time line, point algebra considers an event as a time instance. Motivated by the computational efficiency of point algebra, a subset of IA for which the reasoning tasks can be solved in polynomial time was proposed [6]. This subset is called *pointizable (or simple) interval relations* (SIA). In some domains, an event is considered as a set of recurring events, instead of a single event. For example, *poster sessions* overlap *tea breaks*. In [3], an event (e.g., poster sessions) consisting of a set of interval subevents is defined as a *non-convex interval* (NCI). Multi-Point Event (MPE) framework [9] extends point algebra to model recurring events as *multi-point events*. This framework is further extended to a Generalized Multi-Point Event (GMPE) framework [10] to represent complex relationships such as *discontinuous point relations* which are relations between three point events. For instance, *point I_1 is not between J_1 and J_2, given J_1 is before J_2* [2]. The ability to represent these relations leads GMPE framework to be able to handle the *disjointedness interval relations* (e.g., interval I is either before or after interval J) in point-based framework. Therefore, the MPE and GMPE frameworks improve expressive power of point algebra. These frameworks provide an alternative point based approach to handle information about interval events.

While a large body of literature in temporal reasoning is devoted to theoretical investigations, a little work has been done on experimental studies. The main aim of this paper is to demonstrate that the MPE and GMPE frameworks not merely improved the expressive power of the point algebra but also perform better than the traditional methods.

In temporal reasoning, there is no existing collection of large benchmark problems that actually arise in practise. Our experimental study involved some randomly generated test beds. These tests were generated by using different models for MPE, SIA, IA and GMPE: $S(MPE, k, n, d)$, $S(SIA, k, d)$, and $S(IA, k, d)$, where k is number of nodes, n is number of point events in each node, and d is an average degree of a node. The performance evaluation was focused on solving two major reasoning tasks: finding all feasible relations and a consistent scenario for MPE and GMPE networks. A consistent scenario of a temporal network is a consistent network where all relations are atomic. Our results indicate that the algorithm for finding all feasible relations for MPE networks achieves the solution with about 60 % of the time required by solving the same problem in the PA networks [6]. Precisely, contributions of this paper are:

- an implementation of the algorithms for finding feasible relations and a consistent scenario in the MPE and GMPE networks;
- the design of randomly generated tests to evaluate the performance of the algorithms; and
- an analysis of experimental results with respect to the best known algorithms for PA networks.

2 MPE and GMPE Frameworks

An MPE consists of a series of totally ordered point subevents. The size n of an MPE is the total number of points contained in that MPE. A relation, R, between two MPEs, I and J, is represented as a matrix A of size $n \times m$, where n is the size of I and m is the size of J. Each element, $A_{i,j}$, is a disjunction of basic point relations ($T = \{<, >, =\}$), which is the relation between the points I_i to J_j. To make sure that a relation R is internally path-consistent [4], the matrix A has to be in *Canonical Form*. An MPE matrix relation A is in canonical form when it satisfies the following path-consistency conditions:

1. $A_{i,j-1} \subseteq A_{i,j} \circ \{>\}$ $(\forall i\ 1 \leq i \leq n, \forall j\ 1 < j \leq m)$
2. $A_{i+1,j} \subseteq \{>\} \circ A_{i,j}$ $(\forall i\ 1 \leq i < n, \forall j\ 1 \leq j \leq m)$
3. $A_{i,j+1} \subseteq A_{i,j} \circ \{<\}$ $(\forall i\ 1 \leq i \leq n, \forall j\ 1 \leq j < m)$
4. $A_{i-1,j} \subseteq \{<\} \circ A_{i,j}$ $(\forall i\ 1 < i \leq n, \forall j\ 1 \leq j \leq m)$

There are five operations used when solving reasoning tasks in MPE frameworks. These operations operate between two MPE matrices and the results of these operations can be found in table 1. The symbols $+, \times, ^-, \circ, ^\smile$ are defined in PA and stand for union, intersection, complement, composition and inverse respectively.

Like IA and PA, it is possible to formulate the reasoning task in MPE framework as a *constraint satisfaction problem*. Each node of the network represents a variable which is an MPE. The domain of a variable is a set of sequences of real numbers for

$\forall\, i,j\ (1 \le i,j \le n)$	
Complement $C = \hat{A}$ iff $C_{i,j} = {}^{\neg}A_{i,j}$	
Inverse $\quad C = \breve{A}$ iff $C_{i,j} = {}^{\neg}A_{j,i}$	
Union $\quad\quad C = A \oplus B$ iff $C_{i,j} = A_{i,j} + B_{i,j}$	
Intersection $\;\; C = A \otimes B$ iff $C_{i,j} = A_{i,j} \times B_{i,j}$	
Composition $C = A \odot B$ iff $C_{i,j} = \prod_{k=1}^{n}(A_{i,k} \circ B_{k,j})$	
$\quad = A_{i,1} \circ B_{1,j} \times A_{i,2} \circ B_{2,j} \times ... \times A_{i,n} \circ B_{n,j}$	

Table 1. Operations of Multi-Point Event Relations

every point subevent in that MPE. The label on an arc connecting two nodes is an MPE relation. This is known as an *MPE network*.

In [10], the MPE framework has been generalized to gain higher expressiveness by allowing relations between two MPEs to be a disjunction of MPE relations. By relaxing this, the full set of IA can now be represented. For example, the relation {*before, after*} would be split into two MPE relations, one being {*before*} and the other being {*after*}. The operations used in GMPE and their results are in table 2, where M and N are the numbers of matrices in GMPE relations A and B respectively. The symbols $\oplus, \otimes, \odot, {}^{\wedge}$ and ${}^{\vee}$ are used to denote the union, intersection, and composition of two MPE relations, complement and inverse of a relation, respectively. The reasoning tasks in GMPE framework are also formulated as constraint satisfaction problems.

Complement	$\widehat{\mathcal{A}} = \bigcup_{p=1}^{M} \hat{A}^{p}$
Inverse	$\widecheck{\mathcal{A}} = \bigcup_{p=1}^{M} \breve{A}^{p}$
Union	$\mathcal{A} \oplus \mathcal{B} = \bigcup_{p=1}^{M} \bigcup_{q=1}^{N} A^{p} \oplus B^{q}$
Intersection	$\mathcal{A} \otimes \mathcal{B} = \bigcup_{p=1}^{M} \bigcup_{q=1}^{N} A^{p} \otimes B^{q}$
Composition	$\mathcal{A} \odot \mathcal{B} = \bigcup_{p=1}^{M} \bigcup_{q=1}^{N} A^{p} \odot B^{q}$

Table 2. Operations of the Generalized MPE Relations

3 Experimental Study of MPE Networks

This section presents an experimental study of the algorithms for finding all feasible relations and a consistent scenario of MPE networks.

3.1 Finding All Feasible Relations

The algorithm FEASIBLE_MPE determines if an MPE network is consistent, and computes all feasible relations. There are two parts in FEASIBLE_MPE: the first part is a path- consistency algorithm which determines if the network is consistent. The path-consistency algorithm for MPE proceeds in two steps: (1) converting all MPE matrices into a *canonical form* by checking the path-consistency of each matrix; (2) computing the path-consistency of the network. The second part of FEASIBLE_MPE is used to find *forbidden subgraphs*. See figure 1 for an example of a forbidden subgraph. The relations between any set of three subevents in this subgraph are consistent. However, the relation '=' between subevents S_s and T_t causes the subgraph of four nodes inconsistent. By changing the label between S_s and T_t of all forbidden subgraphs to '<', the MPE network is minimal.

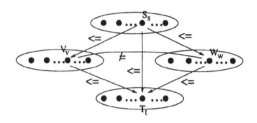

Fig. 1. A forbidden MPE subgraph

MPE vs PA: An MPE network can be transformed into a corresponding PA network, thus the reasoning tasks can be solved by applying the algorithms used for PA networks. Here, we compare the performance of both approaches. We generated random consistent MPE networks from $S(MPE, k, n, d)$ model, described below, then computed all feasible relations by implementing the FEASIBLE_MPE algorithm. To evaluate the PA approach, we converted the MPE networks to the corresponding PA networks. Each point event represents a point subevent in MPE, hence there are $k \times n$ points in the PA network. The relation from point i to $(i + 1, ..., n)$ of the same MPE, in which they are implicitly represented in MPE framework, is expressed as '<' in the corresponding PA network. Certainly, this results in losing connectivity in multi-point events. We applied the FEASIBLE algorithm proposed in [6] to the PA network. The time required to convert the networks was not taken into consideration. Care was taken to always maintain the same base implementation of the algorithms and only the data structures and related operations we were evaluating are different.

$S(MPE, k, n, d)$ **model:** The random instances were generated as follows:

Step 1: Generate an MPE network with k MPEs (nodes) each MPE contains n point subevents, and an average degree of d for each node. With the network of k nodes, we selected $kd/2$ constrained arcs from the total $k(k-1)/2$ possible arcs with uniform distribution. The elements of each matrix constraining an arc were randomly picked up from set of all possible disjunctions of point relations T (excluding the empty label), with equal probability. The unconstrained arcs were labeled with a matrix of "no information" relations (T).

Step 2: Generate a consistent scenario. This enforces the MPE network to be consistent. To do so, we generate a consistent instantiation as follows: Let *Max* be the maximum integer value that our machine can store, and Rdm be a random value obtained from a system random generator. The first point of each MPE, V_1, is $Rdm - n$, when n is the number of points in MPEs. This is to ensure that all n points fit in Max. Then the values of other points, V_i, $(1 < i \le n)$ are:

$$V_i = (Rdm \bmod (Max - (n - i + 1) - V_{i-1})) + V_{i-1} + 1$$

After generating all points, we identified relations between points and represented them in matrices labeling the corresponding arcs. Then we unioned these matrices with the corresponding matrices of the network from step 1. Therefore, the generated network is a consistent MPE network with some infeasible relations.

We experimented on consistent networks of 20 and 50 MPEs generated from $S(MPE, k, n, d)$ by fixing the degree of node[1] to $d = 1/8$. The results show that the MPE approach performed significantly better than PA especially when the sizes of MPEs get larger (see figure 2). This is because MPE requires fewer relations to be stored than PA, due to the implicit representation of the linear ordering relationship of points from the same MPE.

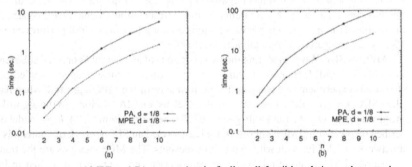

Fig. 2. Performance of MPE and PA approaches in finding all feasible relations when varying sizes of MPEs, 100 instances per data point each from $S(MPE, k, n, 1/8)$: (a) k = 20 (b) k = 50

To evaluate the effect of different degrees of node, d, we generated MPE networks with d varied from $d = 1/8$ (sparse networks), to $d = 1$ (complete networks). The experiments were conducted only on MPEs of size 2 which is the smallest. The results (figure 3) show that finding minimal networks using the MPE approach is more efficient than PA at all degrees of node. MPE required 59 % (figure 3a) and 67 % (figure 3b) of the time that PA took to solve the networks of 50 and 150 nodes respectively.

---

[1] Since the experiments were performed with varying sizes of networks, we normalize the degree of nodes between 0 and 1 to give a clear comparative analysis. Thus, average degree '0' means no constraint, and average degree '1' means complete graph. For example, a network of 20 nodes with $d = 1$ and $d = 1/2$, the number of constrained arcs connecting to a node is 19 and 9 respectively.

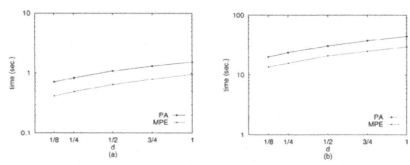

Fig. 3. Performance of MPE and PA approaches in finding all feasible relations of the networks with the smallest MPEs, 100 instances per data point each from $S(MPE, k, 2, d)$: (a) k = 50 (b) k = 150

No matter how small the MPEs are, computing the minimal MPE networks requires some time to handle overheads, e.g., tagging and untagging the matrix elements and conditional checking in the triangle operations. A question arises about the trade-off between these overheads and the effect of the number of ordering relations that MPEs implicitly represent. The results in figure 3 also address this question. That is, with only one ordering relation per MPE omitted in the representation scheme (MPE of size 2), the overheads in manipulating MPE relations do not affect the overall performance of MPE when compared to PA at all degrees of node.

MPE vs SIA: When modeling the two endpoints of an interval as ordered subevents in an MPE, the MPE framework can represent a subset of interval algebra, called SIA [6]. In this experiment, we compare the performance of the MPE algorithm when handling SIA networks (the IA networks with all labels are SIA relations) to the algorithm proposed for IA [1]. We randomly generated SIA networks from $S(SIA, k, d)$ model described below. For the MPE approach, we transformed an SIA network of k intervals to a network of k MPEs each with two point subevents. The MPE relations are the transformation of SIA to point relations between interval endpoints as enumerated in [6]. Then we applied the algorithm FEASIBLE_MPE to the MPE networks, while all feasible relations for the SIA networks were computed using Allen's algorithm. No heuristic was applied in either approach.

$S(SIA, k, d)$ **model:** This model provides random instances of SIA networks which are consistent. Each instance was generated as follows:

Step 1: Generate a consistent scenario: This enforces the generated network to be consistent. To do so, we randomly picked k intervals represented as pairs of real numbers, and then identified relations between pairs of these intervals. If the computed relation does not belong to SIA, we keep regenerating the consistent instance until all labels are SIA relations.

Step 2: Add infeasible relations: If we randomly generate an SIA network and simply merge with the consistent scenario from step 1 (the same as when generating MPE networks), labels of the combined network may not be SIA relations. For example, merging an arc of the scenario labeled with the relation {*after*} to the corresponding arc of a random SIA network with the label {*before,during,overlap*} results in {*before,after,during,overlap*} which is not an SIA relation.

To ensure that the generated network remains an SIA network, we use the scenario generated from step 1 as an underlying network. Then for each constrained arc selected using the degree of node *d*, we extend the atomic relation to non-atomic SIA relations. For instance, if an arc of a solution is labeled with {*after*}, we randomly pick a non-atomic relation from a subset of SIA relations that contains the relation {*after*} such as {*after, overlaped-by, met-by*}. For each non-constrained arc, the label is assigned "no information" representing all of Allen's 13 basic interval relations. Therefore, the resulting network is a consistent SIA network with infeasible relations.

The time required to compute the minimal networks significantly increases when the numbers of intervals get larger (as shown in figure 4). In comparison to IA, the FEASIBLE_MPE algorithm performs slightly better.

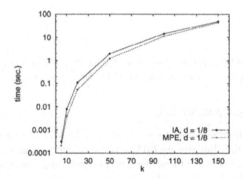

Fig. 4. Performance of MPE and IA approaches when handling SIA networks, from $S(SIA, k, 1/8)$: 10,000 instances for $k = 5$; 1,000 instances or $k = 10, 20$; 100 instances for $k = 50, 100, 150$ per data point

We further experimented on different degrees of node (results are shown in figure 5). The performance of MPE is quite steady when the degrees of node are changed. In comparison to IA, at all degrees of node, MPE performs better when handling the SIA networks of up to 100 nodes, but worse with the larger networks. However, FEASIBLE_MPE provides the exact minimal networks as all forbidden subgraphs are removed, while some infeasible relations still remain in the networks resulting from the IA approach. This is because Allen's algorithm used to solve the SIA network is essentially a path-consistency algorithm. This algorithm is insufficient for SIA networks in which the relation '$\neq$' is allowed in the transformation to point relations [6].

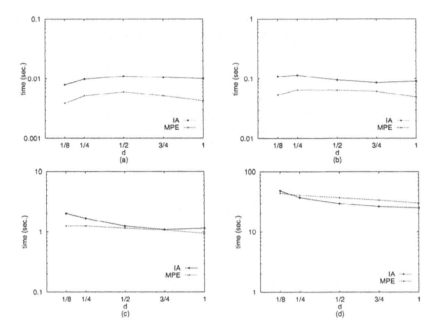

Fig. 5. Performance of MPE and IA approaches when handling SIA networks, from $S(SIA, k, d)$: 1,000 instances for (a) $k = 10$; 100 instances for (b) $k = 50$ (c) $k = 100$ (d) $k = 150$ per data point

3.2 Finding a Consistent Scenario

The algorithm for finding a consistent scenario for an MPE network is based on the backtracking algorithm. Initially, the MPE network is preprocessed by employing FEA-SIBLE_MPE to make sure that the network is consistent, and also remove all infeasible relations. Then apply chronological backtracking method to search for all matrices that the elements are atomic. For each instantiating of the backtracking, FEASIBLE_MPE is called for forward checking.

There are two ways to find an atomic matrix relation to instantiate. Both center on how an MPE matrix is split into an atomic MPE matrix. The first approach assigns each element of the MPE relation an atomic relation from it's set of possible relations. There is no checking to see if the MPE matrix is consistent (in canonical form). This approach is known as *Random Splitting*.

The second approach splits an MPE matrix so that it is still in canonical form. The heuristic search for consistent atomic elements of a matrix starts from the top left non-atomic element and proceeding to the right, row by row. Each element is assigned an atomic relation from it's set of point relations if it is not already atomic. After each assignment, instead of checking if it is consistent with all other matrix elements, the following observations are applied:

Observation I: If element $A_{i,j} = \text{'>'}$, then $A_{i+1,j} = \text{'>'}$,
Observation II: If element $A_{i,j} = \text{'<'}$, then $A_{i,j+1} = \text{'<'}$,
Observation III: If element $A_{i,j} = \text{'='}$, then $A_{i,j+1} = \text{'<'}$ and $A_{i+1,j} = \text{'>'}$.

This approach is known as *Heuristic Splitting*. For example, given a canonical matrix below. If we instantiate $A_{1,2} = \{=\}$, this satisfies $A_{1,3}$ and $A_{2,2}$. Furthermore, from observation III, we also know that $A_{1,3}$ can only be '<', so we do not need to try '=' of $A_{1,3}$. When instantiating $A_{1,3} = \{<\}$, it satisfies $A_{1,4}$ and $A_{2,3}$. If we choose $A_{2,3} = \{<\}$ then $A_{2,4}$ must be '<'. Relation '>' of $A_{2,4}$ do not need to be tried. Finally, the last non-atomic element $A_{3,4}$ can be either '>' or '='.

$$A = \begin{bmatrix} > & \geq & \leq & < \\ > & > & \neq & ? \\ > & > & > & \geq \end{bmatrix}$$

We designed the experiment to evaluate the effects on time of using a heuristic to search locally for a consistent MPE matrix, as opposed to randomly splitting a matrix. We generated an MPE network from the $S(MPE, k, n, d)$ model described in subsection 3.1. Then we computed a consistent scenario of an MPE network as described above using the two splitting methods. Time was counted from the preprocessing until a consistent scenario of the network was found. The results are shown in figure 6.

The effect of heuristic over random splitting is negligible when the sizes of MPEs are small especially with sparse networks. This is because the low sizes of MPEs do favor the random splitting to arrive at a local consistent atomic matrix faster than large sizes. While heuristic splitting requires more time to decompose a matrix than the random method as it always produces a local consistent matrix. At larger sizes of MPEs the results for random splitting become very large. This is because the time it takes to get a local consistent matrix is quite large so it causes a number of backtracking. We also observed that for the heuristic approach there is no backtracking ever detected until

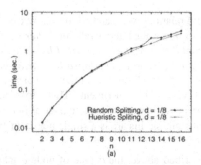 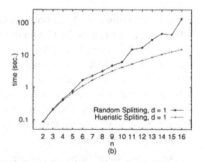

Fig. 6. Effect of heuristics on Average time (sec.) for finding a consistent scenario of MPE networks, 1000 instances per data point each from $S(MPE, 15, n, d)$: (a) d = 1/8 (b) d = 1

reaching a consistent scenario. This reflects in the uniform results for heuristic splitting. The degree of the network also influences the time it takes to find a consistent scenario. At a low degree many relations are the universal relation. Therefore, the decomposed matrix is more likely to be internally consistent.

4   Experimental Study of GMPE Networks

By modeling an interval as an MPE with two point subevents (starting and ending points), an IA network can be translated into the equivalent GMPE network. The GMPE framework has an advantage over IA concerning expressiveness (i.e., it can represent relations over events that happen sequentially without losing connectivity). We evaluated the performance of GMPE in comparison to the IA approach. This is to show the possibility of using GMPE to solve the minimality problem of IA networks.

To compare the performance of GMPE and IA approaches, we adopted the $S(IA, k, d)$ random model [7, 5] described below to generate IA networks. Then we find all feasible relations of the IA networks by implementing the polynomial algorithm proposed by Allen [1]. For GMPE, we converted the generated IA network into the equivalent GMPE network, and applied the algorithm PATH_CON_GMPE. Essentially, PATH_CON_GMPE computes the consistency between all three nodes of the network while maintaining the canonical form of each matrix.

$S(IA, k, d)$ **model:** The random instances were generated as follows:

Step 1: Generate an IA network with k intervals with degree of node d which specifies the number of constrained arcs connecting to an arbitrary node. The labels of constrained arcs are randomly chosen from all possible disjunctions of interval relations (excluding the empty label), with equal probability. The unconstrained arcs are labeled with the universal interval (?) relations.

Step 2: Generate a consistent scenario. This enforces the IA network to be consistent. To do so, we randomly picked k intervals represented as pairs of real numbers, and then identified relations between pairs of these intervals. This results in a consistent atomic labeled network. We then merge together with the network from step 1 to ensure that we have a consistent IA network.

When transforming an IA relation into GMPE relations, we searched for the maximum subsets of SIA that cover the IA relation. For example, the interval relation {*after, equal, during, overlap, start, finish, finished-by, contain, overlaped-by, started-by*} is transformed into three SIA relations which are {*after*}, {*contain, overlaped-by, started-by*} and {*equal, during, overlap, start, finish, finished-by*}. Then each of them is converted to the MPE matrix in the same way as in MPE versus SIA experiments. This is to reduce the number of matrices labeling the arc. For an arc labeled with the universal interval relation, the corresponding MPE matrix constraining this arc is a single matrix of the universal point relations (T).

According to the network generator described above, the degree of node d takes into effect only on the network produced by step 1. When the degree is low, it implies that there are a lot of unconstrained arcs, represented as the universal interval relations. Merging these arcs with the corresponding arcs from step 2 still results in the universal relations. When propagating the consistency check, this network requires less time than the one with more arcs labeled with multiple matrices, due to less number of composition and intersection operations. As a result, at low degree of node GMPE performs significantly better than high degree which is shown in Figure 7.

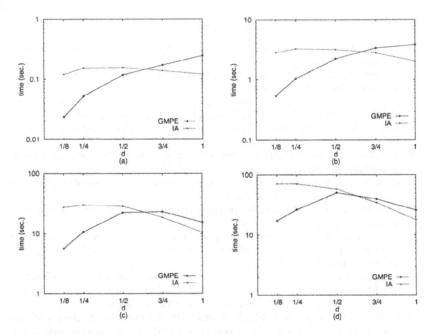

Fig. 7. Performance of GMPE and IA approaches in finding all feasible relations, 1000 instances per data point each from $S(IA, k, d)$: (a) $k = 20$ (b) $k = 50$ (c) $k = 100$ and (d) $k = 130$

5 Conclusion

This paper reports an empirical study that includes implementations and performance evaluations (in comparison to the best known existing results) of the MPE and GMPE algorithms proposed in [9, 10] using randomly generated test beds. We conclude that:

- for finding all feasible relations, MPE based approach performs better than the traditional non-recurring approaches when dealing with recurring events. The reason for this improvement is that the relations between ordered point subevents are implicitly represented in the MPE matrix representation;
- MPE based approach finds the exact minimal SIA network, and performs better than the existing algorithm for finding the approximate minimal SIA network [1], specially when dealing with small size networks;
- for finding a consistent scenario, the proposed heuristics improve the performance of search when the sizes of MPEs are large; and
- finding all feasible relations of IA networks by GMPE approach is shown to be significantly better than by traditional IA with low to moderate degrees of node. However, GMPE performs slightly worse than IA at higher degrees of nodes. Since in practice, we deal with low to moderate degrees of nodes, the GMPE framework can be used as a viable alternative to handle the reasoning tasks involving the full set of interval algebra relations.

References

1. J. Allen. Maintaining knowledge about temporal intervals. *Communication of the ACM*, 26(11):832–843, 1983.

2. A. Gerevini and L. Schubert. On point-based temporal disjointness (reseach note). *Artificial Intelligence*, 70(1):347–361, 1994.

3. L. al Khatib. *Reasoning with Non-Convex Time Intervals*. PhD thesis, Florida Institute of Technology, Melbourne, Florida, 1994. (http://www.cs.fit.edu/~lina/dissertation).

4. A.K. Mackworth. Consistency in networks of relations. *Artificial Intelligence*, 8:99–118, 1977.

5. B. Nebel. Solving hard qualitative temporal reasoning problems: Evaluating the efficiency of using the ord-horn class. *Constraints*, 1:175–190, 1997.

6. P. van Beek and R. Cohen. Exact and approximate reasoning about temporal relations. *Computational Intelligence*, 6:132–144, 1990.

7. P. van Beek and D.W. Manchak. The design and an experimental analysis of algorithms for temporal reasoning. *Journal of AI Research*, 4:1–18, 1996.

8. M. Vilain and H. Kautz. Constraint propagation algorithms for temporal reasoning. In *Proceedings of the 5th National Conference in Artificial Intelligence (AAAI-86)*, pages 377–382, Philadelphia, PA, 1986.

9. R. Wetprasit, A. Sattar, and L. Khatib. Reasoning with multi-point events. In *Lecture Notes in Artificial Intelligence 1081; Advances in AI, Proceedings of the 11th biennial conference on Artificial Intelligence (CSCSI-96)*, pages 26–40, Ontario, Canada, 1996.

10. R. Wetprasit, A. Sattar, and L. Khatib. A generalized framework for reasoning with multi-point events. In *Lecture Notes in Computer Science 1345; Advances in Computing Science, Proceedings of the 3rd Asian Computing Science Conference (ASIAN-97)*, pages 121–135, Kathmandu, Nepal, 1997.

A Mixture of Global and Local Gated Experts for the Prediction of High Frequency Foreign Exchange Rates

D. Hoang and G. Williamson

Basser Department of Computer Science, University of Sydney
doan@cs.usyd.edu.au

Abstract. This paper presents a new mixture of experts neural network architecture for the prediction of the US Dollar Swiss Franc exchange rate. This architecture achieves improved prediction results on noisy and non-stationary data. In contrast to previous efforts the current system was designed with a particular emphasis on solving the problems of local overfitting & underfitting caused by non-stationarity and noise in the data. The cascade correlation constructive neural network training algorithm was used for the fast training of near optimal complexity global & local experts. The Kohonen Self Organizing Map was used to find regions of the data on which to train local experts. Improved results were obtained by using a combination of the outputs of the global & local experts.

1. Introduction

This paper attempts to solve the problem of predicting the US Dollar Swiss Franc exchange rate at a time interval of one minute. People have been trying to do this for as long as markets have existed. Artificial Neural Networks constitute a machine learning tool that is capable of learning an arbitrarily complex function from data examples without any underlying theory of relationships in the data examples. For this reason a number of researchers have hoped that the tool may provide predictions capable of earning great fortunes.

The results for most existing attempts have not been encouraging. Previous efforts that are of particular significance to this study were the two winning entries for the forecasting of the US Dollar Swiss Franc exchange rate in the 1991 Santa Fe time series forecasting competition. Their results barely disproved the random walk hypothesis. Zhang & Hutchinson's [9] entry showed little care for pre-processing & model complexity. Mozer's [7] entry showed some thought towards the pre-processing & model complexity but unfortunately used a training algorithm that was very prone to problems.

The problems that still exist include careless pre-processing and selection of features, the importance of model complexity when learning from a noisy system and the possible variation of underlying system dynamics, complexity and noise.

This study seeks to solve these through careful data selection, pre-processing and feature selection. The use of the constructive training algorithm, cascade correlation, avoids the problems of model complexity by building a near optimal network size for both the global and local experts. The powerful Kohonen self-organizing map allows for the clustering of data and determination of clusters of data with complicated boundaries for which the global network is not optimal. Local experts ensure that local complexity is correctly fitted when the global network does not correctly match the complexity for these regions. Finally the overlap of expertise of the global & cluster networks for the various clusters is exploited using prediction combination rules.

The paper is organized in the following way. Section 2 contains a description of the data and attempts in predicting this data. Section 3 contains a description & justification for the pre-processing. Section 4 describes how the cascade correlation training algorithm works and why it was used. In Section 5 the reason for developing local experts is explained, the Kohonen self-organizing map is described in terms of how it works & why it is useful for this application. Section 6 illustrates the advantages of using both global and local predictive outputs. Section 7 summarises the paper, the results and the contribution it has made.

2. Predicting High Frequency Foreign Exchange Rates

There are many methods that participants may use to try and predict markets. These range from linear macroeconomic models to horoscopes and theories of crowd psychology. Many books and theses have been written on the subject of what determines market prices. Depending on ones belief of the mechanics of the market there are two main approaches that many financial institutions employ.

Fundamental analysis attempts to quantify and model the relationships between fundamental influences to supply and demand and the market in which supply and demand are matched. For instance the relationship between interest rates and currency markets is well understood and recognized (Bailie and McMahon [1]). Attempts to model currency values are often simplistic in their representation of the complex relationships of the economic fundamentals. A number of these models are described in [1]. The other important theory about markets that must be introduced here is that of the Efficient Market hypothesis. Efficient market theorists argue that because new information relating to the market is inherently random the resulting market movement are random. They argue that the time series of the market is simply a random walk and many have attempted to show this empirically. There has been some success in empirically proving this principle in currency markets over periods of hours, days, weeks and months, see [1] for examples.

Random walk theory suggests that the best possible prediction one can make is that the market price will be the same as the current price. The success of a prediction system compared to the random walk hypothesis can be measured by the ratio between the error of the model prediction and the error of using the last price as the prediction. This ratio, which in this study is called the "Better Than Chance ratio", has been used both in this study and others to evaluate the success of predictions over the random walk model.

The data used in this project. The data used in this project was the U.S. Dollar Swiss Franc exchange rate for the period from 20th May 1985 to 12th April 1991. The average time between quotes between one and two minutes. This market has a very large volume, daily volume in 1989 was estimated to be US $650 billion and in 1993 US $1 trillion on busy days. Lequarre [6] reports that 97% of this is speculation and 3% is actual transactions

There are a number of reasons that this data set was selected for this project. These include:The challenge of discovering something from an unknown system in data that has had a number of efforts made on it with only limited success yet an underlying belief that there is more to be discovered, the added benefit that success could be very profitable. Standard statistical tests have already been carried out and were available (LeBaron [5]) and that these tests show signs that there may be some more complex non-linear structure in this data. Large amounts of this data were available. This is extremely important for this sort of research both from the point of view of having lots of training examples but also from the need to have large test sets all providing for greater statistical significance of the results. Because a subset of this data was used for the Santa Fe Time Series forecasting competition the results of the winning entries to this competition are available for both comparison and as leads for further research in this area. The winning competition results appear sub-optimal leaving room for improvement.

Attempts at predicting this data. A subset of the data used in this study was also used in a Santa Fe time series forecasting competition held in 1991. The best entrants to this competition did not achieve results that would allow one to think that the task of predicting this market was very achievable. The approaches taken by the winners were simplistic in terms of either pre-processing or neural network architecture.

Zhang & Hutchinson [9] had the use of a Connection Machine super computer on which they implemented backpropagation networks. The speed of the machine allowed for extensive experimentation. The tick data time series was converted to values 1, 0, or -1 to represent a change in price up, the same and down respectively. This encoding was done without rescaling the irregularly timed ticks to a uniform time scale. This project attempted to use the information contained in the real valued prices and the timing of the ticks were approximated by rescaling to one minute intervals. A network with two hidden layers each with twenty units was used. There is no mention of the method used to determine when to stop training the network. The authors also express concern that their network overfitted the training data. The arbitrary choice of network topology and lack of information regarding point for stopping training indicate that model complexity and overfitting were not important factors to these experimenters. Their results indicate that their predictions beat the random walk hypothesis by a small but statistically significant margin. They make the important point; due to non-stationarity of the underlying system, that there appears to be time periods when the general network does not work very well. This was a problem that the current project aimed to solve. Zhang & Hutchinson also repeated their experiments using radial basis function networks rather than multi layer perceptrons. Little difference in prediction performance was observed.

Mozer [7] attempts to use a recurrent neural network architecture that has a memory in order to try and learn long term relationships in the data. It was mentioned that because the data is high frequency yet the relationships might be long term, a deep memory is required. Mozer adjusts the data to a uniform time grid and uses the real valued differences between two minutes, the time of day and the day of the week of the price recording as inputs to the network. The network was trained using "backpropagation through time" and was stopped when the error on a test set started to increase. Mozer performed considerable re-training using different random starting weights. Unfortunately the test set used to evaluate each network was the same test set that was used as the test set to determine when to stop training. The trained network has an element of bias towards the test set that was used to determine the point at which to stop training. Mozer states that it would be best to have a second test set to evaluate the generalization ability of the network. These results were compared using the measure of the ratio of prediction error to the error if just the last price was the prediction (random walk theory). Both Mozer and Zhang & Hutchinson believe there are more practical measures to evaluate performance.

3. Pre-processing of the data

Conversion to uniform time scale . The tick data is the recording of prices as there are changes in the prices. The prices are recorded in the form of bids and offers. According to Lequarre [6] the spread between these two prices is virtually constant for the duration of the price series. Therefore the bid offer spread is ignored and the bid price alone is used. The quotes are not necessarily recorded at equal intervals of time. The attempt at making predictions for this data by Zhang & Hutchinson; ignored the timing of the ticks. This is equivalent to treating the ticks as though there were a uniform amount of time between the ticks. For comparison purposes the first hour of the time series is shown graphically below with the irregularly timed quotes treated as being at uniform time intervals.

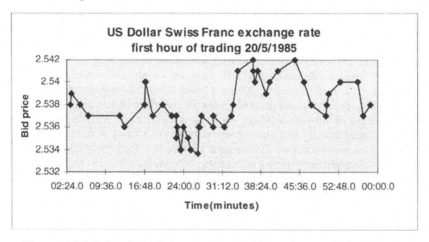

Figure -1 US Dollar Swiss Franc exchange rate first hour of 20/5/85

When plotted according to the times at which the ticks were recorded. There is a noticeable difference in the shape of the time series. This plot is shown below.

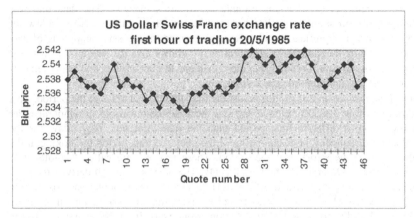

Figure -2 US Dollar Swiss Franc exchange rate first hour of 20/5/85

If the times of the ticks were to be included with the prices in the series of lagged prices that are presented as the input to the machine learning system, it would effectively double the quantity of input data. For memory, dimensionality of the feature space and time complexity reasons it is best to remove these times from the input data if the loss in information is only small. In this case, to make the information loss small, the price quotes were mapped to a uniform time interval of one minute. The time period of one minute was chosen because the average time between ticks is between one and two minutes according to LeBaron

De-trending. Le Baron found that the most likely time scale at which there were temporal relationships in the price series was short term. In order to determine if there are temporal relationships in the price series at a short time scale it is important to examine the data at a short time scale. To de-trend the series the moving average is subtracted from the original bid price series. It was determined that the bid price with the 15 minute moving average subtracted would be used. This choice was arbitrary within the bounds of the justification for de-trending unfeasible.

Windowing. In order to train any machine learning system that will attempt to discover the conditional probability of a future event from some collection of prior events, it is necessary to collect together the features that characterize the prior events and pair these features with the corresponding event. In this application the features are restricted to the prices at each minute for the last ten minutes. In effect this is a sliding window, ten minutes in length. These are paired with the corresponding output which is the price at the next minute i.e. the eleventh minute. In order to maximise the number of such data examples, the sliding window is moved along one minute at a time.

Division of data set into training and test sets. There are a number of factors that must be taken into account when determining the training and test data sets. These are discussed below.

When presented with a very large data set there are practical memory constraints and computational complexity constraints hence it was necessary to take enough data out of the training set to allow the training set to fit in memory. The data that was removed from the training set became the test sets. Having large test sets allow for statistically more significant results. Having a number of test sets comprising of data extracted from the period in different ways allows for the testing of different properties of the data. Testing using more than one test set ensures that improvements are not just specialised to the one test set.

One of the test sets in this project is just the first 400000 examples of the period. This is split into four 100000 example test sets, because these sets are in temporal order and are from a different time period than the other test sets, they allow for the evaluation of temporal non-stationarity of the data over this period by looking at the differences in the errors over the period. These test sets are called "OutofSect1", "OutofSect2", "OutofSect3" & "OutofSect4". The other sets are all derived from the remainder of the complete data set. "Valid1" is created by extracting one observation from every ten, "FinalValid" was created by extracting 10 observations from every 100 and "Valid2" contains 100 observations from every 1000. No example exists in more than one test or training set. The remaining data set after all of these test examples have been extracted is the training set.

4. Using cascade correlation to train the global neural network

In recent years quite a few attempts have been made using neural networks to learn what inputs result in some output in the form of a market prediction. Many of these attempts have either been made with a lack of care for the importance of the data containing certain qualities i.e. not enough training data, too much dimensionality in the data and unintelligent pre-processing. Or it has been approached with a disregard for the need for thoughtful training of the neural network.

How cascade correlation works. Cascade-correlation begins with a minimal network which is just a fully connected input and output layer with no hidden units.

The network, with no hidden units, was trained using the quickprop algorithm over the entire training data set (Fahlman [2]). This training will approach an asymptote where the improvement in error will slow down. A patience parameter controls how long to continue training for small improvements in error. If a reduction in error is still desired a new hidden unit is added to the network, this hidden unit is created using an algorithm described below.

To create a new hidden unit a number of candidate hidden units(eight were used for this project), each with different random initial weights, are trained, they have inputs from all of the networks input units and from the already existing hidden units. The output of the candidate units are trained to maximise the covariance between the output of the candidate unit and the residual error of the output of the so far trained network. When this covariance stops improving the candidate unit with the highest covariance is selected and inserted into the network. Its inputs are frozen and the outputs are trained as described before.

The training. Training was stopped when the error on the "Valid1" test set stopped reducing and started to increase. At this point it was considered that the current network had extracted as much useful structure as possible from the training data set. Any further training would have been learning structure specific to the training data set (noise) which was not correct for the validation set. An assumption being made in choosing the stopping point is that the validation set is representative of the whole data set. Two arguments in favour of making this assumption are that it would be computationally unfeasible to try all different possible combinations of the split between training and test set i.e. it would take too large amounts of computational resources to retrain the neural network with all possible training and corresponding test sets to determine the network that generalizes best to all available data. Secondly, the test sets contain over 20,000 examples. Weiss[8] reports that anything over 1,000 examples approximates being representative of the whole system. Training was stopped where the error on the test set started to increase. At this point the network contained 30 hidden units.

Results of global network on the data sets. The prediction accuracy can be evaluated using a number of different measures. The choice of measure on which to base an evaluation depends on the perspective of the researcher.

- Sum of squared errors

SSE (sum of squared errors) is the measure used by the training algorithm to measure improvements in fit of the model when it attempts a gradient descent in weight space. This gives an indication of the accuracy of the regression to those wanting to predict the actual value of the next value.

$$SSE = \sum \left(observation_t - prediction_t \right)^2$$

- Classification accuracy

Classification accuracy is the measure of the portion of test examples that were correctly classified in terms of direction. Direction could belong to one of three classes up, down or the same.

- Better than chance ratio

BTCR (Better than chance ratio) is a measure of the extent to which the prediction beats the prediction that would be given by the random walk hypothesis. This is the ratio of sum of squared errors of the network prediction to the sum of squared errors if the prediction is simply the last value. In equation form:

$$BTCR = \frac{\sum \left(observation_t - prediction_t \right)^2}{\sum \left(observation_t - observation_{t-1} \right)^2}$$

A BTCR value less than one implies that the random walk hypothesis does not hold and a value greater than one implies that the random walk hypothesis does hold.

- Profit

Profit is measured by the sum of the absolute differences between the last value and the actual outcome for the next value when the prediction was in the correct direction, and the absolute difference is subtracted if the direction was incorrect. This does not reflect real world profitability as no transaction costs are taken into account, market slippage whereby transactions do not actually occur at the price advertised, is also not taken into account and the bid ask spread is not taken into account.

Table - 1 Global neural network prediction results

	Training Set	Test Set 1	Test Set 2	Out of sect1	Out of sect2	Out of sect3	Out of sect4
No. of examples	303484	33720	41600	100000	100000	100000	100000
SSE	12.966	1.4149	1.7423	14.015	6.0910	3.1472	3.5401
Class. Acc.	63.87%	63.66%	64.02%	63.61%	64.60%	64.04%	60.86%
BTCR	0.9541	0.9590	0.9584	0.9572	0.9608	0.9822	1.0672
Profit per min.	0.211%	0.202%	0.198%	0.322%	0.208%	0.153%	0.157%

The results indicate some interesting qualities of the data. The consistency of performance measures across the training data, the test set used to determine stopping and the other test sets (both in and out of sample) indicates a number of things. It indicates that there is not significant overfitting as the results on the training data are not necessarily any better than on the test sets. There still may be local over or underfitting within the data sets, depending on the variance in the complexity of the underlying model. The consistent prediction accuracy, "better than chance ratio" and profit across the data sets indicates that to some extent this data is not merely a random walk. However, the gradual trend in the performance measures across the out of sample test sets indicates that there is a gradual time dependant change in the underlying model, a long term temporal non-stationarity.

An interesting observation is that there is not necessarily a very great correlation (it may be negative) between different performance measures.

Comparison of results with 1991 Santa Fe forecasting competition. The competition entries were evaluated using the "Better Than Chance Ratio" only. The competition involved predictions at a number of time scales. For comparison with the current project, only the one minute time scale results will be considered. The competition entrants only used a subset of the data set used in the current study. Testing for the competition entrants was done using test data that was from the same time period as the training data supplied to entrants. There were 18,465 test examples. The best Mozer achieved was a BTCR of 0.9976 & the best Zhang & Hutchinson achieved was 1.090.

The most equivalent test set in the current project is Test Set 2 which is from the same time period as the training data but was not used at all in the training process. The global neural network achieved a BTCR of 0.9584 for this test set of 41600 examples which clearly beats the competition winners for the time scale of one minute. Both the competition test set and the test set used for the current project are large which means they are representative of the underlying system and therefore the results for both can be compared.

5. Discovery of regions for use of local experts

The problem with training one global network for the whole data set is that it has built a model that treats all parts of the data as the same in terms of the complexity of the underlying structure. For many real world systems there are regime changes during the process. The process is non-stationary, different forces are at work at different times, different features are more or less important at different times. These different regimes may mean that at different times there is a different underlying model. It is therefore not optimal to represent all of these different models with a global network of one size. Because we are learning from the data without a definite theory of how the underlying system or systems work, it is not known how many different regimes there are. There is probably no distinct boundary between different models and the model that best represents the system varies continuously across the feature space.

The approach taken was to firstly train as optimally as possible a global network using the techniques previously mentioned for determining the point at which the network is of optimal size and training. The data is then clustered using a Kohonen self organizing feature map [4]. This essentially makes a non-linear mapping from the n-dimensional feature space to a 2 dimensional feature space, maintaining a topographical ordering of the feature vectors that represent the nodes of the Kohonen map. This enabled the selection of regions of data that were similar in both mechanics and high prediction error, such regions were thought to be suitable candidates for a local expert. The map was chosen to be 15 nodes wide and 20 nodes long. Each time training was repeated starting from a different set of random node vectors, training was conducted for 100,000 cycles.

Choice of high prediction error clusters

Table 1 Average prediction error for data at each node of Kohonen SOM

	3.60	2.93	2.33	3.01			3.48	5.07	5.83	6.51	7.46	8.98	9.60	10.17	
3.20	3.09	3.05	2.08	2.49	2.42	1.75	1.95	4.15	4.47	5.53	5.57	5.99	6.49	9.64	
3.76	3.19	2.71	3.10	2.25	1.81	2.03	1.67	2.50	3.46	3.51	3.87	4.21	5.08	6.06	6.47
2.90	2.77	2.90	2.26	1.74	1.49	1.71	2.05	2.18	3.28	3.61	4.15	3.84	4.65	5.15	7.00
2.60	2.22	2.38	2.58	2.47	2.40	2.15	1.57	2.32	3.06	3.29	3.42	3.75	3.95	4.80	5.53
4.14	4.23	4.00	3.17	2.27	2.08	1.94	1.78	1.12	1.94	2.49	2.80	3.51	3.75	3.72	4.59
3.79	3.64	2.81	2.31	1.76	2.11	2.34	1.40	1.10	1.90	2.91	3.63	3.20	3.14	3.56	4.93
3.95	3.36	3.45	3.19	2.61	1.99	2.16	2.28	2.11	2.47	1.96	2.42	2.34	3.04	3.29	3.68
		3.33	3.30	3.02	2.54	1.96	2.64	2.59	1.55	1.48	1.99	2.39	2.82	3.06	3.38
		3.60	3.47	2.61	2.96	2.62	2.15	2.23	2.39	1.78	2.14	3.08	2.87	3.03	4.04
			3.55	3.41	2.74	3.04	1.81	2.28	2.13	2.23	2.07	2.82	3.28	3.14	3.86
				3.60	3.23	2.89	2.75	1.67	3.07	2.15	2.54	3.01	3.00	4.41	5.50
						3.83	3.21	2.98	3.95	2.78	2.36	2.20	3.09	3.57	5.16

Legend: Bottom Left Cluster (BL), Bottom Right Cluster (BR), Middle Left Cluster (ML), Top Left Cluster (TL), Top Middle Cluster (TM), Top Right Cluster (TR)

The feature vectors that make up any contiguous region in this feature map could be considered a cluster. The average error of prediction by the global network was calculated for each node on the feature map. There were areas of comparatively high error. These regions were assumed to indicate clusters of data for which the global neural network did not optimally model the underlying system. There were initially six clusters. These were named according to their position in the feature map. These names were bottom left (BL), bottom right (BR), middle left (ML), top left (TL) and top right (TR).

Training of cluster specific neural networks. For each of these "high error" clusters of data a separate neural network was trained using the cascade correlation algorithm and the same parameters used as for training the global network

The resulting networks were much smaller than the global network as was expected. The reason for this was that the cluster specific networks have a much more compact input distribution than the global network and also have less training and test data.

Resulting neural networks and their prediction accuracy

Table 2 Comparison of performance of global & cluster neural networks

Data Cluster	Neural Network	Number of examples	SSE	Classification Accuracy	BTCR	Average profit per minute
BL	Global	2745	0.2561	81.38%	0.9194	0.6163%
BL	Cluster	2745	0.2393	82.38%	0.8591	0.6343%
BR	Global	250	0.0186	70.40%	0.9598	0.1761%
BR	Cluster	250	0.0178	73.20%	0.9194	0.4277%
ML	Global	215	0.0117	84.11%	0.9442	0.3362%
ML	Cluster	215	0.0119	69.54%	0.9623	0.2268%
TL	Global	412	0.0307	71.60%	0.9948	0.1023%
TL	Cluster	412	0.0300	71.12%	0.9949	0.2106%
TM	Global	267	0.0241	81.27%	1.0064	0.3044%
TM	Cluster	267	0.0241	73.03%	0.9605	0.3303%
TR	Global	2981	0.3061	78.80%	0.9034	0.6041%
TR	Cluster	2981	0.2977	80.34%	0.8786	0.6638%

There is a clear indication that across all data clusters except for the Middle Left cluster the cluster specific neural networks on their own provide an improvement in performance over the global neural network for the performance measures used.

6   Combination of outputs from global /cluster specific networks

The cluster network and the global network have different perspectives on the same data, the average vector, or centroid, for each networks training data was different. Because of the different perspective each cluster network has on their cluster of data than the global network and the fact that there is some element of noise (i.e. always perfect predictions is impossible) in the data. The global network and the cluster network will give different predictions on the same feature vector. The difference between these two predictions may vary depending on which area of the cluster the feature vector came from. For this reason the difference in the outputs of the two networks to some extent locates the feature vector in the feature space of the cluster. This difference turned out to be useful as a measure to determine which network provides better prediction on different data [3]. Below, each cluster is analysed using the difference between the outputs of the two networks on the same feature vector versus the difference in profitability of the cluster specific and global network. From this rules were developed to determine which network gives a better prediction depending on the difference of the output of the two networks. The advantage of using the rules is shown in terms of profit and classification accuracy.

A linear trendline is calculated for the scatter plot. The x intercept of this line indicates the value of the output difference (global network - cluster network) at which it is best to change the network that is used for prediction to maximise profitability. Due to limited space of the paper, results for only one cluster are presented

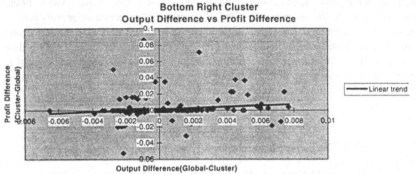

Figure 3 Scatter plot of output difference versus profit difference for BR data

When the rule that the cluster network should be used for output differences (Out_diff) greater than -0.002 and the global network otherwise, the following profits occur:

Table -3 Profits for BR data

	Global	Cluster	Cluster (Out_diff > -0.002)
Total profit	0.22297	0.54151	0.61649
Ave. profit per minute	0.000892	0.002166	0.002466
Ave % profit per minute	0.1761%	0.4277%	0.4869%
Profit over global network	0%	142.86%	176.49%

There is approximately a 177% increase in profitability in using this rule to just using the global network.

Table -4 Classification accuracy for BR data

	Global network	Cluster network	Cluster (Out_diff > -0.002)
Total correct	176	183	190
Classification accuracy	70.4%	73.2%	76%
Improvement over global	0	3.98%	7.95%

For all clusters except for the ML cluster there is an improvement both in profit and in classification accuracy by using the combination rules developed.

It can be seen that even when the cluster specific network on its own achieves a worse score for classification, the combined output rule provides an improved classification score.

7 Conclusion

The main contribution of this paper is a new hybrid neural network architecture and method for building this system that achieves improved prediction results on noisy & non-stationary data, specifically demonstrated on the US Dollar Swiss Franc exchange rate. At the pre-processing and dimensionality reduction stage, this project demonstrates a method for approximating unevenly timed data at a constant time interval and dimensionality reduction techniques that retain more information than previous efforts. Neural network training with an emphasis on complexity control is demonstrated as is the use of the Kohonen self organizing map as a gating network. A method for combining the outputs of experts with overlapping domains is also developed.

8 References

1. Bailie, R.T., and McMahon, P.: The Foreign Exchange Market: Theory and Econometric Evidence. Cambridge University Press, Cambridge, UK (1989)

2. Fahlman S E, Lebiere C.: The Cascade-Correlation Learning Architecture. Carnegie Mellon University, Technical Report CMU-CS-90-100 (1990)

3. Jacobs, R.A. (1995). Methods for combining experts' probability assessments. Neural Computation, 7 (1995) 867-888.

4. Kohonen T, Kangas J, Laaksonen J, Torkkola K. SOM_PAK: The Self-Organizing Map Program Package. 1995

5. LeBaron, B.: Non-linear Diagnostics, Simple Trading Rules and High Frequency Foreign Exchange Rates. In: Weigend, A. S. and Gershenfeld, N. A. (eds.): Time Series Prediction. Forecasting the Future and Understanding the past,. Addison Wesley, (1993)

6. Lequarre J Y : Foreign Currency Dealing: A Brief Introduction. In: Weigend, A. S. and Gershenfeld, N. A. (eds.): Time Series prediction: Forecasting the Future and Understanding the Past, Addison-Wesley, (1993)

7. Mozer M.: Neural network architectures for temporal sequence processing. In: Weigend, A. S. and Gershenfeld, N. A. (eds.): Time Series prediction: Forecasting the Future and Understanding the Past, Addison-Wesley, (1993)

8. Weiss, S.M., & Kulikowski C.A.: Computer Systems that learn: classification and prediction methods from statistics, neural networks, machine learning and expert system., Morgan Kaufmann (1991)

9. Zhang, X. and Hutchinson J.: Practical Issues in Non-linear Time Series Prediction. In: Weigend, A. S. and Gershenfeld, N. A. (eds.): Time Series prediction: Forecasting the Future and Understanding the Past, Addison-Wesley, (1993)

A Neural Network Diagnosis Model without Disorder Independence Assumption

Yue Xu and Chengqi Zhang
School of Mathematical and Computer Sciences
The University of New England
Armidale, NSW 2351, Australia
{yue, chengqi}@mcs.une.edu.au

Abstract. Generally, the disorders in a neural network diagnosis model are assumed independent each other. In this paper, we propose a neural network model for diagnostic problem solving where the disorder independence assumption is no longer necessary. Firstly, we characterize the diagnostic tasks and the causal network which is used to represent the diagnostic problem, then we describe the neural network diagnosis model, finally, some experiment results will be given.

1 Introduction

Finding explanations for a given set of events is an important aspect of general intelligent behaviour. The process of finding the best explanation was defined as *Abduction* by the philosopher C. S. Peirce [8]. Diagnosis is a typical abductive problem. For a set of manifestations(observations), the diagnostic inference is to find the most plausible faults or disorders which can explain the manifestations observed. In general, an individual fault or disorder can explain only a portion of the manifestations. Therefore, a composite hypothesis which consists of several individual hypotheses has to be found. Such composite hypothesis is able to explain all the manifestations. However, finding a composite hypothesis that satisfies some criteria for the best explanation, such as plausibility, parsimony, explanatory coverage and internal consistency, is computationally very expensive. One of the reasons is the large size of the possible combinations of individual hypotheses whose number is exponentially large, thus diagnostic problem solving becomes combinatorially difficulty.

Recent years, the approach on developing neural network diagnosis models has received more and more attention[1,2,3]. For a neural network diagnosis model, generally, it includes three parts: network architecture, activation rules to calculate the node activations, and the network equilibrium which indicates the stop condition of network computing. The activation rules and the network equilibrium vary with different models. Given a set of observations which is the input data to the model, the node activations are calculated by the activation rules repeatedly until the network equilibrium is reached. Thus, a subset of disorders can be determined according to the activations of disorder nodes. The disorder subset is the composite hypothesis to explain the observations, which is one possible solution to the diagnostic problem. By means of the highly parallel local computations of neural networks, the difficulty mentioned above can be alleviated.

For the neural network diagnosis models, the probabilistic causal network is often directly adopted as the network architecture[3,4]. Generally, the disorders in the probabilistic causal network are assumed to be independent of each other, i.e., the disorder independence assumption is one of the basic assumptions for the neural network diagnosis model. With this assumption, the existence of a disorder is assumed not being affected by the existence of other disorders. But for real world diagnosis, very often the disorders are not completely independent, more or less there is some interaction between them. For a diagnosis model with the disorder independence assumption, the interaction between disorders is ignored. In the case that the ignoring of the disorder interaction may cause mistakes, the impact of disorder interaction should be considered. In this paper, we will propose a general neural network diagnosis model where the impact of the disorder interaction is considered and the disorder independence assumption is no longer necessary. We have conducted some experiments to test our model. The experimental results show that for a diagnostic problem with dependent disorders, for the model proposed here, the rate of correct solutions is higher than that of the model which ignores the interaction between disorders. The diagnosis model which considers the impact of disorder interaction is more robust and more applicable to the general diagnostic problems than the models which ignores the disorder interaction.

The remainder of this paper is organised as follows. In Section 2, we characterise the diagnostic tasks and the causal network which represents the diagnostic knowledge, and present the neural network model for solving the diagnostic problems with dependent disorders. In Section 3, the experimental results will be given to demonstrate the efficiency of the model. Finally, Section 4 will summarise the paper.

2 The Neural Network Model for the Diagnostic Task with Dependent Disorders

In this section, firstly we characterise the general diagnostic task and the causal network that is used to represent the diagnostic task, secondly we describe the neural network model including the network architecture, energy function, and the activation rules, and finally the network computing procedure is described.

2.1 Diagnostic Tasks and Causal Networks

A diagnostic task can be characterised as a five-tuple (D, M, e, M_I, D_I), where:

- $D = \{d_i \mid i = 1, \ldots, n\}$ is a finite set of all the individual disorder (or cause) nodes.

- $M = \{m_j \mid j = 1, \ldots, p\}$ is a finite set of all the manifestation (or effect) nodes to be explained.

- e is a map from $\Gamma(D)$ to $\Gamma(M)$, where $\Gamma(A)$ denotes the power set of a set A. $\forall D_s \in \Gamma(D)$, $e(D_s)$ specifies a subset of M which can be explained by D_s.

- M_I is a specific observation set which is a subset of M. It is represented as $M_I = \{mi_j | j = 1, \ldots, p\}$. The value of M_I will not change with time.

- D_I is an explanation to M_I, $e(D_I) = M_I$.

M_I is the observation which is the input. e is the relationship between $\Gamma(D)$ and $\Gamma(M)$ which is the network. The task of diagnosis is to derive D_I based on M_I and e.

A causal network consists of a directed acyclic graph and a conditional probability distribution associated with the graph. It can be characterised as a triplet (H, L, P), where

- H is a finite set of nodes, $H = \{h_1, \ldots, h_n\}$,

- $L \subseteq H \times H$ is a set of links or arcs, where each element in L is a pair of nodes like $< h_i, h_j >$, $h_i, h_j \in H$,

- P is a set of probabilities. For each link $< h_i, h_j >$ in L, there is a conditional probability $P(h_j/h_i)$ accompanying the link which is called the causal strength from h_i to h_j, representing how strongly h_i causes h_j. If there is no causal link between h_i and h_j, $P(h_j/h_i)$ is assumed to be zero.

A class of simplified causal network, the network of disjunctive interaction or noisy-or gates, has received much attention[3,7]. In this paper, not only the disjunctive interaction but also the conjunctive interaction are considered, and a simple version of such causal network is involved. This simple causal network only includes two layers. All the nodes in the causal network are divided into two sets, one is the disorder set $D = \{d_1, \ldots, d_n\}$, the other is the manifestation set $M = \{m_1, \ldots, m_p\}$. In this case, $H = D \cup M$. For each manifestation node $m_j \in M$, the interaction between the nodes in $causes(m_j)$ is either disjunctive such as $d_1 \wedge d_2 \longrightarrow m_j$ or conjunctive such as $d_1 \vee d_2 \longrightarrow m_j$ but not the compound of the two interactions such as $d_1 \vee (d_2 \wedge d_3) \longrightarrow m_j$ or $d_1 \wedge (d_2 \vee d_3) \longrightarrow m_j$, $d_1, d_2, d_3 \in D$. In order to distinguish the two different interactions, for each node $m_j \in M$, there is a node type $TYPE(m_j)$ associated with it, $TYPE(m_j) \in \{OR, AND\}$. $TYPE(m_j) = OR$ indicates that the interaction between the nodes in $causes(m_j)$ is disjunctive, i.e., $d_{i1} \vee \ldots \vee d_{ir} \longrightarrow m_j$, $causes(m_j) = \{d_{i1}, \ldots, d_{ir}\}$. $TYPE(m_j) = AND$ indicates that the interaction is conjunctive, i.e., $d_{i1} \wedge \ldots \wedge d_{ir} \longrightarrow m_j$. The restriction comes from the limitation of the compound of the two interactions.

It should be mentioned that both AND and OR relationships describe how the disorders are combined logically to cause manifestations. Either AND or OR relationship does not refer to the interaction between disorders which is mentioned in Section 1. The disorder interaction refers to some functional relationship between disorders, which describes how the disorders are influenced by some other disorders, while AND or OR relationship gives nothing on the functional relation between disorders.

2.2 The Neural Network Model

2.2.1 Network Architecture

The two-layer causal network described in Section 2.1 is used directly as the network structure. The node set of the network is $D \cup M$. For each node h_i in the network, there is a numeric value $h_i(t)$, called activation, associated with it at time t. The activation $d_i(t)$ of each disorder node d_i represents the possibility of d_i being an element of the solution to the diagnosis problem. The activation $m_j(t)$ of each manifestation node m_j measures the possibility that m_j can be caused by all its causative disorders. The causal strength P is used to represent the link weights. Each link connecting node d_i and m_j is associated with the corresponding probabilistic causal strength c_{ij} which, during the computation, is used to update the activations of nodes d_i and m_j.

For a diagnostic problem, M_I is the input data which are observed before the diagnosis. Generally, if a manifestation m_j is observed as being present, mi_j, the initial value of m_j is marked as being 1, otherwise as being 0. But for real world diagnosis, the presentation of some manifestations may not be clear enough to be recognised, e.g., some manifestations might be presented very clearly or strongly, but others might be presented weakly. For representing the real case, in our model, the initial values of manifestations will no longer be exactly 1 or 0, but will be a value between 1 and 0. That is, $0 \leq mi_j \leq 1$, which demonstrates how strongly the manifestation is presented.

2.2.2 Energy Function

For real world diagnosis, people always try to find the best causes under which the observed manifestations are most likely. That is, the effects of the causes found by the diagnosis should be the same or very similar with the observed manifestations. Let $M(t_e) = \{m_1(t_e), \ldots, m_p(t_e)\}$ be the final manifestation activations derived by the diagnosis model through the neural network computing and $M_I = \{mi_1, \ldots, mi_p\}$ be the observation as described above. According to the idea here, the smaller the difference between $M(t_e)$ and M_I is, the better the inference of the diagnosis model works. We use the following equation to measure the distance between $M(t)$ and M_I at time t.

$$E(t) = \sum_{j=1}^{p} (mi_j - m_j(t))^2 \tag{1}$$

The smaller the $E(t)$ is, the closer the $M(t)$ gets access to M_I. By certain activation rules, $m_j(t)$ can be calculated through the activations of its cause nodes in $causes(m_j)$, that is, $m_j(t)$ is a function of its cause nodes which could be expressed as

$$m_j(t) = f(d_{ij}(t) \mid d_{ij} \in causes(m_j))$$

$E(t)$ hence becomes a function of all the disorder nodes. The equation (1) could be expressed as

$$E(t) = F(d_1(t), \ldots, d_n(t)) \tag{2}$$

For the diagnostic problem modelled by the neural network, to find a solution for a given set of manifestations is to derive a set of disorders whose activations minimise the equation (2).

Let $| D | = n$, if any subset D_I of D is represented as a n-dimensional vector $X = (x_1, \ldots, x_n)$ where $x_i = 1$ if $d_i \in D_I$ and $x_i = 0$ otherwise, then D_I can be considered as one of the 2^n corners of the n-dimensional hypercube $[0, 1]^n$. Thus, a diagnostic problem can be viewed as a discrete optimisation problem, i.e., to find one of the corners of hypercube $[0, 1]^n$ which minimises the equation (2). If X is allowed to go continuously through the interior of the hypercube, i.e., $0 \leq x_i \leq 1$ rather than $x_i \in \{0, 1\}$, the diagnostic problem of finding D_I with the minimum value of equation (2) is transformed into a continuous optimisation problem. The equation (2) is the energy function against which the minimum value is desired.

For our neural network model, the optimisation problem is performed by repeatedly updating $d_i(t)$ and $m_j(t)$ using certain activation rules until $E(t)$ reaches a minimum value which is the equilibrium of the neural network. In order to reach the minimum value of the energy function, $d_i(t)$ is updated based on the current error $E(t)$. The updated $d_i(t)$ will let the error get smaller and smaller. Initially, $d_i(0) = p_i$. When the network approaches its equilibrium, if $d_i(t_e) > \rho$, for instance, $\rho = 0.8$, the disorder d_i is considered to be an element of the solution, otherwise d_i is rejected as a solution. Thus, all the disorders d_i with $d_i(t_e) > \rho$ form a subset of disorders $D_I = \{d_i \mid d_i(t_e) > \rho\}$. D_I is considered as a solution for the given observation.

2.2.3 Activation Rules

(1). Manifestation Activation
Motivated by the results in [5,6], we developed the following activation rules to calculate $m_j(t)$. **Theorem 1** is given in [5,6].

Theorem 1
$$P(E_1 \wedge E_2) = min\{P(E_1), P(E_2)\} \tag{3}$$
$$P(E_1 \vee E_2) = max\{P(E_1), P(E_2)\} \tag{4}$$

The theorem gives the formulas for calculating the probability of a conjunction or a disjunction of dependent propositions. For more than two propositions, formulas (3) and (4) become the following formulas (5) and (6) respectively.

$$P(E_1 \wedge E_2 \ldots \wedge E_n) = min\{P(E_1), \ldots, P(E_n)\} \tag{5}$$
$$P(E_1 \vee E_2 \vee E_n) = max\{P(E_1), \ldots, P(E_n)\} \tag{6}$$

$\forall m_j \in M$, suppose $causes(m_j) = \{d_{i1}, \ldots, d_{ir}\}$. We define the activation rule for m_j as follows.

$TYPE(m_j) = AND$: $m_j(t) = P(d_{i1} \wedge \ldots \wedge d_{ir})P(m_j/d_{i1} \wedge \ldots \wedge d_{ir})$

$TYPE(m_j) = OR$: $m_j(t) = P(d_{i1} \vee \ldots \vee d_{ir})P(m_j/d_{i1} \vee \ldots \vee d_{ir})$

$$= P((m_j \wedge d_{i1}) \vee \ldots \vee (m_j \wedge d_{ir}))$$

Assume $d_{i1}, \ldots, d_{ir}$ are dependent, according to the formulas (5) and (6), the above activation rules for m_j are expressed as

$$m_j(t) = \begin{cases} min(P(d_{i1}), P(d_{i2}), \ldots, P(d_{ir}))P(m_j/d_{i1} \wedge \ldots \wedge d_{ir}) & TYPE(m_j) = AND \\ max(P(m_j \wedge d_{i1}), \ldots, P(m_j \wedge d_{ir})) & TYPE(m_j) = OR \end{cases}$$

For $d_{i1} \wedge \ldots \wedge d_{ir} \longrightarrow m_j$, in the neural network model, the causal strength $c_{i_k j}$ between d_{ik} and m_j is assigned as $P(m_j/d_{i1} \wedge \ldots \wedge d_{in})$, $k = 1, \ldots, r$, i.e., $c_{i_k j} = P(m_j/d_{ik}) = P(m_j/d_{i1} \wedge \ldots \wedge d_{ir})$, and since $P(m_j \wedge d_i) = P(m_j/d_i)P(d_i)$, $P(m_j/d_i) = c_{ij}$ and $P(d_i)$ refers to the current activation $d_i(t)$ of d_i at time t, the activation rules can be expressed as follows.

$$m_j(t) = F(m_j)min_{i=1}^{i=n}(d_i(t)c_{ij}) + (1 - F(m_j))max_{i=1}^{i=n}(d_i(t)c_{ij}) \qquad (7)$$

where $F(m_j) = 1$ if $TYPE(m_j) = AND$, $F(m_j) = 0$ otherwise. Because $c_{ij} = 0$ if $d_i \notin causes(m_j)$, $min_{i=1}^{i=n}(d_i(t)c_{i_1 j}) = min_{d_i \in cause(m_j)}(d_i(t)c_{i_1 j})$, and $max_{i=1}^{i=n}(d_i(t)c_{ij}) = max_{d_i \in causes(m_j)}(d_i(t)c_{ij})$.

Generally, there may be more than one maximum or minimum for $m_j(t)$ at time t. That is, there is $\{d_{i_1}, \ldots, d_{i_q}\} \subseteq causes(m_j)$, $1 \le q \le | causes(m_j) |$, $m_j(t) = d_{i_1}(t)c_{i_1 j} = \ldots \ldots = d_{i_q}(t)c_{i_q j}$. The $d_{i_1}, \ldots, d_{i_q}$ are called the *activation sourses* of m_j at time t, $\{d_{i_1}, \ldots, d_{i_q}\}$ is denoted as $a\_sourse(m_j, t)$. m_j is also called an *activation sourse* of $d_{i_1}, \ldots,$ and d_{i_q}, respectively. Obviously, not all the cause nodes of m_j make contributions to $m_j(t)$, only the *activation sourses* of m_j contribute their activations to calculate $m_j(t)$. In other words, only the *activation sourses* of m_j can affect the value of $m_j(t)$, the activations of other cause nodes contribute nothing to $m_j(t)$.

If the disorder nodes are dependent, there should be some functional relation between them, and the values of all the disorders should meet the functional relation. But usually, the functional relation is hard to be described mathematically. In fact, the disorder interaction is ignored by almost all the existing diagnosis models. If the disorders are independent, there is nothing wrong with the ignoring of disorder interaction. If the disorders are dependent, the ignoring of disorder interaction would cause some errors. If the manifestation activations strongly depend on all the disorder nodes, the errors of the manifestation activations would be very serious because all the disorders contribute their errors to the calculation of manifestation activations. From this point of view, the activation rule described by Equation (7) gets benefits from calculating the manifestation activations only by the disorders with maximum or minimum. The experimental results given in Section 3 will show the effect.

(2). Disorder Activation
From the equations (1) and (7), the energy function can be expressed as

$$E(d_1(t), \ldots, d_n(t)) = \sum_{j=1}^{p}(mi_j - (F(m_j)min_{i=1}^{i=n}(d_i(t)c_{ij}) + (1 - F(m_j))max_{i=1}^{i=n}(d_i(t)c_{ij})))^2$$

$$(8)$$

Initially, $d_i = p_i$, $i = 1, \ldots, n$, the purpose of the network computation is to update $d_i(t)$ until $E(d_1(t), \ldots, d_n(t))$ achieves its minimum. $E(d_1(t), \ldots, d_n(t))$ is the global energy function since it depends on all the disorders. If $d_i(t)$ is the only argument to be considered, and all other $d_k(t)$, $k \neq i$, are considered as parameters with their current values, the global energy function becomes a local energy function denoted as $E_i(d_i(t))$, which only depends on d_i. The local energy function will be used to determine how to update the disorder activations. The general activation rule for updating the disorder activation $d_i(t)$ is given with Equation (9).

$$d_i(t + 1) = d_i(t) + sign\frac{dd_i}{dt}\alpha \tag{9}$$

where $sign$ is a two value variable, $sign \in \{0, 1\}$, $0 < \alpha \leq 1$, and $\frac{dd_i}{dt}$ is the derivative or rate of change of $d_i(t)$. We define $\frac{dd_i}{dt}$ as

$$\frac{dd_i}{dt} = \sum_{m_j \in a\_sources(d_i)} \frac{dd_i^j}{dt} \tag{10}$$

$$\frac{dd_i^j}{dt} = \begin{cases} (mi_j - m_j(t))c_{ij} & m_j \in a\_sources(d_i) \\ 0 & otherwise \end{cases} \tag{11}$$

At time $t + 1$, before updating $d_i(t)$, three values, $E_i(1)$, $E_i(0)$ and $E_i(\mathbf{d_i(t)})$, are calculated with $d_i(t)$ being constrained to 1, 0 and the current activation $\mathbf{d_i(t)}$ respectively. We define a quantity $q_i(t)$ as follows.

$$q_i(t) = \begin{cases} 1 - min(E_i(1), E_i(\mathbf{d_i(t)}))/min(E_i(0), E_i(\mathbf{d_i(t)})) & E_i(0) \neq 0 \text{ and } E_i(\mathbf{d_i(t)}) \neq 0 \\ -1 & E_i(0) = 0 \\ 0 & E_i(\mathbf{d_i(t)}) = 0 \end{cases}$$

$$\tag{12}$$

$q_i(t)$ indicates which value, $E_i(1)$, $E_i(0)$ or $E_i(\mathbf{d_i(t)})$, is the smallest one among the three values. $q_i(t) > 0$, $q_i(t) < 0$ or $q_i(t) = 0$ indicates that $E_i(1)$, $E_i(0)$ or $E_i(\mathbf{d_i(t)})$ is the smallest value, respectively. The smallest value indicates the most promising direction for updating $d_i(t)$. Therefore, in order to let the energy function smaller, $d_i(t)$ should increase, decrease or keep untouched when $E_i(1)$, $E_i(0)$ or $E_i(\mathbf{d_i(t)})$ is the smallest value, respectively. In addition to $q_i(t)$, the derivative of $d_i(t)$, $\frac{dd_i}{dt}$, is also used to determine how to update $d_i(t)$. If $\frac{dd_i}{dt} > 0$, $d_i(t)$ should increase to let the error smaller, otherwise $d_i(t)$ should decrease.

Both $q_i(t)$ and $\frac{dd_i}{dt}$ indicate whether $d_i(t)$ should increase ($q_i(t) > 0$, $\frac{dd_i}{dt} > 0$), decrease ($q_i(t) < 0$, $\frac{dd_i}{dt} < 0$), or untouched ($q_i(t) = 0$, $\frac{dd_i}{dt} = 0$). Note that both $q_i(t)$ and $\frac{dd_i}{dt}$ indicate only the desired direction to update $d_i(t)$ in order to achieve local optimisation, it cannot guarantee that the change of $d_i(t)$ will optimise the global energy function. The local decision is made based on $q_i(t)$ and thus the change of $d_i(t)$ only reflects the current state of the network at time $t + 1$. With the successive parallel computations, such changes are reversible which means that a previously increased activation could be decreased later. This adjustment will let the global energy function towards be optimised.

The variable $sign$ in Equation (9) is defined as the following function.

$$sign = f(q_i(t)\frac{dd_i}{dt}) \tag{13}$$

The function f is defined as follows.

$$f(x) = \begin{cases} 1 & x \geq 0 \\ 0 & x < 0 \end{cases} \tag{14}$$

Equation (13) tells us that, if $q_i(t) > 0$ and $\frac{dd_i}{dt} > 0$, or $q_i(t) < 0$ and $\frac{dd_i}{dt} < 0$, then $sign = 1$. In this case, the change directions of $d_i(t)$ indicated by $q_i(t)$ and $\frac{dd_i}{dt}$ are the same, and $d_i(t)$ will increase by $\frac{dd_i}{dt}\alpha$ if $\frac{dd_i}{dt} > 0$, and decrease by $|\frac{dd_i}{dt}\alpha|$ if $\frac{dd_i}{dt} < 0$. When $q_i(t) = 0$ or $\frac{dd_i}{dt} = 0$, $sign$ is also equal to 1. In the case that $q_i(t) = 0$ and $\frac{dd_i}{dt} \neq 0$, $d_i(t)$ will be updated according to $\frac{dd_i}{dt}$, but the amount of the change is smaller than the amount when $q_i(t) \neq 0$ (see $\delta < \alpha$ in Equation (15)), because the change directions of $d_i(t)$ indicated by $q_i(t)$ and $\frac{dd_i}{dt}$ is not the same, i.e., $q_i(t) = 0$ requires that $d_i(t)$ should keep untouched, and $\frac{dd_i}{dt} \neq 0$ requires that $d_i(t)$ should be updated. When $sign = 0$ which means that the change directions of $d_i(t)$ indicated by $q_i(t)$ and $\frac{dd_i}{dt}$ are opposite, $d_i(t)$ will keep untouched because the change directions of $d_i(t)$ are contradictions. Obviously, when $\frac{dd_i}{dt} = 0$, $d_i(t)$ will keep untouched.

Combining Equation (10) and Equation (14), the activation rule for updating disorder activation $d_i(t)$ is expressed as Equation (16).

$$d_i(t+1) = \begin{cases} d_i(t) + f\left(q_i(t)\frac{dd_i}{dt}\right)\frac{dd_i}{dt}\alpha & q_i(t) \neq 0 \\ d_i(t) + f\left(q_i(t)\frac{dd_i}{dt}\right)\frac{dd_i}{dt}\delta & q_i(t) = 0 \end{cases} \tag{15}$$

where $\delta < \alpha$

With the equation (10), (11) and (15), the activation of d_i can be calculated according to the current activations $d_i(t)$ and $m_j(t)$, link strength P and the observation M_I. To ensure $1 \geq d_i(t+1) \geq 0$, we set it to 0 if $d_i(t+1)$ is less than 0 and to 1 if $d_i(t+1)$ is greater than 1.

2.3 Network Computing Procedure

The network computing procedure consists of a series of iterative computing. Initially, $d_i(0) = p_i$, $m_j(0) = 0$, $i = 1, \ldots, n$, $j = 1, \ldots, p$. Based on the observation data M_I, the activations $d_i(t)$ and $m_j(t)$ are updated with the equations (7), (10), (11) and (15). The computing keeps going repeatedly until the energy function reaches its equilibrium. Here t refers to the times of iteration. Each computing iteration consists of the following steps, initially $t = 0$.

1. Update $m_j(t)$ with the equation (7), $j = 1, \ldots, p$.

2. Update the activation $d_i(t)$ with the equations (10), (11) and (15), $i = 1, \ldots, n$.

3. Determine whether the network reaches its equilibrium, that is, determine whether $| d_i(t) - d_i(t-1) | \approx 0$ for $i = 1, \ldots, n$. If not, t is assigned with $t + 1$, and the computing goes to step 1 for the next iteration, otherwise, the computing stops. If $E(t) \approx 0$, then all the d_i with $d_i(t) > \rho$ forms a solution, otherwise, there is no solution to the observation M_I.

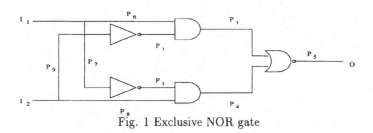

Fig. 1 Exclusive NOR gate

3 Experiments

We have conducted a number of experiments to test the neural network model. All the experiments are performed on a neural network simulator called SNNS (Stuttgart Neural Network Simulator) which provides an efficient and flexible simulation environment for neural network research. The activation rules and the computing procedure are implemented with C program functions which are inserted into SNNS. By means of SNNS, the parallel computation of the neural network model is implemented. A simple example of the digital circuit fault diagnosis is given to show the effect of our model on solving the diagnostic problem with dependent disorders. We will compare the method proposed here with the method proposed in [9].

Fig. 1 is an exclusive NOR gate. I_1 and I_2 are the input signals, and O is the output signal. The state of the circuit is described by $[(I_1, I_2), (O)]$. There are four different inputs to this circuit, they are $(0,0)$, $(0,1)$, $(1,0)$ and $(1,1)$. The correct states for the four inputs are $[(0,0),(1)]$, $[(0,1),(0)]$, $[(1,0),(0)]$ and $[(1,1),(1)]$ respectively. If the circuit faults, the circuit states will not be correct for all the inputs. There are four wrong sates, they are $m_1 = [(0,0),(0)]$, $m_2 = [(1,0),(1)]$, , $m_3 = [(0,1),(1)]$, and $m_4 = [(1,1),(0)]$ which are considered as the manifestations for the example here. There are 9 lines in the simple circuit, denoted as P_1, P_2, P_3, P_4, P_5, P_6, P_7, P_8, and P_9. Two common faults might occur in each line, which are stuck-at-0 and stuck-at-1 faults. $S0(P)$ represents that line P has a stuck-at-0 fault, and $S1(P)$ represents that line P has a stuck-at-1 fault. We only choose the following seven faults as the disorders for the diagnosis example here: $d_1 = S1(P_5)$, $d_2 = S1(P_3)$, $d_3 = S1(P_4)$, $d_4 = S0(P_6) \wedge S0(P_7)$, $d_5 = S1(P_6) \wedge S1(P_7)$, $d_6 = S0(P_6) \wedge S1(P_7)$, and $d_7 = S1(P_8) \wedge S0(P_9)$. Two causal networks are designed, which represent partially the causal relations between some of the disorders and the manifestations. The two networks are illustrated with Fig. 2 and Fig. 3. The disorders in the network Fig.2 are independent each other, and the disorders in Fig. 3 are not completely independent since d_4, d_5 and d_6 are exclusive each other. For simplicity, the network in Fig. 2 is called network 1 and the other is called network 2.

We have proposed a method to solve the diagnostic problem with independent disorders [10]. In order to show that the method reported here is effective on solving the diagnostic problem with dependent disorders, the two methods will be compared here. The difference between the two methods is the different manifestation activation rule. For the method reported in [10], the manifestation activation rule is as follows.

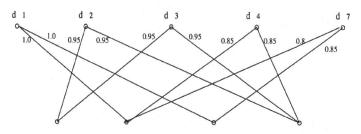

Fig. 2 The causal network with independent disorders

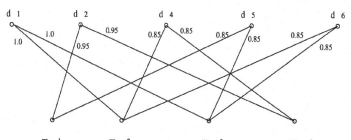

Fig. 3 The causal network with dependent disorders

$$m_j(t) = \begin{cases} d_{i_1}(t)d_{i_2}(t)\dots d_{i_r}(t)c_{i_1 j} & TYPE(m_j) = AND \\ \Delta\big(qiqqiq\dots\Delta(c_{i_1 j}d_{i_1}(t), c_{i_2 j}d_{i_2}(t))\dots, c_{i_n j}d_{i_r}(t)\big) & TYPE(m_j) = OR \end{cases}$$
(16)

Where $causes(m_j) = \{d_{i1}, \dots, d_{ir}\}$.

There are 32 potential disorder subsets for each of the two networks. For different disorder subsets, the manifestations caused by them could be the same. After picking out the disorder subsets whose manifestations are the same, there are 11 disorder subsets left for the two networks. TABLE 2 and TABLE 3 give the experimental result of network 1, and the TABLE 4 and TABLE 5 give the experimental result of network 2.

An important difference between Equation (7) and Equation (16) is that Equation (16) is related to all the disorders in $causes(m_j)$, while Equation (7) is only related to some disorders which have the maximum value or minimum value among $causes(m_j)$. The activation calculated by Equation (16) can be affected by all the disorders in $causes(m_j)$, while the activation calculated by Equation (7) is only affected by some of the disorders. Therefore the manifestation activations calculated by Equation (16) are more accurate than that calculated by Equation (7). This is the reason that the average error of manifestation AEM in TABLE 3 and TABLE 5 is smaller than that in TABLE 2 and TABLE 4 (aem is the average error between M_OBS and the final manifestation activation M_HYP for each case). From Table 1 and Table 2, we can find that, for 11 different observations (M_OBS), there are 11 different disorder hypotheses (D_HYP) being found in Table 2, while there are 6 different disorder hypotheses being found in Table 1, the other 5 hypotheses are duplicates. The reason is also because the sensitivity of Equation (16) to the disorder activations is higher than that of Equation (7). On the other hand, it is because of the insensitivity of Equation (7) to the disorder activations, for the diagnostic problem with dependent disorders, the influences of the disorder interaction to the manifestations can be weakened when using Equation (7) to calculate the manifestation activations. From Table 3 and Table 4, we can find that, there are two hypotheses in Table 4 which are not correct solutions because d_4, d_5 or d_6 occur simultaneously. But in Table 3, there is no such solution, all the hypotheses in Table 3 are correct solutions.

Table 1. The result of the network 1 with the method proposed in this paper

D_HYP					M_OBS				M_HYP				aem	AEM
d_1	d_2	d_3	d_4	d_7	m_1	m_2	m_3	m_4	m_1	m_2	m_3	m_4		
1.00	0.00	0.00	0.00	0.00	0.00	0.85	0.85	0.00	0.00	1.00	1.00	0.00	0.075	
0.00	0.00	0.00	1.00	0.00	0.00	0.85	0.00	0.85	0.00	0.85	0.00	0.85	0.00	
1.00	0.00	0.00	1.00	0.00	0.00	1.00	0.85	0.85	0.00	1.00	1.00	0.85	0.0375	
0.00	1.00	1.00	0.00	0.00	0.95	0.00	0.00	0.95	0.95	0.00	0.00	0.95	0.00	
1.00	1.00	1.00	0.00	0.00	0.95	0.80	0.85	0.95	0.95	1.00	1.00	0.95	0.075	
0.00	1.00	1.00	1.00	0.00	0.95	0.85	0.00	0.95	0.95	0.85	0.00	0.95	0.00	0.024
1.00	1.00	1.00	0.00	0.00	0.95	0.97	0.85	0.99	0.95	1.00	1.00	0.95	0.055	
0.00	1.00	1.00	0.00	0.00	0.99	0.00	0.00	0.99	0.95	0.00	0.00	0.95	0.02	
1.00	0.00	0.00	0.00	0.00	0.00	1.00	1.00	0.00	0.00	1.00	1.00	0.00	0.00	
1.00	0.00	0.000	1.00	0.00	0.00	1.00	1.00	0.85	0.00	1.00	1.00	0.85	0.00	
1.00	1.00	1.00	0.00	0.00	0.95	1.00	1.00	0.95	0.95	1.00	1.00	0.95	0.00	

Table 2. The result of the network 1 with the method proposed in [9]

D_HYP					M_OBS				M_HYP				aem	AEM
d_1	d_2	d_3	d_4	d_7	m_1	m_2	m_3	m_4	m_1	m_2	m_3	m_4		
0.853	0.00	0.00	0.00	0.00	0.00	0.80	0.85	0.00	0.00	0.85	0.85	0.00	0.012	
0.00	0.00	0.00	1.00	0.00	0.00	0.85	0.00	0.85	0.00	0.85	0.00	0.85	0.00	
0.81	0.00	0.00	1.00	0.00	0.00	0.97	0.85	0.85	0.00	0.97	0.81	0.85	0.01	
0.00	0.85	0.85	0.00	0.00	0.95	0.00	0.00	0.95	0.96	0.00	0.00	0.96	0.005	
0.83	0.85	0.85	0.00	0.00	0.95	0.80	0.85	0.95	0.96	0.82	0.82	0.96	0.02	
0.00	0.95	0.95	1.00	0.00	0.95	0.85	0.00	0.99	0.99	0.85	0.00	1.00	0.0125	0.007
0.82	0.86	0.86	0.94	0.00	0.95	0.97	0.85	0.99	0.97	0.96	0.82	0.99	0.015	
0.00	1.00	1.00	0.00	0.00	1.00	0.00	0.00	1.00	1.00	0.00	0.00	1.00	0.00	
1.00	0.00	0.00	0.00	0.99	0.00	1.00	1.00	0.00	0.00	1.00	1.00	0.00	0.00	
1.00	0.00	0.00	1.00	0.96	0.00	1.00	1.00	0.85	0.00	1.00	1.00	0.85	0.00	
1.00	0.90	0.85	0.00	0.96	0.95	1.00	1.00	0.95	0.96	1.00	1.00	0.96	0.005	

Table 3. The result of the network 2 with the method proposed in this paper

D_HYP					M_OBS				M_HYP				aem	AEM
d_1	d_2	d_4	d_5	d_6	m_1	m_2	m_3	m_4	m_1	m_2	m_3	m_4		
1.00	0.00	0.00	0.00	0.00	0.00	0.85	0.85	0.00	0.00	1.00	1.00	0.00	0.075	
0.00	0.00	0.00	1.00	0.00	0.85	0.00	0.85	0.00	0.85	0.00	0.85	0.00	0.00	
0.00	0.00	1.00	0.00	0.00	0.00	0.85	0.00	0.85	0.00	0.85	0.00	0.85	0.00	
0.00	1.00	0.00	0.00	0.00	0.95	0.00	0.00	0.95	0.95	0.00	0.00	0.95	0.00	
0.00	1.00	0.00	1.00	0.00	0.95	0.00	0.85	0.95	0.95	0.00	0.85	0.95	0.00	0.0075
0.00	1.00	1.00	0.00	0.00	0.95	0.85	0.00	0.95	0.95	0.85	0.00	0.95	0.00	
1.00	0.00	0.00	0.00	0.00	0.00	1.00	1.00	0.00	0.00	1.00	1.00	0.00	0.00	
1.00	0.00	0.00	1.00	0.00	0.85	1.00	1.00	0.00	0.85	1.00	1.00	0.00	0.00	
1.00	0.00	1.00	0.00	0.00	0.00	1.00	1.00	0.85	0.00	1.00	1.00	0.85	0.00	
1.00	1.00	0.00	0.00	0.00	0.95	1.00	1.00	0.95	0.95	1.00	1.00	0.95	0.00	

Table 4. The result of the network 2 with the method proposed in [9]

D_HYP					M_OBS				M_HYP				aem	AEM
d_1	d_2	d_4	d_5	d_6	m_1	m_2	m_3	m_4	m_1	m_2	m_3	m_4		
0.87	0.00	0.00	0.00	0.00	0.00	0.85	0.85	0.00	0.00	0.87	0.87	0.00	0.02	
0.00	0.00	0.00	1.00	0.00	0.85	0.00	0.85	0.00	0.85	0.00	0.85	0.00	0.00	
0.00	0.00	1.00	0.00	0.00	0.00	0.85	0.00	0.85	0.00	0.85	0.00	0.85	0.00	
0.00	1.00	0.00	0.00	0.00	0.95	0.00	0.00	0.95	0.95	0.00	0.00	0.95	0.00	
0.00	1.00	0.00	1.00	0.00	0.99	0.00	0.85	0.95	0.99	0.00	0.85	0.95	0.00	0.002
0.00	1.00	1.00	0.00	0.00	0.95	0.85	0.00	0.95	0.95	0.85	0.00	0.99	0.00	
1.00	0.00	0.00	0.00	1.00	0.00	1.00	1.00	0.00	0.00	1.00	1.00	0.00	0.00	
1.00	0.00	0.00	1.00	0.99	0.85	1.00	1.00	0.00	0.85	1.00	1.00	0.00	0.00	
1.00	0.00	1.00	0.00	0.99	0.00	1.00	1.00	0.85	0.00	1.00	1.00	0.85	0.00	
1.00	1.00	0.00	0.00	1.00	0.95	1.00	1.00	0.95	0.95	1.00	1.00	0.95	0.00	

4 Conclusion

In summary, a neural network diagnosis model was presented in this paper. One feature of the model is that the disorder independence assumption is no longer necessary. To the authors' knowledge, the only other neural network diagnostic model which also uses a causal network directly as the neural network is the model proposed by Peng and Reggia [3]. But the causal network used by the model is a noisy-or network, i.e., only independence interaction is involved in the network, and the disorder independence assumption is necessary. This kind network can only represent independent diagnostic problems. Compared with the model of Peng and Reggia, our model can represent the the monotonic diagnostic problem which is more general than the independent diagnostic problem. The second feature is that, the errors between the observations and the current activations of the manifestation nodes are used to guide the network computing. The experimental results show that the correct rate of diagnosis with this method is very high.

References

[1] Benoit H. Mulsant, et al., "A Connectionist Approach to the Diagnosis of Dementia", in Proc. of 12th SCAMC, pages 245-249, 1988.

[2] Jakubowicz, O., et al., "A Neural Network Model for Fault Diagnosis of Digital Circuits", IJCNN, Vol.2, pages 611-614, 1990, Washington D. C.

[3] Peng, Y., and Reggia, J., "A Connectionist Model for Diagnostic Problem Solving", IEEE Trans. On Systems, Man and Cybernetics, 19(2), pages 285-198, 1989.

[4] Goel, A. and Ramanujam, J., "A Neural Architecture for a Class of Abduction Problems", IEEE Transactions on Systems Man and Cybernetics, 26(6), pages 854-860, 1996.

[5] Blockley, D.I., et al., "Measures of Uncertainty", Civil Engineering Systems, 1, pages 3-9, 1988.

[6] Dubois, D. and Prade, H., "A Discussion of Uncertainty Handling in Support Logic Programming", Int. J. of Intelligent Systems, 5(5), pages 15-42, 1990.

[7] Pearl. J., Probabilistic Reasoning in Intelligent Systems : Networks of Plausible Inference, Morgan Kaufmann Publishers, Inc., San Mateo, California, 1988.

[8] Charles Sanders Peirce, Collected Papers of Charles Sanders Peirce (1839-1914). Harvard University Press, Cambridge, MA, 1958.

[9] Yue Xu, Chengqi Zhang, "A Neural Network Model for Monotonic Diagnostic Problem Solving", accepted by the 2nd IEEE International Conference on Intelligent Processing Systems, Gold Coast, Australia, August 4-7, 1998.

Neural Network Based Motion Control and Applications to Non-holonomic Mobile Manipulators

M W Chen [1] and A M S Zalzala [2]

[1] Ngee Ann Polytechnic, Singapore
[2] Sheffield University, UK

Abstract. This paper presents a neural network based motion control approach and its application to a mobile manipulator. The mobile base is subject to a non-holonomic constraint and the base and onboard manipulator cause disturbances to each other. Compensational neural network controllers are proposed to track dynamic trajectories under a non-holonomic constraint and uncertainties. Comparisons were made between neural network controllers with and without model information. It is shown through various simulations and application results that the proposed neural network compensation schemes can achieve good control performances.

1. Introduction

A mobile manipulator is a combination of a robot arm and a mobile base with infinite working space in the horizontal plane. In the case of simultaneous locomotion and manipulation, the robot hand in principle will have the dynamics of the robot arm and the working space of the vehicle[4]. A typical task of a mobile manipulator includes the following two steps: first, move the vehicle in an unstructured environment towards a target either following a prescribed trajectory or going along a collision-free path, second, in the vicinity of the target position, move the vehicle and the onboard arm simultaneously so that the end-effector can follow a trajectory accurately to perform a task, such as doing welding or cutting.

Neural network based controllers have received much attention in recent years[3]. This type of controller exploits the possibilities of neural networks for learning non-linear functions as well as for solving certain type of problems where massive parallel computation is required. The learning capability of neural networks is used to make the controller learn a certain nonlinear function, representing direct dynamics, inverse dynamics or any other mappings in a process.

Neural network control of manipulators or mobile robot is richly addressed in literature[5][1][6], but the research into neural network's application to real mobile manipulators is relatively recent.

This paper deals with neural networks in inverse model learning and compensation to the motion control of a mobile manipulator. The first part of this paper presents the dynamical modelling of mobile manipulators with non-holonomic constraints. Then, based on the model information, a neural network based control scheme is proposed. The second part of the paper shows various simulations under uncertainties and base motion slippage. Lastly, the neural controller is applied to a real mobile manipulator to demonstrate its effectiveness.

2. Dynamical Modelling of a Mobile Manipulator

A mobile robot with an onboard manipulator as shown in Fig. 1 is considered in this paper. The manipulator has one rotational link and two planar links. The mobile base has two driving motors, one for translational moving and one for rotational moving [2].

Fig. 1. A mobile robot with an onboard manipulator

Considering the inertial reference frame in the (X, Y) plane and choosing a point P along the axis of the heading direction on the mobile robot as shown in Fig. 2, the mobile robot at point P can be described by three variables (x, y, θ_p), where (x, y) denotes the Cartesian position and θ_p describes the heading angle, respectively. For the manipulator, the joint angles of the three links are θ_1, θ_2 and θ_3.

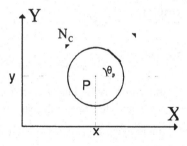

Fig. 2. Top view of the mobile base

Define a vector of coordinates

$$\mathbf{q} = (q_1, q_2, q_3, q_4, q_5, q_6)^T \tag{1}$$

where q_1, q_2 and q_3 denote the base position (x, y) and the heading angle θ_p, respectively, and q_4, q_5 and q_6 denote the manipulator joint angles θ_1, θ_2 and θ_3, respectively.

The mobile base is subject to the following non-holonomic constraint:

$$- \dot{x} \sin \theta_p + \dot{y} \cos \theta_p = 0 \tag{2}$$

i.e., the base can not move in the direction normal to the axis of the heading direction. Note that the position (x, y) and the heading angle θ_p of the base are not independent of each other due to the non-holonomic constraint.

The non-holonomic constraint (1) can be rewritten as a matrix form as:

$$A \dot{q}_p = 0 \tag{3}$$

where $A = \begin{bmatrix} - \sin \theta_p & \cos \theta_p & 0 \end{bmatrix}$, $\dot{q}_p = \begin{bmatrix} \dot{x} & \dot{y} & \dot{\theta}_p \end{bmatrix}^T$.

The Newton-Euler method is used to derive dynamic equations of the mobile manipulator. In order to apply the iteration equations, the base is visualised as having three joints, two prismatic joints (along x and y directions, respectively) and one rotational joint (along the vertical direction). The coordinate system is then built up based on the fictitious joints and the real manipulator joints. Once the complete co-ordinate system is built up, the Newton-Euler iteration equations are applied to obtain the base fictitious joint torques and the manipulator joint torques.

The dynamic equations for the composite base/manipulator system are obtained in the method as outlined above. The dynamic equations for the base X, Y directions are given by

$$m_p \, \ddot{x} = \frac{\cos\theta_p (\tau_r + \tau_1)}{r} - \cos\theta_p \, f_{hm} + \sin\theta_p \, f_{am} - N_c \sin\theta_p \tag{4}$$

$$m_p \, \ddot{y} = \frac{\sin\theta_p (\tau_r + \tau_1)}{r} - \sin\theta_p \, f_{hm} - \cos\theta_p \, f_{am} + N_c \cos\theta_p \tag{5}$$

where f_{hm}, f_{am} denotes the projections of the joint forces from the first manipulator link onto the heading direction and axis direction of the base, respectively.

Differentiating Equation (2), multiplying Equations (4) and (5) by $-\sin\theta_p$ and $\cos\theta_p$ respectively, and adding, we obtain

$$N_c = m_p (\dot{x}\cos\theta_p + \dot{y}\sin\theta_p)\dot{\theta}_p + f_{ma} \tag{6}$$

The composite dynamic equations of the mobile manipulator system can be expressed as

$$\overline{M}(q)\ddot{q} + \overline{K}(q,\dot{q}) = \overline{b}\tau \tag{7}$$

where

$$\overline{M}(q) = \begin{bmatrix} M_{mm} & M_{mp} \\ M_{pm} & M_{pp} \end{bmatrix}, \ \overline{K}(q,\dot{q}) = \begin{bmatrix} K_m + K_{mp} \\ K_p + K_{pm} \end{bmatrix},$$

$$\overline{b} = \begin{bmatrix} I_m & 0 \\ 0 & b_p \end{bmatrix}, \ q = \begin{bmatrix} q_m \\ q_p \end{bmatrix}, \ \tau = \begin{bmatrix} \tau_m \\ \tau_p \end{bmatrix}, \ q_m = \begin{bmatrix} \theta_1 & \theta_2 & \theta_3 \end{bmatrix}^T, \ q_p = \begin{bmatrix} x & y & \theta_p \end{bmatrix}^T;$$

$$\tau_m = \begin{bmatrix} \tau_1 & \tau_2 & \tau_3 \end{bmatrix}^T, \ \tau_p = \begin{bmatrix} \tau_r \\ \tau_1 \end{bmatrix};$$

I_m is an $m \times m$ identity matrix, m is the degree of freedom of the manipulator.

The disturbant couplings between the base and the onboard manipulator are:

$$D_{pm} = M_{pm}\ddot{q}_m + K_{pm} \tag{8}$$

$$D_{mp} = M_{mp}\ddot{q}_p + K_{mp} \tag{9}$$

where the disturbant force D_{pm} from the manipulator to the base consists of the inertial term $M_{pm}\ddot{q}_m$ and the term K_{pm} with centrifugal and Coriolis components in case of the manipulator motion; the disturbant force D_{mp} from the base to the manipulator includes the inertia term $M_{mp}\ddot{q}_p$ and the term K_{mp} with centrifugal and Coriolis components in case of the base motion. Precompensation of D_{pm} and D_{mp} leads to the consequence that the base controller only acts on the base and the manipulator controller only acts on the manipulator.

3. Dynamic Trajectory Tracking by Neural Networks

3.1 Neural Network Compensation Control

When there is no manipulator onboard the mobile base, Equations (4) and (5), can be simplified into the following two equations:

$$\tau_r + \tau_1 = m_p r(\ddot{x}\cos\theta_p + \ddot{y}\sin\theta_p) \tag{10}$$

$$\tau_r - \tau_1 = \frac{2rI}{R}\ddot{\theta}_p \tag{11}$$

or

$$\tau_r = \frac{1}{2}(\frac{2rI}{R}\ddot{\theta}_p + m_p r(\ddot{x}\cos\theta_p + \ddot{y}\sin\theta_p)) \tag{12}$$

$$\tau_1 = \frac{1}{2}(-\frac{2rI}{R}\ddot{\theta}_p + m_p r(\ddot{x}\cos\theta_p + \ddot{y}\sin\theta_p)) \tag{13}$$

From Equations(10)(11), it can be seen that $\tau_r - \tau_1$ directly affects $\ddot{\theta}_p$, and $\tau_r + \tau_1$ directly affects $\ddot{x}$, $\ddot{y}$ and $\ddot{\theta}_p$. Equations (12)(13) show that the input variable affecting τ_r and τ_1 are θ_p, $\ddot{x}$, $\ddot{y}$ and $\ddot{\theta}_p$. Therefore it is not difficult to assume that in order to control the orientation of the base, the difference between the right wheel torque and the left wheel torque is required to be adjusted, while to control the x and y direction motion, the sum of these two torques needs to be changed. Based on this assumption, the outputs in the neural networks proposed for base motion control are chosen as $\tau_r + \tau_1$ and $\tau_r - \tau_1$. The inputs to the neural network are chosen as θ_p, $\ddot{x}$, $\ddot{y}$ and $\ddot{\theta}_p$. For generation of compensation torques $\Delta\tau_r$ and $\Delta\tau_1$, the network outputs are chosen as $\Delta\tau_r + \Delta\tau_1$ and $\Delta\tau_r - \Delta\tau_1$. After the neural network output layer, an additional layer is used to obtain the torques τ_r and τ_1 from $\tau_r + \tau_1$ and $\tau_r - \tau_1$ or to obtain $\Delta\tau_r$ and $\Delta\tau_1$ from $\Delta\tau_r + \Delta\tau_1$ and $\Delta\tau_r - \Delta\tau_1$.

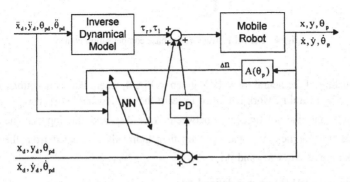

Fig. 3. Structure of neural network control for the base

Based on the above analysis, a neural network compensation control scheme is proposed as shown in Fig. 3. The inputs of the control systems are the desired x, y and θ_p, and their velocities and accelerations. The inverse dynamic equations are applied as feedforward to produce the computed wheel torques and the inputs to the inverse dynamics and the neural network are θ_p, $\ddot{x}$, $\ddot{y}$ and $\ddot{\theta}_p$. The neural network is used as a compensator to generate the compensation torques. When there are tracking errors due to such reasons as uncertainties, or parameter changes. the neural network starts to learn on-line and produce compensation torques to reduce the tracking errors. The second function of the neural network is that when the robot slips, i.e. the non-holonomic constraint is violated and a corresponding constraint error($\Delta n = A \dot{q}$) occurs, the neural network is then trained by using this error to produce corresponding compensation torques to reduce the slippage and the tracking errors.

3.2 Multi-Layered Perceptron Neural Network Compensator

The neural networks used in this paper is a multi-layered perceptron (MLP). The multi-layered perceptron compensator has four layers with four input nodes and two output nodes. The four inputs are θ_p, $\ddot{x}$, $\ddot{y}$ and $\ddot{\theta}_p$. The two outputs are $\Delta\tau_r + \Delta\tau_l$ and $\Delta\tau_r - \Delta\tau_l$. The errors Δx, Δy, $\Delta\theta_p$ and Δn are applied to update the weights of the network. The network is trained using well-known back propagation approach.

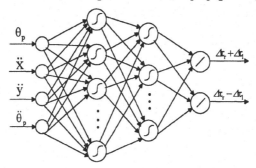

Fig. 4. The MLP structure for base compensation control

The structure of the neural network is given in Fig. 4, where bias connections are not shown. The neural network is trained to learn the relationship between $\Delta\tau_r + \Delta\tau_l$ and the inputs and the relationship between $\Delta\tau_r - \Delta\tau_l$ and the inputs. The wheel compensation torques $\Delta\tau_r$ and $\Delta\tau_l$ are then indirectly calculated from the neural network outputs $\Delta\tau_r + \Delta\tau_l$ and $\Delta\tau_r - \Delta\tau_l$.

The trajectory tracking error is defined as:

$$e = \sqrt{(x_d - x)^2 + (y_d - y)^2 + (\theta_{pd} - \theta_p)^2} \; ; \qquad (14)$$

As the desired outputs of the network are not available, the errors used for updating the weights have to be chosen indirectly. According to the inverse dynamic equations of the base, the errors used to update the weights in the last layer are chosen respectively as:

$$\delta_1 = K_x(x_d - x) + K_y(y_d - y) \qquad (15)$$

$$\delta_2 = K_{\theta_p}(\theta_{pd} - \theta_p) \qquad (16)$$

The weights are updated according to the standard back-propagation algorithm.

4. Simulations

Case 1 A continuous trajectory is given with 30% of base weight error. The initial heading of the base is along x-axis. The task for the neural network compensator is to learn the relationship between the trajectory inputs and the compensation torques. The compensation torques and the torques from the PD control are added to the computed torques to control the robot to follow the given trajectory. The tracking process by MLP compensation and PD control with model information is shown in Fig. 5, which is better than by neural network controller without any model information (Fig. 6).

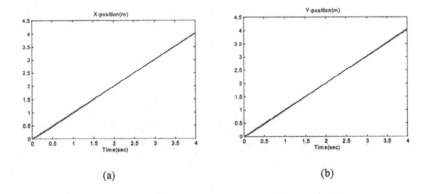

(a)   (b)

Fig. 5. Trajectory tracking by MLP compensation with model information due to 30% base weight error (desired: dashed/dotted, actual: solid)

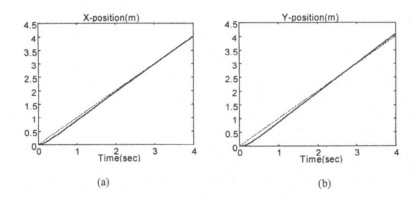

(a)

(b)

Fig. 6. Trajectory tracking by MLP compensation without model information due to 30% base weight error (desired: dashed/dotted, actual: solid)

Case 2 In this case, it is assumed that a slippage happened between the time 1s and 1.2s from the starting point. During this period the non-holonomic constraint is violated. A constraint error is fedback to the neural network to speed the learning process. The tracking process by MLP compensation and PD control with model information is shown in Fig. 7, which is better than by neural network controller without any model information (Fig. 8).

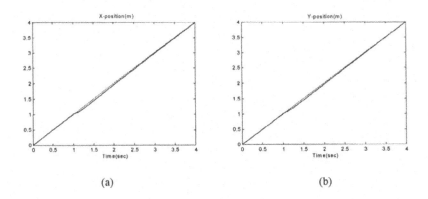

(a)

(b)

Fig. 7. Trajectory tracking by MLP compensation control with model information due to a slippage between the time 1s and 1.2s from the starting point (desired: dashed/dotted, actual: solid)

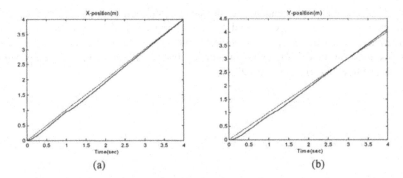

(a)   (b)

Fig. 8. Trajectory tracking by MLP compensation control without model information due to a slippage between the time 1s and 1.2s from the starting time (desired: dashed/dotted, actual: solid)

5. Experiments on the Dynamic Control Using Neural Networks

The proposed control methods are applied to a real mobile manipulator as shown in Fig. 1. This robot is a combination of a mobile base and a two-link arm. The base is subject to a non-holonomic constraint.

In this section, the proposed neural network based control methods are applied to the this real mobile manipulator. Due to the original design, dynamic control can not be applied to the arm, so only base dynamic control is considered. However, the manipulator joints move along given trajectories simultaneously with the base when dynamic control is applied to the base. For comparison, model-based dynamic control are implemented together with the neural network control.

5.1 Model-Based Dynamic Control

The first dynamic control method considered is model-based dynamic control. The structure of model-based neural network control is shown in Fig. 9.

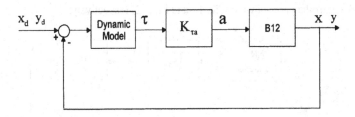

Fig. 9. The structure of the inverse model dynamic control of the base

Fig. 10 shows one implementation results using model only control. Fig. 6.10(a) and (b) show the desired trajectory and the actual trajectory along x direction and y direction, respectively. Due to the unclear structure and unknown parameters of the inverse dynamic model, the control results by inverse dynamic control are not very good. The tracking error norm is 0.071m.

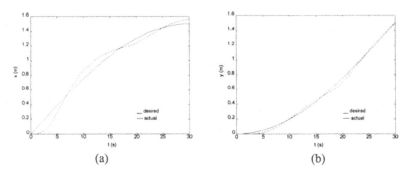

(a)   (b)

Fig. 10. Implementation results with the base following a dynamic trajectory using model only dynamic control

5.2 Neural Network Control

The Structures of the Neural Network Controllers. Because model-based motion control cannot achieve good results, neural network controller is applied to the dynamic control of the base robot to improve the control quality. The poor control quality of the model-based control is mainly due to the fact that the structure and parameters of the real model are unknown. A neural network is used to learn the compensation torques to the uncertainties. The neural network is trained first off-line by giving a variety of unknown model parameters, then it is applied to the real robot to carry on training online.

Two kinds of control structures are proposed. One is neural network only control, and the other is model-based neural network control. The structures of these two neural network controllers are shown in Fig. 11 and Fig. 12, respectively.

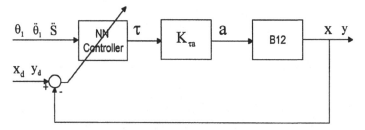

Fig. 11. The structure of the neural network control system

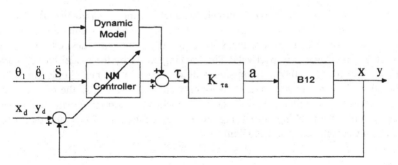

Fig. 12. The structure of model-based neural network control system

Neural Network Only Control . Firstly, a neural network only controller is applied to track the dynamic trajectory given in the simulation. The results are shown in Fig. 13 with a tracking error 0.059m. Fig. 13(a) and (b) show the desired trajectory and the actual trajectory along x direction and y direction, respectively.

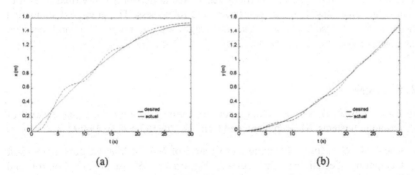

Fig. 13. The practical results when a NN controller is applied to track a dynamic trajectory (tracking error = 0.059m)

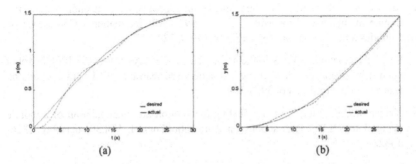

Fig. 14. The practical results when a model-based neural network controller is applied to track a dynamic trajectory (tracking error = 0.037m)

Model-Based Neural Network Control. Secondly, a model-based neural network controller is applied to track the given trajectory. The practical results are shown in Fig. 14. Fig. 14(a) and (b) are, the x direction and y direction desired and actual trajectories over time t, respectively. The tracking errors by the model-based neural network controller is 0.037m. Compared with the results by the model only controller (Fig. 10) and the results by neural network only controller (Fig. 13), the model-based neural network controller achieved the best tracking performance with the lowest tracking error (the tracking error using model only control is 0.071m and that using neural network only control is 0.059m).

6. Conclusions

This paper proposed a neural network compensation controller to a base/manipulator system. The difficulty with the control of such a system is that the base is subject to a non-holonomic constraint and there exist disturbances between the base and manipulator motions. Traditional controllers often fail to achieve good control performances for this type of control systems. Neural networks can virtually learn to compensate any tracking errors and have good robustness. The presented simulation and experiment results showed the advantages of the proposed neural network compensators.

References

1. Borenstein, J., Koren, Y.: Motion control Analysis of a mobile robot. Journal of Dynamic Systems, Measurement, and Control, Vol.109(1987), 73-79.

2. Chen, M. W.: Motion Planning and Control of Mobile Manipulators Using Soft Computing Techniques, PhD thesis, Department of Automatic Control and Systems Engineering, The University of Sheffield (1997).

3. Hunt, K. J., Sbarbaro, D., Zbikowski, R., Gawthrop, P. J.: Neural Networks for Control Systems --- A Survey. Automatica, Vol.28, 6(1992), 1083-1112.

4. Miksch, W., Schroeder, D.: Performance functional based controller design for a mobile manipulator. Proceedings of the 1992 IEEE International Conference on Robotics and Automation, Nice, France(1992), 227-232.

5. Saga, K., Sugasaka, T., Sekiguchi, M., Nagata, S., Asakswa, K.: Mobile robot control by neural networks using self-supervised learning. IEEE Transactions on Industrial Electronics, Vol.39, 6(1992).

6. Yamamoto, Y., Yun, X.: Coordinating locomotion and manipulation of a mobile manipulator. IEEE Transactions on Automatic Control, Vol.39, 6(1994), 1326-1332.

A Geometric Approach to Anytime Constraint Solving for TCSPs

Yeh Hong-ming, Jane Yung-jen Hsu, and Han-shen Huang

Department of Computer Science and Information Engineering
National Taiwan University, Taipei, Taiwan, R.O.C.

Abstract. Temporal constraint satisfaction problems (TCSPs) are typically modelled as graphs or networks. Efficient algorithms are only available to find solutions for problems with limited topology. In this paper, we propose *constraint geometry* as an alternative approach to modeling TCSPs. Finding solutions to a TCSP is transformed into a search problem in the corresponding n-dimensional space. Violations of constraints can be measured in terms of spatial distances. As a result, *approximate* solutions can be identified when it is impossible or impractical to find exact solutions. A real-numbered evolutionary algorithm with special mutation operators has been designed to solve the general class of TCSPs. It can render approximate solutions at any time and improve the solution quality if given more time. Experiments on hundreds of randomly generated problems with representative parameters showed that the algorithm is more efficient and robust in comparison with the path-consistency algorithm.

1 Introduction

A temporal constraint satisfaction problem (TCSP) is a problem that consists of a set of events and a set of constraints on the time points at which the events occur [1]. To solve a TCSP problem is to find a set of assignments, each of which assigns a time point to an event, such that all constraints are satisfied.

When a solution to a TCSP is not available, either because no solution exists or because the algorithms cannot find it in time, an approximate solution may be a good alternative. In fact, there are many practical TCSP applications in which it is acceptable to violate some of the constraints with reasonable costs. Furthermore, there are cases in which a TCSP contains conflicting constraints.

Constraint satisfaction problems are usually formulated as graphs or networks, with algorithms based on graph theory and search [2]. In this paper, a geometric approach, *constraint geometry*, is proposed to model TCSPs. Using this approach, TCSPs can be represented in an intuitive manner, and the concepts of exact and approximate solutions are straightforward. Besides, an evolutionary algorithm based on constraint geometry is also presented here to support *anytime* problem solving for TCSPs.

2   TCSPs

This section introduces a formal definition of TCSPs, which is more rigorous than the one commonly adopted in the literature [1].

Let $X = \{x_1, x_2, \ldots, x_n\}$ be a finite set of variables on $\mathbf{R}$, the set of real numbers. A constraint c over X defines a function $f : X \to \{true, false\}$ which can be represented in the general form below.

$$k_1 x_1 + k_2 x_2 + \cdots + k_m x_m \in [a_1, b_1] \cup [a_2, b_2] \cup \ldots \cup [a_n, b_n]$$

where n is a finite positive integer; for $i = 1, 2, \ldots, n$, we have $a_i, b_i, k_i \in \mathbf{R}$ and

$$a_1 \leq b_1 < a_2 \leq b_2 < \ldots < a_n \leq b_n$$

We call the left-hand side of a constraint c the *characteristic function* of the constraint, denoted by $\Delta[c]$; and the right-hand side the *true range* of the constraint, denoted by $\tau(c)$. For example, let c_1 be the constraint $x_1 - x_2 + x_3 \in [2, 4]$, then $\Delta[c_1]$ is $x_1 - x_2 + x_3$ and $\tau(c_1)$ is $[2, 4]$. The set of all a_i's and b_i's is called the *landmark set* of the true range $\tau(c)$.

A TCSP is a finite set of *temporal constraints* over X. Each constraint is either a unary constraint whose characteristic function is of the form x_i, or a binary constraint whose characteristic function is of the form $x_i - x_j$. A solution to a TCSP is a unifier [5] $\sigma = \{x_1 \leftarrow h_1, x_2 \leftarrow h_2, \ldots, x_n \leftarrow h_n\}$, where $h_i \in \mathbf{R}$, such that all constraints are satisfied. If the unifier $\{x_1 \leftarrow h_1, x_2 \leftarrow h_2, \ldots, x_n \leftarrow h_n\}$ is a solution to a TCSP containing only binary constraints, the unifier $\{x_1 \leftarrow h_1 + k, x_2 \leftarrow h_2 + k, \ldots, x_n \leftarrow h_n + k\}$, for any constant k, is also a solution. More detailed definitions can be found in Yeh [8].

3   Constraint Geometry

Constraint-satisfaction problems are often treated as search problems. Therefore, to solve a TCSP is to search for a solution in the problem space [6] defined by the TCSP. The basic idea of *constraint geometry* is to formulate a problem in an Euclidean space. Subsequently, the constraints and solutions to a TCSP become geometric objects in the space.

Given a TCSP P on the set of variables $X = \{x_1, x_2, \ldots, x_n\}$, the variable space of P, denoted by $\nu(P)$, is the Cartesian product of the domains of all variables in X. The variable space of a constraint, denoted by $\nu(c)$, is a Cartesian product of the domains of all variables occuring in c.

3.1   Geometry of Constraints

For any TCSP problem P with n temporal variables, each constraint is bounded by a set of parallel hyperplanes in the n-dimensional Euclidean space $\nu(P)$.

Definition 1. Boundary. *Let c be a constraint in a TCSP P, and $L(c)$ be the landmark set of $\tau(c)$. The boundary of c at a landmark $l \in L(c)$, denoted by $b(c, l)$, is the set*

$$\{p \mid p \in \nu(c) \text{ s.t. } \Delta[c](p) = l\}.$$

The boundaries of the constraint c, denoted by $B(c)$, is the union of its boundaries at all landmarks, namely

$$B(c) = \bigcup_{l \in L(c)} b(c, l).$$

For example, consider a constraint $c_1 : x_1 - x_2 \in [2, 4]$. Fig. 1 depicts the boundaries $b(c_1, 2)$ and $b(c_1, 4)$, identified by the lines $x_1 - x_2 = 2$ and $x_1 - x_2 = 4$ respectively. The shaded area consists of points that satisfy c_1.

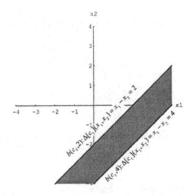

Fig. 1. The boundaries $B(c_1)$ of $x_1 - x_2 \in [2, 4]$.

A point p is said to be *inside* the boundaries of c iff $\Delta[c](p) \in \tau(c)$, or *outside* the boundaries otherwise. A point p is *on* the boundaries iff $\Delta[c](p) \in L(c)$. (Note that $L(c) \subset \tau(c)$.) The *distance* between a constraint c and a point p in the space is the shortest distance between p and the boundaries of c if p is outside the boundaries. The distance is zero if p is inside any of the boundaries.

Definition 2. Distance. *Let c be a constraint with $\Delta[c](x_1, x_2) = k_1 x_1 + k_2 x_2$, and $L(c)$ be the landmark set of $\tau(c)$. Let p be a point in $\nu(X)$. For any landmark $l \in L(c)$, the distance between p and l, denoted by $d(p, l)$, is the minimum of the distance between p and every point in the boundary of c at l. That is,*

$$d(p, l) = \min_{q \in b(c, l)} \{d(p, q)\}$$

where $d(p,q)$ is the Euclidean norm of the vector from p to q. The distance between a point p and the constraint c, denoted by $d(p,c)$, is defined as

$$d(p,c) = \begin{cases} 0 & \text{if } \Delta[c](p) \in \tau(c), \\ \min_{l \in L(c)}\{d(p,l)\} & \text{otherwise.} \end{cases}$$

Take the example from Figure 1. Consider the point $(-1,3)$, which is outside the boundaries of c_1, since $\Delta[c_1](-1,3) = -4 \notin \tau(c_1)$. By definition, the distance between $(-1,3)$ and c_1 is based on the boundary at 2, as shown in Figure 2.

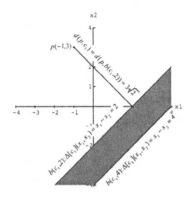

Fig. 2. The distance between (-1,3) and constraint c_1.

Given any point $p = (p_1, p_2)$, we have

$$d(p,l) = \frac{|l - p_1 + p_2|}{\sqrt{2}}$$

When c is a unary constraint, the distance equation can be further reduced into

$$d(p,l) = |l - p_1|$$

These equations are very easy to compute, which makes highly efficient implementations possible.

3.2 Geometry of TCSP

Given a problem P, the variable space $\nu(c)$ of any constraint c in P is a subspace of the variable space $\nu(P)$. To manipulate the constraints with respect to the space $\nu(P)$, two operations, *projection* and *inverse projection*, are necessary.

Let S' be a subspace of a variable space S. The *orthogonal projection* (or simply *projection*) of a point p in the space S unto the space S', denoted by

$\pi[S, S'](p)$, is a point in S', say p', that has the same value as p at every corresponding coordinate. The projection of an object o in S unto S' is the union of the projection of every points of o.

The *inverse orthogonal projection* (or simply *inverse projection*) [4] can be defined in terms of projection. The inverse projection of a point p' in the space S' into S, denoted by $\pi^{-1}[S', S](p')$, is the set $\{p \mid p \in S' s.t. \pi[S, S'](p) = p'\}$. In other words, the inverse projection of p' is the union of all points in S whose projection is p'. It should be noted that distances are invariant through inverse projection.

Given a constraint c for a problem P, we can extend any boundary $b(c, l)$ in the subspace $\nu(c)$ to the variable space $\nu(P)$. The boundary of c at l with respect to the variable space $\nu(P)$ is the inverse projection of every point in $b(c, l)$ into $\nu(P)$, i.e.

$$\{\pi^{-1}[\nu(c), \nu(P)](p) \mid p \in b(c, l)\}.$$

For simplicity, it is denoted by $\pi^{-1}[\nu(c), \nu(P)]\{b(c, l)\}$. The boundaries $B(c)$ in $\nu(P)$ is defined in a similar way.

Let us expand the example of c_1 by adding another constraint $c_2 : x_2 - x_3 \in [1, 4]$. Figure 3 shows the boundaries of c_2 in $\nu(c_2)$, which is an $\mathbf{R}^2$ plane.

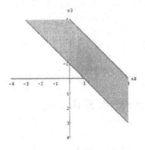

Fig. 3. The boundaries of constraint c_2.

Let $X = \{x_1, x_2, x_3\}$ be the set of variables in the new TCSP P, whose variable space $\nu(P)$ is $\mathbf{R}^3$. To consider c_1 and c_2 in $\nu(P)$, it is necessary to compute the inverse projections of $B(c_1)$ and of $B(c_2)$ into $\nu(P)$. Figure 4 depict $\pi^{-1}[\nu(c_1), \nu(P)]\{B(c_1)\}$ and $\pi^{-1}[\nu(c_2), \nu(P)]\{B(c_2)\}$.

Therefore, any solution to a given TCSP corresponds to a point that is inside the boundaries of all the constraints in its variable space. For instance, for the sample TCSP P presented earlier, a point p is a solution if both $d(p, c_1) = 0$ and $d(p, c_2) = 0$, as shown in Figure 5.

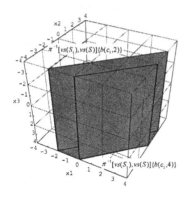
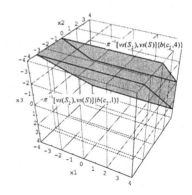

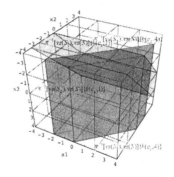

Fig. 4. Inverse projections into $\nu(P)$.

4 Anytime Constraint Solving

Given a TCSP, looking for a solution in its variable space is a daunting task. A good search method should attempt to approach the regions inside the boundaries of all constraints. Intuitively, searching for a solution involves a process of globally minimizing the total potential energy as defined by the distances from the constraints. This section presents an anytime search algorithm, called *Evolutionary Constraint Optimizer* (or ECO), which is a real number genetic algorithm that utilizes the spatial properties of constraint geometry to solve general TCSPs.

4.1 Preprocessing

There are two preparatory tasks before ECO applies genetic algorithms to solve a bounded TCSP: transforming the problem into a canonical form and constricting the domains of the variables. Canonicalization is necessary for the mutation operators described later in this section. The canonicalization procedure is the following:

1. Define a partial order ¡ on the variables such that for any two distinct variables x_i and x_j, if a constraint involving the two variables is in P, then either $x_i < x_j$ or $x_j < x_i$, but not both. If more than one partial order is possible, choose one arbitrarily.
2. Canonicalize binary constraints: For every binary constraint $x_i - x_j \in Q$ in P, if $x_i < x_j$, replace the constraint with an equivalent constraint $x_j - x_i \in -Q$, where $-Q$ is $\{-z \mid z \in Q\}$. For example, if P contains a constraint $x_1 - x_2 \in [1, 2]$ and ECO determines that $x_1 < x_2$, then it is replaced with a new constraint $x_2 - x_1 \in [-2, -1]$.
3. Given constraints with the same characteristic function, ECO will merge them by taking the intersection of their true ranges.

Constricting variable domains helps identify a more reasonable range for the genetic algorithms to explore. For any variable x_i, ECO determines its minimum value $l(x_i)$ and maximum value $u(x_i)$ among all solutions of P. The details of the method can be found in Yeh [8].

4.2 Genetic Encoding

Every individual in ECO consists of a single chromosome representing a possible solution of P. Each gene on the chromosome corresponds to a variable of P: the x_1-gene, the x_2-gene, and so on. Therefore, the number of genes in a chromosome is the same as the number of variables. For ease of presentation, we use the same symbol for a variable and its corresponding gene.

The allele value for a gene g may be either *independent* or *dependent*. The structure of an independent allele is a specific number representing the value assigned to the corresponding variable in P. The strucutre of a dependent allele is a 3-tuple, (h, v, δ), where h is either 0 or another gene, v is a closed interval, and δ is a number indicating an *offset*. Each 3-tuple should satisfy the following conditions:

- The canonicalized problem P contains a constraint c with the characteristic function $\Delta[c] = g - h$.
- The interval v is a component of its true range $\tau(c)$.

The TCSP variable corresponding to g is assigned the value of h plus δ, or simply δ if h is 0. For example, given a TCSP with $x_1, x_2, x_3 \in \mathbf{R}$ and the following constraints (with the partial order $x_1 < x_2 < x_3$):

$$\begin{cases} x_1 \in [-1, 0.18] \cup [0.63, 0.97] \\ x_2 \in [-1, -0.96] \cup [-0.72, -0.49] \cup [0.4, 1] \\ x_3 \in [-0.71, -0.53] \cup [0.31, 0.79] \\ x_2 - x_1 \in [-0.59, -0.36] \cup [0.01, 1] \\ x_3 - x_1 \in [-1, -0.27] \cup [0.35, 0.58] \cup [0.7, 1] \\ x_3 - x_2 \in [-1, -0.72] \cup [-0.25, 0.69] \end{cases}$$

Figure 6 illustrates a chromosome consisting of two dependent alleles and one independent allele.

x_1	$(0,[0.63,0.97],0.72)$
x_2	0.33
x_3	$(x_1,[0.35,0.58],0.4)$

Fig. 6. A chromosome with two dependent alleles.

The allele value of the x_1-gene depends on 0 by an offset of 0.72, thus the value of x_1 is $0 + 0.72 = 0.72$. The allele value of the x_2-gene is independent, thus the variable x_2 is assigned the value 0.33. The allele value of the x_3-gene is dependent on x_1 by an offset of 0.4, so the allele value of the x_3-gene is $0.72 + 0.4 = 1.12$. In other words, this chromosome represents the unifier $\{x_1 \leftarrow 0.72, x_2 \leftarrow 0.33, x_3 \leftarrow 1.12\}$.

4.3 Genetic Operators

ECO adopts the uniform crossover operator [7]. In addition, three mutation operators are defined in ECO: the α-mutation, the β-mutation, and the γ-mutation. The first two apply to genes having either independent or dependent alleles, while the γ-mutation is specially designed for genes with dependent allels only.

The α-Mutation The α-mutation allows ECO to explore the neighborhood of the current individuals. An α-mutated gene has an independent allele. The new allele value is decided by a random variable whose probability distribution is a combination of two normal distributions. More precisely, let x be the gene being α-mutated, $l = l(x)$, $u = u(x)$, and μ be the interpretation of the allele value of x before mutation. The probability density function $\alpha(z; \mu, l, u)$ [3] of the random variable is shown in Equation (1).

$$\alpha(z; \mu, l, u) = \begin{cases} \frac{exp(\frac{-(z-\mu)^2}{2(l-\mu)^2})}{\sqrt{2\pi}|l-\mu|} & \text{if } z < \mu \neq l \\ \frac{exp(\frac{-(z-\mu)^2}{2(u-\mu)^2})}{\sqrt{2\pi}|u-\mu|} & \text{if } z > \mu \neq u \end{cases} \tag{1}$$

Figure 7 shows a sample case of α with $\mu < l$, that is, the interpretation of the original allele value falls outside of the constricted range. Note that by the definition of α-mutation, the farther μ strays from the range between l and u, the more likely for the new allele value to be outside that range. The rationale is that if an individual with a stray allele is reproducing, bearing the straying allele is possibly advantageous for the individual. This is particularly important when ECO faces problems with conflicting constraints.

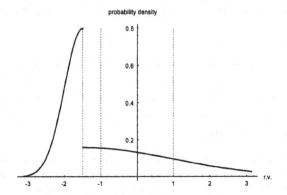

Fig. 7. The probability density function α with $\mu = -1.5, l = -1$, and $u = 1$

The β-Mutation The β-mutation enforces an individual to satisfy a certain constraint. Contrary to the α-mutation, the β-mutation turns the subject gene into having a dependent allele (h, v, δ). Let x be the gene being β-mutated, and $\mathcal{B}$ be the set of all constraints that have x as the first term of their characteristic functions in P. For each constraint c in $\mathcal{B}$, let $y(c)$ be the TCSP variable in the second term of $\Delta[c]$, or 0 if c is a unary constraint; let $K(c)$ be the set of components of $\tau(c)$. We can construct a set Z as

$$Z = \bigcup_{c \in \mathcal{B}} [\{y(c)\} \times K(c)]$$

Choose a random member e from Z with a uniform probability distribution. Now h and v in the new allele (h, v, δ) are decided: h is assigned the first element of e, which represents the variable symbol, or 0; and v is assigned the second element of e, the closed interval. The value of δ is then decided by a random variable with a uniform probability distribution over the interval v.

The γ-Mutation The γ-mutation is very similar to the α-mutation, except that it applies to genes with dependent alleles only and it results in a dependent allele. Assume that a gene having allele value $(h, [p, q], \delta)$ is γ-mutated. The only change is its δ value, which is decided by a random variable with the probability density function $\alpha(z; \delta, p, q)$.

4.4 Measurement of Fitness

The fitness measurement f is defined in terms of the distances between the potential solution corresponding to an individual and every constraint of the given TCSP.

Let i be an individual representing the unifier

$$\sigma = (x_1 \leftarrow a_1, x_2 \leftarrow a_2, \ldots, x_n \leftarrow a_n)$$

and $p = (a_1, a_2, \ldots, a_n)$ be a point in the space. The fitness value of i is defined as

$$f(i) = exp(-\sqrt{\Sigma_{c \in C} d(p,c)^2})$$

where $d(p, c)$ denotes the distance between the point p and the constraint c of the TCSP C. Since $0 \le d(p, c) < \infty$ for each c, it follows that $0 < f(i) \le 1$, and $f(i) = 1$ iff each of the distances is equal to zero, that is, σ is a solution of P.

4.5 Experiment Results

In order to test the performance of ECO, we performed three sets of experiments, examining the influence of the following factors on the performance of ECO: the *number of variables, mean dispersion*, and *constraint density*. The experiments used samples generated from a generic random CSP generator [8] based on a well distributed set of parameters.

The mean dispersion of a TCSP is the algebraic average of the dispersion of each constraint in the problem. The dispersion of a constraint c is the number of intervals that $\tau(c)$ contains. The constraint density of an n-variable TCSP is the number of constraints it has divided by the maximal number of constraints an n-variable TCSP may have.

Number of Variables The goal of the first set of experiments is to test how the number of variables affects the performance of ECO. The experiments tested 70 sample problems, each having 5 to 15 variables. The problems were divided into 7 groups; each group consisted of 10 problems that have the same number of variables. The mean dispersion was 1.5. Figure 8 contrasts the time required by ECO to find an exact solution to the theoretically estimated $O(n^3)$ time required by conventional algorithms based on Floyd-Warshall's algorithm.

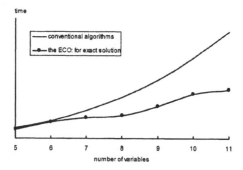

Fig. 8. Time required vs. number of variables

Mean Dispersion The second set of experiments shows how mean dispersion affects the performance of ECO. The experiments tested 150 sample problems with the mean dispersion between 1 and 15. The problems were divided into 15 groups; each group consisted of 10 problems with the same mean dispersion. Each sample problem had 5 variables and 10 constraints. Figure 9 contrasts the time required by ECO to find an individual exact solution to that by conventional algorithms, assuming that path consistency algorithms reduced the mean dispersion by 0%, 50%, 80%, and 95%, respectively.

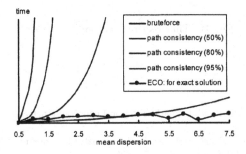

Fig. 9. Time required vs. mean dispersion

Constraint Density The third set of experiments tested 80 sample problems, each having 9 variables, with constraint density from 0.3 to 1. The problems were divided into 8 groups; each group consisted of 10 problems with the same constraint density. Figure 10 contrasts the average time required by ECO to find an individual whose fitness value ≥ 0.8, ≥ 0.9, and $= 1$ (that is, an exact solution) of the sample problems in each of the 8 groups to the (theoretically estimated) time required by conventional algorithm with 50% path consistency and that by the brute-force algorithm.

5 Conclusion

This paper proposes using *constraint geometry* to model TCSPs. The problem of finding a solution becomes a search problem in n-dimensional Euclidean space. An evolutionary algorithm, ECO, has been developed to find exact or approximate solutions. Implementation based on the constraint geometry is relatively straightforward and efficient. Our experiments showed that the time required to find exact solutions is usually much less than exponential (worst case time). The time needed to find good approximate solutions is generally much shorter than finding the exact solutions. Moreover, ECO can return an answer whenever requested, and the quality of the solution improves over time.

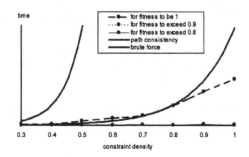

Fig. 10. Time required vs. constraint density

References

1. R. Dechter, I. Meiri, and J. Pearl. Temporal constraint networks. *Artificial Intelligence*, 49:61–95, 1991.
2. R. Dechter and J. Pearl. Network-based heuristic for constraint-satisfaction problems. *Artificial Intelligence*, 34:1–38, 1987.
3. J. L. Devore. *Probability and Statistics for Engineering and the Sciences*. Brooks / Cole Publishing Company, Monterey, California, second edition, 1987.
4. R. M. Haralick and L. G. Shapiro. *Computer and Robot Vision*, page 61. Addison-Wesley, 1993.
5. J. W. Lloyd. *Foundations of Logic Programming*. Springer-Verlag, second, extended edition, 1984.
6. E. Rich and K. Knight. *Artificial Intelligence*, chapter 2. McGraw-Hill, second edition, 1991.
7. G. Syswerda. Uniform crossover in genetic algorithms. In J. D. Schaffer, editor, *Proceedings of the Third International Conference on Genetic Algorithms*, San Mateo, California, 1989. Kaufmann Publishers.
8. H. Yeh. Genetic algorithms for generalized temporal-constraint-satisfaction-problem. Master's thesis, National Taiwan University, June 1995.

Dynamic Constraint Weighting for Over-Constrained Problems

John Thornton[1] and Abdul Sattar[2]

[1] School of Information Technology, Griffith University Gold Coast,
Parklands Drive, Southport, Qld, 4215, Australia
j.thornton@gu.edu.au
[2] School of Computing and Information Technology, Griffith University,
Kessels Road, Nathan, Qld, 4111, Australia
sattar@cit.gu.edu.au

Abstract. Recent research has shown that constraint weighting local search algorithms can be very effective in solving a variety of Constraint Satisfaction Problems. However, little work has been done in applying such algorithms to over-constrained problems with mandatory or *hard* constraints. The difficulty has been finding a weighting scheme that can weight unsatisfied constraints and still maintain the distinction between mandatory and non-mandatory constraints. This paper presents a new weighting strategy that simulates the transformation of an over-constrained problem with mandatory constraints into an equivalent problem where all constraints have equal importance, but the hard constraints have been repeated. In addition, two dynamic constraint weighting schemes are introduced that alter the number of simulated hard constraint repetitions according to feedback received during the search. The results show the dynamic strategies outperform two fixed repetition approaches on a test bed of over-constrained timetabling and nurse rostering problems..

1 Introduction

Recent research has shown that local search techniques can be remarkably effective in solving certain classes of Constraint Satisfaction Problem (CSP) [10]. Particular interest has focussed on the use of GSAT and variants to solve Conjunctive Normal Form (CNF) satisfiability problems [7]. Attempts to improve GSAT have lead to the development of a new class of clause weighting algorithms [6]. These algorithms escape local minimum situations by adding weights to unsatisfied clauses. Further research has looked at applying constraint weights to more general CSPs [8], and at improving the weighting strategy by weighting the *connections* between constraints [9]. Cha et al. [2] have also looked at using clause weighting in solving an over-constrained time-tabling problem. This paper further investigates the use of weighted local search in solving over-constrained problems.

An over-constrained problem is defined as a standard CSP (ie as a set of variables, each with a set of domain values and a set of constraints defining the allowable combinations of domain values for the variables) with the additional proviso that *no* combination of variable instantiations can simultaneously satisfy *all* the constraints. The objective therefore becomes to satisfy *as many as possible* of the constraints [10]. Given all constraints are of equal importance, a standard weighting algorithm can be applied to an over-constrained problem with minimal modification (see section 2). However, most realistic over-constrained problems involve constraints of *varying* levels of importance. Typically there is a set of *hard* constraints that have to be satisfied (otherwise the solution is not *acceptable*) and a set of *soft* constraints whose satisfaction is desirable but not mandatory. The simplest way to represent the relative importance of a constraint is to give it a weight. However, a weighting algorithm already applies weights to constraints during the search when escaping local minima. The question then arises, how can a weighting algorithm add weights to constraints without distorting the original weights that indicate the relative importance of the constraints? The primary purpose of the paper is to answer this question.

Cha et al. [2] proposed an initial answer by calculating fixed hard constraint weights based on an analysis of the problem domain. The present study describes two algorithms that *dynamically* calculate the relative weights of hard and soft constraints during program execution. This means the approach is independent of specific domain knowledge and produces a more extensive search of the problem space. By analysing a set of over-constrained problems, for which there are known optimal answers, the study shows the two dynamic weighting schemes perform at least as well as an ideal weight incrementing scheme that relies on foreknowledge of an optimal answer (a situation not usually found in practice).

The motivation of the study is to encourage the implementation of local search weighting techniques developed in the domain of CNF satisfiability to the more complex 'real-world' of constraint satisfaction. The dynamic weight incrementing algorithms allow constraint weighting to be efficiently applied to over-constrained systems that have *already* been weighted. The remainder of the paper describes the algorithms used in the study, followed by an experimental evaluation of constraint weighting based on a test-bed of real-world staff scheduling and timetabling problems.

2 Constraint Weighting Algorithms

Constraint weighting algorithms are extensions of local search or iterative repair. An iterative repair algorithm starts with an initial instantiation of all problem variables and attempts to improve this solution by repeatedly selecting the 'best' improving local move. The algorithm terminates when no further improving move can be found. This simple approach proves very effective for many problem domains (for instance see [5]). However, a local search frequently terminates on a non-optimal solution or local minimum, and a method is required to escape and continue the search. A simple approach is to restart the algorithm from a different initial position. GSAT accepts moves of equal cost in an attempt to find a better move later in the search. Other approaches include randomly selecting a move (as in simulated annealing and random walk [7]) and selecting the best move that does not repeat a previous move (as in tabu search [4]). Constraint weighting takes the approach of adding a weight to all violated constraints in a local minimum [6]. This changes the cost surface of the problem until a lower cost solution becomes accessible. This is illustrated in the following example:

Example. Consider the over-constrained graph colouring problem in figure 1. The nodes a, b, c and d represent the variables or areas to be coloured, each having a two value domain {red, green}, and the arcs c_{ab}, c_{ac}, c_{bc}, c_{bd} and c_{cd} represent the constraints $a \neq b$, $a \neq c$, $b \neq c$, $b \neq d$ and $c \neq d$ respectively. Using a simple cost function, such that each constraint violation adds a cost of w to the solution, the situation in figure 1(a) represents a local minimum of cost $2w$. A constraint weighting algorithm would continue by adding a further weight w to each violated constraint until the cost of the solution becomes $4w$. This alters the problem so that a choice of lower cost moves become available. Figure 1(b) shows the effect of changing the value of d to green, causing c_{bd} to be violated at a cost increase of w, but satisfying c_{cd} at a cost *decrease* of $2w$. From 1(b) the best cost decreasing move is to change b to red, leading to the (optimal) solution in 1(c) where only one constraint, c_{bc}, is violated.

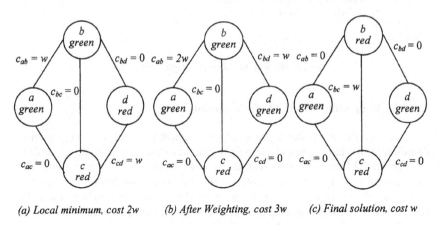

(a) Local minimum, cost 2w   (b) After Weighting, cost 3w   (c) Final solution, cost w

Fig. 1: Graph Colouring CSP

Figure 2 gives the pseudocode for the basic constraint weighting strategy used in the study. As the algorithm solves over-constrained problems, it needs to keep track of the best solution currently found in the search. This is not required for standard CSPs because a clear stopping condition exists (ie when *all* the constraints are satisfied). However, for over-constrained problems, it is generally not known when an optimal solution is found (unless some other complete method has initially solved the problem). Instead, the search terminates when it has continued for sufficiently long without finding an improving move. This means the terminating solution is not necessarily the best solution, hence the need to store each successive best solution as it is found.

In addition, a constraint weighting algorithm may discover an optimum solution during the search, but fail to recognise it because the current constraint weights make another move more attractive. Therefore the algorithm must also calculate the *unweighted* cost of each move and use this measure to evaluate the best solution.

procedure WeightedIterativeRepair
begin
    CurrentState ← *set variables to initial assignments*
    BestCost ← *UnweightedCost(CurrentState), BestState* ← *CurrentState, StuckCounter* ← 0
    while *UnweightedCost(BestState)* > DesiredCost *and StuckCounter* < MaxStucks **do**
        if *CurrentState is not a local minimum* **then**
            for each *variable v_i involved in a constraint violation*
                for each *move m_j in the domain of v_i*
                    if *WeightedCost(CurrentState + m_j)* < *WeightedCost(CurrentState)* **then**
                      CurrentState ← *CurrentState + m_j*
                    if *UnweightedCost(CurrentState + m_j)* < *BestCost* **then**
                      BestState ← *CurrentState + m_j, StuckCounter* ← 0
                      BestCost ← *UnweightedCost(CurrentState + m_j)*
                end for
            end for
        else
            IncreaseViolatedConstraintWeights()
            StuckCounter ← *StuckCounter + 1*
    end while
end

Fig. 2. The Weighted Iterative Repair Algorithm

2.1 Weighting with Hard and Soft Constraints

Constraint weighting was developed as an enhancement to GSAT for CNF problems. Empirical studies have shown clause weighting to be one the best approaches for CNF satisfiability [1] [3] [7]. Further work has looked at applying constraint weighting to more general CSPs such as nurse rostering [8], university timetabling [2], graph colouring and blocks world planning [7]. Several enhancements to weighting have also been proposed, including causing weights to decay over time [3], adding new clauses for CNF problems [1] and weighting connections between constraints [9].

Constraint weighting is therefore recognised as an important and effective technique for solving hard CSP problems. As yet, however, there has been little work in applying constraint weighting to more realistic over-constrained problems involving hard and soft constraints. A pioneering work in this area was Cha et al.'s paper on university timetabling [2]. They converted a small graduate student timetabling problem into CNF format, dividing the clauses into hard and soft constraints. The hard constraint clauses were limited to being either all positive or all negative literals, reflecting the restriction that the problem of satisfying the hard constraints *must be relatively easy*. The greater importance of the hard constraints was then represented by adding a fixed weight to each hard constraint clause.

Thornton and Sattar [8] also looked at solving a set of realistic over-constrained nurse rostering problems using constraint weighting. In their approach *only* violated hard constraint weights are incremented at a local minimum. A soft constraint heuristic is then used to bias the search towards solutions that satisfy a greater number of soft constraints. However, empirical tests showed the soft constraint heuristic, although causing some improvement, was rarely able to find an optimal solution.

Both Cha et al. and Thornton and Sattar's algorithms attempt to satisfy as many as possible soft constraints while looking for a solution that satisfies all hard constraints. Once such a solution is found, a limited search is made for the best soft constraint cost and then the algorithms are either terminated or reset. Cha et al. reset their constraint weights because, in further searching, the distinction between hard and soft constraints weights is lost (due to the weighting action of the algorithm) and the search is no longer able to find acceptable solutions. In Thornton and Sattar's approach the algorithm terminates because there is no mechanism that allows the soft constraint weights to increase, so the search is unable to move out of it's local area.

Maintaining the Hard Constraint Differential. One of the contributions of this study is the extension of Cha et al.'s concept of *repeating* hard constraints [2]. If each hard constraint is *actually* repeated in a problem (say n times) then, when a hard constraint is violated in a local minimum, all n copies of the constraint would receive a weight increment, causing a total increase in cost of $n \times w$. This can be simulated, as with Cha et al., by giving each hard constraint an initial weight of n. The new step is to increment each *hard* constraint violated at a local minimum with a weight of $n \times w$ instead of w (soft constraint violations are still incremented by w). Such a system behaves identically to a system where all constraints have equal weight, with each hard constraint repeated n times. Previous studies have already demonstrated that simple constraint weighting is an effective search strategy. Therefore we should expect our new hard constraint weighting strategy to be equally effective.

In order to adequately explore the search space, a constraint weighting algorithm must be able to move from one area to another where all hard constraints are satisfied, *via intermediate solutions where some hard constraints are violated.* Unlike the previously discussed algorithms, the new hard constraint weighting strategy is able to do this *systematically* rather than accidentally:

Example. Consider the situation in figure 3: A, B, c and d represent four constraints in an unspecified over-constrained problem, where A and B are hard constraints, c and d are soft constraints, and w_A, w_B, w_c and w_d represent the constraint weights of A, B, c and d respectively. Let the number of hard constraint repetitions $n = 3$ and the weight increment $w = 1$. Hence, the soft constraints are given initial weights $w_c = w_d = w = 1$, and the hard constraints are given initial weights $w_A = w_B = n \times w = 3$. Figure 3(a), represents the first local minimum found in the search, where all hard constraints are satisfied and both soft constraints are violated. As yet no weights have been added by the search so the cost of the solution $= w_c + w_d = 2$. A constraint weighting algorithm will now add weight w to c and d, making $w_c = 2$ and $w_d = 2$, and a new solution cost $=$

4. If we assume there is no move available that does not violate both hard constraints, then we are still at a local minimum (as $w_A + w_B > w_c + w_d$) and the soft constraints will be incremented twice more until $w_c + w_d = 4$. In this case the cost of violating both hard constraints (6) is less than the cost of violating both soft constraints (8), so the move which violates both hard constraints will be accepted (shown in figure 3(b)). Assuming this solution is another local minimum, the weights of a and b are now incremented. In Cha et al.'s scheme, w_A and w_B will be incremented by w to 4 (figure 3(c)), whereas in the new constraint weighting scheme w_A and w_B will each be incremented by $n \times w$ to 6 (figure 3(d)). Here the crucial difference between the two approaches is evident. In Cha et al.'s solution all constraints now have the same weight and *there is no way to further distinguish between the hard and soft constraints*. This means the search has no guidance towards solutions which satisfy the hard constraints. In the new constraint weighting strategy, the soft constraints have been allowed to overpower the hard constraints, but as soon as a hard constraint is violated the dominance of the hard constraints is reasserted and the search will now concentrate on finding *another* solution where all hard constraints are satisfied.

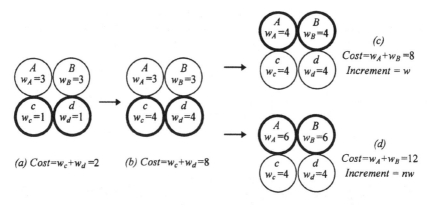

Fig. 3. Weighting Hard and Soft Constraints

Deciding the Initial Hard Constraint Weights. Cha et al. [2] recognised the crucial question for their research was to find the best number of repetitions of the hard constraint clauses. In the extreme case, the weight on each hard constraint can be set to equal the total initial cost of violating all soft constraints plus one (as in the previous example). However, such a scheme when applied to their timetabling problem places very large initial weights on the hard clauses. In practice they found the hard constraint clauses are quickly satisfied with such weights, but high levels of soft constraint violation remain. At the other extreme, giving insufficient weight to the hard constraints results in a search that is unlikely to find *any* solution where all hard constraints are satisfied (although soft constraint satisfaction would be very high).

The issue of the number of repetitions is equally important to the new constraint weighting scheme. The greater the difference between the initial hard and soft constraint weights the slower the search will be, as it will take longer to build up weights on the soft constraints. However, setting the initial hard and soft constraint weights too close together will cause the search to excessively explore areas of hard constraint violation where (by definition) no acceptable solution can exist. Worse still, the search may approach an optimum solution but fail to converge on it because of the over-valuing of the soft constraints. The question therefore arises, how much weight is too much and how much is too little? Cha et al.'s answer was to look at their particular problem and calculate the average number of soft constraint violations that would be caused by satisfying a currently violated hard constraint (they assume that most constraints are already satisfied). They then use this value to set the initial hard constraint weights. Clearly there are problems with this approach. Firstly, the number soft violations caused by the satisfaction of a hard constraint will vary within the search space and secondly, the method requires a detailed analysis of the search space.

2.2 Dynamic Constraint Weighting

A useful property for a hard and soft constraint weighting algorithm would be the ability to learn the correct ratio of hard to soft constraint weights *during the search itself*. Consequently, the second contribution of the paper is the development and empirical evaluation of two such dynamic constraint weighting strategies.

Downward Weight Adjustment (DWA). The first strategy, Downward Weight Adjustment, involves starting the search with the number of repetitions, n, set to the total number of soft constraints + 1 (the maximum value). Then, as soon as a solution is found where all hard constraints are satisfied (an *acceptable* solution), the value of n is adjusted downwards to equal the number of soft constraints currently violated (s_{cur}). Each time a new acceptable solution is found such that $s_{cur} < n$, then n is set to s_{cur} (the new best level of soft constraint violation), ie the number of hard constraint repetitions is *dynamically* adjusted according to the best solution found so far in the search.

This approach is based on the insight that number of hard constraint repetitions, n, should not be set to less than the *optimum* number of soft constraint violations, s_{opt}. If n is less than s_{opt} then the search will tend to prefer a solution where a hard constraint is violated over an optimal solution. If n is close to but greater than s_{opt} then the search may prefer a single hard constraint violation over many *non*-optimal acceptable solutions, but will still prefer an optimal solution. However the value of s_{opt} is generally unknown (unless a complete method has already solved the problem). Therefore, Downward Adjustment Weighting keeps making a closer and closer estimate of s_{opt} by resetting the value of n each time a new *unweighted* cost reducing solution is found. This makes the definition of unweighted cost more complex due to introduction of constraint repetition. Now the unweighted cost equals the *number* of violated constraints *including* repetitions and the weighted cost equals the *sum of the weights* of all violated constraints *including* repetitions. Put more formally, consider an over-constrained problem with a set of hard constraints $H = \{h_1, h_2, h_3, \ldots h_k\}$ and a set of soft constraints $S = \{s_1, s_2, s_3, \ldots s_j\}$. Each hard constraint has a weight wh_i, $i = 1 \ldots k$, and each soft constraint has a weight ws_i, $i = 1 \ldots j$, where the weight i equals the number of times constraint i has been violated in a local minimum. Letting n be the number of hard constraint repetitions, CH be a vector with elements ch_i, where $i = 1\ldots k$, such that element $ch_i = 0$ if h_i is satisfied and $ch_i = 1$ otherwise, and CS be a vector with elements cs_i, where $i = 1 \ldots j$, such that element $cs_i = 0$ if s_i is satisfied and $cs_i = 1$ otherwise, then we have the following definitions:

$$\text{WeightedCost} = n \sum_{i=1}^{k} wh_i\, ch_i + \sum_{i=1}^{j} ws_i\, cs_i \tag{1}$$

$$\text{UnweightedCost} = n \sum_{i=1}^{k} ch_i + \sum_{i=1}^{j} cs_i \tag{2}$$

(Note that n is equivalent to *BestCost* in figure 2). The analysis so far assumes a weight increment of one and that constraints have only two states: satisfied or violated. However, the approach can be easily extended to include different additive or multiplicative weight increments and varying levels of constraint violation.

Flexible Weight Adjustment (FWA). The second dynamic constraint weighting strategy involves adjusting the value of n according to the current state of the search. We start with the smallest differential that distinguishes hard and soft constraints (ie $n = 2$) and then proceed to increase the value of n by 1 each time a non-acceptable local minimum is encountered. n is therefore increased to a level sufficient to cause all hard constraints to be satisfied. Each *acceptable* local minimum encountered, causes n to be reduced by 1, making it easier for hard constraints to be violated and so encouraging the search to diversify out of the current local area. In effect, in non-acceptable areas the search becomes increasingly attracted to acceptable areas and in acceptable areas the attraction moves to the non-acceptable. Using the earlier definitions of n, h_i, s_i, wh_i and ws_i, figure 4 gives the pseudocode necessary to implement FWA (Note IncreaseViolatedConstraintWeights() is called from the main constraint weighting algorithm in figure 2).

```
procedure IncreaseViolatedConstraintWeights()
begin
    TotalHardViolations ← 0
    for each violated hard constraint h_i
        wh_i ← wh_i + 1
        TotalHardViolations ← TotalHardViolations + 1
    end for
    for each violated soft constraint s_i
        ws_i ← ws_i + 1
    end for
    if TotalHardViolations > 0 then n ← n + 1
    else if n > MinRepetitions then n ← n - 1
end
```

Fig. 4. The Flexible Weight Adjustment Algorithm

3 Experiments

The two dynamic weighting strategies were compared to two forms of fixed weighting called MaxIncrement (MAX) and MinIncrement (MIN). MaxIncrement sets the weights of all hard constraints to the total number of soft constraints plus one, and increments all hard constraints by this amount in a local minimum. This is the largest realistic setting for the constraint increment and favours solutions where all hard constraints are satisfied at the expense of satisfying the soft constraints. MinIncrement sets the weights of all hard constraints to the number of soft constraints left unsatisfied in an *optimal* solution (plus one) and again increments by this value. The optimum level of constraint violation is the smallest realistic setting for an increment, otherwise the search is likely to ignore an optimum solution (see section 2.2). An implementation of Cha et al.'s reset algorithm [2] was also tried on our test problems, but in most cases the algorithm was unable to find an acceptable solution. Cha et al.'s approach assumes the initial problem of finding an acceptable solution is relatively easy. In our test problems this was not the case.

3.1 Test Problems

The algorithms were tested on a set of 16 over-constrained nurse rostering problems taken from real situations in a Queensland public hospital. The rostering problem involves allocating a set of pre-generated legal schedules to each nurse in a roster, such that all hard constraints involving numbers of staff for each shift are satisfied. The soft constraints define how attractive a schedule is for a nurse. A typical problem involves 25-35 nurses, each with up to 5,000 legal schedules, and approximately 400 constraints. Further details of the problems are described elsewhere [8]. One attractive feature of the domain is that, although the problems are difficult for a local search algorithm to solve, we have optimal answers for each problem obtained from an integer programming application [8].

The second over-constrained problem was taken from another real-life situation of university timetabling. A single, large problem was considered involving 1237 classes, 287 full-time and part-time staff, 103 rooms and 1511 student groups of 1 to 5 students. In this problem the hard constraints are set to avoid timetable clashes and the soft constraints define the preferred class times for staff members and student groups. The problem proved too large to solve in total, so it was divided into 4 sub problems: firstly laboratories are allocated, then lectures, then tutorials and finally the remaining classes. The results reported here refer to solution times and constraint satisfaction levels for phase two of the problem (laboratories + lectures).

3.2 Results

All problems were solved on a Sun Creator 3D-2000. For the rostering problems, the algorithms were either terminated on finding an optimum solution, or after 250 local minimum were encountered without improvement. The timetable problem, being much larger and with no known optimal solution, was terminated after 75 phase two iterations of the main program loop. The optimum timetabling solution was then defined as the best solution found in all runs.

Table 1 shows the average times and proportion of problems solved for seven runs of each test problem with each algorithm. In all cases the averages are calculated only for those runs that actually found an optimal solution. The results show the Flexible Weight Adjustment algorithm (FWA) has the best overall performance on both problems (ie it equals or exceeds the other algorithms in the proportion of optimal solutions found and has the smallest average execution times). The results also show the MaxIncrement (MAX) algorithm is unable to reliably find optimal solutions (only 51% of roster and 29% of timetable runs were successful), and generally has longer execution times for those problems it can solve.

Method	Roster Results				Timetable Results			
	FWA	MIN	MAX	DWA	FWA	MIN	MAX	DWA
Mean time (secs)	141.3	169.6	306.7	159.5	674	1192	1163	900
% Optimal	79.5	78.6	50.9	76.8	86	86	29	86
% Unsolved	0.9	2.7	0.9	0	0	0	0	0

Table 1. Proportions and Average Solution Times for each Method and Problem

Overall, the dynamic weighting strategies (FWA and DWA) proved more efficient at finding optimal solutions than the fixed weighting strategies (MIN and MAX). However, an important element in evaluating local search is the solution path represented by the so-called 'anytime curve' [10]. This plots the cost of the best solution found in the search against execution time, and represents the quality of solution that would be found if an algorithm were terminated at a particular point. Anytime performance is significant for problems where there is insufficient time to find an optimal solution, or the optimum is unknown, and so is relevant to over-constrained problems. Figures 5 and 6 show the anytime curves for each method and problem type. In these graphs, the y-axis represents the sum of all soft constraint costs of the best solutions found at a given time for all runs of an algorithm.

4 Analysis

Figures 5 and 6 show the evaluation of the algorithms is more complex than a simple comparison of execution times. There is little to distinguish each algorithm in the timetable problem curves (figure 5), but these results are for a *single* problem, repeatedly solved, hence it would be unwise to generalise. With the roster curves in figure 6 (using 16 problem instances), the DWA curve is noticeably lower than the other curves. Although DWA's ability to find an optimal solution is slightly inferior to FWA, the faster descent of DWA indicates it may be more useful when looking for 'good enough' solutions. FWA is more appropriate for longer searches where small cost improvements are considered important. These results can be inferred from the algorithms directly: DWA initially places greater importance on the hard constraints and only slowly reduces these weights. Therefore we would expect DWA to quickly find acceptable solutions of reasonable quality. Then, as DWA approaches an optimum it will find it harder to move by violating a hard constraint, because the relative weights of the hard and soft constraints are only adjusted when a new best solution is found. In contrast, FWA starts by strongly valuing the soft constraints, and so finds acceptable solutions more slowly. However, as FWA's ability to adjust weights remains constant regardless of the distance from an optimum solution, we would expect FWA to be more effective in the later stages of the search.

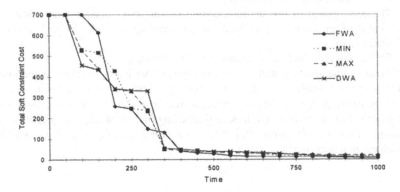

Fig 5. Anytime Curves for the Timetabling Problem

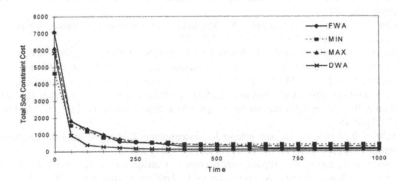

Fig 6. Anytime Curves for the Roster Problems

An interesting result of the study is that both flexible weighting strategies have performed slightly better than the MinIncrement (MIN) algorithm. MinIncrement uses what is *probably* the best fixed increment (ie the optimal solution cost), a value that would typically be estimated from an analysis of the problem domain (as in Cha et al.'s study). In contrast, the dynamic weighting strategies do not rely on domain knowledge, and so avoid the effort and possible errors in using fixed increments, while delivering *at least* comparable performance.

5 Conclusions and Further Work

The main contributions of the paper are as follows

- The development of a constraint weighting strategy that simulates the transformation of an over-constrained problem with hard and soft constraints into an equivalent problem with a single constraint type, where the importance of each hard constraint is represented by repetition.
- The development of two dynamic constraint weighting strategies that adjust the number of repetitions of each hard constraint through dynamic feedback with the search space.
- The empirical evaluation of the new weighting strategies.

The main finding of the study is that both dynamic weighting strategies outperform alternative fixed weighting strategies on a test bed of over-constrained timetable and nurse rostering problems. Further empirical work is required to evaluate proposed algorithms. Future research will look at timetabling in more detail and at comparing dynamic constraint weighting with other local search techniques such as WSAT, simulated annealing and tabu search.

References

1. Cha, B., Iwama, K.: Adding new clauses for faster local search. In: Proc. of AAAI'96, (1996) 332-337
2. Cha, B., Iwama, K., Kambayashi, Y., Miyazaki S.: Local search algorithms for partial MAXSAT. In: Proc. of AAAI'97, (1997) 332-337
3. Frank, J.: Learning short-term weights for GSAT. In: Proc. of AAAI'97, (1997) 384-389
4. Glover, F.: Tabu search - part 1. ORSA Journal on Computing, 1(3) (1989) 190-206
5. Minton, S., Johnston, M., Philips, A., Laird, P.: Minimizing conflicts: a heuristic repair method for constraint satisfaction and scheduling problems. Artif. Intell. 58 (1992) 161-205
6. Morris, P.: The breakout method for escaping local from minima. In: Proc. of AAAI'93, (1993) 40-45
7. Selman, B., Kautz, H.: Domain independent extensions to GSAT: Solving large structured satisfiability problems. In: Proc. of IJCAI'93, (1993) 290-295
8. Thornton, J., Sattar, A.: Applied partial constraint satisfaction using weighted iterative repair. In: Sattar, A. (ed.): Advanced Topics in Artificial Intelligence. LNAI Vol. 1342. Springer-Verlag (1997) 57-66
9. Thornton, J., Sattar, A.: Using arc weights to improve iterative repair. In: Proc. of AAAI '98, (1998) 367-372
10. Wallace, J., Freuder, E.: Heuristic methods for over-constrained constraint satisfaction problems. In: Jampel, M., Freuder, E., Maher, M. (eds.): Over-Constrained Systems. LNCS Vol. 1106. Springer-Verlag (1996) 207-216

Time-Constrained Heuristic Search for Practical Route Finding

Hironori Hiraishi, Hayato Ohwada and Fumio Mizoguchi

Faculty of Sci. and Tech.
Science University of Tokyo
Noda, Chiba, 278-8510, Japan

Abstract. In this paper, we describe a heuristic search algorithm that finds a provably optimal solution subject to a specified time interval. While this algorithm is amenable to previous works on an approximate A^* search with a bounded error (ϵ), it allows us to terminate the search to retain the specified time interval by changing the value of ϵ during the search. Our basic search strategy is that node expansion around the starting node is pessimistic (exact search), and we accomplish the approximate exploration of nodes around the goal by increasing ϵ. This strategy is suitable for real-time route finding in automobile navigation systems. We conducted our experiments to clarify the practical features of the algorithm, using a digital map of a commercial automobile navigation system. The resulting advantage is that the estimation of the finishing time of the search is quite accurate, and optimal solutions are produced by making full use of the permissible search time.

1 Introduction

A heuristic search based on an A* algorithm is one of the most important AI methods. This type of search has been used for eight puzzle and route-finding problems shown in textbooks such as [8]. However, a heuristic search is formulated as an optimal method; thus an A* algorithm tends to be intractable for practical problems in general.

Unlike the above textbook examples, practical problems involve a real-time nature. For example, automatic vehicle control and automobile navigation systems are dynamic; tasks are specified over time and a search program finds a sequence of plans to reach the goals being specified progressively. In such cases, routes should be generated while moving (execution), and the search must be terminated without stopping the movement. This type of the problem can be viewed as an optimization problem with time constraints. If physical systems such as vehicles are regarded as agent systems, the systems are formulated as instances of bounded-optimal agents, as proposed by Russell [7].

Korf introduced a real-time facility into A^*, where planning and execution are interleaved [3]. A heuristic function includes the cost for backtracking to the previously visited node. However, the automobile agents mentioned above have a very high cost for backtracking; therefore, the heuristic function in Korf's

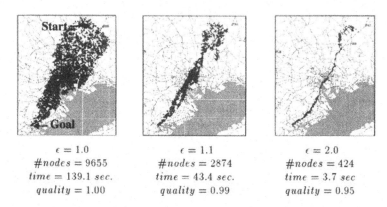

$\epsilon = 1.0$
$\#nodes = 9655$
$time = 139.1\ sec.$
$quality = 1.00$

$\epsilon = 1.1$
$\#nodes = 2874$
$time = 43.4\ sec.$
$quality = 0.99$

$\epsilon = 2.0$
$\#nodes = 424$
$time = 3.7\ sec$
$quality = 0.95$

Fig. 1. Search space of ϵ approximation search (The length of the optimal solution is 67.809 km)

real-time A^* is inadequate. Mobile agents should definitely complete the search before execution.

In this paper we present a new search algorithm to produce a sub-optimal route within a specified time interval. A sub-optimal solution means ϵ approximation one [5][4], and the algorithm is an extension of A^*. The algorithm differs from approximated A^* in that it does not fix the value for ϵ, but dynamically changes its value to keep to the constrained time. In general, a small number of nodes are explored by increasing ϵ; intuitively, it is possible to reach the goal node within a desired search time by controlling the value of ϵ. Such a dynamic change for ϵ has been seen in [6], but our method provides a linkage between the constrained search time and ϵ approximation.

In order to show the applicability of our algorithm, we measured the search time of the algorithm using the digital map of a commercial automobile navigation system. Our experiment clarifies the property of the algorithm, showing the relationships among search time, the number of nodes expanded, the quality of the solution, and the value of ϵ.

We have organized this paper as follows: Section 2 describes the ϵ approximation search, Section 3 shows our constrained optimal search algorithm, Section 4 provides the results of an experimental study, Section 5 describes related work, and the final section contains our conclusions.

2 ϵ Approximation Search

The operation for the ϵ approximation search is the same as that for A^*, and the evaluation function is formulated as follows:

$$f(n) = g(n) + \epsilon h(n) \qquad h(n) \leq h^*(n)$$

where $g(n)$ is the cost of the path between the start node and the node n, and $h(n)$ is the estimated cost from the node n to the goal node. $h^*(n)$ means the real cost from the node n to the goal node, and $h(n)$ is an admissible heuristic.

In the case of $\epsilon h(n) \leq h^*(n)$, $\epsilon h(n)$ guarantees the admissibility of the search, and the ϵ approximation search produces an optimal solution as well as A^*. In case of $\epsilon h(n) > h^*(n)$, the evaluation function f is non-monotonic; therefore it does not produce an optimal solution.

Table 1 shows the characteristics of the ϵ approximation search. For $\epsilon = 0$, the evaluation function becomes $g(n)$, so-called *uniform cost search* [8]. For $\epsilon = \infty$, the $g(n)$ is not material, the evaluation function becomes $h(n)$, and the ϵ approximation search works as the *greedy search*.

Table 1. The characteristics of ϵ approximation search

ϵ	0 ←——————→	∞
Search type	Uniform cost ←— A^* —→	Greedy
Complexity	$O(b^d)$ ←—————→	$O(b*d)$
Optimality	Yes ←—————→	No

As for complexity, both the time and space complexity of the uniform cost search is $O(b^d)$, where b is the branching factor and d is the depth of a solution. In general, the complexity of the greedy search is $O(b^m)$, where m is the maximum depth of a search tree. However, we can expect the complexity $O(b*d)$. Because $h(n)$ is monotonic for the search on the real road map.

Figure 1 shows the expanded nodes according to various values of ϵ in the Tokyo area of Japan. The qualities in this figure are the ratio of the optimal solution (67.809 kilometers) to the computed one. As the ϵ becomes larger, the number of the expanded nodes becomes smaller, and the search time becomes shorter. The search time is shortened to 69% by changing ϵ from 1.0 to 1.1. In the case of 2.0, the search found the solution about 100 times faster. The decrease of the quality is smaller than 5%.

3   Time-Constrained Heuristic Search

One of the most direct methods to finish a search within a given time limit is that which finds the simplest solution at the start, then makes the conditions more strict gradually and finds several solutions in the residual search time. The result of this method is that the best solution will appear among the solutions found.

Our method can search and find one bounded-optimal solution, making full use of the time. It uses the ability of the search time control in the ϵ approximation search. In order to finish the search at the specified time, it estimates the ϵ value, considering the residual search time during its search.

We define the following parameters (Figure 2).

- Distance D : The estimated cost from start node to goal node. $D = h_{start}$.
- Time constrained T : The user-specified time to finish search.
- Average velocity V : The average velocity to finish search on time. It is $V = D/T$.
- Effective distance d : The distance from the expanded nodes toward the goal node. $d = D - \min h_n$.
- Search time t : Current time from beginning of search.
- Effective velocity v : Speed of the expanded nodes toward the goal node. $v = d/t$.

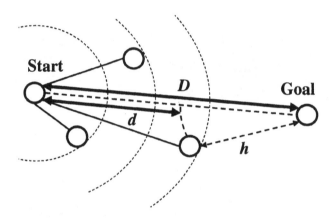

Fig. 2. Parameter for Time-Constrained Heuristic Search

If the search executes at the average velocity, V, at all times, the search will be able to find a solution at the specified time. The control of the ϵ value by V and v allows the effective velocity, v, to retain V, and allows the search to finish on time. Our control strategy is as follows:

1. $v - V < Lower$ then increase the value of ϵ
2. $v - V > Upper$ then decrease the value of ϵ
3. otherwise, no change of ϵ.

The algorithm is shown below.

Time_Constrained_Search($Start$, $Goal$, T)

```
1   ε ← 1.0
2   d ← 0.0, t ← 0.0, v ← 0.0
3   D ← calc_h(Start, Goal)
4   V ← D/T
```

```
5    min_h ← D
6    OPEN ← Start, CLOSE ← φ
7    time_start ← get_time()
8    while true
9        min_node ← get_min_node(ε, Open, Close)
10       min_h ← expand_node(min_node, min_h, Open, Close, Goal)
11       if min_h = 0.0 then
12           return success
13       if d < (D − min_h) then
14           d ← (D − min_h)
15       time ← get_time()
16       t ← (time - time_start)
17       v ← d/t
18       if v − V > Upper then
19           ε ← (ε − δ)
20       else if v − V < Lower then
21           ε ← (ε + δ)
22       if ε < 1.0 then
23           ε ← 1.0
```

We give the algorithm **Time_Constrained_Search** the start node, the goal node and the time-constrained value. Lines 1 through 4 initialize these parameters. The minimum h of all the nodes is set on min_h (line 5), and **get_time** is for finding the current time, which is set on $time_{start}$.

The **get_min_node** in line 9 selects the node which has the lowest f in the set of open nodes, $OPEN$. The selected node returns to the min_node. It has ϵ as its parameter. The evaluation function f must be recalculated with every change of the ϵ value. The heap tree can not be allowed to speed up in finding the minimum node in our algorithm, because the heap has to be restructured when the ϵ value is changed.

The min_node is expanded by the **expand_node** (line 10). min_h is updated as compared to min_h and the h of the expanded nodes from min_node.

Lines 11 and 12 define the goal test. $min\_h = 0$ means to reach the goal node, then the search ends successfully. If min_h is not 0, the effective distance, d, is calculated. If d is increased, then the d is updated.

Lines 15 through 21 control the ϵ value. The effective velocity, v, is calculated by d and the current time, t. The ϵ value is determined by comparing v and V, and it is reevaluated at every step in the algorithm.

The effective velocity, v, becomes slower gradually, because the nodes are expanded from the start node to the goal node elliptically, as in figure 2. The vector to the goal node is large at the start, since the area is small, but as the search area increases, the vector becomes smaller.

The cases in which the search does not finish on time occur because the specified time is greater than the ability of computer to calculate or the *delta* is too small to avoid speeding up.

Practically, we should set the time constrained to more than the search time in $\epsilon = \infty$, considering the ability of the ϵ approximation search. The search time can be shortened as required by increasing ϵ, as described in section 2.

4 Results

We implemented a route-finding program written in Java. We ran the program on a Sun UltraSPARC system with a digital map on its hard disk. The length of the route we selected for practical testing was 67.809 kilometers, and the search time was 139 seconds, using A^*. In this experiment, we set $\delta = 0.05$, because our preliminary test showed that a higher resolution was not meaningful for examining the performance of the algorithm.

Figure 3 shows the relation between the time constrained and the solution quality. The quality rises for 70 seconds. After that, the *quality* has reached 1.0, which is the optimal solution. This indicates that the longer search time yields better solutions.

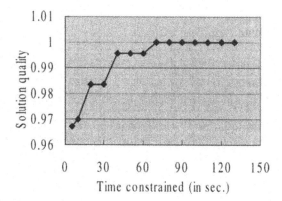

Fig. 3. Slution quality with respect to time constrained

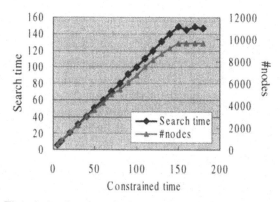

Fig. 4. The relation between time constrained, #nodes and Search time

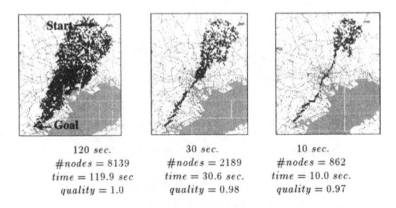

120 sec.	30 sec.	10 sec.
#nodes = 8139	#nodes = 2189	#nodes = 862
time = 119.9 sec	time = 30.6 sec.	time = 10.0 sec.
quality = 1.0	quality = 0.98	quality = 0.97

Fig. 5. Search space of Time constrained heuristic search

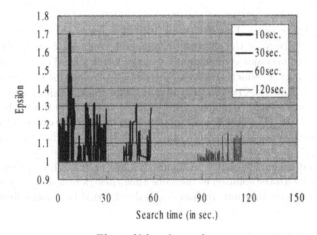

Fig. 6. Value change for ϵ

Figure 4 shows the search time according to the time constrained and the number of expanded nodes. As for the search time, our method finds the optimal solution at the specified time. The number of nodes and the search time rise in the same way. After 140 seconds, each value is established. Because 140 seconds is the search time using A^*, further nodes are not expanded and more time is not needed.

Our algorithm executes a search using the full time, finding the solution precisely on time rather than within the allotted time. It gives support to the result of Figure 3.

Figure 5 shows the expanded nodes in our method. The expanded nodes are smaller, according to the time constrained, as in Figure 1. However, the unique feature is that many nodes are expanded in the area near the start node, and fewer nodes are expanded in the area near the goal node. This is caused by

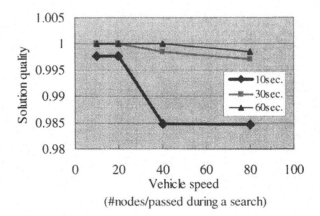

Fig. 7. Solution quality of Real-time search

increasing the ϵ value. Figure 6 shows the changes of the ϵ value during the search. The pattern of the changing ϵ value is that it is 1.0 in the first part of the search and becomes greater than 1.0 in the latter part. This is caused by the effective velocity, v, which is decreased gradually, as described in section 3.

Figure 7 shows the results of real-time route finding using our method for each time constrained. A vehicle executes the search several times while moving from start to goal. The graph is the relation of vehicle speed, which is the number of the passing nodes in one search, and the quality of the distance that vehicle moved.

The solution quality shown in Figure 7 is higher than that shown in Figure 3, compared with the solution of the same time constrained, and they are almost 1.0. This indicates that our method is suitable for real-time route finding.

5 Related Work

Russell provided a general framework for provably optimal agent design with time constraints [7]. The framework we propose here is a time-constrained heuristic search for a practical route-finding domain, and seems to be an instance of bounded-optimal agents. Our framework provides a method and algorithm of time-constrained search, and shows its applicability to real-time automobile navigation. In [7], practical methods were not provided to produce sub-optimal solutions for search problems. We have provided a decision procedure that demonstrates how ϵ can be changed to keep up with the residual search time.

Time-constrained search has this property: longer search time yields better solutions. This property originates from an *anytime* algorithm [1]. This type of algorithm allows an interrupt at any time and produces an optimal answer for that situation. An anytime algorithm is based on the utility function of an action, and the function is monotonic over time. The algorithm has a kind of "meta-level" procedure to decide whether or not a search should be terminated. However, the applicable class of anytime algorithms is not clearly provided, resulting in no experimental (practical) evaluation. While most anytime algorithms fall into iterative deepening, our algorithm controls the degree of approximation for search.

The real-time A^* proposed by Korf allows search and execution to be interleaved, producing a local optimal solution [3]. Real-time A^* eventually backtracks to a previously visited node, but for real applications on vehicle route planning, the real-time search must complete the search and produce an entire solution before execution. This leads to an approximate search method, where node expansion around the starting node is exact, and a greedy-similar search is done around the goal node. The strategy of this method is effective, as shown in Figure 7. Unlike the real-time A^*, our time-constrained search takes search space into account.

Increasing the value of ϵ yields the decrease of branching nodes. This is opposite to the *Iterative Broadening* proposed by Ginsberg [2], where search space becomes larger by incrementing the number of nodes being branched. In our method, the number of branching nodes is dynamically determined, according to the residual search time.

Our motivation for this study originated in the development of route-finding algorithms for commercial automobile navigation systems. Existing algorithms for the commercial systems were not designed to produce optimal solutions. In addition, it is difficult to change a route that has been produced already, when unexpected situations arise. Our algorithm provides a solution to these problems for practical application.

6 Conclusion

We have provided a method for real-time route finding on the digital map used in an automobile navigation system. We formulated the route finding as a time-constrained optimization problem. The proposed algorithm can be viewed as a dynamic version of the previous approximate A^*.

Although the experimental result here was obtained using a map on a hard disk, we also used an Intel 486DX4 computer and a map on a CD-ROM. For such a real situation, the implemented system almost finished within the specified time. This indicates that we can really apply this method to commercial automobile navigation systems.

References

1. Thomas Dean and Mark Boddy, "An Analysis of Time-Dependent Planning," *Proceedings Seventh National Conference on Artificial Intelligence (AAAI-88)*, pp.49-54, 1988.
2. Matthew L. Ginsberg and William D. Harvey "Iterative Broadening," *Proceedings Eighth National Conference on Artificial Intelligence (AAAI-90)*, pp.216-220, 1988.

3. Richard E. Korf, "Real-Time Heuristic Search," *Artificial Intelligence* 42, (1990) 189-211.

4. Andreas L. Köll, Hermann Kaindl, "Bidirectional Best-First Search with Bounded Error: Summary of Results," *Thirteenth International Joint Conference on Artificial Intelligence (IJCAI-93)*, pp.217-223, 1993.

5. Judea Pearl, "Studies in Semi-Admissible Heuristics," *IEEE Transactions on Pattern Analysis and Machine Intelligence*, Vol. PAMI-4, No.4, 1982.

6. Pohl, I., "The avoidance of (relative) catastrophe, heuristic competence, genuine dynamic weighting and computational issues in heuristic problem solving," *Third International Joint Conference on Artificial Intelligence (IJCAI-73)*, pp.20-23, 1973.

7. Stuart J. Russell and Devika Subramanian, "Provably Bounded-Optimal Agents," *Journal of Artificial Intelligence Research*, Vol.2, pp.575-609, 1995.

8. Stuart J. Russell and Peter Norvig, *"Artificial Intelligence: A Modern Approach,"* Prntice Hall

Using Mutual Information to Determine Relevance in Bayesian Networks

A. E. Nicholson and N. Jitnah

School of Computer Science and Software Engineering, Monash University,
Clayton, VIC 3168, Australia
{annn,njitnah}@csse.monash.edu.au

Abstract. The control of Bayesian network (BN) evaluation is important in the development of real-time decision making systems. Techniques which focus attention by considering the relevance of variables in a BN allow more efficient use of computational resources. The statistical concept of *mutual information* (MI) between two related random variables can be used to measure relevance. We extend this idea to present a new measure of arc weights in a BN, and show how these can be combined to give a measure of the weight of a region of connected nodes. A heuristic path weight of a node or region relative to a specific query is also given. We present results from experiments which show that the MI weights are better than another measure based on the Bhattacharyya distance.

1 Introduction

Belief (or Bayesian) networks (BNs) [13] have become a popular representation for reasoning under uncertainty, as they integrate a graphical representation of causal relationships with a sound Bayesian foundation. Belief network evaluation involves the computation of posterior probability distributions, or beliefs, of query nodes, given evidence about other nodes. An introduction to BNs and an example are given in Sect. 2.

The scheduling of BN evaluation is important in the development of real-time decision making systems. Techniques which focus attention by considering the relevance of variables in a BN allow more efficient use of computational resources [13, pp.321-323][14]. The concept of a connection strength between two adjacent nodes in a binary BN was introduced by Boerlage in [3]; this measure was proposed for use when graphically displaying BNs, with a thicker arc indicating higher connection strength. In [10] we proposed new measures for the strength of an arc linking multi-state nodes, which we called the *arc weight*, and showed how it can be used to design an anytime BN belief update algorithm. We used a measure, w_{Bh}, which makes use of the Bhattacharyya distance [2], a statistical measure of the difference between two probability distributions.

In this paper we develop a new measure for the arc weight based on the well-known *Mutual Information* between two related random variables (Sect. 3), extending Pearl's [13, pp.321-323] outline of the possible use of mutual information for "relevance-based control". In Sect. 4 we derive expressions for combining weights over a region consisting of connected nodes. The concept of the *path weight* of a node or of a region relative to a specific query is also described, with appropriate formulas to calculate a heuristic estimate (Sect. 5). An experiment was conducted to compare the accuracy of the arc weight measure based on MI with the Bhattacharyya measure (Sect. 6); this experiment concluded that MI weights are more accurate. In Sect. 7 we discuss how the measure may be used to efficiently control BN evaluation, and place it in the context of related research. We conclude with directions for future work in Sect. 8.

2 Belief Network Example

Belief networks (BNs) [13] are directed acyclic graphs where nodes correspond to random variables. The absence of an arc between two nodes indicates an independence assumption. This framework allows a compact representation of the joint probability distribution over all the variables. Each node has a *conditional probability distribution* (CPD) which gives the probability of each state of the node, for all state combinations of its parents. If a node has no parents its prior distribution is stored. *Evidence* is entered by assigning fixed values to nodes. We *evaluate* a BN by computing posterior probability distributions for some query nodes. These posteriors represent *beliefs* about states of query nodes. Evaluation can be done with or without evidence in the network.

Fig. 1 shows an example network taken from standard BN literature [11]. The structure of the network and the CPDs for each node are shown. We use this BN for numerical examples of weight calculations in Sect. 3, 4, and 5. This network is a simple medical diagnosis model. The nodes have the following meanings. A: *patient visited Asia recently*, T: *patient has tuberculosis*, S: *patient is a smoker*, C: *patient suffers from lung cancer*, O: *tuberculosis or lung cancer are detected*, B: *patient suffers from bronchitis*, D: *dyspnea is present*, X: *x-ray results are normal.* Each node can take two values, true or false.

For polytrees, BN evaluation is computationally straightforward, using a message-passing algorithm [13]. Beliefs can be updated in time linear in the number of nodes by this method, however most real-world BN models have undirected loops, in which case message-passing is not appropriate. The jointree algorithm [11] is the fastest existing method for exactly evaluating a BN containing undirected loops. This algorithm uses clustering to transform the BN into a tree structure i.e. with no loops. Unfortunately this algorithm has expensive memory requirements and is impractical on large networks. In general, both exact and approximate BN evaluation are NP-hard problems [6,7]. One approach to reducing the complexity of evaluation is to focus on the most relevant part of the network, rather than using the complete model. *Arc weights*, as described in this paper, allow us to identify the most relevant nodes, given a specific query.

3 Arc Weight Based on MI

Mutual Information (MI) [15,13] is a measure of the dependence between two random variables. It is the reduction in uncertainty of X due to knowing Y, and

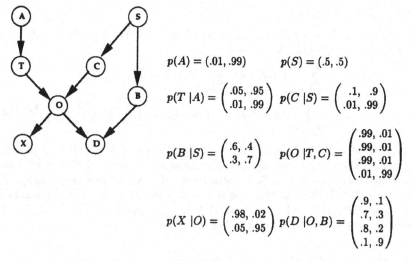

Fig. 1. Example BN and CPDs for medical diagnosis.

vice-versa. The MI between two variables X and Y is given by:

$$I(X,Y) = \sum_{x,y} p(X,Y) \ \log \frac{p(X,Y)}{p(X)p(Y)} \qquad (1)$$

Since $p(X,Y) = p(X)p(Y|X)$, this can be written as:

$$I(X,Y) = \sum_{x} p(X) \sum_{y} p(Y|X) \ \log \frac{p(Y|X)}{p(Y)} \qquad (2)$$

MI is symmetric, i.e. $I(X,Y) = I(Y,X)$. It is a non-negative quantity and is zero if and only if X and Y are mutually independent.

3.1 Single Parent

Given a node Y with single parent X in a BN, the mutual information between X and Y describes the influence of X on Y and vice-versa. The arc weight of $X \rightarrow Y$ is computed as the mutual information between X and Y:

$$w(X,Y) = \sum_{i \in \Omega(X)} p_{pr}(X = i) \sum_{j \in \Omega(Y)} p(Y = j | X = i) \ \log \frac{p(Y = j | X = i)}{p_{pr}(Y = j)} \qquad (3)$$

where $\Omega(X)$ denotes the state space of X and $p_{pr}(X = i)$ denotes the prior probability of X being in state i. If X is a root node, its priors are stored in the BN. Otherwise $p_{pr}(X = i)$ is approximated by averaging the conditional probabilities of X, over all parent state combinations. Similarly, because $p_{pr}(Y = j)$ is not directly available in the BN, it is approximated by averaging the conditional probabilities of Y over all states of X. In the network of Fig. 1, the averaged probability distribution of T is $p_{pr}(T) = (.03, .97)$. Using Eq. 3, $w(A, T) = w(T, A) = 0.009$.

3.2 Multiple Parents

Given a node Y with parent X and a set of other parents $\mathbf{Z} = \{Z_0, \ldots, Z_n\}$, we define the weight of arc $X \to Y$ as:

$$w(X,Y) = \sum_{k \in \Omega(\mathbf{Z})} p_{pr}(\mathbf{Z} = \mathbf{k}) \sum_{i \in \Omega(X)} p_{pr}(X = i)$$

$$\sum_{j \in \Omega(Y)} p(Y = j \mid X = i, \mathbf{Z} = \mathbf{k}) \ \log \frac{p(Y = j \mid X = i, \mathbf{Z} = \mathbf{k})}{p_{pr}(Y = j \mid \mathbf{Z} = \mathbf{k})} \quad (4)$$

$p_{pr}(X = i)$ is obtained as for Eq 3. For each state of Y, $p_{pr}(Y = j \mid \mathbf{Z} = \mathbf{k})$ is approximated by averaging the conditional probabilities of Y over all state combinations of parents in $\mathbf{Z}$. To estimate $p_{pr}(\mathbf{Z} = \mathbf{k})$, we first calculate $p_{pr}(Z)$ for every $Z \in \mathbf{Z}$, then multiply out the joint probabilities for each combination of states, i.e. $p_{pr}(Z_0 = l_0, \ldots, Z_n = l_n) = \prod_{m=0\ldots n} p_{pr}(Z_m = l_m)$. Using Eq. 4, $w(T, O) = 0.602$ in the network of Fig. 1.

4 Weight of a Connected Region

The arc weight measure based on MI described in Sect. 3, like the Bhattacharyya arc weight, W_{Bh}, is *local*; that is, they define the mutual influence between *neighbours*. Sometimes we want to know the informational content of a set of nodes, forming a connected *region*. This section deals with how arc weights are combined to give a total weight to a BN region. We consider regions consisting of converging arcs, chains, subtrees and undirected loops.

The method for combining arc weights is based on the additive property of MI. Given the node configuration $X \to Y \to Z$, the joint probability distribution of $p(X, Y, Z)$ is obtained by applying the Chain Rule:

$$p(X,Y,Z) = p(Z \mid Y)p(Y \mid X)p(X) \quad (5)$$

If the arcs are ignored, then the three nodes would be considered independent and the joint distribution is:

$$p'(X,Y,Z) = p(X)p(Y)p(Z) \quad (6)$$

The informational content of the three variables is the cross-entropy between Eq. 5 and Eq. 6. It is straightforward to show that

$$I(X,Y,Z) = \sum_{x,y,z} p(X,Y,Z) \log \frac{p(X,Y,Z)}{p'(X,Y,Z)} = I(X,Y) + I(Y,Z) \quad (7)$$

This means that the informational content of this group of nodes is simply the sum of the MI between the pairs of neighbours. Because MI is symmetric, the same result holds if the chain arcs were reversed, i.e. $X \leftarrow Y \leftarrow Z$.

Notation: We use $W()$ to denote the combined weight of all arcs in a connected region. For example, if the region $\mathbf{R}$ consists of the set of nodes $\{X, Y, Z\}$, then $W(\mathbf{R}) = W(XYZ)$.

4.1 Weight of Converging Arcs

This section addresses the problem of combining arc weights for a node with multiple converging arcs, i.e. one with many parents. For such a node, we want to estimate the combined effect of all parents. Consider a node Y with parents X and Z: $X \to Y \leftarrow Z$. In this configuration, the weight of the 3-node region is the combined weight of the converging arcs to child node Y from its parents X and Z:

$$W(XYZ) = \sum_{i \in \Omega(X)} p_{pr}(X = i) \sum_{k \in \Omega(Z)} p_{pr}(Z = k)$$

$$\sum_{j \in \Omega(Y)} p(Y = j \mid X = i, Z = k) \ \log \frac{p(Y = j \mid X = i, Z = k)}{p_{pr}(Y = j)} \qquad (8)$$

$p_{pr}(X)$, $p_{pr}(Z)$ and $p_{pr}(Y)$ are obtained using the averaging procedure explained in Sect. 3.1. In general, given node Y with a set of parents $\mathbf{Z}$, the formula is:

$$W(\mathbf{Z}Y) = \sum_{k \in \Omega(\mathbf{Z})} p_{pr}(\mathbf{Z} = \mathbf{k}) \sum_{j \in \Omega(Y)} p(Y = j \mid \mathbf{Z} = \mathbf{k}) \ \log \frac{p(Y = j \mid \mathbf{Z} = \mathbf{k})}{p_{pr}(Y = j)} \qquad (9)$$

Note that the combined weight of the converging arcs is a bound on the sum of the individual arc weights as calculated previously by Eq. 4:

$$W(Z_0 \ldots Z_n Y) \leq w(Z_0, Y) + \ldots + w(Z_n, Y) \qquad (10)$$

In Fig. 1, the weight of the region consisting of nodes T, O and C is $W(TOC)$ = 1.212.

4.2 Weight of a Chain

Since mutual information can be added over a chain of nodes, we can add arc weights over chains. This section presents formulas for the combined weight of arcs along chains of nodes.

Simple Directed Chain and Chain with a Diverging Node. For the chains of length n, $Z_0 \to \cdots \to Z_n$ and $Z_0 \leftarrow \cdots \leftarrow Z_m \to \cdots \to Z_n$, the weight of the chain from Z_0 to Z_n is:

$$W(Z_0 \ldots Z_n) = w(Z_0, Z_1) + \cdots + w(Z_{n-1}, Z_n) \qquad (11)$$

Summing over all arc weights on the chain between Z_0 and Z_n gives a measure of the combined effect of the intervening nodes. In Fig. 1, the weight of the simple directed chain S $\to$ C $\to$ O $\to$ X is $W(SCOX) = .022 + .618 + .555 = 1.195$. The weight of the chain with a diverging node, O $\leftarrow$ C $\leftarrow$ S $\to$ B is $W(OCSB) = .618 + .022 + .046 = .686$.

Head-to-head Node on a Chain. Consider the chain containing a head-to-head node: $Z_0 \rightarrow \cdots \rightarrow Z_{m-1} \rightarrow Z_m \leftarrow Z_{m+1} \leftarrow \cdots \leftarrow Z_n$. If all parents of the head-to-head node Z_m are on the chain, then Eq. 8 for converging arcs is used to calculate $W(Z_{m-1}Z_mZ_{m+1})$. The combined weight of the chain is then:

$$W(Z_0 \ldots Z_n) = W(Z_0 \ldots Z_{m-1}) + W(Z_{m-1}Z_mZ_{m+1}) + W(Z_{m+1} \ldots Z_n) \qquad (12)$$

For example, consider in Fig. 1 the chain $A \rightarrow T \rightarrow 0 \leftarrow C \leftarrow S$. 0 is a head-to-head node and all its parents are on the chain. The chain weight is $W(ATOCS)$ $= .009 + 1.212 + .022 = 1.243$.

However, if Z_m has parents which are not on the chain, then Eq. 4 should be used to calculate separately the weights of arcs into Z_m. Therefore,

$$W(Z_0 \ldots Z_n) = W(Z_0 \ldots Z_{m-1}) + w(Z_{m-1}, Z_m) + w(Z_m, Z_{m+1}) + W(Z_{m+1} \ldots Z_n) \quad (13)$$

4.3   Weight of a Subtree

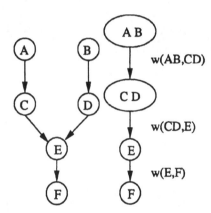

Fig. 2. (a) Subtree S in a BN. (b) Clusters in jointree of S and associated arc weights.

Consider a subtree S of a BN as shown in Fig. 2(a). To calculate the combined weight of the subtree, we transform the subtree into a jointree of clusters as shown in Fig. 2(b); this jointree has a chain structure. Applying Eq. 11 to the jointree, the subtree weight is:

$$W(S) = w(AB, CD) + w(CD, E) + w(E, F) \qquad (14)$$

where $w(CD, E)$ is calculated as the combined weight $W(CDE)$ of the converging arcs into E, as shown in Eq. 8, and $w(E, F)$ is computed as in Eq. 3. The weight of arc $AB \rightarrow CD$ can be regarded as the cross-entropy between the joint distributions $p(A, B, C, D) = p(A)p(C \mid A)p(B)p(D \mid B)$ and $p'(A, B, C, D) = p(A)p(C)p(B)p(D)$. Therefore,

$$w(AB, CD) = \sum_{a,b,c,d} p(A)p(C \mid A)p(B)p(D \mid B) \ \log \frac{p(C \mid A)p(D \mid B)}{p(C)p(D)} \qquad (15)$$

which simplifies to: $w(AB, CD) = w(A, C) + w(B, D)$.

The method used to calculate the subtree weight of this simple example can be generalised in a straightforward manner to any subtree of a BN. In Fig. 1, the weight of the subtree given by the nodes A, T, O, C, S and X is $W(ATOCSX) = w(A, T) + w(S, C) + W(TOC) + w(O, X) = .009 + .022 + 1.212 + .555 = 1.798$.

4.4 Weight of a Loop

In this section we derive a formula for the combined weight of arcs in a BN region consisting of an undirected loop. A simple example of such a loop is presented, then we propose a general formula for arbitrary loops. Fig. 3(a) shows a simple example of a group of nodes that form an undirected loop L_1 in a BN.

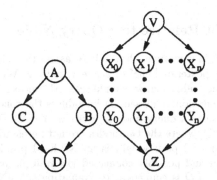

Fig. 3. (a) Loop L_1 in a BN. (b) General Loop L in a BN, where $X_i \ldots Y_i$ is a chain.

The weight of loop L_1 is the cross-entropy between the joint distributions $p(A, B, C, D)$ and $p'(A, B, C, D)$:

$$W(L_1) = \sum_{a,b,c,d} p(A, B, C, D) \ \log \frac{p(A, B, C, D)}{p'(A, B, C, D)}$$

$$= \sum_{a,b,c,d} p(A)p(B \mid A)p(C \mid A)p(D \mid B, C) \ \log \frac{p(A)p(B \mid A)p(C \mid A)p(D \mid B, C)}{p(A)p(B)p(C)p(D)}$$

$$= \sum_{a,b} p(A)p(B \mid A) \ \log \frac{p(B \mid A)}{p(B)} + \sum_{a,c} p(A)p(C \mid A) \ \log \frac{p(C \mid A)}{p(C)} +$$

$$\sum_{b,c,d} p(D \mid B, C) \ \log \frac{p(D \mid B, C)}{p(D)} \ p(B)p(C)$$

$$= w(A, B) + w(B, C) + W(BC, D) \tag{16}$$

In the simplest general case of a loop L as shown in Fig. 3(b), where $X_i \ldots Y_i$ is a chain, the weight can be calculated as follows. The combined weight of the diverging nodes from V is:

$$W(V, X_0 \ldots X_n) = \sum_{v, x_0 \ldots x_n} p(V)p(X_0 \mid V) \ldots p(X_n \mid V) \; \log \frac{p(X_0 \mid V) \ldots p(X_n \mid V)}{p(X_0) \ldots p(X_n)}$$

$$= w(V, X_0) + \cdots + w(V, X_n) \qquad (17)$$

Each chain weight $W(X_i, Y_i)$ can be calculated as shown in Sect. 4.2. Finally the combined weight $W(Y_0 \cdots Y_n, Z)$ of the converging arcs into Z is found using Eq. 8. Therefore, the loop weight is:

$$W(\mathbf{L}) = w(V, X_0) + \cdots + w(V, X_n) +$$
$$W(X_0, Y_0) + \cdots + W(X_n, Y_n) + W(Y_0 \cdots Y_n, Z) \qquad (18)$$

In Fig. 1, the weight of the loop given by the nodes **S, C, O, D** and **B** is $W(SCODB) = w(S, C) + w(S, B) + w(C, O) + W(OBD) = .022 + .046 + .618 + .164 = .85$.

5 Path Weight Relative to a Query Node

In BN evaluation, it is sometimes desirable to assess the relative impact of selected nodes on the posterior belief of a query node Q. When performing approximate or anytime evaluation, we should select the most informative nodes to include in the computation. This section introduces the concept of *path weight* of a node X, relative to a query node Q, written $W_Q(X)$. It is an estimate of the impact of X on Q, where the two nodes are not necessarily neighbours.

Exact computation of path weight is an NP-hard problem. When X and Q are widely spaced and possibly connected via multiple paths, assessing the exactly effect on X on Q is equivalent to evaluating the BN, with all possible values of X entered as evidence. Such an exhaustive procedure is impossible in practice. It is preferable to use a heuristic measure that can be evaluated quickly.

Path Weight of a Node relative to Q. Consider the node configuration $X \rightarrow Y \rightarrow Q$. Boerlage's [3] bound on the connection strength (CS) of such a Markov Chain is given by the inequality:

$$tanh(\tfrac{1}{4}CS(X, Q)) <= tanh(\tfrac{1}{4}CS(X, Y)) \; tanh(\tfrac{1}{4}CS(Y, Q)) \qquad (19)$$

For arc weights based on mutual information, we define the path weight of X relative to Q as:

$$W_Q(X) = w_Q(X, Y) + w(Y, Q) \qquad (20)$$

where $w_Q(X, Y)$ is $\frac{w(X,Y)}{pl(X,Q)}$, and $pl(X, Q) = 2$ is the path length from X to Q. We divide $w(X, Y)$ by the path length to get the weight of arc $X \rightarrow Y$ w.r.t. to Q, since the impact of a node is generally attenuated by distance. This provides a heuristic estimate of the informational value of arc $X \rightarrow Y$ relative to node Q. In general, for a chain of nodes $Z_n \rightarrow Z_{n-1} \rightarrow \cdots \rightarrow Z_1 \rightarrow Z_0 \rightarrow Q$, the path weight of Z_n w.r.t. Q is defined by:

$$W_Q(Z_n) = \frac{w(Z_n, Z_{n-1})}{pl(Z_n, Q)} + \frac{w(Z_{n-1}, Z_{n-2})}{pl(Z_{n-1}, Q)} + \cdots + w(Z_0, Q) \qquad (21)$$

The direction of arrows on the chain does not matter since $w()$ is a reversible measure. In Fig. 1, the path weight of S relative to X is $W_X(S) = .859$.

Path Weight of a Region relative to Q. Consider a region **R** consisting of several connected nodes and linked to Q via a path through node X on the boundary of **R**. We define the path weight of **R** relative to Q as:

$$W_Q(\mathbf{R}) = W_Q(X) + \frac{W(\mathbf{R})}{pl(X, Q) + \frac{pl(\mathbf{R})}{2}} \tag{22}$$

where $pl(\mathbf{R})$ is the distance between the nodes nearest and furthest from Q and we divide by 2 to take the average. $W(\mathbf{R})$ is calculated as in Sect. 4. If there are multiple paths between **R** and Q, we may substitute for $W_Q(X)$ the average, the minimum or the maximum of the individual path weights, or the path weight measured along heaviest arcs [1]. In Fig. 1, the path weight of the region (loop) given by the nodes S, C, O, D and B, relative to the query node X, is $W_X(SCOBD) = .895$. Here, O is the nearest node to X on the boundary of the region.

6 Results

In this section we compare the arc weight measure w, based on MI, with the measure, w_{Bh}, based on the Bhattacharyya distance. The measures describe the influence between the two linked nodes.

We repeated the following experiment for the ALARM [1] and hailfinder [4] networks. For each incoming arc of every node N, the arc was deleted and the network evaluated. The error in the node's belief of N was recorded, as well as the weights of the deleted arc, in terms of the w_{Bh} and w arc weight measures. The error is the Kullback-Leibler [13] distance between the belief of N after deleting the arc, $bel'(N)$, and the exact belief of N, $bel(N)$ [2].

Finally, we calculated the correlation between error and arc weight. The results are shown in Tab. 1. If a particular measure of arc weight has a high correlation with the error induced by removal of the arc, then we consider this to be a good measure. For each network, the correlation was calculated after grouping the nodes according to their numbers of parents; the first two columns of the table show the number of nodes, #N, with #P parents. All nodes of ALARM (46 nodes) and hailfinder (66 nodes) have at most four parents. Tab. 1 also shows the correlation over all nodes of each network. The correlation data of Tab. 1 indicates a higher correlation between w and error, than between w_{Bh} and error. The z *statistic* [5] of the correlation values is also shown. This is obtained using Fisher's r *to z transform*, which produces a statistic whose distribution is approximately normal, assuming the variables are themselves normally, or almost normally, distributed. In each network, the mean of z is higher for the

---

[1] Draper [8] uses the heaviest path through the loop, which is suitable for LPE since arcs are added in a greedy way.

[2] The exact belief is obtained by evaluating the complete network.

Network: **ALARM**

#N	#P	Corr(wt,err)		z statistic		Z test	
		w_{Bh}	w	w_{Bh}	w	w_{Bh}	w
8	1	.424	.534	.452	.596	1.011	1.333
28	2	.475	.613	.517	.713	2.585	3.565
6	3	.620	.967	.725	2.049	1.256	3.549
4	4	.807	-.276	1.119	-.283	1.119	-.283
46	[1-4]	.505	.654	.556	.783	3.646	5.143
Mean				.674	.772	1.923	2.661

Network: **hailfinder**

#N	#P	Corr(wt,err)		z statistic		Z test	
		w_{Bh}	w	w_{Bh}	w	w_{Bh}	w
20	1	-.348	.678	-.363	.825	1.497	3.402
26	2	.436	.663	.467	.798	2.240	3.827
12	3	.698	.709	.864	.886	2.592	2.658
8	4	.159	.842	.160	1.227	.358	2.744
66	[1-4]	.262	.554	.268	.625	2.128	4.961
Mean				.279	.872	2.128	3.518

Table 1. Correlation, z statistic and Z test.

arc weight w based on MI than for the w_{Bh} weight. The "Z test" column in Tab. 1 indicates how significantly different from zero the correlation values are. The conventional critical values are -1.96 and 1.96; correlation values outside this range indicate that the variables being measured are not independent. Most of the Z values in Tab. 1 are outside the critical range for w, hence we can conclude the error is correlated to arc weight w based on mutual information. The negative correlation for 4-parent nodes is unexpected but since the sample has only four values, it is not significant and we can disregard it. [3]

7 Discussion and Related Work

Pearl [13, pp.321-323] briefly looked at the possible use of mutual information to measure impact, as part of "relevance-based control". In this paper we have provided formulas to calculate a mutual information measure for various configurations; exact measures for arcs and connected regions, and an estimate for the path weight relative to a query node. Unlike the Bhattacharyya distance based weight measure, w_{Bh} developed in earlier work, weights using MI are symmetric, which is intuitively appealing. As Pearl pointed out, the disadvantage of a measure based on MI is that it gives equal penalty to all errors, and does not reflect ordering or scale information about variable values. However, as we have shown, the arc weight based on MI is correlated with the error if that arc was removed.

Arc weights in BNs have many uses. The concept of *connection strength* was first introduced by Boerlage [3], who proposed the use of arc weights to draw a

---

[3] The negative correlation of error to w_{Bh} for 1-parent nodes in hailfinder is also unexpected. Of the 20 arcs measured, 5 had a very low weight but caused a large error if they were deleted. If these outliers are ignored, the correlation is about .65.

contour map of a BN, showing areas of high and low connectivity between nodes. He also suggested the use of connection strengths in a method of approximate BN evaluation. However, Boerlage's measure is limited to binary nodes. Draper [8] uses arc weights to search for the best nodes to include in the active set in Localized Partial Evaluation. In [9], we describe a framework for anytime evaluation of a BN by best-first traversal, using arc weights based on the Bhattacharyya measure as part of the search criterion. Wellman and Liu in [12] suggest that a measure of informativeness be used when selecting nodes to coarsen or refine in State-Space Abstraction, which is another technique for anytime BN evaluation. The weights based on MI presented in this paper are suitable for all these purposes.

The complexity of the calculation of the w measure is typically exponential in the joint state-space size of a node and its parents. For the very large majority of BNs, this is not a problem. Only when nodes have hundreds of parents, each with very large state-spaces, will the computation of arc weights be infeasible. This exponential complexity is also a feature of most BN algorithms. In addition, we envisage that the weights would be computed and stored off-line, then loaded on demand in real-time decision making situations, to control network evaluation.

8 Conclusions and future research

We have introduced a new measure of arc weights in a Bayesian Network, based on the well-known statistical concept of mutual information between two related random variables. Expressions are given to calculate the weight of an arc, given the values in the child node's CPD. Rules are also given for combining weights over a region consisting of connected nodes. The concept of the path weight of a node or of a region relative to a specific query is also described, and the formulas for calculating the path weight are given. The arc weight and the region weight are exact measures, while the *path weight* is a heuristic estimate used for comparative purposes. The use of these formulas is illustrated by some numerical examples. Experiments conducted to compare the accuracy of the arc weight measure based on MI with another measure show that MI weights are more accurate in terms of correlation with the error.

While the initial experimental results look promising, we have yet to provide formal analysis of the relationship between weights based on mutual information and the error. We are also investigating the performance of these weights with existing techniques for anytime BN updating, such as best-first traversal [10, 9] and state-space abstraction [12], and also with the jointree evaluation algorithm.

References

1. I. Beinlich, H. Suermondt, R. Chavez, and G. Cooper. The alarm monitoring system: A case study with two probabilistic inference techniques for belief networks. In *Proc. of the 2nd European Conf. on Artificial Intelligence in medicine*, pages 689–693, 1992.

2. A. Bhattacharyya. On a measure of divergence between two statistical populations defined by their probability distributions. *Bulletin of the Calcutta Mathematics Society*, 35:99–110, 1943.

3. B. Boerlage. Link strengths in Bayesian networks. Master's thesis, Dept. of Computer Science, U. of British Columbia, 1995.

4. John Brown. Hailfinder: Bayesian system that combines meteorological data and models with expert judgment to forecast severe summer weather in ne colorado. INFORMS Atlanta, November 3-6, 1996. Talk. See http://www.informs.org/Conf/ATL96/TALKS/SD12.html, 1996.

5. Paul R. Cohen. *Empirical Methods for Artificial Intelligence*. MIT Press, Cambridge, Massachusetts, 1995.

6. G.F. Cooper. The computational complexity of probabilistic inference using bayesian belief networks. *Artificial Intelligence*, 42:393–405, 1990.

7. P. Dagum and M. Luby. Approximating probabilistic inference in belief networks is NP-hard. *Artificial Intelligence*, pages 141–153, 1993.

8. Denise Draper. *Localized Partial Evaluation of Belief Networks*. PhD thesis, Dept. of Computer Science, University of Washington, 1995.

9. N. Jitnah and A. Nicholson. A best-first search method for anytime evaluation of belief networks. In *ICONIP'97: International Conference on Neural Information Processing (ICONIP'97)*, pages 600–603, 1997.

10. N. Jitnah and A. Nicholson. treenets: A framework for anytime evaluation of belief networks. In *First International Joint Conference on Qualitative and Quantitative Practical Reasoning, ECSQARU-FAPR'97*, 1997. Lecture notes in Artificial Intelligence, Springer-Verlag.

11. S.L. Lauritzen and D.J. Spiegelhalter. Local computations with probabilities on graphical structures and their application to expert systems. *Journal of the Royal Statistical Society*, 50(2):157–224, 1988.

12. C. Liu and M. Wellman. On state-space abstraction for anytime evaluation of bayesian networks. In *IJCAI 95: Anytime Algorithms and Deliberation Scheduling Workshop*, pages 91–98, 1995.

13. Judea Pearl. *Probabilistic Reasoning in Intelligent Systems*. Morgan Kaufmann, San Mateo, Ca., 1988.

14. K. L. Poh and E Horvitz. A graph-theoretic analysis of information value. In *Proceedings of the Twelfth Conference on Uncertainty in AI*, pages 427–435, 1996.

15. C. E. Shannon and W. Weaver. *The mathematical theory of communication*. University of Illinois Press, 1949.

Context-Specific Independence, Decomposition of Conditional Probabilities, and Inference in Bayesian Networks

Nevin L. Zhang

Department of Computer Science
Hong Kong University of Science & Technology
lzhang@cs.ust.hk,
http://www.cs.ust.hk/~lzhang

Abstract. Three kinds of independence are of interest in the context of Bayesian networks, namely conditional independence, independence of causal influence, and context-specific independence. It is well-known that conditional independence enables one to factorize a joint probability into a list of conditional probabilities and thereby renders inference feasible. It has recently been shown that independence of causal influence leads to further factorizations of some of the conditional probabilities and consequently makes inference faster. This paper studies context-specific independence. We show that context-specific independence can be used to further decompose some of the conditional probabilities. We present an inference algorithm that takes advantage of the decompositions and provide, for the first time, empirical evidence that demonstrates the computational benefits of exploiting context-specific independence.

1 Introduction

The probabilistic approach to reasoning under uncertainty has grown to prominence in the last fifteen years or so. It models a problem domain using a set of random variables, represents uncertain knowledge and beliefs as probabilistic assertions, and makes inference, i.e. computes posterior probabilities, according to the laws of probability.

In principle, arbitrary queries about posterior probabilities can be answered if there is a joint probability over all variables. The amount of numbers it takes to specify a joint probability is exponential in the number of variables. For this reason, probabilistic inference was thought to be infeasible until the introduction of Bayesian networks (BNs) [1] [9], [5]. Making use of conditional independence, a BN factorizes a joint a probability into a list of conditional probabilities: the joint probability can be recovered by multiplying the conditional probabilities. The factorization renders knowledge acquisition and inference feasible because each of the conditional probabilities involves only a fraction of the variables.

---

[1] Also known as probabilistic influence diagrams and belief networks.

Recently, there is much interest in exploiting structures in the conditional probabilities. One major source of structures is independence of causal influence (ICI) [2] [4] . ICI refers to situations where multiple causes influence a common effect independently. Olesen *et al* [7] and Heckerman [4] point out that ICI can be used to simplify the topology of a BN and hence speed up inference. A more efficient approach is developed by Zhang and Poole [15]. The approach is based on the observation that ICI allows one to further factorize a conditional probability into a list functions: the conditional probability can be recovered by combining the functions using a convolution-like operator. While the conditional probability might involve a number of variables, each of the functions involve only two variables. Knowledge acquisition and inference are therefore made easier.

This paper is concerned with another major source of structures, namely context-specific independence (CSI) [1]. CSI refers to conditional independencies that hold only in specific contexts. We observe that CSI allows one to further decompose a conditional probability into a list of partial functions: the conditional probability can be recovered by taking the "union" of the partial functions. The partial functions require fewer numbers to specify than the conditional probability and hence knowledge acquisition and inference becomes easier. We develop an inference algorithm that takes advantage of the further decompositions and provide, for the first time, empirical evidence that demonstrates the computational benefits of exploiting CSI.

The rest of this paper is organized as follows. We will start with a brief review of BN (Section 2) and a brief review of CSI (Section 3). The notions of partial function and decomposition will be formally defined in Section 4. In Section 5 we will present a high level inference algorithm that works with the decompositions induced by CSI and in Section 6 we briefly discuss the issue of preserving structure during inference. Empirical results will be reported in Section 7, related work discussed in Section 8, and conclusions provided in Section 9.

2 Bayesian networks

A *Bayesian network* (BN) is an annotated directed acyclic graph, where each node represents a random variable and is attached with the conditional probability of the node given its parents. In addition to the explicitly represented conditional probabilities, a BN also implicitly represents conditional independence assertions. Let $x_1, x_2, \ldots, x_n$ be an enumeration of all the nodes in a BN such that each node appears before its children, and let π_{x_i} be the set of parents of a node x_i. The following assertions are implicitly represented:

For $i = 1, 2, \ldots n$, x_i is conditionally independent of variables in $\{x_1, x_2, \ldots, x_{i-1}\} \backslash \pi_{x_i}$ given variables in π_{x_i}.

The conditional independence assertions and the conditional probabilities together entail a joint probability over all variables. As a matter of fact, by the

---

[2] Also known as causal independence.

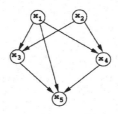

Fig. 1. A Bayesian network.

chain rule, we have

$$P(x_1, x_2, \ldots, x_n) = \prod_{i=1}^{n} P(x_i | x_1, x_2, \ldots, x_{i-1}) = \prod_{i=1}^{n} P(x_i | \pi_{x_i}), \qquad (1)$$

where the second equation is true because of the conditional independence assertions. The conditional probabilities $P(x_i | \pi_{x_i})$ are given in the specification of the BN. Because of (1), we say that the BN *factorizes* the joint probability $P(x_1, x_2, \ldots, x_n)$ into conditional probabilities $p(x_1 | \pi_{x_1})$, $p(x_2 | \pi_{x_2})$, ..., and $p(x_n | \pi_{x_n})$ and that the conditional probabilities constitute a *multiplicative factorization* of the joint probability. The BN in Figure 1, for instance, gives us the following multiplicative factorization of $P(x_1, x_2, \ldots, x_5)$:

$$P(x_1), P(x_2), P(x_3 | x_1, x_2), P(x_4 | x_1, x_2), P(x_5 | x_1, x_3, x_4). \qquad (2)$$

We will use this network as a running example through out the paper.

3 Context-specific independence

Let C be a set of variables. A *context* on C is an assignment of one value to each variable in C. We denote a context by $C = \gamma$, where γ is a set of values of variables in C. Two contexts are *incompatible* if there exists a variable that is assigned different values in the contexts. They are *compatible* otherwise.

This following definition of context-specific independence (CSI) is due to Boutilier *et al* [1]. Let X, Y, Z, and C be four disjoint sets of variables. X and Y are *independent given Z in context $C = \gamma$* if

$$P(X | Z, Y, C = \gamma) = P(X | Z, C = \gamma)$$

whenever $P(Y, Z, C = \gamma) > 0$. When Z is empty, one simply says that X and Y are *independent in context $C = \gamma$*.

The following example of CSI first appeared in [13]. Consider three variables: gender, age, and number of pregnancies. Number of pregnancies depends on age for females. It does not depend on age for males. In other words, number of pregnancies is independent of age in the context "gender=male".

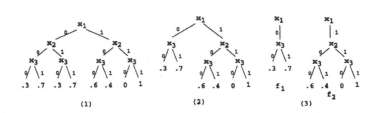

Fig. 2. CSI and compact representations of conditional probabilities.

Here is another example. Consider four variables: income, profession, weather, and qualification. A farmer's income depends on weather and typically does not depend on his qualification. On the other hand, a office clerk's income depends on his qualification and typically does not depend on weather. In other words, income is independent of qualification in the context "profession=farmer" and it is independent of weather in the context "profession=office-clerk".

Boutilier *et al* [1] point out that one can use CSI to come up with compact representations of conditional probabilities. In our running example, suppose all variables are binary and suppose the conditional probability $P(x_3|x_1, x_2)$ is represented by the tree shown in Figure 2 (1). The tree consists of 8 paths. Because x_3 is independent of x_2 in context $x_1=0$, the conditional probability can be represented more compactly by the tree in Figure 2 (2), which consists of 6 paths.

This paper takes a different view on the structures that CSI has to offer. We regard CSI as providing one with opportunities to decompose conditional probabilities into smaller components. In the above example, the fact that x_3 is independent of x_2 in context $x_1=0$ enables one to decompose the conditional probability $P(x_3|x_1, x_2)$ into the two trees shown in Figure 2 (3) (in a sense to be formally defined in the next section).

4 Partial functions

Before showing why CSI can be helpful in inference, this section formally defines the notion of partial functions and introduces an operation for manipulating partial functions. We also formally define the concept of decomposition and generalize the notion of factorization.

Let X be a set of variables. A *partial function* of X is a mapping from a proper subset of possible values of X to the real line. In other words, it is defined only for some but not all possible values of X. The set of possible values of X for which a partial function is defined is called the *domain* of the partial function. A *full function* of X is a mapping from the set of all possible values of X to the real line. In other words, it is defined for all possible values of X. In the rest of a paper, we use the term "function" when we are not sure whether the function under discussion is a partial function or a full function.

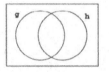 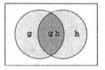

Two Functions   Union-Product

Fig. 3. Union-product: The two circles in the left figure represent the domains of two functions g and h. The domain of the union-product $g \uplus h$ is the union of those of g and h. The union-product equals the product of g and h in the areas where both g and h are defined; it equals g in the area where only g is defined; and it equals h in the area where only h is defined.

The tree f_1 in Figure 2 (3) represents a partial function of variables x_1 and x_3. It consists of two *paths* $[x_1{=}0, x_3{=}0]$ and $[x_1{=}0, x_3{=}1]$, each representing a context in which the partial function is defined. The numbers at the leaf nodes are the values for the contexts. We also refer to them as *values of the paths*. The partial function is not defined in all other contexts, namely $[x_1{=}1, x_3{=}0]$ and $[x_1{=}1, x_3{=}1]$.

4.1 Union-products

Suppose X, Y, and Z are three disjoint sets of variables and suppose $g(X, Y)$ and $h(Y, Z)$ are two functions. The *union-product $g \uplus h$ of g and h* is the function of variables in $X \cup Y \cup Z$ given by

$$(g \uplus h)(X, Y, Z) = \begin{cases} \texttt{undefined} & \text{when both } g(X, Y) \text{ and } h(Y, Z) \text{ undefined} \\ g(X, Y) & \text{when } g(X, Y) \text{ defined, } h(Y, Z) \text{ undefined} \\ h(Y, Z) & \text{when } g(Y, Z) \text{ undefined, } h(X, Y) \text{ defined} \\ g(X, Y)h(Y, Z) & \text{when both } g(X, Y) \text{ and } h(Y, Z) \text{ defined} \end{cases} \quad (3)$$

The operation is illustrated in Figure 3. We sometimes write $g \uplus h$ as $g(X, Y) \uplus h(Y, Z)$ to make explicit the arguments of f and g. When the domains of g and h are disjoint, we call $g \uplus h$ the *union* of g and h and write it as $g \cup h$.

4.2 Decompositions

A list $\mathcal{F}$ of functions with disjoint domains is *decomposition* of a function f if $f = \cup \mathcal{F}$. A decomposition is *proper* if no two functions in the decomposition share the same set of arguments. A decomposition of a function f is *nontrivial* if there is at least one that has fewer arguments than f itself. A function is *decomposable* if it has a nontrivial decomposition.

The conditional probability shown in Figure 2 (1) is decomposable. The two partial functions shown in Figure 2 (3) constitute a nontrivial proper decomposition of the conditional probability.

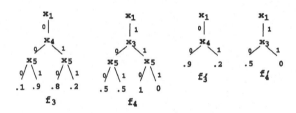

Fig. 4. Decomposition of $P(x_5|x_1, x_3, x_4)$ and evidence absorption.

4.3 Union-product factorizations

A list $\mathcal{F}$ of functions is a *union-product factorization*, or simply a *UP-factorization*, of a function f if $f = \uplus \mathcal{F}$. Note that functions in a decomposition must have disjoint domains whereas domains of functions in a UP-factorization might intersect. A decomposition is a UP-factorization but not vice versa.

For any variable z, let $\mathcal{F}_z$ be the set of functions in $\mathcal{F}$ that contain z as an argument. A UP-factorization $\mathcal{F}$ is *normal* if $\uplus \mathcal{F}_z$ is a full function whenever $\mathcal{F}_z \neq \emptyset$. The following theorem, which we state without proof, lays the foundation for making inference with UP-factorizations.

Theorem 1 *Suppose $\mathcal{F}$ is a normal UP-factorization of a full function f and z is an argument of f. Then $\mathcal{G} = (\mathcal{F} \setminus \mathcal{F}_z) \cup \{\sum_z \uplus \mathcal{F}_z\}$ is a normal UP-factorization of $\sum_z f$.*

5 CSI and inference

This section explains why CSI can be helpful in inference and presents a high level inference algorithm that takes advantage of CSI.

5.1 Finer-grain factorization

A BN factorizes a joint probability into a list of conditional probabilities. CSI can be helpful in inference because it allows one to further decompose some of the conditional probabilities into smaller pieces. In our running example, we have assumed earlier that x_3 is independent of x_2 in context $x_1 = 0$ and that the conditional probability $P(x_3|x_1, x_2)$ is decomposed into the two partial functions f_1 and f_2 shown in Figure 2 (3). Now further assume x_5 is independent of x_3 given x_4 in context $x_1 = 0$ and x_5 is independent of x_4 given x_3 in context $x_1 = 1$. Also assume $P(x_5|x_1, x_3, x_4)$ is decomposed into the two partial functions f_3 and f_4 shown in Figure 4 because of CSI. Then we get the following list of functions:

$$P(x_1), P(x_2), f_1, f_2, P(x_4|x_1, x_2), f_3, f_4. \tag{4}$$

Those functions constitute a UP-factorization of the joint probability $P(x_5|x_1, x_3, x_4)$ because

$$P(x_1) \uplus P(x_2) \uplus f_1 \uplus f_2 \uplus P(x_4|x_1, x_2) \uplus f_3 \uplus f_4$$
$$= P(x_1) \uplus P(x_2) \uplus [f_1 \uplus f_2] \uplus P(x_4|x_1, x_2) \uplus [f_3 \uplus f_4]$$
$$= P(x_1) \uplus P(x_2) \uplus P(x_3|x_1, x_2) \uplus P(x_4|x_1, x_2) \uplus P(x_5|x_1, x_3, x_4)$$
$$= P(x_1, x_2, x_3, x_4, x_5),$$

where the first equation is true because the union-product operation is associative and the third equation is true due to the first property of the operation. The factorization is also normal. For example, $\mathcal{F}_{x_3} = \{f_1, f_2, f_4\}$. Since $f_1 \uplus f_2 = P(x_3|x_1, x_2)$ is a full function, so must be $\uplus \mathcal{F}_{x_3}$ by the second property of union-product.

Note that this UP-factorization is of finer-grain than the multiplicative factorization shown by (2). In the multiplicative factorization, one has the full function $P(x_5|x_1, x_3, x_4)$, which requires 16 numbers to specify. In the UP-factorization, the full function is replaced by partial functions f_3 and f_4. The two partial functions require only 8 numbers to specify.

In general, let $\mathcal{F}$ be the set that consists of, for each variable in a BN, the conditional probability of the variable or, when the conditional probability is decomposed, its components. Then $\mathcal{F}$ is a normal UP-factorization of the joint probability of all variables in the BN. It is of finer-grain than the multiplicative factorization given by the BN if at least one conditional probability is decomposed.

5.2 Evidence absorption

Let $h(z, X)$ be a function of variable z and of variables in a set X. For any value α of z, *setting z to α in h* results in a new function, denoted by $h_{|z=\alpha}$, of variables in X. For any value β of X, $h_{|z=\alpha}(X=\beta)$ is defined if and only if $h(z=\alpha, X=\beta)$ is defined. When this is the case, it equals $h(z=\alpha, X=\beta)$. Note that $h_{|z=\alpha}$ is a function of variables in X only; variable z is not an argument of $h_{|z=\alpha}$. If h is full function, so is $h_{|z=\alpha}$. For convenience, let $h_{|z=\alpha}$ be h itself when h does not contain z as an argument.

Suppose a list R of variables are observed and we are interested in the posterior probability $P(Q|R=R_0)$ of a set Q of query variables after obtaining evidence $R=R_0$, where R_0 is the list of observed values. To compute the posterior probability, the first step is to absorb evidence. *Absorbing evidence* means to set observed variables to their observed values in all functions of $\mathcal{F}$. Denote the resulting list of functions by $\mathtt{absorbEvidence}(\mathcal{F}, R, R_0)$.

In our running example, suppose x_5 is observed to take value 1. After absorbing this piece of evidence, the partial functions f_3 and f_4 become the partial function f_3' and f_4' shown in Figure 4. There are no changes otherwise.

5.3 The variable elimination algorithm

Let Z be the set of variables outside $Q \cup R$ and use $h_{|R=R_0}$ to denote the function obtained by setting the observed variables to the observed values in a function h. Since $\mathcal{F}$ is a normal UP-factorization of the joint probability $P(Z, Q, R)$, absorbEvidence($\mathcal{F}, R, R_0$) is a normal UP-factorization of the function $P(Z, Q, R)_{|R=R_0}$. Because of Theorem 1, the posterior probability $P(Q|R=R_0)$ can be obtained using the following procedure.

Procedure VE-CSI($\mathcal{F}, Q, R, R_0$):

1. $\mathcal{F} \leftarrow$ absorbEvidence($\mathcal{F}, R, R_0$).
2. For each variable z outside $Q \cup R$,
3. $g \leftarrow \uplus \mathcal{F}_z$;
4. $h \leftarrow \sum_z g$;
5. $\mathcal{F} \leftarrow (\mathcal{F} \setminus \mathcal{F}_z) \cup \{h\}$.
6. $f \leftarrow \uplus \mathcal{F}$.
7. Return $f(Q)/\sum_Q f(Q)$ (Renormalization).

The operations carried out at lines 3-5 are usually referred to as *eliminating variable z*. In particular, line 3 *combines* all functions that contain z using the union-product operator and line 4 *sums out z* from the combination. The algorithm is named VE-CSI because it eliminates variables outside $Q \cup R$ one by one and it exploits the finer-grain factorization induced by CSI.

5.4 Discussions

When the first input is a multiplicative factorization instead of a UP-factorization, the union-products at lines 3 and 6 reduce to multiplications and VE-CSI therefore reduces to the VE algorithm [15]. Like VE, the complexity of VE-CSI is heavily influenced by the ordering by which variables are eliminated. Assume functions are represented as trees. Define the *size* of a function to be the number of paths in its tree representation. We suggest the following heuristic: as the next variable to eliminate, choose the variable such that the sum of the sizes of functions that contain the variable is the minimum.

In both VE and VE-CSI, the elimination of a variable involves those and only those functions that contain the variable. The input functions of VE-CSI are of finer-grain than the input functions of VE. Consequently, VE-CSI deals with fewer numbers than VE when eliminating a variable.

As an example, consider the problem of computing the posterior probability $P(x_2|x_5=1)$ in our running example. To solve the problem, VE-CSI starts with the UP-factorization given by (4). After absorbing evidence, f_3 and f_4 becomes f_3' and f_4' (Figure 4). Suppose the first variable to eliminate is x_3. To eliminate x_3, VE-CSI first combines the partial functions f_1, f_2, and f_4'. The amount of numbers involved is $2+4=6$. On the other hand, VE starts with the multiplicative factorization given by (2). To eliminate x_3, it needs to combine $P(x_3|x_1, x_2)$ and $P(x_5|x_1, x_3, x_4)_{|x_5=1}$. This involves $8+8=16$ numbers.

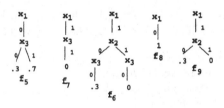

Fig. 5. Elimination of variable x_3.

This is a good place to discuss the advantage of our view on the structures CSI has to offer over the view advocated by Boutilier *et al* [?]. Using CSI, we have decomposed the conditional probability $P(x_5|x_1, x_3, x_4)$ into two partial functions f_3 and f_4, the first of which is not required when eliminating variable x_3 because it does not contain x_3 as an argument. Boutilier *et al*, on the other hand, would represent the conditional probability compactly as *one* tree, which is a simply the merge of f_3 and f_4 (see Figure 2 for another example). While the tree has the same representational complexity as the two partial functions, it makes inference less efficient; The elimination of x_3 requires the entire tree, even though the portion of the tree that corresponds to f_3 is not really needed.

6   Preserving structures during inference

VE-CSI eliminates a variable in two steps. It first combines all functions that contain the variable and then sums out the variable from the combination. Two full functions are produced, one at each step. The two full functions are often decomposable. To eliminate x_3 in the running example, VE-CSI first computes the union-product of f_1, f_2, and f_4' and then calculates $\sum_{x_3} f_1 \uplus f_2 \uplus f_4'$. As it turns out, the three partial functions f_5, f_6, and f_7 in Figure 5 constitute a decomposition of the union-product $f_1 \uplus f_2 \uplus f_4'$ and the two partial functions f_8 and f_9 constitute a decomposition of $\sum_{x_3} f_1 \uplus f_2 \uplus f_4'$.

By preserving structures we mean that, when the aforementioned two full functions are decomposable, we find a decomposition of each of them instead computing the functions themselves. It is desirable to preserve structures for two reasons. First, decomposition simplifies future computations. Second, it is often less expensive to obtain a decomposition of a function than to compute the function itself.

VE-CSI needs to be modified in order to preserve structures. At line 3, one should find a decomposition of the union-product of functions that contain the variable being eliminated, instead of computing the union-product itself. A procedure for this task is developed in a longer version of this paper [16]. It is named decompUP for obvious reasons. At line 4, one should start with the decomposition obtained at line 3 and find a decomposition of the function h. A procedure for this task is also developed in [16]. It is named decompSumOut again for obvious reasons. Finally, the singleton set $\{h\}$ at line 5 should be replaced by the decomposition found at line 4. After the modifications, VE-CSI reads as follows.

Procedure VE-CSI$(\mathcal{F}, Q, R, R_0)$:

1. $\quad \mathcal{F} \leftarrow$ absorbEvidence$(\mathcal{F}, R, R_0)$.
2. $\quad$ For each variable z outside $Q \cup R$,
3. $\quad\quad \mathcal{G} \leftarrow$ decompUP$(\mathcal{F}_z)$;
4. $\quad\quad \mathcal{H} \leftarrow$ decompSumOut$(\mathcal{G}, z)$;
5. $\quad\quad \mathcal{F} \leftarrow (\mathcal{F} \setminus \mathcal{F}_z) \cup \mathcal{H}$.
6. $\quad f \leftarrow \uplus \mathcal{F}$.
7. $\quad$ Return $f(Q)/\sum_Q f(Q)$.

7 Empirical results

Experiments have been conducted to demonstrate the computational benefits of VE-CSI. The experiments were designed to compare VE-CSI with VE — an algorithm that is identical to VE-CSI except that it does not exploit CSI (see Section 5.4). This section describes the experiments and reports the results.

7.1 Implementation issues

VE-CSI works with both partial and full functions while VE works with only full functions. Partial functions should obviously be presented as trees, while full functions can be represented as either trees or tables. To be consistent, both partial and full functions are represented as trees in the implementation of VE-CSI. The choice between tree and table representations is not clear for VE. On one hand, tree representation allows VE to prune zero-valued paths. One the other hand, table representation provides faster access to function values and requires fewer memory allocations. We tried both representations. In the following, we will use VE-TABLE to refer to the implementation of VE where full functions are represented as tables and use VE-TREE to refer to the implementation where full functions are represented as trees.

7.2 The testbed

A BN named Water [6] was used in the experiments [3]. Water is a model for the biological processes of a water purification plant. It consists of 32 variables. Strictly speaking, conditional probabilities of the variables are not decomposable. To make them decomposable, some of the probability values were modified. The induced errors are upper bounded by 0.05. Using a decision tree-like algorithm [11], we were be able to decompose some of the modified conditional probabilities and thereby reduce their representation complexities drastically [4].

---

[3] Obtained from a Bayesian network repository at Berkeley.

[4] Modifications of probability values actually take place during the decomposition process. We choose to describe them as two separate steps here for presentation clarity.

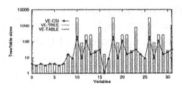

Fig. 6. Representation complexities of conditional probabilities in VE-CSI, VE-TREE, and VE-TABLE.

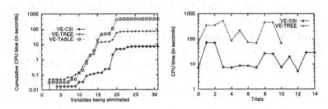

Fig. 7. Performances of VE-CSI, VE-TREE, and VE-TABLE.

In all experiments, the inputs to VE-CSI were the decompositions of the modified conditional probabilities while the inputs to VE were the modified conditional probabilities themselves. In VE-TABLE, the conditional probabilities were represented as tables. In VE-TREE, they were represented as trees and the zero-valued paths were pruned. The representation complexities of the conditional probabilities in the three algorithms are shown in Figure 6.

7.3 Experiments and results

The experiments were performed on a SUN ULTRA 1 machine. The task was to eliminate all variables according to a predetermined elimination ordering. In the first experiment, an ordering by Kjærullf was used [5]. The the amounts of times in CPU seconds that VE-CSI, VE-TREE, and VE-TABLE took to eliminate the first n variables for n running from 0 to 31 are shown in left chart of Figure 7. We see that VE-CSI significantly outperformed VE-TREE, which in turn significantly outperformed VE-TABLE. In particular, VE-CSI completed the entire elimination process in about 7 seconds, while VE-TREE took about 70 seconds and VE-TABLE took about 460 seconds.

In the second experiment, only VE-CSI and VE-TREE were considered. We generated 14 new elimination orderings by randomly permuting pairs of variables in Kjærullf's ordering. A trial was conducted with each ordering. The performances of VE-CSI and VE-TREE accross all the trials are summarized in the right chart of Figure 7. We see that VE-CSI significantly outperformed VE-TABLE in all trials.

---

[5] The ordering was also obtained from the Berkeley repository

The speedup was more than one magnitude on average. Moreover, there are four trials where VE was not able to complete due to large memory requirements. On the other hand, VE-CSI completed each of those four trials in less than 30 seconds.

8 Related work

CSI has its origins in both the BN literature and the influence diagram literature. In the influence diagram literature, CSI arises in the study of asymmetric decision programs and can be traced back to Olmsted [8]. Olmsted introduces a notion of coalescence within influence diagrams, which is slightly more general than CSI. Fung and Shachter [2] propose to explicitly represent CSI by associating each variable with a collection of contingencies and decompose the conditional probability of the variable according to the contingencies. Smith *et al* [14] extend this work so that coalescence and impossible contexts, i.e. contexts with zero probability, can both be represented [6]. Both of these two papers emphasize more on representational issues and less on inferential issues. They provide no general methods for exploiting and preserving structures induced by CSI.

Several methods for exploiting CSI in BN inference have been proposed. Santos and Shimony [12] show that CSI can speed up search-based methods for approximating posterior probabilities. Geiger and Heckerman [3] propose to make use of CSI at the time when a BN is being constructed. A set of local networks is obtained instead of one global network. The set of local networks is called a Bayesian multinet. One can either carry out inference directly in the multinet or convert the multinet into a global network before making inference. This approach requires a predetermined set of conditioning variables and CSI due to other variables is not exploited. Boutilier *et al* [1] present two methods. One method makes use of CSI to reduce the size of the cutset in the cutset conditioning algorithm. The cutset conditioning algorithm reduces a loopy BN into polytrees by conditioning on a set of variables. It is usually less efficient than algorithms such as VE and clique tree propagation that work on the loopy BN itself. The other method proposed by Boutilier *et al* coverts CSI statements into conditional independence statements by introducing auxiliary variables. This method creates many auxiliary variables and structural information can be lost during the conversion [10]. Poole [10] proposes a rule-based method, which bears strong similarity to the method developed in this paper. Our method is conceptually clearer and computationally more efficient than Poole's method. See [16] for detailed discussions.

9 Conclusions

We have studied the role of context-specific independence in Bayesian network inference. Making use of conditional independence, a Bayesian network factorizes a joint probability into a list of conditional probabilities that involve fewer

---

[6] Impossible contexts are another main source of asymmetries for decision problems.

variables. This paper points out that context-specific independence allows one to further decompose some of the conditional probabilities into partial functions that take fewer numbers to specify, resulting in a finer-grain factorization of the joint probability. An inference algorithm that exploits the finer-grain factorization has been developed. The algorithm preserves structures during inference. Experiments have demonstrated that exploiting context-specific independence with our algorithm can bring about significant computational gains.

References

1. C. Boutilier, N. Friedman, M. Goldszmidt, and D. Koller (1996), Context-specific independence in Bayesian networks, *Proceedings of the Twelfth Conference on Uncertainty in Artificial Intelligence*, pp. 115-123.
2. R. M. Fung and R. D. Shachter (1990), Contingent Influence Diagrams, Advanced Decision Systems, 1500 Plymouth St., Mountain View, CA 94043, USA.
3. D. Geiger and D. Heckerman (1996), Knowledge representation and inference in similarity networks and Bayesian multimets, *Artificial Intelligence*, 92, pp. 45-74.
4. D. Heckerman (1993), Causal independence for knowledge acquisition and inference, *Proceedings of the Ninth Conference on Uncertainty in Artificial Intelligence*, pp. 122-127.
5. R. A. Howard, and J. E. Matheson (1984), Influence Diagrams, *The principles and Applications of Decision Analysis*, Vol. II, R. A. Howard and J. E. Matheson (eds.). Strategic Decisions Group, Menlo Park, California, USA.
6. F. V. Jensen, U. Kjærulff, K. G. Olesen, and J. Pedersen (1989), Et forprojekt til et ekspertsystem for drift af spildevandsrensning (An expert system for control of waste water treatment — A pilot project), Technical Report, Judex Datasystemer A/S, Aalborg, Denmark (in Danish).
7. K. G. Olesen and S. Andreassen (1993), Specification of models in large expert systems based on causal probabilistic networks, *Artificial Intelligence in Medicine* 5, pp. 269-281.
8. S. M. Olmsted (1983), Representing and solving decision problems, Ph.D. Dissertation, Department of Engineering-Economic Systems, Stanford University.
9. J. Pearl (1988), *Probabilistic Reasoning in Intelligence Systems: Networks of Plausible Inference*, Morgan Kaufmann Publishers, Los Altos, CA.
10. D. Poole (1997), Probabilistic partial evaluation: exploiting rule structure in probabilistic inference, *Proceedings of the Fifteenth International Joint Conference on Artificial Intelligence*, pp. 1284-1291.
11. J. R. Quinlan (1986), Induction of decision trees, *Machine Learning*, 1, pp. 81-106.
12. E. Santos Jr. and S. E. Shimony (1996), Exploiting case-based independence for approximating marginal probabilities, *International Journal of Approximate Reasoning*, 14, pp. 25-54.
13. G. Shafer (1996), *Probabilistic Expert Systems*, SIAM.
14. J. E. Smith, S. Holtzman, and J. E. Matheson (1993), Structuring conditional relationships in influence diagrams, *Operations Research*, 41, No. 2, pp. 280-297.
15. N. L. Zhang and D. Poole (1996), Exploiting causal independence in Bayesian network inference, *Journal of Artificial Intelligence Research*, 5, pp. 301-328.
16. N. L. Zhang (1998), Inference in Bayesian networks: The role of context-specific independence, Technical Report, HKUST-CS98-09, Department of Computer Science, University of Science and Technology, Hong Kong. Available at http://www.cs.ust.hk/ lzhang/paper/csitr.html.

Derivational Grammar Approach to Morphological Analysis of Japanese Sentences

Yasuhiro OGAWA[1], Muhtar MAHSUT[2], Katsuhiko TOYAMA[1]
and Yasuyoshi INAGAKI[1]

[1] Graduate School of Engineering, Nagoya University
Furo-cho, Chikusa-ku, Nagoya, 464-8603, Japan
[2] Faculty of Engineering, Mie University
1515, Kamihama-cho, Tsu, 514-8507, Japan
{yasuhiro, muhtar, toyama, inagaki}@inagaki.nuie.nagoya-u.ac.jp

Abstract. This paper proposes a new simple Japanese morphological analysis system which we call MAJO. Of course, many Japanese morphological analyses have been proposed and used in the wide area of Japanese language processing. But they are rather complicated because their analysis methods are based on conjugations of verbs and adjectives. On the other hand, it is known that the derivational grammar, which does not use the concept of conjugations, makes morphological analysis simple. Although there are some literatures which discuss Japanese morphological analysis used derivational grammar, all of them has modified their grammar to utilize existing systems. MAJO is constructed directly from the derivational grammar, so that it has a smaller number of grammar rules than the previous systems. We have evaluated its performance on the EDR corpus and MAJO succeeded with 97.9% ratio.

1 Introduction

Morphological analysis is the most important task of natural language processing of many Asian languages such as Japanese, Korean, and so on, because no spaces are placed between words. In linguistic typology, many Asian languages are classified as agglutinative languages in which verbs usually do not conjugate and words are derived from other words by mechanically appending affixes to invariable stems. Thus treatment of the word derivation is one of the important problems in morphological analysis of those languages.

Although the Japanese language is an agglutinative language, traditional Japanese grammars claim that Japanese verbs conjugate and that verbal stems and suffixes vary in six conjugation forms, viz. "imperfect(*mizen*)", "continuative(*renyou*)", "conclusive(*shuushi*)", "attributive(*rentai*)", "provisional(*katei*)" and "imperative(*meirei*)" forms. And there are many complex connection rules between conjugation forms and other words. For example, *kakaseru* [make one write] is segmented into *kaka-seru*, in which *kaka-* is an imperfect form of *kaku* [write] and *-seru* is a conclusive form of causative auxiliary verb *seru* which is connectable only with imperfect form of verbs. Traditional Japanese grammars also classify the verbs into "quadri-grade(*yodan*)", "mono-grade(*ichidan*)" and "irregular" verbs, where quadri-grade verbs are subclassified into 9 conjugation types by conjugational endings which begin with k, g, r, t, w, b, n, m or s. For example, *kaku* belongs to quadri-grade verbs whose conjugation type is k and *taberu* belongs to mono-grade verbs.

Since almost all of former Japanese morphological analysis systems are based on such Japanese grammars, they need to deal with conjugations of verbs. They use many kinds of techniques to process them so that they are forced to have quite complex morpheme grammars.

On the other hand, there have been another approach, called a phonological approach, which originated with Bloch[1]. In his paper, Japanese verbal variants are considered to be verbal stems followed by verbal suffixes. In the view of morphological analysis, this consideration makes the analysis system quite simple, because both verbal conjugations and subclassification of verbs by conjugational endings become unnecessary. Although, there have been proposed some Japanese grammars based on the phonological approach, derivational grammar[2] which pays attention to agglutinative features of the Japanese language succeeds in dealing with verbal variants including auxiliary verbs systematically.

Also, there are some Japanese morphological analysis systems which is based on derivational grammar[3][4]. However, they modified derivational grammar to use existing systems which assume conjugations of verbs, so that they did not make the best of derivational grammar.

In this paper, we propose a new Japanese morphological analysis system which we call MAJO. By being constructed directly from derivational grammar, MAJO became simpler system than previous ones. In order for the system to be simple, it is desired that the system does not deal with conjugations. For this reason, we analyze morphemes by phonological approach based on derivational grammar. However, pure phonological approach can not analyze sandhi forms and irregular verbs. So, we introduce backward search and supplementation with phonemes which realize an analysis without verbal allomorphs or complicated phonological rules. In results, the connection matrix of MAJO is smaller than the one of previous systems, which means that MAJO has a simple morpheme grammar. MAJO succeeds analysis of EDR corpus[5] with 97.9% ratio.

Our approach is also applicable to other agglutinative languages such as Korean, Uighur and so on, because derivational grammar pays attention to agglutinative features of them.

This paper is organized as follows; Section 2 introduces derivational grammar. In Section 3, the problems when derivational grammar is used for morphological analysis are pointed out and we show how MAJO solves the problems. Features of MAJO in comparison with other systems and evaluations of MAJO by experiments are shown in Section 4 and 5, respectively.

2 Derivational Grammar

The Japanese language is commonly said to be one of agglutinative languages which usually have no conjugations of verbs. Words of the languages are derived

Table 1. Connections between a verbal stem and suffixes

conjugation form in traditional grammar	segmentation in derivational grammar		suffix
imperfect form	*kak-ana-i*	*tabe-na-i*	*-(a)na-i*
	kak-are-ru	*tabe-rare-ru*	*-(r)are-(r)u*
	kak-ase-ru	*tabe-sase-ru*	*-(s)ase-(r)u*
	kak-ou	*tabe-you*	*-(y)ou*
continuative form	*kak-imas-u*	*tabe-mas-u*	*-(i)mas-(r)u*
	kaφ-ita	*tabe-ta*	*-(i)ta*
conclusive form	*kak-u*	*tabe-ru*	*-(r)u*
attributive form	*kak-u*	*tabe-ru*	*-(r)u*
provisional form	*kak-eba*	*tabe-reba*	*-(r)eba*
imperative form	*kak-e*	*tabe-ro*	*-e / -ro,-yo*
	kak-una	*tabe-runa*	*-(r)una*

from other words by adding affixes to invariable stems. That is, there are no internal changes of sounds in agglutinative languages as there are in inflectional languages such as Indo-European.

On the other hand, traditional Japanese grammars say that Japanese verbal stems and suffixes conjugate although Japanese is classified as agglutinative languages. Does Japanese really have conjugations ?

To answer this problem, G. N. Kiyose proposed derivational grammar[2] which claimed Japanese verbs did not conjugate and Japanese verbal variants were made up by appending suffixes to verbal stems. In this section, we explain derivational grammar focusing on verbal formations.

2.1 Union Consonant and Union Vowel

The invariable part of a verb is called a verbal stem. For example, *tabe-* in *tabe-ru* [eat] and *kak-* in *kak-u* [write] are both verbal stems in Japanese. There are two sorts of verbal stems; the one ending with a vowel, e.g. *tabe-*, which is labeled a vowel stem, and the one ending with a consonant, e.g. *kak-*, which is labeled a consonant stem. The verb whose stem is a vowel stem corresponds to the "mono-grade conjugation" verb in traditional grammar and the verb whose stem is a consonant stem corresponds to the "quadri-grade conjugation" verb in traditional grammar. Note that, in case of such verbs as *kaw-u* (romanized as *kau*) [buy], its verbal stem is *kaw-*, which is classified in consonant stems.

Traditional grammars say that Japanese verbs vary in six conjugation forms, viz. "imperfect(*mizen*)", "continuative(*renyou*)", "conclusive(*shuushi*)", "attributive(*rentai*)", "provisional(*katei*)" and "imperative(*meirei*)" forms. On the other hand, derivational grammar says that a verbal variant consists of a verbal stem and some following suffixes. The correspondence between two grammars are shown in Table 1.

As shown in Table 1, the verbal suffixes of *tabe-ru* and *kak-u* are *-ru* and *-u*, respectively. And verbal stems of them are a vowel stem and a consonant stem, respectively. The verbal suffix *-ru* follows only a vowel stem and the suffix *-u* follows only a consonant stem. Derivational grammar says those suffixes are the environmental variants of the suffix *-(r)u*. The consonant *r* appears when appended to a vowel stem and disappears when appended to a consonant stem. A consonant of this kind is called a union consonant.

Verbs *tabe-na-i* [do not eat] and *kak-ana-i* [do not write], are imperfect forms which represent negative actions, the negative verbal suffixes of them are *-na-* and *-ana-*, respectively. Those suffixes are also the variants of the suffix *-(a)na-*. The vowel *a* appears when appended to a consonant stem and disappears when appended to a vowel stem. A vowel of this kind is called a union vowel.

To summarize above, derivational grammar has following two rules about connections between verbal stems and verbal suffixes.

Connection rule 1 : When the suffix beginning with a union consonant is appended to a consonant stem, the union consonant disappears.

Connection rule 2 : When the suffix beginning with a union vowel is appended to a vowel stem, the union vowel disappears.

2.2 Derivational Suffixes and Syntactical Suffixes

As shown Table 1, the negative verbal suffix *-(a)na-* can be followed by other verbal suffixes, for example, *kak-ana-i* [do not write] and *kak-ana-katta* [did not write]. This shows that the verbal suffix appended to verbal stems derives a new stem which is called a secondary stem. The suffixes which derive new stems are called derivational suffixes. The Japanese language has several derivational suffixes, viz. *-(r)are-* which derives passive, potential or honorific secondary stems, *-(s)ase-* which derives causative secondary stems, *-(i)mas-* which derives polite secondary stems, *-(i)ta-* which derives desiderative secondary stems and *-(a)na-* which derives negative secondary stems.

Other verbal suffixes which do not derive new stems are called syntactical suffixes. Syntactical suffixes form various verbal forms, which are classified into finite, participle, converb and imperative forms. For example, the suffix *-(r)u* mentioned in above subsection is a syntactical suffix and it forms a finite form. Japanese verbal stems can follow several suffixes, but syntactical suffixes are always appended last.

2.3 Internal Sandhi Form

The verbal suffix *-(i)ta* is a syntactical suffix which denotes that an action or an movement has been already performed before a certain point of time. For example, *tabe-ta* means 'ate'. There is no problem when *-(i)ta* is appended to a vowel stem, because its union vowel *i* has lost and *-ta* is suffixed as seen in *tabe-ta*. This suffixation is entirely regular. However, problems arise when *-(i)ta*

Table 2. Internal sandhi form of verbs

ending of stem		sandhi form		example
–k	-(i)ta	-ϕ	-ita	ki-ita
–g	-(i)ta	-ϕ	-ida	oyo-ida
–r	-(i)ta			kit-ta
–t	-(i)ta	-t	-ϕta	tat-ta
–w	-(i)ta			kat-ta
–b	-(i)ta			ton'-da
–n	-(i)ta	-n'	-ϕda	sin'-da
–m	-(i)ta			yon'-da
–s	-(i)ta	-s	-ita	kas-ita

A mark ϕ points out vanishing the phoneme
at that position.

is appended to a consonant stem. For example, when -*(i)ta* is appended to *kak-*
, according to regular suffixation, it would be *kak-ita*, but in fact it is *ka-ita*.
This change is internal sandhi and it takes place when -*(i)ta* is appended to
a stem ending with consonants other than *s*. The internal sandhi in this case
always depends on ending consonants of a stem and it follows fixed rules shown
in Table 2.

The only exception to the sandhi rules in Table 2 is a verb *ik-u* [go]. According
to the rules, when appended -*(i)ta*, it would be *iϕ-ita* but in fact *it-ϕta*.

It should be noted here that this regular internal sandhi can apply to the
syntactical verbal suffixes with the initial -*(i)t-* such as -*(i)ta*, -*(i)te*, -*(i)tara*,
-*(i)temo*, etc.

2.4 Irregular Verbs

The aspect in which derivational and syntactical suffixes are appended to the
verbal stems is extremely regular and the appearance or disappearance of union
consonants and union vowels is solely mechanical. However, there are a few
exceptions of those connection rules. Verbs *ku-ru* [come] and *su-ru* [do] are one
of those exceptions called irregular verbs. Derivational grammar says irregular-
verbal stems change forms according to following suffixes. *ku-ru* has 3 forms–*ko-*,
k-, *ku-* and *su-ru* has 4 forms–*se-*, *s-*, *si-*, *su-* and those stems are followed by
suffixes according to the following rules.

Connection rule 3.1 : The suffixes beginning with a union vowel *i* and the
suffixes beginning with a union vowel *u* are appended to a stem *k-* or *s-*.
Connection rule 3.2 : The suffixes beginning with a union consonant *r* are
appended to a stem *ku-* or *su-*.
Connection rule 3.3 : The negative derivational suffix -*(a)na-* and the imperative suffix -*ro* are appended to a stem *si-*.

Connection rule 3.4 : All other suffixes not mentioned above are appended to a stem *ko-* or *se-*.

When verbs that are honorific words showing the speaker's respects to the agent as a referent, namely *nasar-u* [(esteemed one) do], *kudasar-u* [(id.) give to me] and so on are followed by the polite suffix -*(i)mas-*, while still keeping the feature of consonant stems (i.e., while having the union vowel *i* in -*(i)mas-* remain), they regularly delete their stem-final consonant *r* to form *nasaφ-imas-u* [(esteemed one) do, sir], *kudasaφ-imas-u* [(id.) give to me, sir]. These types of verbs are specifically labeled anomalous verbs.

The verb *ar-u* [exist] follows connection rules except that the negative derivational suffix -*(a)na-* is not appended.

3 Morphological Analysis System–MAJO

We propose a new Japanese morphological analysis system based on derivational grammar, which we call MAJO(<u>M</u>orphological <u>A</u>nalyzer of <u>J</u>apanese based <u>O</u>n derivational grammar). MAJO takes phonological approach in order to make the best of derivational grammar. Since Japanese sentences are usually written by kanji and kana, MAJO romanizes the parts written by kana in the sentences to clarify internal structures of verbs.

Derivational grammar was designed for word generation, so that there are some problems when using it for morphological analysis. In this section, we point out the problems and show the solutions on MAJO.

3.1 Parts of Speech and Morpheme Grammar on MAJO

MAJO defines parts of speech by combinations of left connective attributes and right connective attributes. The left/right connective attribute of a part of speech prescribes which morpheme can appear before/after the part of speech. If we define that all verbal stems have same right connective attributes no matter whether those endings are consonants or vowels, we need to deal with disappearance of union consonants and union vowels according to connection rule 1 and 2. In word generation, we make verbal phrases easily according to those rules. In analysis, however, the restoration of union consonants or union vowels is troublesome. Thus, instead of applying connection rule 1 and 2 directly, we also register allomorphs of suffixes into the dictionary in which a union consonant or a union vowel is disappeared. For example, for the non-perfective finite and participle -*(r)u*, we register both -*ru* and -*u*. Similarly, for the negative derivational suffix -*(a)na-*, we register both -*ana-* and -*na-*. We also define two left connective attributes for verbal suffixes— a consonant-stem suffix and a vowel-stem suffix. For example, the left connective attributes of -*ru* and -*na-* are vowel-stem suffixes which means the suffixes can be appended to vowel stems, and those of -*u* and -*ana-* are consonant-stem suffixes which means the suffixes can be appended to consonant stems.

Table 3. Examples of parts of speech used in MAJO

part of speech	left connective attribute	right connective attribute
consonant-stem verb	verb	consonant stem
vowel-stem verb	verb	vowel stem
participle consonant s.s.	consonant-stem suffix	participle
converb consonant s.s.	consonant-stem suffix	converb
participle vowel s.s.	vowel-stem suffix	participle
converb vowel s.s.	vowel-stem suffix	converb
consonant-consonant d.s.	consonant-stem suffix	consonant stem
vowel-consonant d.s.	vowel-stem suffix	consonant stem
consonant-vowel d.s.	consonant-stem suffix	vowel stem
vowel-vowel d.s.	vowel-stem suffix	vowel stem

s.s. = syntactical suffix   d.s. = derivational suffix

Table 4. Connectability matrix in MAJO

	verb	consonant stem suffix	vowel stem suffix	noun	nominal suffix	case suffix
consonant stem	-	5	-	-	-	-
vowel stem	20	-	5	20	-	20
participle	20	-	-	10	-	25
converb	10	-	-	20	-	-
nominal stem	20	-	-	15	5	5
case suffix	10	-	-	10	-	30

MAJO has 24 left connective attributes and 26 right connective attributes whose combinations define 56 parts of speech. Examples of parts of speech used in MAJO are shown in Table 3.

We give the morpheme grammar to MAJO in terms of connectability between left connective attributes and right ones, and add costs to the connectability in order to use the minimum connective-cost method[7]. A part of connectability matrix in MAJO is shown in Table 4. For example, the connective-cost is 5 when a part of speech whose right connective attribute is a consonant-stem is followed by a part of speech whose left connective attribute is a consonant-stem suffix.

3.2 Treatment of Sandhi Forms

MAJO is able to analyze connections between verbal stems and verbal suffixes without conjugation processing. That is, MAJO only checks the connectability matrix. However, as mentioned in section 2.3, since sandhi forms of verbs are irregular, we need specific techniques to deal with them.

Table 5. Supplementing a verbal stem with a consonant

allomorph of suffix	supplementing consonant	word example		
-ita	k	kiita	→	kik-ita
-ida	g	oyoida	→	oyog-ida
-tta	r	kitta	→	kir-tta
	t	tatta	→	tat-tta
	w	katta	→	kaw-tta
-n'da	b	ton'da	→	tob-n'da
	n	sin'da	→	sin-n'da
	m	yon'da	→	yom-n'da
-ita	ϕ	kasita	→	kas-ita

The technique used in previous systems[4] is registration of all allomorphs. For example, allomorphs *ka-* and *kat-*, which correspond to *kak-* and *kaw-* respectively, are registered in the dictionary. Obviously, this technique is simple but needs a vast amount of allomorphs. In contrast, the techniques used in MAJO are backward search and supplementation with phonemes, which does not need to register allomorphs of verbs in the dictionary.

The reason of registration of allomorphs is that sandhi forms of verbs are different from the forms registered in dictionary and not able to be analyzed by pure matching. But, if a verb is searched backward, the allomorph of a suffix can be found before the allomorph of the verb is found. For example, when *kaita* [wrote] is searched backward, *-ita* is found first. In case of verbal phrases ending with verbal suffix *-ita*, backward search would find *-ita*, *-ida*, *-tta* or *-n'da* which are shown in Table 2. Then MAJO supplements the verbal stem with a consonant which would be disappeared according to Table 5. This process is illustrated in Figure 1. Although there are several consonants with which the verbal stem can be supplemented for allomorphs *-tta* and *-n'da*, in this case, MAJO supplements the stem with each consonant and selects an appropriate verb by checking the dictionary.

Note that, this process does not need verbal allomorphs. Although allomorphs of verbal suffixes are needed as mentioned in section 2.3, such allomorphs are limited to the syntactical suffixes which begin with *-(i)t-*. Thus only a few allomorphs are registered in the dictionary. In addition, *ik-u* [go] is irregular at sandhi. Since there are few such irregular verbs, we registered an allomorph *it-* into the dictionary.

3.3 Treatment of Irregular Verbs

As mentioned in section 2.4, stems of irregular verbs are varied and can not be analyzed in the similar way. To overcome this problem, MAJO registers allomorphs of irregular verbal stems. However, if *k-* or *s-*, which consists of one

```
kaita              backward search
   ←
            ⇓
ka + ita           found -ita
            ⇓
ka k̲ + ita         supplemented with a consonant k for -ita
            ⇓
kak + ita          analyzed as "kak-" + "-ita"
```

Fig. 1. Processing of internal sandhi by MAJO

phoneme, is registered, the number of analysis patterns will increase and analysis will not be efficient. So, MAJO registers allomorphs *ko-*, *ku-* and *ki-* for verb *ku-ru* [come] and registers *se-*, *su-* and *si-* for verb *su-ru* [do]. For example, *kita* [came] is analyzed as *ki-ta* not as *k-ita*. Thus, all allomorphs of irregular verbal stems end with vowels and MAJO registers those as vowel-stem verbs. In this approach, the connection rules from 3.1 to 3.4 mentioned in section 2.4 are not considered, but these rules are only needed for word generation. For analysis, the sentences which deviate from these rules are considered not to appear and MAJO does not deal with these rules.

The Japanese language has other verbs that vary irregularly. Verb *ik-u* [go] is irregular about sandhi form and anomalous verbs are irregular when a verbal suffix which begins with vowel *i* is appended. But, there are few verbs that classified as those kinds. For example, in EDR Japanese dictionary[5], which contains 26,091 verbs as a whole, only 14 verbs which are the kind sort as *ik-u* and only 18 anomalous verbs appear. Thus, we registered the allomorphs of those verbs into MAJO. Also, verb *ar-u* is irregular because derivational suffix *-(a)na-* does not append it. But irregular variants such as *aranai* does not exist in the Japanese language, so we don't consider this irregularity.

4 Characteristic Features of MAJO

In this section, we describe the characteristic features of MAJO in comparison with other morphological analysis systems.

4.1 Treatment of Word Variation

The analysis of *kakaseraretagatta* [wanted to be caused to write] by JUMAN[6] and MAJO are shown in Figure 2 and Figure 3, respectively.

JUMAN is a popular morphological analysis system which assumes verbal conjugations. Its dictionary has verbal stems and conjugation types of them. Finding a verb in an input sentence, JUMAN supplements the sentence with candidates for conjugational endings according to its conjugation type and decides a conjugation form by comparing with the input sentence.

input word	part-of-speech	conjugation type	conjugation form
kaka	verb	consonant verb type *ka* (*ka-gyo*)	imperfect form
se	verbal suffix	vowel verb	imperfect form
rare	verbal suffix	vowel verb	basic attributive form
ta	adjectival predicative suffix	*i*-adjective *a,o,u*	stem
gatta	verbal suffix	consonant verb type *ra* (*ra-gyo*)	*ta* form

Fig. 2. An example of analysis by JUMAN[6]

word	part of speech
kak-	consonant-stem verb
-ase-	consonant-vowel d.s.
-rare-	vowel-vowel d.s.
-ta-	vowel-qualitative d.s.
-gar-	qualitative-consonant d.s.
-tta	participle consonant s.s.

Fig. 3. An example of analysis by MAJO

On the other hand, MAJO does not need to decide conjugation forms, because it is based on derivational grammar and does not assume verbal conjugations. MAJO can analyze input sentences by checking the connectabilities between two morphemes. But, when MAJO finds an allomorph of suffixes, it has to supplement a verbal stem with a consonant.

Compared these two systems, MAJO needs less supplementing processing than JUMAN. JUMAN always needs the supplementation whenever it finds verbs, while MAJO needs the supplementation only when it finds allomorphs of verbal suffixes. In addition, the number of candidates for supplements is greater than 10 in JUMAN, but at most 3 in MAJO.

4.2 Complexity of Morpheme Grammar

Compared MAJO with JUMAN on the morpheme grammar, JUMAN needs connection rules for each conjugation form, while MAJO does not need such trivial rules since assuming no conjugations.

The size of the connection matirx, which are usually used as a measure for complexity of morpheme grammar, is 195×165 in JUMAN. At the approach which apply derivational grammar to JUMAN[3], the size of connextion matirx is improved to be 63×71. But MAJO is simpler than those systems, in fact, the size of connextion matirx is 24×26 .

The morphological analysis systems usually use minimum connective-cost method[7] which assigns costs to each connection rule. When the method used, we need to adjust connective-costs. MAJO also has an advantage at this point, because it has smaller number of connection rules.

4.3 The Number of Words in the Dictionary

The method which uses derivatinal grammar for syntactical analysis[4] deals with sandhi forms by registration of verbal allomorphs. Although this method makes the action of the system simple, it needs a vast number of verbal allomorphs. For example, when using EDR Japanese dictionary[5] which contains 26,091 verbs(include 14,353 consonant verbs), this method needs 9,247 verbal allomorphs. And it also needs additional connection rules for each verbal allomorph, which makes the morhological grammar more complicated.

On the other hand, MAJO analyze sandhi forms by backward search and supplementation with a consonant, so it needs only allomorphs of suffixes. In fact, MAJO has only 40 allomorphs for processing of sandhi forms. In addition, MAJO does not need additional rules because supplemented verbal stems are the same form as normal verbal stems and follow normal rules.

4.4 Treatment of Colloquial Expressions

The Japanese language has many colloquial expressions which deviate from traditional grammars for literary expressions. MAJO can deal with colloquial expressions easily because it uses phonological approach. Especially, MAJO can deal with many of those by adding one morpheme for each colloquial expression. For example, the colloquial expression such as *tabereru* [can be eaten] is known as *ra-nuki kotoba* [lacking *ra* expression], while the regular expression of that is *taberareru*. MAJO can analysis these expressions by only registration of a derivational suffix *-(r)e-* into the dictionary.

MAJO can also analysis other colloquial expressions such as *kak-as-u* and *tabe-sas-u*, whose regular expressions are *kak-ase-ru* and *tabe-sase-ru* respectively, by registration of a derivational suffix *-(s)as-*.

5 Experiments

We used 1,000 sentences from EDR Japanese Corpus[5] to evaluate performance of MAJO. Since MAJO uses minimum connective-cost method[7], we adjust the connective-costs by hand. We compared the results of analysis by MAJO with the one by hand.

We use an error ration as a measure of performance. It is calculated as dividing the number of word segmentations which assigned wrong part of speech tags by the number of total word segmentations. We compared performance of MAJO with two other systems[8][3] as shown in Table 6. This shows that MAJO can analyze Japasese sentences as correctly as former morphological analysis systems, in spite of having the simple grammar and the simple system.

Table 6. Comparison of morphological analysis systems

system	input sentences	morphemes	wrong assignments	error ratio
MAJO	1,000	25,082	522	2.08%
Maruyama[8]	1,016	29,024	687	2.36%
Fuchi[3]	10,000	207,547	2,040	0.98%

6 Conclusion

In this paper we proposed a new Japanese morphological analysis system MAJO. MAJO is based on derivational grammar and makes the best use of simpleness of the grammar. In addition, MAJO eliminates complicated grammar rules of verbal variants by registration of some allomorphs and supplementation with phonemes.

Since derivational grammar pays attention to agglutinative features of the Japanese language, MAJO is applicable to morphological analysis of other agglutinative languages such as Korean, Uighur and so on, and be used for machine translation between these languages. We are studying of machine translation from Japanese to Uighur by using MAJO and the detail is described elsewhere[9].

References

1. Bloch, B.: Studies in Colloquial Japanese, Part I, Inflection, Journals of the American Oriental Society, Vol. 66 (1946).
2. Kiyose, G. N.: Japanese grammar –A new approach–, Kyoto university press, Japan (1995).
3. Fuchi, T. and Yonezawa, M.: A morpheme grammar for Japanese Morphological Analyzers, Journal of Natural Language Processing, Vol. 2, No. 4, pp. 37–65 (1995).
4. Nishino, H., Washikita, K. and Ishii N.: Syntax analysis of Japanese Sentences using Derivational Grammar, IPSJ SIG Notes, NL 87-6, pp. 43–50 (1992).
5. EDR: EDR Electronic Dictionary version 1.5 Technical Guide (1996).
6. Matsumoto, Y., Kurohashi, S., Utsuro T., Myoki, Y. and Nagao, M.: Japanese Morphological Analysis System JUMAN Manual version 3.0, Nara Institute of Science and Technology (1996).
7. Hisamitsu, N., Nitta, Y.: Morphological Analysis by Minimum Connective-Cost Method, IEICE Technical Report, NLC 90-8, pp. 17–24 (1990).
8. Maruyama, H. and Ogino, S.: Japanese Morphological Analysis Based on Regular Grammar, Transactions of Information Processing Society of Japan, Vol. 35, No. 7, pp. 1293–1299 (1994).
9. Ogawa, Y., Muhtar, Toyama, K. and Inagaki, Y.: Japanese-Uighur Machine Translation based on Derivational Grammar —A Translation of Verbal Suffixes—, IPSJ SIG Notes, NL 120-1, pp. 1–6 (1997).

An Automatic Thai Lexical Acquisition from Text

Chuleerat Jaruskulchai

Department of Computer Science, Faulty of Science, Kasetsart University,
Bangkok, Thailand
fscichj@nontri.ku.ac.th

Abstract. The Thai writing system has no natural marks to indicate words or sentences. This is one of the causes for many machine leaning researches including the automatic indexing in Information Retrieval to identify keywords for searching. A new method for constructing lexicons from a corpus text is presented. This method is based on the basic Thai morphologies and Bayesian networks concept. The Bayesian networks are based on the well-known minimal description length (MDL) principle. The MDL concepts allow us to construct the Thai lexicons and are used for segmenting the Thai texts. The segmentation effectiveness in terms of recall/precision is 59/51 while the effectiveness of dictionary procedure has 71/54 of recall/precision. However, this new algorithm does not require any lexicon patterns for training.

1 Introduction

The Thai writing system, like the Chinese and the Japanese system, has no delimiters to indicate word boundaries. There is a space in the written texts, but this space is not used to determine the end of a word, a phrase or a sentence. However, the Thai word formation is similar to English. Determining the word boundary, most research is done by consulting a dictionary. This is not practical in many computer research areas, especially in Information Retrieval, since it is costly to maintain, and the domain of vocabularies is changed from application to application. Even with vocabularies, the segmentation ambiguity still can not be fully solved. Additionally, in information retrieval systems, it is not necessary to get perfect segmentation. The Chinese and the Japanese Text Retrieval systems use bi-gram mutual information to determine a keyword search [1]. In [2], however, it was shown that the number of consecutive character of the n-gram for Thai Text retrieval is 4 which is not effective in both space and time complexity.

Generally, the previous works of segmentation can be classified into pure dictionary, morphology and statistical approaches. The primitive dictionary approach is simply the table lookup [4], [5], [8]. There are some variations of the algorithms for solving the segmentation ambiguity such as longest match or backtracking. In the morphological approach, most of the segmentation is achieved in the syllable level. Recently, the statistical and dictionary approaches are incorporated in order to solve the segmentation ambiguity, for example, by applying word frequencies [4] or Markov model [5].

Other Asian segmentation schemes are more varied. However, most of them still require some lexicon patterns, heuristics' rule or morphology for learning the word patterns. The Chinese word segmentation presented by Sproat et al. [11] also incorporate lexical knowledge, morphologies and stochastic finite-state. Another probabilistic automaton proposed by Ponte and Croft [7] also requires lexicons to obtain the statistics.

The pure statistical segmentation has shortcomings in that it lacks of linguistic knowledge. For example, some of the orthographies can not be segmented without some well-defined orthography preceding or following. In fact, Thai word formations are very unique. The word formations are similar to English in that Thai words are composed of consonants and vowels but without inflection and tense. Thai grammar in [6 pp. 59] states that Thai words are also similar to Chinese words but the writing system is not pictograph. Learning of the Thai language starts from understanding where the sounds come from. Then symbols for representing sounds are taught. The basic monosyllable words are also taught. The more complicated words are formed by combing the monosyllable words. In this last step, human beings have to accumulate his/her previous knowledge to determine where the word boundaries are. In some degree, humans have to read the whole phrase and pre-process it with their previous knowledge to determine the word boundaries from the contexts.

This work emulated the human learning processes. Texts are segmented by the morphological rules, then forming the more complicated words is determined by statistics. The minimal description length (MDL) [14] is used to construct the Thai lexicons' network. The number of states' model can be treated as number of monosyllables for combining a compound word. Therefore, our objective is to distribute the basic monosyllables into different states with satisfying the MDL criteria.

In this paper, a brief basic background of the characteristic of Thai written texts is discussed. The Bayesian statistical concepts which are used to form the problem formulation will be discussed in Section 3. In Section 4, an algorithm for learning the structure and parameters model for the lexicons is presented. The final results are reported in Section 5.

2 Characteristics of Thai Written Text and Related Research

The Thai writing system has its root from the ancient Indian Bhrami and the Thai written texts are done in a sequence of continuous symbols with no natural word boundary or any sentence marker similar with other Asian languages. However, there exists spaces in the written text. These spaces are used by the writers to emphasis the content, and there is no exact rule how to use these spaces. Nonetheless, if space is used in a wrong place, the interpretation will be different.

The basic word formation is based on the phonetic rules. The smallest linguistic unit in Thai is called syllable. The syllable may or may not have a certain meaning. In general, a syllable must consist of at least three different phonemes, an initial consonant, vowel and tonemic phoneme. Each syllable also can be added the a fourth phoneme which is called the final or ending consonant. However, if the ending phoneme does not want to be pronounced, it can be canceled by placing cancellation mark at the ending phoneme. Furthermore, the initial and final consonant can be represented by double consonant phoneme (Fig.1, the first case). It is not necessary that these double consonants have to be pronounced every phoneme.

Most original Thai words are monosyllables. However, Thai words also are formed by combining monosyllables to form compound words. Since Thai has no inflection and tense, the word structure may be in the form of noun + noun, noun + verb, or noun + verb + object (See Fig. 2). These word structures make it more difficult to detect the sentence.

IC	V	T	FC	Word	Meaning
กล	ใ	-	-	ใกล้	near
จ	ะ	-	-	จะ	may
พ	เ-ื่อ	-	-	เพื่อ	for
พ	เ-ื่อ	-	น	เพื่อน	friend

Fig. 1. An Example of Thai Words, where IC is initial consonant, V is vowel, T is tone marker and FC is Final Consonant.

Compound words	Word	Meaning
ปัญญาประดิษฐ์	ปัญญา (ปัญ/ญา) /intellect, ประดิษฐ์ (ประ/ดิษฐ์)/ to invent	Artificial Intelligence
เครื่องเย็บผ้า	เครื่อง /machine, เย็บ / sew, ผ้า / cloth	Sewing machine

Fig. 2. Thai Compound Words

The Thai writing system is also an alphabetic system similarly to the English writing system. Usually, the alphabetic system represents each phoneme by a single character. In the Thai writing system, not all phonemes are represented by a single character. Some of the vowel phoneme is represented by four characters. Furthermore, some phonemes may not require any character for representing their phoneme due to the reduction grammar rules. In general, the minimum number of characters for a word appearance is two, with one of them being a consonant[1].

There are 44 symbols for representing the 20 consonant phonemes. Nineteen symbols are used to construct the 32 vowel phonemes. Finally, four symbols is used for five tonemic phonemes where one of them does not required a symbol. Consonants can be placed before, after or in between the vowel sound as shown in Fig. 1.

Despite of the inconsistencies between the phonology and writing system, the Thai linguistics and computer experts had compiled a set of morphological rules to detect the word boundaries [3], [6], [9], [10]. However, the morphological rules are achieved in the syllabic level.

Most of the machine learning community determines the word boundaries by using the dictionary [4], [5], [8]. Practically, the process of segmentation is simply matching the sequence of string text into words. Various dictionary approaches have been proposed; however, none of them can achieve the perfect segmentation. More importantly, lexicons are changed from application to application, and therefore it is very time consuming to build the dictionary.

However, the segmentation process is more difficult due to the language itself. The sequence of string text can be segmented in different ways. For example, "โคลง" can consider as a verb or a sentence in which a sentence can be segmented into two words. Both morphological rules and dictionary give the same results.

In this research, the Thai morphological rules were compiled from the previous research [3],[6], [10]. The double consonants rules are also vigorously checked. More details our morphological rules can be found in [12]. Nonetheless, the monosyllables which are segmented according to our Thai morphological rules, do not necessary to get prefect segmentation. For example, the compound noun "น้ำมันแบบอื่น" can be segmented as shown in Fig. 3, and the correct segmentation should be in case 1 and 2.

However, the case 3 get the corrected segmentation but no related to meaning to the original word. Furthermore, each monosyllable word can be placed in any positions to form compound words as shown in Fig.4. From these examples, the Bayesian Networks is used to construct a lexicon network. The compound words are explored by utilized the minimal description length as depicted in Fig. 5.

3 Automatic Lexical Acquisition From Text

In this section, the definition of Thai text segmentation and the basic concept for statistics are discussed. The basic concept of Bayesian networks can be found in [17]. A complete foundation for understanding information theory also be found in [18].

3.1 Problems definition

The problem of automatic lexical acquisition from text can be stated as follows. Given any text, a word, a phrase or a sentence, $< T_s >$, is segmented by Thai grammar into $(m_1,...,m_j)$. Each m_j will be placed in the left-to-right model as shown in Fig. 6. The algorithm will learn the number of states in the model and also the possible values in each state. Therefore, a compound word will be formed in $<m_{i1}, m_{i2},..., m_{ik}>$ where k is a number of monosyllable words. However, at the end of each m_{ij} may be a word which has a certain meaning as well. In this case, it means that the next monosyllable is a null value. The unseen monosyllable at each state also handle with some degree.

The Bayesian networks concept is used to construct the model for automatic acquisition Thai lexicons. A Bayesian network is annotated directed acyclic graph that encodes joint probabilities' distribution of a set of random variables. Formally, the notation of Bayesian Networks is written as $B(\Theta, M_h)$, where M_h is structure of the network, and Θ is a set of parameters that encode the local probability distribution. The joint probability distribution for the lexicons in Thai writing system can be encoded in some network structure. The joint probability distribution this network is given as follow:

$$p(s|\theta_M, M_h) = \prod_{i=1}^{n} p(s_i|pa_i, \theta_i, M_h) .$$ (1)

Where n is a number of states or number of monosyllables to compose a word.

Finding the best network in order to fit the training data is based on the principle of minimal description length (MDL) [14]. The MDL measure the model structure in the information theory in that the best model must satisfy the minimum of (1) the encoding of the model size and (2) the encoding of the model given data as shown in Eq. (2).

$$Acc(P, P_M^*) = \sum_i (v(s_i) * v(ps_i)) + E(s_i|ps_i) .$$ (2)

Where $v(s_i)$ is the possible values of state i and $v(ps_i)$ is the possible values of its previous state. The second term in Eq. (2) is measured of the uncertainly contents of an information and was original proposed by Shannon [19] and define as

$$E(s_i|ps_i) = \sum_{s_i, ps_i} P(s_i, ps_i) * \log_2 P(s_i|ps_i) .$$ (3)

1	น้ำมันเบนซิน/Gasoline, petrol			
2	น้ำมัน/Gasoline, fuel, oil		เบนซิน/Gasoline, petrol	
3	น้ำ/water	มัน/fat, yams	เบน/no meaning	ซิน/ no meaning
4	น้ำ/water	มัน/fat, yams	เบ/ no meaning	นซิน/no meaning

Fig. 3. The Possible Segmentation for 'น้ำมันเบนซิน'

Words	Meaning	Monosyllable
น้ำร้อน	hot water	น้ำ-water, ร้อน-hot
กาน้ำ	a kettle	กา-a crow, น้ำ-water
กระโดดน้ำ	water jumping	กระ-spotted, โดด- jump, น้ำ-water, กระโดด-jump

Fig. 4. Examples of a Monosyllable Word Which Can Be Placed in Any Places

1. Original string เบนซินธรรมดา (Regular Gas soline), เบนซินพิเศษ (Super Gas)

2. Segmented by Morphological เบน/ซิน/ธรรม/ดา/พิ/เศษ/ and the initial mode has probability $P(X|M_0) = -16\log 2$

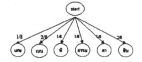

3. Connected nodes according to their probability and $pP(X|M_1) = -4 \log 2$

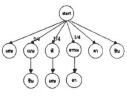

4. Model M_2 with $P(X|M_2) = -3 \log 3$

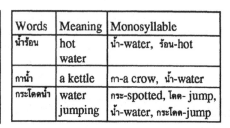

5. Model M_3 with $P(X|M_3) = -2 \log 2$

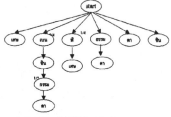

Fig. 5. Sequence of Constructing the Dictionary Model

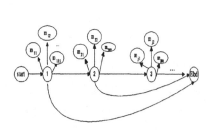

Fig. 6. Bayesian Net for Acquiring Lexicons.

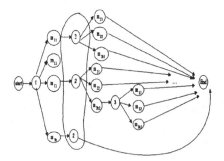

Fig. 7. Details of Bayesian Net with Their Previous Values.

Where $E(s_i|ps_i)$ is conditional probability of the true model. In theory, the smallest of $E(s_i|ps_i)$ is more certainly contents of an information. In practice, the true model is unknown. Since this formula is a measurement of the best model given data, the best constructed model should give the closest number to the true model. Thus, this measure can be calculated in the form of cross entropy or Kullback-Leibler cross entropy.

$$Dist_L(P,P_M) = \sum_{s \in sate} p(s)\log_2 \frac{P(s)}{P_M(s)} \; . \tag{4}$$

Where P_M is the distribution of training model. In general, if the training model is the same as the true model, the $Dist_L(P,P_M)$ will be zero. However, this measure will be left for users to decide how large a distance is acceptable in the model. Therefore, the equation Eq.2 can be rewritten as

$$Acc(P,P_M{}^*) = \sum_i v(s_i) * v(ps_i) + Dist(P,P_M{}^*) \; . \tag{5}$$

It had been proved in [14] that $Dist(P,P_M{}^*)$ will be minimized if and only if

$\sum_{s=1,ps_i \neq 0}^{n} M(s_i,ps_i)$ is maximized. Where $\sum_{s=1,ps_i \neq 0}^{n} M(s_i,ps_i)$ is the mutual information between any random variable and its parents. This mutual information is the relation of the monosyllable k and its parents.

$$E(x_i^k|ps_i) = \sum_j P(x_i^k,ps_i^j)\log_2 \frac{P(x_i^k,ps_i^j)}{P(x_i^k) * P(ps_i^j)} \; . \tag{6}$$

Thus, the prior structure is constructed from the relation of the monosyllables which give the highest MDL score and with the minimum increasing of model entropy. The initial parameters have Dirichlet distribution :

$$p(\theta_{ij}|\zeta) = Dir(\theta_{ij}|\alpha_{ij1},...,\alpha_{ijr_i}) \; . \tag{7}$$

Where r_i is number of all possible values at state i, and are discovered at the time of being constructed the model and θ_{ij} are the vector model parameters. Thus, the probability for seeing word k at state i having seen word j is defined as :

$$\theta_{ijk} = \frac{\alpha_{ijk}}{\alpha_{ij}} \; . \tag{8}$$

Where α_{ijk} is also discovered at the time of being constructed the model.

In summarize, corpus text is segmented by using Thai morphological rules. Then relationship between any two monosyllables is calculated using Eq. (6) These relationships are used to initial the model. Decision for extending the word length will consider from the Eq.(5). The model parameters are also initialized by Eq.(8). The next section will describe the training and recognizing algorithms.

3.2 Training and Recognizing

When the initial model is constructed, concept of sequential update of Bayesian Networks [15] and conjugate priors are used to refine the parameters. The network structure will be extended according to the new score.

In the process of refining the parameters, the new observation N_{ijk}, can not be directly obtained from the training data since word boundaries do not appear in the training data. The algorithm which is similar to the stack decoding [16] is used to search through all possible word boundaries of a given phrase. The new observation (N_{ijk}) will be estimated from the expectation with respect to the joint distribution on the configuration of θ_M and known data. This formula is given as :

$$E_{p(x|y_l,\theta_M,M_h)}(N_{ijk}) = P(x_i^k, pa_i^j|y_l, \theta_M, M_h) \ . \tag{10}$$

Since word boundaries and correct word patterns can not be obtained, all possible words from the stack decoding algorithm will be assumed correct words. Thus, the expectation of the new observation will be normalized according to the data.

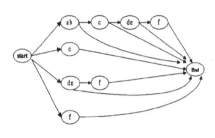

abcdef	4 monosyllables word
abc/def	each of them comprises of 2 monosyllables
abc/de/f	3 words, where abc is 2 monosyllable word
abcde/f	2 words, where abcde is 3 monosyllable words
ab/c/def	3 words, where def is 2 monosyllable words
ab/c/de/f	4 words where each word is one monosyllable word

Fig. 8. Sample Topology of Phrase "abcdef"   **Fig. 9.** All Possible Segmented for "abcdef"

3.2.1 Searching All the Possible Paths

Since model is not constructed from the word patterns and no further knowledge for consideration the possible word strings, all possible paths for segmentation are explored. Thus a phrase can be segmented in different ways depending on the model topology. At the same time, a word may be formed from the different monosyllables. For example, word strings 'abcde' might come the different monosyllables patters, 'ab' + ' cde', 'abc' + 'de' or 'abcd' + 'e'. In the second case, it is not difficult to solve due to the TRIE data structure which is a special kind of data structure. Stack linguistic decoding [16] algorithm is used to explore all possible paths.

First, the shortest words are extracted and put in a stack. The stack is a data structure which can be insert at any entries as shown in Fig. 10. A word which starts at a new position will be inserted in a vertical stack. In contrast, a word starts at the same position as other words in stack will be horizontally inserted. Backward search starts at the second last of the top stack, and explore differently longer word pattern. If there exists a longer word pattern and the successive word starts with different symbols from the stack, the process will continue search new word pattern and search until the end of phrase. The new word pattern will be inserted according to the word order in a given phrase.

For example, in Fig. 10, a word is longer than 'ab' is 'abc' and will be horizontally inserted in stack after word 'ab'. The successive word 'abc' is already in the stack, therefore no needs to search for the next word. On the other hand, a word is longer than 'c' is 'cd'. The successive word of 'cd' may be 'e' or 'ef' will be vertically inserted after word 'de' and move word 'f' to the end of stack as shown in 10.d.

Search all possible paths does not apply any cost function for considering the most likely path, since the characteristic of word pattern and model differ from the speech recognition application. However, the computation is feasible and the worse case for this algorithm is $(1+n)/2$ where n is the string length.

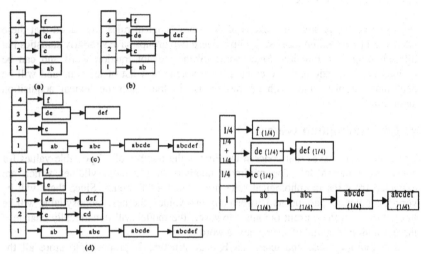

Fig. 10. The Sequence of Finding All the Possible Paths

Fig. 11. An Example of Normalization Factor.

3.2.2 Search the Most likely Path

In the algorithm for search all possible path, every time step that gets new word, the mostly word in the horizontal stack will be recalculated. For example, in Figure 10, every word in Fig.10. a gets a highest probability. When in (b), a new word insert at state 3, these two words in this state will be recalculated the probability and marked the one that gives the highest probability.

When the all possible paths have been discovered, search the most likely path simply searches horizontal in the stack and looks for a word which has been marked. The process continues vertical search for the next word.

3.2.3 Updating Parameters

Search all possible paths increases a number of shortest word length in each phrase. For example, word 'f' in Fig.10.c appears more than three times than word 'abcdef'. In stead to update using the expectation of the joint distribution using Eq.10, the expectation of this joint distribution of each word will be multiplied by normalization factor to equalize the segmentation paths at each stack. For example, the possible segmentation for 'abcdef' as shown in Fig. 9 and stack decoding in Fig. 10.c. will be normalized by multiplied with ¼ as shown in Fig. 11.

The procedure to calculate the normalization factor is follows:

1. Normalization factor at the being stack is assigned to 1. Each branch to the being of word is equal to normalization factor divides by number of branch.
2. The normalization factor at each word will be update to the successor word at next stack.

3.3 Adding Knowledge

We examine the preliminary tokens of the morphological rules and found that these tokens can be classified into two groups. These two groups have similarly statistics but different linguistic function. Since some tokens are not fraction word and can be defined the linguistic unit, we created these tokens as a list of lexicons and will be determine linguistic unit with no further use in the automatic lexical acquisition algorithm.

4. Implementation Issues

There are many issues that concern us. First is the number of all possible values for constructing the model. The minimum numbers of the monosyllables which are extracted from the morphological rules are around 4200 values. Since there will be very few potential parameters between any two values, the next monosyllable will be limited only on the current outputs. However, the model will dynamically change if there is a high potential of seeing next a word.

The multi-variable characters TRIE data structure is proposed to store all the related parameters. This TRIE helps us to reduce the number of step to recalculate the model probability. The full algorithm can be found in [12]. A single hash table is used to look up the starting search in the TRIE data structure.

The next issue is the calculation of the probabilistic model in which the values are closed to zero. Instated of calculating probabilities, the log probabilities are used. Therefore, each time, the multiplication of the path probabilities is simply done by adding the logarithms.

5 Results and Discussion
5.1 Available Text

The data set is downloaded from the Internet. Mostly the text contents are in the Thai current social, economic, and foreign affairs from the Thai news, the *Daily News*. Some of the foreign words, for example, foreign names and places are transliterated to Thai scripts.

This data set is hand segmented by an expert into two sets: longest hand-segmented and shortest hand-segmented. The shortest hand-segmented are segmented text into the smallest unit where the smallest unit still has related meaning to the original meaning. For example, words in Fig. 2. will be segmented into the smallest unit as its shown second column for the shortest hand-segmentation. On the other hand, longest hand-segmented words are a group of words that use to represented a specific object or abstract idea as shown in the first column in Fig. 2. The basic characteristic of the hand segmented text is shown in Fig 12.

	Shortest words	Longest words
Number of sentences	16,957	16,957
Number of words	66,298	65,249
Number of unique words	6,307	6,591
Average words per a phrase	3.91	3.85
Average character per word	5.14	5.22
Average frequency per word	10.51	10.01
No. of term with frequency equal to 1	45%	46%

Incorrect	ราย/งา/นรา/คา/ชาย/ปลี่/ก น้ำ/มัน/สำ/เร็จ/รูป
Correct	ราย/งาน/รา/คา/ชาย/ปลีก/น้ำ/มัน/สำ/เร็จ/รูป
Incorrect	ล้าน/เม/ตริ/กตัน
Correct	ล้าน/เม/ตริก/ตัน

Fig. 12. Characteristics of the Hand Segmented Thai News

Fig. 13. An Example of Morphological Ambiguity

5.2 Morphological Correctness

In this section, the effectiveness of the morphological rules which are used to segmented before applying the statistics is evaluated. As demonstrated in [12], the morphological rules can not be covered every case. In this studies, it is observed the double consonants are not limited in a specific set of the Thai double consonants rules. Therefore, a list of double consonants is created and added to the morphological rules. As a result, the algorithm failed the detect the final consonant as shown in Fig. 15.

Another constraint is the minimum monosyllable length. It is observed that the morphological rules have tendency to produce one character syllable. This phenomenon is effected from the Pali and Sanskrit words which have their root from the Indian language. As a result, the two characters monosyllable is added to the rules.

These constraint also caused a segmentation ambiguity; however, it is not clear that it effected the segmentation algorithm. If Pali or Sanskrit words are segmented according to the Thai morphological rules, they might be combined later on when constructing the model. It might have side effect. However, we did not examine theirs errors here.

The segmentation effectiveness of morphological rules is compared with the syllable hand segmented files. The comparison is 90% of recall and 91% of precision. Additionally, the effectiveness is compared with the shortest hand segmented words. The morphological rules can be able to segment text with 56% of recall and 34% of precision.

5.3 Experiment Results

The general evaluation is done by comparing our results with the results of "Useg" which is borrowed from the University of Massachusetts [7] Amherst. The Useg is constructed using lexicons from the Thai dictionary and obtained the parameters from the data set in our algorithm. The results are compared with the hand-segmented data sets using recall and precision. The results of our algorithm are not much different from the Useg.

5.4 Error Analysis

Fig. 16 shows the segmentation errors from the different approaches. All the example words shown in this figure are appeared in the dictionary train text for the Useg which should be able to detect. As we stated earlier that the statistical word-based lack of the linguistic knowledge, therefore the tokens which are extracted the statistical word-based is not useable.

Judges	Recall/Precision
Syllable Hand-segmented	90/91
Shortest word Hand-segmented	56/34

Fig. 14. Morphological Correctness

Methods	LHS	Dict.	Useg	BayN
SHS	96/98	71/54	69/43	59/51
LHS		70/52	69/42	57/50
Dict.			61/50	53/63
Useg.				37/53

Fig. 15. Recall/Precision Ratio from Different Segmentation Methods.

Corrected Segmentation	Dictionary Approach	Useg	BayNet	Morphology	Meaning in English
รั่วไหล	รั่ว / ไหล	รั้ /-้ / า /ไหล	รั่ว/ไหล	รั่ว/ไหล	to leak
เร่งระดม	เร่ง/ ระดม	เร/-้ /ง/ ระด/ ม	เร่ง/ระดม	เร่ง/ระ/ดม	to mobilize
วิจัย	วิจัย	วิจ/-้/ย	วิ/จัย	วิ/จัย	to research
อำเภอ	อำเภอ	อ/้า/เ/ภ/อ	อำเภอ	อำ/เภอ	an administrative sub-division of province
อุปกรณ์	อุปกรณ์	อุ/ปก/ร/ณ์/	อุป/กรณ์	อุป/กรณ์	Equipment

Fig. 16. The Segmentation Errors from Different Approaches.

6. Conclusion

We have shown that Thai writing system has its own unique problems. Only the statistic method can not achieve the Thai segmentation problems. The basic linguistics still play an important part for the segmentation problem.

We presented a new approach for segmentation Thai text. Our approach incorporated the linguistic and new statistical technique. The performance results are reasonable. Our approach is able to learn new lexicons with the minimum word patterns. This approach will contribute to the information retrieval since the most importance in the information retrieval are the retrieval effectiveness. Therefore, one of our future work, the retrieval performance will be investigated.

There a number of approach in Bayesian net can be refined the model and parameters. More complicated language model might be added to improve the segmentation instead only lexicons patterns.

References

1. Chen A., He J., Xu L., Gey F., and Meggs J., Chinese Text Retrieval Without Using a Dictionary, Proc. of the 20th Annual International ACM SIGIR Conference on Research and Development in Information Retrieval, Philadelphia, Pennsylvania, USA, July 27- July 31, 97, pp. 42 - 49.

2. Jaruskulchai C. Thai Text Retrieval: Simply Term Weight and Basic Thai Morphological Rules, Technical Report, Dept. of Computer Science, George Washington University, USA, Jan, 1998.

3. Shibayama M. and Hoshino S., Thai Morphological Analyses Based on the Syllable Formation Rules, Journal of Information Processing, Vol. 15, No. 4, pp. 554- 563, 1992.

4. Varakulsiripunth R., Suchichit W., Juwan S., and Thipchaksurat S., An Analysis on Correct Sentence Selection by Word's General Usage Frequency, Papers on Natural Language Processing: Multi-lingual Machine Translation and Related Topics (1987-1994), pp. 291-300, 1994.

5. Kawtrakul A., Thumkanon C. and Seriburi S., A Statistical Approach to Thai Word Filtering, Proc. SNLP'95, The 2nd Symposium on Natural Language Processing, pp.398-406, August 2-4, 1995, Bangkok, Thailand.

6. Phraya Uphakit Silapasan, Thai Grammar, Reprinted in 1989. (อำมาตย์เอก พระยาอุปกิตศิลปสาร 'หลักภาษา ไทย - อักษรวิธี วจีวิภาค วากยสัมพันธ์ ฉันทลักษณ์ พ.ศ. 2461)

7. Jay M. Ponte and W. Bruce Croft, Useg: A Retargetable Word Segmentation Procedure for Information Retrieval, Computer Science Department Amherst, MA, USA.

8. Somlertlamvanich V., Word Segmentation for Thai in Machine Translation System, National Electronics and Computer Technology Center, National Science Technology Development Agency, Ministry of Science, Technology and Environment (In Thai).

9. Vilas Wuwongse and Ampai Pornprasertaskul, Thai syntax Parsing, Proceedings of the Symposium on Natural Language Processing in Thailand, pp. 446-467, 11-17 Mar, 1993.

10. Sinthupunprathum D. and Buntitanon T (เดือน สินธุพันธ์ประทุม และ ชัยศิริ บัณฑิตานนท์), Thai word Processing, Proc. of the Symposium on Natural Language Processing in Thailand, Mar 17-21, 1993, Thailand.(In Thai)

11. Sproat R., Shih C., Gale W., and Change N., A Stochastic Finite-State Word-Segmentation Algorithm for Chinese, cmp-lg/940508, 5 May, 94.

12. Jaruskulchai C., An Automatic indexing for Thai Text Retrieval, Doctor's Thesis, George Washington University, USA, July 22, 98.

13. Rissanen J., Universal Coding, Information, Prediction, and Estimation, IEEE Transactions on Information Theory, vol. IT-30, No. 4, Julay 1984.

14. Lam W., and Bacchus Fahiem, Learning Bayesian Belief Networks An approach based on the MDL principle, Computation Intelligence, Vol. 10:4, 1994.

15. Friedman Nir and Goldszmidt Moises, Sequential Update of Bayesian Network Structure, Uncertainty in Artificial Intelligence, Proc. of the 13th Conference, Edited by Dan Geiger and Prakash Pundalik Shenoy, August 1-3, 1997, pp.165-174.

16. Bahl L. R., Jelinek F., and Mercer R. L., A Maximum likelihood approach to continuous Speech Recognition, IEEE Transactions on Pattern Analysis and Machine Intelligence, Vol. PAMI-5, No. 2, page 179-190, 1983.

17. Heckerman D., A Tutorial on Learning Bayesian Networks, Technical Report MSR-TR-95-06, Microsoft Research, 1995.

18. Cover T.M., and Thomas J.A., Elements of Information Theory, John Wiley and Sons, Inc., New York, New York, 1991.

19. Shannon C.E., Prediction and Entropy of printed English, Bell Systems Technical Journal, 30:50-64, 1951.

Knowledge Representation Issues
in Information Extraction

Wee Li Kwang Angela[1], Tong Loong Cheong[1], Tan Chew Lim[2]

[1]Kent Ridge Digital Labs, 21 Heng Mui Keng Terrace, Singapore 119613
{angela, tonglc}@krdl.org.sg
[2]School of Computing, National University of Singapore, Kent Ridge, Singapore 119260
isctancl@nus.edu.sg

Abstract. The advent of computing has exacerbated the problem of overwhelming information. Advanced information management strategies such as Information Extraction, Information Filtering, Information Retrieval, and Text Categorization are becoming important to manage the deluge of information. Information Extraction (IE) systems can be used to automatically extract relevant information from free-form text for update to databases or for report generation. This paper describes the major challenge of knowledge representation issues in an information extraction task – representing the meaning of the input text, the knowledge of the field of application (or domain application) and the knowledge about the target information to be extracted. In this research, we have chosen a directed graph structure to represent the input text meaning, a domain ontology to represent the domain application and a frame representation to capture the target information to be extracted. We discuss in this paper how these knowledge structures interplay to perform the task of information extraction.

1. Introduction

Information is pertinent in today's society. Having the right information at the right time is critical for decision-making. But while information is a valuable resource, overwhelming information can pose a serious problem of time wastage in sorting through the disorganized textual mass for the relevant information.

This information deluge will escalate further with the advent of computers and Internet. It is vital to leverage on advanced information management technology aids for a fast way of sieving through these texts for meaningful information. The most common information management strategies are Text Categorization [13,21,25,27], Information Filtering [6,20], Information Extraction [6,7,8,9,12,15,19], Text Summarization [22,23] and Personalized Information Dissemination [20].

Information Extraction is the extraction of relevant information from free-form text (or unrestricted text) based on a set of pre-defined template of what information is to be extracted (or what is relevant for extraction). The template specification constrains the relevancy of the information to be extracted, which could be about pre-specified types of events, entities or relationships. For example, in a financial transaction, an information extraction system could extract the transaction type, date, customer, principal, currency, interest rate, and so on.

The extracted information is usually formatted as a database record suitable for subsequent processing, which may include database update for on-line access or data trend analysis, abstract, summary or report generation, text categorization, and message routing. Fig 1 shows extraction of information from a financial telex to update fields within a database record.

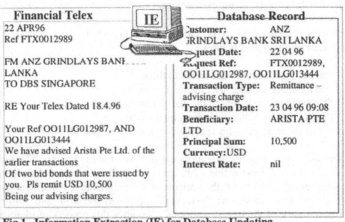

Fig 1. Information Extraction (IE) for Database Updating

Practical Natural Language Processing applications in IE are exemplified by work on the Tapestry projects [15,19,22] and by publications in the Message Understanding Conferences (MUC) [6,7,8,9].

A wide range of techniques for IE have been reported, ranging from statistics [14] and lexical pattern matching [1,16,21] to full text understanding [11,15]. Whichever techniques used, the issues of representing knowledge required in IE have to be addressed.

This paper will first present the knowledge representation issues and their proposed knowledge structures in detail. After which, it describes how these knowledge structures interplay to perform the task of information extraction.

2. Knowledge Representation Issues

One of the major challenges in Information Extraction is how to represent the 3 different types of domain knowledge that is required in this task, namely:

a) the meaning of the input text,
b) the knowledge of the field of application (domain application),
c) the target information that is to be extracted

2.1 Message Intermediate Representation (MIR)

Traditionally, input text is represented as syntax trees where the branching of the trees is governed by the syntax rules of the language grammar. Such syntax representation has an obvious weakness in its syntax-dependency, making it difficult to handle flexibility of language expressions.

The following sentences, S1 to S5, have different grammatical constructs and hence have different syntax tree structures.

S1 - "The manager sent the document to the staff."
S2 - "The manager sent the staff the document."
S3 - "The document was sent to the staff by the manager."
S4 - "The staff was sent the document by the manager."
S5 - "It was the manager who sent the document to the staff."

These sentences are semantically equivalent and state the same facts. The variants of syntax structures made extraction of information difficult. In order to identify the person who sent the document, the variants of the grammatical constructs have to be considered. In some cases, the "manager" appears at the front and sometimes, it appears at the back of the tree structure. To simplify this process of identifying the required concept for information extraction, there needs to be a less syntax-dependent way of representing the input text that is also able to express the meaning of the text. Here, we have chosen semantic graph structures to represent the text meaning. We refer to this semantic graph structures as *Message Intermediate Representation (MIR)*.

The MIR is a directed acyclic labeled graph with nodes that represent the concepts that occur in the text. Concepts could range from simple keywords, terms, and phrases to more complex patterns, which represent real-world entities that have been discovered during the text analysis. These concepts could be events, activities, transactions, attributes, circumstances, facts, incidents, milestones, occasions, outcome, etc.. The nodes of the graphs (referred to as MIR-nodes) are inter-connected through labeled directed links (referred to as MIR-links), that represent the relationships between these concepts. The MIR is a more neutral representation, independent of syntax or linear ordering, more meaningful semantic representation (sometimes referred to as logical form or deep structures) yet preserving syntactic information for reconstruction back to its syntactic tree structure.

The sentences S1-S5 have different syntax tree structures but will have the same MIR structure as shown in Fig 2. The main concepts that appear in the sentences are "manager", "send", "document", and "staff" and they are represented as nodes of the graph structure. The relationships between these concepts are "ARG0", "ARG1", and "ARG2". With the MIR, identifying the person who sent the document becomes much easier with a single representation.

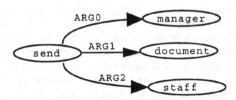

Fig 2. Message Intermediate Representation (MIR)

The designed and implemented MIR is very similar to the PEGASUS semantic representation [10] which also provides a definitive move from syntax to semantics, based on the definition of case frames or thematic roles (or predicate-argument relations). The PEGASUS structure is also a labeled, directed graph. The MIR and PEGASUS differ in argument assignments from the identification of meaningful relationships between head words of phrases and their modifiers or adjuncts. Hence, both representations also differ in the concepts and the set of relations. PEGASUS is similar to MIR in adopting the notion of "deep" cases or functional roles. For example, deep subject of ARG0 for MIR and DSUB for PEGASUS; ARG1 for MIR and DOBJ for PEGASUS.

The MIR is also similar to Schank's conceptual dependency (CD) notion [17]. However there are subtle differences. The basic entity in a CD is the event, or conceptualization whereas a basic entity in a MIR is the node, which could be an event or an entity. The CD has only a limited number of cases such as ACTOR which is similar to ARG0 of MIR. It also has a limited number of action types or primitives based on the abstract notion of transfer: ATRANS, abstract transfer (such as of possession of an object); PTRANS, physical transfer; and MTRANS, mental transfer (such as talking). It also includes primitive actions of bodily activity such as PROPEL (apply force), MOVE (move a body part), GRASP, INGEST, and EXPEL, as well as a few mental actions such as CONC (conceptualize or think) and MBUILD (perform inference).

2.2 Domain Ontology

The second important piece of knowledge required in an Information Extraction system is the knowledge of the domain application, i.e. the domain ontology. A *domain ontology* defines the set of basic terms comprising the vocabulary of the domain area and the relationships that bind these terms. For example, in an automobile domain, the set of vocabulary includes motorcar, motorist, engine, chassis, body, wheel, steering, light, brake, fuel system, gearbox, wiper, etc. These terms have some relationships to one another, example, a motorist is a person operating a motorcar; the glove compartment and the boot are reserved spaces in an automobile for storage of things.

In this research, for pragmatic reason, we have selected to model a single restrictive domain, using a simple yet process-able ontology. The domain knowledge is organized in object-centered hierarchies with inheritance, with the objects representing the terms and concepts in the domain, and the relationships of these concepts through the hierarchy. In this hierarchy, the subordinate concepts, in addition to having their own attributes, will inherit characteristics and features from the super-ordinate concepts. However, if the subordinate concept has an attribute that has a different value from that inherited from its super-ordinate parent, its attribute value takes precedence.

Fig 3 shows an ontology on the concept of delivery node of documents. The term "delivery-mode" comprises of all the various concepts which are lower level in the hierarchy, such as, mail, airmail, surface mail, registered mail, express mail, courier, Federal Express, DHL, local urgent mail, and LUM. All these subordinate concepts will inherit all characteristics of the term "delivery-mode".

Such an ontology facilitates reasoning. For example, the system through its inference reasoning "understands" that the concept "DHL" is a kind "courier", which is in turn a kind of "express mail" of "mail", and a type of "delivery-mode". From the larger ontology that encompasses this ontology, when "DHL" is being used in a different sense, such as a verb in "Pls DHL the documents to the issuing bank", the concept of "send" is implied.

This ontology representation also facilitates the knowledge specification of the target information to be extracted. As super-ordinate concepts of a concept could be automatically inferred from the ontology, there is no need to specify all possible concepts in the knowledge specification of the target information to be extracted.

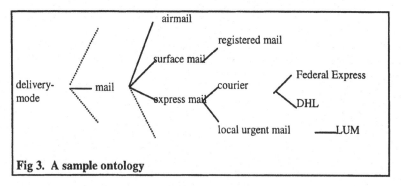

Fig 3. A sample ontology

2.3 Frame for Extracting Information from Messages (FEIM)

After having represented the meaning of the input text and the application domain field, the third piece of information that needs to be represented in an Information Extraction application is the target information to be extracted (refer to interchangeably as *target-information*).

In this research, a frame approach to represent the target information to be extracted has been chosen. The frame system is called *Frame for Extracting Information from Messages (FEIM)*.

Frames or templates are common knowledge representation tools in AI applications [2,4,5,13]. However the FEIM system employs templates for the specific purpose of extracting information from input messages. The design of FEIM is very much influenced by the Framekit [13], GUS [3] and KRL [2] frame representations. It has similar basic features such as slot, demon and inference as well as similar operators such as creation, access and update of slot values. In particular, the FEIM structures have been designed to handle practical issues in an Information Extraction application. FEIM provides convenient means for the knowledge coder (or the user) to specify common phenomena in Information Extraction applications like relationships between target-information.

The following table summarizes the attributes of the FEIM system.

Attributes	Explanations
Slot-Name	Name of the slot
Slot-Description	Description of the slot
Slot-Content	Content value of the slot
Default	Default value to Slot-Content
Invalid-Content	The value of Slot-Content will be transferred here and the Slot-Content will be reset to nil if its value fails the validation test.
Discrepancy	Records the failed validation test
Single	Determines if the Slot-Content is single-valued or multi-valued
Compulsory	Determines if the Slot-Content value is optional or compulsory
Validate	Tests to validate the Slot-Content value
To-Fill	Demon on how to fill the Slot-Content value
Normalize	Demon on how to manipulate the Slot-Content value
When-Filled	Demon on what instructions to perform after the Slot-Content value is determined
Modifiable	Determines if the Slot-Content value can be manually modified

Knowledge on what constitutes relevant information that is to be extracted from the input text is stored as a set of FEIM specifications. A FEIM specification can be viewed as a template of slots with each slot corresponding to a piece of relevant information that is to be extracted. Associated with each slot is a set of attributes with values of one of the following types: *descriptive* that describes the slot; *status* that contains characteristics of the target-information; *constraint* that spells the type specifications of the slot value; and *demon* that contains the function and macro calls that manipulate the slot value.

Fig 4 shows a sample of a FEIM slot specification. The FEIM slot named *Dispatch-of-Document-Slot* specifies that the target-information to be extracted could correspond to a MIR subgraph of the input text, if this MIR subgraph is identified and matched by a GML-rule *document-to-send-rule*. GML is a graph manipulation language cum graph pattern matcher developed for matching specified conditions against graph structures such as the MIR structure. The FEIM slot also specifies that the information may be absent in the input text, but a warning is to be reported if the GML rule identifies more than one such information in the input text. Also specified is the relationship between the *Dispatch-of-Document*-Slot and the other slots, *Available-Document-Slot* and *Delivery-Mode-Slot* in the When-Filled demon. The information for these two slots is to be inferred from the extracted information of *Dispatch-of-Document-Slot.*

```
(FEIM-SLOT Despatch-of-Document-Slot
        (content nil)
        (to-fill (gml-rule document-to-send-rule
                        (a r1 b r2 c r3 d r4 e)
                        ((a despatch)
                        (r1 object->)
                        (b document)
                        (r2 beneficiary->)
                        (c (or person organization))
                        (r3 means->)
                        (d delivery-mode)
                        (r4 agent->)
                        (e (or person organization))))
                        (extract)))
        (when-filled (infer FEIM-SLOT
                                (Available-Document-Slot
                                Delivery-Mode-Slot)))
        optional
        single
        modifiable)

Fig 4. A FEIM Slot
```

The design of FEIM has incorporated practical operational requirements of *Inferencing, Cross-Checking, Discrepancy* Highlighting, and *Change Propagation.*

Cross-checking is a special type of inferencing but with a different purpose. The aim of cross-checking is for verification of consistency across slots. A special slot, known as the *Cross-Checking-Slot* (similar to Inferee slot) is created to verify consistency of one or more of the *To-Be-Cross-Checked-Slots* (similar to Inferer slots). If the consistency check fails, the *Discrepancy* attribute value will be filled. *For* example, in a loan application domain, a Cross-Checking-Slot "Check-Credit-Limit" is a Inferee slot derives its value of whether credit limit extended to customer is exceeded by cross-checking that the Inferer slot "Credit-Limit-Extended" is less than or equal to 2 times the Inferer slot "Monthly-Salary". If the cross-checking finds that the check fails, the "Check-Credit-Limit" will have its *Discrepancy* attribute value filled.

This will serve to highlight to the user to do a check on the credit limit that is extended to the customer.

Similar to the Inferee slots, the Cross-Checking-Slot does not have a TO-FILL attribute. Instead, it has a special attribute of *Cross-Check* and the TO-FILL attribute will be automatically generated during compilation of the FEIM specification. The following shows a Cross-Checking-Slot "type-of-tenor" which cross-checks the To-Be-Cross-Checked-Slots "type-of-tenor" and "tenor" through a predicate function "type-tenor-agree-p".

```
(FEIM-SLOT type-of-tenor
    (cross-check type-tenor-agree-p type-of-tenor tenor))
```

FEIM highlights any discovered discrepancies in the Slot-Content of slots through its *Discrepancy* attribute of the slots. Three types of discrepancies can be discovered through the FEIM system. They are *missing information* (through the Compulsory and Slot-Content attributes), *excess information* (through the Single and Slot-Content attributes) and *wrong information type* (through the Invalid-Content attribute). This discrepancy feature of FEIM conveniently highlights to the user of potential incorrectness in the financial transaction or inaccuracy in the information that has been automatically extracted by the system.

The discrepancy feature enables the user to more quickly detects incorrectness and allows him to make the necessary modifications. Only the slots with the Modifiable attribute can be modified by the user. For ensuring integrity of some Slot-Content of slots, the slots are marked intentionally with unmodifiable attribute and hence the user will not be able to modify these slots. Most of the Inferee slots are intentionally marked unmodifiable as their values are inferred. As FEIM caters for the flexibility of inferencing, once the Slot-Content value of a Inferer slot is modified, FEIM has a Change-Propagation mechanism to propagate changes to other Inferee slots that are affected by this change. The Change-Propagation mechanism will re-infer and re-validate the values of all the Inferee slots. Without this mechanism, it will be difficult to ensure the consistency and integrity of the Slot-Content values of all the Inferer and Inferee slots through manual changes.

3. Interplay of the Knowledge Structures in Information Extraction

Fig 5 below shows how the various knowledge structures interplay to perform the task of information extraction. For example, the text "All transcripts are to be DHLed to the personnel department.", it would be pre-processed and analyzed to a MIR with entities of 'transcript', 'DHL' and 'personnel department'.

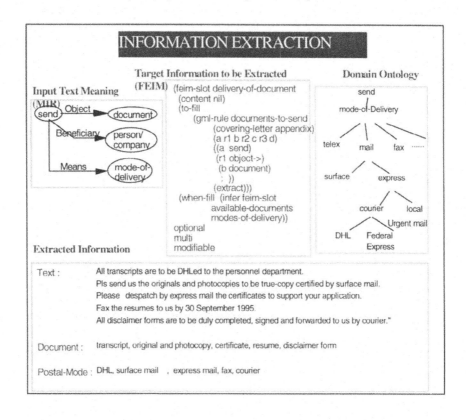

Fig 5. Interplay of Knowledge Structures in Information Extraction

Through the general and domain ontology, it is derived that 'transcript' is a type of 'document', 'DHL' is a mode of 'send', and 'personnel department' is part of a 'company'.

When the system attempts to fill up the FEIM slot 'delivery-of-document', it searches the MIR through the GML-rule and matches successfully the MIR represented by the text. Hence, the relevant portion of the MIR is extracted. The relevant portion of the MIR to be extracted is determined by the text document layout hierarchical structure. However, the user can overwrite the default by specifying in the <return-function> of the GML-rule to return the entity discovered instead of the determined section, paragraph, or sentence of the text document layout hierarchical structure. For example, if the user is only interested to know the documents that were discussed in the text, he can specify in the GML-rule to return the particular node corresponding to the matched document.

The extracted information can then either be updated into databases, or could be used to generate a summary or for subsequent text processing such as Text Categorization.

These knowledge structures have been implemented in the context of a practical IE Architecture - the Generic Information Extraction (GIE). The GIE Architecture was deployed in a few practical IE systems, including a financial application within one of the largest local banks in Singapore - DBS Bank. The Message Formatting Expert (MFE) system [19] has been operational in the bank since early 1997. It was the joint development of the Kent Ridge Digital Labs and DBS Bank. The MFE system processes some finance package application forms from the customers and automatically extract relevant information as database records. The bank officers verify these extracted database records before final update into the bank's central database. The average recall of extraction is 95% and the average precision of extraction is 83%. In the operational MFE system, total recall is ensured with a "miscellaneous" feim-slot that extracts all unextracted information. This feim-slot allows the bank officer to verify that the unextracted information is irrelevant to the extraction.

4. Conclusion

We discussed in this paper, the major challenge of knowledge representation issues in an information extraction task – representing the meaning of the input text, the knowledge of the field of application (or domain knowledge) and the knowledge about the target information to be extracted. In this research, we have chosen a directed graph structure to represent the input text meaning, a domain ontology to represent the domain knowledge and a frame representation to capture the target information to be extracted. We discuss in this paper how these knowledge structures interplay to perform the task of information extraction. These structures have been implemented in the context of a practical IE Architecture.

References

1. Appelt D E, J Bear, J R Hobbs, D Israel and M Tyson (1992). "SRI International FASTUS System" Proc. MUC-4, Morgan Kaufmann : 143-147.
2. Bobrow G. Daniel and Winograd Terry (1977). "An Overview of KRL, a Knowledge Representation Language". Cognitive Science 1(1), 1977,3-46.
3. Bobrow G. Daniel, R M Kaplan, M Kay, D A Norman, H Thompson and T Winograd (1977). "GUS, A Frame-Driven Dialog System" Artificial Intelligence, North-Holland Publishing Company 1977: 155-173.

4. Brachman R.J. and Schmolze J.G. (1985). "An Overview of the KL-ONE Knowledge Representation System". Cognitive Science 9 : 171-216.

5. Charniak Eugene (1978). "On the use of framed knowledge in language comprehension". Artificial Intelligence 11 :225-265

6. DARPA (1991). Proc. of Third Message Understanding Conference (MUC-3). Morgan Kaufmann Publishers Inc.

7. DARPA (1992). Proc. of Fourth Message Understanding Conference (MUC-4). Morgan Kaufmann Publishers Inc.

8. DARPA (1993). Proc. of Fifth Message Understanding Conference (MUC-5). Morgan Kaufmann Publishers Inc.

9. DARPA (1995). Proc. of Sixth Message Understanding Conference (MUC-6). Morgan Kaufmann Publishers Inc.

10. Jensen Karen, Heidorn E. George, Richardson D. Stephen 1993 Natural Language Processing : The PLNLP Approach. Kluwer Academic Publishers, Boston/Dordrecht/London. Chapter 16 : 203-214. Chapter 21 : 273-283.

11. Krupka G, P Jacobs, L Rau, and L Iwanska (1991). "The GE NLToolset System" Proc. MUC-3, Morgan Kaufmann.

12. Marco Costantino, Richard G. Morgan, Russell J. Collingham, Roberto Garigliano (1997). " Natural Language Processing and Information Extraction: Qualitative Analysis of Financial News Articles" Proc. of Conference on Computational Intelligence for Financial Engineering (CIFEr '97), New York City, March 23-25, 1997.

13. Nyberg H. Eric (1988). "The FrameKit User's Guide Version 2.0", Carnegie Mellon University, 1988.

14. Tan Sian Lip, Tong Loong Cheong (1993). "A statistical approach to automatic text extraction." Asian Libraries, Vol 3 No 1, Mar 1993: 46-54.

15. Tan Sian Lip, Aw Ai Ti (1993). "Domain specific information Extraction - a NLP-Enable application." Proc. of the First Symposium on Intelligent Systems Applications (SISA '93), Singapore, Nov 1993.

16. Tong Loong Cheong, Wee Li Kwang, Goh Ann Loo, Lee Chee Qwun, and Teo Pit Koon (1992). "A Telex Destination Identification System." Proc. First Singapore Int. Conf. on Intelligent Systems (SPICIS 92), Sep 1992: 281-287.

17. Allen James (1987). "Natural Language Understanding". University of Rochester. Menlo Park: The Benjamin/Cummings Publishing Company, Inc..

18. Wan Kwee Ngim, Tong Loong Cheong, Lynda Ang Seok Lay (1993). "Automatic Categorisation of Cargo Descriptions." Proc. of the First Symposium on Intelligent Systems Applications (SISA '93), Singapore, Nov 1993.

19. Tong Loong Cheong, Angela Wee Li Kwang, Augustina Gunawan, Goh Ann Loo, Lee Chee Qwun, and Shu Huey Leng (1994). "A Pragmatic Information Extraction Architecture for the Message Formatting Expert (MFE) System". Proc. Second Singapore Int. Conf. on Intelligent Systems (SPICIS 94), Nov 1994: B371-377.

20. Wee Li Kwang Angela, Tong Loong Cheong, Chng Tiak Jung (1997). "DeNews - A Personalized News System." Journal of Expert Systems with Applications, Vol. 13, 1997, Elsevier Science Ltd, UK 0957-4174/97.

21. Dolan C P, S R Goldman, T V Cuda and A M Nakamura (1991). "Hughes Trainable Text Skimmer" Proc. MUC-3, Morgan Kaufmann : 155-162.

22. Tong Loong Cheong, Low Poh Lian (1991). "Automatic Text Abstraction - Prospects and a Proposed R&D Plan" Information Technology, Journal of SCS, Vol 4 No 2, Sep 1991: 85-94.

23. Julian Kupiec, Jan O. Pedersen, Francine Chen (1995). "A Trainable Document Summarizer". Proc. of the 18th ACM/SIGIR Conference,1995: 68-73.

Structuralization of Case-Bases, Using Concept Hierarchy

Toyohide Watanabe and Masataka Yamada

Department of Information Engineering,
Graduate School of Engineering, Nagoya University
Furo-cho, Chikusa-ku, Nagoya 464-8603, Japan
Phone: +81-52-789-4409, Fax: +81-52-789-3808
E-mail: watanabe@nuie.nagoya-u.ac.jp

Abstract. *The case-based reasoning makes it possible to construct easy management mechanism for manipulating knowledge resources successfully. Some prototyping systems have been developed and applied to individual domains. However, it is important to structuralize effectively the organization in point of retrieval efficiency. In this paper, the structuralization method is addressed. Our structuralization method is characterized with regard to two concepts: categorization with knowledge about concept hierarchy; and organization based on the common features among two or more attributes. Our case categorization structure is represented by a direct acyclic graph, and can be organized automatically on the basis of the above concepts. This paper describes a case structuralization method and evaluates the retrieval efficiency through experiments.*

1 Introduction

The case-based reasoning provides a framework that the knowledge can be automatically acquired and the reasoning can be done incrementally on the basis of the existing instance-specific knowledge. This framework resolves the problems of knowledge acquisition and knowledge refinement successfully[1-3]. Namely, in the case-based reasoning the most suitable case, which is similarly applicable to retrieval request, is selected from many accumulated case-bases(a set of practically observable facts) and then is used to interpret the retrieval request inferentially with the similarly selected case. In this case, it is important to retrieve the most applicable case from the case-bases and control this retrieval process easily/rapidly.

In order to overcome these subjects the configuration of case base has been investigated, and many proposals focused on the hierarchical configuration on the basis of commonly shared attribute values among individual cases, with respect to categorization concept. For example, Shared Feature Network is one of hierarchical structures [1]. In this structure, individual cases are divided into categories whose cases have commonly shared features. However, these proposals could not always support sufficient retrieval facilities because the structure to specify various features of each case is strongly limited[4]. It is very important to be able to categorize various volumns of cases effectively and retrieve the most similar case fastly, in accordance with common features to be shared inherently, but not owing to only the explicitly represented attribute values. Namely, the semantic-based approach takes an important role of case manipulation in point of the similarity retrieval and case categorization. The knowledge about concept hierarchy is regarded as a keypoint to establish such a framework.

MEDIATOR, which is an extension of Redundant Discrimination Network, is one of hierarchical case-bases, using the knowledge about concept hierarchy as the domain knowledge for contructing case-bases[5]. Individual cases are classified by each attribute into attribute-specific sets. In the case retrieval the similar cases are first searched with similarity computation, owing to attributed structures, and then the most suitable case is selected from their searched cases under additional retrieval conditions. However, the case categorization is not always sufficient because the case classification is derived from only the similarity, based on only one attribute, though in many cases the similarity among cases is dependent on the combination among some related attributes.

In this paper, we propose an experimental method to organize a hierarchical structure of case-bases, using the knowledge about concept hierarchy. Our idea is that the case categorization strategy is applied under the generalization mechanism with respect to several different attributes, shared commonly between two cases. Namely, the nodes in our hierarchical structure are composed of several common category-dependent attributes though in the traditional approaches only one attribute is usable in each node.

2 Approach

Usually, the case structure is composed of several features as pairs of attribute and its value, and the categorization method classifies into several classes with inclusive relationship hierarchically, which is dependent on the attribute value. Thus, the categorization method determines the case-base structure directly. The case-base structure takes critical roles of supporting high retrieval efficiency and selecting correct retrieval effects. From a viewpoint of retrieval efficiency and retrieval effect, we propose a case-base structure, based on two concepts: categorization with knowledge about concept hierarchy; and organization with respect to common features among two or more attributes[6].

The case categorization, based on the knowledge about concept hierarchy, makes it possible that the attribute values in individual cases are not dependent on explicit representations directly but are distinguished implicitly with respect to the semantical information. Therefore, individual cases are classified meaningfully in the categorization structure, and also the interrelated cases have similar features: the traditional concept of similarity may be alternatively defined as the function of distances among cases. Additionally, our organization method for constructing the case-base with common features among two or more attributes is integrated into categorization method, based on the knowledge about concept hierarchy. We call this integration method of categorization and organization as the structuralization method based on the minimum generalization with common features: hereafter, this method is abbreviated as CMGS method.

In our CMGS method, the case-base structure is hierarchically organized: the terminal nodes are practical cases and non-terminal nodes are category nodes with common features between two terminal nodes and/or two non-terminal nodes. Namely, non-terminal node attends with features, shared commonly among two lower nodes. We consider two cases, shown in Figure 1. **Case-1** and **Case-2** are composed of two attributes "figure" and "color". We assume that the knowledge about concept hierarchy for "figure" and "color" is organized respectively as shown in Figure 2. Under such an assumption, our CMGS method integrates **Case-1** and **Case-2** into the only one upper category in Figure 3: the common upper attribute value for "square" in **Case-1** and "pentagon" in **Case-2** is "polygon"; and also the common attribute value for "yellow" in **Case-1** and "orange" in **Case-2** is "warm-color". Thus, when **Case-3**, **Case-4** and **Case-5** in Figure 4(a) are inserted into the case-base newly, the final case-base is organized as illustrated in Figure 4(b).

Our case-base is defined as a directed acyclic graph because the lower nodes in our case-base structure are not linked to only one upper node but also may be related to two or more different upper nodes at once. It is clear that the upper node is more generalized than the lower node with respect to the knowledge about concept hierarchy. Moreover, our CMGS method is so clear that since the category nodes can keep two or more attributes at once in comparison with the traditional categorization strategies our categorization ability is more excellent.

3 Similarity Retrieval

In the case-based reasoning, the similarity retrieval is one of important facilities. Our retrieval procedure is as follows:

[Similarity Retrieval Algorithm]

Step1: Select all non-termial nodes, which matched with attribute value of retrieval request(as an input term) from our case-base of directed acyclic graph by setting the root node to a starting point of this search.

Step2: Find out all terminal nodes linked from the selected non-terminal node.

Step3: Retrieve the most suitable terminal node from these linked nodes, using the following similarity computation,

$$\textbf{Case-sim} = \sum_{a_i \in C_1, a_j \in C_2} \textbf{Attr-sim}(a_i, a_j)$$

$$\textbf{Attr-sim}(a_i, a_j) = 2 * D_c/(D_i + D_j)$$

where D_i and D_j are the path lengths(the number of path edges from the root node to the terminal node), and D_c is the path length to the lowest common non-terminal node from the root node. Of course, when two attribute values have no common non-terminal node, Attr-sim is 0.

Step4: If the retrieved node is terminal node, finish. Otherwise, goto Step2.

In this procedure, the matching process is not realized by the traditional string-direct matching method, but performed on the basis of inclusive relationship between attribute values in the appropriate concept hierarchy. For example, we find out the most similar case from directed acyclic graph, illustrated in Figure 4, with respect to the input retrieval case: $\langle\langle figure : square\rangle, \langle color : red\rangle\rangle$.

In Step1, **Category-3**, **Category-4** and **Category-5** are selected. Here, **Category-3** is only the first retrieved set of cases because **Category-3** is the lower node in them. Thus, in Step2 **Case-4** and **Category-1** are found out. Next, compute the similarity for **Case-4** and **Category-1**. Here, **Category-1** is more similar to the input retrieval case than **Case-4**(in Step3). However, repeat again the matching process for **Category-1** because **Category-1** is not terminal. In Step2, **Case-1** and **Case-2** are selected because they are linked from **Category-1**. In Step3, compute the similarity for **Case-1** and **Case-2**, and retrieve **Case-2** because **Case-2** is more similar to the input retrieval case. And, **Case-1** is the final result since this is a terminal node in Step4.

4   Case-base Structure

Our categorization method on the concept hierarchy can construct successfully the case-base structure, based on the common features among two or more attribute values and the concept hierarchy.

4.1   Incremental Construction

The new cases are inserted into the existing case-base one by one even if many cases are added. This is because our CMGS method maintains the case structure on the basis of common features among several attribute values of two cases or categories. Thus, the case-base is incrementally updated. When a new case is registered to the existing case-base, the following procedure is applicable:

1) Select the most similar case for the new case.
2) Compose a category, generated from common attribute values between these two cases.
3) Link two related cases(such as the new case and the most similar existing case) to the composed category.
4) Compose an upper category between the generated category and existing category, and link these two related categories to the upper category.
5) Repeat Step 4) until the upper category becomes the uppest node.

Steps 2), 3), 4) and 5) may be not always usual phases: in our viewpoint, the new case is linked to the most similar existing case as a child node. In some cases, the subtree, composed of the newly generated category in Step 2) and two mutually related cases in Step 3), may replace a pair of nodes. These variations are dependent on the concept hierarchy between attribute values of the new case and the similar existing case. However, the update is stepwisely performed as category generation process from the lower node to the upper node. The linking ways of newly generated category(in the above Step 2)) are judged independently in accordance with the inclusive relationship between the parent node of the most similar existing node and newly generated category.

1) When there is an existing node with the same attribute values as newly generated category, the new category is deleted and the new case is set as a child node to the existing node.
2) When the parent node linked from the most similar case includes the newly generated category, the category is set as a child node to the parent, and is attached with the most similar case and newly inserted case.

3) When the newly generated category includes the parent node of the most similar case, the subtree, which is composed of the category, its inserted case, and similar case, replaces the node position of the most similar case, and also this replacement is repeated until this process reaches to the root node.

4) When the newly generated category is compatible to the parent node of the most similar case, first the most similar case and newly inserted case are linked to the new category as child nodes. Next, one or more categories are generated from the new category and grandparent of the most similar case. Then, one of the above phases 1), 2) and 3) is selected between the new category and the grandparent, and repeated.

The processing flow for the above four phases is illustrated in Figure 5, imaginarily. We consider an example. Figure 6(a) is an initial case-base structure: this structure is composed of **Category-1**, **Case-1** and **Case-2** so that **Category-1** is the root node. Figure 6(b) is a newly input case **Case-3**. Under such a situation, **Case-2** is retrieved as the most similar case for **Case-3**. Thus, a new category **Category-2** is composed of **Case-2** and **Case-3**, as shown in Figure 6(c). Next, the inclusive relationship between **Category-2** and **Category-1**, as the upper node of **Case-1**, is checked up. Here, since **Category-1** includes **Category-2**, **Category-1** is set as a parent node to **Category-2**, and the final structure is updated as Figure 6(d).

4.2 Structure Modification
Under the above processing flow, our case-base structure is organized. Moreover, the structure is not always optimal because the structuralization is applied to only one related node among linked neighboring nodes with respect to the most similar case. Thus, the modification is necessary to make the structure effective from a viewpoint of constructiveness and meaningfulness.

Modification of inclusive relationship Generally, the inclusive relationship may be created among the lower node of new link and other child nodes of the newly linked upper node. If the inclusive relationship is observed the corresponding link must be modified. Of course, this process must be repeated until all inclusive relationships are got off for the newly linked nodes and the corresponding nodes along the edge path. This is illustrated in Figure 7.

Deletion of redundant link Another link may be generated duplicatedly in addition to the existing links. Such links are happened in three cases as shown in Figure 8. These are checked and the corresponding links are removed. Here, N_d is the lower node for newly generated link, and N_u is the upper node.

1) When the upper link from N_d to N_u is existing, the new link is redundant.
2) When the upper link from child node of N_u to N_d is existing, the link between N_u and its child node is redundant.
3) When the upper link from N_u to the parent node of N_d is existing, the link between N_d and its parent node is redundant.

Removement of minimum generalization By reducing nodes with almost similar attribute values, it is necessary to support high retrieval performance. Our CMGS method introduces a criterion for generating extra-nodes on the basis of the minimum generalization principal[7]. The minimum generalized nodes are defined as nodes with almost equal similarity. These nodes do not always take important plays to organize a hierarchical structure. Thus, it needs to check up whether the upper and lower nodes with the minimum generalization are generated when a new link is set. Figure 9 shows such an illustration. In our research the minimum generalization nodes are dependent on whether the similarity between the corresponding nodes is in excess of some thresholds. If the nodes are on the minimum generalization, the lower node, connected by the link, and the link, related to the lower nodes, are removed. Then, the child node of the lower node is reset as the child node of the upper node.

5 Experiments

Here, we show experimental results for our CMGS method.

5.1 Experiment with Practical Data

We used 200 samples of Q&A about Kana-Kanji translation system, cited from Internet news. Each case is composed of a question and the answer, and the retrieval of similar case was applied to the attribute values of question term. Each case was represented by case-frame structure: the representation form for question term is illustrated in Figure 10. Our representation form is the nested structure, based on pairs of attribute and value. The knowledge about concept hierarchy was edited from Roget thesaurus[8] with some modification, and the threshold value for minimum generalization was set as 0.85. By removing the nodes of the minimum generalization, the number of categories was reduced to 398 from 592 under the total 220 cases.

Retrieval time We compared the processing times of similarity retrieval for flat-structure and our directed acyclic graph structure. Figure 11 shows the result. The vertical axis is the retrieval time, and the horizontal axis is the number of registered cases(per 10 units). In the flat-structure, the time grows up drastically according to the number of cases, while in our structure the time is not so. Clearly, our method is better than the flat-structure method.

Next, the numbers of searched nodes are shown in Figure 12. The vertical axis is the number of nodes, and the horizontal axis is the number of registered cases(per 10 units). The direct line is the number of cases to be used for similarity computation in the flat-structure method. In our method, the number of cases used for similarity computation is much better(as the lowest graph).

Retrieval hit ratio Generally, it is not always observed that the most similar cases are found out in the hierarchical structure. In our method, the number that the most similar cases were found out is 120 for the total retrieval trials 219. Table 1 shows the retrieval result. In this table, we conclude that our method can retrieve the appropriate cases by the high retrieval hit ratio when the cases with high similarity are accommodated in the case-base.

5.2 Experiment with Artificial Data

In order to check up that our method is successful even if the number of cases is too many, this experiment was done. However, since it is difficult and time-consuming to register many cases by manual, we used artificial data. Each case is associated with four attributes for the knowledge about concept hierarchy: the level of hierarchy is 5; the number of edges in each node is 3; and the number of terminal nodes is 273. Figure 13 shows the similarity retrieval times for flat-structure method and our method. The vertical axis is the retrieval time and horizontal axis is the number of cases(per 100 units). We can observe explicitly that our method is better than flat-structure method.

6 Conclusion

In this paper, we proposed CMGS method, which categorizes two cases with two or more attribute values at once on the basis of knowledge about concept hierarchy. Also, we made it clear that our method is better through some experiments. Of course, our evaluation is not always sufficient. We must compare our method with other hierarchical case-base structure methods such as MEDIATOR.

As our future work, we must investigate the following subjects, first of all:

1) Evaluation in comparison with other hierarchical structure methods;
2) Processing for maximum generalization principal though in this paper only the minimum generalization principal was considered;
3) Generalization refinement in the same level of hierarchical structure.

Acknowledgements

The authors are very grateful to Prof. T.Fukumura of Chukyo University, and Prof. Y.Inagaki and Prof. J.Toriwaki of Nagoya University, and also wish to thank our research members for their cooperative remarks.

References

[1] J.Koloduer: "Case-Based Reasoning", *Morgan Kaufmann*(1993).

[2] A.Aamodt and E.Plaza: "Case-Based Reasoning: Foundational Issues, Methodological Variation, and System Approaches", *AI Communications*, Vol.7, pp.39-59(1994).

[3] D.B.Leake (ed.by): "Case-Based Reasoning: Experiences, Lessons, and Future Directions", *AAAI Press/MIT Press*(1996).

[4] R.H.Stottler, A.L.Henke and J.A.King: "Rapid Retrieval Algorithms for Case-Based Reasoning", *Proc.of IJCAI'89*, pp.233-237(1989).

[5] R.L.Simpson: "A Computer Model of Case-Based Reasoning in Problem Solving: An Investigation in the Domain of Dispute Mediation", *Georgia Institute of Technology, School of Information and Computer Science Technical Report*, No.GIT-ICS-85/18(1985).

[6] M.Yamada and T.Watanabe: "A Categorical Case Structure in Case-based Reasoning System", *Proc.of VSMM'96*, pp.462-466(1996).

[7] H.-D. Burkhard, and M.Lenz: "Case Retrieval Nets: Basic Ideas and Extensions", *KI-96: Advances in Artificial Intellegence*(eds.by G.Gurz and S.Hulldobler)(1996).

[8] R.Chapman: "Roget's International Thesaurus, 4th ed.", *Harper and Row*(1977).

Table 1: Evaluation of retrieval results

A	B	C	D	E
0.9 - 1.0	25	22	3	0.88
0.8 - 0.9	30	26	4	0.86
0.7 - 0.8	24	16	8	0.66
0.6 - 0.7	42	23	19	0.54
0.5 - 0.6	37	13	24	0.35
0.4 - 0.5	32	10	22	0.31
0.0 - 0.4	29	9	20	0.31

(Note)
A: similarity between retrieval case and
   selected cases
B: number of retrievals
C: number of what most similar cases
   were found out in our method
D (=B-C): number that most similar cases
   were not found out in our method
E (=C/B): ratio that most similar cases
   were found out in our method

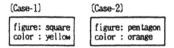

(Case-1)
figure: square
color : yellow

(Case-2)
figure: pentagon
color : orange

Figure 1: Examples of cases

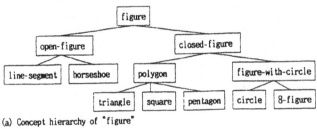

(a) Concept hierarchy of "figure"

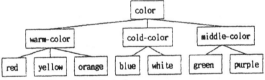

(b) Concept hierarchy of "color"

Figure 2: Concept hierarchy

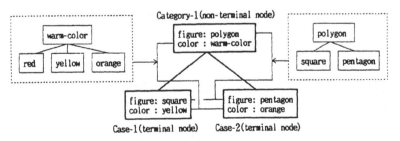

Figure 3: Example of common minimum generalization

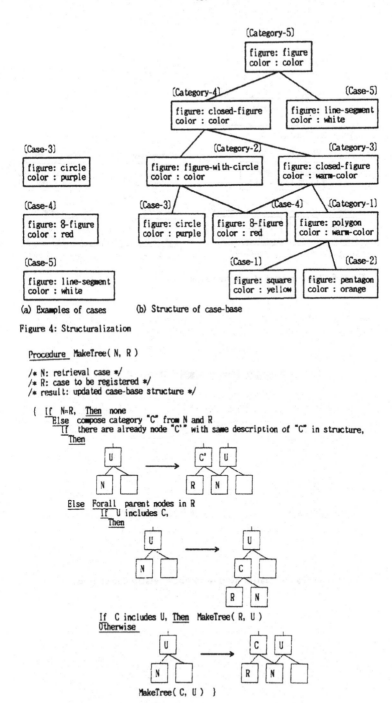

(a) Examples of cases   (b) Structure of case-base

Figure 4: Structuralization

Procedure MakeTree(N, R)

/* N: retrieval case */
/* R: case to be registered */
/* result: updated case-base structure */

(If N=R, Then none
  Else compose category "C" from N and R
    If there are already node "C'" with same description of "C" in structure,
    Then

Else Forall parent nodes in R
    If U includes C,
    Then

If C includes U, Then MakeTree(R, U)
Otherwise

MakeTree(C, U) }

Figure 5: Update algorithm of case-base structure

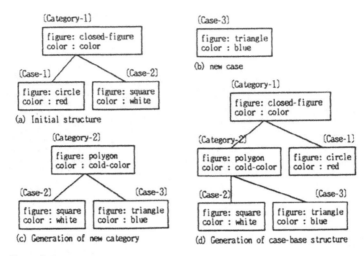

Figure 6: Update process of case-base structure

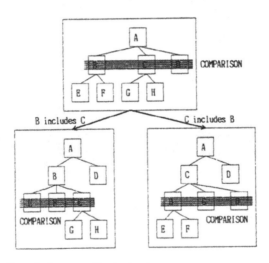

Figure 7: Restructuralization based on inclusive relationship of links

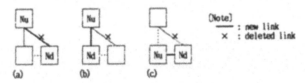

Figure 8: Deletion of redundant link

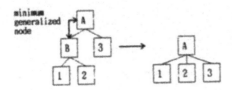

Figure 9: Movement of minimum generalized node

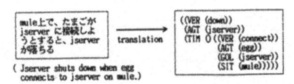

Figure 10: Example of case representation

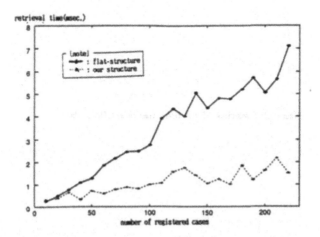

Figure 11: Comparison of retrieval time by practical data

number of nodes

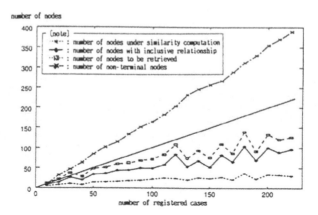

Figure 12: Number of searched nodes

retrieval time(msec.)

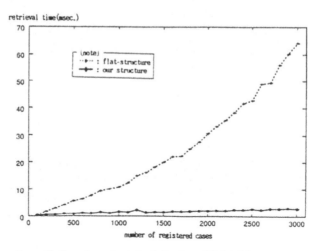

Figure 13: Comparison of retrieval time by artificial data

A Closer Look at Preduction

Allen Courtney and Norman Foo

Knowledge Systems Group
School of Computer Science and Engineering
University of New South Wales
Sydney, Australia 2052
allenc|norman@cse.unsw.edu.au

Abstract. In a recent paper Jun Arima formalises the idea of *preduction* – a non-monotonic schema providing a common basis for inductive and analogical reasoning. We examine some of the implications of this schema, as well as its connections with prototypes and conceptual spaces. A generalised version of his schema is motivated and developed to address difficulties with asymmetry and disjuncts.

1 Introduction

Most of our common forms of reasoning involves the use of deduction, induction or analogy. Deduction and *mathematical* induction are well understood methods which guarantee licensed conclusions. Less clear is the process of *scientific* induction (to be referred to simply as induction in the remainder of this paper) – inferring a general case from specific examples; and analogy – inferring common properties of individuals based upon a similarity between them. Both allow conclusions that may later be invalidated by new information. In traditional mathematics, this potential invalidation has caused induction and analogy to be poor cousins of the highly venerated deduction. Nevertheless, their roles in creative science and mathematics were so obvious that they could not be ignored. Polya [Polya54] has given a masterly exposition of this role in mathematics. A *formal* account that can rival that of deduction was however missing. In AI, the fact that new information can invalidate previous inferences has been successfully accounted for by many forms of *non-monotonic* logics. All of them are essentially second-order, and that is perhaps the clue to how induction and analogy can receive a formal account. This has indeed been achieved in a recent paper by Jun Arima [Arima97], which offers a formalisation of these methods and reveals potential connections between them. He suggests that analogy and induction can be split into two steps. The first is a defeasible inference, called the *preductive* step, allowing a property to be propagated along all points given by a specified relation. Analogical or inductive conclusions follow by a secondary step of deduction or mathematical induction respectively. We reproduce below some examples essentially due to [Arima97] that illustrate the key features of preduction and indicate how it subsumes induction and analogy.

Induction
1. $P(0) \wedge ... \wedge P(n)$ Hypothesis
2. $\forall x(P(x) \rightarrow P(s(x)))$ Preduction
3. $\forall x P(x)$ Mathematical Induction

Analogy 1
1. $P(b) \wedge b \sim t$ Hypothesis
2. $\forall xy(P(x) \wedge x \sim y \rightarrow P(y))$ Preduction
3. $P(t)$ Deduction

Analogy 2
1. $P(b) \wedge S(b) \wedge S(t)$ Hypothesis
2. $\forall x(S(x) \rightarrow P(x))$ Preduction
3. $P(t)$ Deduction

The first line in each example (denoted as hypotheses) is the base or "root" case. In each example an instance of the preduction schema is invoked in the second line. It essentially authorises the propagation of the property P along "paths" defined by a binary relation that has differing interpretations in particular contexts. The binary relation in the first example is simply that which relates an element to its successor. Here, the preduction pattern yields the familiar axiom of mathematical induction. In the second example the relation $\sim$ is one that can be interpreted as formalising "similarity", so $a \sim b$ would be saying that object a is similar to object b in the context of the discourse. In this case preduction has the following intuitive interpretation: if x has property P and y is similar to x, then y also has property P. This is of course a familiar method of analogical reasoning. Another kind of analogical inference is captured by the third example. Here, $S(x) \wedge S(y)$ can be interpreted to say that objects x and y share some underlying property, and preduction is used to project it to the possibly dependent property P. The concrete case that Arima [op. cit.] adduces is when $S(x)$ is "x is human", and $P(x)$ is "x is mortal".

As will be seen when we outline Arima's ideas in section 2, the preduction schema is second-order, and as with many other second-order schemas meant to complete knowledge or information, it is not only non-monotonic but its effective use demands judicious choices of formulas for substitution. Moreover, we shall see that there are possibly a number of viable schemas (much like there are various forms of circumscription). We will therefore examine in this paper some of the consequences of preduction, intended or otherwise, along with a generalisation of Arima's preductive schema (A-schema) and corresponding model theory. The paper is organised as follows: Section 2 reviews the schema as originally presented. Section 3 discusses connections with *conceptual spaces* for representing natural types. Section 4 looks at some difficulties with the A-schema and proposes a generalisation. Section 5 gives some model theoretic results, section 6 concludes.

2 Preduction

Preduction formally represents the concept "If every entity known to be P can be traced back to some roots of P along a relation R, then the unknown descendants of their roots will satisfy P similarly"[Arima97].

For this we take $P\cdot$ to be an n-ary predicate and $\cdot R\cdot$ to be a $2n$-ary relation. There is no distinction between arguments indexing entities or arguments holding values. Implicit in the informal definition of preduction is that the relation we trace back along is transitive. To ensure this, we introduce a new relation $\prec_R$, defined as the minimal predicate satisfying

$$\forall xy(xRy \to x \prec_R y) \land \forall xyz(x \prec_R z \land z \prec_R y \to x \prec_R y)$$

expressed by $Tr(R; \prec_R)$. This can be formally expressed by a second order sentence which *circumscribes* $Tr(R; \prec_R)$ in $Tr(R; \prec_R)$[McCarthy80], giving "$x \prec_R y$ iff x transitively-R y".

Arima's preductive sentence (A-schema) is now defined as

$$\exists \Phi(\forall x(\Phi(x) \to P(x)) \land \exists xy(\Phi(x) \land x \prec y \land P(y))$$
$$\land A[P(x)/\lambda x(\Phi(x) \lor \exists z(\Phi(z) \land z \prec x))])$$
$$\to \forall xy(P(x) \land x \prec y \to P(y))$$

The notation $A[X/Y]$ means Y is uniformly substituted for X throughout A, where A is the theory hypotheses.

His interpretation is that Φ is meant to represent the *root* of P things with respect to $\prec$. The first conjunct expresses that Φ is a subclass of P. The second confirms that Φ contains an ancestor of P. The third expresses that P can be interpreted as a set of entities with their roots in Φ. This interpretation and the necessity of these conjuncts is argued against in the next section, but kept for the examples following. The consequent tells us every $\prec$-descendant of an entity satisfying P also satisfies P.

The preduction of P on R from A is then

$$A \land Tr(R; \prec_R) \land A\text{-schema}$$

Adapting a concrete example presented by Arima [op. cit.]

Example 1. Let A and S be

$$A \equiv G(4) \land G(6)$$

$$xSy \equiv y = s(x)$$

where the numbers are shorthand for $s(s(...s(0)...))$ and $G(x)$ is to be interpreted as x is greater than 3. Let $\prec_S$ be the transitive closure of S by $Tr(S; \prec_S)$. We then get

$$\exists \Phi(\forall x(\Phi(x) \to G(x)) \land \exists xy(\Phi(x) \land x \prec_S y \land G(y))$$
$$\land(\Phi(4) \lor \exists z(\Phi(z) \land z \prec_S 4))$$
$$\land(\Phi(6) \lor \exists z(\Phi(z) \land z \prec_S 6))$$
$$\to \forall xy(G(x) \land x \prec_S y \to G(y))$$

Substituting $\Phi(x) \equiv x = 4$, the left hand side becomes

$$G(4) \wedge \exists y(4 \prec_S y \wedge G(y)) \wedge 4 \prec_S 6$$

which follows from $A \wedge \text{Tr}(S; \prec_S)$, and by $\forall xy(y = s(x) \to x \prec_S y)$, we conclude

$$\forall x(G(x) \to G(s(x)))$$

From $4 > 3$ and $6 > 3$ we infer "the successor of each number greater than 3 is greater than 3", and get $G(4), G(5), G(6), \dots$.

The use of a one place predicate G as > 3 is for simplicity – choosing $G(x, y)$ to mean $x > y$, and $xpSyq \equiv y = s(x) \wedge p = q$, we can deduce

$$\forall xn(G(x, n) \to G(s(x), n))$$

To demonstrate the non-monotonic nature of the A-schema, we extend the previous example and show the earlier conclusions are no longer warranted.

Example 2. Let S be as before, and A

$$A \equiv G(4) \wedge G(6) \wedge \neg G(5)$$

we now get the previous left hand side plus

$$\neg\Phi(5) \wedge \neg\exists z(\Phi(z) \wedge z \prec_S 5)$$

This says anything $\prec_S 5$ is not in Φ, contradicting the substitution for $G(4)$ (4 or something $\prec_S 4$ is in Φ). Thus for any Φ the preductive sentence is a tautology.

When looking at analogy, a simpler version of the preductive schema is available. For an S not containing P, let the similarity relation be defined as $xCy \equiv S(x) \wedge S(y)$. Then a theorem of the A-schema is

$$\exists z(P(z) \wedge S(z)) \wedge A[P/S] \to \forall x(S(x) \to P(x))$$

The proof is in [Arima97]

Example 3. Let A be

$$human(tom) \wedge human(sue) \wedge mortal(sue)$$

and $xCy \equiv human(x) \wedge human(y)$. The first conjunct follows from A, as does the replacement of $mortal(sue)$ with $human(sue)$, and so can conclude $\forall x(human(x) \to mortal(x))$.

Whilst this schema is simple apply, there are cases discussed later where it fails to produce a conclusion. For these, the standard A-schema (or proposed new version) must be used.

3 Prototypes and Concepts

One of the interesting consequences of the A-schema is that it can account for certain features of conceptual spaces that are evidently beyond the expressive power of first-order logic. As the schema is second-order, this is perhaps not surprising. We will describe two highly persuasive approaches to conceptual spaces by way of illustration.

The linguist George Lakoff, in his seminal work "Women, Fire and Dangerous Things" [Lakoff87], argues that first-order semantics is inadequate to capture mental categories and natural language. Likewise, Peter Gardenfors [Gardenfors90] also criticised classical semantics, including modal ones, for their weakness in meeting the challenge of formalising natural kinds. Both of them have suggested remedies that are essentially topological in character, and we will show that the A-schema can be adduced to support them.

We will now briefly recount those ideas of Lakoff's and Gardenfors' that can be explained by preduction. Lakoff based a number of his arguments on prior work by Rorsch who observed that natural concepts manifest *prototypical effects*. For instance, he cites the concept *mother* as one with a *central case* – "a mother who is and has always been female, and who gave birth to the child, supplied her half of the child's genes, nurtured the child, is married to the father, is one generation older than the child, and is the child's legal guardian" [op. cit.]. Other mother concepts are deviations from this central case, and include as examples adoptive mother, surrogate mother, etc. He further asserts that the deviant concepts are derived from the central case by convention, implying a *radial* structure for the concept space. One may describe a topology for such a radially structured space using an algebraic notation arising from the work of Gardenfors. Let $\prec$ be a transitive binary relation on some space S, to be interpreted in the Lakoff context as the relation "can derive", so that $x \prec y$ would be read sub-concept y can be derived from sub-concept x. A concept space C (a subset of S) is *radial* if there exists a central concept c in C such that if $c \prec y$ and y is in C, then for all x such that $c \prec x \prec y$, x is in C. Gardenfors calls such radial structures "star-shaped". Consider an ostensibly weaker structure C_0 which consists of exactly the c-reachable points, i.e. $C_0 = \{c\} \cup \{x | c \prec x\}$, where initially only c is known to be in the space C. Call such a set *c-reachable*. The following lemma exhibits the power of the A-schema in permitting us to propagate membership in a conceptual space from a central member via derivation closure – which is the essence of radial structuring. To avoid triviality, we assume that there are at least two elements in the space.

Lemma 1 *Assuming the A-schema, every c-reachable structure is a radial structure with the same central concept.*

Proof In schema A we let $P(x)$ be the relation $x \in C$, $A(x)$ be just $P(c)$, and $\Phi(x)$ be the equality $x = c$.

Observation 1 *The above is a "nonlinear" analog of the standard induction on numbers. Another difference is that there is no restriction that the $\prec$ relation be* *non-circular; if it is circular with c in the circuit, then any other point in the circuit can also serve as a central concept.*

In [Gardenfors90] Gardenfors introduces *convexity* as the topological structure that is natural for a conceptual space to be "projectible", i.e., which can be subject to induction. For instance, he gives an account of how the well-known Grue Paradox [Goodman65] of induction can be resolved using a topological argument that blocks the unwanted induction. In effect, he asserts that natural kinds correspond to convex subsets of topological spaces where the coordinates are perceptual or cognitive dimensions. It turns out that the A-schema, with a minor restriction on the $\prec$ reachability relation, will extend the above lemma to convex structures. We recall that a structure C is convex with respect to the relation $\prec$ if for every pair x, y of elements in C, if $x \prec z$ and $z \prec y$, then z is also in C.

Lemma 2 *Assuming the A-schema, every symmetric $\prec$-reachable structure is a convex structure.*

Proof Let the structure be reachable from some point c. Then by symmetry c itself is reachable from any other point, and hence every pair of points are mutually reachable. Then use the previous lemma.

4 Observations and Modifications

In the previous sections it was shown how a property can be transfered forwards along $\prec$, yet by taking the contrapositive of the preductive consequent it can be seen how negative properties can be transfered backwards. Continuing the greater-than-3 example

Example 4.

$$A \equiv G(4) \wedge G(6) \wedge \neg G(2)$$

Taking $\Phi(x) \equiv x = 4$, and the left side of the preduct of $G(4) \wedge G(6)$ as ψ gives

$$\psi \wedge (4 \neq 2) \wedge \neg(4 \prec_S 2) \to \forall xy(G(x) \wedge x \prec_S y \to G(y))$$

As the left hand side holds, we can conclude $\forall x(G(x) \to G(s(x)))$ and $\forall x(\neg G(s(x)) \to \neg G(x))$, and thus $\neg G(2), \neg G(1), ...$ as well as $G(4), G(5), ...$, with $G(3)$ unknown.

One way of viewing this result is to look at $\prec$ as fitting a path, or a possibly disjoint directed graph, through points in the domain. The preductive sentence then determines if it is consistent to assign such points to P or $\neg P$, such that there is at most one transition point for each disjoint subgraph where $\neg P$ changes to P. In the above example, such a graph might be:

$$\xleftarrow{\quad} \neg G | G \xrightarrow{\quad}$$
$$0 \to 1 \to 2 \to 3 \to | 4 \to 5 \to 6 \to ...$$

Alternately, 3 may belong to G. The set of such graphs corresponds to an *expansile set*, explained in the next section. Of course, if $\prec$ is symmetric or forms a cycle there can be no transition point as this would allow a change from P to $\neg P$.

As given, the preductive sentence restricts this model to those paths passing through at least two points known to be P (one if $\prec$ is reflexive), thus preventing propagation of negative properties over *symmetric* relations. Such a restriction breaks symmetry, and forces a representational bias towards positive predicates. *notfly*(x) can be propagated, whilst $\neg fly(x)$ can not.

This problem can be rectified by removing the first two conjuncts from the preductive sentence, namely $\forall x(\Phi(x) \rightarrow P(x)) \wedge \exists xy(\Phi(x) \wedge x \prec y \wedge P(y))$. This both removes the necessity for ground positive instances of P as well as freeing the restriction that Φ is a *known* sub-class of P. Φ should still be interpreted as roots for P, however Φ need only be consistent with P, not known to be in P. This holds with the intuition that the earliest example of P we know about need not be the actual roots of P over $\prec$. $\Phi(x) \equiv x = 3$ would then be an alternate choice with the modified schema in the above example. To propagate negative properties, Φ can either be after known instances of $\neg P$, or empty, indicating no transition point to P.

Example 5. let A and S be

$$A \equiv \neg fly(a) \wedge snail(a)$$

$$xSy \equiv snail(x) \wedge snail(y)$$

then by taking $\Phi \equiv$ false, we get

$$\neg \text{false} \wedge \neg\exists z(z \prec_S a \wedge \text{false}) \rightarrow \forall xy(fly(x) \wedge x \prec_S y \rightarrow fly(y))$$

yielding $\forall xy(\neg fly(y) \wedge snail(x) \wedge snail(y) \rightarrow \neg fly(x))$ and then $\forall x(snail(x) \rightarrow \neg fly(x))$ from A.

A further consequence of this simplification is that if A does not mention P then $\forall xy(P(x) \wedge x \prec y \wedge P(y))$ can be deduced for any $\prec$. This is analogous to mathematical induction without a base case – the *process* of induction is always valid, however no useful results can be concluded until a base is provided. Likewise, the preduction allows P and $\neg P$ to be assigned along $\prec$, but without a known instance of P $(\neg P)$, no further point can be deduced to be P $(\neg P)$.

There are still difficulties with this solution, which can occur when A contains disjunctive information. This is illustrated in the following example

Example 6. let A be

$$A \equiv gold(m) \wedge \forall x(gold(x) \rightarrow expensive(x))$$

We now try to propagate gold over some relation (say wedding-rings). The second conjunct of A is given, however it could have been produced by a previous application of the preductive schema if gold(m)∧expensive(m) was known. Now:

$$\Phi(m) \lor \exists z(z \prec m \land \Phi(z)) \land$$
$$\forall x((\neg \Phi(x) \land \neg \exists z(z \prec x \land \Phi(z))) \lor expensive(x)) \to \ldots$$

Any choice of Φ satisfying the first conjunct will fail to satisfy the substituted section of the second conjunct, as all x is $\neg \Phi$. Take $\Phi(x) \equiv x = m$. then

$$\text{true} \land \forall x(\text{false} \lor expensive(x)) \to \ldots$$

Since we can't deduce expensive(x), the preduction fails even though the consequent is consistent with A.

The problem occurs because *expensive(x)* could be *false* and allow a potential inconsistency with the preduction. We alleviate this by allowing substitutions for all predicates in A, not just P. If the substitutions are consistent and provable, then the consequent of the peductive sentence can be proved from A.

We now define the preductive sentence as:

$$\exists \Phi(A[P(x)/\gamma, \ \alpha_0/\beta_0, \ \alpha_1/\beta_1, ..., \ \alpha_n/\beta_n]) \to$$
$$\forall xy(P(x) \land x \prec y \to P(y))$$

where γ is $\lambda x(\Phi(x) \lor \exists z(\Phi(z) \land z \prec x))$, $\alpha_0, ..., \alpha_n$ are predicates in A, ($\prec$ is not included) and $\beta_0, ..., \beta_n$ are arbitrary formulas. All substitutions are assumed to be in parallel and obey standard logical "free-for" rules (no capturing of variables).

From the previous example

Example 7. A as before, let $\Phi(x) \equiv x = m$ and substitute true *for expensive(x). Then*

$$\text{true} \land \forall x(\text{false} \lor \text{true}) \to \ldots$$

allowing gold(x) to be propagated and non-monotonically concluding, for example, that wedding-rings are gold and expensive.

In all examples given so far an implicit assumption has been that whenever $P(p)$ is mentioned in A, p is a point in $\prec$. This assumption is naive when working with complex domains, where we may wish to transfer a property over one class of objects but not over another. Interpreting $\prec$ as a graph, it is clear that for each disjoint subgraph, a separate root is needed to propagate positive properties along it (not necessary for negative properties). Any point p not reachable through $\prec$ is a single point subgraph, and must be in Φ if $P(p)$ is in A. From the human-mortal example

Example 8. Let A be

$$human(tom) \land human(sue) \land mortal(sue)$$
$$\land cat(topaz) \land mortal(topaz)$$

and $xCy \equiv human(x) \wedge human(y)$. *Simply substituting human for mortal as in the earlier example would require us to prove* $human(topaz)$. *Instead we need to use* $\Phi(x) \equiv x = sue \vee x = topaz$, *giving*

$$human(tom) \wedge human(sue) \wedge cat(topaz)$$
$$\wedge(sue = sue \vee sue = topaz)$$
$$\wedge(topaz = sue \vee topaz = topaz) \rightarrow ...$$

to conclude $\forall x(human(x) \rightarrow mortal(x))$.

In simple cases as above, the choice for Φ is obvious. This may not always be the true, with the complexity of Φ increasing with additional unconnected points. Another option is to choose a different $\prec$ which covers these areas – say *isalive* instead of *human* above. However this is not always easy or desirable. The choice for Φ and $\prec$ in general remains a problem.

5 Model Theory

In this section we demonstrate the soundness of our proposal by providing semantics for it. Let U and φ be sets such that $\varphi \subseteq U$, and $\prec$ a transitive relation on U. Define the *expansile set* of φ with respect to $\prec$ as:

$$\varphi \cup \{e \mid z \in \varphi, z \prec e\}$$

For a predicate P and a given universe, let E be the set of all models such that the extension of P in any model is an expansile set of some φ. Equivalently, $E = Mod(\forall xy(P(x) \wedge x \prec y \rightarrow P(y)))$. Let A represent either a set of first-order sentences, or its models where the usage of such is unambiguous. We define the *preductive set* of models A' of A in the following manner:

If $A \cap E = \emptyset$ then $A' = A$, otherwise, $A' = A \cap E$

For all proofs it is assumed that there are no substitutions made on $\prec$, and $Product(A; P; R)$ is taken to mean the new preductive sentence with $A \wedge Tr(R; \prec_R)$.

Theorem 1 (substitution rule). *For any formulae* T, *if* $T \Leftrightarrow T'$, *and* S *and* S' *are produced from* T *and* T' *respectively by a uniform parallel substitution of formulae for predicates in* T (T'), *such that the standard "free-for" conditions are satisfied, then* $S \Leftrightarrow S'$.

If $T \Leftrightarrow T'$, then $T \leftrightarrow T'$ is a theorem. Any proper substitution of formulae for predicates will guarantee only theorems are obtained from theorems [Kalish80]. Thus, $S \leftrightarrow S'$ is a theorem, so $S \Leftrightarrow S'$.

Theorem 2 (soundness). *For a preductive set of models* A' *of* A *and a sentence* ϕ, $A' \models \phi$ *if* $\text{Product}(A; P; R) \vdash \phi$.

Let the preductive sentence after substitution be $\psi \rightarrow \beta$

1. $A \cap E = \emptyset$ $(A' = A)$: As $E = Mod(\beta)$ and A contains no E models, $A \vdash \neg\beta$. By the substitution rule, $\psi \Leftrightarrow \psi'$, where ψ' is produced by substitution from $A \wedge \neg\beta$ $[= A \wedge \exists xy(P(x) \wedge x \prec y \wedge \neg P(y))]$. Choosing Φ as the "roots" of P, $\psi' = \psi \wedge \exists xy(\Phi(x) \vee \exists z(\Phi(z) \wedge z \prec x) \wedge x \prec y \wedge \neg\Phi(y) \wedge \neg\exists z(\Phi(z) \wedge z \prec y))$, which is equivalent to *false* by transitivity of $\prec$. ($x \prec y$, x or something $\prec x$ is in Φ, nothing $\prec y$ is in Φ) Therefore $\psi \to \beta \Leftrightarrow \psi' \to \beta \Leftrightarrow true$, so $Mod(A \wedge \psi \to \beta) = Mod(A)$

2. $A' = A \cap E$: $E \subseteq Mod(\psi \to \beta)$ as $E = Mod(\beta)$, thus $(A \cap E) \subseteq (A \cap Mod(\psi \to \beta))$ $[= Mod(A \wedge \psi \to \beta)]$

Corollary 1 (partial completeness). *If $A \vdash \psi$ or $A \vdash \neg\beta$, then for any sentence ϕ, $A' \models \phi$ only if* Preduct$(A; P; R) \vdash \phi$.

If $A \vdash \psi$, then $Mod(A \wedge \psi \to \beta) = Mod(A \wedge \beta) = A \cup E = A'$. Otherwise, if $A \vdash \neg\beta$, $Mod(A \wedge \psi \to \beta) = A = A'$ (from soundness proof).

Corollary 2 (consistency). *A is consistent iff* Preduct$(A; P; R)$ *is consistent.*

From the definition of a set of preductive models, $A = \emptyset$ iff $A' = \emptyset$ (as $E \neq \emptyset$). Thus if *Preduct*$(A; P; R)$ is inconsistent, $A' = A = \emptyset$. If A is inconsistent, then *Preduct*$(A; P; R)$ is inconsistent by monotonicity.

6 Conclusion

In this paper we analysed some of the mechanics and consequences of Arima's preductive schema. When representing knowledge as topological spaces over concepts, the preductive sentence proved to be a powerful tool in working with radial and convex structures, transferring a property throughout the space from a single instance. Closer examination revealed the nature of this propagation by means of fitting paths through points in the domain. By generalising the schema around this idea we were better able to deal with domains where information was not represented by positive ground instances, and provide a model theory for our results. Yet while this schema allows us to make consistent analogical and inductive inferences, it offers little in helping choosing when such inferences are justified. In common with many other second-order schemas, it requires careful choice in formulae for substitution to prove the desired results. It does however, provide a good first step towards understanding the nature of analogy and induction in a logical environment. Currently we are looking at stronger connections between knowledge representation, conceptual spaces and *coherence* by attempting to "lift" analogical reasoning from transferring properties to analogy between formulae and inferences.

References

[Gardenfors90] Gardenfors, P., "Induction, Conceptual Spaces and AI", *Philosophy of Science*, 57, pp 78-95, 1990.

[Goodman65] Goodman, N., "Fact, Fiction and Forecast", Bobbs-Merril, 1956.

[Lakoff87] Lakoff, G., "Women, Fire, and Dangerous Things : what categories reveal about the mind", University of Chicago Press, 1987.

[Arima97] Arima, J., "Preduction: A Common Form of Induction and Analogy", In *Proceedings of the fifteenth International Joint Conference on Artificial Intelligence*, pp 23-29, 1997.

[Kalish80] Kalish, D., Montague, R., and Mar, G., "Logic: Techniques of Formal Reasoning" second ed., pp 349-355, 1980.

[Polya54] Polya, G., "Mathematics and Plausible Reasoning", Princeton, N.J., Princeton University Press, 1954.

[McCarthy80] McCarthy J., "Circumscription–A Form of non-monotonic reasoning" in *Artificial Intelligence* 13, pp27-39, 1980.

Learning Linearly-Moded Programs
from Entailment

M. R. K. Krishna Rao   and   A. Sattar

School of Computing and Information Technology
Faculty of Information and Communication Technology
Griffith University, Brisbane 4111, Australia.
e-mail: {krishna,sattar}@cit.gu.edu.au

Abstract. Logic programs with elegant and simple declarative semantics have become very common in many areas of artificial intelligence such as knowledge acquisition, knowledge representation and common sense and legal reasoning. For example, in Human GENOME project, logic programs are used in the analysis of amino acid sequences, protein structure and drug design etc. In this paper, we study exact learning of logic programs from entailment and present a polynomial time algorithm to learn a rich class of logic programs that allow local variables and include many programs from Sterling and Shapiro's book [20] such as add, append, merge, split, delete, insert, member, prefix, suffix, length, quick-sort, merge-sort, insertion-sort, preorder and inorder traversal of binary trees, polynomial recognition, derivatives, sum of a list of natural numbers etc.

1   Introduction

Starting with the seminal work of Shapiro [18, 19], the problem of learning logic programs from examples and queries has attracted a lot of attention in the last fifteen years. Many techniques and systems for learning logic programs are developed and used in many applications. See [13] for a survey. In this paper, we consider the framework of *learning from entailment* [1-7,10,14,15] and present a polynomial time algorithm to learn a rich class of logic programs that allow local variables and include many programs from Sterling and Shapiro's book [20].

The framework of *learning from entailment* has been introduced by Angluin [1] and Franzier and Pitt [6] to study learnability of propositional Horn sentences. In this framework, an oracle (teacher) that answers the following types of queries from the learner is employed. The oracle answers 'yes' to an *entailment equivalence query* $EQUIV(H)$ if H is equivalent to the target program H^*, i.e., $H \models H^*$ and $H^* \models H$. Otherwise, it produces a clause C such that $H^* \models C$ but $H \not\models C$ or $H^* \not\models C$ but $H \models C$. A *subsumption query* $SUBSUME(C)$ produce an answer 'yes' if the clause C is subsumed by a clause in H^*, otherwise answer 'no'. Besides, equivalence and subsumption queries, the learner is also *allowed to ask for hints*. If C is a clause $A \leftarrow B_1, \cdots, B_n$ such that $H^* \models C$, the request-for-hint query $REQ(C)$ returns (1) an answer 'subsumed' if $A \leftarrow B_1, \cdots, B_n$

is subsumed by a clause in H^*, otherwise returns (2) an atom (hint) B in the proof of $H^* \models C$. Recently, this framework of learning from entailment has been used in learning first order Horn programs by Page [?] and Arimura [3]. The main restriction imposed in [?, 3] is that all the terms in the body of a clause are subterms of the terms in the head. This means that local variables are not allowed. However, local variables play an important role of *sideways information passing* in the paradigm of logic programming and hence there is an urgent need to extend the results for classes of programs which allow local variables.

In this paper, we extend the results of Arimura [3] for one such class of programs, using moding annotations and linear predicate inequalities. This class is a major fragment of linearly-moded programs, which were shown to be learnable (not necessarily polynomial time) from positive data in Krishna Rao [9]. In other words, we present a subclass of linearly-moded programs that are learnable in polynomial time from entailment. Our learning algorithm takes at most polynomial (in the size of the largest counterexample/hint provided by the oracle in response to the equivalence queries) number of queries.

The rest of the paper is organized as follows. The next section gives preliminary definitions and section 3 defines the class of simple linearly-moded programs. Section 4 presents a few results about subsumption and entailment and section 5 presents the learning algorithm for finely-moded programs. Section 6 provides correctness proof of the learning algorithm and section 7 compares our results with the existing results.

2 Preliminaries

Assuming that the reader is familiar with the basic terminology of first order logic and logic programming [12], we use the first order logic language with a finite set Σ of function symbols and a finite set Π of predicate symbols including Prolog builtins $=, <, >, \leq, \geq, \neq$. The arity of a predicate/function symbol f is denoted by $arity(f)$. Function symbols of arity zero are also called constants.

Linearly-moded Programs

We are primarily interested in programs operating on the following recursive types used in Sterling and Shapiro [20].

```
Nat ::= 0 | s(Nat)
List ::= [ ] | [item | List]
ListNat ::= [ ] | [Nat | ListNat]
Btree ::= void | tree(Btree, item, Btree)
```

Definition 1 For a term t, the *parametric size* $[t]$ of t is defined recursively as follows:

- if t is a variable x then $[t]$ is a linear expression x,

- if t is the empty list $[\,]$ or the natural number 0 or the empty tree **void** then $[t]$ is zero,

- if $t = f(t_1, \ldots, t_n)$ and $f \in \Sigma - \{0, [\,], \textbf{void}\}$ then $[t]$ is a linear expression $1 + [t_1] + \cdots + [t_n]$.

The parametric size of a sequence $\mathbf{t}$ of terms $t_1, \cdots, t_n$ is the sum $[t_1] + \cdots + [t_n]$.

For a term t (or a sequence $\mathbf{t}$ of terms), the sum of coefficients and constants in its parametric size $[t]$ ($[\mathbf{t}]$ resp.) is denoted by $[\![t]\!]$ ($[\![\mathbf{t}]\!]$ resp). If t is a ground term, $[t]$ and $[\![t]\!]$ coincide.

Example 1 The parametric sizes of terms a, [ ], [a], [a,b,c], [X] are 1, 0, 2, 6, $X + 1$ respectively. □

Definition 2 A *mode* m of an n-ary predicate p is a function from $\{1, \cdots, n\}$ to the set $\{in, out\}$. The sets $in(p) = \{j \mid m(j) = in\}$ and $out(p) = \{j \mid m(j) = out\}$ are the sets of input and output positions of p respectively.

A moded program is a logic program with each predicate having a unique mode associated with it. $p(\mathbf{s}; \mathbf{t})$ denotes an atom with input terms $\mathbf{s}$ and output terms $\mathbf{t}$.

Definition 3 Let P be a moded program and I be a mapping from the set of predicates occurring in P to sets of input positions satisfying $I(p) \subseteq in(p)$ for each predicate p in P. For an atom $A = p(\mathbf{s}; \mathbf{t})$, we denote the linear inequality

$$\sum_{i \in I(p)} [s_i] \geq \sum_{j \in out(p)} [t_j] \tag{1}$$

by $LI(A, I)$.

Definition 4 Let P be a moded program and I be a mapping from the set of predicates occurring in P to the sets of input positions satisfying $I(p) \subseteq in(p)$ for each predicate p in P. We say P is *linearly-moded w.r.t.* I if each clause

$$p_0(\mathbf{s_0}; \mathbf{t_0}) \leftarrow p_1(\mathbf{s_1}; \mathbf{t_1}), \cdots, p_k(\mathbf{s_k}; \mathbf{t_k})$$

$k \geq 0$, in P satisfies the following:

1. $LI(A_1, I), \ldots, LI(A_{j-1}, I)$ together imply $[\mathbf{s_0}] \geq [\mathbf{s_j}]$ for each $j \geq 1$, and

2. $LI(A_1, I), \ldots, LI(A_k, I)$ together imply $LI(A_0, I)$,

where A_j is the atom $p_j(\mathbf{s_j}; \mathbf{t_j})$ for each $j \geq 0$.
A program P is *linearly-moded* if it is linearly-moded w.r.t. some mapping I.

Example 2 Consider the following **reverse** program.

moding: app(in, in, out) and rev(in, out).

app([ ], Ys, Ys) ←
app([X|Xs], Ys, [X|Zs]) ← app(Xs, Ys, Zs)

rev([ ], [ ]) ←
rev([X|Xs], Zs) ← rev(Xs, Ys), app(Ys, [X], Zs)

We can prove that this program is *linearly-moded* w.r.t. the mapping $I(\text{app}) = in(\text{app})$; $I(\text{rev}) = in(\text{rev})$ as follows. The first clause satisfies the requirements of Definition 4 as $LI(\text{app}([\,], Ys, Ys), I)$ is $Ys \geq Ys$, which trivially holds. Now consider the second clause. $LI(\text{app}(Xs, Ys, Zs), I)$ is

$$Xs + Ys \geq Zs \tag{2}$$

and $LI(\text{app}([X|Xs], Ys, [X|Zs]), I)$ is

$$1 + X + Xs + Ys \geq 1 + X + Zs. \tag{3}$$

It is easy to see that inequality 2 implies inequality 3 satisfying the requirement 2 of Definition 4. The requirement 1 of Definition 4 trivially holds as $1 + X + Xs + Ys \geq Xs + Ys$.

It is easy to check that the third clause satisfies the requirements of Definition 4. Now consider the fourth clause.

$LI(\text{rev}(Xs, Ys), I)$ is

$$Xs \geq Ys, \tag{4}$$

$LI(\text{app}(Ys, [X], Zs), I)$ is

$$Ys + 1 + X \geq Zs \tag{5}$$

and $LI(\text{rev}([X|Xs], Zs), I)$ is

$$1 + X + Xs \geq Zs. \tag{6}$$

It is easy to see that inequalities 4 and 5 together imply inequality 6 satisfying the requirement 2 of Definition 4. The requirement 1 of Definition 4 holds for atoms rev(Xs, Ys) and app(Ys, [X], Zs) as follows. $1 + X + Xs \geq Xs$ trivially holds for atom rev(Xs, Ys). For atom app(Ys, [X], Zs), inequality 4 implies $1 + X + Xs \geq Ys + 1 + X$. Therefore, **reverse** is a linearly-moded program. □

The characteristic property of linearly-moded programs is given below.

Theorem 1 (From [9]) Let P be a linearly-moded program w.r.t. a mapping I and $\leftarrow q(\mathbf{s}; \mathbf{t})$ be a goal such that $\mathbf{s}$ is ground. If there is an SLD-refutation G with answer substitution σ, then $\mathbf{t}\sigma$ is ground and $LI(q(\mathbf{s}; \mathbf{t})\sigma, I)$ is valid. Further, $[\mathbf{s}] \geq [\mathbf{u}\sigma] \geq [\mathbf{v}\sigma]$ for each atom $r(\mathbf{u}; \mathbf{v})$ in G.

3 Simple Linearly-moded Programs

In this section, we introduce the class of simple linearly-moded programs, for which a learning algorithm is presented in a later section.

Definition 5 A linearly-moded program P is *simple* if each non-unit clause

$$p_0(s_0; t_0) \leftarrow p_1(s_1; t_1), \cdots, p_k(s_k; t_k)$$

$k \geq 1$, in P satisfies the following: for each $i \in [1, k]$, every term in s_i is a subterm of a term in $s_0, t_1, \cdots, t_{i-1}$ or is of the form $f(u_1, \ldots, u_n)$ such that $u_1, \ldots, u_n$ are subterms of terms in $s_0, t_1, \cdots, t_{i-1}$.

Example 3 It is easy to see that the reverse program given above is a simple linearly-moded program. □

Example 4 Consider the following quick-sort program.

> moding: app (in, in, out); part (in, in, out, out) and
> qs (in, out)
>
> app($[\,]$, Ys, Ys) ←
> app($[X|Xs]$, Ys, $[X|Zs]$) ← app(Xs, Ys, Zs)
>
> part($[\,]$, H, $[\,]$, $[\,]$) ←
> part($[X|Xs]$, H, $[X|Ls]$, Bs) ← X ≤ H, part(Xs, H, Ls, Bs)
> part($[X|Xs]$, H, Ls, $[X|Bs]$) ← X > H, part(Xs, H, Ls, Bs)
>
> qs($[\,]$, $[\,]$) ←
> qs($[H|L]$, S) ← part(L, H, A, B), qs(A, A1), qs(B, B1), app(A1, $[H|B1]$, S)

Input terms of each atom (except app(A1, $[H|B1]$, S) in the last clause) are subterms of input terms of head and output terms of the atoms before that. For atom app(A1, $[H|B1]$, S) in the last clause, the term $[H|B1]$ is of the form $f(u_1, \ldots, u_n)$ such that $u_1, \ldots, u_n$ are subterms of input terms of head and output terms of the earlier atoms. Therefore, this program is simple linearly-moded. □

Definition 6 A predicate p defined in a moded program P is *deterministic* if $t_1 \equiv t_2$ whenever $P \models p(s; t_1)$ and $P \models p(s; t_2)$ for any sequence of ground input terms s.

A program P is *deterministic* if each predicate defined in it is deterministic.

In this paper, we only consider deterministic programs.

4 Subsumption and Entailment

Definition 7 Let C_1 and C_2 be clauses $H_1 \leftarrow Body_1$ and $H_2 \leftarrow Body_2$ respectively. We say C_1 *subsumes* C_2 and write $C_1 \succeq C_2$ if there exists a substitution θ such that $H_1\theta \equiv H_2$ and $Body_1\theta \subseteq Body_2$.

Definition 8 A program P_1 is a *refinement* of program P_2, denoted by $P_1 \sqsubseteq P_2$ if $(\forall C_1 \in P_1)(\exists C_2 \in P_2)C_2 \succeq C_1$. Further, P_1 is a *conservative refinement* of P_2 if there exists at most one $C_1 \in P_1$ such $C_2 \succeq C_1$ for any $C_2 \in P_2$.

Definition 9 A program P *entails* a clause C, denoted by $P \models C$, if C is a logical consequence of P.

The relation between subsumption and entailment is discussed below.

Definition 10 A *derivation* of a clause C from a program P is a finite sequence of clauses $C_1, \ldots, C_k = C$ such that each C_i is either an instance of a clause in P or a resolvent of two clauses in $C_1, \ldots, C_{i-1}$. If such a derivation exists, we write $P \vdash_d C$.

The following theorem is proved in Nienhuys-Cheng and de Wolf [14].

Theorem 2 (Subsumption Theorem)
Let P be a program and C be a clause. Then $P \models C$ *if and only if one of the following holds: (1) C is a tautology or*
(2) there exists a clause D such that $P \vdash_d D$ and D subsumes C.

When C is ground, the above theorem can be reformulated as follows.

Theorem 3 Let P be a program and C be a ground clause $A \leftarrow B_1, \cdots, B_n$. Then $P \models C$ *if and only if one of the following holds.*
(1) C is a tautology.
(2) C is subsumed by a clause in P.
(3) There is a minimal SLD-refutation of $P' \cup \{\leftarrow A\}$, where $P' = P \cup \{B_i \leftarrow \mid i \in [1, n]\}$.

Definition 11 An SLD-refutation is *minimal* if selected atoms are resolved with unit clauses whenever possible.

Even though (2) is covered by (3) in the above theorem, we explicitly mention (2) in view of its importance in our learning algorithm.

Lemma 1 If C_1 and C_2 are two simple linearly-moded clauses, $C_1 \succeq C_2$ is decidable in polynomial time over the sizes of C_1 and C_2.

5   Learning Algorithm

In this section, we present an algorithm **Learn-LM**$_l$ for exact learning of **terminating** simple linearly-moded programs, whose clauses have no more than l atoms in the body, from entailment using equivalence, subsumption and request-for-hint queries. The oracle (teacher) answers 'yes' to an *entailment equivalence query* $EQUIV(H)$ if H is same as the target program H^*, except for the renaming of variables. Otherwise, it produces a ground atom A such that $H^* \models A$ but $H \not\models A$ or $H^* \not\models A$ but $H \models A$. A *subsumption query* $SUBSUME(C)$ produces an answer 'yes' if the clause C is subsumed by a clause in H^*, otherwise answer 'no'. When C is a ground clause $A \leftarrow B_1, \cdots, B_n$ such that $H^* \models C$, the request-for-hint query $REQ(C)$ returns (1) an answer 'subsumed' if $A \leftarrow B_1, \cdots, B_n$ is subsumed by a clause in H^*, otherwise returns (2) an atom (hint) $B\theta$ in a minimal adapted SLD-refutation of $H^* \cup \{\leftarrow A\}$ with answer substitution θ such that $B\theta \notin \{B_1, \cdots, B_n\}$. As we are interested in polynomial time learnability, we consider programs for which the above types of queries can be answered in polynomial time.

Algorithm **Learn-LM**$_l$ uses the notions of saturation [8, 17] and least general generalization (lgg).

Definition 12 A clause C is a saturation of an example E w.r.t. a theory (program) H if and only if C is a reformulation of E w.r.t. H and $C' \Rightarrow C$ for every reformulation of E w.r.t. H. A clause D is a reformulation of E w.r.t. H if and only if $H \wedge E \Leftrightarrow H \wedge D$.

We are concerned with simple linearly-moded programs/clauses and define saturation of an example E w.r.t. a program H as $E \leftarrow Closure_H(E)$, where $Closure_H(E)$ is the following set of ground atoms.

Definition 13 The closure of an example $E \equiv p_0(s_0; t_0)$ w.r.t. a program H is defined as $Closure_H(E) = S_1 \cup S_2 \cup \cdots \cup S_l$, where

1. for $1 \leq i \leq l$, $S_i = \{p(\mathbf{u}; \mathbf{v}) \mid H \models p(\mathbf{u}; \mathbf{v}), [\![\mathbf{u}]\!] \leq [\![s_0]\!]\}$ and each term in $\mathbf{u}$ is either a subterm of a term in T_i or of the form $f(\mathbf{w})$ such that each term in $\mathbf{w}$ is a subterm of a term in T_i and f is a function symbol in Σ $\}$,

2. $T_1 = \{s \mid s$ is a term in $s_0\}$ and

3. for $1 \leq i < l$, $T_{i+1} = T_i \cup \{s \mid s$ is an output term of an atom in $S_i\}$.

Definition 14 Let C_1 and C_2 be two clauses $A_1 \leftarrow Body_1$ and $A_2 \leftarrow Body_2$ respectively. The least general generalization $C_1 \sqcup C_2$ of C_1 and C_2 is defined as a clause $A \leftarrow Body$ if σ_1 and σ_2 are two least general substitutions such that (1) A is the least general generalization of $A_1 \equiv A\sigma_1$ and $A_2 \equiv A\sigma_2$ and (2) $Body = \{B \mid B\sigma_i \in Body_i, i \in [1, 2]\}$.

Now, we are in a position to present our algorithm **Learn-LM**$_l$.

Procedure **Learn-LM$_l$**;
begin $H := \phi$;
while $EQUIV(H) \neq$ 'yes' **do**
  begin $A := EQUIV(H)$;
    $C := A \leftarrow Closure_H(A)$;
    while $REQ(C)$ returns a hint B **do** $C := B \leftarrow Closure_H(B)$;
    % This **while** loop exits when C is subsumed by a clause in H^*. %
    $C := \textbf{Reduce}(C)$;
    if $SUBSUME(C \sqcup D)$ returns 'yes' for some clause $D \in H$
      then $H := H \cup \{\textbf{Reduce}(C \sqcup D)\}$
      else $H := H \cup \{C\}$
  end;
return H
end Learn-LM$_l$;

Procedure **Reduce**$(A \leftarrow Body)$;
begin
    for each atom $B \in Body$ **do**
        if $SUBSUME(A \leftarrow (Body - \{B\}))$ **then** $Body := (Body - \{B\})$
end Reduce;

Example 5 We illustrate the working of **Learn-LM$_l$** by considering the standard quick-sort program given in Example 4. Due to space limitations, we cannot present full details, but only outline the trace of **Learn-LM$_l$** run on this problem. For this example, we take $l = 4$. **Learn-LM$_l$** starts with $H = \phi$ as the initial hypothesis and query $EQUIV(H)$ returns a counterexample, say $A = $ qs$([3,1,5],[1,3,5])$. The inner **while** loop asks $REQ(A \leftarrow Closure_H(A))$, which results in a hint, say $B = $ part$([1,5],3,[1],[5])$. Then, it asks $REQ(B \leftarrow Closure_H(B))$ and continue. This loop terminates with a unit clause part$([\,],3,[\,],[\,]) \leftarrow$ which will be added to H in the **if** statement.

The outer **while** loop asks $EQUIV(H)$ and gets a counterexample, say $A_1 = $ qs$([5,2],[2,5])$. The inner **while** loop terminates with unit clause part$([\,],5,[\,],[\,]) \leftarrow$. The **if** statement replaces the clause part$([\,],3,[\,],[\,]) \leftarrow$ in H by the lgg of this clause and the above clause, i.e., part$([\,],\textsf{H},[\,],[\,]) \leftarrow$.

The outer **while** loop asks $EQUIV(H)$ and gets a counterexample, say $A_2 = $ qs$([5,2,7,3],[2,3,5,7])$. The inner **while** loop asks $REQ(A_2 \leftarrow Closure_H(A_2))$, which results in a hint, say $B_2 = $ part$([3],5,[3],[\,])$. In the next iteration, it asks $REQ(B_2 \leftarrow Closure_H(B_2))$ and gets answer 'subsumed' as $Closure_H(B_2)$ includes part$([\,],5,[\,],[\,])$ as well as $3 \leq 5$. The clause part$([3],5,[3],[\,]) \leftarrow 3 \leq 5,$ part$([\,],5,[\,],[\,])$ will be added to H.

The outer **while** loop asks $EQUIV(H)$ and gets a counterexample, say $A_3 = $ qs$([3,1,8,2],[1,2,3,8])$. The inner **while** loop asks $REQ(A_3 \leftarrow Closure_H(A_3))$, which results in a hint, say $B_3 = $ part$([2],3,[2],[\,])$. In the next iteration, it asks $REQ(B_3 \leftarrow Closure_H(B_3))$ and gets answer 'subsumed' as $Closure_H(B_3)$ includes part$([\,],3,[\,],[\,])$ as well as $2 \leq 3$. Now, **Reduce**(C) is part$([2],3,[2],[\,]) \leftarrow 2 \leq 3,$ part$([\,],3,[\,],[\,])$.

The **if** statement replaces the clause $\text{part}([\,], \text{H}, [\,], [\,]) \leftarrow$ in H by the lgg of these two clauses, i.e., $\text{part}([\text{X}], \text{H}, [\text{X}], [\,]) \leftarrow \text{X} \leq \text{H}, \text{part}([\,], \text{H}, [\,], [\,])$.

Similarly, a clause $\text{part}([\text{X}], \text{H}, [\,], [\text{X}]) \leftarrow \text{X} > \text{H}, \text{part}([\,], \text{H}, [\,], [\,])$ will be added to H. At some later stages, these two clauses will be replaced by their generalizations:
$\text{part}([\text{X}|\text{Xs}], \text{H}, [\text{X}|\text{Ls}], \text{Bs}) \leftarrow \text{X} \leq \text{H}, \text{part}(\text{Xs}, \text{H}, \text{Ls}, \text{Bs})$
$\text{part}([\text{X}|\text{Xs}], \text{H}, \text{Ls}, [\text{X}|\text{Bs}]) \leftarrow \text{X} > \text{H}, \text{part}(\text{Xs}, \text{H}, \text{Ls}, \text{Bs})$
The clauses for app will be learnt in a similar fashion. Now, we explain the generation of clauses for qs.

The outer **while** loop asks $EQUIV(H)$ and gets a counterexample, say $A_4 = \text{qs}([3, 1, 8], [1, 3, 8])$. The inner **while** loop terminates (after asking some REQ queries) with a unit clause $\text{qs}([\,], [\,]) \leftarrow$ and this clause will be added to H.

The outer **while** loop asks $EQUIV(H)$ and gets a counterexample, say $A_5 = \text{qs}([6], [6])$. The inner **while** loop asks $REQ(A_5 \leftarrow Closure_H(A_5))$ and gets answer 'subsumed' as $Closure_H(A_5)$ has atoms $\text{part}([\,], 6, [\,], [\,])$, $\text{qs}([\,], [\,])$, $\text{app}([], [6], [6])$ in it and the clause $\text{qs}([6], [6]) \leftarrow \text{part}([\,], 6, [\,], [\,]), \text{qs}([\,], [\,]), \text{app}([\,], [6], [6])$ will be added to H. This clause will be later replaced by a generalization
$\text{qs}([\text{X}], [\text{X}]) \leftarrow \text{part}([\,], \text{X}, [\,], [\,]), \text{qs}([\,], [\,]), \text{app}([\,], [\text{X}], [\text{X}])$.

The outer **while** loop asks $EQUIV(H)$ and gets a counterexample, say $A_6 = \text{qs}([2, 1, 3], [1, 2, 3])$. The inner **while** loop asks $REQ(A_6 \leftarrow Closure_H(A_6))$ and gets answer 'subsumed' as $Closure_H(A_6)$ includes atoms $\text{part}([1, 3], 2, [1], [3]), \text{qs}([1], [1])$, $\text{qs}([3], [3]), \text{app}([1], [2, 3], [1, 2, 3])$. Now, $\textbf{Reduce}(C)$ is the clause $\text{qs}([2, 1, 3], [1, 2, 3]) \leftarrow \text{part}([1, 3], 2, [1], [3]), \text{qs}([1], [1]), \text{qs}([3], [3]), \text{app}([1], [2, 3], [1, 2, 3])$. The **if** statement replaces $\text{qs}([\text{X}], [\text{X}]) \leftarrow \text{part}([\,], \text{X}, [\,], [\,]), \text{qs}([\,], [\,]), \text{app}([\,], [\text{X}], [\text{X}])$ by the lgg of these two clauses, i.e., $\text{qs}([\text{H}|\text{L}], \text{S}) \leftarrow \text{part}(\text{L}, \text{H}, \text{A}, \text{B}), \text{qs}(\text{A}, \text{A1}), \text{qs}(\text{B}, \text{B1}), \text{app}(\text{A1}, [\text{H}|\text{B1}], \text{S})$. □

6 Correctness of the Learning Algorithm

In this section, we prove that the learning algorithm **Learn-LM$_l$** exactly identifies simple linearly-moded programs in polynomial time. Let H^* be the target program, $H_0, H_1, \cdots$ be the sequence of hypotheses proposed in the equivalence queries and $A_1, A_2, \cdots$ be the sequence of counterexamples returned by those queries. The following theorem states an important property of the hints returned in the inner **while** loop of **Learn-LM$_l$**.

Theorem 4 Let A be a positive example and $B_1, \cdots, B_n$ be the sequence of hints returned in the inner **while** loop of **Learn-LM$_l$**. Then *there is an SLD-refutation $G_0, G_1, \cdots, G_{n1}$ of $H^* \cup \{\leftarrow A\}$ with answer substitution θ such that for each $i \in [1, n]$, $B_i \equiv B_i'\theta$, where B_i' is the selected atom in goal G_{k_i} and $1 < k_1 < k_2 < \cdots < k_n \leq n1$. Further, $H^* \models B_i$ for each $i \in [1, n]$.*

Proof : Induction on i. See full paper [11]. □

Theorem 5 For each $i \geq 0$, hypothesis H_i is a conservative refinement of H^* and counterexample A_{i+1} is positive.

Proof: Induction on i. See full paper [11]. □

It is easy to see that any conservative refinement H of a deterministic program H^* is deterministic and $H \models A$ is decidable in polynomial time if $H^* \models A$ is decidable in polynomial time.

Now, we establish polynomial time complexity of **Learn-LM$_l$**.

Theorem 6 For any counterexample A of size n, the number of iterations of the inner **while** loop of **Learn-LM$_l$** is bounded by a polynomial in n.

Proof: By assumption, the request query $REQ(A \leftarrow Closure_H(A))$ is answered in polynomial (in n) time and hence the length of the minimal SLD-refutation of $H^* \cup \{\leftarrow A\}$ is bounded by a polynomial in n. By Theorem 4, the number of hints returned (and hence the number of iterations of the inner **while** loop of **Learn-LM$_l$**) is bounded by a polynomial in n. □

Theorem 7 If $A \equiv p_0(\mathbf{s}_0; \mathbf{t}_0)$ is a counterexample such that $n = [\![\mathbf{s}_0]\!]$ and C is the clause $A \leftarrow Closure_H(A)$, each iteration of the inner **while** loop
$\quad\quad$ **while** $REQ(C)$ returns a hint B **do** $C := B \leftarrow Closure_H(B)$;
takes polynomial (in n) time.

Proof: Omitted. See full paper [11]. □

The following lemma is needed in proving polynomial time complexity of the learning algorithm **Learn-LM$_l$**.

Lemma 2 If C is a clause of size n, then the sequence $C = C_0 \prec C_1 \prec C_2$ is of length no more than $2n$.

Proof: Omitted. See full paper [11]. □

Now, we can prove the main result of the paper.

Theorem 8 The algorithm **Learn-LM$_l$** exactly identifies any simple linearly-moded program with m clauses in a polynomial time over m and n, where n is the size of the largest counterexample provided.

Proof: Termination condition of the main **while** loop is $EQUIV(H)$. Therefore **Learn-LM$_l$** exactly identifies the target program H^* if **Learn-LM$_l$** terminates. Now, we prove that the number of iterations of the main **while** loop is bounded by a polynomial over m and n.

By Theorem 5, H is always a conservative refinement of H^* and hence H has at most m clauses. The size of each clause in H is bounded by a polynomial in n. Each iteration of the main **while** loop either adds a clause to H or generalizes a clause in H. By Lemma 2, the number of times a clause can be generalized is bounded by twice the size of the clause. Therefore, the number of iterations of the main **while** loop is bounded by $m.poly(n)$, where $poly(n)$ is a polynomial in n. Each iteration takes polynomial time as (1) saturation and lgg are polynomial time computable, (2) each query is answered in polynomial time and (3) by Theorem 6, the number of iterations of the inner **while** loop is bounded by a polynomial in n and by Theorem 7, each iteration takes polynomial time. Therefore, **Learn-LM$_l$** exactly identifies any simple linearly-moded program with m clauses in a polynomial time over m and n. □

7 Comparison

We compare the results of this paper with three recent works [3, 10, 16] on learning first order acyclic (terminating) Horn programs. Each of these works provides a class of deterministic and terminating programs that can be learnt in polynomial time from entailment.

In [3], Arimura presents the class of acyclic constrained Horn (ACH) programs. The main restriction ACH-programs is that each term occurring in the body of a clause is a subterm of a term in the head. This excludes all the programs using local variables.

In [10], Krishna Rao and Sattar present the class of finely-moded programs, that properly contains the class of ACH programs. The main restriction of finely-moded programs is the following: if a local variable occurs in an output position of an atom A in the body, then each input term of A is a subterm of an input term in the head. This excludes programs like **quick-sort** and **merge-sort**. However, this class contains programs like **multiplication** and **exponentiation** which are not linearly-moded.

In [16], Reddy and Prasad present the class of acyclic Horn (AH) programs. The main restriction AH-programs is that each term occurring in the head of a clause is a subterm of a term in the body. This is a strong restriction from the programming point of view and excludes even simple programs like **append** and **member**. However, Reddy and Tadepalli [16] argue that the class of acyclic Horn (AH) programs is quite useful for representing planning knowledge.

The relationship between various classes discussed above is depicted below.

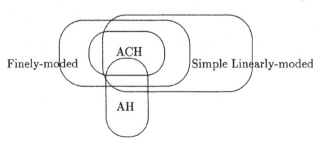

8 Conclusion

In this paper, we considered exact learning of logic programs from entailment and present a polynomial time algorithm to learn a rich class of logic programs that allow local variables. The naturality of this class and applicability of our results in practice can be infered from the fact that our class contains a substantial portion of the set of programs given in Sterling and Shapiro's book [20].

References

1. D. Angluin (1988), *Learning with hints*, Proc. COLT'88, pp. 223-237.
2. D. Angluin (1988), *Queries and concept learning*, Machine Learning **2**, pp. 319-342.
3. H. Arimura (1997), *Learning acyclic first-order Horn sentences from entailment*, Proc. ALT'97, Lecture Notes in Artificial intelligence **1316**, pp. 432-445.
4. W. Cohen and H. Hirsh (1992), *Learnability of description logics*, Proc. COLT'92, pp. 116-127.
5. S. Dzeroski, S. Muggleton and S. Russel (1992), *PAC-learnability of determinate logic programs*, Proc. of COLT'92, pp. 128-135.
6. M. Frazier and L. Pitt (1993), *Learning from entailment: an application to propositional Horn sentences*, Proc. ICML'93, pp. 120-127.
7. M. Frazier and L. Pitt (1994), *CLASSIC learning*, Proc. COLT'94, pp. 23-34.
8. P. Idestam-Almquist (1996), *Efficient induction of recursive definitions by structural analysis of saturations*, pp. 192-205 in L. De Raedt (ed.), *Advances in inductive logic programming*, IOS Press.
9. M.R.K. Krishna Rao (1996), *A class of Prolog programs inferable from positive data*, Proc. of Algorithmic Learning Theory, ALT'96, LNAI **1160**, pp. 272-284. Revised version to appear in *Theoretical Computer Science* special issue on ALT'96.
10. M.R.K. Krishna Rao and A. Sattar (1998), *Learning from entailment of logic programs with local variables*, to appear in Proc. of ALT'98.
11. M.R.K. Krishna Rao and A. Sattar (1998), *Learning linearly-moded programs from entailment* – full paper with proofs, see http://www.cit.gu.edu.au/~krishna.
12. J. W. Lloyd (1987), *Foundations of Logic Programming*, Springer-Verlag.
13. S. Muggleton and L. De Raedt (1994), *Inductive logic programming: theory and methods*, J. Logic Prog. **19/20**, pp. 629-679.
14. S.H. Nienhuys-Cheng and R. de Wolf (1995), *The subsumption theorem for several forms of resolution*, Tech. Rep. EUR-FEW-CS-96-14, Erasmus Uni., Rotterdam.
15. C.D. Page and A.M. Frish (1992), *Generalization and learnability: a study of constrained atoms*, in Muggleton (ed.) Inductive Logic programming, pp. 29-61.
16. C. Reddy and P. Tadepalli (1998), *Learning first order acyclic Horn programs from entailment*, to appear in Proc. of ICML'98.
17. C. Rouveirol (1992), *Extensions of inversion of resolution applied to theory completion*, in Muggleton (ed.) Inductive Logic programming, pp. 63-92.
18. E. Shapiro (1981), *Inductive inference of theories from facts*, Tech. Rep., Yale Univ.
19. E. Shapiro (1983), *Algorithmic Program Debugging*, MIT Press.
20. L. Sterling and E. Shapiro (1994), *The Art of Prolog*, MIT Press.

Learning First-Order Rules from Image Applied to Glaucoma Diagnosis

Hayato Ohwada†, Makiko Daidoji†, Shiroaki Shirato‡ and Fumio Mizoguchi†

† Faculty of Sci. and Tech.
Science University of Tokyo
Noda, Chiba, 278-8510, Japan

‡University of Tokyo
Bunkyo-ku, Tokyo, 113-8654, Japan

Abstract. Computer-based diagnosis from image data is important for medicine. In particular, for the glaucoma diagnosis we target here, the ocular fundus image can be easily obtained and can be used to automatically identify whether an eye is glaucomatous or not. However, the image has a two-dimensional distribution, and it is difficult to feature the whole image through some real-valued parameters in general. This paper proposes a machine learning method using a set of expert's decision cases that identify local abnormalities of an image. This method finds regularities between an image set and the decision cases using Inductive Logic Programming (ILP). Unlike decision-tree learning and neural networks, ILP allows relational learning between concepts. Learned rules are abstract enough to absorb noisy data obtained directly from image analysis. We applied the method to detecting early glaucomatous eyes. Our ILP system, GKS produced 30 rules from 2000 positive and negative examples that were obtained by segmenting 39 glaucomatous eyes. A 10-fold cross validation assessment shows about 80% sensitivity and 65% accuracy of the rules, resulting in the high performance comparable with human-level classification.

1 Introduction

Image data is very important for medical consultation. CT-scan, X-ray photographs, and sonar sensor images provide invaluable data for dramatically improving the performance of diagnosis. Such images are digitized and processed automatically by computers, yielding a practical tool for screening large volumes of data. Our objective here is glaucoma diagnosis where ocular fundus images are easy to take compared with other data obtained from expensive instruments. The ultimate goal of this paper is to develop diagnostic systems that can handle such images with performance comparable to that of human experts.

However, automatic diagnosis from images only is very difficult for the following reasons:

- Locality of abnormal parts
  Since an image has a two-dimensional distribution, it is difficult to feature the whole image. Instead, abnormalities are detected locally.

– Context-sensitive noisy data

Images are very sensitive to conditions of patients, physicians and instruments. Also, they are analyzed by human manually, yielding noisy data.

– Abstracting raw data

There is a major gap between a digital image and decision rules. No general method exists to compute a small set of feature values by abstracting raw data.

To solve the above problems, we exploit the results of image analysis by a human expert. More specifically, using decisions specifying local abnormalities of the image by the expert, we employ a machine-learning method to extract the regularity in abnormal parts. This method extracts the underlying relationships between an image and the expert decision cases and can be regarded as a datamining method for images. Such relationships reflect how the expert reads the image, and the machine-produced rules are used to simulate the expert's image analysis.

The proposed method divides the original image into several segments and computes feature values for each segment. It then constructs relational features such as differences and trend patterns between single features. Given a set of an expert's decision cases, our inductive logic programming (ILP) system, GKS[5], produces a set of rules that associates the decision cases with some of the relational features. The rule set is used to detect abnormal parts of a new image.

Unlike decision-tree learning and neural network, ILP allows relational learning between concepts. ILP enables us to abstract image data and increase the comprehensibility of learned rules. Thus, it is possible to conduct interactively refine the rules through the expert[7]. Furthermore, the rules are abstract enough to absorb noisy data, yielding stable performance of the rule application.

We applied the method to diagnosing an eye disease, glaucoma. There are several glaucoma consultation systems such as CASNET[9], EXPERT[4] and DG4[3]. These work in a question-answer method and require appropriate interpretation by experts. In contrast, an image is a directly measured data set and is used to identify glaucomatous eyes without the need of experts. This suggests a screening tool for detecting glaucomatous eyes from a large data set.

2 Relational features of images

Our data-mining method provides a bridge between low-level image data and high-level knowledge representation based on the first-order formalism. Data transformation is introduced to construct useful feature values obtained from image analysis, and such values are combined to construct relational features for inductive learning.

2.1 Heuristic image segmentation

Our image analysis focuses on the geometrical or topological structure of the target domain and constructs features based on this structure. The structure allows us to decompose the original image into several segments and to extract the features for each segment.

An image is specified by a set of pixels. Let $P_n(I)$ be a decomposition function mapping image I to set of n images S_i. The function holds the following equalities:

$$P_n(I) = \{S_1, S_2, ..., S_n\}$$
$$I = S_1 \cup S_2 \cup .... \cup S_n$$
$$\forall_{i,j} S_i \cap S_j = \phi$$

As the third equality shows, there is no intersection between segments.

Heuristic image analysis is not always automatic, but reflects the target structure sought by the human operator. For example, ocular fundus image should be circularly divided according to the underlying medical knowledge. This segmentation can be done by human assistance where the human specifies the central position of the ocular being segmented. Using a certain guideline, procedure or manual, such assistance is possible for non-experts, resulting in a semi-automatic process. Our heuristic image analysis indicates somewhat interactive image analysis without experts.

To extract meaningful feature values from the segments, irrelevant regions are eliminated, and some features are defined on the remaining image region. Vessel parts of an ocular fundus image are irrelevant for detecting glaucomatous eyes. Filtering function g for image S generates a subset of S, defined as follows:

$$g(s) \subseteq S$$

Approximation feature function $\hat{f}(s)$ for image S is an eliminated version of S:

$$\hat{f}(s) = f(g(s))$$

This indicates that feature function f is applied to a subset of a decomposed image set.

Images can be segmented using a regular pattern, but filtering is applied in an irregular manner, with the human eliminating a small part of the image. In this sense, various image processing techniques are used for filtering, and we use a commercial image processing system in analyzing ocular fundus images. It is possible for non-experts to filter the image using the system through interactive operations.

2.2 Relations for qualitative differences and trends

In general, geometrical and topological relations for k segments can be defined. For example, mesh-based segmentation has four relations (east, west, north and south) for the adjacent segments. Let s_1 and s_2 be adjacent segments for relation R. The difference between those feature values is regarded as a new feature called the relational feature. Focusing on the ordering relation for the difference, such a feature represents the qualitative difference or trend.

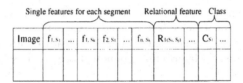

Fig. 1. Table representation

To derive relational features, we define them as a logic program consisting of background knowledge in inductive learning. For example, the following rule defines the predicate **up** stating that the feature values for two adjacent segments are increasing:

```
up(Relation, Image, Segment1, Segment2, Feature) ←
    adjacent(Relation, Segment1, Segment2),
    data(Image, Segment1, Feature, Value1),
    data(Image, Segment2, Feature, Value2),
    Value1 ≤ Value2.
```

where the predicate **adjacent** states that **Segment1** and **Segment2** are adjacent. The **up** predicate holds true if for the feature values **Value1** and **Value2**, the inequality **Value1** ≤ **Value2** is satisfied. The predicate **down** can be defined in a similar manner.

It is possible to define higher-order relations by combining qualitative difference relationships. These relations represent a trend for a sequence of adjacent segments. Suppose that there is a sequence of three adjacent segments where the first and second segments hold the down relation and the second and third segments hold the **up** relation.

3 Inducing relational rules

In propositional learning, single and relational features can be described as a table as shown in Figure 1. However, such representation causes the following problems:

(1) Features are specific to particular segments.
    For a produced decision tree, edges are conditions for specific segments. Existentially quantified variables should be used to represent segments.
(2) It is impossible to distinguish segments of the same image from those of other segments.
    To solve problem (1), we construct a case mixing its image ID and segment number. In this treatment, an induced rule is produced which subsumes facts for several segments. However, such segments may come from different images.

(3) A very large number of attributes are required for each case.

An image consists of single features and relational features for specific segments. If we have k segments and a relational feature with m arity, this feature constructs a very large number of potential attributes (m-combinations of the k segments).

ILP solves all the problems, and relational features can be user-defined as a simple logic program as mentioned in the previous section. A variable for a segment is existentially quantified in the conditional part of the produced rule.

3.1 First-order learning

First-order learning produces a set of hypotheses H from a set of examples E and background knowledge B where each element in H, E and B takes a first-order clausal form. We separate E into a set of positive examples E^+ and negative examples E^-. A set of hypotheses H satisfies the following condition:

$$B \wedge H \models E^+$$

A hypothesis is a rule for a target corresponding to a class in propositional learning. For learning from images, a hypothesis is a rule for deciding whether a segment is abnormal or not. In this case, positive and negative examples are described as follows:

$$\texttt{abnormal(Image, Segment)}$$

In contrast, a hypothesis is of the following form:

$$\texttt{abnormal(Image, Segment)} \leftarrow \texttt{C}_1, \ \ldots, \ \texttt{C}_n.$$

where $\texttt{C}_i$ is a condition and all $\texttt{C}_i$ must be satisfied to show the abnormality of **Segment** in **Image**. The variables **Image** and **Segment** are universally quantified.

As a first-order learning system, our GKS system [5][6] is used for application to glaucoma diagnosis. In GKS, a hypothesis and an element of background knowledge are described as a definite clause, and each example, as a unit clause. We developed three versions of GKS implemented in a constraint logic programming language, a concurrent logic programming language and Java language. Given a source file including background knowledge and a set of examples, GKS loads the file and produces a set of rules. Although GKS allows learning from numerical data, we focus on learning from relational features in this paper.

4 Application to glaucoma diagnosis

4.1 Input and output for GKS

Input data to GKS consists of feature values obtained from image analysis and expert's analysis, and background knowledge described as a logic program. The feature values for image analysis are put on the background knowledge, and

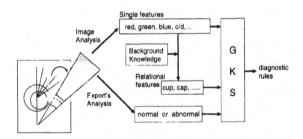

Fig. 2. Constructing input data

abnormality labeling for expert's analysis yields positive and negative examples. Figure 2 shows how input data are constructed. Although single features are extracted from each segment, relational features are derived from the background knowledge and the single feature values. Whereas this derivation is done at GKS run time, the figure shows, in a comprehensive manner, that GKS takes as input the derived relational features. GKS then generates a set of rules that associates the abnormality for each segment with single and relational features.

In this study, we focus on 39 early glaucomatous eyes and construct input data for both 36 segments and 26 segments (These segmentations are due to previous empirical studies on glaucoma diagnosis.). Background knowledge consists of RGB information and the C/D ratio for each segment, adjacent relationships between segments, and relational feature definitions. The numbers of elements in the background knowledge are shown in Table 1 and 2.

A produced rule is as follows:

```
% { Pos = 48/162, Neg = 48/1242 }
abnormal(Image, Segment)  ←
    down2cup5(Image, Segmet, red),
    cuup(Image, Segment, green).
```

The rule means that for all **Image** and **Segment**, **Segment** of **Image** is **abnormal** if the trend of the feature **red** is **down2up5** and the trend of the feature **green** is **cuup**. Since no specific segment is used, the rule is general enough to predict abnormalities for unseen images. The prediction is performed by searching for a segment matching with the **down2cup5** trend for the **red** feature and matching with the **cuup** trend for the **green** feature. The annotated part indicates the ratios of positive and negative examples covered by the rule.

4.2 Performance

We adopted k-fold cross validation to investigate the performance of produced rules. K-fold cross validation divides a given example set into k mutually exclusive test partitions of approximately equal size. In this setting, the set of residual

Table 1. Examples and background knowledge for the 36 segments

Positive and negative examples	Number
abnormal(+image, +segment)	162
\+ abnormal(+image, +segment)	1242
Background knowledge	
data(+image, +segment, +feature, -value)	5616
adjacent(+segment, -segment)	35
Derived relational features	
cup(+image, +segment, +feature)	2712
cap(+image, +segment, +feature)	2769
cuup(+image, +segment, +feature)	4172
caap(+image, +segment, +feature)	4176
cup2up/up2cap(+image, +segment, +feature)	5136
cap2down/down2cup(+image, +segment, +feature)	5487

Table 2. Examples and background knowledge for the 26 segments

Positive and negative examples	Number
abnormal(+image, +segment)	146
\+ abnormal(+image, +segment)	868
Background knowledge	
data(+image, +segment, +feature, -value)	5616
adjacent(+segment, -segment)	35
Derived relational features	
cap(+image, +segment, +feature)	2109
cuup(+image, +segment, +feature)	2348
caap(+image, +segment, +feature)	2952
cup2up/up2cap(+image, +segment, +feature)	2877
cap2down/down2cup(+image, +segment, +feature)	3677

examples, excluding each partition, is used as a training set.

The performance of the rules produced by GKS varies in the permissible ratio of negative examples covered by the rule (apparent error rate). As shown in Table 1, 2, there are 80 ~ 90% negative examples, and the default accuracy is very high where a simple classifier always concludes negative, However, sensitivity approaches zero, and a higher permissible ratio should be set with high sensitivity and reasonable accuracy. In particular, medical diagnosis needs high sensitivity because a false negative error is very critical.

Figure 3 is a graph for changes of sensitivity and accuracy with respect to the permissible ratios from 1% to 40%. Sensitivity goes beyond 60% when the permissible ratio exceeds 3%. Sensitivity and accuracy converge at a ratio of 5%. Our minimum requirement sets 50% accuracy, and we experimented with the learning performance for ratios from 5% to 10%.

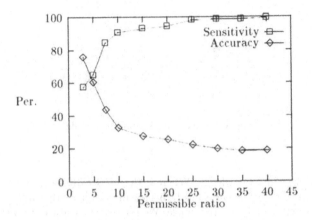

Fig. 3. Performance change for various permissible ratios

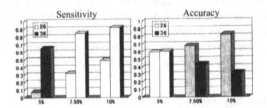

Fig. 4. Performances of 26-segment and 36-segment methods

We investigated the performances for the two image segmentation methods; the performances are shown in Figure 4. It is evident that the 36-segment method has higher performance than the 26-segment method. The next section analyzes the detail of the performance with respect to the 36-segment method.

5 Analysis and insight

5.1 Utility of background knowledge

The learning performance varies with the relevance of background knowledge in ILP. In addition to measurement data, medical knowledge can be explicitly coded in the background knowledge. Owing to the progress in medicine, new medical knowledge can be added to the background knowledge to produce more reliable rules.

So far, the input data includes RGB values and the C/D ratio extracted from ocular fundus images. In this section, we compare the learning performances for

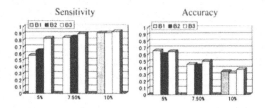

Fig. 5. Utility of background knowledge

different background knowledge. Whereas the C/D ratio is an indicator of the cupping state of the optic nerve head, this feature is inherently three-dimensional and is not reliable based on the image. We remove the feature from the original background knowledge (B2). In contrast, we add the rim abnormality identified by three-dimensional measurement into B2. Figure 5 shows the performances of B2, B1 (removed version), and B3 (added version). For most cases, B3 has better performance, and the performance of B2 is not better than that of B1. The result indicates that the reliable data increases the learning performance, but unreliable data added into the background knowledge is immaterial. The progress of medical knowledge and measurement instruments makes data more reliable and increases the learning performance.

5.2 Screening big data

The problem in using our diagnostic system for screening large volumes of data is the inability of automatic image analysis. Although our image analysis can be done by even non-experts, some manual operations such as vessel exclusion are time-consuming, and the analysis is not suitable for image analysis. We now present the learning performance for background knowledge constructed by automatic image analysis. Figure 6 compares automatic and manual image analyses. It is straightforward to see the advantage of manual image analysis. However, the automatic analysis has 65% sensitivity and 40% accuracy with respect to 10% permissible ratio. This performance is not bad for screening data. The problem is the balance between the inspection cost indicating the accuracy and the false negative error making decisions critical. Setting the best break-even-point for good balance corresponds to deciding the best permissible ratio of negative examples covered. Figure 7 shows the learning performance of the automatic image analysis in changing the permissible ratio. For ratios from 5% to 10%, sensitivity and accuracy change drastically. This indicates that the best permissible ratio is in this range.

The present study uses high-resolution image data to detect early glaucomatous eyes. However, most image data obtained from a mass examination seems to be rough, and the reliability of a single feature value is lower. For such an

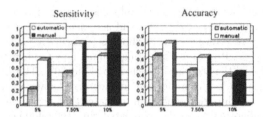

Fig. 6. Comparison with automatic image analysis

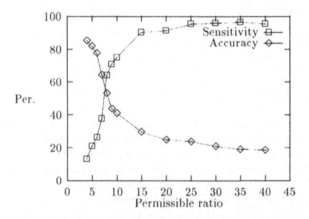

Fig. 7. Performance change for various permissible ratios

application, a small number of ocular fundus images are not sufficient for producing useful diagnostic rules. We need at least 10,000 images because a single glaucomatous eye may be found in 40 men or 50 women, and most cases are negative examples. We should carefully consider statistical analysis, inspection cost and false negative error for screening.

5.3 Extracting human expertise

The advantages of ILP are that produced rules are readable and that the validity of the rules can be checked easily. However, some experts are not interested in rules themselves, but prefer statistical measures such as sensitivity and accuracy. This is because they focuses on the usability of the rules and take different clinical approaches using the results of the measures. In this respect, the experts view the rule application as a black box and need the reliability measure of the result of the rule application, irrespective of which rules are applied.

In contrast, from the perspective of young doctors acting as assistants, the rules reflect experts' decision cases, and they are interested in the rule themselves. If there are some highly successful rules compared with their own rules, they may see the meaning of the rules and use them to enhance their decisions. The performance of young doctors is about 60% accuracy for early detection of a glaucomatous eye. However, after being trained how to identify glaucomatous image by an expert, the accuracy increases to about 80%. This implies that even machine produced rules are important for doctors. As an example, the following rule provides high performance and indicates that nerve fiber layer defect is caused by the abnormality of the associated rim. By refining such a rule progressively, it is possible to make experts' clinical know-how explicit.

```
% { Pos = 50/162, Neg = 58/1242 }
abnormal(A, B) ←
    rim(A, B),
    cuup(A, B, green),
    cup(A, B, blue).
```

6 Related work

An initial experiment applying ILP to ocular fundus image was conducted in [6]. This trial has the same motivation, but in this paper we challenge the detection of early glaucomatous eyes as a hard and real problem. We introduce relational features for abstracting image data, while our initial framework deals with measurement data directly. Thus, our new approach provides a data-mining method including image analysis, and ILP-based learning.

A method based on neural networks was applied to identifying a glaucomatous eye [2]. Although both sensitivity and accuracy are higher than ours, input data is more reliable based on expert's interpretation and other measurement data. In contrast, our image analysis can be done in a certain procedure by non-experts.

The major difference from neural network is the ability to easily describe background knowledge. The advent of highly successful measurement instruments improves the background knowledge. Furthermore, produced rules are reusable and evaluable by different experts.

Relational features are derived by differentiating single feature values similarly as in time-series data analysis. Our method differs from handling a sequence of two-dimensional data. The qualitative difference proposed here is based on the qualitative reasoning framework and is close to Bratko's work for ILP-based qualitative synthesis of dynamic system modeling[1]. Our work integrates image analysis, and inductive learning to extract qualitative spatial relationships from the underlying image in medicine.

7 Conclusions

This paper presented a method for extracting diagnostic rules from images. The method integrates image analysis and inductive learning as a new data-mining method. Heuristic image analysis is semi-automatic under a certain procedure. Relational features are derived from single features generated by the image analysis. Inductive learning associates abnormal image segments with these relational features.

Our ILP system, GKS, generated a set of rules that are expressive compared with propositional learning. The performance of these rules was investigated through cross-validation assessment and was comparable with that of human-level classification.

References

1. Bratko, I., Applications of Machine Learning: Towards Knowledge Synthesis, *New Generation Computing*, Vol. 11 pp. 343-360, 1993.
2. L. Brigatti, D.Hoffman, and J.Caprioli, Neural Networks to Identify Glaucoma With Structural and Functional Measurements, American Journal of Oohthalmology, Vol.121, 1996, pp.511-521.
3. Kitazawa, Y., Shirato, S., Mizoguchi, F., A new computer-aided glaucoma consultation system (G4-Expert), *Royal Society of Medicine International Congress and Symposium Series*, No.44, pp.161-168, 1981.
4. Mizoguchi, F., Maruyama, K., Kitazawa, Y. and Kulikowski, C. A., A case study of EXPERT formalism: An approach to a design of medical consultation system through EXPERT formalism, *Proc. of IJCAI*, pp. 583–585, 1979.
5. Mizoguchi F., Ohwada H., Constrained Relative Least General Generalization for Inducing Constraint Logic Programs, *New Generation Computing*, vol.13, 1995.
6. Mizoguchi F., Ohwada H., Daidoji M., Sirato S., Using Inductive Logic Programming to Learn Rules that Identify Glaucomatous Eyes, *Intelligent Data Analysis in Medicine and Pharmacology*, Kluwer Academic Publishers, 1997, pp. 227-242.
7. N. Lavrac, E. Keravnou, B. Zupan, Intelligent Data Analysis in Medicine and Pharmacology, Kluwer Academic Publisher, 1997.
8. Rissanen, J.A.Modeling by Shortest Data Description, Automatica, Vol. 14, 1978, pp.465-471.
9. Weiss, S. M., Galen, Kulikowski, C.A., Amarel, S., and Safir, A., A model-based method for computer-aided medical decision making, *Artificial Intelligence*, Vol. 11, 1978, pp. 145-172.
10. Sholom M. Weiss, Nitin Indurkhya, Predictive Data Mining, Morgan Kaufmann,San Mateo,Califolnia, 1998.

Knowledge-Based Formulation of Dynamic Decision Models

Chenggang Wang, Tze-Yun Leong

Medical Computing Laboratory, School of Computing,
National University of Singapore, Lower Kent Ridge Road, Singapore 119260
{wangcg, leongty}@comp.nus.edu.sg

Abstract. We present a new methodology to automate decision making over time and uncertainty. We adopt a knowledge-based model construction approach to support automated and interactive formulation of dynamic decision models, i.e., models that explicitly consider the effects of time. Our work integrates and extends different features of the existing frameworks. We incorporate a hybrid knowledge representation scheme that integrates categorical knowledge, probabilistic knowledge, and deterministic knowledge. We provide a set of knowledge-based modification operations for automatic and interactive generation, abstraction, and refinement of the model components. We have built a knowledge base in a real-world domain and shown that it can support automated construction of a reasonable dynamic decision model. The results indicate the practical promise of the proposed design.

1 Introduction

Dynamic decision modeling is a very challenging task. The multitude of problems, the domain-specificity, the uncertainty, and the temporal nature of the underlying phenomena all contribute to the intricacy of the dynamic decision modeling process [5]. To automate the model construction process, efforts in developing knowledge-based model construction (KBMC) systems have emerged in recent years. The relevant works include ALTERID [1], Frail3 [4], SUDO-PLANNER [14], and DYNASTY [9]. These systems advocate that the decision models for different problems should be constructed on demand from a knowledge base [13]. This approach facilitates scalability and reusability of the knowledge base. Moreover, the resulting decision models are parsimonious and most relevant to the problems at hand.

An important issue in KBMC research is the choice of the target model. All of the existing KBMC systems synthesize only one type of decision models; influence diagram or its variants are the choice in all the systems mentioned. Since each type of decision models can convey only certain information explicitly, some important characteristics of the decision situations are lost when the models are completed. Moreover, most of the existing frameworks do not support knowledge-based model modification. The model construction process terminates when an initial model is completed. If the user is not satisfied with the resulting model, he has to manually modify it separately.

We propose a KBMC framework that adopts a new dynamic decision modeling language, DynaMoL [5], to model target decisions, and provides a set of knowledge-based modification operations for interactive generation, abstraction, and refinement of the model components. The framework incorporates a hybrid knowledge base representation scheme that integrates categorical knowledge, probabilistic knowledge, and deterministic knowledge. We have tested the design by building a knowledge base in a real-world domain and demonstrating how it can support automated formulation of a reasonable dynamic decision model. We illustrate the proposed design and address some future research issues in this paper.

2 System Architecture

The proposed system architecture is depicted in Figure 1. Given as input a dynamic decision problem description, the model constructor will access the knowledge base via the KB-manager to formulate a model. Further modification operations can be applied interactively by the user. The final model is then evaluated or solved, with respect to some pre-specified optimality and evaluation criteria, e.g., life expectancy, monetary cost, and/or desirability or utility, by DYNAMO, a prototype implementation of DynaMoL, to determine an optimal course of action.

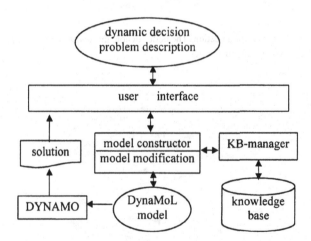

Figure 1. The system architecture

3 An Example Problem

For illustration, we consider a simplified dynamic decision problem in colorectal cancer management [2]. In managing the follow up of colorectal cancer patients, a series of diagnostic tests are performed to detect possible recurrence, metastasis, or both recurrence and metastasis of the cancer; treatment is prescribed if cancer is detected. The diagnostic tests available are different in terms of monetary cost, sensitivity, and specificity. The decision is to determine the optimal course of diagnostic tests for effective disease detection so that timely treatment can be given.

4 The Target Language: DynaMoL

DynaMoL has four major components. First, the decision grammar supports problem formulation with multiple interfaces. Second, the presentation convention, in the tradition of graphical decision models, governs parameter visualization in multiple perspectives; two graphical representations are currently included: *transition view* which corresponds to the Markov state transition diagram, as shown in Figure 2, and *influence view* which corresponds to the dynamic influence diagram [12] without decision nodes or value nodes, as shown in Figure 3. Third, the mathematical representation, in terms of a Semi-Markov Decision Process (SMDP), provides a concise formulation of the decision problem; it also admits various solution methods. Fourth, the translation convention establishes automatic transformations among the different graphical representations, and from these representations into an SMDP [5].

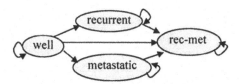

Figure 2. Transition view for an action. The nodes denote the states; the links denote the possible transitions from one state to another

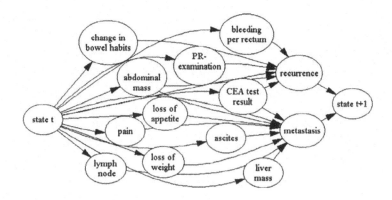

Figure 3. Influence view for an action. The nodes depict the possible event or chance variables, each with a possible set of outcomes or values, that affect the state transitions, and the links the probabilistic dependences. The states are captured as outcomes of the state variables

DynaMoL makes a good target decision modeling language because the high-level modeling constructs and the multiple graphical perspectives allow simple and explicit specification of the decision factors and constraints, thus facilitating automated formulation. DynaMoL also supports incremental language extension, which allows the scope of the dynamic decision problems addressed to be gradually expanded.

5 Knowledge Base Representation

Our knowledge base representation design is based on the first-order logic-like representations [1, 4, 7, 9] and the fluid multilevel representation [14] in existing KBMC systems. We adopt a hybrid framework that integrates categorical knowledge, probabilistic knowledge and deterministic knowledge. The categorical knowledge captures the definitional and structural relations of the domain concepts. This type of knowledge provides the power of abstraction and inheritance; it supports modeling at multiple levels of details. The probabilistic knowledge captures the interactions (probabilistic dependencies) among the concepts. These relations are needed to support the derivation of missing information in model construction. The deterministic knowledge expresses deterministic rules and declaratory constraints about the domain.

5.1 Categorical Knowledge

We use knowledge frames to describe domain concepts, e.g., diseases, tests, treatments, and other entities related to the decision problems. All the concepts may be instantiated as actions and event variables in the probabilistic knowledge base. Every concept definition has at least an attribute indicating the specialization relation, AKO. For all concepts a and b and all individuals α, AKO = {(a, b) | a$\subseteq$ b, i.e., $\forall \alpha$, $\alpha \in$ a $\Rightarrow$ $\alpha \in$ b}. The AKO relation imposes a hierarchy or partial ordering of the domain concepts. Figure 4 shows part of such a hierarchy for the example problem. The AKO links will always point upward. A parent of a concept indicates a concept immediately above the given concept in the hierarchy. An ancestor of a concept is situated somewhere above the given concept. A child and a descendent of a concept are analogously defined, but downward in the hierarchy. The lowest common ancestor of a set of concepts $\{C_1, C_2,... C_n\}$ is a concept C which is an ancestor of these concepts, and for all children $S_1, S_2,...S_q$ of C, there exists a C_k, $1 \leq k \leq n$, where S_j, $1 \leq j \leq q$, is not a parent of C_k. The lowest common ancestors of a set of concepts may not be unique.

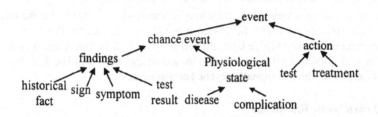

Figure 4. Domain knowledge base hierarchy

5.2 Probabilistic Knowledge

To represent the probabilistic knowledge, we must be able to model the action effects, the relations among event variables, and the temporal nature of the decision environment. We use timed concept instances to represent actions and event variables. For example, test-A(t) represents the action to perform test-A at time t. Similarly, test-A-result(t), which can take either the positive or negative value, represents the event variable test-A-result at time t. It follows that test-A-result(t, positive) is an event.

Probabilistic dependency statements, similar to those in [1] except that we separate the logic program clauses as the preconditions in the probabilistic statements for representational clarity and inferential efficiency, represent the action effects and probabilistic relationships among the event variables. They have the form $E_0|_p E_1,..., E_n = Pr(\omega_{E0}|\omega_{E1}, \omega_{E2}... \omega_{En}) \leftarrow C_1, C_2, ... C_m$ where n>=0, m>=0. E_i, i = 1,..., n, is an event variable and C_j, j = 1,..., m, is a conditioning literal, which could be an event or an action taken. ω refers to one of the alternative outcomes of the event variables. The left hand side of the equality indicates the possible probabilistic dependence between $E_1, E_2,..., E_n$ and E_0. The right hand side indicates the conditional probability distribution over the alternative outcomes of the event variable E_0 given the outcomes for the event variables $E_1,..., E_n$. The last part is a logical expression which must be true for this probabilistic relation to be applicable. If P is the above probabilistic sentence, we define *precondition*(P) to be the conjunction $C_1, C_2, ... C_m$, *(probabilistic) antecedent*(P) to be the conjunction $E_1,...,E_n$, and *(probabilistic) consequent*(P) to be E_0. As an example, consider the following dependency, which expresses the probability distribution of metastasis at time t+1 given the outcome of loss-of-appetite at time t when action "observation" is taken and the Dukes' stage of the patient is C.

metastatic(t+1)$|_p$loss-of-appetite(t)=Pr($\omega_{metastatic(t+1)}|\omega_{loss-of-appetite(t)}$)

	metastasis (t+1, present)	metastasis(t+1, absent)
loss-of-appetite(t, yes)	0.6	0.4
loss-of-appetite(t, no)	0.3	0.7

$\leftarrow$ observation(t), duke-stage(t,C)

A probabilistic knowledge base is a finite set of probabilistic dependency statements. Event variable e_1 directly influences e_2, denoted $e_1 \rightarrow e_2$, if there exists a probabilistic rule P such that $e_1 \in$ antecedent (P) and e_2 = consequent (P). There is a directed path from e_1 to e_2, if there exists a sequence $e_1 \rightarrow I_1$, $I_1 \rightarrow I_2,..., I_n \rightarrow e_2$, where $I_1, I_2,... I_n$ are the intermediate nodes on the path between e_1 and e_2.

Since an influence view is a directed acyclic graph, we must ensure that the knowledge base contains no cycles [6]. Since it is not easy to enforce this "acyclicity" requirement for the knowledge base, the KB-manager will include a function which, after new probabilistic rules are added to the knowledge base, will check if they will lead to any cycles in the originally acyclic knowledge base.

5.3 Deterministic Knowledge

A deterministic knowledge base is a set of logical statements, called deterministic dependency statements, of the form $L_0 \leftarrow L_1$ and $L_2 \ldots$ and L_n, or $L_0 \leftarrow L_1$ or $L_2 \ldots$ or L_n n>=0, where $\leftarrow$ stands for implication, L_i, i = 1, ..., n, is a condition literal, which can be an event or an action. A deterministic dependency statement expresses the logical relationship or constraint among the events and/or actions; it allows deduction of the implicit values for the preconditions. For example, if a patient is assumed to be dead after having two successive metastasis, the following rule can be included: status(t,dead) $\leftarrow$ metastasis(t, yes) and metastasis(t-1, yes).

5.4 Inferences Supported by the KB-Manager

With reference to Figure 1, the model constructor can access the knowledge base via some general queries to the KB-manager. This implies that the knowledge base representation is modular with respect to the inferences supported. Therefore, when new constructs are added to the knowledge base representation, or when the structure of the knowledge base is changed, we need not re-implement the model constructor. An example of the queries supported is "what are the event variables that directly influence <event variable x> given <action a > at <time t>?" If the knowledge base contains two different rules with identical consequent, the KB-manager will select the more specific rule or just combine the antecedents with some canonical forms, such as noisy-OR [8], generalized noisy-OR [11], noisy-AND, and noisy-ONEOF.

6 Dynamic Decision Model Formulation

Based on the example problem, we automate the construction of a dynamic decision model. The resulting well-formed model can then be solved for the optimal course of action by the DYNAMO system.

Step 1. Eliciting Decision Context Information

The process begins with the model constructor asking the user for some background or context information about the decision problem, e.g., the characteristics of the group of patients concerned, with the help of knowledge base. The problem is to determine a course of optimal actions for the follow-up patients. The *decision horizon T* is a finite-horizon of 8 time units, with constant decision stage duration of 6 months, and the *evaluation criterion* is subjective utilities of the final health states for the patients.

Step 2.Defining the Action Space

The model constructor will then prompt for the alternative actions by showing the user an action hierarchy generated from the categorical knowledge base, as shown in Figure 5. The general concept action for the follow-up problem has two subtypes, test and treatment. A test can be the test for local recurrence, test for metastasis, or test for both. There are different combinations of these tests, leading to different testing strategies. For the example problem, the *action space A=* {CEA, Ultrasound, Colonoscopy, Sigmoidscopy, Ba-enema, CT-scan, LFT, CXR, None}, which denotes performing a diagnostic test such as CEA, Ultrasound, and Colonscopy to detect metastasis or recurrence, or just do nothing.

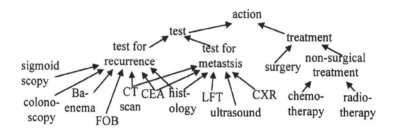

Figure 5. Action hierarchy generated from the knowledge base

Step 3. Defining the State Space

The model constructor will first identify the state attribute variables, which denote the different characteristics that constitute and distinguish the states, and define the states in terms of these variables. Some irrelevant states will be reduced according to the domain knowledge and the user's feedback during the process. For the example problem, the *state attribute variables* are *recurrence*, which indicates the presence or absence of recurrence, and *metastasis*, which indicates the presence or absence of metastasis. A total of 4 states are defined, which are well, recurrent, metastatic, both recurrent and metastatic (rec-met). At this time, the system also generates the state function. A state function is an expression of the form $s = \Phi(\omega_{A1}, \omega_{A2}, \ldots \omega_{An})$, where s is a state variable, ω_{Ai} is an outcome of the state attribute variable A_i, and Φ is a state-valued function which specifies each state variable outcome for every possible combination of outcomes of the state attribute variables. For the above example, state function is such that well := {recurrence = absent, metastasis = absent}, metastatic := {recurrence = absent, metastasis = present}, recurrent := {recurrence = present, metastasis = absent}, rec-met := {recurrence = present, metastasis = present}.

The system will then proceed to ask the user about a set of value functions with respect to the utility values defined for each state. For the example problem, we have V(well)=1, V(recurrent)=0.4, V(metastatic)=0.2, V(rec-met)= 0.

Step 4. Transition View Construction

To specify the transition characteristics, a transition view is constructed for each action defined in the action space for the follow up problem. Figure 1 shows the general structure of the transition view for all the actions.

The model constructor will first try to find if there are relevant probabilistic dependency statements, i.e., state-attribute-variable$_i$ (t+1) $|_p$ state-attribute-variable$_i$ (t) defined for all the state attribute variables for a certain action. For any two states, S_1, $S_2 \in S$, $S_1 = \Phi (A_1 = a_{11}, A_2 = a_{21}, \ldots, A_n = a_{n1})$, $S_2 = \Phi (A_1 = a_{12}, A_2 = a_{22}, \ldots, A_n = a_{n2})$, A_i (i=1..n) is a state attribute variable, S_2 is accessible from S_1 given an action a at time t if for each state attribute variable A_i (i=1..n), $P (A_i(t+1, a_{i2})| A_i(t, a_{i1})) > 0 \leftarrow a(t)$, i.e., each constituent state attribute of S_2 is accessible from the corresponding constituent state attribute of S_1. The transition probability from S_1 to S_2 at time t, P (state (S_2, t+1) | state (S_1, t)), is defined as $\prod_{i=1}^n P(A_i(t+1, a_{i2})| A_i(t, a_{i1}))$. This computation method of transition probabilities is a reasonable approximation as long as the state attribute variables are conditionally independent given the action.

However, such probabilistic dependency statements may not exist for all the actions. In this case, if the user can assess such transition functions directly for an action, the transition view is completed. Otherwise, the system will try to identify a set of event variables that constitute the effects of each action and a set of probabilistic influences among the event variables, i.e., the system will specify the transition functions in terms of the influence view components.

Step 5. Influence View Construction

Influence view construction begins with the incipient influence view, as shown in Figure 6 for the example problem. The basic operation performed by the influence view constructor is backward chaining. The constructor chains backward from each state attribute variable at time t+1, along all the influence relations until reaching the terminating nodes. The terminating nodes can be state attribute variables at time t, event variables at time t-1, or event variables with a marginal probability distribution. By simply backward chaining on the state attribute variables, the constructor generates all the relevant nodes, and avoids generating those nodes which are not the intermediate nodes between the state variables at time t and time t+1. Such nodes are irrelevant in the computation of transition probabilities. The final influence view for the action CEA test in the example problem is shown in Figure 3.

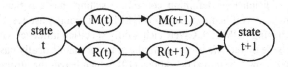

Figure 6. The incipient influence view for an action in the example problem

7 Model Modification Operations

We define three sets of model operations to help the user modify the influence view. The model modification process starts with the initial influence view and is complete when two criteria are met. First, the influence view appropriately represents the user's understanding of the decision problem. Second, the influence view is well-formed with all the appropriate information provided for each node.

7.1 Abstraction Operations

A detailed influence view may be too complicated to solve or understand; abstraction on the model is sometimes necessary to omit or suppress detail, for computational tractability and for comprehensibility. Unlike most of the existing work which focus on abstracting the state space [3, 15], we focus on abstracting and refining the network structure, including abstracting and refining a group of event variables based on concept taxonomies, and summarizing the influence path based on node reduction. In the following discussions, the nodes to be abstracted or the node to be refined are referred to as "original node(s)", and the node to be abstracted into or the nodes to be refined as "target node(s)".

7.1.1 Event Variable Abstraction

The event variable abstraction operation groups a set of similar variables into a single variable which is a generalization of such variables in the hierarchical knowledge base.

Consider the initially constructed influence view, which contains variables such as loss of appetite (LOA), loss of weight (LOW), lymph node involvement (LNI), liver mass (LM), pain and ascites. The user may want to have a more general model. He may choose to group LOA, LOW, LNI, LM, pain and ascites together; and then the system, according to the concept taxonomies in the knowledge base, will suggest that these six variables be abstracted into symptoms of metastasis (SOM).

The procedure will first identify the target abstraction variable which is one of the lowest common ancestors of the original nodes. Then, in order to accomplish the probability updating task automatically, the procedure will add the target variable into the influence view, which has no successors and has the original nodes as its only predecessors. In Figure 7, this step is illustrated by dotted lines. The probability distribution P(abstraction node | original nodes), e.g., P(SOM(t, present)|LOA(t, present)), can be inferred from the AKO definition in the hierarchical knowledge base, which is 1. The overall probability distribution table for the abstraction node can be expressed by incorporating a disjunctive definition constraint, stating that a patient will have a symptom of metastasis if he has LOA, LOW, LM, LNI, pain or ascites; otherwise, the probability of having SOM is 0. Given such a fully specified influence view, the original nodes can be removed one by one from the graph probabilistically based on the arc reversal and barren node removal operations [10], which leaves the abstraction node in place of the original nodes in the new graph.

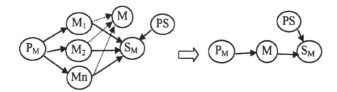

Figure 7. A simplified event variable grouping operation example

7.1.2 Influence reduction

The influence reduction operation abstracts away the intermediate details (both event variables and relationships among them) between two event variables. Therefore, the final diagram contains only a direct influence between the two original nodes with modified probability distributions. We use an algorithm similar to probabilistic node reduction in [10] to accomplish this task.

7.2 Event Variable Refinement

Event variable refinement is the reverse operation to event variable abstraction. The user can "emphasize" the important event variables by refining them or "de-emphasize" less important, similar variables by abstracting them [3]. For example, in the follow-up model, an influence view which models only the symptoms of metastasis (SOM) may need to be refined to differentiate loss of appetite (LOA), loss of weight (LOW), lymph node involvement (LNI), liver mass (LM), pain, and ascites. Hence, the SOM node needs to be split into nodes of LOA, LOW, LNI, LM, pain, and ascites. All the children of an original node in the concept hierarchy constitute the refinement of the original node. We adopt a strategy similar to that in the event variable abstraction to facilitate the assessment of probability distributions of the variables involved. However, this time the user needs to interactively specify the probability distribution for P (target node | original node), e.g., P (LOW|SOM). This requirement may be relaxed by pre-storing some relevant numbers in the knowledge base.

7.3 Node addition / deletion operations

It is possible that new nodes may need to be added to, or existing nodes deleted from, the influence view. In node addition, the knowledge base will be consulted to determine which nodes could be added. In node deletion, the arcs from the node to be removed will be reversed into each successor in order [10]. When the node has no successors and is barren, the node will just be deleted from the model.

8 Related Work

Our KBMC design integrates many desirable features of the existing frameworks; it differs from these frameworks mainly by providing a set of knowledge-based model modification operations to support interactive extension and modification of the automatically constructed model.

There are some similarities between our framework and Breese's Alterid [1]. However, Alterid does not consider hierarchical knowledge, so it can not support modeling at different levels of detail; it does not consider time in knowledge representation, so it can not handle dynamic decision model construction. Alterid's model construction procedure includes both backward chaining and forward chaining. Our influence view constructor employs only backward chaining to avoid the generation of nodes that are irrelevant in the computation of transition probabilities. We have proven that backward chaining is sufficient to generate all relevant event variables in the influence view.

Provan's DYNASTY [9] includes model updating operations to update model components form time interval t to t'. It also incorporates a method for automatic probability updating for such operations; we will explore the feasibility of this method in our future work. However, the system does not consider abstracting an influence path. Since there is no hierarchical knowledge in DYNASTY, the refinement and coarsening operations mainly depend on the progression or reduction of findings over time.

In Wellman's SUDO-PLANNER [14], domain descriptions can also be expressed at multiple levels of detail. However, in our representation of probabilistic knowledge, the predecessors of a variable are bundled together, rather than represented as a collection of individually asserted predecessors as in SUDO-PLANNER. Illuminated by the elaboration operation in SUDO-PLANNER, which replaces the direct relationship between the two event variables with a more detailed path, we are now exploring if we can introduce similar refinement operation into our framework. Since there is significant difference in the semantics between the *probabilistic dependency* in our framework and the *qualitative influence* defined in SUDO-PLANNER, the final definition of the operation may be quite different.

9 Discussion

We have presented the design of a knowledge-based dynamic decision model formulation framework. We are now working on the prototype implementation to assess the practical promise of the proposed framework. The overall performance of the framework will then be evaluated based on the scope of decision problems addressed, the ease of encoding domain knowledge in the knowledge base, the speed of model construction, the ease of model revision, and the quality of the resulting model in terms of accuracy, conciseness, and clarity.

One potential disadvantage of our influence view construction control strategy is that it cannot avoid exhaustive inclusion in the influence view of all the relevant variable in the knowledge base. Therefore, the influence view may become quite complex sometimes. Although the user can perform abstraction on the model components to reduce the model size, a better solution is to define a set of stopping criteria which takes into account the relative significance of the available information, and the relative utility of further expanding the model.

A future research issue of this work involves incorporating a machine learning module into the system, which will learn probabilities from large data sets, so as to reduce the work on the estimation and specification of the numerical parameters involved. Another interesting issue is to extend the framework to handle automated decision model formulation from multiple knowledge sources. Integration of expertise from multiple sources is critical to constructing a comprehensive model. However, the KBMC system should then also address such issues as the wide variety of available information sources, their imprecision, and possible disagreements or inconsistencies among the different sources.

Acknowledgments

This work is supported by a strategic research grant no. RP960351 from the National Science and Technology Board and the Ministry of Education in Singapore.

References

1. Breese, J. S.: Construction of belief and decision networks. *Computational Intelligence*, 8(4): 624-647 (1992)

2. Cao, C. and Leong, T. Y.: Learning Conditional Probabilities for Dynamic Influence Structures in Medical Decision Models, In *Proceedings of the 1997 AMIA Annual Fall Symposium* (formerly SCAMC), AMIA (1997)

3. Chang, K. C. and Fung, R.: Refinement and Coarsening of Bayesian Networks, *Uncertainty in Artificial Intelligence*, pages 435-445 (1991)

4. Goldman, R. P. and Charniak, E.: Dynamic construction of belief networks. In *Proceedings of the seventh Conference on Uncertainty in Artificial Intelligence*, pages 90-97 (1990)

5. Leong, T. Y.: Multiple perspective reasoning. In Aiello, L. C., Doyle, J., and Shapiro, S. (eds) *Principles of Knowledge Representation and Reasoning: Proceedings of the Fifth International Conference (KR'96)*, pages 562-573, Morgan Kaufmann (1996)

6. Ngo, L. and Haddawy, P.: A Knowledge-Based Model Construction Approach to Medical Decision Making. In James J. Cimino, editor, *Proceedings of 1996 AMIA Annual Fall Symposium*, Washington (1996)

7. Ngo, L., Haddawy, P. and Helwig, J.: A Theoretical Framework for Context-Sensitive Temporal Probability Model Construction with Application to Plan Projection. *Uncertainty in Artificial Intelligence: Proceedings of the Eleventh Conference*, pages 419-426. Morgan Kaufmann (1995)

8. Pearl, J.: *Probabilitic Reasoning in Intelligent Systems: Networks of Plausible Inference*. Morgan Kaufmann, San Mateo, CA (1988)

9. Provan, G. M.: Dynamic network updating techniques for diagnostic reasoning. In James Allen, Richard Fikes, and Erik Sandewall, editors, *Principles of Knowledge Representation and Reasoning: Proceedings of the Second International Conference (KR91)*, pages 279-286, San Mateo, CA (1991)

10. Shachter, R. D.: Probabilistic Inference and Influence Diagrams. *Operations Research*, 36:589-604 (1988)

11. Srinivas, S. (1992). Generalizing the noisy or model to n-ary variables. Technical Memorandum 79, Rockwell International Science Center, Palo Alto Laboratory, Palo Alto, CA

12. Tatman, J. A. and Shachter, R. D.: Dynamic programming and influence diagrams. *IEEE Transactions on Systems, Man, and Cybernetics*, 20(2):365-279 (1990)

13. Wellman, M. P., Breese, J. S. and Goldman, R. P.: From Knowledge Bases to Decision Models. *The Knowledge Engineering Review*, 7(1):35-53 (1992)

14. Wellman, M. P.: *Formulation of Tradeoffs in Planning Under Uncertainty*. Pitman and Morgan Kaufmann (1990)

15. Wellman, M. P. and Liu, C.: State-Space Abstraction for Anytime Evaluation of Probabilistic Networks. *Uncertainty in Artificial Intelligence: Proceedings of the Tenth Conference*, pages 567-574. Morgan Kaufmann (1994)

An Intelligent Job Counseling System

James Liu, Thomas Mak, Brian Tang, Katie Ma, Zikey Tsang

Department of Computing, Hong Kong Polytechnic University
csnkliu@comp.polyu.edu.hk

Abstract. Job finding process is a high human-resource utilization process. The applicant needs to search for all the jobs that he is interested in. After the searching and filtering process, the applicant's qualification and personal information, such as working experience, fields interested in and so on, are necessary to be matched with the basic requirements of the job so as to see whether he is suitable for applying the job. To enhance this process, an Intelligent Job Counseling System (IJCS) is developed in the present paper. The IJCS aims at performing job finding and matching process. It is designed to be an expert system with rule-based reasoning.

1. Introduction

The proposed system attempts to match people to suitable jobs and fitness of job matching is ensured by evaluating the general ability, numeral reasoning skills, language skills, spatial reasoning ability and personality factors. According to [2], the Harvard Business Review published the result indicates that personality factors are a critical factors to determine whether a person fits to a job. Therefore, the job matching concept of the system is not simply matching people to job based on education, experience, training and basic skills. It requires us to evaluate all the characteristics of an individual. The concept derived here is the Total Person. Under this concept, the aim is to match people with jobs in which both of their needs are met.

Generally speaking, to attain this goal, there have three steps to go through. The first step is to qualify the skills and experience a person possessed. The next step is interviewing. It is to judge the candidate based on how he or she performs in the interview. Finally, it is testing and job matching. For every job, there is a combination of abilities, interests and personality traits that will contribute to success on that job. The employers have to identify them out and benchmark them. Then these findings will be used as the criterions for matching people to jobs.

In the design of our system, it will include these two parts: qualifying skills and experience as well as testing and job matching. The first part requires users to state some personal background information and expectations on a job with ranking. The second part requires users to conduct a test by answering a list of multiple choice questions in order to determine the personalities and skills possessed by them. After that, result measured will be used to match with the criterions for the jobs and those appropriate jobs will be selected.

2. Development of IJCS

This is an expert system (Figure 1) which provides job matching to applicants based on their personality. The methodology which based on the background studies [1], [4], [5], has been integrated and implemented by Database Development Tools.

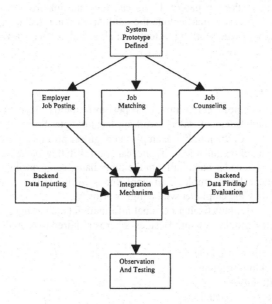

Fig. 1. System architecture of IJCS

3. Components of IJCS

In the IJCS, there have four components to form the whole system. They are: job posting, job matching, aptitude test and job analysis. The details of these components are as follows:

3.1 Job Posting

This option is provided for the employers to post their jobs into our database. The system will then provide these jobs to the job applicants if they match with the job requirement.

The system will first need the employer to fill in some background information of the company and the job such as the company name and contact methods. Then the job information such as the position supplied, the number of vacancy, job location, salary given, the job nature including whether the job needs the employee to work overtime, outdoor working or shift duties.

Then the requirement of the job is needed in order to let our system match the job with the job applicants. The requirement includes the education background, previous experience required, required skills such as the PC knowledge, language, accounting qualification and typing skills.

At last, we require the employer to fill in the ranking part. The ranking is used to let us know more about the job nature. Users can rank the job from 1-10 to show the importance of the criteria which include the outdoor working, technical, observation / analysis, innovation, paper working, interpersonal, social services, awareness and on-call stand by.

3.2 Job Matching

Our database allows employers to input their post information. A post contains several attributes such as qualification, salary, working location, etc. Some of these attributes are basic requirement of the job. For example, an engineer post may need the applicants to have a diploma of engineering. If one cannot fulfil this basic requirement, the employers will not consider one at all. On the other hand, some attributes of a post are optional requirement. For example, if an employee is willing to take oversea trips, s/he will be considered by the employer with a higher priority.

The applicant first inputs his/her personal information (such as age, salary expected, qualification ...etc) into the system. Besides, s/her is required to provide preference for the following items:

- i) Overtime available
- ii) Working location
- iii) Shift duty
- iv) Oversea trip (station)
- v) Outdoors working
- vi) Salary expected

The preference is ranked from 1 to 6. A ranking of 1 denotes that the applicant considers this item with the highest preference while that of 6 refers to the lowest preference. Our system will first find out the posts which s/he matches the basic requirements. Then it will sort these posts by the ranking order of the applicant. For example, if a job finder ranks the optional items as shown in Table 1:

Table 1. Personal preference

Optional Items	Ranking	Score
i) Overtime available	2	500
ii) Working location (HK Island preferred)	3	400
iii) Shift duty not preferred	4	300
iv) Oversea trip(station)	5	200
v) Outdoor working preferred	1	600
vi) Salary expected (7000-10000)	6	100

Suppose post A has the following item that matches his/her requirements,
i) Overtime needs
ii) Not require shift duty
iii) Outdoor working required

Post B has the following items that match his/her requirements.
i) Work at HK Island
ii) Need oversea trip
iii) Salary (7000-10000)

Then the match of ranking 1 will score 600, the match of ranking 6 will score 100. Therefore,

Post A has score: 500 + 300 + 600 = 1400
Post B has score: 400 + 200 + 100 = 700

So, Post A has a higher order than Post B.

3.3 Aptitude Test

When the applicant fails to find a suitable job in Job Matching System, s/he can use this Job Counseling System for verifying whether the jobs are suitable for her/him according to some personal characteristics. The applicant needs to have two tests: Character Test and Favourite Occupation Test.

3.3.1 Character Test

Character Test is used to identify what kind of personality the applicant possesses. When the applicant finished the test, a conclusion will be drawn for him/her accordingly, as shown in Table 2.

Table 2. Four groups of personalities

Group	Conclusion
Aa	You possess strong social power, especially in affecting and leading others, which is your advantage. You also possess the ability to direct and organize people.
Ba	You have high power of data analysis, especially tedious and complex work. You are suitable for working procedural and repeatable job. In addition, you can have good performance in controlling tools or machines.
Ab	You have agility thinking and so you have many fresh ideas. In other words, your thinking is very creative. Moreover, you are self-expressive and so this can make you good in social relation.
Bb	You are self-center and good in thinking alone systematically and logically. You also possess the high power of problem investigation and analysis.

The conclusion is drawn by rule-based reasoning. There are 4 rules established as shown below.

3.3.2 Favourite Occupation Test

The test requires the applicant to rank 9 groups of occupation. One of the groups is shown in Table 3. After the applicant finished the ranking, the system will put the 9 sets of ranking data into the second table correspondingly. The first elements of each set are needed to put into the boxes marked by asterisks (*), and the remaining elements will be put in order by following the box of the first element. When finishing the second table, total marks for the 9 different factors can be calculated by summing up the marks in the same row.

Table 3. Group of occupations with different rankings

Occupation	D
Dancing Teacher	3
Script-writer	7
Hotel Manager	5
Labor Inspector	4
Pharmacist	9
Foremen	2
Urban Designer	6
Stenographer	1
Chemist	8

An example is shown in Table 4. The asterisks * in set D is in the fourth block and so the applicant needs to copy the foremost digit in set D to the fourth block, and fill in the remaining blocks in order. The applicant will come back to the first copied block when he/she fills the last block. The process repeats until all sets of ranking are copied. Finally, by having the row sums computed, the applicant can derive the highest mark representing that class of jobs most suitable for him/her.

Table 4. Sample for Favourite Occupation Test

Class of jobs	A	B	C	D	E	F	G	H	I	Total
Outdoors	*2	8	1	6	9	3	6	4	3	42
Mechanical	7	*2	2	1	1	5	3	5	1	27
Archaeology	6	1	*3	8	6	1	9	2	4	40
Art	8	7	6	*3	5	9	4	7	8	57
Literature	9	6	9	7	*4	6	8	9	5	63
Interpersonal	5	5	8	5	3	*2	7	1	2	38
Social Services	3	4	5	4	8	4	*2	3	9	42
Medical	1	9	7	9	7	8	5	*8	7	61
Realistic	4	3	4	2	2	7	1	6	*6	35

3.4 JOB ANALYSIS

After the result of the latter test has been evaluated, we obtain a set of total scores for each individual job types. Then, these figures are converted to the values of range between 1 to 10 for job types matching in the next session. Let the score for an individual job type be X, since the possible range for X is between 9 to 81. To convert the score to an integer ranging from 1 to 10, simply substitute the score into the formula below and calculate the mark M for an individual item:

$$M = [(X / 81 * 10) + 0.5]$$

The parenthesis pair [] means taking the integral part of a value. Results are given in Table 5.

Table 5. Sample for aptitude test

Job Types	Total Score(X)	Mark(M)
Outdoors	42	5
Mechanical	27	3
Archaeology	40	5
Art	57	7
Literature	63	8
Interpersonal	38	5
Social Services	42	5
Medical	61	8
Practical	35	4

After that, we will take a job from the jobs set which fulfills the basic requirements specified by the user and performs the following matching.

Job Matching Percentage – 96%

(Factor 80%)   (Factor 90%)

Table 6. Matching between job and personality

Job Types	1	2	3	4	5	6	7	8	9	10	
Outdoors											100%
Mechanical			3								62%
Archaeology											100%
Art											100%
Literature											100%
Interpersonal											100%
Social Services											100%
Medical											100%
Practical											100%
										Overall % :	96%

For each individual job, the employer will specify the degree of required job type attributes. Consider the above example, employer specifies that the degree of a candidate required to be willing for outdoor work is 5 to 7 as indicated in shadow boxes of Table 6. If the mark (M) falls within the requirement (i.e. 5 to 7), the matching percentage is claimed to be 100%. Otherwise, the matching percentage is calculated by the following three steps. As an example, consider the job type - Mechanical:

a) Calculate the mean of the range
   mean $= (6 + 4) / 2 = 5$

b) Calculate the ratio of distance to the range in this case
   d = (mean $-$ M) / greatest distance
   $= (5 - 3) / 9$
   $= 2/9$

c) If M is lower than the required score, using factor 80% or 90% otherwise. Since the mark (M) is lower in this case, we take factor as 80%

   Matching % $= (1 - d)$ * factor
   $= (1 - 2/9)$ * 80%
   $= 62$ %

d) Finally, the matching percentage for this job is determined by the following formula:

   Overall % $= \Sigma$matching % / maximum distance
   $= (8 * 100 + 62) / 9$
   $= 96$ %

Rules ID Convention

Table 7a: Aptitude group
Jobfinder's Aptitude
A

Table 7b: Job classes	
Job Required Characteristics	
II	I
III	IV

The aptitude of a person is divided into 4 main categories. Table 7b contains job characteristics required for the position. If the applicant's aptitude (Table 7a) falls into the same category with the job required characteristics, i.e. A with I, it is the best match for the applicant. However, if the applicant's aptitude falls into the opposite category with the job required characteristics, then the job may not be suitable for the applicant. If the fallen category is next to the applicant's aptitude, then the job may have some area matched with the applicant's aptitude.

The categorization of job required characteristics is performed using the following method. Based on the nature and necessity of the job, the ranking of each factor given should be ranged between 1 and 10, where 1 represents the least importance and 10 represents the opposite.

Since there are 4 groups of jobfinder, the job also needs to be divided into 4 groups so that the system can try to match the group of jobs to that of jobfinder. By using the range of each ranking factor given by the employer, the job will be distributed to one of the groups accordingly.

Table 8. Mean range value corresponding to class

Range	Class
1.0 – 2.5	1
2.6 – 5.0	2
5.1 – 7.5	3
7.6 – 10.0	4

TABLE 9: JOB CLASS VS JOB REQUIRED CHARACTERISTICS

Group Job Class	I	II	III	IV
Outdoors	3	1	2	4
Mechanical	2	4	3	1
Archaeology	1	3	4	2
Art	1	2	3	4
Literature	1	2	4	3
Interpersonal	4	2	1	3
Social Services	3	1	2	4
Medical	1	3	4	2
Realistic	2	4	3	1

The mean of the range value given by the employer will be checked to see which classes it falls into. Then the group that has the same class will have 1 mark. For example, the range of 'Outdoors' is 3 to 6 and its mean is 4.5, it falls into class 2 (Table 8). Since Group III is also in Class 2 for 'Outdoors' (Table 9), 1 mark is placed in Group III. Finally the total mark will be calculated for each group. The job will then be classified to the group that has the highest mark as shown in Table 10.

Table 10. Scoring the group of jobs

Group Job Class	I	II	III	IV
Outdoors			1	
....	....	....	....	....
Total Marks:	4	2	3	0

Finally, the explanation of matching between an individual job and the personality of the job finder can be derived from matching the rules in Table 11. Making use of the rule stated in Table 12, the system can also indicate what common characteristics both the job finder possessed and this individual required. Moreover, the system can also provide explanation in detail about what the personality of the job finder is using the rule in Table 2.

Table 11. Rules set for matching job with personality

Aptitude Category	Job Required Characteristics	Rule Description
A	I	A perfect Job matching. You are capable of working within your own specialty. Your characteristics and interests fit to the job.
A	II	A good job matching. You possess almost all the required skills and personality for the job.
A	III	The required personality of the job is extremely different from your aptitude. It indicates that you have a role conflict. Your aptitude is quite different from your personal interests.
A	I, II	The job nature matches with your own personality. But the job requires you to have some extra characteristics to make you fit into it.
A	I, III	This job requires a person who possesses two extremely different personalities at the same time. You possess one side of the characteristics and you must be quite adaptive in your working environment.
A	II, III	The required personality of the job has some characteristics being the common ground with your personality. You have to overcome difficulties, problems and challenges in the job.
A	II, IV	You possess almost all the required skills and personality for the job. But you need to have some improvement for better match with the job nature.
A	I, II, IV	You have the main characteristics that match the job. But the job may need some other characteristics that you marginally bear.
A	II, III, IV	You possess some characteristics that the job needed. However, you may lack of the main characteristics.
A	I, II, III, IV	This job should suitable to people with any kind of personalities. It may not suitable for people who want specific development.

Table 12. Similar and opposite characteristics between groups

Group	Characteristics		Similarity	Opposite
Aa	1.	Strong social power	Ab	Bb
	2.	Direct people		
	3.	Good organizing power	Ba	
	4.	Good leadership		
	5.	High influence of others		
Ba	6.	Good organizing power	Aa	
	7.	Good analytical power	Bb	
	8.	Good control in tools or machines		
	9.	Procedural and repeatable works		Ab
Ab	10.	Strong social power	Aa	
	11.	Agility thinking	Bb	
	12.	Creative thinking		Ba
	13.	Self-expressive		
Bb	14.	Good analytical power	Ba	
	15.	Agility thinking	Ab	
	16.	Logical thinking		
	17.	Creative thinking	Ab	
	18.	Self-center		Aa

4. Implementation and Operation of IJCS

The implementation of this system was on Windows95 platform using Visual FoxPro Version 5.0. Rules are stored in table format in Visual FoxPro. Since this system can be divided into 4 components, we implement each of them separately and then integrate them into a single system.

Screen 1 allows the user to enter his/her personal information and education background in order to let the system match the applicant's information with the job requirement.

Screen 1

Screen 2 allows for inputting the skills of the job applicants. The skills include the PC knowledge, language, typing skills and the accounting education background.

Screen 2

Screen 3 allows the applicants to provide ranking of these requirements. For example, if the applicant finds that the salary is the first priority when looking for a job, then the applicant should give the rank 1 to the salary field. The system will take the salary requirement as the first matching criteria.

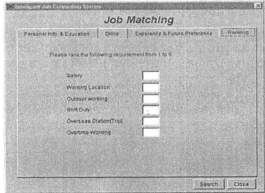

Screen 3

Screen 4 gives one of the aptitude tests. This test is used to let the system know more about the personality of the applicant. The test contains 10 questions and the applicant needs to answer all the questions.

Screen 4

5. Evaluation

Four test cases were used to verify and validate our system's functionality. In the first test cases, we illustrated that the job requirement was matched with the applicant's background and experience. In the other three test cases, the system showed that if the applicant did not satisfy with the first search result, he/she could do the aptitude test that was provided in our system. After the two aptitude testes, the applicant could find many jobs that were close to his/her aptitude. Our system also gives the percentage to the user according to the matching percentage of the job with the applicant's aptitude. Also some comments on the job selected with the personality of the applicant, the similarity of the job with the applicant's aptitude will also be given. In the analysis result, we illustrated that the aptitude test could help the applicant select more jobs that the applicant would not have considered before. And our system can also let the applicant know more about the job and his/her personality, so that he/she can evaluate whether the job is suitable for him/her or not. From the 4 test cases, it demonstrates that our system functions quite well and is correctly developed.

6. Comments and Conclusion

Finding a post is easy, but to find a suitable post is not a piece of cake. An applicant needs to consider lots of things. Most jobs matching system will just look into the basic requirements of a vacancy and then find a qualified person for that post. Our system handles this at ' Job matching '. It selects a list of jobs available in order of scores, derived from the ranking input by the user. This will help the user get into the first sight of the available posts.

The second part of the system will provide an aptitude test that analyses the personality of the applicant. According to the analysis result, we not only provides jobs within his interesting field, but also the alternative ones that deem to be suitable.

The system also allows the employer to input the required 'personality factors' for the related post. Thus, the post at the backend database contains the 'personality requirements' information. This allows the system to make decision from the point of view of the employer and ensure 'employer-employee' match in the final outcome.

Nevertheless, in the Job Matching part of the system, the requirements specified for a job are limited in several areas. If an employer wants to have a requirement which is not concerned in our Job Matching part, the employer will need to give up the particular requirement. In addition, the aptitude test used in the system might have been simplified a bit, such that a person's character could not be concluded absolutely.

It is therefore recommended to provide the flexibility and versatility for employers to enter some specific or inexact job requirements. Some kind of uncertainty and similarity measures are necessary to empower the intelligent system for problem solving in complicated domain [3].   Moreover, if a more generic aptitude test can be used for replacing the currently one, a more precise result before matching jobs to individuals shall be achieved. This is the subject of future paper.

References

1.   Editorial Section of Job Finder: A Book for Job Finder. ONE Publisher Limited. 2 (1997).
2.   Internet Resource
     http : // world.std.com/~bunt/advantages.html
3.   Liu, J., Yung, K.W.: An Intelligent System for Respiratory Protection. Expert Systems with Applications, Vol. 11, 3 (1997) 309-322.
4.   Peskin, D.B.: Human Behavior and Employment Intervening. American Management Association (1971).
5.   Pritchard, D., Murns, H.: Job's, Roles & People -The New World of Job Evaluation. Nicholas Brealey (1992).

The Layout Problem: Investigation and Aggregation of Artificial Intelligence and Optimization Techniques

Hamdy Elwany[1]. Mohamed G. Abou-Ali[2]. Nermeen A. Harraz[3]

Alexandria University, College of Engineering, Production Engineering Department,
Alexandria 21544, Egypt
[1] Elwany@Dataxprs.com.eg
[2] M_abouali@Frcu.eun.eg
[3] Helal@Dataxprs.com.eg

Abstract. Various solution techniques and solution procedures for the facility layout problem are reviewed and compared on a basis of general characteristics, inputs, limitations and type of output. A computer system working in a tandem mode, combining artificial intelligence tool, with an improvement algorithm for solving cellular layout problems is presented. The system handles the qualitative and the quantitative aspects via a knowledge-based system and an improvement Simulated Annealing (SA) global optimization algorithm. The problem solving strategy is illustrated with a set of reasonable number of numerical examples under different boundary conditions.

1 Introduction

In cellular layout analytical models are not generally applicable. They consider only quantifiable factors and are difficult to implement. Also, due to the computational complexity of the facility layout problem, optimization algorithms, normally, are not suitable for large problems. It was found that knowledge-based systems could address the totality of factors involved in the problem. Several articles in the past decade described knowledge-based systems that dealt with the layout problem [1-3]. The emphasis of the literature survey presented in this paper is on the inter-cell layout problem. The block layout design problem seeks the best arrangement of cells based on their inter-relationships and involves their relative location of cells within the available area. The scope of this work is to handle the multicriteria aspect that affects the idealized relative location of cells within a floor plan. The problem in perspective is an inter-cell layout problem, static, single floor, affected by multicriteria (qualitative and quantitative), it is also a multigoal problem. The number of cells and sites is equal. As the problem of optimizing a facility layout is combinatory difficult, the number of possible configurations for the layout increases factorially with the increasing number of cells, and the task becomes tedious to human beings especially if the criteria affecting the problem conflicts with each other.

This paper describes a knowledge-based system for cellular layout built by using an object oriented expert system shell. It combines the qualitative and the quantitative criteria that affect the problem. The solution obtained can be improved by seeding it to a global optimization Simulated Annealing (SA) algorithm adopting the quadratic assignment programming (QAP) for the formulation.

2 Investigation of the Facility Layout Problem

2.1 Features of the General Layout Problem

There is a wide range of techniques that can be used in solving the layout problem depending on the major feature(s) of the problem. The most common features of the layout problem are described in Table 1.

Table 1. Different features of the layout problem

Feature	Description	Remark
Number of facilities	a) Single b) Multiple	
Site presentation	a) Discrete b) Continuous	Summation Integration
Relationship between Variables	a) Linear b) Non-linear	Such as in FMS Interaction between facilities (QAP)
Planning horizon	a) Static b) Dynamic (Multiperiod)	
Number of criteria	a) Single b) Multiple	
Criterion type	a) Quantitative b) Qualitative c) Combination	Objective Subjective (Safety, noise level, etc.)
Number of floors	a) Single b) Multiple	
Sector	a) Private b) Public c) Quasi-public	The scope is mainly to increase profit The scope is to give services The scope is to give services and realize a minimum profit
Function	a) Allocation b)Minimization of the maximum variable (minimax problem) c) Facility layout	such as in the case of allocating schools or fire stations
Solution quality	Optimal, Sub-optimal	a) For small problems b) Large problems

Researchers are trying to find the most appropriate solution as the problem is till now unsolved. In early to mid fifties, the traditional schematic techniques, which depended on the judgment and intuition of the analyst, dominated, so the solution was subjective. The analyst used tools such as flow diagrams, templates, iconic models, etc. During mid fifties to early sixties the graphical systematic technique appeared [4]. Muther introduced the systematic layout planning (SLP) technique [5]. Also this period was characterized by the beginning of the mathematical modeling [6,7]. The mathematical modeling and computer based algorithms emerged in the late sixties, the problem is mainly presented by a quadratic model. Heuristic algorithms used to solve the model were branch and bound and computerized algorithms. Mid to late seventies special attention was given to the graph theory. The graph theory is more appropriate in the case of new layouts, it gives flexibility to the designer, but it may be not valid in certain cases. With early to mid eighties a great evolution in the mathematical modeling took place, interactive packages appeared, use of graphics, and the problem is treated as a multigoal problem. The use of the global optimization technique "The Simulated Annealing" is introduced [8]. Mid eighties, the general trend affects the problem and the emerging artificial intelligence tools are used to solve the problem, knowledge bases and expert systems are used. In the late eighties, the Fuzzy Set theory begun to be used in solving the problem.

The authors conducted a comprehensive study [47] aiming at comparing seven solution procedures namely: quadratic assignment formulation [9-20], nonlinear [21-23], multicriteria [24-27], dynamic aspects [28-33], expert systems and decision support systems [34-41], simulated annealing [42-45] and fuzzy sets [46]. The base of comparison are the general characteristics, the inputs required, the limitations and the type of output.

2.2 Theoretical Background

The problem considered is the layout of machine cells within a floor plan, the cells may be product layout cells or process layout cells, hence the quadratic assignment formulation can represent the problem.

Classical quadratic assignment. Traditionally the problem has been formulated as:

$$Z = \sum_{i=1}^{n} \sum_{j=1}^{n} \sum_{k=1}^{n} \sum_{l=1}^{n} f_{ij} d_{kl} x_{ik} x_{jl} \tag{1}$$

$$\text{S.T.} \quad \sum_{i=1}^{n} x_{ik} = 1, k = 1,2,\ldots,n \tag{2}$$

$$\text{S.T.} \quad \sum_{k=1}^{n} x_{ik} = 1, i = 1,2,\ldots,n \tag{3}$$

$$x_{ik} \in \{0,1\} \forall i, k \tag{4}$$

Where

f_{ij} flow between facility i and j	X_{ik} integer 0,1 variable
d_{kl} distance between sites k and l (from center to center as the facilities dimensions are assumed to be the same)	$X_{ik} = 1$ if facility i is assigned to location k $= 0$ otherwise.

Constraint (2) assures that each location is assigned one facility. Constraint (3) assures that only one facility will be assigned to one location. Number of facilities and sites is the same other wise dummy facilities were used with flow equal to zero with all other facilities.

Inclusion of the qualitative and quantitative criteria. There have been few attempts to handle the two types of criteria in the same function, for example,[24-27]. According to the model of Harmonosky and Tothero[25] the objective becomes:

$$\text{Min } Z = \sum_i^n \sum_k^n \sum_j^n \sum_l^n \sum_m^t \alpha_m T_{ijm} d_{kl} x_{ik} x_{jl} \tag{5}$$

$$\text{S.T.} \quad \sum_i^n \sum_j^n T_{ijm} = 1 \qquad \text{For all m} \tag{6}$$

$$\text{S.T.} \quad \sum_{i=1}^n x_{ik} = 1 \qquad k = 1,..., n \tag{7}$$

$$\text{S.T.} \quad \sum_{k=1}^n x_{ik} = 1 \qquad i = 1,...., n \tag{8}$$

$$x_{ik} = 0 \text{ or } 1 \ \forall i, k \tag{9}$$

Where

α_m = weight for factor m	d_{kl} = distancbetween location k and l
t = number of factors	x_{ik} = 1 if department i is assigned to location k
n = number of departments	0 otherwise
i, j stands for department numbers	k, l stands for location numbers

The above mathematical model will be used in the improvement part of this work to evaluate the alternate configuration, the model proposed by Harmonsky and Tothero [25] is appropriate as it incorporates the qualitative and quantitative criteria in the same function. They defined S_{ijm} as the relationship value between departments i and j for factor m, T_{ijm} as the normalized relationship value between departments i and j for factor m ($T_{ijm} = S_{ijm} / \sum_i^n \sum_j^n S_{ijm}$), and α_m as the weight representing the relative importance of each factor.

3 Aggregation of AI and Optimization Techniques

The layout problem is a multicriteria problem, incorporates quantitative criteria and qualitative criteria. Knowledge-based systems, one of the artificial intelligence (AI) techniques, is used a tool for solving the problem in perspective.

3.1   The Structure and Performance of the System

The system mainly comprises an interface, inference engine, database and an improvement algorithm. The elements as flow chart of the structure of the system is shown in Fig. 1. The inputs to the system include the number of departments, the inter-departmental flow, the desired adjacency relationship between departments. The system generates a layout configuration that respects the priority given to the qualitative or the quantitative criterion meanwhile respects the other one. When a configuration is generated the rule that calls the graphical module is triggered and the relative locations of cells within the floor plan are illustrated. The system interfaces with a global optimization algorithm that can adjust the solution quality whenever the end user is not satisfied.

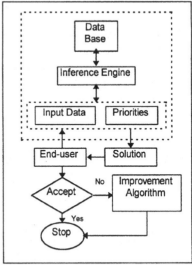

Fig. 1 The system structure and elements

3.2   Knowledge Acquisition, Representation and Implementation

The knowledge base is developed containing heuristics and expertise, most of this experience and knowledge is documented in published work [5],[7]. A protocol analysis of experts' behavior and reports was used to express facts about concepts and practices, and rules. An adequate amount of knowledge was elicited verbally to justify and reason a number of the concepts adopted.

Experience concerning the allocation of cells is transformed into steps structured in a logical way. The steps are represented in the form decision trees that is composed of eight principle branches.

Knowledge related to the domain is transformed into the form of a knowledge base in two steps: transformation of knowledge to clauses and transformation of the clauses to the LEVEL5 shell syntax.

4   The System Knowledge-base

4.1   The Knowledge-base Architecture

The rule-based is structured in three levels, as shown in Fig. 2. The first level is the controlling level that causes the system to chain to the appropriate knowledge-base.

The second level comprises the data-input module and the allocation procedure module. The third level comprises modules for the priorities of sites, priorities of the cells, and distances between assumed sites. The function of each module is:

Data-input module: The system is first initialized by introducing the number of cells to be handled, this is done by asking the end-user. The system then chains to the appropriate knowledge base and another display appears which asks the user to input the flow of materials, and the adjacency relationships.

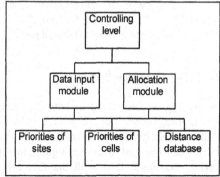

Fig. 2 Architecture of the knowledge-base

Allocation module: This module consists of a number of structured rules and demons used to allocate the cells.

Priorities of cells: The priorities of cells determine the order in which they are allocated

Priorities of sites: The priorities of sites determine the rode in which they are assigned

Distance database: The distance database determines the distance from site to site.

4.2 The Knowledge-base Development

There are three user-defined classes, and one system class. The user-defined classes contain information about the number of cells, the size of the arrays representing the flow of material and the adjacency relationship. The system class "domain" contains the "shared" attributes. The shared attributes are those attributes that are shared between the islands of knowledge. The shell enables the developer to link more than one knowledge base using the command "CHAIN" that invokes a knowledge- base from within a different knowledge base. When the CHAIN command is executed, the current knowledge base ends, and a new knowledge base begins, example of a rule to demonstrate chaining:

```
IF number of cells := 5
THEN CHAIN "knb5"
```

There is eight control rules to chain between islands of knowledge, in each island there is two general "housekeeping" rules, one to call the improvement algorithm, the other is a rule-set (group of rules) to allocate cells in the appropriate locations (sites), one group for if the priority is assigned to the quantitative criteria, and the other for if it is assigned to the quantitative one. The size of the group varies from one island to another according to the problem size. Example of a rule (see rule listing in the Appendix):

IF Tflow[3] OF cells = MAX(Tflow[1] OF cells, Tflow[2] OF cells, Tflow[3] OF cells, Tflow[4] OF cells, Tflow[5] OF cells)
THEN site number [1] OF Sites := 3

4.3 The Allocation Procedure

Inferencing is carried out in both the forward chaining and the backward chaining modes. The procedure of allocation held by the inference engine as follows:

If the priority of the quantitative criteria is the first, the total flow for each cell is calculated. The cell with the highest total flow is allocated in the first site. The cell having maximum flow with the first cell allocated in site one is allocated in a neighbor site, if more than one site are neighbors, it is allocated in the site with lower order. If more than two cells have the same flow, the adjacency relationship matrix is consulted. The one with the highest value is allocated first. The procedure is repeated till all cells are allocated and a solution is obtained. This solution can be seeded to the global optimization algorithm "simulated annealing", in order to perform any adjustments required to cope with the change in the weight of the different criteria.

5 Tests Results and Discussion

The facility layout problem is practical as well as a methodological problem. A number of test problems, common in the literature, in addition to a set of hypothetical problems are tested to assess the performance of the developed system.

The multicriteria aspect characterizes the test problems. An example of the test problems is shown in Fig. 3 (a,b) to illustrate the system's performence; the problem is a 5-cell layout case. Fig. 3 (a) represents the flow data (above diagonal), and the adjacency data (below diagonal). Fig. 3 (b) represents the distance between cells centroid.

When the end-user assigns the first priority to the quantitative criteria, the rule-based system generates the solution shown in Table 2. It can be seen that the layout produced by the system is intuitively correct. For example, cells 1 and 2

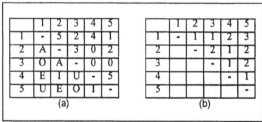

Fig. 3 Flow, adjacency and distance data

where maximum flow exists are neighbors. The resulted solution may not satisfy all qualitative criteria, and the end user may call the improvement algorithm and assign different weights to the quantitative criteria $\alpha 1$, and to the qualitative criteria $\alpha 2$.

Table 2. The initial layout and the generated alternate layouts for a five-cell problem

Initial Layout		Improvement phase					
Layout	Score	α1	α2	Layout	Time (sec)	Score	% improvement
1 2 / 4 3 5	3.00	1	0	2 3 / 1 4 5	0.49	2.63	12.12
	3.97	0.9	0.1	2 3 / 1 4 5	0.49	3.66	7.70
	4.94	0.8	0.2	2 3 / 1 4 5	0.49	4.69	5.08
	5.91	0.7	0.3	2 3 / 1 4 5	0.49	5.72	3.29
	6.88	0.6	0.4	1 2 / 4 5 3	0.49	6.72	2.30
	7.85	0.5	0.5	1 2 / 4 5 3	0.49	7.71	1.70
	8.82	0.4	0.6	1 2 / 4 5 3	0.49	8.71	1.20
	9.79	0.3	0.7	1 5 / 4 2 3	0.49	9.63	1.60
	10.8	0.2	0.8	1 5 / 4 2 3	0.49	10.5	2.10
	11.7	0.1	0.9	1 5 / 4 2 3	0.49	11.4	2.40
	12.7	0.0	1.0	1 5 / 4 2 3	0.49 Av. 0.49	12.3	2.70 Av. 3.84

From the consultation of the algorithm for other eight test problems, varying in size from 5-cell to 12-cell problem the trade-off curves for the effect of the change of α1 and α2 on the percentage improvement in the OFV can be detected (Fig. 4). From Fig. 4, it can be seen that, although the designation of the priorities for the different criteria, the rule-based heuristic generates a solution that considers the qualitative and quantitative criteria equally. This is deduced from the fact that the minimum

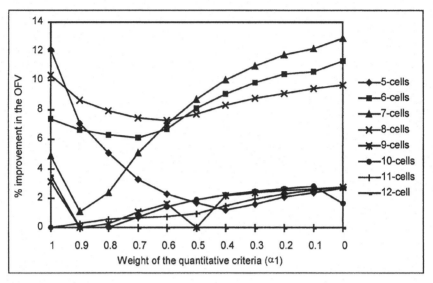

Fig. 4 The effect of the change of α1 and α2 on the percentage improvement in the OFV

percentage improvement occurs between α1= 0.6 or 0.5 when applying the global optimization algorithm. The 9-cell problem illustrates this comment: at α1= .5 the percentage improvement is zero but at α1 = 0.4 (which means at the same time that the weight of the qualitative criteria α2 = 0.6) the curves jumped to a value of 2.2.

6   Conclusions and Further work

The system developed in this paper describes a rule-based system working in a tandem mode, i.e. it combines the expert system with an optimization algorithm, the two parts are capable of solving the problem for more than two factors handling the qualitative and quantitative criteria similarly. In the first part, the expert system generates the solution using the rules that act in a way to satisfy the requirements and the designated priorities. The solution obtained from the first part serves as a seed solution for the second part, which is the improvement algorithm. The improvement algorithm -Simulated annealing- is a global optimization algorithm. Another advantage of the algorithm used in the methodology is that the exchanges is performed according to the two-way exchange procedure, which has been proven in the literature to outperform the tree-way exchange procedure in the CPU time. This replaces the random exchange of the locations, which can increase the CPU time.

The comparably inferior quality solution is overcomed by the use of the simulated annealing technique. The facility layout problem implies long hours to perform manual iterations, that subjects humans to extreme mental stress, and prone to calculation errors. The suggested methodology economizes time as it produced law computations time in comparison with existing heuristics. It also economizes human effort that can be abused in solving the multidisciplinary problem.

The layout problem in general and the cellular manufacturing layout problem in particular possess many areas to be investigated and incorporated in the study such as the noise considerations, the selection of the material handling device, the illumination, the ergonomic considerations. All those factors are subject to study by the authors in order to normalize their effect and to incorporate them in the knowledge base and in the objective function of the improvement algorithm.

References

1. Abdou, G., Dutta, S.P.: An Integrated Approach to Facilities Layout Using Expert System. Int. J. Prod. Res. Vol. 28, No. 4 (1990) 685-708
2. Chen, C.S., and Kengskool, K.: An Autocad-Based Expert System for Plant Layout. Computers and Industrial Engineering, Vol. 19, No 1-4 (1990) 299-303
3. Heragu, S.S., Kusiak, A.: Machine Layout:an Optimization and Knowledge Based Approach. Int. J. Production Research, Vol. 28, NO. 4 (1990) 615-635
4. Foulds, L.R., Gibb, P.B., Giffin, J.W.: Facilities ayout djacency etermination: n Experimental Comparison of Three Graph Theoretic Heuristics. Operations Research, Vol. 33, No. 5 (1985) 1091-1105
5. Francis, R.L., White, J.A.: Facility Layout and Location: An Analytical Approach. Prentice Hall (1974)
6. Lockyer, K.G.: Factory and Production Management. ELBS, 1st edition (1978)
7. Muhlemann, A., Oakland, J., Lockyer, K.,: Production and Operation Management. Pitman, Sixth edition (1993)
8. Burkard, R.E., Rendl, F.,: A Thermodynamically Motivated Simulation Procedure for Combinatorial Optimization Problems. European J. of Operational Research, Vol. 17 (1984) 169-174
9. Nugent, C.E., Vollmann, T,E, Ruml, J.: An Experimental Comparison on Techniques for the Assignment of Facilities to Locations. Operation Research, Vol. 16, No. 1 (1968) 150-173
10. Hurter, A.P., Jr., Schaefer, M.K., Wendell, R.E.: Solution of Constrained Location Problems. Management Science, Vol. 22, No.1 (1975) 51-56
11. Chan, A.W., Francis, R.L.: A Least Total Distance Facility Configuration Problem Involving Lattice Points. Management Science, Vol.22, No.7 (1976) 778-787
12. Erlenkotter, D.: Facility Location with Price Sensitive Demands: Private, Public and Quasi Public. Management Science, Vol.24, No. 4 (1977) 378-386
13. Dokmeci V.F.: A Quantitative Model to Plan Regional Health Facility Systems. Management Science, Vol.24, No.4 (1977) 411-419
14. Drezner, Z.: DISCON: A New Method for the Layout Problem. Operations Research, Vol.28, No. 6 (1980) 1375-1384
15. Johnson, R.V.: Spacecraft for Multi-floor Layout Planning. Management Science, Vol.28, No.4 (1982) 407-417
16. Picone, C.J., Wilhelm, V.E.: Solution to the Facilities Layout Problem. Management Science, Vol. 30 (1984) 1238-1249
17. Drezner, Z.: A Heuristic Procedure for the Layout of A Large Number of Facilities. Management Science, Vol. 33, No. 7 (1987) 907-915

18. Golany, B., Rosenblatt, M.J.: A Heuristic Algorithm for the Quadratic Assignment Formulation to the Plant Layout Problems. Int. J. Production Research, Vol.27, No.2 (1989) 293-308

19. Rosenblatt, M.J.: The Dynamics of Plant Layout. Management Science, Vol. 32, No. 1 (1986) 76-86

20. Bozer, Y.A., Meller, R.D., Erlebacher, S.J.: An Improvement Type Layout Algorithm for Single and Multiple-Floor Facilities. Management Science, Vol. 40, No.7 (1994) 918-932

21. Heragu, S.S., Kusiak, A.: Efficient Models for the Facility Layout Problem. European J. of Operational Research, Vol. 53 (1991) 1-13

22. Riopel, D., Langevin, A.: Optimizing the Location of Material Transfer Stations within Layout Analysis" Int. J. Production Economics, Vol. 22 (1991) 169- 176

23. Van Camp, D.J., Carter, M. W., Vannelli, A.: Nonlinear Optimization Approach for Solving Facility Layout Problems. European J. of Operational Research, Vol. 57, No.2 (1992) 174-189

24. Jacobs, F. R.: A Layout Planning System with Multiple Criteria and a Variable Domain Representation. Management Science, Vol. 33, No. 8 (1987) 1020-1034

25. Harmonosky, C.M., Tothero, G.K.: A Multi-Factor Plant Layout Methodology. Int. J. Production Research, Vol. 30, No.8 (1992) 1773-1789

26. Sarin, S.C., Loharjun, P., Malmborg, C.J., Krishnaumar, B.: Multiattribute Decision-Theoretic Approach to the Layout Design Problem. European J. of Operational Research, Vol. 57, No. 2 (1992) 231-242

27. Shang, J.S.: Multicriteria Facility Layout Problem : An Integrated Approach. European J. of Operational Research, Vol. 66 (1993) 291-304

28. Wesolowsky, G.O., Truscott, W.G.: The Multiperiod Location-Allocation Problem with Relocation of Facilities. Management Science, Vol. 22, No. 1 (1975) 57-65

29. Sweeney, D.J., Tatham, R.: An Improved Long Run Model for Multiple Warehouse Location. Management Science, Vol. 22, No. 7 (1976) 748-758

30. Rosenblatt, M.J.: The Dynamics of Plant Layout. Management Science, Vol. 32, No. 1 (1986) 76-86

31. Montreuil B., Venkatadri U.: Strategic Interpolative Design of Dynamic Manufacturing Systems Layouts. Management Science, Vol. 37, No. 6 (1991) 682-694

32. Balakrishnan, J., Jacobs, F.R., Venkataramanan, M.A.: Solution for the Constrained Dynamic Facility Layout Broblem. European J. of Operational Research, Vol.57 (1992) 280-286

33. Palektar, U.S., Batta, R., Bosch, R. M., Elhence, S.: Modeling Uncertainties in Plant Layout Problems. European J. of Operational Research, Vol 63 (1992) 347-359

34. Kumara, S.R.T., Kashyap, R.L., Moodies, C.L.: Expert System for Industrial Facilities Layout Planning and Analysis. Computers and Industrial Engineering, Vol. 12, No. 2 (1987) 143-152

35. Malakooti, B., Tsurushima, A.: An Expert System Using Priorities for Solving Multiple-Criteria Facility Layout Problems. Int. J. of Production Research, Vol. 27, No. 5 (1989) 793-808

36. Abdou, G., Dutta, S.P.: An Integrated Approach to Facilities Layout Using Expert System. Int. J. of Production Research, Vol. 28, No.4 (1990) 685-708

37. Chen, C.S., Kengskool, K.: An Autocad-Based Expert System for Plant Layout. Computers Industrial Engineering, Vol. 19, No. 1-4 (1990) 299-303

38. Golany, B., Rosenblatt, M.J.: A Heuristic Algorithm for the Quadratic Assignment Formulation to the Plant Layout Problems. Int. J. of Production Research, Vol.27, No.2 (1989) 293-308

39. Worrall, B.M., Gibbs, H.P.: Design of a Facility Layout Decision Support System. International Industrial Engineering Conference Proceedings, Institute of Industrial Engineers, (1990) 218-223

40. Pham, D.T., Onder, H.H.: A Knowledge-Based System for Optimizing Workplace Layout Using a Generic Algorithm. Ergonomics, Vol. 35, No. 12 (1992) 1479-1487

41. Repede, J.F., Bernardo, J.J.: Developing and Validating a Decision Support System for Locating Emergency Medical Vehicles in Louisville, Kentucky. European J. of Operational Research, Vol. 75 (1994) 567-581

42. Burkard, R.E., Rendl, F.: A Thermodynamically Motivated Simulation Procedure for Combinatorial Optimization Problems. European J. of Operational Research, Vol. 17 (1984) 169-174

43. Heragu, S.S., Alpha, A.S.: Experimental Analysis of Simulated Annealing Based Algorithms for the Layout Problem. European J. of Operational Research, Vol. 57, No. 2 (1992) 190-202

44. Jajodia, S., Minis, I., Harhalakis, G., Proth, J.: CLASS : Computerized Layout Solutions Using Simulated Annealing. Int. J. of Production Research, Vol.30, No. 1 (1992) 95-108

45. Kouvelis, P., Chiang, W., Fitzsimmons, J.: Simulated Annealing for Machine Layout Problems in the Presence of Zoning Constraints. European J. of Operational Research, Vol. 57, No. 2 (1992) 203-223

46. Raoot, A.D., Rakshit, A.: A "Fuzzy" Approach to Facilities Layout Planning. Int. J. of Production Research, Vol.29, No.4 (1991) 835-857

47. Elwany, M.H., Abou-Ali, M.G., Harraz, N.A.: The Development of a Decision-Support Expert System for Solving Facilities Layout Problems. Alexandria Engineering Journal, Vol. 36, No.2 (1997) 136-147.

Appendix

Rule-sets: An example of a rule-set containing 3 rules:

```
IF site number [1] OF Sites = 3
AND flow[1] OF cells = MAX (flow[1] OF cells, flow[2] OF cells, flow[4] OF cells, flow[5] OF cells)
THEN site number [2] OF cells := 1
IF site number [1] OF Sites = 3
AND site number [2] OF Sites = 1
AND flow[4] OF cells = MAX (flow[2] OF cells, flow[4] OF cells, flow[5] OF cells)
THEN site number [3] OF Sites := 4
IF site number [1] OF Sites = 3
AND site number [2] OF Sites = 1
AND site number [3] OF Sites = 4
AND flow[2] OF cells = MAX (flow[2] OF cells, flow[5] OF cells)
THEN site number [4] OF  Sites := 2
AND site number [5] OF Sites := 5
```

Displays: Displays can be attached to attributes, rules, or procedures, example:

```
INSTANCE  pushbutton 2 ISA pushbutton
WITH location := 313, 178,432,224
WITH label := "Proceed"
WITH attribute attachment := call algorithm
```

Logical Fiction: Real vs. Ideal

Roderic A. Girle

Department of Philosophy, University of Auckland
Auckland NEW ZEALAND
r.girle@auckland.ac.nz

Abstract: Formal systems for knowledge and belief, from Lemmon[13] and Hintikka[11] to present day Belief Revision systems[5], have often been described as models of "ideal rational agents." From the first, there has been extensive controversy about the validity of the models.[12, 14, 18] A series of topics have given focus to the controversy. They include distinguishing knowing from believing, formalising positive and negative introspection, omniscience of various kinds, the contrast between finite and infinite, and contradictory belief. We consider the extent to which a range of formal models of knowledge and belief are reasonable and realistic. We conclude with comments on the persistence of unreal models and the lack of discussion of their structure.

1   Introduction

Even before the appearance of Knowledge Representation (KR) as a major area of Artificial Intelligence (AI) research, there were formal systems for the representation of knowing and believing. The early works of Lemmon[13] and Hintikka[11] were precursors of KR. Lemmon's logic was based on the system **S0.5**, a sub-normal modal logic. Hintikka's logic was based on the system **S4**, a normal modal logic. Lemmon recognised that there were features of formal systems for knowing and believing which made the systems unrealistic. He suggests an ideal, a "logical fiction" – that we re-interpret the epistemic logician's 'X knows that':

> We may make a start, however, by treating X as a kind of logical fiction, the rational man. ... (A rational man knows (at least implicitly) the logical consequences of what he knows.)

But, there are some infelicities:

> There are some queer consequences: X knows that T, let us say, where T is some very long tautology containing 396 propositional variables. But this is not to worry us ...

Lemmon's ideal rational agents are assumed to have considerable logical powers. In axiomatic **S0.5**, these powers are given expression by the inference rule (interpreted for epistemic logic by replacing the $\Box$ of modal logic with K_X, read as "X knows that"):

> *If T is a tautology, then* $\vdash K_X T$

We might note that Lemmon's agent could be said to be an ideal *Cartesian* agent.

Descartes[3] says that there are some eternal truths which dwell in our minds:

> To this class belong: *It is impossible that a given thing should at once be and not be;* ... and countless others. It would not be easy to enumerate them all; but one is not either likely to be ignorant of them when occasion arises to think of them and when we are not blinded by prejudice. (pg 191)

Such an agent is just like Lemmon's ideal. The rational agent is the rationalist's agent.

The ideal rational agent is not much discussed in recent knowledge representation literature. The focus is more on the languages used to represent knowledge or belief.

Gärdenfors[5] claims that any epistemological theory will have two major features. There will be an account of epistemic states, and an account of how those states *change* as a result of epistemic input. Epistemic inputs can be either the addition of belief content to an epistemic state (*expansion*) or the derogation of belief content (*contraction*). In the standard AGM[1] (Alchourrón, Gärdenfors, Makinson) theory of belief revision, an account is given of the expansion and contraction of the epistemic states of ideal belief agents.

In this paper we consider several *idealisations* of epistemic agents, and indicate the features of the idealisation which bear on the reality or unreality of the system. There are two major cases to consider. The first are what we call the "logico-philosophical systems". Second there are the recent Belief Revision (BR) systems. We conclude with remarks about the present situation.

2　Logico-philosophical Systems

We begin with a consideration of the formal systems which were the precursors of recent KR and BR systems. Two of the major contributors were Lemmon and Hintikka. A survey by Lenzen[14] in 1978 gives other contributers. The major contributions were philosophically motivated, and the discussions were methodologically philosophical.

2.1　Five Features

We note five features of those formal systems. First, there was a determination to distinguish knowledge from belief. The formal systems were based on both epistemic (knowledge) and doxastic (belief) logics. In some cases the two were interlinked. The approach to knowledge and belief reflected the philosophical orthodoxy which accepted some form of the *justified true belief* (JTB) account of knowledge. Knowledge was a species of belief. On this account, knowing that P entailed believing that P. So, knowing and believing were both kept apart and linked in terms of the prevailing JTB epistemology.

Alternative epistemologies had no serious impact on the relationship, in formal systems, between epistemic and doxastic logic. We also note in passing that very few recent, computationally motivated and oriented systems display a distinction between knowing and believing. The major interest, if there is one, is in believing[19].

The second feature of the logico-philosophical systems is the seriousness with which introspection was taken. This reflects the notion of the incorrigibility of introspection. There is a sense in which we might trace this back to Decartes' *cogito ergo sum*. The debate centred around the **S4** axiom (interpreted for epistemic logic):

$$K_X P \supset K_X K_X P$$

When Hintikka proposed this *KK-thesis*, now known as the *positive introspection thesis*, there was intense, mostly adverse, reaction and prolonged debate.

In the logico-philosophical systems no serious consideration was given to the acceptance of the *negative introspection thesis*.

$$\sim K_X P \supset K_X \sim K_X P$$

The third feature of the logico-philosophical systems was their *omniscience*. This feature was not then discussed at anywhere near the intensity of the *KK-thesis*. But it was considered to be problematic. It is argued elsewhere[10] that there are in fact three kinds of omniscience, logical omniscience, deductive omniscience, and factual omniscience. The definitions are:

> Where the knowledge agent automatically knows all the logical truths defined by some logic the agent is *logically omniscient*.

> Where the knowledge agent automatically knows all the logical consequences of known propositions, the agent is *deductively omniscient*.

> Where the knowledge agent automatically knows, for any proposition *A*, whether *A* is true or not, the agent is *factually omniscient*.

The last of these is not to be found in any of the logico-philosophical systems. The systems have logical and deductive omniscience features. Some recent systems[4], in much the same tradition, have managed to shed deductive omniscience.

The fourth feature of the logico-philosophical systems is their *infinite* nature. This follows from omniscience. The knower knows infinitely many things.

The fifth feature of the logico-philosophical systems is their *classicality*. The systems, per their era, were non-relevant. The strong motivations for non-classical and non-intuitionist logics had not emerged then with the forcefulness of the last twenty years.

In drawing attention to these features we do not mean to suggest that these are *automatically* defects. We simply wish to point out, at this stage, that these features are worthy of attention.

Given these features of the logico-philosophical systems, we proceed to consider the extent to which these features make the ideal agent non-real.

2.2   Unrealistic Features

The five features of the philosophico-logical systems are: distinguishing knowing and believing, formalising introspection, logical and deductive omniscience, infinite knowledge, and classicality.

2.2.1 Knowing and Believing

The first of these features reflects a common facility exercised by human agents, even children. Though we may argue about the manner of making the distinction, the distinction is commonly and routinely made in everyday human life. If a formal system could make this distinction in a similar way, then we can hardly claim that this is an idealisation which gives us a formal system which is somehow unlike real agents.

But this is too quick! What is important here? For example, say that the systems distinguish between knowing and believing in the following way. (We'll call it the "R-way".) It is only logical and mathematical propositions that can be known, contingent truths can only be believed. In this case one could not *know* that one's bank balance is only $27-50, nor could one *know* that this is the PRICAI Conference.

But the R-way of distinguishing knowledge is certainly not in accordance with the common practice of the "man on the Clapham bus", or the "everyday person". Even the ardent philosophical and po-mo skeptic will find themselves slipping into the talk of *knowing* what their bank balance is, and of *knowing* what conference they are attending.

So, the R-way of distinguishing knowing from believing departs from the everyday person, and approaches the view of the post-modern skeptic. Who is to be our measure here – the everyday person, or the skeptical philosopher? In what follows we will eschew the theorising of the radical philosophers and look for everyday cases, countercases, and experiences to inform us as to "real" agents, "real" knowledge, and "real" belief. If it be pointed out out that this is nothing other than anglo-saxon common-sense philosophy, ingenuously disguised, there will be no vigorous denial.

But, that is not the end of the matter. The formal distinction between knowing and believing in Hintikka, especially, does not rely upon some analytic definition of knowledge. The distinction is revealed by the ways in which epistemic logic differs from doxastic. There are two important differences. First there is the *Veridicality Principle* in epistemic logic:

$$K_X P \supset P$$

This principle has no doxastic analogue. The conditional:

$$B_X P \supset P$$

is not a valid principle of any doxastic logic, especially not of Hintikka's.

The second difference is that epistemic logic contains the principle of the *transmissability of knowledge*:

$$K_X K_Y P \supset K_X P$$

This principle has no doxastic analogue.

These seem to accord with the everyday situation. To the extent to which the philosopico-logical systems base the knowing/believing difference on these principles, they are realistic systems. To the extent to which systems do not make the distinction at all, to that extent they are impoverished.

2.2.2 Positive and Negative Introspection

The second of the features, the introspection theses, breaks into two theses. There are the positive and negative introspection theses. Neither of these reflects a common facility which human agents have. There is not enough space to deal thoroughly with this topic here, but something must be said.

We begin with the positive introspection thesis, the *KK-thesis*. We note that the standard counter-examples to the *KK-thesis* are self-deception examples. They are of a kind with the case where someone claims, "I knew that he was being unfaithful, but I did not know that I knew." The claim is that both of the following are (or were) true:

$$K_I P \qquad \sim K_I K_I P$$

If Hintikka's epistemic logic was in accord with everyday realities then everyday agents would know the *KK-thesis* to be true in practice. If everyday agents knew the *KK-thesis* to be true then they *could not* believe that there was a counter-example. Since they do believe there are counter-examples, it follows that the *KK-thesis* is not everyday realistic.

If it's counter-claimed to our argument above, that everyday agents do really know the *KK-thesis*, but are in denial, then the counter-claim is providing yet another counter-example to the *KK-thesis*. With this cursory discussion we leave the *KK-thesis* with the judgement that it is an unrealistic thesis.

The negative introspection thesis is:

$$\sim K_X P \supset K_X \sim K_X P$$

If X does not know that P, then X knows that X does not know that P

The negative introspection thesis, if accepted into an epistemic logic, converts the logic from an **S4** logic into an **S5** logic, a logic which is often thought of as the logic of logical possibility and necessity. The use of **S5** principles for epistemic logic is a serious problem in KR.

Unfortunately, the negative and positive introspection principles together give the following:

$$\sim P \supset K_X \sim K_X P$$

If P is false, then X knows that X does not know that P

This is sometimes called *Plato's principle*.[6] It asserts that the mere falsity of a proposition is enough for the agent to *know* that they do not know the proposition. The weaker, reasonable idea that if a proposition is false, then a person cannot know it, is nowhere as strong as *Plato's Principle*. The principle is far too strong for any agent other than a divinity. It is very unrealistic, and no human could ever aspire to it. If someone responds to this point that they only want the "weaker" principle, then they just cannot have the weaker principle alone in an **S5** logic.

But there are other considerations. The **S4** logics are often seen as the proper basis for logics of provability. The **S4** contrast with **S5** is often seen to match the contrast between necessity and provability, particularly with regard to first-order logics. It is worth noting that Hintikka draws a strong link between knowledge and provability in his work, but not between knowledge and necessity.

One way to see the contrast is to interpret the two crucial axioms for provability, especially as it applies to first-order logic, and with proof linked to computability. We get, for any P:

S4   *If there's a proof that P then there is a proof that there is a proof.*

S5   *If there is no proof that P then there is a proof that there is no proof.*

The **S4** principle is fine, but the **S5** principle is not true in every case. If the **S5** principle were correct we would not have undecidability or incompleteness.

2.2.3 Omniscience

The third of the features is the combination of logical and deductive omniscience. In both S4 and S5 systems, and in many weaker systems, there is automatic knowledge of all logical truths, automatic knowledge of the epistemic principles, and automatic knowledge of all the consequences of what is known. This kind of automatic knowledge does not reflect a common facility which human agents have. We will not delay arguing over this claim. It seems clear that everyday realities are dead-set against omniscience.

2.2.4 Infinite Knowledge

One of the consequences of deductive omniscience is that the agent knows the infinitely many consequences of their knowledge. This is puzzling in many ways. It is clear that no mind or physical data base could contain an infinite amount of material.

But, it might be argued that, for example, the knowledge of one tautology gives us knowledge of the substitution class. If we know that *If it's hot then it's hot*, then we know that *If P then P* for all *P*. The filler for *P* can be as complex as we like. It can contain, to slightly correct Lemmon, 396 atomic indicative sentences properly compounded. But, if *P* is that complex, then it would be too complex for us to comprehend. It's doubtful that we would know that *If P then P*.

The other cases to consider, cases which are not substitution instances of relatively simple tautologies, are the classes of equivalences which are not substitution instances. These are more problematic. Even a machine agent working in first-order languages cannot guarantee to decide on what is equivalent to what. The equivalence class case is more unrealistic than the substitution class cases.

Given the problems with making infinitistic knowing explicable, it would seem to be far less complicated and more realistic if we were to confine our accounts of knowledge to finite domains.

2.2.5 Classical Consistency

The fifth of the features, classical consistency, is somewhat more problematic. The more traditional view is that knowledge must be consistent, that one cannot *know* contradictory content. As well, although everyday belief might be inconsistent, the rational agent will endeavour to have consistent beliefs.

In terms of the orthodoxy, classical consistency will be realistic for knowledge, but somewhat unrealistic for belief. This raises questions about the extent to which unrealistic features are, in fact, desirable features. We may well want our machine agents to be consistent in both knowledge and belief, even if consistency is not a feature of everyday agents.

But that is not the end of the matter. There is a view that classical consistency is not only unrealistic but is also undesirable. In a recent paper, Priest[17] argues for just this view. There is an ongoing stream of publications[7, 9, 16] on paraconsistent and dialethic systems.

Paraconsistent systems are systems which lack the *ex falso quodlibet* inference rule:

$$(P \& \sim P) \vdash Q$$

Paraconsistency allows for non-trivial contradictory sets of propositions.

Priest argues that there are several difficulties with classical systems which are alleviated by paraconsistency. These include changing from inconsistent to consistent belief, overwhelming evidence for both of an inconsistent pair of propositions, and the undecidability of the consistency of sets of propositions. We return to these matters later.

Dialethic systems are those in which some contradictions are both false (as expected) and true (as not expected). "True contradictions" is the catch-call of dialethic philosophy. We do not engage in further discussion about dialethism.

2.3 Real and Unreal

We have taken as our standard of realism the everyday epistemic and doxastic agent. On that standard we have claimed that the five features of logico-philosophical systems fare differently.

One of the four features of the systems is realistic, namely, the knowing/believing distinction feature. Two other features, positive introspection, and logical and deductive omniscience, are unrealistic. The fourth and fifth features, classical consistency and infinitistic knowledge are, at best, problematic.

3 Belief Revision

We turn to the standard AGM belief revision system. Although this system has been the subject of considerable modification since it first appeared[1], the basic principles which bear on its realism have hardly changed. The changes to AGM are changes by improvement, not changes by radical new approaches. There are some exceptions, but they are rare.

For our purposes, consideration of the AGM system will form a basis for deciding about the realism of a typical belief revision system. We consider the five features discussed above, looking at the extent to which AGM has or lacks these features.

3.1 Five Features

According to Gärdenfors[5], a chief proponent of the AGM theory, any epistemological theory will have two major features. There will be both an account of epistemic states, and an account of how those states change as a result of epistemic input. The epistemic states are modelled in propositional fashion by *belief sets*. AGM theory begins with classical propositional logic in a deductive form, and builds its model of belief states as closed deductive theories which include all the theorems of the base logic. So, AGM belief sets are infinitely large, classically consistent sets of sentences (expressing the believed propositions).

3.2.1 Knowing and Believing

There is no facility in AGM, nor in most BR systems, for distinguishing between knowing and believing. This impoverishment of these knowledge representation systems is not necessarily an unalterable feature.

If one were to adhere to the JTB account of knowledge, knowledge sets for any agent would be sub-sets of belief sets. Of course, the beliefs in the knowledge sub-set could not be contracted or revised. One could only ever expand knowledge. This contrast between knowledge and belief raises some interesting issues which we can only point towards here.

The JTB account of knowledge, if applied to either the logico-philosophical or the BR accounts, requires a permanence for knowledge which might well seem unconscionable. It also requires appropriate justification for propositions in the knowledge set. The latter might set us on the course for an unpopular "foundationalism," where some material is considered utterly beyond doubt.

The application of the JTB account of knowledge may well commit us, in BR, to too many things which are too difficult to accept. There are other accounts of the knowledge/belief distinction which are less draconian in what they commit us to. One such is John Austin's[2] so called "performative" account. This is discussed in earlier papers.[6, 8]

At this point we leave this feature, noting that, although AGM theory is presently presented in an impoverished form, it does not have to remain in that form.

3.2.2 Positive and Negative Introspection

There is nothing in AGM theory which commits the theory to either positive or negative introspection. Some other recent KR systems do commit to both kinds of introspection. We have already commented on the unreality of both the positive (*KK-thesis*) and negative (*Plato's Principle*) introspection principles.

3.2.3 Omniscience

The agents of AGM theory are logically and deductively omniscient, according to our earlier definitions. Although Gärdenfors[5] writes that:

> An important feature of belief sets is that they need not be *maximal* in the sense that for every sentence A either A belongs to the belief set or −A belongs to it. The epistemic interpretation of this is that an individual is mormally not *omniscient*. (page 25)

this is a far too restrictive an approach to omniscience. It gives the misleading impression that there is no other kind of omniscience. The literature around this topic shows that there are other views. The kind of omniscience which Gärdenfors correctly claims is not a feature of AGM belief sets is factual omniscience.

3.2.4 Infinite Belief Sets

We have seen that AGM belief sets are infinite. This provides us with a *prima face* case of an unrealistic modelling, especially if we accept the finitistic nature of cognitive states.

A certain amount of work has been done on finitistic belief revision. Finitistic approaches are clearly more realistic than infinitistic.

3.2.5 Classical Consistency

AGM theory is classical, and the postulates to do with expansion are monotonic. But, it does not follow that it is not possible to have a non-classical AGM style of belief revision theory. It just happens that there is not a lot of work in the area.

We have already listed Priest's suggested difficulties with classical theory, difficulties which are alleviated by paraconsistency. The first was the problem of changing from inconsistent to consistent belief. Under classical principles, if a belief set contains an inconsistency then it is trivial. How is one going to distinguish the "core" of consistent belief?

Of a realistic situation, Priest[17] says:

> If, by oversight, I believe both that I will give a talk on campus at noon, but also that I will be in town at noon, this hardly commits me to believing that the Battle of Hastings was in 1939.

It seems even more bizarre to respond to such a case that the ideal *rational* agent would most certainly conclude that the Battle of Hastings was in 1939.

The realistic rational agent would not conclude what the inferential idiocy of classical logic dictates. So, classical logic provides, on this count, an unreal model. The realistic model would enable us to start with inconsistent belief sets, clarify and expand.

The second difficulty was when there is overwhelming evidence for both of an inconsistent pair of propositions. This is common problem in science, law, logic, philosophy, and everyday life. For example, in the late 19th century, evolutionary and thermodynamic evidence about the age of the earth was contradictory. In such a situation the good scientist does not normally throw away one set of information for the sake of rationality.

The third difficulty is the undecidability of the consistency of sets of propositions. If we maintain the centrality of classical consistency, and if we use first-order logic in our belief sets, then we will be caught in the position where, for infinite sets, we cannot determine consistency in all cases. So, at any point we may well be unknowingly trivialised.

Paraconsistent systems release KR from the tyranny of these difficulties. The key is that, even if our belief sets are inconsistent, triviallity does not follow automatically. So, to the extent that BR systems, AGM or AGM modified, are classical, to that extent they are unrealistic.

3.3   Real and Unreal

It is clear that AGM theory has inherited many of the unrealistic features of the logico-philosophical sytems. In standard AGM theory, only the introspection theses are avoided.

4 Conclusion

It seems strange that these unrealistic features continue in KR. A generation of logicians and researchers have been and gone since Lemmon. All their debate seems to have been lost. The cynical view might be that researchers are not prepared to participate in the difficult semi-philosophical debates. The inconclusiveness of philosophical debate can be very frustrating.

But the cynical view is too simple. In some cases there is the deliberate aim of being unrealistic. Some of the features which are unreal, when compared to human abilities, are desirable in machine agents. There is an understandable drive in AI to make machines more reliable and more competent than everyday people. Theoretical models reflect this drive.

Consider the unrealistic features one by one. First, there is introspection. Although we might baulk at negative introspection, it is not unreasonable to require a machine agent to be unable to decieve itself. Its knowledge should be transparent to itself. We might require a machine to be an S4 agent in order to avoid self deception.

Second, there is omniscience. It may be better for a machine agent to be deductively powerful than to have a weak deductive ability. The latter may be human, but it may also build unreliability into machine performance. Given the remarks above about the contrast between S4 and S5, we might prefer the S4 provability model rather than the S5 logical necessity model.

Third, there is the infinitistic approach. This is not such an immediate problem if we accept the provability approach. It simply becomes the idea that of any of the infinitely many things the machine agent can prove from what it knows, any one can be proved on demand. That may be too strong for standard first order languages, but realistic for a suitable fragment. So, the infinitistic approach is still debatable.

Even so, there are risks. The risks are nowhere more evident than in the machine-human interface. The major risk is that the machine structure will be so alien, so powerful, and the machine concepts so contrasting, that a major failure in communication and understanding could occur. Michie and Johnston[15] argue that:

> In order for any beings, human or machine, to talk to each other, they must share the same mental structures. (pg 72)

They claim that failure to observe this sharing has already caused serious practical consequences.

Michie and Johnston's claims need to be taken with utmost seriousness. They indicate that we need much more debate of these issues. We need to bring assumptions and implicit operating principles to light.

5 References

1. Alchourrón, C.E., P. Gärdenfors, and D. Makinson. 1985. "On the logic of Theory Change: Partial meet functions for contraction and revision." *Journal of Symbolic Logic* 50: 510-530

2. Austin, J.L. 1961. "Other Minds", in *Philosophical Papers*, Clarendon Press, Oxford, 44-84.

3. Descartes, R. *Principles of Philosophy*, in *Descartes, Philosophical Writings* 1964. translated by Anscombe, E. and Geach, P.T. Nelson, Melbourne.

4. Fitting, Melvin C. Marek, V. Wictor and Truszczynski, Miroslaw 1992. "The Pure Logic of Necessitation", *Journal of Logic and Computation* 2 (3), 349-373.

5. Gärdenfors, P. 1988. *Knowledge in Flux: Modeling the Dynamics of Epistemic States*, The MIT Press, Cambridge, Mass.

6. Girle, R.A. 1989. "Computational Models for Knowledge", *Proceedings of the Australian Joint Artificial Intelligence Conference*, Melbourne, Vic, Nov. 14-17, 104-119

7. Girle, R.A. 1990. "Weak Para-consistent Logics for Knowledge and Belief" *Proceedings of the Third Florida Artificial Intelligence Research Symposium* Cocoa Beach, Florida, April 3-6, 117-121.

8. Girle, R.A. 1990. "Knowledge, Belief and Computation", *Pacific Rim International Conference on Artificial Intelligence*, Nagoya, Japan, November 14-16, 748-753

9. Girle, R.A. 1992. "Contradictory Belief and Logic", *Advances in Artificial Intelligence Research, Volume II*, (Eds. M.B. Fishman and J.L. Robards), JAI Press, London, 23-36.

10. Girle, R.A. 1998. "Delusions of Omniscience" *Proceedings of the Florida Artificial Intelligence Research Symposium* Sanibel Beach, Florida, May 18-20, (forthcoming).

11. Hintikka, J.J. 1962. *Knowledge and Belief: An Introduction to the Logic of the two Notions*, Cornell University Press, Ithaca.

12. Hocutt, M.O. 1972. "Is Epistemic Logic possible?", *Notre Dame Journal of Formal Logic* 13 (4), 433-453

13. Lemmon, E.J. 1959. "Is there only one correct system of modal logic?" *Aristotelian Society Supplementary Volume XXXIII*, 23-40

14. Lenzen, W. 1978. "Recent Work in Epistemic Logic", *Acta Philosophica Fennica* 30, (1), North-Holland, Amsterdam.

15. Michie, D. and Johnston, R. 1985. *The Creative Computer*, Penguin Books, Harmondsworth.

16. Priest, G. 1987. *In Contradiction*, Martinus Nijhoff, Dordrecht.

17. Priest, G. 1998. "Paraconsistent Belief Revision", unpublished paper.

18. Schotch, P.K. and Jennings, R.E. 1981. "Epistemic Logic, Skepticism, and Non-Normal Modal Logic", *Philosophical Studies*, 40, 47-67.

19. Segerberg, K. 1994. "Belief Revision from the point of view of Doxastic Logic" *Bulletin of the IGPL*, Vol 2 No 3, 3-21.

Coherence Measure Based on Average Use of Formulas

Rex Kwok[1], Abhaya Nayak[2] and Norman Foo[1]

email: rkwok@cse.unsw.edu.au, abhaya@u2.newcastle.edu.au, norman@cse.unsw.edu.au

[1] Knowledge Systems Group,
School of Computer Science and Engineering,
University of New South Wales, Sydney, Australia 2052
[2] Information Systems Group,
School of Management,
University of Newcastle NSW, Australia 2308

Abstract. Coherence is a positive virtue of theories, and its importance in theory construction is beyond debate. Unfortunately, however, a rigorous and computable definition of coherence is conspicuously lacking in the literature. This paper attempts to remedy this situation by formalising this notion of coherence and suggesting a measure. Roughly speaking, we suggest that a theory is coherent to the degree that its members (read formulas) are required to account for the intended class of observations. This approach is motivated by Bonjour's account of coherence. We also generalise this notion of coherence to work in the context of a potentially infinite long sequence of observations.

1 Introduction

Intelligent behaviour (read decision making) involves, among other things, selecting the "right" hypothesis from a set of competing hypotheses that are equally efficacious in explaining the observed data in question. One might think that the subjective element in this choice behaviour can be eliminated by acquiring more data so that only the "correct" hypothesis will pass the scrutiny. This hypothetical position is flawed on at least two counts: firstly, the bounds on available resources (time, cost, etc.) often do not allow such luxury; secondly, and more importantly, Quine [Qui60] has demonstrated that no amount of data can eliminate enough of the alternative hypotheses to leave just one, since *theory is inherently underdetermined by facts*. Hence theory choice would inevitably involve, apart from the ability to explain observations, pragmatic factors such as coherence, simplicity, etc.. The aim of this paper is to formally articulate and examine our notion of coherence – in particular, to propose a metric on the coherence measure of theories and examine how this metric fares *vis a vis* the received accounts of coherence found in the relevant literature.

Coherence is a positive virtue of a good scientific theory.[1] Parts of a coherent theory "hang together", lending each other mutual support; they are also supposed to be

---

[1] Coherence is also a property of text or speech; perhaps the primary usage of "coherent" is in the context of speech, and its use in the context of theories is a derived usage. In this paper, however, we are concerned with the coherence of theories. We are not making any claim about the applicability of our account in the context of textual coherence.

"organised"and "well structured". In contrast, an incoherent theory is a "helter skelter collection" of "conflicting subsystems". That, roughly, is as far as our intuitive notion of coherence goes.

However, there are several accounts of coherence in the literature , e.g. [Bon85,Tha89,Leh90]. In this introductory section we will briefly outline Bonjour's account which comes close to capturing our intuitive notion of coherence. Then we will point out the connection among the coherence of theories, theory replacement and machine learning. We will close this section with a brief outline of the paper.

Bonjour's Account of Coherence

Bonjour [Bon85] offers a very intuitive account of coherence of theories. We suggest that any attempt at formally capturing our intuitive notion of coherence should validate conditions specified by Bonjour. Bonjour suggests that coherent theories have elements which share a number of subject matters and can be connected using inference rules. Consider, for instance, two sets of propositions: $A = \{$"this chair is brown", "electrons have a negative charge", "today is Thursday"$\}$ and $B = \{$"ravens are black", "this bird is a raven", "this bird is black"$\}$. A is less coherent than B because while the statements in A refer to different subject matters, elements of B share some subject matter and can be connected via inference rules.

Furthermore, according to Bonjour, coherence should increase in proportion to the number and strength of inferential connections between components while a theory should be less coherent if it can be divided into subsystems which are relatively unconnected by inferential relations. The coherence of individual elements of a theory should also be definable and the measure should be dependent on the degree to which the element is involved in different inferential relations. One of the consequences of our formalisation in Section 2 is a rigorous validation of this intuition.

Coherence and Theory Replacement

It is well known from history of science that theories do not get rejected in face of counter-evidence – auxiliary hypotheses are added to the current theory to account for the hitherto unaccounted for evidence instead. To account for the gain of weight in the process of burning (the extra oxygen, as we know now), the propounders of the phlogiston theory had suggested as auxiliary hypothesis that phlogiston has negative mass; more and more epicycles were added to the Ptolemaic cosmology to explain away newly discovered counter examples; existence of more planets were postulated (Pluto) in order to salvage Newtonian mechanics in face of anomalous evidence (aberrance with the orbit of Uranus).

Popper [Pop68] imposed the condition that auxiliary assumptions were justified if their addition did not render the resultant theory unfalsifiable. This restriction is very mild indeed, since such eventuality (unfalsifiability of the expanded theory) is rare in practice [Grü59]. We propose the restriction instead that the auxiliary assumption in question should not be *ad hoc,* as in the case of successive additions of epicycles in the Ptolemaic cosmology. We suggest that the *ad hoc*-ness of an auxiliary hypothesis is linked to the increased incoherence in the resultant theory. The purpose of an auxiliary hypothesis is not just to explain the new evidence, but also to increase the the over all coherence of the theory in question. Once we have a metric for the coherence of a theory, we can use it to judge whether or not the addition of a particular auxiliary hypothesis to the current theory is acceptable or not.

Coherence and Machine Learning

In computer science in general, and AI in particular, machine learning comes closest to theory construction (via inductive learning). It is not surprising that the tradition in machine learning conforms to our intuition about coherence. Many machine learning systems, including C4.5 [Qui93], FOIL [Qui90], CIGOL [MB88], and GOLEM [MF90], accept as input a set of facts and output general theories. While the input generally consists of unconnected facts, the output consists of a relatively small number of highly connected generalisations. Quinlan's [Qui87] method for simplifying decision trees is another example of a policy which increases coherence. Branches in a decision tree can become highly complex and specialised, leaving the theory highly susceptible to noisy data. The process of pruning a decision tree removes such specialised branches in favour of more general principles.

Paper Outline

In the next section (§2) we present the formal account of our theory of coherence. Coherence measures the extent to which the elements (formulas) in a theory are necessary to account for the observation sequence in question. We also show how our formalism captures Bonjour's account of coherence. Section §3 explores the connection between redundancy and coherence. Perhaps surprisingly, it turns out that on occasion redundant elements in a theory help increase its overall coherence. In section §4 we explore the effect that merging of two or more theories has on coherence. This is interesting as scientific revolutions are characterised by unification of seemingly unconnected theories into more general theories. Finally, in section §5 we consider the issue of infinite observational sequences. We conclude with a short summary.

2 Measuring Coherence

When we talk of the coherence of a theory, we do not take it to be an intrinsic property of the theory. A theory is coherent or otherwise only with respect to our knowledge of the domain that the theory is about – for our purpose, with respect to a particular class of observations. (Compare with the consistency of a theory.) A theory acquires its coherence property from its ability to neatly systematise and explain past observations, as well as predict future phenomena. Hence the formal account of coherence we are about to present will, of necessity, be parametrised by observations.

We will assume a first order language $\mathcal{L}$, its (classical) semantic entailment relation $\models$ and a consequence function Cn defined $x \in Cn(X)$ iff $X \models x$ for every member x and subset X of $\mathcal{L}$. By $\mathcal{L}_o$ we will denote the maximal, observational sub-language of $\mathcal{L}$. By a theory T (perhaps with decorations) we will mean any finite subset of $\mathcal{L}$ consisting of clausal formulas only (the reason for this restriction will become clear later). Similarly, by an *observation set* O we will denote a subset of $\mathcal{L}_o$. The *size* of a theory T is its cardinality, namely $|T|$. We will denote the observational consequences of a theory

T, namely $Cn(T) \cap \mathcal{L}_o$ by $Cn(T)|_{\mathcal{L}_o}$. Furthermore, for every subset Γ and O of $\mathcal{L}$, we will use $\Gamma \models O$ to signify that $\Gamma \models o$ for every element o of O; analogously, $\Gamma \not\models O$ signifies that $\Gamma \not\models o$ for some member o of O. Two theories T and T' will be said to be *empirically equivalent* if, and only if, they have the same observational content, i.e., $Cn(T)|_{\mathcal{L}_o} = Cn(T')|_{\mathcal{L}_o}$. Finally, a theory T will be termed *empirically adequate* just in case the contextually defined set of observations O is included in $Cn(T)|_{\mathcal{L}_o}$. Equipped with this formal apparatus, we can now attempt to capture our intuitive notion of coherence.

As we pointed out in section §1, introduction of *ad hoc* auxiliary assumptions can decrease the coherence of a theory. Consider, for instance, an initial theory $T_0 = \{\forall x(swan(x) \to white(x))\}$. If a black swan, sw_1, were to be observed then this observation would contradict T_0. An *ad hoc* method of revising the theory is to treat the black swan as an exception by weakening the sentence in T_0 to assert that all swans, except sw_1, are white and add that sw_1 is a black swan. This gives the following theory:

$$T_1 = \{\forall x(swan(x) \wedge x \neq sw_1 \to white(x)), swan(sw_1), black(sw_1)\}.$$

As more black swans are observed, the theory can be successively revised in this *ad hoc* manner so as to remain empirically adequate. Suppose that n swans, $sw_1, sw_2, \ldots, sw_n$, have been observed to be black. If theory is revised in the same manned as above for each swan, the resulting theory would be:

$$T_n = \{\forall x(swan(x) \wedge \bigwedge_{i=1}^n x \neq sw_i \to white(x))\} \cup \bigcup_{i=1}^n \{swan(sw_i), black(sw_i)\}.$$

We would like to claim that this resultant theory, which is primarily about the colour of swans, is highly incoherent in the sense that only one or two elements in the theory of size $2n + 1$ are required to determine the colour of any one swan. For instance, suppose that $Janice$ is a constant in the language and that the unique names assumption is implicit, then to arrive at the conclusion that if $Janice$ is a swan then $Janice$ is white, only one element, $\forall x(swan(x) \wedge \bigwedge_{i=1}^n x \neq sw_i \to white(x))$, is necessary out of the $2n + 1$ elements of T_n.

What seems to be at issue here is the proportion of a theory which is necessary for entailing certain observational consequences. As a first approximation, we say that a theory T is "necessary" for implying its observational consequence o to the extent that its members play an active role in the derivation of o. Thus, if most members of T participate in some minimal proof of o or other in T, then T is by and large necessary for the implication of o. On the other hand, if very few members of T play such a role, then a large part of T is superfluous as far as implication of o is concerned. Accordingly, we define a minimal proof or support set as follows:

Definition 1. Let T be a theory and let O be an observation set. The set of supports of T for O, namely $S(T, O)$, is defined by

$$S(T, O) = \{\Gamma \mid \Gamma \subseteq T \text{ and } \Gamma \models O \text{ and for every } \Gamma' \subset \Gamma \, (\Gamma' \not\models O)\}$$

Continuing with the swan example, consider the following observation set, $O = \{swan(sw_1), black(sw_1)\}$. The subset, $\Gamma = \{swan(sw_1), black(sw_1), swan(sw_2)\}$, of T_n would not be a support set of T_n for O because its strict subset, $\Gamma' = \{swan(sw_1), black(sw_1)\}$ also entails every element of O. Further, since no other subset of T_n entails O, the set of supports of T for O contains only Γ'. Notice that if a theory, T, does not entail all of the elements in an observations set, O, that the set of supports of T for O is the empty set because first order logic is monotonic.

In the next definition we define the *utility* $U(\alpha, T, O)$ of an element α of a theory T with respect to a certain observation set O is defined as the proportion of support sets of T for O that contain α as an element. Notice that this is necessarily a partial function defined only if $T \models O$ since when $T \not\models O$, the proportion of support sets which contains a certain element will be undefined. In order to avoid having to specify such a condition continually, henceforth, when observation sets are mentioned in the same context as a theory the implicit assumption will be that support sets exist.

Definition 2. Let T be a theory and let O be an observation. For every $\alpha_i \in T$, the utility of α_i in T for O, denoted by $U(\alpha_i, T, O)$, is defined by:

$$U(\alpha_i, T, O) = \frac{|\{\Gamma \mid \Gamma \in S(T, O) \text{ and } \alpha_i \in \Gamma\}|}{|S(T, O)|} \text{ if } S(T, O) \neq \emptyset$$

Consider the observation set, $\{swan(sw_1), black(sw_1)\}$, and the theory T_n. For such an observation set, only one support set exists which is a subset of T_n, i.e. the observation set itself. Thus, the utility of the element $swan(sw_1)$ (respectively $black(sw_1)$) is 1 because all support sets for the observation set in question contain this element. However, for all other elements of T_n, since they are not present in any support sets, the utility in question is zero.

Since the utility of an element of a theory is a proportion, it can be easily shown that utility values range from zero to one. Further, as shown in Lemma 3 the utility of a theory element equals one if and only if every support set contains that element. This result accords well with Bonjour's principle which asserts that the coherence of individual components of a theory should be dependent on the degree to which the element appears in different inferential relations.

Lemma 3. *Let T be a theory and O_j an observation set. Then, for any $\alpha_i \in T$, $0 \leq U(\alpha_i, T, O_j) \leq 1$. Further, $U(\alpha_i, T, O) = 1$ if and only if $\alpha_i \in \Gamma$ for every $\Gamma \in S(T, O)$.*

With the utility of a theory element measuring the use of that element in entailing an observation set, summation over the elements of the theory and normalisation with respect to the size of the theory gives the *average use* of theory elements in entailing an observation set. Summing this value for each observation set in the sequence and then normalising with respect to the number of observation sets in the sequence gives the average use of theory elements in entailing all the observation sets. The coherence of a theory for a finite sequence of observation sets is defined as the sum, over all elements of the theory and observation sets in the sequence, of the utility of each theory element for that observation set normalised with respect to the number of elements in the theory and the number of observation sets in the sequence.

Definition 4. Let $T = \{\alpha_1, \alpha_2, ..., \alpha_n\}$ be a theory and let $O = (O_1, O_2, ..., O_m)$ be a finite sequence of observations. The coherence of T with respect to O, denoted by $C(TO)$, is defined by:

$$C(T, O) = \frac{1}{nm} \sum_{i=1}^{n} \sum_{j=1}^{m} U(\alpha_i, T, O_j)$$

Consider a sequence of observation sets which contains only one observation set, $O_1 = \{swan(sw_1), black(sw_1)\}$. With the theory T_n, the utility of $swan(sw_1)$ and $black(sw_1)$ in the theory is one while for all other elements of T_n, the utility is zero. Thus, the coherence of T_n for (O_1) is $\frac{2}{2n+1}$. This accords well with the intuition that T_n is not a very coherent theory since T_n attempts to hold on to the idea that all swans are white except all the exceptions observed. As more black swans are observed and T_n is revised using the *ad hoc* recipe specified previously, the coherence of the theory for observation sets like O_1 tends to zero. A more coherent theory for explaining the colour of swans may contain assertions about genetic traits and inheritance rules.

The reason why we restricted formulation of theories to clausal formulas alone is now clear. Since this restriction disallows conjunction of formulas, we prevent artificial hiking of the coherence measure of a theory that would result if one were to conjoin several formulas in a theory into a single formula.

. Since the utility of theory elements ranges from zero to one, the coherence of a theory for a sequence of observation sets, the normalised sum over utilities, also ranges from zero to one. Further, it can be shown that a maximally coherent theory has, for any observation set, one support set which consists of the entire theory itself.

Lemma 5. Let $T = \{\alpha_1, \alpha_2, ..., \alpha_n\}$ be a theory and let $O = (O_1, O_2, ..., O_m)$ be a finite sequence of observations. Then, $0 \leq C(T, O) \leq 1$. Further, $C(T, O) = 1$ if and only if $S(T, O_j) = \{T\}$ for every j, $1 \leq j \leq m$.

Recall the original theory about swan colour, T_0, which merely asserts that all swans are white. Such a theory is in fact maximally coherent for observation sets containing elements which assert that certain swans are white. The single element of the theory is necessary in entailing such observation sets.

Coherence as defined here can be viewed in other ways. As it turns out coherence for a single observation set is equivalent to the average size of the support sets of the theory for the observation set normalised by the size of the theory. Thus, for a sequence of observation sets, coherence is equal to the average of the average size of support sets for the observation sets.

Theorem 6. Let $T = \{\alpha_1, \alpha_2, ..., \alpha_n\}$ be a theory and let $O = (O_1, O_2, ..., O_m)$ be a finite sequence of observations. Then,

$$C(T, O) = \frac{1}{nm} \sum_{j=1}^{m} \frac{1}{|S(T, O_j)|} \sum_{\Gamma \in S(T, O_j)} |\Gamma|$$

3 Redundancy and Coherence

In this section we examine whether or not, and if so, how, the coherence of a theory changes when we remove from it elements that are deemed superfluous. Intuitively elimination of superfluous formulas should increase the coherence of a theory. But as it turns out on occasion the presence of superfluous elements in a theory can positively contribute to its coherence. Accordingly, first we define what it is for a theory to contain *redundancy*, and what elements of it are deemed *redundant* or *superfluous*.

Definition 7. Let T be a theory. T has *redundancy* iff there exists $\alpha \in T : Cn(T \setminus \{\alpha\}) |_{\mathcal{L}_o} = Cn(T) |_{\mathcal{L}_o}$ Further, we say that $\alpha \in T$ is *redundant* iff $Cn(T \setminus \{\alpha\}) |_{\mathcal{L}_o} = Cn(T) |_{\mathcal{L}_o}$.

This notion of redundancy can be expressed in terms of the utility of theory elements and the observational consequences of the theory. The following result shows that an element of a theory is redundant if and only if the utility of that element is less than one for every observational consequence of the theory.

Lemma 8. *Let T be a theory. T has redundancy if and only if there exists element α in T such that for every $\gamma \in Cn(T) |_{\mathcal{L}_o}$ $U(\alpha, T, \gamma) < 1$.*

The relationship between the coherence of subsets of a theory and the coherence of the theory itself can be established by showing how the removal of elements from a theory contracts the set of supports for arbitrary observation sets. It turns out that the support sets for a theory without a certain element are simply the support sets of the original theory which do not contain that element.

Lemma 9. *Let T be a theory, O an observation set, and α an element of T. Then $S(T \setminus \{\alpha\}, O) = \{\Gamma \mid \Gamma \in S(T, O) \text{ and } \alpha \notin \Gamma\}$.*

A consequence of it is that elements of a theory which have zero utility, relative to certain observation sets, can be removed to increase the coherence of the theory relative to those observation sets. An element of a theory which has a utility of zero does not appear in any of the support sets. As such, by Lemma 9, the support sets for the contracted theory are exactly the support sets of the original theory. The gain in coherence comes from the decrease in the size of the theory while the average size of the support sets remains unchanged. Examples of theory elements which have zero utility include formulae which contain only theoretical predicates which cannot be used by the rest of the theory to derive observational consequences.

Corollary 10. *Let $T = \{\alpha_1, \alpha_2, \ldots, \alpha_n\}$ be a theory and $O = (O_1, O_2, ..., O_m)$ be a finite sequence of observations. Let $U(\alpha, T, O) = \frac{1}{m} \sum_{j=1}^{m} U(\alpha, T, O_j)$. If $\mid T \mid \geq 2$, $C(T, O) > 0$, and $U(\alpha, T, O) = 0$ then $C(T, O) < C(T \setminus \{\alpha\}, O)$. Further, $C(T \setminus \{\alpha\}, O) = \frac{n}{n-1} C(T, O)$.*

A sufficient condition for the existence of an element of a theory with zero utility is that the theory contains redundancy and that for the observation sets under consideration, the set of supports of the theory for each observation set is a singleton.

Lemma 11. *Let T be a theory and $O = (O_1, O_2, ..., O_m)$ be a finite sequence of observations. If T has redundancy and for every $j, 1 \leq j \leq m, | S(T, O_j) | = 1$ then there exists $\alpha \in T$ such that $U(\alpha, T, O) = 0$.*

In general, however, the removal of redundant elements of a theory does not always guarantee an increase of coherence because redundant elements can be part of relatively large support sets for the observation sets under attention. For example, consider the following theory and observation set:

$$T = \{a, a \vee b, \neg b \vee c, \neg c \vee d\}$$
$$O = \{a \vee d\}$$

In T, $a \vee b$ is clearly redundant since another element of the theory, a, entails $a \vee b$. But, for the particular observation set which consists of $a \vee d$, T has two support sets for O, $\{a\}$ and $\{a \vee b, \neg b \vee c, \neg c \vee d\}$, giving T a coherence of $\frac{1}{2}$. If the redundant formula is removed, the resulting coherence would fall to $\frac{1}{3}$.

4 Theory Union and Coherence

A number of major achievements in science have coincided with the formulation of theories which unify and explain a number of previously disparate fields of study. These scientific achievements range from the discovery of the connection between magnetism and electricity to the formulation of plate tectonics theory. Since scientific revolutions tend to unify a number of previously disparate fields it is of interest to consider how the coherence measure presented here behaves when theories are joined together.

Given two theories that do not share common elements of language and have their coherence measured with respect to two finite sequences of observation sets, the following result shows the connection between the coherence of each of the two theories and the coherence of the union of the two theories on the concatenation of the two sequences of observation sets.

Theorem 12. *Let $\mathcal{L}_1$ and $\mathcal{L}_2$ be the respective languages for theories, $T_1 = \{\alpha_1, \alpha_2, \ldots, \alpha_n\}$ and $T_2 = \{\alpha'_1, \alpha'_2, \ldots, \alpha'_{n'}\}$ and suppose that $\mathcal{L}_1 \cap \mathcal{L}_2 = \emptyset$. Let $O_1 = (O_1, O_2, \ldots, O_m)$ and $O_2 = (O'_1, O'_2, \ldots, O'_{m'})$ be two sequences of observation sets such that the observation sets of O_1 and O_2 are subsets of the observational language of $\mathcal{L}_1$ and $\mathcal{L}_2$ respectively. Let $O_1 \circ O_2$ be the concatenation od O_1 and O_2, then, $C(T_1 \cup T_2, O_1 \circ O_2) =$*

$$\frac{1}{(n + n')(m + m')}(nmC(T_1, O_1) + n'm'C(T_2, O_2))$$

The relationship between the coherence of two theories and the coherence of union of the two theories is similar to that between the velocity of a combined object with that of the initial objects having different masses. To gain a better understanding of the result, considers the effect of combining two theories of equal size when accounting for the same number of observation sets and which have the same coherence in doing so. This gives that $C(T_1 \cup T_2, O_1 \circ O_2) = \frac{1}{2}C(T_1, O_1)$ which means that the coherence is halved. The main reason for this is that the size of the theory is doubled while the average size of support sets remain unchanged. Although not presented formally here, another corollary is that the coherence of the union of the two theories is strictly less than the maximum of the coherence of the two theories.

In general, when two theories are placed together, without the constraint that languages of the theories haven an empty intersection, the coherence of the union of the theories may increase as well as decrease. As an example, consider the following theories and observation set:

$$T_1 = \{a, b \rightarrow c, c \rightarrow d, d \rightarrow e, e \rightarrow f\} \quad T_2 = \{b, g, h, i, j\}$$
$$O = \{a \lor f \lor g\}$$

Then the coherence of T_1 with respect to O is $\frac{1}{5}$ and T_2 with respect to O is $\frac{1}{5}$. But the coherence of the union of T_1 and T_2 with respect to O equals $\frac{1}{10} \cdot \frac{7}{3} = \frac{7}{30}$ which is greater that $\frac{1}{5}$.

5   Infinite Observational Sequences

One of the major results demonstrating the eliminability of theoretical terms from logical theories is Craig's theorem [Cra53]. Given a recursive axiomatisation of a theory, which may contain theoretical terms, Craig presents a construction of another recursive axiomatisation which does not contain theoretical terms but which agrees exactly with the first axiomatisation on observational consequences. However, the extralogical axioms of the axiomatisation consists of formulas of the form $A\&A\&\dots\&A$ where the number of conjunctions of A encodes the Gödel number of the proof of A in the original theory and A is any non-trivial consequence of the original theory. Craig himself describes the method by which axioms of the observational axiomatisation are generated as "artificial". It is interesting that the coherence measure we have defined implies that theories which consist of a finite number of observations, under minor constraints, are highly incoherence and that, in the limit, this coherence approaches zero. Craig's description of "artificiality" would therefore appear to a formal interpretation in our approach.

Theorem 13. *Let $O = (O_1, O_2, \dots)$ be an infinite sequence of observation sets, each O_i being a singleton Let $O|_n$ denote the finite subsequence of O consisting of the first n observation sets and $T_n = \{\alpha | \alpha \in O_i \text{ for some } i, 1 \leq i \leq n\}$ for any positive integer n. Suppose for every j, $\{O_i \mid j \neq i\} \not\models O_j$. Then $C(T_n, O|_n) = \frac{1}{n}$. Further,*

$$\lim_{n \to \infty} C(T_n, O|_n) = 0$$

In the above result, a sequence of theories is defined such that T_n consists of the elements of the first n observation sets in the infinite sequence. The constraint that no observation set in the sequence is entailed by the remaining observation sets ensures that there is no redundancy in the sequence of observation sets and that each observation set tests the coherence of the theory on something new. The coherence of the theory, T_n, on the first n observation sets is $\frac{1}{n}$ because T_n has only one support set for any observation set, O_i where i is less than n, and that consists of the observation set itself.

Since scientific theories tend to have an infinite number of observational consequences, without redundancy, it is important that a measure of coherence should be able to handle an infinite sequence of observation sets. The simplest way of extending the current definition of coherence is to define the coherence of a theory for an infinite sequence of observation sets as the limiting value of coherence as coherence is measured for more and more observation sets.

Definition 14. Let T be a theory and $O = (O_1, O_2, ...)$ be an infinite sequence of observations. Say that $C(T, O)$ exists if $\lim_{n \to \infty} C(T, O \mid_n)$ exists.

The limiting value of coherence may not always exist. The following result considers the case when observation sets can be partitioned into a finite number of *observation types*. Each observation type determines an average size for its support sets. Given these assumptions, the following result defines the coherence of a theory in terms of the asymptotic proportions of each observation type within all observation types. In many scientific theories, certain observational consequences arise from the same parts of the theory giving the same support sets for the observational consequences. For example, in Newtonian mechanics, the same portions of the theory will be used to calculate the trajectory of projectiles while another portion will be used to determine planetary orbits.

Theorem 15. *Let T be a theory such that $|T| = n$ and $O = (O_1, O_2, ...)$ be an infinite sequence of observations. Further, let $0 < c_1, c_2, ..., c_l \leq n$ and $0 < p_1, p_2, ..., p_l \leq 1$ such that $\sum_{k=1}^{l} p_i = 1$. Suppose that $\forall_{\epsilon > 0} \exists_{m \in Z+} \forall_{m' \geq m}$*

$$\left(\left| \frac{\mid \{O_j : j \leq m' \text{ and } C(T, O_j) = \frac{c_k}{n}\} \mid}{m'} - p_k \right| < \epsilon \right).$$

Then, $C(T, O) = \frac{1}{n} \sum_{k=1}^{l} p_k c_k$.

In the above result, each c_k corresponds to the average size of support sets of the theory when entailing observations of type k. Thus, for observations of type k, the coherence of the theory on such observation sets is $\frac{c_k}{n}$. Each p_k represents the proportion of observation sets in the sequence which correspond to observations of type k. Since this represents a probability distribution, individual values of p_k range between zero and one and the sum of such values is equal to one. A value of zero for p_k is excluded because this would mean that the observation type is not present in the sequence of observation sets. The major constraint on each observation type, k, where k ranges from 1 to l, is that:

$$\forall_{\epsilon > 0} \exists_{m \in Z+} \forall_{m' \geq m} \left(\left| \frac{|\{O_j : j \leq m' \text{ and } C(T, O_j) = \frac{c_k}{n}\}|}{m'} - p_k \right| < \epsilon \right)$$

To interpret this, first consider the following set for an arbitrary positive integer, m', and a value of k between 1 and l:

$$\{O_j : j \leq m' \text{ and } C(T, O_j) = \frac{c_k}{n}\}$$

This sets contains all the observation sets, out of the first m', for which the coherence of the theory on the observation set is $\frac{c_k}{n}$. Thus, since observations of type k correspond to the theory having a coherence of $\frac{c_k}{n}$, the cardinality of this set corresponds to the number of observation sets, out of the first m', which correspond to observations of type k. Dividing by m' gives the proportion of the first m' observation sets which are of type k. Since the intended interpretation of p_k is that p_k is the proportion of observation sets in the sequence of type k, for any deviation, there should exist a point in the sequence beyond which the difference between p_k and the proportion of k type observation sets is less than the deviation.

Thus with each c_k representing the average size of support sets in accounting for observation of type k and with p_k representing the proportion of k type observation sets in the sequence, the coherence of the theory on the infinite observation sequence is given by summing, over the types of observations, the product of c_k and p_k and normalising with respect to the size of the theory.

6 Summary and Future Work

We started with the guiding principle that *ad hoc* revision of theories result in their loss of coherence. Based on this principle we defined a measure of coherence for theories that calculates the average proportion of a theory necessary for proofs of observational consequences. The greater the necessity of theory elements in entailing observational consequences, the higher the coherence of the theory. We then examined how elimination of superfluous elements from a theory affects coherence. We also explored the effect of theory merger on coherence. Finally we generalised our account to take care of infinite observation sequences.

A shortcoming of the coherence measure presented here is that new non–observational propositions can be used to increase coherence. By making the new propositions necessary for the derivation of any observational consequence, the average utility of theory elements increases. This is achieved by weakening each clause in the theory by disjoining it with the negations of each new proposition. As more propositions are invented and used in this way, the coherence of a theory approaches arbitrarily close to 1. Such a problem provides one avenue for further research. A second avenue for research would address the question of: Which observation sets should be used to measure the coherence of a theory? An answer to such a question is important because the coherence of a theory will vary depending on which observational consequences are used to measure coherence. There should be some criteria for determining which observation sets are appropriate for measuring the coherence of a theory. Finally, a common view [Bon85] is that a coherent theory should unify several fields of study and be able to explain seemingly disparate observations. While the coherence measure presented here was used to show that coherence decreases when two linguistically unrelated theories are joined by set union, the problem of measuring the unifying properties of a theory has yet to be addressed.

References

[Bon85] L. Bonjour. *The Structure of Empirical Knowledge*. Harvard University Press, 1985.

[Cra53] W. Craig. On axiomatizability within a system. In *The Journal of Symbolic Logic vol. 18*, pages 30–32, 1953.

[Cra56] W. Craig. Replacement of auxilliary expressions. In *Philosophical Review, 55(1)*, pages 38–55, 1956.

[Grü59] Adolf Grünbaum. The falsifiability of lorentz-fitzerald contraction hypothesis. In *British Journal for the Philosophy of Science, 39*, pages 48–50, 1959.

[Leh90] Keith Lehrer. *The Theory of Knowledge*. Routledge, London, 1990.

[MB88] S. Muggleton and W. Buntine. Machine invention of first-order predicates by inverting resolution. In *Proceedings of the 5th International Machine Learning Workshop*, pages 339–352. Morgan Kaufman, 1988.

[MF90] S. Muggleton and C. Feng. Efficient induction of logic programs. In *Proceedings of the Fifth International Conference on Machine Learning*. Morgan Kaufman, 1990.

[Pop68] Karl R. Popper. *The Logic of Scientific Discovery*. London: Hutchinson, 1968.

[Qui60] W. V. Quine. *Word and Object*. MIT Press, 1960.

[Qui70] W. V. Quine. On the reasons for indeterminacy of translation. In *The Journal of Philosophy, LXVII 6*, pages 178–183, 1970.

[Qui87] Ross Quinlan. Simplifying decision trees. In *International Journal of Man-Machine Studies 27*, pages 221–234, 1987.

[Qui90] Ross Quinlan. Learning logical definitions from relations. In *Machine Learing, 5(3)*, pages 239–266, 1990.

[Qui93] J. R. Quinlan. *C4.5: Programs For Machine Learning*. Morgan Kaufmann, 1993.

[Tha89] P. Thagard. Explanatory coherence. In *Behavioural and Brain Sciences, 12*, pages 435–467, 1989.

Diagrammatic Reasoning About Linked Lists

Norman Foo

Knowledge Systems Group
Department of Artificial Intelligence
School of Computer Science and Engineering
University of New South Wales, Sydney NSW 2052, Australia

Abstract. A recently developed theory of local reasoning with diagrams is applied to a practical domain, that of inserting a node into a singly linked list, to illustrate its explanatory power. Prior to this demonstration there was only an informal feel as to why diagrams used to explain the generation of imperative code for similar applications should work. This paper is a partial answer to the charge that theory in artificial intelligence is remote from application. On the contrary, it shows that properly constrained theories can assist in underpinning cognitive tools.
Keywords: diagrammatic reasoning, imperative programming, linked lists, finite models, actions.

1 Introduction

In explaining algorithms on data structures one habitually resorts to diagrams of one kind or another. The role of this informal method of communication has not been seriously examined from the viewpoint of artificial intelligence (AI), presumably because the intersection of interests between algorithm designers and diagrammatic reasoning researchers is meagre. However, with the increasing interest of both the AI and software engineering communities in discovering effective methods of communication and understanding why they work (or fail), the time is ripe to apply rigorous techniques to supplement theories from cognitive science to this enterprise.

In this paper we will introduce new ideas in diagrammatic reasoning to formalize and justify common practice in the use of diagrams in conveying the semantics of algorithms on data structures.

A representative sample of approaches to diagrammatic reasoning is the collection edited by Glasgow, et.al. [Glasgow, et. al. 95]. Of the papers in this collection, the ones closest in spirit to our work are [Myers and Konolige 95] and [Barwise and Etchemendy 95]. Both the papers use logic as the textual mode but make the point that it is not intended that one should regard diagrams as merely a more convenient mode of expression that can in principle be replaced by logic. In other words, diagrams can convey information not expressible in the logic. Likewise, in this paper we will provide a semantics for the diagrams that, if translated to logic, will have to be supplemented with extra-logical conventions.

2 Linked Lists

For expository purposes, we will confine our attention here to one data structure — linear lists. It will be clear from the exposition that the techniques, insights, and results obtained here will translate to other data structures.

2.1 Updating Linear Lists

Perhaps the simplest linear list is the *sorted* singly linked list. Let us assume a structure as *partially* illustrated in the top part of figure 1. Such a list is composed from nodes, each of which has a *value* (which has an ordering relation $<$) and a *link* field. The value field records information or data, while the link field has the reference to the next node. We may express this in logic by declaring the atom $node\_value(N, Val)$ to mean the node with reference N has Val in its value field, and the atom $node\_link(N, Link)$ to mean that it has $Link$ in its link field. Thus, the diagram in figure 1 will have four atoms declared, viz., $node\_value(n1, v1)$, $node\_value(n2, v2)$, $node\_link(n1, n2)$ and $node\_link(n2, n3)$. The null link is declared as the constant *nil*, and this is also identified with the empty list. Indeed, we intend that a partial semantics of data structure diagrams be identified with the standard semantics of *logic programs* so that questions of soundness and completeness for such diagrams can be relegated to the latter semantics. This being so, each diagram will be partially translated to a finite collection of atoms. For subsequent reference, let us name the logic program consisting of the above four atoms P_0. Not all of a diagram may be so translatable, nor is it necessarily desirable to do so for reasons that will become clear. The part of the diagram in figure 1 that is not translated by the four atoms above are the indicated prefix and suffix of the list that respectively precede and succeed the two explicitly displayed nodes. As the prefix and suffix are not named, nor are their extent known, it is impossible to assert a collection of atoms corresponding to them. This is suggested by figure 4. Issues to do with the compactness of first-order logic intrude subtly here to caution us against supposing that there might be a clever declarative logic programming way to circumvent this. There are however procedural ways of simulating "lazy" node-by-node extensions of the list beyond the two explicitly displayed.

Figures 2 and 3 are diagrams that display the sequential updating stages in the insertion of a new node that contains a value v such that $v1 < v < v2$, where $<$ is the assumed ordering on the entries in the value field of the nodes and that there are no other nodes with values closer to v. The latter condition is automatically satisfied in the sorted list whenever the two values $v1$ and $v2$ are in successive nodes. These diagrams are typical of the ones used to instruct novice programmers on the sequence of imperative code that should be written to mirror the updates indicated by the diagrams. The logic programs, say P_1 and P_2 respectively, corresponding to these two diagrams are related to the P_0 above as follows: $P_1 = P_0 \cup \{node\_value(n, v), node\_link(n, n2)\}$, and $P_2 = P_1 \cup \{node\_link(n1, n)\} \setminus \{node\_link(n1, n2)\}$. These set-theoretic operations can be translated directly into the meta-operations of *assert* and *retract* on the logic programs, which we will address in a later section. Of course node insertion in a linked list is so simple that one may ask why should we bother with examining the use of diagrams to guide code generation. Our response is that the theory developed here can handle situations much more complex than this, but we have chosen a very familiar case to illustrate the key ideas and to show that they are natural.

2.2 Why Do They Work?

Such diagrams are unquestionably effective instructional devices. They are the precursors of a wide variety of similar sequential diagrams that convey state dynamics in many situations. We wish to understand why they work.

The first thing to observe is that the three diagrams are really *finite schemas*. The particular entries for links or values are not significant, even though their relative orderings may be critical. The finiteness is important, as all diagrams are of necessity finite. Intimations of infiniteness have to be suggested by convention, e.g., as in elliptical dots in the sequence $2, 4, 6, 8, \ldots$. But on the other hand, since the node insertion algorithm has to work on lists of arbitrary length, how does one determine the "size" of the finite sub-list that can be used to illustrate the update procedure? Programmers have intuitive ways of doing this even if they find it difficult to explain how they do it.

It is the main thesis of this paper that recent research in the logic of actions can shed light on this process. Node insertion can be considered to be an action on an object that yields another. This action may be named *insert(n,v)* where v is the value in a new node n that is to be inserted into the linked list. The *pre-condition* of this action is the search condition alluded to above is formalizable by:

$$\exists v1 \exists v2 (v1 < v < v2 \wedge node\_value(n,v) \wedge \exists n1 \exists n2 (node\_value(n1,v1) \wedge node\_value(n2,v2) \wedge node\_link(n1,n2)).$$

While the constants n and v are given as constants of the action, in the pre-condition formula other constants are eventually instantiated for the variables $v1$, $v2$, $n1$ and $n2$. These latter instantiations are specific to the particular linear list structure for the given state.

Observation 1 *Note that the pre-condition comprises sub-formulas of a certain form. The atoms are (i) partly grounded in the constants n and v, and (ii) if at all quantified, the quantification is nested, and either existential or the negation of an existential.*

Such formulas are important enough to merit a formal description. We reproduce a simplified version of such a description from [Foo 98].

Definition 1 (EnE sentences) *A EnE sentence of width n based on $\bar{c}$ is* $\pm \exists \bar{x}_1 \phi_1(\bar{x}_1)$ *where:*
$\phi_1(\bar{x}_1)$ *is* $P_1(\bar{c}, \bar{x}_1) \wedge \pm \exists \bar{x}_2 \phi_2(\bar{x}_2)$;
$\phi_2(\bar{x}_2)$ *is* $P_2(\bar{x}_1, \bar{x}_2) \wedge \pm \exists \bar{x}_3 \phi_3(\bar{x}_3)$;

⋮

$\phi_n(\bar{x}_n)$ is $\pm\exists\bar{x}_n P_n(\bar{x}_{n-1}, \bar{x}_n)$.

The notation $\bar{x}$, etc, means a sequence of x variables. P_i can be a conjunction of predicates.

By this definition the pre-condition formula above is an EnE sentence of width 2, where, e.g. $\bar{c}$ is $\{n, v\}$ and $P_1(n, v, v1, v2)$ is $v1 < v < v2 \wedge node\_val(n, v)$. Actions which have a local character, i.e. depend only on a "small" region of the state space for testing pre-conditions, have the character that it suffices to reason about them using only diagrams that correspond to this small region. It turns out that this region can be determined precisely for pre-conditions that are EnE sentences and they are typical of many applications. The paper [Foo, et.al. 97] initiated investigations into the localness of actions, and these were subsequently embellished in [Foo 98]. The relevant definitions and results from the latter paper are paraphrased below for completeness.

Definition 2 *Suppose $\mathcal{L}$ is a first-order language with equality but no function symbols. An $\mathcal{L}$-structure $\mathcal{U}$ is a triple $\langle \mathcal{A}, \mathcal{R}, \mathcal{C} \rangle$ where $\mathcal{A}$ is a non-empty set called the domain of $\mathcal{U}$, $\mathcal{R}$ is a map that assigns relations of the appropriate arity on $\mathcal{A}$ to predicate symbols in $\mathcal{L}$, and $\mathcal{C}$ is a map that assigns elements of $\mathcal{A}$ to constant symbols in $\mathcal{L}$.*

Definition 3 *If $\mathcal{U}_1$ and $\mathcal{U}_2$ are $\mathcal{L}$ structures with domains $\mathcal{A}_1$ and $\mathcal{A}_2$ respectively such that $\mathcal{A}_1 \subseteq \mathcal{A}_2$, and the relation and constant assignment maps of $\mathcal{U}_1$ are that of $\mathcal{U}_2$ restricted to $\mathcal{A}_1$, then $\mathcal{U}_1$ is a substructure of $\mathcal{U}_2$, and conversely $\mathcal{U}_2$ is an extension of $\mathcal{U}_1$.*

Definition 4 *Two $\mathcal{L}$ structures $\mathcal{U}_1$ and $\mathcal{U}_2$ are elementarily equivalent, written $\mathcal{U}_1 \equiv \mathcal{U}_2$, if for every sentence $\phi \in \mathcal{L}$, $\mathcal{U}_1 \models \phi$ iff $\mathcal{U}_2 \models \phi$.*

These three definitions are standard [Chang and Keisler 73]. Two elementarily equivalent structures satisfy exactly the same set of sentences, and are therefore indistinguishable by sentences. This is an extremely strong condition. Ideally, we would like a situation suggested by figure 4 in which a "cut-out" (the dashed boundary) portion of a state is a substructure of the entire state and yet nothing is lost in confining reasoning to that substructure. We wish to get as close to elementary equivalence as possible for the case when $\mathcal{U}_1$ in definition 4 is a substructure of $\mathcal{U}_2$ (i.e., an elementary substructure). The main result in this paper is that a version of this will hold for formulas *relativised* to particular substructures and pre-condition syntax.

The intuition we wish to formalize about diagrams applied to list algorithms is that these diagrams represent substructures with a property that is analogous to but substantially weaker than elementary equivalence. Let us dwell a little on this intuition before introducing the formalization.

Figure 4 suggests that no more than the *relevant* or *active* portion of the linked list is being represented. Further, this portion is in some sense *generic* or *typical* — it is representative of an entire class of similar situations, so it is a *diagram schema*. Any particular instance of a list insertion can be obtained by grounding the variables in the schema to constants of the instance.

To look ahead a little, our interest in substructures arises from the intuition that they are the "windows" within pictures of states to which actions are locally applied. The construction of these windows is determined by the arguments or parameters of the action pre-condition, and the objects of relevance are accumulated via a closure operation. This closure has the effect of accruing, to the constants that instantiate a pre-condition, other constants that may be needed to evaluate predicates in the pre-condition. For instance, if $\exists X P(X, b)$ is a component of a pre-condition and b is a constant instantiated into it as an action parameter, we would need to accrue all constants c in the (domain of the) structure for which $P(c, b)$ holds in order to evaluate the component. This motivates the closure definition below (reproduced from [Foo 98]).

Definition 5 (Closure) *Given a set S of constants in $\mathcal{U}$, the 1-expansion of S by n-ary predicate P in $\mathcal{U}$, denoted $closure(\mathcal{U}, S, P, 1)$, is*
$\bigcup\{\{a_1, \ldots, a_n\} \mid$ *some a_i is in S, and $\mathcal{U} \models P(a_1, \ldots, a_n)\}$.*
Inductively, the j+1-expansion of S by P, $closure(\mathcal{U}, S, P, j + 1)$, is
$\bigcup\{\{a_1, \ldots, a_n\} \mid$ *some a_i is in $closure(\mathcal{U}, S, P, j)$, and $\mathcal{U} \models P(a_1, \ldots, a_n)\}$*
$\cup \, closure(\mathcal{U}, S, P, j)$.*
The notation $closure(\mathcal{U}, S, P_1, \ldots, P_k, n)$ is the obvious generalization to several predicates in which any of them can be used at any stage.

For the linked list the primary objects of interest are the nodes and values. They are the constants in the structure $\mathcal{U}$, and in the figures shown the closure constants will turn out to be precisely the set $\{n1, n, n2, v1, v, v2\}$. The initial set $\{n, v, \}$ of constants for the closure is determined by the pre-condition formula of the *insert(n,v)* action. This formula is then used, in conjunction with definition 5, to accrue the constants $v1$, $v2$, $n1$ and $n2$ using the *node_value* and *node_link* predicates which occur in it. Thus, the window of this insert action has as domain the set $\{n1, n, n2, v1, v, v2\}$ which would be denoted, in the notation of definition 5 above, $closure(\mathcal{U}, \{n, v\}, \{node\_link, node\_val\}, 2)$.

The accrual of the new constants in two stages beyond n and v are sugggested in the second picture in figure 1. This is a representation of the logical status of the first diagram. The inner dashed boundary marks $closure(\mathcal{U}, \{n, v\}, \{<, node\_value, node\_link\}, 1)$. In this stage of the closure, the predicate *node_link* is not actually used. The outer dashed boundary marks the second stage $closure(\mathcal{U}, \{n, v\}, \{<, node\_value, node\_link\}, 2)$ and is the extent of the window.

We record this window notion as the formal construction of a *substructure* as follows:

Definition 6 *Let the pre-condition of action A be $\phi(X_1, \ldots, X_n)$, an EnE sentence of width n. If A applies in state $\mathcal{U}$ with substitutions $a_1, \ldots, a_n$ for $X_1, \ldots, X_n$ respectively, construct a sub-structure (called the window of A in this state) $\mathcal{W}$ of $\mathcal{U}$ by letting the domain of $\mathcal{W}$ be*

$closure(\mathcal{U}, \{a_1, \ldots, a_n\}, \{P_1, \ldots, P_k\}, n)$ *where* $P_1, \ldots, P_k$ *are the predicates that occur in* ϕ.

In order to emphasize the origins of $\mathcal{W}$, it is convenient to also write it as $window(\phi[a_1, \ldots, a_n], \mathcal{U})$ or alternatively by $window(A[a_1, \ldots, a_n], \mathcal{U})$, being careful to remember that the domain of this structure includes constants beyond $a_1, \ldots, a_n$ by virtue of closure.

3 Cut and Paste

The key idea behind our explanation for the efficacy of the diagrams in linked list node insertion is that they determine the extent of the smallest window necessary for a *cut and paste* operation. Using the pre-condition and the extension closure in definition 5, any linked list into which a node is to be inserted can have that portion matching the window *cut out*. This cut-out portion can be successively updated and eventually *pasted back* into the original linked list.

Technically, the validity of this operation is confirmed by the Pre-condition and Post-condition Conservative Extension theorems below. They are only valid for actions with pre-conditions that have the EnE syntax described above (or more generally, any Boolean combinations thereof). For proofs, we refer the reader to [Foo 98].

Theorem 1 (Pre-condition Conservative Extension) *Let an EnE formula* $\phi[a_1, \ldots, a_n]$ *be a pre-condition of an action instance to be applied to state* $\mathcal{U}$. *If* α *is any* $\{a_1, \ldots, a_n\}$-*formula, then* $\mathcal{U} \models \alpha$ *iff* $window(\phi[a_1, \ldots, a_n], \mathcal{U}) \models \alpha$.

This is why we can "cut" a piece out of a diagram, such as the dashed boundary in figure 4. In this figure, $\mathcal{U}$ is indicated by the suggested full extent of the linked list, and $window(\phi[a_1, \ldots, a_n], \mathcal{U})$ is the region indicated by the dashed boundary. The theorem says that if the action pre-condition is an EnE formula — which it is for the *insert* action — then this pre-condition for the whole state (e.g., entire list) may be tested by looking at the window (e.g. dashed region) alone.

The validity of "pasting" relies on an assumption that is satisfied in practice. This is the insistence that the post-condition, which amounts to the sequence of asserts and retracts in the logic program corresponding to the list alterations, do not refer to objects not already implied in the pre-condition. This does not preclude predicates not in the pre-condition from appearing in the post-condition.

Assumption 1 (Post-condition Assumption) *If* $A[a_1, \ldots, a_n]$ *is an action instance with pre-condition* $\phi[a_1, \ldots, a_n]$, *then all constants of this instance in the post-condition are among the* $a_1, \ldots, a_n$, *and all the predicates in the post-condition are among those of the pre-condition.*

We should remark that it is not hard to relax the post-condition assumption. The definition of closure can be modified to accommodate it. However, granted the assumption we have the "paste" counterpart of the "cut" theorem. Here, we have summarized the post-condition as an EnE formula ψ which, in the logic program mirroring the list operations, expresses the effect of the asserts and retracts (i.e., conjoining atoms of the asserts and negated atoms for the retracts). In the theorem below $\mathcal{U}_1$ refers to the structure which is the (entire) state after the execution of action A.

Theorem 2 (Post-condition Conservative Extension) *If ϕ and ψ are the pre- and post-conditions of action instance A respectively, with the notation above and the Post-condition Assumption, then (i) the domain of $window(\psi, \mathcal{U}_1)$ is a subset of the domain of $window(\phi[a_1, \ldots, a_n], \mathcal{U})$, and (ii) the Pre-condition Conservative Extension theorem also holds for $window(\psi, \mathcal{U}_1)$ with respect to $\mathcal{U}_1$.*

These two theorems justify rigorously the correctness of reasoning about singly linked list insertion using only the window defined by the pre-condition. To be complete in our demonstration that these properly capture node insertion we actually have to argue that they model the logic programs before and after the insertion action. As this is routine and not particularly instructive we shall omit it. However we should record it as a corollary to the theorems.

Corollary 1 *The cut-and-paste procedure in the finite figures 1, 2 and 3 correctly reflect the node insertion logic for the potentially unbounded figure 4.*

As a matter of some interest we mention that in work on conceptual graphs, a diagrammatic logic introduced by Sowa [Sowa], there is also a version of a cut-and-paste theorem but geared toward proofs.

The genericity of the windows, and the schema-like semantics of action specifications is captured by the following observation, which is a corollary of the preceding theorems.

Observation 2 *Any two windows $\mathcal{W}$ and $\mathcal{V}$ of two action instances A are isomorphic.*

4 Imperative Code

Traditionally pictures like those in figures 1, 2 and 3 are drawn to illustrate the *sequence* of statements that one should write in an imperative programming language like Pascal to implement the node insertion. Since we intend to use logic programs to provide (partial) semantics for diagrams, it is important that we have constraints for such programs to correctly reflect features peculiar to imperative code. In fact it is easy to say informally what these should be if the constants in the pre-condition and (instantiated) constants in the post-condition are known. We simply require that at no stage in the sequence of asserts and retracts is it the case that the bindings corresponding to these constants are lost. Imposing this constraint will guarantee safety. As an example, consider the logic program sequence in section 2.1. There we exhibited the two programs — following the initial P_0 which represented the precondition window — as $P_1 = P_0 \cup \{node\_value(n, v), node\_link(n, n2)\}$, and $P_2 = P_1 \cup \{node\_link(n1, n)\} \setminus \{node\_link(n1, n2)\}$. With the translation to asserts and retracts, the constraint says that *retract(node_link(n1,n2))* cannot be performed before *assert(node_link(n,n2))*, or in other words the sequence P_0, P_1, P_2 cannot have the last two reversed.

5 Conclusion

We provided a model-theoretic justification for reasoning with diagrams in data-structure updates, exposing in particular the assumptions that are apparently necessary for correctness of the cut-and-paste operations on such diagrams. While the cognitive significance of our proposal is not yet clear, the results suggest that connections with computational complexity are highly plausible given that the notion of a window introduced here is really part of finite model theory. If the graph in figure 1 is regarded as a representation of the local structure generated by an intial set of constants, then the window construction (equivalently, the closure procedure) is essentially that of finding shortest paths from that set. That this can be accomplished by low-polynominal algorithms may be suggestive of why windows are natural.

6 Acknowledgements

Without the stimulating discussions with my colleagues in the Knowledge Systems Group, particularly Yan Zhang, Pavlos Peppas, Maurice Pagnucco and Abhaya Nayak, this work would not have see the light of day.

This research is supported in part by a grant from the Australian Research Council.

References

[Barwise and Etchemendy 95] Barwise, J. and Etchemendy, J., *Heterogeneous logic*, in Diagrammatic Reasoning: Cognitive and Computational Perspectives, eds. J. I. Glasgow, N. H. Narayanan and B. Chandrasekaran, MIT Press, 1995, 209-232.

[Chang and Keisler 73] Chang, C.C., and Keisler, H.J., *Model Theory*, North Holland, 1973.

[Foo, et.al. 97] Foo, N., Nayak, A., Pagnucco, M., Peppas, P., and Zhang, Y., *Action Localness, Genericity and Invariants in STRIPS*, Proceedings of the Fifteenth International Joint Conference on Artificial Intelligence, IJCAI'97, pp. 549-554, Nagoya, August 1997, Morgan Kaufmann.

[Foo 98] Foo, N., *Local Extent in Diagrams*, Proceedings of the AAAI Fall Symposium on Formalizing Reasoning with Visual and Diagrammatic Representations, Orlando, Oct 1998. URL:

573

[Glasgow, et. al. 95] Glasgow,J.I., Narayanan, N.H. and Chandrasekaran, B. (eds), *Diagrammatic Reasoning: Cognitive and Computational Perspectives*, MIT Press, 1995.

[Myers and Konolige 95] Myers, K. and Konolige, K., *Reasoning with Analogical Representations*, in Diagrammatic Reasoning: Cognitive and Computational Perspectives, eds. J. I. Glasgow, N. H. Narayanan and B. Chandrasekaran, MIT Press, 1995, 273-301.

[Sowa] Sowa, J., *Conceptual Structures*, Addison Wesley, 1984.

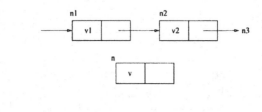

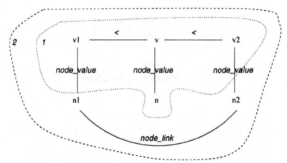

Fig. 1. Initial Substate and Closure Stages

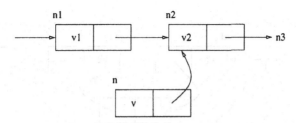

Fig. 2. Intermediate Substate

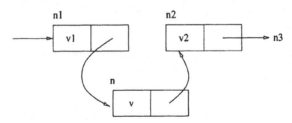

Fig. 3. Final Substate

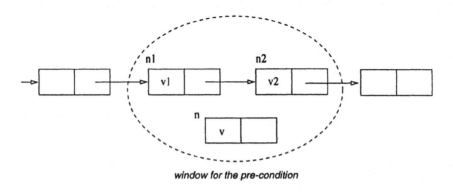

window for the pre-condition

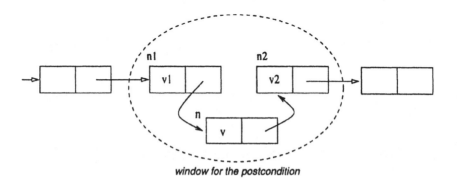

window for the postcondition

Fig. 4. Substates/Windows for the Pre- and Post-condition

A Decision-Theoretic Approach
for Pre-sending Information on the WWW

A.E. Nicholson, I. Zukerman, and D.W. Albrecht

School of Computer Science and Software Engineering
Monash University
Clayton, VICTORIA 3168, AUSTRALIA
{dwa,annn,ingrid}@csse.monash.edu.au

Abstract. We present a decision-theoretic model which determines
whether to pre-send web documents a user is likely to request. Our model
balances the cost of transmitting information with the inconvenience
or cost to a user caused by having to wait for information. It uses a
Markov model built from web-access data to predict which documents
are likely to be requested next. A comparative evaluation of our pre-
sending scheme identifies circumstances in which our scheme is beneficial
for users.

1 Introduction

Users typically have to wait for information they require from the World Wide
Web (WWW). If the waiting time is excessive, this results in increased costs and
user dissatisfaction, and, for work-related tasks, loss of productivity. The aim of
this research is to develop a system that reduces a user's expected waiting time
by pre-sending information s/he is likely to request. However, there is an obvious trade-off between the cost of possibly pre-sending an unrequired document
(which incurs unnecessary transmission costs) and the reduction in the user's
waiting time due to pre-sending a required document. This motivates our development of a decision-theoretic approach which combines cost models (Sect. 5)
with prediction models that anticipate which document will be requested next
by a user (Sect. 6). The system then chooses the action with the highest expected
utility; this action may be pre-sending a document or it may be doing nothing.
The prediction model used in this paper is a Markov model built from observations of document requests for WWW pages at a particular site (the School
of Computer Science and Software Engineering at Monash University). We have
evaluated our system using several values for transmission rate, transmission cost
and waiting cost (Sect. 7). Our evaluation shows that for most configurations
of these parameters, our pre-sending scheme gives a positive cumulative benefit,
which confirms the feasibility of our approach.

2 Related Work

The recent growth in the WWW and on-line information sources has inspired
research in the development of agents to help users derive the most benefit from

the vast quantities of available facilities and information. Many of these agents (WebWatcher[2,5], Letizia [7], Syskill & Webert [9] and DICA [11]) fall into the category of *recommender systems*. These systems acquire user features relevant to a particular domain (by combining machine learning techniques with explicit knowledge elicitation from the user), and then recommend facilities or information items which are likely to be of interest to the user. However, these systems do not take any action on behalf of the user, rather they let the user determine a course of action. In contrast, the system described in [3] considers two policies, exploitation versus exploration, to select web documents to be delivered to a user; the user's profile is represented by a linear function of the term vectors [10] of the documents of interest to the user. Likewise, the system described in [4] pre-sends to a user web pages in which the user is likely to be interested. This system is the most closely related to the work described in this paper. However, it differs from our system in the following aspects: (1) Bestavros' system pre-sends any number of pages which satisfy certain conditions (their predicted probability of being requested within a particular time window is above a threshold, and their size is below another threshold), while we send only one ("best") page; and (2) in choosing pages to send to a user, Bestavros' system takes into account the communication cost between client and server, the server's load and the bandwidth, while our system uses a utility function which considers the waiting cost as well as the transmission cost and transmission rate. The first aspect affects the evaluation of our system's performance, since our system's predictions are considered successful only if the predicted document is the document requested next by the user. In contrast, the predictions of Bestavros' system are considered successful if a pre-sent document is requested within a time window.

3 The Domain

Consider the server on an internet WWW site which handles requests for documents from users, either from the local site or from other internet sites. There is a cost to the user associated with receiving a requested document: (1) the cost of transmitting the page from the server where the document is located to the user's server; and (2) the cost of the delay to the user while waiting to receive the requested document. The transmission cost (which is shared between the requesting user and the server supplying the document) typically depends on the number of bytes being transmitted, and hence is a function of the size of the document. The cost per byte may vary with the network load (and hence with the time of day at the location of the requesting user and the supplying server). The cost of waiting is a function of a number of factors. The user may be paying for internet access per logged on time unit, in which case the cost of waiting is a function of the size of the document and the transmission speed of the network. Other less easily quantified factors include the user's dissatisfaction at having to wait, and the loss of productivity while waiting for work-related information.

Analysis of the WWW server information yields the following features. (1) Unlike other work done in plan recognition for domains such as the Multi-User Dungeon (MUD) [1] and UNIX [6], we cannot directly observe the actions performed by a user in his/her system.[1] Our observations consist of records of visited pages (locations) in the WWW, and our aim is to predict the next location to be visited by a user. (2) It is extremely difficult to obtain a perspicuous representation of the domain. Typically there are huge numbers of documents located on a server and many links between them. There may be any number of links to pages from external locations, which we cannot model. The existence, location and size of documents are all subject to continual change, as are the links to and between them. (3) There is no obvious clear objective that applies to all users (unlike, for example, quests in a MUD domain). Some users may be browsing, others may be seeking specific information but may not be sure how to get to it. Because links between documents form a graph, there may be many candidate paths from a document to the desired information. (4) The sequence of requests from a user observed by the server providing the documents is only a partial record of the users' movements through the internet, since the users' movements to external locations are not observed. (5) Finally, most WWW servers cache documents received by a user. The cache size and the duration of documents in the cache may vary. This means that a user's requests for previously supplied documents are not observed (in Sect. 4, we discuss the need for the client to provide this information to the server).

The server logs access data for the requests it receives for documents. This data is of the form {client referer requestedDoc date ACTION CODE size}. The client is the internet WWW server site that is requesting the document (data corresponding to requests made by empty sites are deleted during pre-processing). The referer is the current internet location (an http address) of the user requesting the document. The referer may have one of the following values: (1) a local location, that is, a (previously requested) web page on the system server; (2) an external location, that is, a web page on another internet site (this sometimes, but not always, indicates the start of a new session); or (3) empty (represented by '-'), because the information has not been provided (neither by the user's browser nor the client server). The requestedDoc is the http address of the document being requested by the client. This field may also be empty (represented by '-'), indicating that the client has requested a document which does not exist on the server (in this case an error code is generated). The date is a (local) time stamp indicating when the request was received. ACTION and CODE indicate particular information noted by the system server which pertains to the handling of the request, such as the success of the document transfer. The current system uses data items with ACTION=GET and CODE=200; this corresponds to a situation where a file is requested from the server, found and sent. The size is the number of bytes in the requested document.

The data points are divided into *sessions* during pre-processing. Each session contains the temporal sequence of requests from a single client, where a request takes the form {time referer requestedDoc size} (time is given in seconds

---

[1] Such observations would be very limited in terms of the range of actions. Most actions would be document requests, either by opening a new page or moving forward or back through previously requested documents.

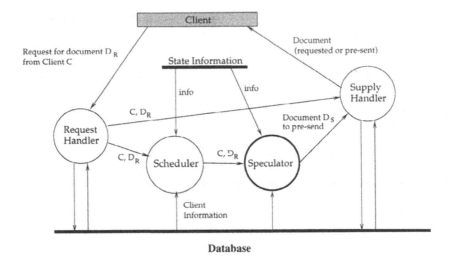

Fig. 1. System architecture.

elapsed since the startup of the system). This grouping of the data points into client-specific sessions supports the development of a request model based simply on the temporal sequence of requested documents, i.e., a Markov model (Sect. 6). A session is considered terminated if there are no further requests from a client within a particular time interval. During pre-processing we also handle problems created by certain WWW phenomena which generate server traffic that distorts prediction models; more specifically, we remove data generated by search engines and web-crawlers.

We logged our web server over a 15 month period. The results presented in this paper are based on a one-week time window of that data. After pre-processing, the following data were obtained: 131153 document requests, where 14263 clients requested 11698 documents from 4490 referer locations. The data include 2557 referers which are also requested documents and 25379 different referer/document combinations.

4 The Architecture

The pre-sending system sits on an internet WWW server site, the *server*, and handles the provision of documents to other sites, the *clients*. It handles document requests received by the server from various clients, sending requested documents (when able to do so). In addition, our system identifies a document that may be requested next by a client who has just made a request for a particular document. The system has the following components.

Request Handler: The Request Handler performs various book-keeping functions, updating the database to record a request which has just been received, checks whether the document exists and, if so, passes on the request to both the Supply Handler module and the Scheduler.

Scheduler: The Scheduler decides whether, given the current server load and the client profile, our system should speculate or not (that is, whether the Speculator module should be activated). This module is not yet implemented; at present the Speculator module is triggered after each document request.

Speculator: The Speculator calculates the utility of sending each document in the server site. This involves calculating the probability that the client will request a document and estimating the cost of pre-sending this document. This cost is a function of the user's waiting time and the transmission cost (for client and server), which in turn depend on the size of the document, the server load, the network traffic and the client's cache size and caching policy. For the results in this paper, we assume a constant server load and network traffic, and we do not consider the client cache size and caching policy. The document with the highest expected utility is pre-sent if this utility is better than the expected utility of simply waiting for the next request (Sect. 5). The current model considers only the prediction of the next request. In Sect. 8, we discuss an extension to this model which involves predictions that a document will be requested within a particular time window (such predictions are also considered in [4]).

Supply Handler: The Supply Handler module sends documents to clients based on directives received from the Request Handler (in response to a client request) or from the Speculator. In this paper we assume that if the system receives a request for a document, and the Supply Handler is in the process of pre-sending a different document, the transmission will be discontinued and the requested document sent instead. In the future, we will consider other protocols (Sect. 8).

Client-Server Protocol: The first time our system receives a request from a particular client, it initiates a dialogue to establish whether the client wants to take advantage of the pre-sending facility. If the client declines to participate, it can request this facility in the future. If the client chooses to participate, it must agree that all user requests for a document from the server shall be passed on to the server. In particular, if a document is already in the client's cache (because the client has previously requested it or because the system has present it), the request must be passed on with a "don't send" flag to indicate that the request took place (even though it was trivially satisfied). There are several reasons why the client must agree to this notification protocol: (1) it facilitates the building of the database; (2) the speculation phase can be terminated by this next request and no further time is wasted speculating based on an earlier, now out-of-date, document request; and (3) it enables the system to evaluate its pre-sending policy.

5 Decision-Theoretic Model

Consider a situation where we are dealing with a single client who has requested a document D_R at time T_R; the document chosen by the Speculator to pre-send is D_S, and it is sent at time T_S. Now, at time $T_{R'}$ ($T_{R'} \geq T_S$) the client requests another document $D_{R'}$. If $D_S = D_{R'}$ then we have saved the user

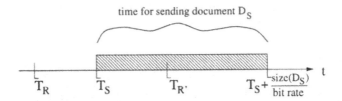

Fig. 2. Time line.

some time, as we have already started sending the desired document. The time line corresponding to this situation is shown in Fig. 2. If $D_S \neq D_{R'}$ then the transmission of D_S is interrupted when the request for $D_{R'}$ is received, and $D_{R'}$ is sent instead. In this case, the user has not wasted any time compared to a situation where s/he did not use the pre-sending service, but s/he has incurred some cost for the unnecessary transmission.

These considerations are incorporated into a utility function which is used to determine whether it is worthwhile to pre-send a document. As indicated in Sect. 1, this function is affected by the following factors: (1) the cost of transmitting a document, and (2) the cost of waiting for the desired document.

For the calculation of our utility function we designate the documents in our database $\mathbf{D} = \{D_1, \ldots, D_n\}$, and adopt the convention that D_0 represents the null document; $D_S = D_0$ means not pre-sending any document, and $D_{R'} = D_0$ means receiving no further request from the client in question. Further, we assume that the distribution of the time for requesting a document is independent of the actual document that is requested. In the future, we propose to investigate whether this assumption should be relaxed and how to do so.

5.1 Cost of transmission

The cost of sending a document is a function of the document size (in bytes) and the cost per byte, *cpb*, expressed in cents/byte. In practice, the cost per byte may vary with the network load, but in the current implementation we assume that it is constant. Thus, the cost of pre-sending a document D_S at time T_S when $D_{R'}$ is requested by the client at time $T_{R'}$ is

$$
C_{S,R'} = \begin{cases}
cpb \times size(D_S) & \text{if } D_{R'} = D_0 \\
cpb \times size(D_{R'}) & \text{if } D_{R'} = D_S \\
cpb \times [bps \times (T_{R'} - T_S) + size(D_{R'})] & \text{if } T_{R'} < T_S + size(D_S)/bps \\
cpb \times [size(D_S) + size(D_{R'})] & \text{otherwise}
\end{cases}
$$

where *bps* is the transmission rate, expressed in bytes/sec. The top line of this formula reflects a situation where no further requests are made by the client. The second line reflects the normal cost of transmitting a document. The third line reflects the notion that if the request for the correct document arrives before the transmission of the wrong document is completed, then the user will be charged only for the portion of the wrong document that was transmitted plus the cost of transmitting the correct document. Finally, if the request for the correct document arrives after the transmission of the wrong document has been completed, then the user will be charged for both documents.

5.2 Cost of waiting

If the system pre-sends the document the client requests next, then the waiting time is reduced or removed altogether. Since our formulation of the utility of pre-sending a document is in terms of cost, we multiply the formulas for waiting time by the cost in cents per second (cps) of a timed internet connection. Let $W_{S,R'}$ represent the user's cost due to waiting for the desired document $D_{R'}$ requested at time $T_{R'}$, after document D_S was pre-sent at time T_S. This cost is

$$W_{S,R'} = \begin{cases} 0 & \text{if } D_{R'} = D_0 \\ cps \times \max\{0, [T_S + size(D_{R'})/bps - T_{R'}]\} & \text{if } D_{R'} = D_S \\ cps \times size(D_{R'})/bps & \text{otherwise} \end{cases}$$

That is, if no further requests are made by the client, then the waiting cost is zero. If the pre-sent document is requested next, the user will have to wait only for the portion of the document that still remains to be sent at the time the request was made. Hence, as indicated in the second line, if $T_{R'} \geq T_S + size(D_{R'})/bps$ then $W_{S,R'} = 0$. If the pre-sent document is not the one that is requested next, then the user will have to wait for the entire document.

5.3 The utility function

The utility of pre-sending a document D_S at time T_S when the next document $D_{R'}$ is requested at time $T_{R'}$ is simply composed of the transmission cost of the requested document and the waiting cost. The higher these costs, the lower the utility and vice versa.

$$U_{S,R'} = -C_{S,R'} - W_{S,R'}$$

The utility of not pre-sending any document is

$$U_{0,R'} = -[cpb + cps/bps] \times size(D_{R'})$$

The Speculator pre-sends the document whose transmission yields the highest expected utility, so long as this utility is higher than the expected utility of not pre-sending any document. The expected utility of pre-sending a document D_S at time T_S is [2]

$$EU_S = -\sum_{i=0}^{n} [EC_{S,i} + EW_{S,i}] \times \Pr(D_i \text{ is requested next})$$

---

[2] In our data set each client has a single run. Therefore, $\Pr(D_{R'} = D_0)$ is approximated by $\frac{\# \text{ of clients}}{\# \text{ of requests}} \simeq 0.10875$.

where $EC_{S,i}$ and $EW_{S,i}$ are, respectively, the expected transmission cost and the expected waiting cost.[3] The expected utility of not pre-sending any document is

$$EU_0 = -[cpb + cps/bps] \sum_{i=1}^{n} size(D_i) \times \Pr(D_i \text{ is requested next})$$

5.4 Benefit of pre-sending

Once a request for the next document $D_{R'}$ is made at time $T_{R'}$, we can compute the actual benefit from having pre-sent document D_S at time T_S. This benefit is the difference between the utility of having pre-sent this document and the utility of not pre-sending any document

$$B_{S,R'} = U_{S,R'} - U_{0,R'}$$

We measure the success of our system by computing the cumulative benefit of our pre-sending policy over some period of time.

6 Prediction Models

The decision-theoretic model described in the previous section requires the following two prediction models: (1) $\Pr(D_{R'}$ is requested at time $t)$, required for the calculation of both $EC_{S,R'}$ and $EW_{S,R'}$; (2) $\Pr(D_i$ is requested next), required for the calculation of EU_S and EU_0.

6.1 Probability of receiving a request at a particular time

For our current database (based on one week of data), the time between successive requests from a client ranges from 0 to 600,000 seconds (approximately one week): $0 \leq T_{R'} - T_R \leq 600,000$. We approximate $\Pr(D_{R'}$ is requested at time $t)$ by the conditional probability distribution $P(T_{R'} - T_R | \mathbf{D})$, which can be estimated by fitting functions to the data (see [8]).

$$\Pr(T_{R'} - T_R = t | \mathbf{D}) = \begin{cases} 0 & t = 0 \\ 0.13 \times \ln(t) + 0.22 & t \in [1, 82) \\ 0.04 \times \ln(t) + 0.615 & t \in [82, 318) \\ 0.007 \times \ln(t) + 0.805 & t \geq 318 \end{cases}$$

6.2 Probability of the next requested document

We view the link(s) from one requested document to the document(s) requested next as a graph, which in turn may be considered an approximation to the graph composed of all the links between documents in the WWW. Let G be the directed graph constructed from successive documents requested, that is, $D_i \rightarrow D_j$. Each requested document D_i is a vertex in the graph, with the arcs

---

[3] The formulas for $EC_{S,i}$ and $EW_{S,i}$ are given in [8]

in the graph from D_i to D_j indicating that a client's request for D_i was followed by a request for D_j (by the same client) during a session. Each arc $D_i \rightarrow D_j$ has an associated weight, $w(D_i, D_j)$, which is the frequency of the pair of successive requests across all sessions plus a small number (0.5) that is added to adjust the frequencies for unseen requests.

Let us define the set of successors of a node D_i in the graph G to be $succ(D_i)$. An examination of the data indicates that, given the current requested document D_i, 72.2% of the time $D_j \in succ(D_i)$ in G. This high figure motivates our time-Markov model for the prediction of the next request. When $D \in succ(D_R)$:

$$\Pr(D = D_{R'}|D_R) = \frac{w(D_R, D)}{\sum_{D_i \in succ(D_R)} w(D_R, D_i) + 0.5}.$$

7 Results

The results in this section were obtained from the one week of logged data from our server. The utility model was tested using 80% of the data for training (i.e., constructing the database) and 20% of the data (20171 requests) for testing. These results were obtained with a C++ implementation of the Speculator running on a SGI Indy R5000, using the DiamondBase C++ database engine.[4] A number of runs were done to test the effect of different configurations of the cost per second (cps), cost per byte (cpb) and bytes per second (bps) parameters.

In the testing phase, given each data item (that is, document request), the Speculator used the time-Markov prediction model to obtain the estimated probability for the next requested document. The Speculator then computed the expected utility of pre-sending all documents which had a predicted probability greater than a threshold value of 0.1, and pre-sent the document with the highest expected utility, providing it was greater than the utility of not pre-sending any document. When computing the expected utilities, we assumed that the speculation computation would take no time, that is, we took the time when a document was pre-sent, T_S, to be T_R. This is a reasonable approximation for the current implementation and database size (131153 requests of 11698 documents), since the speculation time is less than 0.03 seconds. We assess the accuracy of the time-Markov prediction model by considering the probability with which it predicted the actual documents that were requested next. The percentage of requested documents that were predicted with a particular probability were as follows: 2% with probability greater than 0.8, 20% with probability greater than 0.5, while 53% were predicted with probability greater than 0.2.

Fig. 3 shows the cumulative benefit over a test run for several configurations of the cps, cpb and bps parameters. Note that the scale of the y-axis varies for the different graphs. Fig. 3(a) shows that if the transmission rate is slow and the user's waiting cost is low, then if the transmission cost is high ($cpb=1$), pre-sending is clearly worse than not pre-sending. Other values for cpb for this configuration result in a positive total benefit, which increases as cpb decreases.

---

[4] See http://www.cs.monash.edu.au/~kevinl/diamond/.

Fig. 3(b) shows that for a slow transmission rate and a high waiting cost, the benefits of pre-sending for all values of *cpb* are positive and higher than with other scenarios. When a higher waiting cost is combined with a fast transmission rate, as shown in Figure 3(c), the cumulative benefits for a high transmission cost become negative again. Note that the cumulative benefit when $cpb = 0$ is very close to the cumulative benefit when $cpb = 0.01$ for all four cases (the graphs overlap in Fig. 3(b)); the largest difference occurs when both the waiting cost and the transmission rate are high (Fig. 3(c)). More results illustrating the performance of the speculator are given in [8].

8 Discussion and Future Work

In this paper we have developed a decision-theoretic model which selects documents for pre-sending based on a prediction model for the next requested document. However, most client sites maintain a cache of received documents. Thus, if at some later time, the client server receives a request from a user for a previously pre-sent document, the user may benefit from this document (depending on the size and duration of the client cache). In order to account for this situation, we intend to extend our models and evaluation procedures to cover a window of future requests as described in [4], and incorporate a client cache profile. We also intend to consider a preemptive-resume transmission strategy, whereby the transmission of a pre-sent document that is not the next requested document is temporarily discontinued in order to send the requested document, but is resumed after the transmission of the requested document has been completed.

Our decision-theoretic model allows the Speculator to adapt to different cost factors and different transmission rates. If the transmission cost is low but the waiting cost is high, users derive more benefit from the Speculator if it pre-sends large files; this behaviour contrasts with Bestavros' speculation procedure, which gives best results when limited to documents with a maximum size of 30KB [4].

Most documents have few time-Markov successors compared to the number of documents in the database, and currently our prediction model only uses successors with predicted probabilities above the 0.1 probability threshold (Sect. 7). This means that the Speculator needs to compute the expected utility of only a few candidate documents, and compare these utilities with each other and also with the utility of not pre-sending. This is the basis of the current negligible speculation computation time of less than 0.03 seconds. However, certain parts of the speculation process, such as searching for a document in the directed graph, depend on the size of the database; we will test the Speculator's scalability experimentally using the full 15 months of logged data.

Our decision-theoretic model is based on the assumption that a client requires the whole requested document. This assumption may not always be valid; for example, the user may receive part of the document, see a link to another document in which s/he is interested, and request that document, at the same time terminating the transmission of the first requested document. We intend to analyse the interrupted transmissions recorded in our data with a view to extending our utility model to incorporate a prediction of such request cancellations.

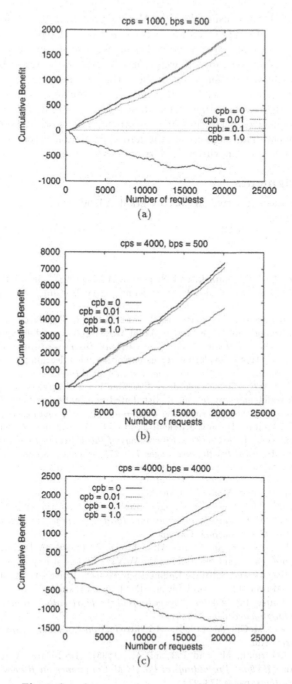

Fig. 3. Set of test runs for a range of cost factors.

The results obtained using the time-Markov prediction model show that it provides an adequate approximation of document request patterns, and allows the Speculator to accumulate a positive benefit for several combinations of cost factors and transmission rates. However, nearly 28% of the time the next requested document is *not* a successor of the current request, and the inaccuracy of the prediction model may lead to a negative cumulative 'benefit' in some situations. Further examination of the data logs shows that 97% of the next requests correspond to pages that have a common referer with the current requested document. This suggests an alternative prediction model based on the referer information; we are currently developing such a model.

Acknowledgments

This research was supported in part by grant A49600323 from the Australian Research Council.

References

1. Albrecht, D. W., Zukerman, I., and Nicholson, A. E. (1998). Bayesian models for keyhole plan recognition in an adventure game. *User Modeling and User-Adapted Interaction*.
2. Armstrong, R., Freitag, D., Joachims, T., and Mitchell, T. (March, 1995). Web-Watcher: A learning apprentice for the World Wide Web. In *AAAI Spring Symposium on Information Gathering from Heterogeneous, Distributed Environments*.
3. Balabanović, M. (1998). Exploring versus exploiting when learning user models for text recommendation. *User Modeling and User-adapted Interaction*.
4. Bestavros, A. (1996). Speculative data dissemination and service to reduce server load, network traffic and service time in distributed information systems. In *ICDE'96 – Proceedings of the 1996 International Conference on Data Engineering*.
5. Joachims, T., Freitag, D., and Mitchell, T. (1997). Webwatcher: A tour guide for the world wide web. In *IJCAI97 – Proceedings of the Fifteenth International Joint Conference on Artificial Intelligence*, pages 770–775, Nagoya, Japan.
6. Lesh, N. and Etzioni, O. (1995). A sound and fast goal recognizer. In *IJCAI95 – Proceedings of the Fourteenth International Joint Conference on Artificial Intelligence*, pages 1704–1710, Montreal, Canada.
7. Lieberman, H. (1995). Letizia: An agent that assists web browsing. In *IJCAI95 – Proceedings of the Fourteenth International Joint Conference on Artificial Intelligence*, pages 924–929, Montreal, Canada.
8. Nicholson, A. E., Zukerman, I., and Albrecht, D. W. (1998). A Decision-theoretic approach for pre-sending information on the WWW. Technical Report 98/15, School of Computer Science and Software Engineering, Monash University, Australia.
9. Pazzani, M., Muramatsu, J., and Billsus, D. (1996). Syskill & Webert: Identifying interesting web sites. In *AAAI96 – Proceedings of the Thirteenth National Conference on Artificial Intelligence*, pages 54–61.
10. Salton, G. and McGill, M. (1983). *An Introduction to Modern Information Retrieval*. McGraw Hill.
11. Starr, B., Ackerman, M., and Pazzani, M. (1996). Do-I-Care: A collaborative web agent. In *CHI'96 – Proceedings of the ACM Conference on Human Factors in Computing Systems*, pages 273–274.

Dynamic Non-uniform Abstractions for Approximate Planning in Large Structured Stochastic Domains

J. Baum and A.E. Nicholson

School of Computer Science and Software Engineering
Monash University, Clayton, VICTORIA 3168, Australia
phone: +61 3 9905-5225   fax: +61 3 9905-5146
{jirib,annn}@cs.monash.edu.au

Abstract. The theory of Markov Decision Processes (MDPs) provides algorithms for generating an optimal policy. For large domains these algorithms become intractable and approximate solutions become necessary. In this paper we extend previous work on approximate planning in large stochastic domains by using automatically-generated non-uniform abstractions which exploit the structure of the state space. We consider a state space expressed as a cross product of sets, or dimensions. We obtain approximate solutions by varying the level of abstraction, selectively ignoring some of the dimensions in some parts of the state space. We describe a modification of a standard policy generation algorithm for the now non-Markovian decision process, which re-calculates values for nearby states based on a locally uniform abstraction for each state. We present methods to automatically generate an initial abstraction based on the domain structure and to automatically modify the non-uniform abstraction. The changes to the abstraction are based on both the current policy and the likelihood of encountering particular states in the future, thereby taking into account the agent's changing circumstances.

1   Introduction

For small to medium sized stochastic domains, the theory of Markov decision processes provides algorithms for generating the optimal plan [2, 3]. However, as the domain becomes larger, these algorithms become intractable and approximate solutions become necessary [9, 7]. In particular where the state space is expressed in terms of dimensions, or as a cross product of sets, its size and the resulting computational cost is exponential in the number of dimensions. On the other hand, fortunately, this results in a fairly structured state-space where effective approximations often ought to be possible. Dearden and Boutilier use this structure [6, 4] to obtain an exact solution or [5, 8] an approximate solution by ignoring particular dimensions, however, their abstractions are fixed throughout execution. The solution presented in this paper is based on selectively ignoring some of the dimensions, in some parts of the state space, some of the time. In other words, we obtain approximate solutions by dynamically varying the level of abstraction in different parts of the state space.

This paper deals with control error exclusively. Sensor error is not considered and it is assumed that the agent can accurately discern the current world state. It is also assumed that the agent accurately knows the state space, the goal or reward function, and the distribution over the effect of its actions.

The remainder of this paper is organised as follows. In Sect.2 we briefly explain classical planning in MDPs and the structure of the agent, and present an example domain to facilitate explanation. Section 3 presents the idea of non-uniform abstraction, and discusses how it might be relatively simply represented. Section 4 deals with the modifications to classical MDP planning necessitated by this approximation, involving re-calculation of values based on a locally uniform abstraction. In Sect.5 we present methods to automatically generate an initial abstraction based on the domain structure and to automatically modify the non-uniform abstraction. The changes to the abstraction are based on both the current policy and the likelihood of encountering particular states in the future, thereby taking into account the agent's changing circumstances. Finally, we discuss the approach and indicate directions for future research in Sect.6.

2 Planning in Stochastic Domains

A Markov Decision Process (MDP) is a tuple $\langle S, A, T, R, s_0 \rangle$, respectively the *state space, set of available actions, transition function, reward function* and *initial state*. The agent begins in state $s_0 \in S$. At time n, the agent selects an action $a \in A$, which, together with the current state s_n and T gives a distribution over S for s_{n+1}, the current state at time $n+1$. It also receives a reward of $R(s_n)$; the agent aims to maximise the expected discounted sum of these rewards. It is well-known that in a fully-observable MDP, where the agent knows T, R and s_n when selecting an action, the optimal solution can be expressed as a policy $\pi : S \to A$ mapping from the current state to the optimum action. The planning problem, then, is the calculation of this π.

The standard algorithms for computing the policy are policy iteration [11] and value iteration [2]. Each consists of two iterative interrelated parts, one dealing with changing the policy, the other with computing the values. The iterative steps are:

$$\pi(s) \leftarrow \arg\max_a \sum_{s'} \Pr(s, a, s') V(s') \tag{1}$$

and

$$V(s) \leftarrow R(s) + \gamma \sum_{s'} \Pr(s, \pi(s'), s') V(s') \tag{2}$$

where γ the discounting factor is a parameter ($0 \leq \gamma < 1$), the probabilities are specified by T, and $V : S \to \Re$ is the *value function*, calculated as a byproduct of the algorithm. The value function gives the expected discounted sum of reward for each state. In this paper we use the value iteration algorithm, in which (1) and (2) are iterated together.

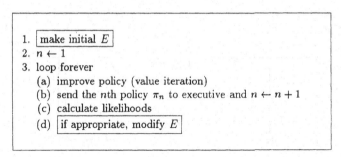

Fig. 1. Planner algorithm

As S becomes larger, the calculation of the optimal policy becomes more computationally expensive. If the state space is represented as a cartesian product of dimensions, each of which is a set, $|S|$ will be exponential in the number of dimensions. To obtain at least an approximate solution, one can approximate the MDP with a MDP with a smaller state space E. For example, Dean *et al.* [7] use a subset of S, based on the notion of locality, and plans only for those states that are likely to be reached. If the state space has structure, however, the planner ought to be able to do better by taking advantage of this structure to focus the computation and improve the approximations. One possibility is to make the reduced state space (or *envelope*) E the cartesian product of a subset of these dimensions [8, 14]. Excluding a dimension from E in this way is called 'uniform abstraction' or simply 'abstraction'. It is also possible to exclude different dimensions from different parts E — this is called 'non-uniform abstraction', and is the focus of the research presented in this paper.

We assume an agent which has processing power available while it is acting. Architecturally, the agent is split into a *planner* and an *executive*; the planner continually improves policy, modifies the approximation and updates the focus based on the current state, while the executive selects actions based on the current state and current policy. This means that the agent does not need to plan so well for unlikely possibilities, and can therefore expend more of its planning on the most likely paths and on the closer future, expecting that when and if it reaches other parts of the state space, it can improve the approximation as appropriate. Dean *et al.* [7] call this *recurrent deliberation*, and use it with their locality-based approximation. A similar architecture is used by the CIRCA system [13, 10] to guarantee hard deadlines; in CIRCA terminology, the planner is the AIS, and the executive is the RTS.

The algorithm for the planner is shown in Fig.1. The key steps are Step 1 and Step 3d, for the initial choice and modification of E almost exclusively determine the quality of the approximation. The other parts of the algorithm require only minor changes.

Example Domain The example domain used in this paper is a simple robot navigation world, similar to the **RN1** world of [12] but with the addition of two walls and three doors (see Fig.2(a)). It is a 10×10 grid, with one wall between

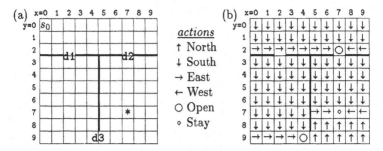

Fig. 2. Example domain. (a) Initial situation with starting location s_0, goal $*$, all three doors ($d1$, $d2$ and $d3$) closed and no damage; (b) Part of an optimal policy obtained using value iteration on the complete state space, with $\gamma = 0.99999$

$y = 2$ and $y = 3$ and the other, for $y \geq 3$, between $x = 4$ and $x = 5$. The doors are (in order) south of $\langle 2, 2 \rangle$ and $\langle 7, 2 \rangle$ and east of $\langle 9, 4 \rangle$; each can be either open or closed. There is also a 'damaged' dimension dmg, which may take the values true (T) or false (F), which indicates whether the robot or some other part of the world (a door, or wall) has been damaged; this is used to discourage the agent from attempting to walk through a closed door. More formally, $S = S_x \times S_y \times S_{d1} \times S_{d2} \times S_{d3} \times S_{dmg}$ where $S_x = S_y = \{0, 1, \ldots 9\}$, $S_{d1} = S_{d2} = S_{d3} = \{\text{open}, \text{closed}\}$ and $S_{dmg} = \{\text{T}, \text{F}\}$. Note that the full state space of this example contains $|S| = 10^2 \times 2^3 \times 2 = 1600$ states. The initial state consists of the agent in the location marked s_0 with no damage and all doors closed, that is, $\langle 0, 0, \text{closed}, \text{closed}, \text{closed}, \text{F} \rangle$.

There are six actions in A: movements in all four cardinal directions, OpenDoor, which opens the immediately adjacent door, and Stay, which is a do-nothing action. Each action may fail with some specified probability. The reward function R corresponds to a goal of achieving a particular location while avoiding damage. It gives 0 for a goal state ($x = 7, y = 7, dmg = \text{F}$), -2 for damage and -1 for all other states. The reward necessary to force the agent to definitely avoid damage, corresponding to a CIRCA [13] control-level goal, depends on the probabilities. However, since the intended domains of application do not have guaranteed actions, guaranteed control-level goal satisfaction will usually not be possible anyway. We use discounting factor $\gamma = 0.99999$ in this paper. An optimal policy for the grid locations with all doors closed and no damage is shown in Fig.2(b).

3   Non-uniform Abstraction

Non-uniform abstraction is based on the intuitive idea of ignoring some dimensions in *some parts* of the state space. For example, a door is only of interest when the agent is about to walk through it, and can be ignored in those parts of the state space which are distant from the door. This is not a question of lack of knowledge about the dimensions in question, but wilful conditional ignorance of them during planning as a matter of computational expediency.

We will use the following terminology in the remainder of this paper. Members of E are called *envelope states*. Members of S are *specific states*. E is a partition of S, which means that each envelope state is a set of specific states.

Representation of the Envelope. Since E is a partition of S, an envelope state $e \in E$ is a subset of S. Therefore the representation of the envelope states parallels the structure of S. As S is a cross product of several state space dimensions, so each e is represented as a cross product of several envelope state dimensions. In the example domain, each e is $e_x \times e_y \times e_{d1} \times e_{d2} \times e_{d3} \times e_{dmg}$.

Each envelope dimension is either (1) a singleton subset of the corresponding state space dimension; the dimension is then taken into account, that is, the state is *concrete* in the dimension; or (2) the entire state space dimension; the dimension is then ignored, that is, the state is *abstract* in that dimension. Note that when state e is abstract in one or more dimensions, it effectively groups a number of specific states in S.

For example the envelope state having $x = 7$, $y = 2$, $d2 = \mathtt{closed}$, $dmg = \mathtt{F}$ and ignoring the dimensions $d1$ and $d3$, would be represented as $\{7\} \times \{2\} \times S_{d1} \times \{\mathtt{closed}\} \times S_{d3} \times \{\mathtt{F}\}$ and groups together four specific states, corresponding to the four combinations of open and closed for $d1$ and $d3$. For brevity, we write $\langle 7, 2, ., \mathtt{closed}, ., \mathtt{F} \rangle$, dispensing with the set notation and using a period to denote an ignored dimension. It is not inherent in this representation that E is a partition of S; this needs to be maintained as an invariant through all manipulations.

To quantify the abstractness of a state, we use its a priori probability. This is an overall distribution over the states in the state space, without regard to the initial state or the agent's policy. We specify the a priori probability of a specific state, $\Pr(s)$, as the product of the a priori probabilities of its dimensions. The a priori probability of an envelope state, $\Pr(e)$, on the other hand, is the product of the a priori probabilities of its *concrete* dimensions, or, equivalently, the sum of the a priori probabilities of its members. In the example, the a priori probabilities are uniform, so $\Pr(s)$ is the same for all s and $\Pr(e) = |e| \Pr(s)$.

Tree Domain Representation. As the intended domains of application have a large S, it will not be possible to specify the transition function T directly due to its size. The transition probabilities must therefore be specified in some other, more compact manner. In the current implementation, the transition function probabilities for each action are written in the form of a decision tree [15], enriched to allow non-determinism by allowing some nodes to decide at random rather than based on a particular dimension. The reward function R, is specified as an ordinary decision tree. No non-determinism is required, even for the abstracted state space, since the leaves can simply be combined linearly (averaged).

4 Policy Generation

Given an envelope of non-uniformly abstracted states, we can compute a policy using the standard value iteration (or policy iteration) algorithm described in Sect. 2. Note that this section pre-supposes the envelope; we discuss how to go about devising this envelope automatically in Sect. 5. The policy π becomes a

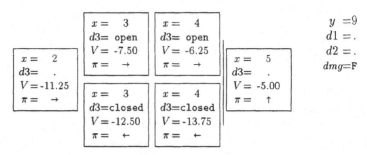

Fig. 3. Ostrich effect

mapping $E \to A$ and the value function becomes $V : E \to \Re$. Equations (1) and (2) then read:

$$\pi(e) \leftarrow \arg\max_a \sum_{e'} \Pr(e, a, e') V(e') \tag{3}$$

and

$$V(e) \leftarrow R(e) + \gamma \sum_{e'} \Pr(e, \pi(e'), e') V(e') \tag{4}$$

where $R(e)$ and $\Pr(e, a, e')$ are specified by the abstracted reward function and abstracted transition function, respectively. Before the policy is used by the executive, it is translated back into $S \to A$ form by setting $\pi(s) = \pi(e)$ whenever $s \in e$. Note that there are likely to be problems as the non-uniformly abstracted approximation will not in general satisfy the Markov property. However, the algorithm can be run, though it will sometimes compute incorrect values and hence return non-optimal policies. The main anomaly, which we call the *ostrich effect*, is discussed below.

Ostrich Effect. When the agent plans to move from a relatively concrete state e_1 to a more abstract state e_2 and thence to e_3, it may need to know that e_2 was reached from e_1 in order to identify the correct e_3, which violates the Markov property. If the abstracted approximation is simply treated as a MDP in which the agent doesn't know which e_3 it will reach, it won't correspond to the underlying process, which might reach a particular e_3 deterministically. The problem is especially obvious when the actual e_3 that will be reached is in fact e_1 — the planner will plan a loop.

For a specific example of this, consider Fig.3 which shows a small part of a sample E, part of the southernmost row in the vicinity of $d3$. Each box represents one envelope state, showing the x and $d3$ dimensions, the value V and the policy π for that state. For clarity, the other dimensions ($y = 9$, $d1 = .$, $d2 = .$, $dmg = $ F) are omitted from the diagram. Since the goal is to the East of door $d3$, an optimal policy would be the $\to$ action at all the depicted states except the one with $x = 4$ and $d3 = $ closed, where the optimal action is $\bigcirc$ to open the door. The door, which is between $x = 4$ and $x = 5$ (suggested by a vertical line in the diagram), is relatively difficult to open, with only a 10% probability of success. On the other hand, when moving from $x = 2$ (e_2 in the general description) to $x = 3$ (e_3) the a priori probability that the door is already open is 50%. When the calculations are performed, this turns out to be preferable to attempting to open the door.

Locally-uniform Abstraction. The ostrich effect occurs when states of different abstraction are considered, the problem being, as noted above, that the DP given by the abstraction is non-Markovian. The solution is to make the abstraction locally uniform, and therefore locally Markovian. In this way, the iterative step of the policy generation algorithm does not have to work across the edge of an abstract region, and, since the same information is available in all the states being considered at each point, there is no impetus for any of them to be favoured or avoided on that basis.

Specifically, let $O(e)$ denote the set of all possible outcomes of all actions in the state e, i.e. $O(e) = \{e' \in E : (\exists a \in A) \Pr(e, a, e') > 0\}$. For example, for Fig.3 (listing only x and $d3$ for each state and only states shown in Fig.3):

e	$O(e)$	comment
3, closed	$\{3, \text{closed}; 4, \text{closed}; 2, .; \text{etc}\}$	one outcome is abstract in $d3$
4, closed	$\{4, \text{closed}; 3, \text{closed}; 4, \text{open}; \text{etc}\}$	all at equal level of abstractness

Then, when calculating $\pi(e)$ for a particular e, if any member of $O(e)$ is abstract in a dimension in which e is concrete, e and all members of $O(e)$ are temporarily abstracted in that dimension. Note that E itself is not changed, and that different abstracting will occur to the same states depending on the e that is currently being planned for. Values for this local additional abstraction, $\bar{V}$, are the averages of the original V weighted by the relative a priori probabilities of the new and original states. These are used in the π update formula instead of the original Vs. The values V are calculated from T, π and R in the usual fashion.

Continuing with the example above, consider first the state with $x = 3$, $d3 = $ closed. Since the corresponding O contains the state with $x = 2$, $d3 = .$ (i.e., in which $d3$ is abstract), all members of O are reduced to $d3 = .$ The resulting values $\bar{V}$, calculated from the V, are shown in Fig.4 between the states they correspond to (note that the values V are different from those in Fig.3, since the policy is different). The correct action, East ($\rightarrow$), is selected. On the other hand, consider the state with $x = 4$ and $d3 = $ closed. Since the whole corresponding O is already at the same level of abstractness (the state with $x = 5$, $d3 = .$ cannot be reached as it is on the other side of the closed door), no reduction is necessary. The action selected, Open (O), is again correct.

Effects and Consequences. As can be seen from the above description, the door is only partially considered at $x = 3$. This means that, in most cases, the more concrete region must extend one step beyond the region in which the dimension is immediately relevant. For a dimension to be fully considered at a state, the possible outcomes of all actions at that state must also be concrete in that dimension. Another, less obvious problem arises when the concrete region is insufficient. In some cases, the policy does not converge, instead oscillating between two possibilities. One must be careful, therefore, with the envelope to avoid these situations, or else to detect them and modify the envelope accordingly.

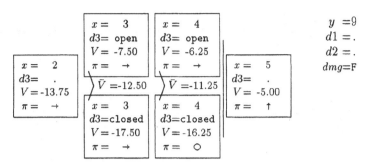

Fig. 4. Locally-uniform abstraction

At present, it appears that the algorithm described in Sect.5 below ensures the envelope is sufficient.

5 Dynamic Envelope Abstraction

Before planning, an initial abstracted envelope E must be selected; as noted earlier, how this is done is crucial. As planning and execution progress, the envelope abstraction may need to be changed. Changes occur both as the planner gains a better idea of the best path to the goal, and as the agent itself moves from one part of the state space to another. The general strategy of our approach is that the envelope should be mostly concrete near the agent and its planned path to the goal, to allow detailed planning, but mostly abstract elsewhere, to conserve computational resources. The planner must balance *refinement*, making states more concrete, and *coarsening*, making them more abstract, so that it makes the best possible use of the available computational resources. This section presents the initial envelope selection first, followed by two possible methods of envelope modification: one based on the policy calculated, the other on the likelihood of encountering particular states in the future, given the current state.

Selecting the Initial Envelope Abstraction As we have discussed earlier, real-world domains are too large for the transition function to be specified exhaustively, so a higher-level description will always be available. This description can therefore be used to construct the initial envelope by inferring the nexus[1] between the dimensions (that is, linking points, those points at which the dimensions interact). Intuitively, the structure of the solution is likely to resemble the structure of the problem. The incorporation of the reward function reflects the assumption that the dimensions on which the reward is based will be important.

The two steps in deriving the initial envelope from the high-level domain descriptions are as follows. Firstly, all the dimensions mentioned in the reward tree are to be concrete throughout the envelope. In the sample domain, these are the x and y coordinates and the dmg dimension. Secondly, for each leaf node

---

[1] Note that 'nexus' is both singular and plural.

in each action tree, the states matching the corresponding pre-state are to be concrete in all the dimensions mentioned in the ancestors of that leaf node. We call this a *nexus* between dimensions. In the sample domain, nexus involving dimensions not already concrete are on both sides of each door, in the two locations immediately adjacent. This makes a total of 12 significant nexus, derived from 3 doors $\times$ 2 sides $\times$ {open, closed}. After the reward dimensions are included $|E| = 10 \times 10 \times 2 = 200$, and after the nexus are taken into account $|E| = 212$ (compared to $|S| = 1600$ specific states). While the more concrete states will be taken into account only to a very minimal extent after reduction to the locally-uniform abstraction form (Sect.4), it is sufficient to trigger the policy-based envelope refinement algorithm below where necessary.

Policy-based Envelope Refinement. Consider two (or more) envelope states which differ only in the value of a single dimension and have a different policy, and have an adjacent state which is abstract in that dimension. The difference in the policy of the two states indicates that the dimension is important there, yet by the reduction to the locally-uniform abstraction form, undertaken to avoid the ostrich effect, it will not be taken into account fully. This suggests a test for refining the envelope: whenever there are three states c_1, c_2 and a in the envelope such that $\pi(c_1) \neq \pi(c_2)$, $a \in O(c_1)$, and c_1 and c_2 differ in the values for a concrete dimension d in which a is abstract, but not in any dimensions in which a is concrete, add the dimension d to state a. This algorithm, together with the one presented in 5 above, is how E was obtained for Sect.4. It increases the number of envelope states from the initial 212 to 225.

In some cases, this policy-based envelope refinement propagates beyond the immediate vicinity.[2] One way to solve this problem is to combine this refinement test with the envelope modification strategy described in next section.

Likelihood-based Envelope Modification We noted above that the envelope should be mostly concrete near the agent and its planned path to the goal, to allow detailed planning, but mostly abstract elsewhere, to conserve computational resources. Likelihoods are one way to realise this concept; they can be described as 'discounted sum of probabilities'. The likelihood of a state decreases both as the state is further in the future and as it is less probable. Unlike the measure used by [12] and [7], likelihoods are independent of planning cycle length.

The formula for the likelihood l is similar to the formula for value, except the reward for the state is replaced with an 'is current state' function, *cur*, and the transition probabilities are reversed. That is,

$$l(s) \leftarrow \text{cur}(s) + \gamma_l \sum_{s'} \Pr(s', \pi(s'), s) l(s') \tag{5}$$

where γ_l is the likelihood discounting factor ($0 \leq \gamma_l < 1$) and

$$\text{cur}(s) = \begin{cases} 1 - \gamma_l & \text{if } s \text{ is the current state} \\ 0 & \textit{otherwise} \end{cases} \tag{6}$$

---

[2] Example described in [1].

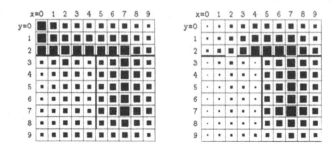

Fig. 5. Likelihoods for the initial state, $\langle x = 0, y = 0 \rangle$, and a state later in the execution, $\langle x = 4, y = 2 \rangle$. Symbol size based on logarithm of likelihood.

This can be equally applied to the variously-abstract envelope: s is simply replaced by e in (5) and (6). For many purposes, however, the likelihoods will then need to be inversely scaled by the a priori probabilities to compensate for variation due to the varying abstractness. To take into account further planning, and ensure that nearby absorbing states are kept in mind even if the current policy deterministically avoids them, (5) is modified to use an estimated future policy $\hat{\pi}$ instead of π. In this estimate, $\hat{\pi}(e)$ is a distribution over actions which assigns some constant probability to the current $\pi(e)$ and distributes the remaining probability mass among the other actions equally. This distributed probability mass corresponds to the probability that the policy will change sometime in the future. This can also be expressed and solved as a set of linear equations; in matrix notation, the equation solved is $(I - \gamma_l T_{\hat{\pi}}^T)l = \text{cur}$ where $T_{\hat{\pi}}$ is the transition matrix induced by the policy $\hat{\pi}$. There are two parameters for the likelihood calculation, the discounting factor γ_l and the probability of policy change.

Likelihoods for the initial situation $(\langle 0, 0, \texttt{closed}, \texttt{closed}, \texttt{closed}, \texttt{F} \rangle)$ and a possible situation later in the execution $(\langle 4, 2, \texttt{closed}, \texttt{closed}, \texttt{closed}, \texttt{F} \rangle)$, with $\gamma_l = 0.95$ and probability of policy change 10%, are shown in Fig.5. Larger symbols correspond to higher likelihood; size is based on the logarithm of the likelihood since the likelihoods shown in the figure range from 2^{-37} to $2^{-1.4}$.

One interesting feature of the resulting numbers is that they emphasise absorbing and near-absorbing states somewhat more than might be intuitively expected. However, considering that absorbing states are in general important, this is probably a good feature, especially since normally the planner will try to minimise the probability of entering an absorbing state. This feature should help ensure that absorbing states are kept in mind as long as there is any chance of falling into them. With the measure of [12] and [7], absorbing states along the path to the goal tend to come up as candidates for removal from the envelope, as they are unlikely to be reached with the current policy, and special accommodation must be made for them so they are not removed from the envelope. With likelihood emphasising these states, such special handling is not necessary in our approach.

With the choice of $1 - \gamma_l$ as the constant for the current state, $\sum_s l(s) = 1$. In fact, l is the probability distribution for the current state of the agent in the near future, provided it follows the policy $\hat{\pi}$ and 'near future' is suitably defined (probability of checking at time t is $(1 - \gamma_l)\gamma_l^t$).

6   Discussion and further work

The solution presented in this paper is based on selectively ignoring some of the dimensions in some parts of the state space. In other words, we obtain approximate solutions by varying the level of abstraction in different parts of the state space. This has strong implications, since the resulting approximation is no longer Markovian. However, the approach is both intuitively appealing and, as we have shown in the examples presented, appears to be a useful method of approximation. The robot only considers a door dimension when it is about to walk through the door; if it has to walk through a dozen doors, it can focus on each door as it approaches, and forget about those already passed.

This paper deals with control error exclusively. Sensor error is not considered and it is assumed that the agent can accurately discern the current world state. The relaxation of the assumption of observability will require the investigation as to the potential of applying the idea of non-uniform abstraction used in this paper to work being done in the area of Partially Observable MDPs (POMDPs). It is also assumed that the agent accurately knows the state space, the reward function, and the transition function. Given a transition function representation based on decision trees, it may be possible to adapt existing techniques for learning decision trees [15].

The classical MDP policy generation algorithm, applied to a non-uniformly abstracted envelope, may result in a policy where the agent goes to particular states depending on whether it seems better to know or not to know. This is because the DP given by the abstraction is non-Markovian. We have described modifications to the policy generation algorithm, whereby we re-calculate values for nearby states based on a locally uniform abstraction for each state. This ensures that the resulting policy is not based on value of information, although it may still be suboptimal.

The most crucial part of the approach is envelope selection and modification. The quality of the initial envelope is important since it provides the basis for the modification algorithms. The policy-based refinement only extends the envelope, by adding dimensions to envelope states in particular situations. It requires a 'seed' of a more concrete area before it is triggered and only works along the edges of more concrete regions.

The current method makes all the dimensions mentioned in the reward tree concrete throughout the initial envelope. In domains where the reward is a function of many (or all) dimensions, obviously this strategy would no longer be applicable and some sort of sensitivity analysis would need to be applied to determine which of the dimensions most influence the reward.

We make the assumption that the agent continues computation as it is acting ('recurrent deliberation' of [7]). This means the agent can focus more closely on planning for the most likely paths and the closer future, expecting that it can later improve the approximation for other parts of the state space as needed. This is the basis for the likelihood-based envelope modification. The potential problem of too much propagation of the policy-based refinement is addressed when that method is combined with the likelihood calculation. This is because the states which are not near the shortest path are made abstract using the likelihood calculation, and states on the shortest path are made concrete. The interaction between the methods is currently being investigated.

References

[1] J. Baum and A. E. Nicholson. Dynamic non-uniform abstractions for approximate planning in large structured stochastic domains. Technical Report TR 98/18, Department of Computer Science, Monash Uni., 1998.

[2] R. Bellman. *Dynamic Programming*. Princeton Uni. Press, 1957.

[3] D. P. Bertsekas. *Dynamic Programming*. Prentice-Hall, Englewood Cliffs, N.J., 1987.

[4] C. Boutilier. Correlated action effects in decision theoretic regression. In *Proc. of UAI*, pages 30–37, 1997.

[5] C. Boutilier and R. Dearden. Approximating value trees in structured dynamic programming. In *Proc. of 13th Int'l Conf. on Machine Learning*, pages 54–62, Bari, Italy, 1996.

[6] C. Boutilier, R. Dearden, and M. Goldszmidt. Exploiting structure in policy construction. In *Proc. of IJCAI*, pages 1104–1111, Montreal, 1995.

[7] T. Dean, L. P. Kaelbling, J. Kirman, and A. E. Nicholson. Planning under time constraints in stochastic domains. *Artificial Intelligence*, 76(1-2):35–74, 1995.

[8] R. Dearden and C. Boutilier. Abstraction and approximate decision theoretic planning. *Artificial Intelligence*, 89(1):219–283, 1997.

[9] M. Drummond and J. Bresina. Anytime synthetic projection: Maximizing the probability of goal satisfaction. In *Proc. of AAAI-90*, pages 138–144. AAAI, 1990.

[10] R. P. Goldman, D. J. Musliner, K. D. Krebsbach, and M. S. Boddy. Dynamic abstraction planning. In *Proc. of AAAI 97*, 1997.

[11] R. A. Howard. *Dynamic Programming and Markov Processes*. MIT Press, Cambridge, Massachusetts, 1960.

[12] J. Kirman. *Predicting real-time planner performance by domain characterization*. PhD thesis, Brown Uni., 1994.

[13] D. J. Musliner, E. H. Durfee, and K. G. Shin. World modeling for the dynamic construction of real-time plans. *Artificial Intelligence*, 74:83–127, 1995.

[14] A. E. Nicholson and L. P. Kaelbling. Toward approximate planning in very large stochastic domains. In *Proc. of Spring Symposium on Decision Theoretic Planning*, 1994.

[15] J. R. Quinlan. *C4.5: Programs for Machine Learning*. Morgan Kaufmann, San Mateo, California, 1993.

A Characterization of Contrastive Explanations Computation

Alex Kean

Department of Computer Science
Hong Kong University of Science & Technology
Clear Water Bay, Kowloon, Hong Kong
kean@cs.ust.hk

Abstract. Abduction in artificial intelligence in a narrow sense is a methodology for finding explanation to a question in a deductive model. The problem of selecting which explanation is *better suited* to explaining a question is still unresolved. This paper proposes a computational model of explanation selection based on the concept of *contrastive explanation* popularly known in literature of *inference to the best explanation*. The proposed model of explanation finding for the question *why P* is replaced by finding the explanation for the question *why P instead of Q* given a particular contrast *Q*.

1 Introduction

Aristotle (384-322 B.C.) (Ross, 1952) first introduced the term *abduction* as an inference that given a major premise, forms a plausible minor premise such that together they sanctions the consequence. Another variant is the inference of *induction* where given the minor premise and the consequence, the task is to discover the major premise such that this newly discovered major premise together with the minor premise sanctions the consequence. Both abduction and induction are not truth preserving. In the case there is no distinction between a major and a minor premise, abduction and induction is best called, following the proposal by Harman (1965), the *inference to the best explanation.*

However, in artificial intelligence the distinction between a major and minor premises is important as it reflects the typical organization of an intelligent system where there are an explicit knowledge base (major premise) and accumulated facts (minor premises) as input to the system. The distinction also plays the role in separating the task of inquiry (abduction) and discovery (induction). In the process of inquiry, given a knowledge base (major premise) and an observation (consequence), ask what facts (minor premises) must present in order for the observation to hold; and in induction, given some facts (minor premise) and an observation (consequence), ask what general knowledge (major premise) do we need to establish the logical relationship between the facts and the observation.

Abduction is formulated as finding a suitable minor premise as an *explanation* such that together with a knowledge base logically entails a consequence. Hereon, abduction and explanation appear in this paper is to mean the model used in artificial intelligence.[1]

Much work have been done in abduction of computing an explanation for a query(Reiter and de Kleer, 1987; Kean and Tsiknis, 1992). Let K be a knowledge base, a set of facts if true, is an explanation for a query with respect to the knowledge base if together they logically entails the query. And to be meaningful, they better be consistent. In this sense, *to explain* a query is to have a set of premises, if true, will necessarily entail the truth of the query. First, this form of explanation is rather restrictive in which there is no room for premises that *possibly but not necessarily* entail the query. Second, as the formulation indicates, there can be many such explanations that satisfy the logical entailment and consistency requirements, for instance, any such explanation plus a true proposition about the sun rises in the morning. There is no mechanism in selecting a *better* explanation other than those that satisfy the entailment and consistency requirements. There is no natural method for choosing the most *critical* or *prominent* one among these explanations, which are all necessary conditions in the deductive sense in explaining the query.

The first problem of explanation possibility can be addressed by probabilistic or approximation methods. The second problem, which is the focus of this paper, can be addressed using *contrastive analysis* to refine the explanations generated. The notion of a *contrastive explanation* (Lipton, 1990; Lipton, 1991) is well known and popular in the literature of the *inference to the best explanation* (Harman, 1965; Lipton, 1991). Contrastive explanation basically points out that when a question *why P* is posed, there is an unspoken context assumed where the expected explanation is circumscribed. When asked why did you eat chicken, the question really is why did you eat chicken instead of beef, or instead of fish. The expected explanation should explain eating chicken in the context of beef or fish, not in other context like the sky is blue.

I shall borrow this idea and attempt to formulate a computational model for computing contrastive explanation. The notion of a contrast is reviewed and argued briefly first, then I shall propose a model of abduction in the artificial intelligence framework using contrast.

2 Contrastive Explanation

2.1 Explanation

When a question is asked by an *enquirer* to an *explainer*, an explanation for the question provided by the explainer is referential to the enquirer. The explanation provided is delineated by the explainers inference ability and the appropriateness of the explanation is dictated by the enquirer's explanatory preference (or interest). I asked a 5-year old child why there are images on the television screen

---

[1] Note that the AI approach is concerned with finding ordinary explanation which may or may not be law like scientific explanation.

and her explanation is because I have turned on the television. A similar question posed to my physicist colleague yields the explanation on the working of a cathode-ray tube and the transmission of television signals. If the role of the enquirer and explainer are reversed, the 5-year old child would probably accept turning on a television as a better explanation than the workings of a television. Thus, the explainer's inference is guided by the enquirer's explanatory preference and the explanation derived by the explainer is delineated by her own inference ability.[2]

Such context dependent task of explaining is beyond the ability of our present day knowledge based system's technology. To limit our discussion, I shall assume the explainer is in her earnest way to find the *best*[3] explanation, and the enquirer's explanatory preference must be explicitly communicated to the explainer. Equally important, I shall assume both the enquirer and the explainer are knowledgeable in the same domain of discourse.

In the framework of abduction in artificial intelligence, a question why A is to mean why A is a logical consequence of a given knowledge base describing a particular domain. Thus, explanation generation in artificial intelligence is based on the inference of deduction. That is, given the consequence, find the premise (explanation) such that if true, can possibly yield the truth of the consequence.

Naturally, there can be many such explanations given a consequence, including any inconsistent explanation with its knowledge base. Furthermore, some explanation is more specific, in the sense of sufficiency of its truth status in entailing the consequence than others. For instance, if both statements *"if I have money then I will go to Hawaii"* and *"if I have money and won a lottery then I will go to Hawaii"* are both true propositions in the knowledge base, then the explanation *"I have money"* together with the first statement is sufficient to entail the consequence *"I will go to Hawaii"* regardless of whether I won a lottery. This principle of *Occum's Razor* shall be termed the *logical minimality* of explanation. To summarize, an explanation for a consequence in abduction must be consistent with its knowledge base, logically minimal with respect to its knowledge base, and deductively entails the consequence.

Can the above properties of explanation sufficiently provide us with the *best* explanation? Apparently not since there still can be many consistent and logically minimal explanations for a given consequence. It has been argued that the onus of selecting which is a better explanation for a consequence is on the enquirer since it is the enquirer's explanatory preference that really determine the goodness of an explanation. Thus, scheme such as preference ordering or cost functions is used in such task. Most of these schemes are context dependent and lack a discipline in its design. I shall offer another scheme called contrastive

---

[2] Whether the explanatory preference is customary or un-customary, with or without a purpose, or emotional preference, for example, and whether the inference is logical or fallacious.

[3] I have failed to define what *best* means. As the reading progresses, the reader will discover the definition is appealing to the reader's interpretation of naturalness in explanation.

explanation borrowed from philosophy, not as an argument against the existing scheme, but rather as an additional scheme that is natural and useful.

2.2 Contrast

When the enquirer asks me why did I go to Hawaii, she really has in mind, not stated explicitly, why did I choose to go to Hawaii instead of not going to Hawaii, or instead of going to Europe, or instead of going to the library? The observation is that when a question is asked, it is usually accompanied by a *contrast*[4] that reflects the context in which the explanation for the question is to be provided (Lipton, 1990; Lipton, 1991). Typically, a contrast is of the same type with its question. A question about an entity is accompanied by a contrast about an entity and an action accompanied by an action. For instance, normally we are interested in why is the forest looks brown instead of green. The contrast tells us that we are conjecturing the forest to look green, and all the assumptions that would support a green forest comes into the context: including being in the summer season, there is sufficient rain, there is no forest fire and so on. Any explanation that supports a brown forest but *does not support* (or deny to support) a green forest is *better* in explaining the forests brown looking color. On the contrary, the assumption that someone spray paint on the forest, although probable, does not come into mind likely.

In circuit diagnosis many components are interconnected. When asked why did component X failed, we are faced with many possibilities, and after selecting those that are consistent and logically minimal, they are all explanations. Truly when an engineer is performing fault finding, she is really thinking of why did component X failed instead of component Y, probably components X and Y are contrasted because they come from the same circuit module.

If our explainer is a computerized knowledge base system, it is only fair we insist the enquirer must submit the contrast to her question explicitly. In the absence of a contrast, we could assume the negation of the question being a contrast, although it may not serve the purpose sometimes.

There is a propensity to axiomatized the relationship between the question and the contrast (the *instead of* relation) in a logical form. For instance, using the conjunction of the question Q and the contrast C, or the material implication $Q \vee C \rightarrow Q$. In the former, the conjunction of the question and its negation as a contrast is simply an inconsistent question. In the latter, it is too strong because it is equivalent to $(Q \rightarrow Q) \wedge (C \rightarrow Q)$, or the contrast must play a role in the deduction to entail the question.

Lipton (1991) proposed the notion of comparing the question and the contrast via their *causal difference*. To better aid the design of our computing procedure, I shall redefine the notion as the *difference* between the causal explanation for the question and the causal explanation for the contrast and is what we will call a contrastive explanation. The causal difference method is after John Stuart Mill's

---

[4] Some argue that there are questions devoid of contrast, especially in the scientific realm (Ruben, 1990).

Method of Difference (Copi, 1982, pp 419). Mill's motivation was in inductive inference:

> If an instance in which the phenomenon under investigation occurs, and an instance in which it does not occur, have every circumstance in common save one, that one occurring only in the former; the circumstance in which alone the two instances differ, is the effect, or the cause, or an **indispensable**[5] *part of the cause, of the phenomenon.*

In our deductive framework, we can loosely define a contrastive explanation as the *difference* between the consistent and logically minimal explanations that entails the question, and the consistent and logically minimal explanations that entails the contrast. Nevertheless, in order to design a computing procedure, we have to be more precise than the above intuitive description.

3   Contrastive Explanation in Abduction

We shall assume a set of sentences over a vocabulary and the normal interpretation of logical truth and falsity, connectives and entailment. The standard set operations on its syntactic membership is also assumed.[6]

Definition 1 (Explanation). *Let K be a knowledge base and Q a question. A sentence E is an **explanation** for Q with respect to K if $K \models E \rightarrow Q$ and $K \wedge E$ is consistent. E is logically minimal explanation for Q with respect to K if no other E' satisfies $\models E' \rightarrow E$ is an explanation for Q with respect to K.*

Thus, together with the knowledge base, an explanation entails the question and is consistent with the knowledge base. We can define a similar definition of an explanation for the contrast.

When asked why the question Q instead of the contrast C, a causal difference of Q with respect to C is, roughly speaking, those explanations involved in explaining the question Q is not essential in explaining the contrast C. These explanations of Q are inessential to the contrast C in precisely the sense that they are irrelevant to C but are relevant to Q. These explanations tell us that they are necessary (but not sufficient) explanation in entailing the question Q, but are neither necessary nor sufficient in the case of the contrast. Let us illustrate the causal difference in the following example in propositional sentences representing the knowledge base K:

---

[5] I have added the boldface to highlight the property of being different in Mill's Method.

[6] It is worth noting here that the set operation on its syntactic membership is only a convenience and is insufficient to capture the full meaning intended. For instance, the *syntactic set difference* $A - B = \{a | a \in A \wedge \forall b \in B, b \neq a\}$ do not distinguishes the possibly semantically equivalent propositions a and b. To extend this is to have the definition of a *semantic set difference* defines as $A - B = \{a | a \in A \wedge \forall b \in B, b \not\equiv a\}$. *Semantic set intersection* can be defined analogously. In the propositional case, such equivalence can be computed via rewrite rules.

$$
\begin{array}{rcl}
has\_time & \rightarrow & goto\_library \\
has\_money & \rightarrow & buy\_car \\
has\_time \wedge has\_money & \rightarrow & goto\_Hawaii \\
win\_lottery & \rightarrow & has\_money
\end{array}
$$

Let us ask why $goto\_Hawaii$ instead of $goto\_library$? Two possible explanations for $goto\_Hawaii$ are $(has\_time \wedge win\_lottery)$ and $(has\_time \wedge has\_money)$ corresponding to

$$K \models (has\_time \wedge win\_lottery) \rightarrow goto\_Hawaii$$

and

$$K \models (has\_time \wedge has\_money) \rightarrow goto\_Hawaii.$$

On the other hand, a possible explanation for $goto\_library$ is has_time corresponding to $K \models (has\_time) \rightarrow goto\_library$. Intuitively, the *real* reason I went to Hawaii instead of the library is because I won the lottery, or because I have money. We reason that since having free time is needed in explaning both going to Hawaii and the library, thus having free time alone does not *really* explain why I go to Hawaii instead of the library. Also, having won the lottery or have money are irrelevant to whether I go to the library but are relevant to me going to Hawaii. Hence the difference between going to Hawaii and going to library is *best explained* by the fact that I won a lottery or I have money.

If we consider why $goto\_Hawaii$ instead of buy_car then the causal difference in this case is the explanation has_time. This is because $win\_lottery$ and has_money share the same status as explanations for both the question $goto\_Hawaii$ and the contrast buy_car. The real difference, or the remaining difference, is that of the explanation has_time. That is, not only we need to have money, we also need to have free time in order to explain the journey to Hawaii. Thus, the contrast buy_car enters into the context in which wining a lottery and have money are the commonality and the difference (or why we favour one over the other) is because of the factor of free time. Whereas in the previous example the contrast $goto\_library$ enters into the context in which having free time is the commonality, and winning lottery and have money are the most important reasons why I went to Hawaii.

The above example illustrates that by explicitly stating the contrast, the enquirer's explanatory preference can be roughly incorporated into the explainer's inference ability. However, there can be many interpretation on how to differ in its explanations between the question and the contrast. We shall enumerate some of the interpretations of contrastive explanation in more detail using the model theorectic approach.

A *variable* is a name and the set of all variables is the vocabulary $\mathcal{V}$. A *literal* is either a variable or a negated variable. An interpretation I is a function that assign literals to *true* or *false*. The truth value of a sentence is calculated according to the interpretation of the literals in the sentence and the meaning of the connectives (disjunction $\vee$, conjunction $\wedge$ and negation $\neg$). A *model M* is a set of *true* literals collected from the interpretation that makes a sentence K *true*, denoted by the relation $M \models K$. Literals that are not in the model are *false*.

We shall assume the knowledge base (a set of sentences) and all of the sentences hereon are built using the same vocabulary $\mathcal{V}$. Let K be a knowledge base and Q a sentence. The entailment relation $K \models Q$ means that for all interpretations (models) that make K *true* also make Q *true*. For a particular such model M, notationally we shall write $K \models_M Q$.

Definition 2 (Essential Model). *Let K be a set of sentences, Q a sentence and let M be a model of $K \models Q$. The model $M_K \subseteq M$ is an **essential model** for $K \models Q$ if $K \models_{M_K} Q$ and no other $\Delta \subset M_K$ satisfies $K \models_\Delta Q$.*

The property of an essential model[7] reveals that it is the smallest set of *true* literals that satisfies the relation $K \models Q$. If we were to alter the truth value of a literal in the essential model M_K it will no longer satisfies $K \models Q$. Intuitively, an essential model defines the smallest relevant world, smallest in terms of membership and relevant in terms of participation in truth preservation in describing the relationship between the knowledge base and the consequence. The intention here is obvious since a model could be infinite if the vocabulary is infinite. In the propositional case an essential model is finite.

The motivation behind defining an essential model is to provide a structure to circumscribe the relevant model that describe the explanation which will be used in performing causal difference operation in computing contrastive explanation. Intuitively, we want to extract a partial model from the essential model that describe the explanation for a question and similar one for the contrast, thus giving us the precise causal knowledge to perform the difference operation.

Definition 3 (Explanation Model). *Let K be a set of sentences, Q a sentence and E an explanation of Q with respect to K. Let M_K be an essential model for $K \models E \rightarrow Q$. The model M_Q is an **explanation model** of $K \models E \rightarrow Q$ if $M_Q \subseteq M_K$, $M_Q \models E \rightarrow Q$ and no other $\Delta \subset M_Q$ satisfies $\Delta \models E \rightarrow Q$.*

An explanation model is the smallest part of the essential model that describe the relationship between the explanation and the consequence. The existence of these models (essential and explanation) is garanteed by the entailment relationship in the definition of an explanation expressed by the following corollary.

Corollary 1. *Let the knowledge base K be a set of sentences and a question Q a sentence. If E is an explanation for Q with respect to K than there is an essential model M_K that satisfies $K \models E \rightarrow Q$, and an explanation model $M_Q \subseteq M_K$ satisfies $M_Q \models E \rightarrow Q$.*

3.1 Non-Preclusive Contrastive Explanation

Let K be the knowledge base, a question Q and a contrast C. Also, let E_Q be the explanation for the question Q and E_C be the explanation for the contrast C. By the definition of an explanation and the existence of an explanation model,

---

[7] To be precise, it is a partial model.

we can construct the appropriate explanation models M_Q for $K \models E_Q \rightarrow Q$ (the question) and M_C for the contrast $K \models E_Q \rightarrow C$ with the subscript appropriately indicates its belongings. Thus, one possible causal difference is that of the difference between a particular M_Q from a particular M_C, that is $M_Q - M_C$. Let's call this difference a *non-preclusive contrastive explanation* (M_{Q-C}) for the question Q instead of C with respect to the knowledge base K. More formally,

Definition 4 (Non-Preclusive Contrastive Explanation). *Let the knowledge base K be a set of sentences, a question Q and a contrast C both are a sentence, and E_Q and E_C are the corresponding explanations for Q and C, and M_Q and M_C be the explanation models for $K \models E_Q \rightarrow Q$ and $K \models E_C \rightarrow C$ respectively. The model $M_{Q-C} = M_Q - M_C$ is a **non-preclusive contrastive** explanation for the question Q instead of C with respect to K.*

This definition of a non-preclusive contrastive explanation differs in its role between the question and the contrast in the sense that it is irrelevant to the model of explaining the contrast C but is different and necessary in the model of explaining the question Q. It is necessary in the model of explaining the question Q because M_{Q-C} is a subset of its explanation model M_Q. It is different because all of the propositions that are involved in explaining both the question and the contrast are eliminated. And it is irrelevant to the model of explaining the contrast C simply because this newly constructed model is absent in the contrast's explanation model. Thus, a non-preclusive contrastive explanation for the question Q instead of C is a contrastive explanation that is necessary in explaining Q but is absent in the need to explain C, and no more. It does not tell us more about explaining or not explaining the contrast and it could very well be the case that the contrast is also explainable by its own explanation. In other word, the non-preclusive contrastive explanation is an improtant reason for Q to be a consequence but does not preclude C being a consequence. For example, let K be

$$has\_red\_wine \wedge mushy\_peas \quad \rightarrow \quad eat\_steak$$
$$has\_white\_wine \wedge mushy\_peas \quad \rightarrow \quad eat\_fish.$$

To explain why *eat_steak* instead of *eat_fish*, one non-preclusive contrastive explanation is the reason that *has_red_wine*, or to be more precise, the explanation model for the question *eat_steak* is $M_Q = \{has\_red\_wine, mushy\_peas, eat\_steak\}$. Conversely, the explanation model for the contrast *eat_fish* is $M_C = \{has\_white\_wine, mushy\_peas, eat\_fish\}$. The difference between these two models is $M_{Q-C} = \{has\_red\_wine, eat\_steak\}$. Even though mushy peas is a part of an explanation for eating steak but it does not distinctly explain the preference over fish since it is also involves in explaining the choice of fish eating. Note that *eat_steak* is also a non-preclusive contrastive explanation but it is a trivial explanation. If both red wine and white wine were present, the non-preclusive contrastive explanation does not tell us whether we eat fish or steak. A non-preclusive contrastive explanation is not a prediction but simply a reason of great importance. This is best used in characterizing preferences that are non-preclusive.

3.2 Preclusive Contrastive Explanation

The model of the non-preclusive contrastive explanation is similar to John Stuart Mill's Method of Difference. This is a simple minded method of difference in the constituent of their explanations. This may prove to be sufficient for certain classes of applications in non-law like intelligent knowledge-based system.

For example, what if we are interested in a contrastive explanation for a question that conjecturally precludes its contrast? This type of question occurs in finding explanation for consequences that cannot both exist, like in some events. For instance, ask why is the concert being held in the sport Colosseum instead of being held in the theater? Since both events cannot occur at the same time, the explanation must explains the the reason why the concert occurs at the Colosseum (the question) and also precludes the concert from happening at the theater (the negation of the contrast). However, to simultaneously explain the question and also explain the negation of the contrast for all types of knowledge requires a lot of luck in knowledge acquisition. A weaker form is to have an explanation that explains the question and conjecturally denies the contrast. The caveat is that this explanation only conjecturally denies the contrast, it does not decisively preclude the contrast from being a consequence.

Lipton proposed such a notion of contrastive explanation with his Difference Condition (1991, pp 43) as follows:

> To explain why Q rather than C, we must cite a causal difference between Q and $\neg C$, consisting of a cause of Q and the absence of a corresponding event in the history of $\neg C$.

To the best of my interpretation, this Liptonian style of preclusive contrastive explanation consists of two parts: a cause of Q is the non-preclusive explanation for Q instead of C, and the absence of a corresponding event in the history of $\neg C$ is the consequence of $\neg C$ that is consistent with explaining Q. In the case of the contrast, if $\neg C \rightarrow \neg E$, taking its contra-positive yields $E \rightarrow C$, that is, E is an explanation for the contrast C. Thus, the Liptonian notion of precluding the contrast can be constructed by finding the explanation for the contrast and negate it. However, to ensure this construction is consistent with its partner, we can rephrase the construction as the negation of the non-preclusive explanation of why C instead of Q.

Lipton did not give an account on how his contrastive explanation can be computed because his interest is in modeling epistemically how scientist can search for new explanation, that is, scientific discovery. However, a computer knowledge base cannot infer what is not already inferable from the knowledge base, hence my rough interpretation is intended to capture the essence of Lipton's Difference Condition, rather than providing an exact account on how Lipton's model can be computed.

For example, this morning Alex is late for work and Mary is not. If Alex's train was late, then Alex would be late for work and if Mary's bus was late then Mary would be late for work.

$$Alex's\_train\_late \quad \rightarrow \quad Alex\_is\_late$$
$$Mary's\_bus\_late \quad \rightarrow \quad Mary\_is\_late$$

A non-preclusive contrastive explanation for the question why $Alex\_is\_late$ instead of $Mary\_is\_late$ is the difference in their explanation models, namely $Alex's\_train\_late$ (we shall leave the trivial explanation $Alex\_is\_late$ aside). However, that does not say anything why Mary was not late for work. In fact, there is nothing in the above statements can help us in inferring decisively why Mary was not late for work. The next best explanation would be to conjecture that Mary's bus was not late. By doing so, we have weaken the possibility of the contrast $Mary\_is\_late$. Note that this conjecture is not to assert the equivalence (hence their truth values) between $Mary's\_bus\_late$ and $Mary\_is\_late$. It is merely a conjecture, explicitly reconstructed for the purpose of presenting an explanation.

Such a preclusive contrastive explanation can be constructed by augmenting the non-preclusive contrastive explanantion for why $Alex\_is\_late$ instead of $Mary\_is\_late$, by the negation of why $Mary\_is\_late$ instead of $Alex\_is\_late$. That is, the preclusive contrastive explanation becomes $Alex's\_train\_late$ and not $Mary's\_bus\_late$.

Intuitively, a reason why Q instead of C that precludes C is conjectured to be the reason why Q instead of C and not the reason why C instead of Q. If we were interested in conjecturing preclusively why did I go to the library instead of Hawaii, there is no non-preclusive contrastive explanation for it and what remains is the negation of the reason why I go to Hawaii instead of the library, which is, because I did not win lottery or did not have money. Again, not having the luck or fortune does not sanction decisively why I did not go to Hawaii. I see that this form of conjecture making preclusive contrastive explanation is especially useful in the case where there is a lack of a better explanations (no non-preclusive contrastive explanation).

In model theorectic terms, Let M_Q nad M_C be the explanation models for the question part $K \models E_Q \rightarrow Q$ and the contrast part $K \models E_C \rightarrow C$ respectively and the two difference models $M_{Q-C} = M_Q - M_C$ and $M_{C-Q} = M_C - M_Q$. A *preclusive contrastive explanation* for Q instead of C is the model $M_{Q-C} \cup \neg M_{C-Q}$. The notation $\neg M_{C-Q}$ means to flip positive literal into negated literal and vice versa for every literal in the model M_{C-Q}.

Definition 5 (Preclusive Contrastive Explanation). *Let the knowledge base K be a set of sentences, a question Q and a contrast C both are a sentence, and E_Q and E_C are the corresponding explanations for Q and C. Let M_Q and M_C be an explanation model for $K \models E_Q \rightarrow Q$ and $K \models E_C \rightarrow C$ respectively. Let $M_{Q-C} = M_Q - M_C$ and $M_{C-Q} = M_C - M_Q$ be the non-preclusive contrastive explanations for the statement Q instead of C and the statement C instead of Q*

*respectively. A **preclusive contrastive explanation** for Q instead of C is the model $M_{Q-C} \cup \neg M_{C-Q}$.*

Intuitively, M_{Q-C} is the necessary model for explaining Q but not needed in explaining C. Conversely, M_{C-Q} is the necessary model for explaining C but not needed in explaining Q. Hence, M_{Q-C} is the necessary model in explaining Q and $\neg M_{C-Q}$ will preclude the contrast C (by falsifying its justification). The constructed model of the preclusive contrastive explanation comprises the part which is a non-preclusive contrastive explanation for the question and the part which is the negated model of the contrast. Since these two part models are constructed using set difference, the intersection between them is empty, ensuring the union of them is consistent — no complementary literals exist in the constructed model.

Corollary 2. *A **preclusive contrastive explanation** for Q instead of C is consistent.*

Using the previous example on being late for work, a non-preclusive contrastive explanation for why $Alex\_is\_late$ instead of $Mary\_is\_late$ is the preclusive contrastive explanation expressed by the new model $\{Alex's\_train\_late, \neg Mary's\_bus\_late\}$.

4 Computing Contrastive Explanation

The characterization of contrastive explanations based on their corresponding logical models lays the framework for a computational model. Extracting an explanation model can be approximated by a *Clause Management System* (CMS) (Reiter and de Kleer, 1987; Kean and Tsiknis, 1992; Kean and Tsiknis, 1993), a tool designed for abductive reasoning. In the syntactic approach of the CMS, an explanation E for Q with respect to a knowledge base K is a clause (a set of disjunctive literals) such that $K \models E \rightarrow Q$ and $K \wedge E$ is consistent. A minimal explanation is the smallest such clause. It can be shown that an explanation model correspond to such a minimal explanation. Thus, The difference between explanation models can be approximated by the set difference among the minimal explanations represented in clausal form. In a full paper, we shall explore in detail the algorithms needed for such computation.

5 Conclusions

The knowledge base cannot infer what is not already inferable from the knowledge base. A close minded human can only be as intelligent as a static knowledge base. What we can hope for is to have the knowledge base system ask us human intelligent questions, in order to provide us with intelligent answer to our original question. Query and explanation are the two major components in a constructive discussion, and the discussion must be an iterative process. Incorporating contrastive explanation computation into an intelligent knowledge base system bring us a step forward towards this goal. In a full paper, we shall explore the properties of contrastive explanations (intutively it is irreflexive, asymetric and intransitive), their preference orderings (loveliest and likeliest contrastive explanations), a model for multiple contrasts (for example, in a disjunctive compound contrast, why did you eat salad instead of beef or fish?), and examining the opposite of contrast: **consonance** (Mill's method of agreement).

References

Irving M. Copi. *Introduction to Logic.* Macmillian, New York, sixth edition, 1982.

Gilbert H. Harman. The Inference To The Best Explanation. *Philosophical Review*, 74, 1965.

Alex Kean and George Tsiknis. Assumption based Reasoning and Clause Management Systems. *Computational Intelligence*, 8(1):1–24, 1992.

Alex Kean and George Tsiknis. Clause Management Systems (CMS). *Computational Intelligence*, 9(1):11–40, 1993.

Peter Lipton. Contrastive Explanation. In Dudley Knowles, editor, *Explanation and its Limits*, pages 247–266. Cambridge University Press, Cambridge, Great Britain, 1990.

Peter Lipton. *Inference To The Best Explanation.* Routledge, London, 1991.

Sigmund Stephen Miller, editor. *Funk & Wagnalls Family Medical Guide.* Funk & Wangnalls, Inc., USA, 1976.

Raymond Reiter and Johan de Kleer. Foundations of Assumption-Based Truth Maintenance Systems: Preliminary Report. In *Proceeding of AAAI-87*, pages 183–188, Seatle, Washington, 1987.

W. D. Ross. *The Works of Aristotle.* William Benton, Publisher, 1952.

David-Hillel Ruben. *Explaining Explanation.* Routledge, London, 1990.

SL Method for Computing a Near-Optimal Solution Using Linear and Non-linear Programming in Cost-Based Hypothetical Reasoning

Mitsuru Ishizuka and Yutaka Matsuo

Dept. of Information and Communication Eng.
School of Engineering, University of Tokyo
7-3-1, Hongo, Bunkyo-ku, Tokyo 113-8656, Japan

Abstract. Hypothetical reasoning is an important framework for knowledge-based systems because it is theoretically founded and it is useful for many practical problems. Since its inference time grows exponentially with respect to problem size, its efficiency becomes the most crucial problem when applying it to practical problems. Some approximate solution methods have been proposed for computing cost-based hypothetical reasoning problems efficiently; however, for humans their mechanisms are complex to understand. In this paper, we present an understandable efficient method called *SL (slide-down and lift-up) method* which uses a linear programming technique, namely simplex method, for determining an initial search point and a non-linear programming technique for efficiently finding a near-optimal 0-1 solution. To escape from trapping into local optima, we have developed a new local handler which systematically fixes a variable to a locally consistent value when a locally optimal point is detected. This SL method can find a near-optimal solution for cost-based hypothetical reasoning in polynomial time with respect to problem size. Since the behavior of the SL method is illustrated visually, the simple inference mechanism of the method can be easily understood.

1 Introduction

By handling incomplete hypothesis knowledge which possibly contradicts with other knowledge, hypothetical reasoning tries to find a set of element hypotheses which is sufficient for proving (or explaining) a given goal (or a given observation) [Poole 88]. Because of its theoretical basis and its practical usefulness, hypothetical reasoning is an important framework for knowledge-based systems, particularly for systems based on declarative knowledge. However, since hypothetical reasoning is a form of non-monotonic reasoning and thus an NP-complete or NP-hard problem, its inference time grows exponentially with respect to problem size. In practice, slow inference speed often becomes the most crucial problem.

There already exist several investigations trying to overcome this problem. (For example, see [Ishizuka 91, 94, Kondo 93, 96, Ohsawa 97] for authors' work.)

Besides symbolic inference methods which have been exploited mostly in AI field, search methods working in continuous-value space have recently shown promising results in achieving efficient inference for hypothetical reasoning as well as for SAT problems and CSP (constraint satisfaction problem). This approach is closely related to mathematical programming, particularly with 0-1 integer programming. When we consider a cost-based propositional hypothetical-reasoning problem, it can be transformed into an equivalent 0-1 integer programming problem with a set of inequality constraints. Although its computational complexity still remains NP-hard, it allows us to exploit a new efficient search method in continuous-value space. One key point here is an effective use of the efficient simplex method for linear programming, which is formed by relaxing the 0-1 constraint in 0-1 integer programming. Also, non-linear programming formation provides us another possibility. These approaches may be beneficial particularly for developing efficient approximate solution methods, for example, in cost-based hypothetical reasoning [Charniak 90].

The pivot-and-complement method [Balas 80] is a good approximate solution method for 0-1 integer programming. Ishizuka and Okamoto [Ishizuka 94] used this method to realize an efficient computation of a near-optimal solution for cost-based hypothetical reasoning. Ohsawa and Ishizuka [Ohsawa 97] have transformed the behavior of the pivot-and-complement method into a visible behavior on a knowledge network, improved its efficiency by using the knowledge structure of a given problem, and consequently developed networked bubble propagation (NBP) method. NBP method can empirically achieve a polynomial-time inference of $N^{1.4}$ where N is the number of possible element hypotheses, to produce a good quality near-optimal solution in cost-based hypothetical reasoning.

The key point of these methods is the determination of an initial search point by using simplex method and efficient local searches around this point in continuos space for eventually finding a near-optimal 0-1 solution. However, in order to avoid trapping into locally optimal points, a sophisticated control of the local search is required; as a result, the inference mechanisms have become complicated and for humans they are difficult to understand.

On the other hand, Gu [Gu 93, 94] exploited an efficient method to solve SAT problems by transforming them into unconstrained non-linear programming; the SAT problem is related to propositional hypothetical reasoning. There are several methods for unconstrained non-linear programming, i.e., the steepest descent method, Newton's method, quasi-Newton method, and conjugate direction method. The mechanisms of these local search methods are easy to understand as they basically proceed by descenting a valley of a function. However, since those methods simply try to find a single solution depending upon an initial search point, they cannot be used for finding a (near) optimal solution for the folowing reason: if they are trapped into local optima, they have to restart from a new initial point that is to be selected randomly.

In order to find a near-optimal solution using the simple non-linear programming technique, we combine a linear programming, namely simplex method, to determine the initial search point of the non-linear programming. The search, however, often falls into local optima and an effective method escaping from these local optima is required. In this paper, we present an effective method named *variable fixing method* for this problem. Variable fixing corrects a local inconsistency at each locally optimal point and allows to restart the search. Unlike conventional random restart schemes, this method permits to direct the search systematically using the knowledge structure of a given problem.

As sliding-down operations toward a valley of a non-linear function and lifting-up operations are repeated alternately, we call this method **SL (Slide-down and Lift-up) method**. By illustrating its behavior visually, we show that its mechanism is easily understandable and also achieves good inference efficiency that is close to the efficiency of the NBP method.

In this paper, we will treat hypothetical reasoning problems that are represented in propositional Horn clauses; we will also allow for (in)consistency constraints among hypotheses.

2 Transformation into Linear and Non-linear Programming and their Combination

First we show how to transform a hypothetical reasoning problem into linear and non-linear programming problems. These transformations become the basis of the SL method. As for the transformation into linear programming, there are several ways of replacing logical knowledge by an equivalent set of linear inequalities. Among them, we adopt the following transformation used in [Santos 94].

Associating the true/false states of logical variables such as $p1$, $p2$, q, etc. with 1/0 of the corresponding numerical variables represented by the same symbols, we transform a Horn clause

$$q \leftarrow p1 \wedge p2. \tag{1}$$

into a set of inequalities

$$q \leq p1, \ q \leq p2, \ p1 + p2 - 1 \leq q \tag{2}$$

and also

$$q \leftarrow p1 \vee p2. \quad \text{(combination of } q \leftarrow p1 \text{ and } q \leftarrow p2) \tag{3}$$

into

$$p1 \leq q, \ p2 \leq q, \ q \leq p1 + p2 \tag{4}$$

This transformation is advantageous in that it allows to produce a 0-1 solution only by using simplex method for a certain type problem [Santos 96], though the number of generated inequalities becomes large.

For the constraint representing inconsistency, the head of its Horn clause is set to false which is translated to 0 in the corresponding inequality. As the goal of hypothetical reasoning has to be satisfied, it is set to true which becomes 1 in the inequality.

Let the weights of possible element hypotheses $h1, h2, h3, \cdots$ be $w_1, w_2, w_3 \cdots$, respectively. Moreover, let the element hypothesis $hi(i = 1, 2, \cdots)$ become $hi = 1$ if it is included in the solution hypothesis, and $hi = 0$ otherwise. Then we can define the cost of the solution as

$$\mathrm{cost} = w_1 h1 + w_2 h2 + w_3 h3 + \cdots,$$

which expresses the sum of the weights of the element hypotheses included in the solution. Let us set cost as the objective function; then if we compute the optimal solution to minimize this function under the generated inequalities, it indicates the optimal solution in the cost-based hypothetical reasoning problem.

In this way, hypothetical reasoning becomes a 0-1 linear integer programming. In the pivot-and-complement method (Balas 80), an efficient approximate solution method for 0-1 integer programming, the optimal real-number solution is obtained as follows: first the simplex method is used by relaxing the 0-1 constraint on the variables, then a near-optimal 0-1 solution is searched in a sophisticated manner around the optimal real-number solution. This local search mechanism for the 0-1 solution is rather complicated because it incorporates several heuristics that have been obtained empirically. For our new method here, while we utilize this optimal real-number solution obtained by the simplex method as the initial search point, we try to develop a new simple and understandable method of the local search using a non-linear programming technique.

Gu [Gu 93, 94] presented a method for SAT problems by transforming them into unconstrained non-linear programming problems. According to this transformation, the transformation of propositional Horn clauses to clauses that can be processed by our hypothetical reasoning can be realized as follows.

- If the same variable appears in head part of a cluse, we introduce new variables and produce a rule clause with disjunctive body as exemplified below. [ex.] In case of $q \leftarrow p1 \wedge 2$, and $q \leftarrow p3 \wedge 4$, replace them by $q1 \leftarrow p1 \wedge 2$, $q2 \leftarrow p3 \wedge p4$, $q \leftarrow q1 \vee q2$. (This is to make the following completion operation effective even for OR-related rules.)
- Apply completion for each rule. (Completion is an operation that changes $q \leftarrow p$ to $q \leftarrow p$ and $q \rightarrow p$, interpreting $\{q$ if $p\}$ as $\{q$ if and only if $p\}$. In the definition of material implication (used in formal logic), $q \leftarrow p$, for instance, is interpreted as true if q is true regardless of p's truth value; this makes backward inference impossible which is required in the hypothetical reasoning. Thus completion is needed here.)

After the above operations, a given problem is transformed to the problem of finding the minimal value 0 of a non-linear function constructed as follows.

- Associate the true/false states of each logical variable with $1/-1$, respectively, of the corresponding numerical variable.
- Replace the literals x and $\neg x$ by $(x-1)^2$ and $(x+1)^2$, respectively.
- Replace conjunction ($\wedge$) and disjunction ($\vee$) in the logical formula by arithmetic operation $+$ and $\times$, respectively, assuming that all the clauses are connected by conjunction.

For example, consider the following hypothetical reasoning problem.

$$1 \leftarrow g. \text{ (the goal } 'g' \text{ shall be satisfied.)}$$

$$g \leftarrow a \wedge b., \ a \leftarrow h1 \wedge c., \ b \leftarrow h2 \wedge c., \ c \leftarrow h3 \wedge h4.,$$

$$c \leftarrow h5 \wedge h6., \ inc \leftarrow h1 \wedge h4.$$

('inc' stands for inconsistent which is equivalent to the empty clause.)

After applying completion, the following set of formulae is generated.

$$1 \leftarrow g., \ g \leftarrow a \wedge b., \ a \leftarrow g., \ b \leftarrow g., \ a \leftarrow h1 \wedge c., \ h1 \leftarrow a., \ c \leftarrow a.,$$

$$b \leftarrow h2 \wedge c., \ h2 \leftarrow b., \ c \leftarrow b., \ c1 \vee c2 \leftarrow c., \ c \leftarrow c1., \ c \leftarrow c2.,$$

$$c1 \leftarrow h3 \wedge h4., \ h3 \leftarrow c1., \ h4 \leftarrow c1., \ c2 \leftarrow h5 \wedge h6., \ h5 \leftarrow c2.,$$

$$h6 \leftarrow c2., \ inc \leftarrow h1 \wedge h4.$$

Then the following non-linear function is to be constructed, for which a solution achieving the minimal value 0 is searched.

$$\begin{aligned}
f = &(g-1)^2 + (g-1)^2(a+1)^2(b+1)^2 + (g+1)^2(a-1)^2 + (g+1)^2(b-1)^2 \\
&+ (a-1)^2(h1+1)^2(c+1)^2 + (a+1)^2(h1-1)^2 + (a+1)^2(c-1)^2 \\
&+ (b-1)^2(h2+1)^2(c+1)^2 + (b+1)^2(h2-1)^2 + (b+1)^2(c-1)^2 \\
&+ (c+1)^2(c1-1)^2(c2-1)^2 + (c-1)^2(c1+1)^2 + (c-1)^2(c2+1)^2 \\
&+ (c1-1)^2(h3+1)^2(h4+1)^2 + (c1+1)^2(h3-1)^2 + (c1+1)^2(h4-1)^2 \\
&+ (c2-1)^2(h5+1)^2(h6+1)^2 + (c2+1)^2(h5-1)^2 + (c2+1)^2(h6-1)^2 \\
&+ (h1+1)^2(h4+1)^2
\end{aligned} \tag{5}$$

The weight of each element hypothesis is not considered here; thus, even if a 0-1 solution achieving $f = 0$ is found, it will not necessarily be an optimal or near-optimal one. However, if local search is conducted starting from the real-value optimal point determined by the simplex method with respect to the linear inequality constraints and the objective function, it will reach a near-optimal 0-1 solution.

One feature of the non-linear function thus generated is that it is at most quadric with respect to one variable. This is due to the fact that one variable never appears twice in one propositional Horn clause.

3 Improvement of the Construction of the Non-linear Function

Although the above computational mechanism using both the linear and non-linear programming techniques provides us with an understandable scheme for cost-based hypothetical reasoning, we have to solve one crucial problem, namely trapping into local optimal points where f is strictly above 0. To cope with this problem, we first reconsider the form of the above non-linear function.

The following example shows a simple case of trapping into a local optimal point.

$$\cdots$$

$$a(\text{false}) \leftarrow b(\text{true}) \wedge c(\text{false}) \wedge d(\text{true}) \tag{6}$$

$$c(\text{false}) \leftarrow e(\text{false}) \vee p(\text{true}) \tag{7}$$

$$\cdots$$

where **true/false** inside ( ) indicates the truth value of the variable in a state. In this example, Eq.(7) is in a false state; this prevents the non-linear function covering all the logical formulae or constraints to become 0. After completing Eqs.(6) and (7), the non-linear function obtained as a result of the proposed replacements becomes Eqs.(8) and (9), respectively:

$$(a-1)^2(b+1)^2(c+1)^2(d+1)^2 + (a+1)^2(b-1)^2 + (a+1)^2(c-1)^2 + (a+1)^2(d-1)^2 \tag{8}$$

$$(c+1)^2(e-1)^2(p-1)^2 + (c-1)^2(e+1)^2 + (c-1)^2(p+1)^2 \tag{9}$$

Suppose that c appears in these two clauses of the knowledge base. Then, to consider the effect of c's change, we compute the partial derivatives of Eqs.(8) and (9) with respect to c as

$$(-1-1)^2(1+1)^2(2(c+1))(1+1)^2 + (-1+1)^2(2(c-1)) = 128(c+1) \tag{10}$$

$$2(c+1)(-1-1)^2(1-1)^2 + 2(c-1)(-1+1)^2 + 2(c-1)(1+1)^2 = 8(c-1) \tag{11}$$

As these are summed to compute $\partial f/\partial c$ as in Eq.(5), we obtain $\partial f/\partial c = 136c + 120$. Since f is quadratic with respect to one variable, f becomes minimal at $c = -120/136$. This suggests that c tends to stick to -1(**false** state).

This example indicates that the non-linear function proposed by Gu [Gu 93, 94] is problematic when a parent node[1] has many child nodes[1] and the truth status of a clause is determined by its one child node. That is, since the coefficient of the variable corresponding to this node increases with the involution of 2 in the non-linear function, as seen in Eq.(8), this effect becomes too large so as to prevent the same variable appearing in the head part of another Horn clause moving away from its incorrect status. The problem here is that if p is **true**, then $(p+1)^2$ becomes 2^2; that is, the coefficient of one variable in a certain state varies with the involution of 2, depending on the number of body atoms in the Horn clause.

Hence, rather than associating **true/false** states with $1/-1$, respectively, we associate them with $0.5/-0.5$, respectively, and transform x and $\neg x$ to $(x-0.5)^2$ and $(x+0.5)^2$, respectively, to construct a new non-linear function. Thereby,

---

[1] In this paper, 'variable' and 'node' are used interchangeably since a propositional variable constitutes one node in the proof tree.

when p is **true**, $(p + 0.5)^2$ becomes 1; the unbalance among the coefficients of the product terms in a certain state can be avoided.

The following list summarises the way of constructing the new non-linear function.

- Associate the **true/false** states of each logical variable with $0.5/-0.5$, respectively, of the corresponding numerical variable.
- Replace the literals x and $\neg x$ by $(x - 0.5)^2$ and $(x + 0.5)^2$, respectively.
- Replace conjunction ($\wedge$) and disjunction ($\vee$) in the logical formula by the arithmetic operations $+$ and $\times$, respectively.

4 Variable Fixing Scheme for Escaping from Local Optima

There remains the possibility that the search is trapped into local optima and can not go to the minimal point of $f = 0$ even if we use the new non-linear function. For example, consider the following simple case. If all the values are **false** (namely, -0.5) at the initial stage, this becomes a locally optimal point. As $h1$, $h2$, $h3$ and $h4$, which are all in a **false** state, pull a and b toward their **false** states, the goal g can not go to a **true** state.

$$g \leftarrow a \wedge b. , \ a \leftarrow h1 \wedge h2. , \ b \leftarrow h3 \wedge h4 .$$

In large complex problems, the non-linear functions tend to have many locally optimal points of this and other sorts.

To solve this problem, consider again the following case of a locally optimal state.

$$\cdots$$

$$a(\text{false}) \leftarrow b(\text{true}) \wedge c(\text{true}) \wedge d(\text{false}). \tag{12}$$

$$d(\text{false}) \leftarrow e(\text{true}) \wedge p(\text{true}) \wedge q(\text{true}). \tag{13}$$

$$\cdots$$

When the non-linear function does not reach 0, the minimum value, it indicates that at least one Horn clause is not satisfied. In this example Eq.(13) is not satisfied, since two restrictions, one from an upper node (d shall be **false**) and one from a lower node (d shall be **true**), contradict each other. This situation can not simply be resolved because a might be requested to be **false** from its upper node, and also e, p and q might be requested to be **true** from their lower nodes.

We thus determine the state of d to be **true** or the state of either e, p or q to be **false**, so as to escape from the locally optimal point. There are two cases in unsolved states where the goal is unsatisfied: first, some of element hypotheses which are needed to prove the goal are missing, and secondly, selected hypotheses violate the consistency constraint. Since the former case arises more often empirically in the search process starting from the initial point, which is obtained as the real-number optimal point by the simplex method, we adopt the strategy of resolving the former case first. In this case, if the restrictions from the upper node and from the lower node contradict, the central node is set to true.

In addition, after restarting from a new state, the search often falls into the same local optimal point since the non-linear function is quadratic with respect to one variable. Thus, if one variable is changed to 0.5 (true state) to resolve the local inconsistency, we don't change it anymore in the search process; that is, we consider it a constant rather than a variable afterwards. As this implies the substitution of 0.5 in a strong sense, we call this operation **variable fixing**. The effect of variable fixing propagates to other variables through the minimization process of the non-linear function.

The target nodes (variables) for the variable fixing operations are as follows. Here, we evaluate the state of each node by rounding its value to -0.5 (**false**) or 0.5 (**true**).

1. the goal node in a **false** state.
2. a parent node in a **false** state such that its AND-related child nodes are all in a **true** state.
3. a parent node in a **false** state such that one of its OR-related child node is in a **true** state.
4. an AND-related child node in a **false** state such that its parent node is in a **true** state.
5. one of the OR-related child nodes in a **false** state such that its parent node is in a **true** state.

When fallen into a locally optimal point, we find one of the target nodes (variables) as listed above sequentially in order of numbers (1) - (5), apply the variable fixing operation to that variable and restart the search. The reason for applying variable fixing to one target variable at a time rather than to multiple target variables is to avoid moving apart far from the real-number optimal point which is obtained by the simplex method.

In (2) and (3) above where the restriction from the lower nodes is considered, variable fixing does not contribute to satisfy the goal and hence causes inconsistencyin rare case, since the states of the lower nodes are determined by considering the consistency constraints.

On the other hand, in (4) and (5)above, although variable fixing may contribute to satisfy the goal, it possibly causes inconsistency by changing a **false** child node to **true**. Thus, we place priority on (2) and (3) over (4) and (5).

In (5), the selection of one target node is not uniquely determined; however, we select the one with the largest analog value as it may affect the states of its lower nodes the least. We call this process an "OR-node selection phase".

Experiments show that the order of (2), (3) and (4) above causes no big difference on the performance. The algorithm always stops in finite steps, since one variable fixing operation always decreases one free variable. Also, as the variable fixing operation increases the number of **true** nodes, it guarantees to produce a solution if the given problem has no consistency constraint. Redundant element hypotheses in the solution can be removed in an improvement phase in order to obtain a near-optimal solution.

Yet, there are cases where a solution can not be obtained due to variable fixing of wrong nodes (variables) which contradict with the consistency constraint. These cases arise the following situations.

i. The node which shall be **false** is fixed to **true**.

ii. In the OR-node selection phase one wrong node, which is different from one to be **true**, is fixed to **true** and causes inconsistency.

For case (i), try to remove the redundant element hypotheses from the resulting solution hypothesis set so that the inconsistency can be resolved (redundancy detection phase). For case (ii), keep other possible OR-related child nodes not selected in a stack, and if the search is failed, restart the OR-node selection phase by picking another child node from the stack. Although this operation causes inefficient backtracking, it almost never occurs in our experiments and therefore does not become a serious problem.

In our system, the OR-nodes are usually selected in the minimization process of the non-linear function. Here, if a wrong OR-node is selected, there is no way to remedy it. Then the search proceeds via the local optima by the variable fixing operations; redundant element hypothesis in the solution hypothesis can be removed in the improvement phase to be described below.

The variable fixing operation is effective only when the new non-linear function introdced in this paper is used. If Gu's non-linear function is used, it is not useful since the probabilities of the wrong selection in the OR-node selection phase and of fixing wrong nodes in other steps become large due to the coefficient unbalance of the terms in the non-linear function.

5 Improvement Phase of Solution Cost

The solution obtained after the search undergoes an improvement phase taking into account its cost. A simple algorithm is employed here; that is, each element hypothesis included in the solution hypothesis set is checked in order according to its weight to see whether or not it can be removed without undercutting the provability of the goal. If it can, then the element hypothesis is removed from the solution. This operation, which is also employed in the pivot-and-complement method [Balas 80] for 0-1 integer programming, seems to be the most effective in terms of its computational cost and its performance.

6 Algorithm of SL Method

Summarizing above descriptions, we show below the algorithm of the SL method for cost-based hypothetical reasoning. The steepest descent method is currently employed for the minimization of the non-linear function.

i. **Initial Phase** Constitute a set of linear inequalities from a given problem. Relaxing the 0-1 constraint, obtain the optimal real-number solution by the simplex method and set this as the initial search point for the subsequent 0-1 solution search. (The range of $[0, 1]$ of the variables at this initial search point is shifted to $[-0.5, 0.5]$ when used in the subsequent minimization of the non-linear function.)

ii. **Constitution of Non-linear Function** Constitute the non-linear function as described previously.

iii. **Search Phase** Execute the search for finding the minimal value 0 of the non-linear function. If rounding the variables into $0.5/-0.5$ makes the non-linear function be 0, then stop and go to (vi). If a local optimum is detected, then go to (iv).

iv. **Variable Fixing** In order to escape from the local optimum, select one target node according to the order of (1)-(5) described in the section of variable fixing, apply variable fixing to this node, and go back to (iii). If there is no target node found, then go to (v).

v. **Redundancy Detection Phase** If there is no target node in (iv), it means that all the Horn clauses being related to the proof of the goal are satisfied except the consistency constraints. Thus, keeping the goal node `true`, try to reduce the `true` hypothesis so as to remove the inconsistency among hypotheses. If this succeeds, go to (vi). Otherwise, restart from the OR-node selection phase in (iv) by picking up one of the remaining OR-nodes in the stack. If there is no such OR-node in the stack, the search fails.

vi. **Improvement Phase** Try to temporally change each `true` element hypothesis to `false` without spoiling the proof of the goal. If this succeeds, then change this element hypothesis and its associated intermediate nodes to `false`; that is, remove this element hypothesis from the solution hypothesis as a redundant one.

7   Visual Illustration of the Behavior of the SL Method

Unlike other efficient methods for (cost-based) hypothetical reasoning, one salient feature of the SL method is its simple and understandable mechanism, which is basically based on the minimization of the non-linear function starting from the initial search point which is determined by the simplex method. Here, we illustrate its behavior visually.

For visual illustration, we have to find an effective way of mapping the behavior in multi-dimensional space into two or three-dimensional space; simple display methods such as one using two axes of two variables are not good enough. For effective display, we choose here two axes such that one axis corresponds to the vector from the current search point to the previous point determined by variable fixing or the minimization process, and another corresponds to the vector from the current search point to the optimal solution point. We set the current search point, the previous point and the optimal solution point at $(0, 0)$, $(0, 1)$ and $(1, 0)$, respectively, and that the height represents the shape of the non-linear function.

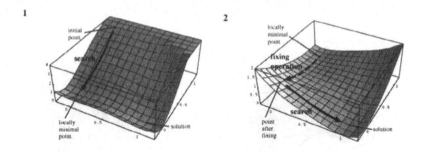

Fig. 1. A behavior of search (example 1).

Figure 1 shows an example in which a solution with function value 0 can be found after only one variable fixing operation. Starting from an initial search point, the search first falls into a locally minimal point, from which it can not proceed to the solution point as there is a small hill between them. One can observe from the figure on the right that variable fixing changes the form of the function and allows the search to go to the solution point.

Figure 2 illustrates a more complicated case, in which four variable fixing operations are required before reaching the solution. It can be seen well that the minimization (Slide-down) and variable fixing (Lift-up) operations are repeated. (These illustrations are produced using Mathematica.)

We want to emphasize that this visualization facilitates comprehension of the simple inference mechanism of the SL method; the simplicity is important to grasp the inference behavior and to trust it. For a computer, visualization is not necessary to execute the search.

8   Experimental Results and Evaluation

Figure 3 shows the experimental results of the inference time of the SL method. The system is implemented in C and runs on Sun Ultra and SGI workstations. The number of body atom in each Horn clause is 2-7, and the number of the occurences of each atom in one experimental knowledge set is at most 10. The horizontal axis is the number of nodes, as the SL method carries out the search on the nodes. Since in practice, the simplex method produces its optimal solution in polynomial time, the average data excluding cases in which the 0-1 solutions were obtained only using simplex method are plotted in 3. Also, the times spent for the simplex method are excluded from the plotted data.

As illustrated in Fig. 3, the SL method can compute a near-optimal solution in a polynomial-time of approximately $n^{1.8}$ where n is the number of nodes. Failure of finding a solution was one case out of 111 problems. The near-optimality of the obtained solution is as good as that of the NBP method [Ohsawa 97], in which at least the third nearest solution to the optimal one is obtained for all the cases where the system finds the solution.

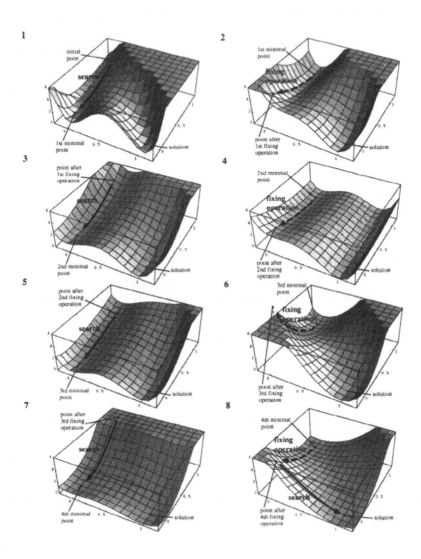

Fig. 2. A behavior of search (example 2).

inference time (s)

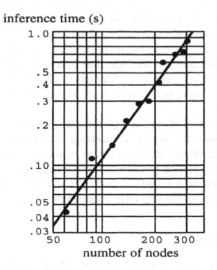

number of nodes

Fig. 3. Inference time of SL method.

9 Related Work

ATMS [deKleer 86] is an efficient method for dealing with possibly hypothetical knowledge. It is used as a caching mechanism for the working memory of a production system and to maintain inferred data that are supported by consistent hypotheses ('label' in ATMS terminology). Although its mechanism is also useful partially for logical problem solving, it is not enough for problem solving in general. The logic-based framework of hypothetical reasoning was presented in [Poole 88]. Since then, several schemes have been developed to improve its slow inference speed. A method using an inference-path network [Ishizuka 91] where network compilation phase is based on the linear-time algorithm of Dowling & Gallier [Dowling 84] for propositional Horn logic, has achieved nearly ultimate speed for propositional hypothetical reasoning. As for predicate-logic hypothetical reasoning, effective fast inference methods have been presented in [Kondo 93, 96], which use a deductive database technique.

On the other hand, the effectiveness of using mathematical programming techniques for logical problem solving has been advocated by [Hooker 88]. Recently, Santos showed that many problems of cost-based hypothetical reasoning (or abduction) [Charniak 90] can be solved using only the simplex method [Santos 94, 96]; however, the hypothetical reasoning problem there does not permit any inconsistency among possible hypotheses. Cost-based hypothetical reasoning is closely related to 0-1 integer programming. Both are NP-hard problem in general; however there exists a good approximate solution method called pivot-and-complement method [Balas 80] for 0-1 integer programming. This method was applied in [Ishizuka 94] for computing a near-optimal solution in polynomial time with respect to problem size to cost-based hypothetical reasoning. In network bubble propagation (NBP) method [Ohsawa 97], the behavior of the pivot-and-complement method has been transformed into a visible behavior on a knowledge network and the efficiency has been improved by using the knowledge structure of a given problem. Although the NBP method can achieve high efficiency, i.e., a low-order polynomial-time inference, its mechanism has become complicated.

As another approach of applying mathematical programming techniques, Gu [Gu 93, 94] exploited the use of unconstrained non-linear programming techniques for SAT problems, which are closely related to logical inference and CSP (constraint satisfaction problem). These techniques provide simple efficient mechanisms for finding a single solution. Yet it is not appropriate to find the (near) optimal solution, for example, in cost-based hypothetical reasoning.

10 Conclusion

We have presented the SL (slide-down and lift-up) method for cost-based hypothetical reasoning, which can find a near-optimal solution in polynomial time in cost-based hypothetical reasoning. It uses both linear and non-linear programming techniques. Moreover, it incorporates a local handler to escape from trapping into locally optimal points. The notable feature of this method is its simple and understandable search behavior as visually illustrated here, though at present it speed performance is slightly lower than that of the NBP method [Ohsawa 97]. The mechanism of the SL method may also be useful to develop systematic polynomial-time methods for finding near-optimal solutions in other problems such as the constraint optimization problem.

References

[Balas 80] E. Balas and C. Martin: Pivot and Complement – A Heuristic for 0-1 Programming, Management Science, Vol.20, pp.86-96 (1980).

[Charniak 90] E. Charniak and S. Shimony: Probabilistic Semantics for Cost Based Abduction, Proc.AAAI-90, pp.106-111 (1992).

[deKleer 86] J. deKleer: An Assumption-based TMS, Artif. Intelli., Vol.28, pp.127-162 (1986)

[Dowling 84] W. F. Dowling and J. H. Gallier: Linear-time Algorithm for Testing Satisfiability of Propositional Horn Formulae, Jour. of Logic Programming, Vol.3, pp.267-284 (1984)

[Gu 93] J. Gu: Local Search for Satisfiability (SAT) Problem, IEEE Trans. on Systems, Man and Cybernetics, Vol.23, No.4, pp1108-1129 (1993).

[Gu 94] J. Gu: Global Optimization for Satisfiability Problem, IEEE Trans. on Knowledge and Data Engineering, Vol.6, No.3, pp.361-381 (1994).

[Hooker 88] J. N. Hooker: A Quantitative Approach to Logical Inference, Decision Support Systems, Vol.4, pp.45-69 (1988)

[Ishizuka 91] M. Ishizuka and F. Ito: Fast Hypothetical Reasoning System using Inference-path Network, Proc. IEEE Int'l on Tools for AI (TAI'91), pp.352-359 (1991)

[Ishizuka 94] M. Ishizuka and T. Okamoto: A Polynomial-time Hypothetical Reasoning employing an Approximate Solution Method of 0-1 Integer Programming for Computing Near-optimal Solution, Proc. Canadian Conf. on AI, pp.179-186 (1994)

[Kondo 93] A. Kondo, T. Makino and M. Ishizuka: Efficient Hypothetical Reasoning System for Predicate-logic Knowledge-base, Knowledge-Based Systems, Vol.6, No.2, pp.87-94 (1993)

[Kondo 96] A. Kondo and M. Ishizuka: Efficient Inference Method for Computing an Optimal Solution in Predicate-logic Hypothetical Reasoning, Knowledge-Based Systems, Vol.9, pp.163-171 (1996)

[Ohsawa 97] Y. Ohsawa and M. Ishizuka: Networked Bubble Propagation: A Polynomial-time Hypothetical Reasoning for Computing Near Optimal Solutions, Artificial Intelligence, Vol.91, No.1, pp.131-154 (1997).

[Poole 88] D. Poole: A Logical Framework for Default Reasoning, Artif. Intelli., Vol.36, pp.27-47 (1988)

[Santos 94] E. Santos, Jr.: A Linear Constraint Satisfaction Approach to Cost-based Abduction, Artificial Intelligence, Vol.65, pp.1-27 (1994).

[Santos 96] E. Santos, Jr. and E. S. Santos: Polynomial Solvability of Cost-based Abduction, Artificial Intelligence, Vol.86, pp.157-170 (1996).

Image Retrieval System Using KANSEI Features

Hideyuki Kobayashi, Yoriyuki Okouchi and Shunji Ota

OMRON Corporation, Information Technology Research Center
Shimokaiinji, Nagaokakyo-city
Kyoto, 617-8510, Japan
{Hideyuki_Kobayashi, Yoriyuki_Okouchi, Shunji_Ota}@omron.co.jp

Abstract. We have developed an Image Retrieval System using KANSEI(feeling or sensitivity) features. This system can search the same sensuous image from a large image storage not using text or word but an image. Therefore it doesn't need indexing on each image for preparing image retrieval. Out system extracts the KANSEI features from each image, and sets adequate weights for combining those features. In order to decide the weights, we introduce a new value called "adaptability". It judges how much the features are extracted from the image. As a result, adaptability makes it possible to construct a KANSEI model according to each image and to calculate similarity between images.

1 Introduction

Recently, contents of multimedia have been changed from text-based data to data combined with text, sound and image material. Especially, image data play an important role in multimedia information processing. However, we have had a problem of dealing with image data efficiently because a volume of image data is much bigger than text data. It is also difficult to interpret images by words because contents of image are ambiguous for computers.

One of well-known image retrieval systems is QBIC system developed by IBM corp.[1]. It deals with not only still images but also video images. Its search/match engine uses color, texture and shape features as image content parameters. It considers with plural objects, a rough sketch and an arrangement of each object as information of a target image. This system is based on a relational database, then it can also use indexed text data.

Another representative retrieval system is Chabot, which was developed by University of California at Berkeley[2]. Its main feature from image is color, especially color histogram data. This system uses this image feature as one of parameters in the database for a large collection of images.

One of image retrieval systems which pay attention to a human subjective visual perception, is TRADEMARK system developed by Electrotechnical Laboratory (ETL: one of Japanese national laboratories)[3]. This system extracts about ten features from each image data and converts them into a subjective field. In this field, the system calculates similarity between images.

Our system focuses on human subjective decision. Then we adopt a "composition" pattern method which was hardly used on the former systems. Our system selects the best pattern, which represents an original image, of the four. And we think that this process is approximated to a human visual recognition process, especially a letter or simple pattern recognition. Our system uses simple composition patterns, calculates an adaptability between each pattern and original image as a search key and selects the best pattern. After using this best one, it calculates similarity between images.

Our approach is based on a KANSEI model with features to deal with image data easily. KANSEI is a Japanese word, which means sensitivity, feeling, and comfort. The KANSEI features are extracted from images and represent an impression or a feeling of atmosphere. For human beings, the KANSEI features are much easy to acquire. We apply this ability to information processing.

We join a human media project directed by the Ministry of International Trade and Industry (MITI) of Japan. The purpose of the project is to establish a human centered media technology rather than machine-oriented one. In this project, we take part in the KANSEI factory working group, and take charge of KANSEI image retrieval. This report is a result of the human-media project.

Formerly our laboratory has developed a needlework image retrieval system using a fuzzy technology. Design patterns of needlework are used by industrial apparel makers. This system extracts the distribution of black and white pixels, aspect ratio of width and height, thickness of line and so on. We have analyzed a relationship between features and KANSEI-words such as "simple", "soft", "realistic". We apply this technology and extend to the various images into a new system.

Our system extracts two perceptual features: color features and shape features. Our KANSEI model is based on a combination of the two perceptual features, so this model is applied for similarity measurement of images.

2 Extraction of KANSEI Features

We define color and shape features as the KANSEI features which express the characteristic elements of image data.

2.1 Extraction of color feature

Concerning the color feature, we analyze compositions, which are very important when human beings impressed from images.

Our system uses four basic composition templates (see Fig.1). These templates are introduced from standard compositions of photographs and paintings. Horizontal and Vertical division types are very simple, popular and useful compositions. Circular division type is effective when an object is on the center of images. And, the radiation division type is effective when the image includes an infinity point on the center. All the templates divide the image into 12 regions in our system [4].

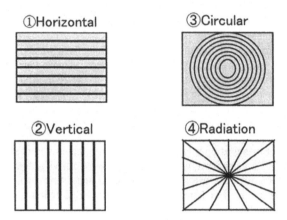

Fig. 1. Our system uses four composition templates. They are referred from a basic composition of paintings and photographs.

After an image is divided into the regions, the average color is calculated on each region. In our system, the RGB color space is adopted.

The color features of each template have 36 elements: 12(regions)x3(RGB colors). Fig.2 shows an example of extracting color features using our method.

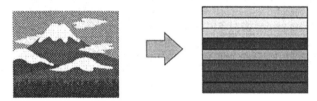

Fig. 2. Example of extracting color features from the image using the horizontal composition template.

2.2 Extraction of shape feature

Shape features are based on graphical features in the TRADEMARK system developed by ETL, this system retrieves monochrome trademark images from the image database[5].

We combined the algorithm for monochrome images with the one dealing with the color contents. Fig.3 shows the procedure of extracting the shape features.

At first, the RGB data are converted to brightness from an equation:

$$\text{Brightness} = 0.299 \times R + 0.587 \times G + 0.114 \times B \tag{1}$$

Then, brightness are converted to binary (black or white pixels), based on the threshold value which is set on the average value of the brightness. This binary image is divided into 8 by 8 blocks, and the number of black pixels on each region are counted. These numbers on each region are defined as the shape features. In Fig.3, the last image is shown by gray scale.

Fig. 3. Procedure of extracting shape feature. The first one is an original image, the second one is binalized image and last one represents a number of black pixels as a gray scale.

3 KANSEI model combining features

We have developed the method of calculating similarity between images using the KANSEI model. This KANSEI model includes with the color and shape features, and simulates the human being's perception. This model will be changed dynamically referring to a key image. This change is related to the human perception, and it is an important characteristic point of our method.

3.1 Comparison with the color feature

In order to find the best fitted composition template of the four, our system calculates the variance of 12 regions and selects the template which has the maximum variance. It represents the characteristic color features. Fig.4 shows an example of this procedure. In this case, the horizontal division template (the left one) is the best because it shows the separate color bands clearly and it has the maximum variance.

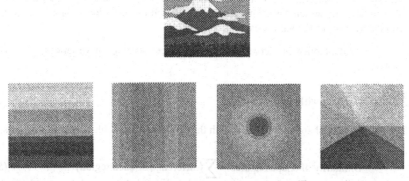

Fig. 4. The procedure of choosing the best composition template. The upper image is the original image. The lower images are converted ones with each composition template.

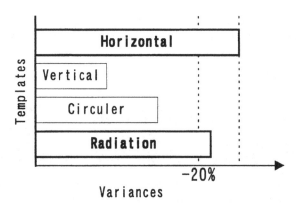

Fig. 5. Comparison with the four composition templates.

After the selection of the best template, another template will be also used, if the variance of another template is close to the one of the best. This threshold is set on 80% of the maximum variance in our system. Fig.5 shows an example to compare the variances. In this example the horizontal template is the best, and the variance of the radiation template is close to the best one, then the radiation one is also adopted.

The distance in the RGB color space is a scale of the similarity. Our system calculates the distance between colors of the same regions.

$$\text{Similarity on each template} = \sum (\text{Distance of each region}) \qquad (2)$$

If more than two composition templates are selected, the same calculation is carried out. They are combined with the weight which are the same as the color variance of the selected templates. The color similarity is calculated by combining the distance of each region. The simple addition is applied.

$$\text{Similarity of color features} = \sum (\text{Weight} \times \text{Similarity on each template}) \qquad (3)$$

We introduce the value which decides the weight. This value is called adaptability and means how much it gets the characteristic feature from images. Our system calculates the similarities as well as the adaptability between a key image and all the other images in the database. This judgment is based on the color variance compared with the average of the variances in all images.

$$\text{Adaptability of color features} = \text{Variance}/(\text{Average of variances}) \qquad (4)$$

3.2 Comparison with shape feature

The similarity of shape is calculated with the difference of the black pixel's numbers.

$$\text{Similarity of shape features} = \sum (\text{difference of each region}) \qquad (5)$$

The adaptability of shape features is calculated as the one of color features, and is used by the variance of the shape similarity.

$$\text{Adaptability of shape features} = \text{Variance}/(\text{Average of variances}) \qquad (6)$$

3.3 KANSEI model combining features

The synthetic similarity measurement is based on the color and shape features. We use the KANSEI model which controls the weights depending on the key image. Our system uses the color and shape features, then it is decided by the weights for those similarity.

The weights are separately decided by comparing the average of each adaptability. In order to consider the balance of each weight, we introduce a fuzzy method for deciding the weights. Fig.6 shows a simple function model. The maximum and minimum weights are decided. The change range of adaptability is also fixed beforehand.

Our system decides the weights for combining each feature and uses the color variance of regions on composition template as this information. But their weights on features become unbalanced because the method doesn't consider other feature's information. So, we set a limitation of maximum and minimum weight values. This limitation is represented by a function.

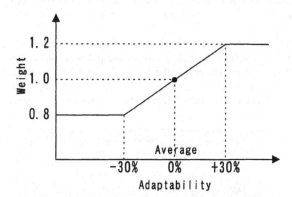

Fig. 6. Convert function model from adaptability to weight.

The synthetic similarity is combined using each similarity and weight.

$$\text{Syntehtic Similarity} = \sum (\text{weight} \times \text{similarity}) \qquad (7)$$

After the other KANSEI features are added, those procedures are adopted. The system needs two values. The one is similarity on each feature. It indicates how close each other on the point of its feature. The other is adaptability. It calculates the weight and shows the KANSEI model referring to all features. Our system shows the simple example of this approach. Our main proposal is this approach for making the KANSEI model.

4 KANSEI image retrieval system

We have developed on image retrieval system using the KANSEI model. Our system consists of a server and clients. The server provides extracting the KANSEI features and calculating the similarities. The clients are web browsers as the interface between the users and the server. This connection can be used with the network.

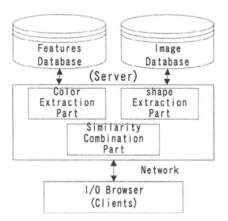

Fig. 7. Construction of KANSEI image retrieval system. It consists of a server and clients system. The server includes a search engine and an image database. Clients are user interface.

As the color image contents of the database, Japanese stamp(about 1500 images), national flag(400) and butterfly (200) images are provided. After the user picks up one of the images as a key image, similar images in the database can be retrieved.

Fig.8 shows the interface of our system. The lower right large frame displays all image in the database and the result. Our system shows top 20 images in a similarity order.

Fig. 8. GUI of KANSEI image retrieval system. The majority field is a browsing area. The user can find some image and pick it up as a search key.

4.1 Results

Figs.9 -11 are the results of our image retrieval system. A key image is at the upper left corner. The closer to the key image, the more similar.

Fig.9 shows an example that the color feature is affected. The key image is the stamp that consists of a big dark-brown train in the center against a light blue background. In this case, the best composition template is the horizontal type, and the circular type is the second one. Our system uses the two composition templates at this time. The comparison with the color and shape features, the adaptabilities of both features are bigger than the threshold, and their weights are set by 1.2 each other. As a result, our system deals with the features by the weights.

Fig.10 shows the result that the shape feature is effected. The key stamp has a typical Japanese old style that is a fine pale red pattern. In this case, the selected composition patterns are horizontal (weight:1.0) and circular (weight:0.83). The adaptability of the color feature is smaller than the average. The weights are 0.80 for color and 0.96 for shape. As a result, the most similar stamp has a different color and the same pattern(shape) stamp as the key stamp, because the system regards color feature as more important than the shape's at this time.

Fig.11 is one of good examples. The key image is the stamp that an old brown house is in the center against the blue sky. This example shows that the KANSEI model is effective. The series of stamps that have the same composition and color are searched. But our system never understands that the object in the stamp is an old house. The system can find the similar images only by the shape and color features.

Fig. 9. Result 1:An example that the color feature is affected.

Fig. 10. Result 2: An example that the shape feature is affected.

Fig. 11. Result 3: One of good example in our system.

5 Conclusion

The KANSEI model is based on the color and shape features from images. We introduce the adaptability which judges how much characteristics or special features are extracted. This KANSEI model is changed referring to the key image like human being's perceptions. It controls the weights of the color and shape features. As a result, our system can retrieve the similar image like a human being's perception.

Our system is not enough to simulate a human being's complicated perception. The methods of extracting features from images, methods of calculating adaptability and an objective evaluation for results are our important topics.

Especially, the evaluation is our current interest. KANSEI model deals with human being's perception, but it is much difficult to measure our sense. If an established evaluation method doesn't exist, we can not understand the performance of models. We need a good evaluation method.

Concerning the KANSEI model, we are analyzing many simple composition templates. The calculating adaptability is also improved. We also introduce a fuzzy technology into the combination method, then an advanced KANSEI model will simulate the parallel processing in human brains and become much closer to the human being's perception.

Acknowledgments

This paper was prepared under a re-entrustment contract with the Laboratories of Image Information Science and Technology (LIST) from the New Energy and Industrial Technology Development Organization (NEDO), concerning the Human Media Technology program under the Industrial Science and Technology Frontier Program (ISTF) of MITI of Japan.

References

1. Flickner, M., Sawhney, H. Niblack, W. and et.al.: Query by Image and Video Content: The QBIC System, IEEE Computer Magazine, Vol.28, No.9(1995)23-32

2. Ogle, V.E., Stonebraker, M.: Chabot: Retrieval from a Relational Database of Images, IEEE Computer Magazine, Vol.28, No.9 (1995) 40-48

3. Kato, T., Shimogaki, H., Mizutori, T. and Fujimura, K.: TRADEMARK : Multimedia database with Abstracted Representation on Knowledge Base, Proc. Of 2nd Int. Symp. On Interoperable Info. (1988) 245-252

4. Hashimoto, M., Sato, K. and Chihara, K.: Content Based Image Retrieval using Color Features, The 40th Annual Conf. of the Institute of Systems, Control and Information Engineers (1996) 103-104

5. Kurita, T. and Kato, T.: Learning of Personal Visual Impression for Image Database Systems", IEEE Computer Society, Proc. of Int. Conf. on Document Analysis and Recognition [ICDAR'93] (1993) 547-552

A Robust Front-End for Telephone Speech Recognition

Hoon-Young Cho, Sang-Mun Chi, and Yung-Hwan Oh

Department of Computer Science,
Korea Advanced Institute of Science and Technology
{nymph,smchi,yhoh}@bulsai.kaist.ac.kr

Abstract. In this study, we propose an effective front-end technique to improve the performance of telephone speech recognition. Many works have been concentrated on compensating the noise and the channel distortions contained in telephone speech at the front-end stage of speech recognition. Based on RASTA processing which is well known for its channel robust feature parameters, we tried to further improve this method using the channel estimation power of cepstral mean subtraction and maximum likelihood method. As a hybrid method of channel estimation and RASTA processing, the proposed method was proved to be effective by experiments performed on real telephone speech data.

1 Introduction

The speech recognition on public telephone network has a lot of useful applications such as remote control systems and reservation systems. But its performance suffers from many degrading effects contained in telephone speech. A clean speech signal is contaminated by many kinds of background noises which are additive in the spectral domain and distorted by the linear filtering effect of the telephone line which is additive in the cepstral domain.

For the compensation of the additive ambient noises of telephone speech, we can consider the application of general speech enhancement techniques such as spectral subtraction [1], nonlinear spectral subtraction [2], short term modified coherence [3] and so on. These methods work quite well on the stationary noises like car noise or white noise. But, since most of the real telephone speech data include nonstationary additive noises, the application of the above techniques sometimes degrades the recognition performance. Therefore, in case that signal to noise ratio is high enough, most of the studies have been concentrated on compensating channel distortion [5].

To compensate for the channel effect of telephone line, methods based on the subband filtering of filterbank energy trajectory such as RASTA (RelAtive SpeTrAl) processing [6], CMS (cepstral mean subtraction) [7] and high-pass filtering [8] have been studied. Such methods as MAP (maximum a posteriori) and ML (maximum likelihood) channel estimation [9] are based on statistical estimation. Linear discriminant analysis, signal bias removal or model adaptation

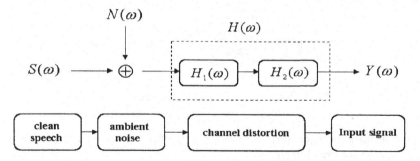

Fig. 1. distortion model of telephone speech

are also known to be effective for the compensation of the channel distortion. Among the techniques mentioned above, RASTA and CMS are widely spread front-end channel compensation methods because of their simplicity and powerfulness. And there have been several trials to improve these two methods [10–12]. As for the experiment performed on real telephone data, CMS performed slightly better than RASTA processing [10]. The reason is that RASTA can not remove channel distortion properly since it uses the same filter for every input signal, while the channel response of the telephone line varies on each input [4,5]. On the other hand, CMS estimates the channel distortion of the input signal and removes it, although the estimation is quite rough.

In this paper we propose a method which improves RASTA processing by adapting RASTA filter to input channel environments. The proposed algorithm estimates channel bias that maximizes likelihood and removes it from the time trajectory of the feature vector sequence to obtain a reference signal. Then it searches a shifted RASTA filter coefficient with the reference signal. The resultant filter reflects the channel condition of current input speech. By applying this filter to the input speech again, we can extract more robust feature parameters.

This paper is organized into 7 sections. In Section 2, we model telephone speech and channel distortion. Section 3 describes feature parameter extraction process in brief and discusses on RASTA processing. In section 4 and 5, the proposed RASTA filter adaptation algorithm is explained in depth. Experimental results are evaluated and discussed in section 6. Section 7 makes the concluding remarks.

2 Modeling the Telephone Speech

The speech changes to an electrical signal by the handset and transfers through the PSTN (public switched telephone network) to the recognizer running on the remote server. The input speech to the recognizer can be modeled as shown in Fig. 1. The ambient noise $n(k)$ is added to the clean speech $s(k)$. Then the signal is distorted by the impulse response $h_1(k)$ of a handset. Later, when it passes through the telephone line, the impulse response $h_2(k)$ of the line is convoluted

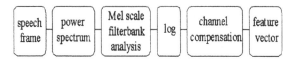

Fig. 2. feature parameter extraction procedure

and it distorts the signal further as shown in the Eq. 1 in the time domain and Eq. 2 in the spectral domain.

$$y(k) = (s(k) + n(k)) * h_1(k) * h_2(k)$$
$$= (s(k) + n(k)) * h(k) \tag{1}$$
$$Y(\omega) = (S(\omega) + N(\omega)) \cdot H(\omega) \tag{2}$$

The log power spectrum of each frame can be represented as in Eq. 3 where m denotes the time index of a speech frame. Assuming that SNR is high enough, the second term of Eq. 4 can be regarded as zero. So, Eq. 5 approximates Eq. 3.

$$\ln |Y_m(\omega)| = \ln |S_m(\omega) + N_m(\omega)| + \ln |H(\omega)| \tag{3}$$
$$= \ln |S_m(\omega)| + \ln \left| 1 + \frac{N_m(\omega)}{S_m(\omega)} \right| + \ln |H(\omega)| \tag{4}$$
$$\cong \ln |S_m(\omega)| + \ln |H(\omega)| \tag{5}$$

In Eq. 5, $H(w)$ is the channel distortion of the telephone speech. And it is assumed to be time invariant and independent of mth frame. It is because the channel distortion remains almost fixed during a call, while it varies from call to call [4, 5].

3   RASTA processing

As mentioned in the previous section, RASTA is one of the most widely spread methods among the researchers studying on the telephone speech recognition. It is applied during the feature parameter extraction process and it supplies robust features to the recognizer. A common feature parameter extraction procedure is shown in Fig. 2. Frist, the input speech frames are processed by discrete fourier transform. From the power spectrum, mel-scaled triangular filterbank energy trajectory is extracted [12]. The time trajectory of each filterbank output energy is log transformed and compensated by the RASTA or other compensation methods to produce channel robust feature parameters.

In RASTA processing, RASTA filter suppresses slowly varying factors like channel distortion and quickly changing parts in speech signal so that it can stress the speech portion of the distorted input signal. The transfer function of

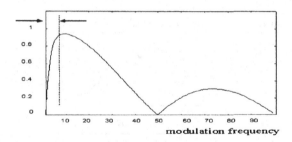

Fig. 3. frequency response of RASTA filter

the filter is as shown in Eq. 6, where α is a filter coefficient that determines the first peak frequency of RASTA filter in Fig. 3. In the figure, the left side of the first peak frequency (marked with arrows) reduces the slowly varying channel distortion [6], and the position of the first peak frequency determines the amount of channel reduction. Therefore, by controlling the coefficient α properly according to the channel environment of the current input, we can reduce the distortion well.

$$H(z) = \frac{0.2 + 0.1z^{-1} - 0.1z^{-3} - 0.2z^{-4}}{1 - \alpha z^{-1}} \tag{6}$$

In RASTA processing, for the α value, $\alpha = 0.98$, $\alpha = 0.94$ or some other fixed values have been used. In this case, RASTA filter can not remove the telephone channel distortion which is variable in each input speech. We can expect a better performance, if the coefficient α changes properly as the channel varies. In the following section, we describe a method to adapt this coefficient to the input channel condition.

4 Adaptation of the RASTA filter

Assuming that we have a channel-free reference trajectory $d(t)$ for the filterbank output trajectory of Fig. 2, α in Eq. 6 can be calculated by gradient descent method (note that RASTA filter is one of IIR filters). After minimizing the error between the reference trajectory and the filtered output with varying α, we can reduce the channel distortion better with the resulting α. Figure 4 shows the block diagram of the proposed method. At iteration n, RASTA filter can be described as Eq. 7 and α_n is the filter coefficient that moves to the local optimal value as the iteration count increases.

$$H_n(z) = \frac{0.2 + 0.1z^{-1} - 0.1z^{-3} - 0.2z^{-4}}{1 - \alpha_n z^{-1}} \tag{7}$$

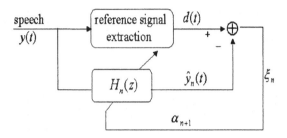

Fig. 4. filter adaptation by gradient descent method

Mean squared error ξ_n between the reference $d(t)$ and the filter output $\hat{y}_n(t)$ can be computed as in Eq. 8.

$$\xi_n = E\{|d(t) - \hat{y}_n(t)|^2\}$$
$$= \frac{1}{T} \sum_{t=1}^{T} [d(t) - \hat{y}_n(t)]^2 \tag{8}$$

We calculate the derivative of ξ_n with respect to α_n. Then, move the value α_n by the step size μ to the negative direction of the derivative to decrease ξ_n. The derivative is calculated by Eq. 9 and 10.

$$\frac{d\xi_n}{d\alpha_n} = -\frac{2}{T} \sum_{t=1}^{T} \left(d(t) - \hat{y}_n(t) \right) \cdot \frac{d\hat{y}_n(t)}{d\alpha_n} \tag{9}$$

$$\frac{d\hat{y}_n(t)}{d\alpha_n} = \hat{y}_n(t-1) + \alpha_n \frac{d\hat{y}_n(t-1)}{d\alpha_n}$$

$$\vdots$$

$$= \sum_{k=0}^{t-2} \alpha_n^k \hat{y}_n(t-k-1) \tag{10}$$

In brief, the algorithm first initializes with reference trajectory extraction, $\alpha_0 = 0.98$ and $\mu = 0.05$. μ is determined experimentally. At iteration n, it calculates the filter output $\hat{y}_n(t)$, and the derivative in Eq. 9. Then it calculates α_{n+1} by Eq. 11. It iterates until ξ_n converges. The algorithm is summerized in Fig. 5.

$$\alpha_{n+1} = \alpha_n - \mu \frac{d\xi_n}{d\alpha_n} \tag{11}$$

5   Obtaining the Reference Signal

Most of the telephone speech data pass through a single channel. Therefore, it is needed to estimate the channel bias and remove it from the input speech to

Algorithm

1. Initialization : $d(t)$, $\mu = 0.05$, $\alpha_0 = 0.98$

2. At n-th iteration

   calculate $\hat{y}_n(t)$, $\dfrac{d\xi_n}{d\alpha_n}$, ξ_n

3. Calculate α_{n+1}

4. Iterate step 2 , 3 until ξ_n converge

Fig. 5. filter adaptation algorithm

obtain a reference signal. We can use the cepstral mean subtraction or the maximum likelihood channel estimation method based on the HMM (hidden Markov model) to obtain a reference. The former simply assumes the cepstral mean of the input signal as the channel distortion and operates with little overhead. The latter gives us a better reference with relatively a large amount of calculation. Let the input vector sequence be represented as $Y = y_1, y_2, \cdots, y_T$, and Viterbi decoded state sequence as $S = s_1, s_2, \cdots, s_T$. Then, the maximum likelihood channel vector can be calcalated as shown in Eq. 12 [9]. μ_{S_t}, Σ_{S_t} are the mean vector and the covariance matrix of the HMM state S_t at time t. The reference trajectory is then calculated by Eq. 13.

$$\hat{h}_{ML} = \left(\sum_{t=1}^{T} \Sigma_{s_t}^{-1} \right)^{-1} \left(\sum_{t=1}^{T} \Sigma_{s_t}^{-1}(y_t - \mu_{s_t}) \right) \tag{12}$$

$$d(t) = y_t - \hat{h}_{ML} , \quad t = 1, 2, \cdots, T \tag{13}$$

The restriction of the ML estimation [9] is that it is dependent on recognition model, i.e, a continuous HMM. In this study, to make ML estimation possible for discrete HMM-based recognition system without changing its structure, we calculate the statistics μ_S, Σ_S for each state of DHMM as follows. After training all the models, we perform Viterbi decoding on the training data for each word model and collect the data vectors for each DHMM state and calculate μ_S, Σ_S and store them. We use them when the Eq. 12 is needed for the calculation of $\hat{h}_{ML}$.

6   Experimental Results

Recognition experiments were performed to demonstrate the effectiveness of the proposed method. The speech data are 8kHz sampled, collected on real public telephone network with various handsets located in office, street, underground, supermarket and so forth. These data are parts of database for the voice dialing service system of Korea Telecom Research Center. For the experiments, 50 isolated Korean words of 10 males and 10 females were used for training data, and

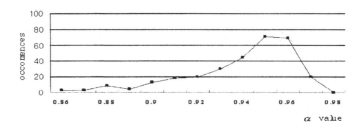

Fig. 6. The distribution of α at 10th feature vector trajectory

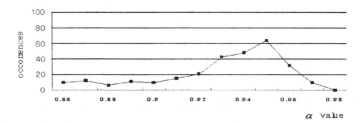

Fig. 7. The distribution of α at 15th feature vector trajectory

333 speaker independent data collected in the similar environment were used for recognition test.

The front-end process follows Fig. 2 and 17 static feature vectors, 17 difference vectors with $\delta = 2$, 17 acceleration vectors with $\Delta = 2, \delta = 3$, and energy and delta energy with $\delta = 2$ were used as the feature parameters. The meaning of Δ and δ follows that in [14]. For recognition model, left-to-right discrete hidden Markov model with 5 states per a syllable was used.

Baseline was set to MFCC which is known to be more robust than linear prediction cepstral coefficient. We compared the proposed method with CMS, RASTA and ML estimation. For the proposed method, reference signals using CMS and using ML estimation were also compared. The maximum iteration number in Fig. 5 was set to 300, but in most case 100 iterations were enough for the convergence of error. Figure 6 and 7 shows the distribution of the filter coefficients after the convergence. In the figure, the estimated suboptimal filter coefficients are spread out instead of concentrating on a single value, because the channel distortions vary in each speech data.

The recognition results are described in table 1. CMS (2) performed slightly better than RASTA filtering (3) because CMS estimated the channel and removed it on each input, while RASTA filter was the same on every channel variations. This result corresponds to the result of the other researchers [13]. ML estimation gave better result than CMS because ML estimates the channel more accurately and this result is also reflected in (5, 6) when the proposed

Table 1. comparison of proposed method with conventional ones

	method	1st	2nd
(1)	MFCC	69.67	77.78
(2)	MFCC + CMS	75.38	83.48
(3)	MFCC + RASTA	74.17	84.08
(4)	MFCC + ML	76.88	84.08
(5)	CMS + RASTA adaptation	80.78	85.89
(6)	ML + RASTA adaptation	82.28	87.39

method used CMS or ML to obtain the reference signal. Because the proposed method (6) reduced the channel distortion equally as ML estimation (4) and stressed the speech portion of input signal like the RASTA does (3), it showed better performance than the other methods compared with and confirmed the effectiveness of it.

The proposed method is not a real time algorithm because it extracts the reference signal with ML estimation and iterates many times. But, for the application based on isolated word recognition and in the domain that recognition performance is more important than real time processing the proposed method can be useful.

7 Conclusion

In this paper, we adapted the RASTA filter which was independent of variable telephone channel environments. Proposed method estimates channel bias in each telephone speech by ML estimation and extracts a reference signal which is channel-free. From this reference signal, we determined a shifted RASTA filter coefficient that is able to remove the channel distortion better. Even though the algorithm needs much calculation, it can remove the variant channel distortion better than the RASTA while preserving the merit of RASTA filter, which is to stress the speech portion of distorted signal. Experiments on real telephone data confirmed the effectiveness of the proposed method as a successful front-end technique.

References

1. S. F. Boll, "Suppression of acoustic noise in speech using spectral subtraction," *IEEE Trans. Acoust. Speech Signal Processing*, Vol. ASSP-27, no. 2, pp 113-120, 1979.
2. P. Lockwood and J. Boudy, "Experiments with a nonlinear spectral subtractor (nss), hidden markov models and the projection, for robust speech recognition in cars," *Speech Communication*, 11:215-228, 1992.
3. D. Mansour and B. H. Juang, "The short-time modified coherence representation and its application for noisy speech recognition," *Proc. ICASSP*, pp. 525-528, 1988.

4. P. J. Moreno, "Speech Recognition in Telephone Environments," MS. Thesis, Carnegie Mellon University, 1992.

5. C. Mokbel, J. Monne and D. Jouvet, "On-line adaptation of a speech recognizer to variations in telephone line conditions," *Proc. EUROSPEECH*, pp. 1247 - 1250, 1993.

6. H. Hermansky, N. Morgan, A. Bayya and P. Kobn, "Compensation for the effect of the communication channel in Auditory-like analysis of speech (RASTA-PLP)," *Proc. EUROSPEECH*, pp. 1367 - 1370, 1991.

7. A. Acero, "Environmental Robustness in Automatic Speech Recognition," *Proc. ICASSP*, pp. 849 - 852, 1990.

8. B. A. Hanson and T. H. Applebaum, "Subband or cepstral domain filtering for recognition of Lombard and channel-distorted speech," *Proc. ICASSP*, pp. 79 - 82, 1993.

9. J. T. Chien, H. C. Wang and L. M. Lee, "Estimation of channel bias for telephone speech recognition," *Proc. ICSLP*, pp. 1840 - 1843, 1996.

10. J. D. Veth and L. Boves, "Comparison of channel normalization technique for automatic speech recognition over the phone," *Proc. ICSLP*, pp. 2332 - 2335, 1996.

11. C. Avendano, S. V. Vuuren and H. Hermansky, "Data Based Filter Design for RASTA-like Channel Normalization in ASR," *Proc. ICSLP*, pp. 2087 - 2090, 1996.

12. J. L. Shen, W. L. Hwang and L. S. Lee, "Robust Speech Recognition Features Based on Temporal Trajectory Filtering of Frequency Band Spectrum," *Proc. ICSLP*, pp. 881 - 884, 1996.

13. J. D. Veth and L. Boves, "Comparison of channel normalization technique for automatic speech recognition over the phone," *Proc. ICSLP*, pp. 2332-2335, 1996.

14. B. A. Hanson and T. H. Applebaum, "Robust speaker-independent word recognition using static, dynamic and acceleration features: Experiments with Lombard and noisy speech," *Proc. ICASSP*, pp. 857 - 860, 1990.

Author Index

Springer
and the
environment

At Springer we firmly believe that an
international science publisher has a
special obligation to the environment,
and our corporate policies consistently
reflect this conviction.

We also expect our business partners –
paper mills, printers, packaging
manufacturers, etc. – to commit
themselves to using materials and
production processes that do not harm
the environment. The paper in this
book is made from low- or no-chlorine
pulp and is acid free, in conformance
with international standards for paper
permanency.

Springer

Lecture Notes in Artificial Intelligence (LNAI)

Vol. 1397: H. de Swart (Ed.), Automated Reasoning with Analytic Tableaux and Related Methods. Proceedings, 1998. X, 325 pages. 1998.

Vol. 1398: C. Nédellec, C. Rouveirol (Eds.), Machine Learning: ECML-98. Proceedings, 1998. XII, 420 pages. 1998.

Vol. 1400: M. Lenz, B. Bartsch-Spörl, H.-D. Burkhard, S. Wess (Eds.), Case-Based Reasoning Technology. XVIII, 405 pages. 1998.

Vol. 1404: C. Freksa, C. Habel. K.F. Wender (Eds.), Spatial Cognition. VIII, 491 pages. 1998.

Vol. 1409: T. Schaub, The Automation of Reasoning with Incomplete Information. XI, 159 pages. 1998.

Vol. 1415: J. Mira, A.P. del Pobil, M. Ali (Eds.), Methodology and Tools in Knowledge-Based Systems. Vol. I. Proceedings, 1998. XXIV, 887 pages. 1998.

Vol. 1416: A.P. del Pobil, J. Mira, M. Ali (Eds.), Tasks and Methods in Applied Artificial Intelligence. Vol. II. Proceedings, 1998. XXIII, 943 pages. 1998.

Vol. 1418: R. Mercer, E. Neufeld (Eds.), Advances in Artificial Intelligence. Proceedings, 1998. XII, 467 pages. 1998.

Vol. 1421: C. Kirchner, H. Kirchner (Eds.), Automated Deduction – CADE-15. Proceedings, 1998. XIV, 443 pages. 1998.

Vol. 1424: L. Polkowski, A. Skowron (Eds.), Rough Sets and Current Trends in Computing. Proceedings, 1998. XIII, 626 pages. 1998.

Vol. 1433: V. Honavar, G. Slutzki (Eds.), Grammatical Inference. Proceedings, 1998. X, 271 pages. 1998.

Vol. 1434: J.-C. Heudin (Ed.), Virtual Worlds. Proceedings, 1998. XII, 412 pages. 1998.

Vol. 1435: M. Klusch, G. Weiß (Eds.), Cooperative Information Agents II. Proceedings, 1998. IX, 307 pages. 1998.

Vol. 1437: S. Albayrak, F.J. Garijo (Eds.), Intelligent Agents for Telecommunication Applications. Proceedings, 1998. XII, 251 pages. 1998.

Vol. 1441: W. Wobcke, M. Pagnucco, C. Zhang (Eds.), Agents and Multi-Agent Systems. Proceedings, 1997. XII, 241 pages. 1998.

Vol. 1446: D. Page (Ed.), Inductive Logic Programming. Proceedings, 1998. VIII, 301 pages. 1998.

Vol. 1453: M.-L. Mugnier, M. Chein (Eds.), Conceptual Structures: Theory, Tools and Applications. Proceedings, 1998. XIII, 439 pages. 1998.

Vol. 1454: I. Smith (Ed.), Artificial Intelligence in Structural Engineering. XI, 497 pages. 1998.

Vol. 1455: A. Hunter, S. Parsons (Eds.), Applications of Uncertainty Formalisms. VIII, 474 pages. 1998.

Vol. 1456: A. Drogoul, M. Tambe, T. Fukuda (Eds.), Collective Robotics. Proceedings, 1998. VII, 161 pages. 1998.

Vol. 1458: V.O. Mittal, H.A. Yanco, J. Aronis, R. Simpson (Eds.), Assistive Technology in Artificial Intelligence. X, 273 pages. 1998.

Vol. 1471: J. Dix, L. Moniz Pereira, T.C. Przymusinski (Eds.), Logic Programming and Knowledge Representation. Proceedings, 1997. IX, 246 pages. 1998.

Vol. 1476: J. Calmet, J. Plaza (Eds.), Artificial Intelligence and Symbolic Computation. Proceedings, 1998. XI, 309 pages. 1998.

Vol. 1480: F. Giunchiglia (Ed.), Artificial Intelligence: Methodology, Systems, and Applications. Proceedings, 1998. IX, 502 pages. 1998.

Vol. 1484: H. Coelho (Ed.), Progress in Artificial Intelligence – IBERAMIA 98. Proceedings, 1998. XIII, 421 pages. 1998.

Vol. 1488: B. Smyth, P. Cunningham (Eds.), Advances in Case-Based Reasoning. Proceedings, 1998. XI, 482 pages. 1998.

Vol. 1489: J. Dix, L. Fariñas del Cerro, U. Furbach (Eds.), Logics in Artificial Intelligence. Proceedings, 1998. X, 391 pages. 1998.

Vol. 1495: T. Andreasen, H. Christiansen, H.L. Larsen (Eds.), Flexible Query Answering Systems. Proceedings, 1998. IX, 393 pages. 1998.

Vol. 1501: M.M. Richter, C.H. Smith, R. Wiehagen, T. Zeugmann (Eds.), Algorithmic Learning Theory. Proceedings, 1998. XI, 439 pages. 1998.

Vol. 1502: G. Antoniou, J. Slaney (Eds.), Advanced Topics in Artificial Intelligence. Proceedings, 1998. XI, 333 pages. 1998.

Vol. 1504: O. Herzog, A. Günter (Eds.), KI-98: Advances in Artificial Intelligence. Proceedings, 1998. XI, 355 pages. 1998.

Vol. 1510: J.M. Zytkow, M. Quafafou (Eds.), Principles of Data Mining and Knowledge Discovery. Proceedings, 1998. XI, 482 pages. 1998.

Vol. 1515: F. Moreira de Oliveira (Ed.), Advances in Artificial Intelligence. Proceedings, 1998. X, 259 pages. 1998.

Vol. 1529: D. Farwell, L. Gerber, E. Hovy (Eds.), Machine Translation and the Information Soup. Proceedings, 1998. XIX, 532 pages. 1998.

Vol. 1531: H.-Y. Lee, H. Motoda (Eds.), PRICAI'98: Topics in Artificial Intelligence. XIX, 646 pages. 1998.

Lecture Notes in Computer Science